GUERRILLA AND TERRORIST ORGANISATIONS:
A WORLD DIRECTORY AND BIBLIOGRAPHY

GUERRILLA AND TERRORIST ORGANISATIONS: A WORLD DIRECTORY AND BIBLIOGRAPHY

Peter Janke

Head of Research, Control Risks Ltd., London
Formerly Head of Research, Institute for the Study of Conflict, London

with
Richard Sim

Macmillan Publishing Company
New York

Macmillan Publishing Company, 866 Third Avenue, New York, NY 10022

ISBN 0-02-916150-9

Printed in Great Britain

Contents

274371

France   **25**

AFRICA

MIDDLE EAST

Contents

Contents

FAR EAST INCLUDING OCEANIA

NORTH AMERICA

LATIN AMERICA

Contents

Chile 443

Colombia 449

Dominican Republic 461

El Salvador 465

Guatemala 475

Honduras 483

Mexico   485

Nicaragua   493

Paraguay   499

Peru   501

Uruguay   507

Preface

To call a book a directory of 'Guerrilla and Terrorist Organisations' at once raises a question which neither the League of Nations nor the United Nations has been able to resolve satisfactorily: namely, who or what a guerrilla is. The definition depends somewhat on one's point of view, and, if one is engaged in the struggle, on the side for which one is fighting.

In this Directory the reader will find listed those movements which have attempted to pose a threat to established governments since the end of the Second World War.

Some have come to power, mostly in colonial circumstances where the metropolitan governments felt compelled, after a brief struggle, to grant independence. Often these movements, whether or not they deserve the title, are now popularly known as national liberation movements. Obvious examples are the *Front de Libération Nationale* (FLN) in Algeria, or the *Mau Mau* in Kenya. In Namibia and the Republic of South Africa, similar but not identical struggles are being waged.

Besides the colonial complex, a different complex of movements draws its inspiration primarily from ideological convictions. Such movements have almost invariably failed to win power, although they have brought about the collapse of democratic government, and in Latin America sometimes provoked right-wing military dictatorships. For a time, during the 1960s, it appeared they might indeed pose a serious revolutionary challenge, but even in the wake of Fidel Castro's victory in Cuba none took power.

Still other groups have sprung up to challenge the authority of central government, seeking for ethnic reasons a greater degree of regional autonomy or even to win complete independence for a region. The Third World has been affected by this phenomenon, as have industrialised states such as Canada and Spain. In the absence of major wars which galvanise a greater nationalism, separatism appears to engage the loyalty and enthusiasm of an increasing number of minorities.

Often enough, dictatorship of the right or of the left has caused men to seek freedom abroad from the tyranny of authoritarian or totalitarian rule. On occasions the more militant in exile have set up organisations dedicated to overturning the home government. These may embark on political violence and even receive the support of either neighbouring states which see in the destruction or weakening of a neighbour their own advantage, or of countries which, pursuing an expansion of their own influence, are sympathetic to the organisation's ideological stance. In such cases these organisations are found in the Directory if they are of more than a transitory nature.

Within some industrial societies — Italy, for instance — weak democratic government has given rise to a truly astonishing number of miniscule groups, many of which practise terrorism on the streets. So it was in Paris during and after the heady days of 1968, when Europe underwent its student revolution. Since those involved act under a variety of names, such *groupuscules* have not been included in the Directory. Only substantial organisations, like the Red Brigades, which have stood the test of time, appear.

Violent seizure of political power comes in many forms. There is no place in this Directory for the movements or organisations set up by military officers before or after they have attempted a *coup d'état*, nor is there any record of Marxist-Leninist political parties as such. Those that have been included are listed because they have waged a violent political campaign over a period of time and on a level to warrant more than the occasional attention of the security forces.

The Directory is divided into seven geographical regions, each with a short introduction that explains the broad political context in which violence operates. Then, under the country in which they operate, or in which they aim to seize power, guerrilla movements and terrorist groups appear alphabetically. Each country has a brief introductory explanation of the specific political context relating to violence. For readers at a loss as to which country the group operates in, an index of movements in their original language as well as in English appears at the back of the book. For ease of reference I have also included an alphabetical list of the more widely used acronyms.

Care has been taken to render the original language most properly into English — where this conflicted with established usage, in the interest of reducing ambiguity I have preferred the accustomed form. The group appears in English unless the overwhelmingly accepted usage in the English-speaking world is in the original tongue. Thus Colonel Grivas' movement in Cyprus is listed as EOKA and not as the National Organisation of Cypriot Fighters.

My long-standing colleague Richard Sim undertook the research for the South Asian and Far Eastern sections of the Directory, for which I am grateful. Other friends whom I should like to thank include James Anderson, Claude Eichhorn, Hans Horchem, Brian Jenkins, Abbas Kelidar and Paul Wilkinson. Throughout the preparation of the manuscript the research department of Control Risks in London provided a highly stimulating and friendly intellectual environment. Especial thanks go to Debbie Sherrin and Sharon Cheal, on whom so much depended.

EUROPE

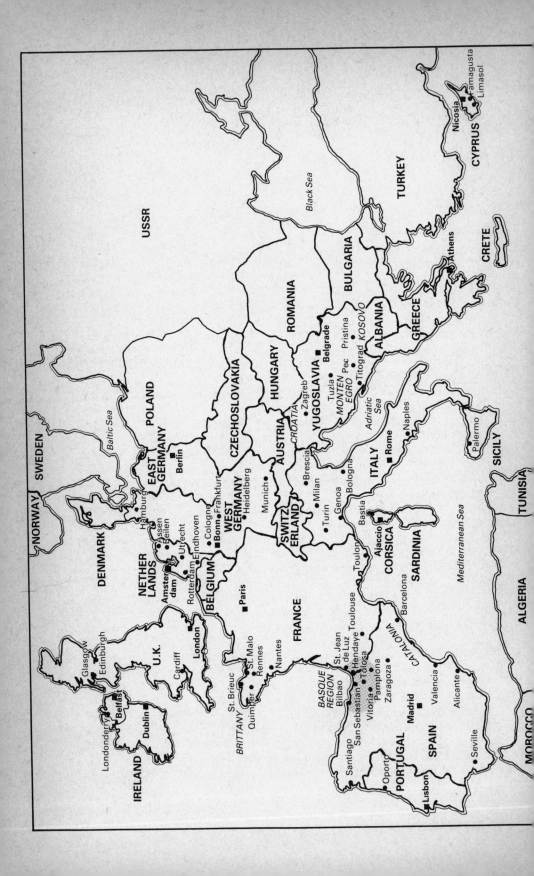

Introduction

In Europe over the last 20 years two over-riding issues have compelled men, rightly or wrongly, to commit acts of terrorism against the state and the law of the land in pursuit of political and social aims. The first was nationalism, a thing of the heart, the second was an ultra-leftist chimera, a thing of the brain.

The nationalism of ethnic minorities has posed the greater threat. Europe witnessed acts of terrorism motivated by Scottish nationalism, Welsh nationalism, Ulster nationalism, Irish nationalism, Breton nationalism, Corsican nationalism, Basque nationalism, Catalan nationalism, Flemish nationalism, Albanian nationalism, and from outside Europe the continent has suffered terrorist acts from frustrated Palestinian, Croat and Armenian nationalism. Some of these campaigns have proved more intransigent and resistant to political amelioration than others — those that seemed likely to persist virulently into the mid-1980s were the Irish, the Basque, and the Corsican.

What strikes the eye from this list is that three great and historic nations, Britain, France and Spain, have had to face similar problems, albeit in varying degrees of severity. Although other motives lay behind the acts of other indigenous terrorist groups in these countries, insofar as the state had been challenged by terrorism the most serious threat undoubtedly emanated from nationalism.

Of secondary import, so far as terrorist acts were concerned, was terrorism arising from ultra-leftist ideological motivation — that which inspired the Angry Brigade in Britain, the Patriotic Anti-Fascist Revolutionary Front (FRAP) in Spain or the ultra-leftist *groupuscules* of a Trotskyist or Maoist persuasion in France.

But in the two other great nation states of Western Europe, Italy and Germany, although in the case of the Federal Republic it is of course regrettably a divided nation, the reverse is true. The primary terrorist problem arose from political motivation of an ultra-leftist variety, which did not concern itself with nationalism. It found expression in the Red Army Faction and the Italian Red Brigades. The secondary problem was indeed nationalistically motivated, although not in the particularistic fashion of Bavarian separatism or South Tyrolean separatism in Alto Adige, but in the ultra-patriotic form of neo-fascism.

Britain, France and Spain all suffered from terrorist acts of the neo-fascist ultra-right, but only to a tertiary degree of importance. Of course the incidence of terrorist acts from any of these sources did not at all reflect the political importance which they enjoyed: indeed the inverse order more frequently applied. For instance, the leftist *groupuscules* in France were hardly involved in terrorist acts in the 1960s and yet contributed greatly to the major events of 1968. Spain lay in greater danger from a right-wing coup than it did from Freedom for the Basque Homeland (ETA) bombing the Basque country into independence.

None of these terrorist campaigns, neither the amateur revolutionary ambitions of the Angry Brigade, nor the ruthless and privately disenchanted bitterness of members of the Red Army Faction (RAF), nor the hard core of the Irish Republican Army (IRA), nor ETA, nor the Red Brigades came remotely near to achieving their designs.

Equally clear from the most cursory glance at the European map of political violence is the unclouded tranquillity of Scandinavia and the communist countries of Eastern Europe. In Denmark, Norway, Sweden and Finland an ethnic and religious homogeneity prevails; that in itself reduced the potential for conflict. Democratic socialism furthermore provided for the welfare of all, reducing the inequalities of class and profession, which elsewhere in Europe prompted a handful of men to embrace revolutionary solutions to social disparity. Only occasionally did the actions of foreign terrorist groups disturb Scandinavian peace. Yet the outlook for the 1980s suggested that environmental issues, and particularly that of nuclear power, possibly exploited by ultra-leftist activists from abroad, could bring about the extension to northern Europe of at least violent demonstrations, and at worst sabotage.

Political violence in the Soviet bloc is not dealt with in this directory. It goes without saying that the great national uprisings against Soviet hegemony in 1956 (Hungary), in 1968 (Czechoslovakia) and in 1981 (Poland) exhibited the most serious political violence in all of Europe. It was equally apparent that the Soviet Union was by the 1980s losing its freedom of action to intervene militarily: Poland's problems were not such as could be rectified by Soviet military force. As the traditional methods of Soviet control became obsolete and Moscow's capacity to devise new ones was in doubt, for the system lacked political imagination and flexibility, the post-Second World War Soviet empire began to crumble. Under these circumstances there were indications that Eastern Europe would increasingly suffer from acts of terrorism against the state. Furthermore, it appeared unlikely that in its present form Marxism-Leninism within the Soviet Union would for much longer be able to contain the mounting pressures from nationalist sentiment, from the yearning for spiritual nourishment, Christian and Islamic, and for the right to participate in political decision-making. If these forces, which contribute powerfully to the current of political movement, continue to be capped rather than canalised, the Soviet Union too can expect to suffer from the whole spectrum of political violence.

Bibliography

Behind all political violence lies a motivation. On the left, Leszek Kolakowski definitively described the breakdown of Marxism-Leninism in Vol. 111 of *The Main Currents of Marxism* (Oxford, 1978). The attitudes and composition of European communist parties are found in Neil McInnes' brilliantly brief *The Communist Parties of Western Europe* (London, 1975); on the Trotskyists, see Pierre Frank's *The Fourth International* (London, 1979), which takes account of the upheavals of 1968.

On the right, Stanley Payne's introductory *Fascism* (Wisconsin, 1980) can be followed by *Fascism: A Reader's Guide* (Penguin, 1979) edited by Walter Laqueur. Paul Wilkinson considered contemporary ultra-rightist violence in *The New Fascists* (London, 1981). For anarchism, the two classic introductions are George Woodcock's *Anarchism* (Penguin, 1979) and James Joll's *The Anarchists* (London, 1964). See also *The Anarchist Reader* (London, 1977) edited by George Woodcock. Kenneth Minogue wrote on *Nationalism* (London, 1977). E.J. Hobsbawm's *Revolutionaries* (London, 1977) contains fascinating essays on communists and anarchists, but also on violent politics. More generally, see Hannah Arendt *On Revolution* (London, 1964).

A judicious selection of basic texts can be found in Walter Laqueur's two anthologies *The Guerrilla Reader* (London, 1978) and *The Terrorism Reader* (London, 1975), which he published after *Guerrilla* (London, 1976) and *Terrorism* (London, 1977). See also the texts selected by S. Sarkesian in *Revolutionary Guerrilla Warfare* (Chicago, 1973). For an overview of terrorism in Germany, France, Italy, Netherlands, and Northern Ireland, see Juliet Lodge *Terrorism: A Challenge to the State* (Oxford, 1981). For separatism, see *Nations without a State* (New York, 1980) edited by Charles Foster. Paul Wilkinson defined the subject in *Political Terrorism* (London, 1974) and considered the West's reaction in *Terrorism and the Liberal State* (London, 1977). See also Alona Evans and J. Murphy (eds.) *Legal Aspects of International Terrorism* (Lexington, 1978) and Robert Friedlander's *Terrorism: Documents of International and Local Control* (New York, 1979).

On the psychological and social dimensions of violence, see Eugene Walter *Terror and Resistance* (New York and Oxford, 1969) and, at a popular level based upon interviews, Gerald McKnight *The Mind of the Terrorist* (London, 1974). For hijacking, see Peter Clyne *An Anatomy of Skyjacking,* (London, 1973), which considers three Arab hijackers, and David Hubbard *The Skyjacker* (New York, 1971), a profile of 16 American hijackers. Hostage taking has been examined by Caroline Moorehead in *Fortune's Hostages: Kidnapping in the World Today* (London, 1980), by Richard Clutterbuck in *Kidnap and Ransom* (London, 1978), and by Carol Baumann *Diplomatic Kidnappings — A Revolutionary Tactic of Urban Terrorism* (The Hague, 1973). For weaponry, see *The Weapons of Terror* (London, 1979) by the journalists Christopher Dobson and Ronald Payne.

The question of terrorism affecting nuclear facilities was given excellent consideration by M. Willrich and T.B. Taylor in *Nuclear Theft: Risks and Safeguards* (Cambridge, Mass., 1974) and by R.W. Mengel, H. Greisman, P.A. Karber, G.S. Newman, E. Novotny, and A.G. Whitley in *Analysis of the Terrorist Threat to the Commercial Nuclear Industry* (Vienna, 1975). Mengel published *Terrorism and New Technologies of Destruction: An Overview of the Potential Risk* (Vienna) the following year. See also A.R. Norton and M.H. Greenberg *Studies in Nuclear Terrorism* (New York, 1979) and Bernard Feld's paper 'Nuclear Violence at the Non-Governmental Level' in D. Carlton and C. Schaerf (eds.) *Contemporary Terror* (London, 1981).

The facts of contemporary terrorism can be found in the Facts on File publication *Political Terrorism* Vols I and II (Oxford, 1975 and 1978) edited by Lester Sobel, in the *Annual of Power and Conflict* (ISC, London) from 1976 to 1982, and in the chronologies of Brian Jenkins published by the Rand Corporation, Santa Monica, USA. Well researched articles on terrorism can be found in all issues of Yonah Alexander's quarterly journal *Terrorism* (Crane Russak, New York) from 1977, and on political violence in George Tanham's journal *Conflict* from the same publisher.

Cyprus

The violent hostility of two communities — Greek (80 per cent) and Turkish (20 per cent) — which caused the present division of the island by Turkish military intervention in 1974 arose from EOKA's campaign in the mid-1950s for union with Greece (*enosis*). True, EOKA's leader, George Grivas (1900-74), did his best to focus Greek attention upon British rule rather than upon the minority population, but the nationalist stimulus led in June 1958 to serious outbreaks of communal strife.

Such hostilities were in the minds of those who drafted the new republic's constitution, which with care safeguarded minority rights. In 1960 Archbishop Makarios (1913-77), the Greek Cypriot nationalist leader, became president, but there was a Turkish Cypriot vice-president with powers of veto. From the start the two ethnic groups disputed the integration of the armed forces, the composition of the civil service, the municipal system, taxation and expenditure. By late 1963 the quarrels were accompanied by violence in the streets, which escalated to civil war the following year, when both Greek and Turkish governments clandestinely supplied their compatriots with arms, thereby promoting the growth of irregular armed forces. To control the conflict the Cyprus government asked for a United Nations peacekeeping force (7000), which arrived in May 1964.

Two months later General Grivas returned to Cyprus from Greece in the hope of imposing some order upon the violent armed factions that opposed the Cypriot government. He was given control of the National Guard and also commanded a number of Greek volunteers from the mainland. Suspicion and distrust marked the new relationship between Grivas and Makarios. Nor did the general's presence do anything to revive the confidence of the Turkish community, which in December 1967 established its own *de facto* government. Meanwhile, UN troops remained on the island.

Following a dreadful massacre of Turkish civilians in November 1967, Grivas, disgraced, was recalled to Greece. Thereafter Greek Cypriot nationalist elements organised themselves in terrorist bands in the National Front, which in 1969 embarked on terrorism to achieve union with Greece. Politically they achieved nothing, for when elections were held in July 1970 in the Greek part of the island, only one candidate favouring union with Greece was returned. A year later Grivas, who still cherished his dream of *enosis*, returned secretly, established contact with the National Front and set about reorganising EOKA-B, as it became known. The new guerrilla force attacked the government of President Makarios.

Makarios condemned violence as a means of achieving union with Greece, fearful that it would provoke a Turkish military reaction. In this he was supported by Athens. When put to the vote, he and his policy were supported by the majority of Greek Cypriots in presidential elections in February 1973. Throughout the rest of the year he contended with bombs set off by Grivas's supporters, in fact until the old man died in January 1974. In a gesture of reconciliation Makarios then released 100 of his supporters from jail.

Still the old antagonisms survived, and, with Greek backing, a military coup forced Makarios to leave hurriedly, if briefly, for London in July. The take-over provoked a Turkish military intervention which effectively partitioned the island. The occupation of the north caused many Greeks to leave their homes and to become refugees in the remaining Greek sector of the island. Three years later Makarios died and was succeeded by President Kyprianou. Thereafter, rather than along nationalist lines, Greek Cypriot politics divided between left and right, and the island remained divided.

Bibliography

The editor of the *Cyprus Times*, Charles Foley, published his critical observations of the Cypriot conflict in *Island in Revolt* (London, 1962) and *Legacy of Strife* (London, 1964). For an informed synopsis of later events, see Kenneth Mackenzie, editor of the *Cyprus Mail*, *Cyprus: The Ideological Crucible* (ISC, London, 1972). The whole story of Cypriot independence is recounted around the life of *Makarios* (London, 1981) by Stanley Mayes. On EOKA, *The Memoirs of General Grivas* (New York, 1964) and *Guerrilla Warfare and Eoka's Struggle* (London, 1964) by George Grivas himself are essential. Three further books might be recommended, W. Byford Jones *Grivas and the Story of EOKA* (London, 1959), Robert Stephens *Cyprus — A Place of Arms* (London, 1966) and Doros Alastos *Cyprus Guerrilla — Grivas, Makarios and the British* (London, 1960). See also Frank Kitson's *Bunch of Five* (London, 1977).

Ethniki Organosis Kyprion Agoniston — EOKA
(National Organisation of Cypriot Fighters)

In 1951 George Grivas (b.1900) determined upon armed struggle to oust the British from Cyprus and to bring union (*enosis*) with Greece. His vehicle was EOKA, a nationalist organisation which specifically rejected all contact with Marxist-Leninist organisations or governments.

Grivas spent several years in preparations before arriving on the island in 1954, prior to launching his guerrilla campaign in April 1955. At the time EOKA numbered no more than 200 activists, who sabotaged government offices and buildings, but who also simultaneously under-took rural actions. The Greek population (80 per cent) solidly supported the organisation, whose members, although ruthless in taking revenge upon informers, behaved with the utmost correctness towards local people.

EOKA activity, whilst not reaching the level of civil war in 1955, caused the British government that year to seek a political compromise through talks with the Greek nationalist leader, Archbishop Makarios. They were broken off in February 1956 and the British deported the Archbishop to the Seychelles Islands. Thenceforth EOKA had to contend with a new military governor, Field Marshal Sir John Harding, who concentrated his efforts upon a military solution to the conflict. He disposed of 5000 police and 25,000 troops against some 300 hard-core EOKA activists who were helped by 750 armed sympathisers in the villages.

EOKA organised the population through first showering them with leaflets and then addressing rural villages through loudspeakers at night. Later a clandestine youth organisation (ANE) and a covert civilian front (PEKA) were set up, but the Greek population gave its support willingly enough, since it had long desired union with Greece.

By the end of 1956 EOKA was able at its height to carry out 416 terrorist incidents in one month. This relatively high incidence continued into 1957, although in so exposing its members EOKA suffered a relatively heavy toll in deaths — 60 in the first three months of the year. It then offered a truce in return for Makarios' release, which the British accepted although the Archbishop was not allowed to return to Cyprus: he resided in Athens.

Towards the end of the year and into 1958 EOKA engaged in sporadic actions, but by this time the Turkish population (20 per cent) of the island had organised itself to resist union with Greece, making independence or partition the only practical political alternative to British rule. With civil war between the communities a real possibility, EOKA was com-pelled to give up its political pretensions of union with Greece and accept in 1959 the course leading to independence in 1960. Grivas disbanded EOKA, and turning in his arms withdrew to Greece, where he became a national hero.

Ethniki Organosis Kyprion Agoniston -B — EOKA-B
(National Organisation of Cypriot Fighters)

General Grivas reactivated a guerrilla force in Cyprus in September 1971, when he returned secretly from Greece to give support to the terrorist activities of the National Front. He used a network identical to the original EOKA organisation. His followers, knitted together in under-ground cells, professed an absolute devotion to Grivas. They penetrated the National Guard and the police, and in all may have numbered 3000. For arms they raided police stations and gunsmiths, and for explosives turned to local quarries.

Thus equipped, EOKA-B embarked upon a campaign of terrorism in response to the presidential elections of February 1973, when President Makarios was returned unopposed and with majority support. Hitherto Grivas had worked primarily through a loosely knit organisation — the Committee for the Coordination of the Enosis Struggle (ESEA); henceforth he turned to violence in a fashion similar to his earlier campaign in the 1950s.

To reinforce its political demands EOKA-B kidnapped Cristos Vakis, the Cypriot minister of justice, in July 1973, but the tactic backfired: public disapproval led Grivas within a month to release Vakis. Grivas was concerned that no one should die in the campaign, but there was no certainty that accidental deaths would not occur from the bombings, which targeted government and administrative buildings. In police raids plans were certainly discovered to assassinate the president, but Grivas and his second-in-command, Georghios Karousos, eluded all attempts at capture.

EOKA-B survived the death from a heart attack of its founder in January 1974. It had infiltrated the island's administration, or, at least, members of the administration had approached EOKA-B for membership. Influential leaders of the Greek establishment also favoured the movement. Karousos, who inherited the leadership, returned to Greece, leaving the organisation in the hands of Greek mainland officers stationed in Cyprus. EOKA-B thus played a crucial role in the coup of 15 July, when Makarios was temporarily ousted from power. Nicos Sampson, a former EOKA terrorist who had joined EOKA-B, became at Greek instigation a short-lived (eight-day) president, but he was subsequently arrested for his role and jailed in 1976 for 20 years.

No other figure emerged as leader: the organisation became a factor of diminishing importance, involved from time to time in armed clashes with the Makarios government. At the time, fears were expressed that it might develop an offensive terrorist capacity aimed against Turkish occupation of northern Cyprus. Such a development never materialised. A few dozen activists were imprisoned for terrorist offensives, the memory of Grivas faded, and finally in early 1978 the group announced its dissolution, but not before attempting unsuccessfully to achieve their colleagues' release from jail by kidnapping the president's son in December 1977.

National Front
(Ethniki Parataxis)

A militant Greek-Cypriot nationalist organisation, the National Front was active in the island in 1969. Through terrorism and political violence it sought to impose union with Greece upon the Cypriot people, as EOKA had done before it. Members raided police posts for arms and bombed not only Cypriot targets, but British military buildings and vehicles attached to the British bases on the island. It shot and wounded the Cyprus police chief, and in March 1970 attempted to assassinate President Makarios. Other ministers had been targeted for bomb attacks. The National Front's campaign was not supported by the Greek government. The organisation was overtaken by the arrival in Cyprus of General Grivas, who promptly organised EOKA-B, which succeeded the Front.

Federal Republic of Germany

Despite the past, post-Second World War Germany has not been as seriously disturbed by ultra-rightist violence as by ultra-leftist activity. Indeed, neo-fascism had a stronger appeal in Italy and Spain than it did in the Federal Republic. Not surprisingly, nostalgia for the past lived on in the minds of a high percentage of the older population, but it was given no political expression. Young people in general were not attracted to the German National Democratic Party (NPD), which dwindled from an initial fringe popularity in the 1960s to a rump of a few thousand fractious members in the 1980s. As the party declined its leaders tried hard to prove its democratic credentials but by so doing alienated its younger members, who in small numbers took to violence, adopting an extravagant political stance of their own.

More substantial, and of greater sociological interest, was the emergence of a new left among young people, who contributed to a fundamental change of attitudes in the late 1960s. Ideologically the attraction was heterodox, ranging from anarchism to alternative Marxism-Leninism, derivatives of orthodox collectivist dogma. Life-style played as important a part as intellectual enquiry. Most representative of this new and essentially amoral order were Red Army Faction members Andreas Baader (1943-77) and Ulrike Meinhof (1934-76), both of whom committed suicide in jail. They had emerged from the student revolution of the late 1960s, best characterised by the international activities of Rudi Dutschke.

Whilst in terms of numbers the RAF core could be counted on fingers, a wider band of support ensured recruits to it and to the Second of June Movement and the Revolutionary Cells, which developed a little later. There were signs in the 1980s that the new generation of terrorists, demoralised by the complete lack of success in making any political impact, had reached a point where they would happily renounce a life on the run.

The existence of a terrorist phenomenon in the midst of the material satisfaction which the liberal Federal Republic provided for its citizens caused Germans to think hard and deeply about the nature of their democracy. It led them also to develop highly skilled responses, which contributed to containing the terrorist problem.

In addition to indigenous German groups, society was plagued by extremist in-fighting among the large numbers of foreign guest workers, in whose midst exiled separatists and leftists of every variation at-

tempted to recruit for their respective causes back home. These groups,
where they engaged in political violence, are described under their
countries of origin, which include Turkey, Italy, Yugoslavia, Spain and
Portugal.

Bibliography

In English the German terrorist problem was analysed by Jillian Becker in
Hitler's Children: The Story of the Baader Meinhof Terrorist Gang (London,
1978). See also her essays in *Contemporary Terror* (London, 1981) edited
by David Carlton and Carlo Schaerf, and in *British Perspectives on Terrorism* (London, 1981) edited by P. Wilkinson.A Second of June Movement
member, Michael Baumann, translated his *Terror or Love: Bommi Baumann's Story of his life as a West German Urban Guerrilla* (New York, 1979).
Of greater interest are the memoirs of Hans Joachim Klein *Rückkehr in die
Menschlichkeit* (Hamburg, 1979). Hans J. Horchem provided a short
analysis in *West Germany's Red Army Anarchists* (ISC, London, 1974) and
a year later in the same Conflict Studies series analysed the ultra-right in
Right Wing Extremism in Western Germany. Melvyn J. Lasky wrote a
purposeful essay in June 1975 in *Encounter*, 'Ulrike Meinhof and the
Baader Meinhof Gang'.

The German Ministry of the Interior in Bonn published the handiest
documentary evidence, *Dokumentation über Aktivitäten anarchistischer
Gewalttäter in der Bundesrepublik Deutschland*. For the Schleyer case, see
*Dokumentation zu den Ereignissen und Entscheidungen im Zusammenhang
mit der Entführung von Hanns Martin Schleyer und der Lufthansa Maschine
'Landshut'* (Bonn, 1977). Klaus Croissant, the defending lawyer, pub-
lished *A propos du procès Baader Meinhof Fraction Armée Rouge: La torture
dans les prisons en RFA* (Paris, 1975), a frankly polemical account. Of
greater interest is Daniel Cohn Bendit and Heinrich Böll, *Tupamaros
Berlin Ouest* (Munich, 1975). O. Rammstedt also compared and con-
trasted the RAF with the Tupamaros and the Brazilian followers of
Marighella in 'Stadtguerilla und soziale Bewegung' in J. Niezing (ed.)
*Urban Guerrilla — Studies on the Theory, Strategy and Practice of Political
Violence in Modern Societies* (Rotterdam, 1974). A. Stumper analysed RAF
motivation in 'Considérations à propos de l'affaire Baader Meinhof' in
Revue de Droit Pénal et de Criminologie (October, 1973). See also R. Rauball
(ed.) *Die Baader-Meinhof-Gruppe* (Berlin, 1973).

There are three outstanding books in German which deal with the
problem of terrorism generally in that country, *Terrorismus* (Bonn, 1978)
by the SPD spokesman and former mayor of Berlin, Sepp Binder, the
more detailed *Terrorismus* (Munich, 1977) by the respected TV journalist,
Frans Woerdemann, and the collection of essays in Manfred Funke's
Terrorismus (Düsseldorf, 1977). On combatting terrorism, see Josef Aug-
stein and others in *Terrorismus contra Rechtsstaat* (Darmstadt,
1976).

Black Cells
(Schwarze Zellen)

Black cells were formed in 1970/71 in Berlin by young students and working people who had adopted anarchism as their political credo. They believed in the possibility of establishing a society without the framework of a state, and defended passionately the unlimited freedom of the individual. Through their publications *883* and *Fizz* they openly propagated violence and displayed solidarity with the Red Army Faction. Membership amounted to no more than a hundred sympathisers.

Black Help
(Schwarze Hilfe)

The name was taken in the early 1970s by groups of German anarchists who worked alongside Red Help, in the hope of winning converts to the anarchist cause from the Red Army Faction. They did not succeed: the new wave of terrorists sprang from a different tradition from that of historic anarchism.

German Action Groups
(Deutsche Aktionsgruppen — DA)

The DA was the first ultra-rightist group to cause death, when in 1980 militants set alight a Hamburg hostel for foreigners. Two Vietnamese died. Foreign workers were a target for the German neo-Nazis, a handful of whom looked to a former lawyer, Manfred Roeder (b. 1930), for leadership. In 1978 Roeder was jailed for incitement; he subsequently spent a period abroad, before his arrest in 1980 and subsequent sentencing to 13 years' imprisonment in June 1982. His two colleagues, Raymond Hörnle and Sybille Vorderbrugge, were sentenced to life imprisonment, the first neo-Nazis to be so punished.

German Empire Party
(Deutsche Reichspartei — DRP)

Founded in 1946, the DRP remained until 1964 the principal ultra-conservative party in the Federal Republic, where its main following was in Lower Saxony. The British authorities disliked its National Socialist programme, and on more than one occasion intervened in DRP activities.

In the 1953 Federal Parliamentary elections it won 1.1 per cent of the votes. In state elections it won 3.8 per cent in Lower Saxony in 1955, and 5.1 in Rhineland Palatinate in 1959. In 1963 support dwindled to 1.5 per cent in Lower Saxony and 3.2 per cent in Rhineland Palatinate. Adolf von Thadden was the party's chairman. In 1964 von Thadden contributed to the founding of the National Democratic Party of Germany (NPD), which assumed the role of spokesman for the far right. In 1967 he became chairman, a post he was forced to relinquish in 1971.

German Socialist Student Association
(Sozialistischer Deutscher Studentenbund — SDS)

The SDS which cut in 1961 all its original links with the Socialist Party (SPD) rose to prominence at the Free University of West Berlin in the mid-1960s. Although representing only a small minority of students, the ultra-left SDS promoted the struggle to reform university education in West Germany. Led by Rudi Dutschke, SDS students were behind serious rioting in 1967, when the Shah of Iran visited Berlin. The death of one student, shot by police in the demonstration, transformed the situation into a nation-wide student revolt, which included high-school children. In March 1968 in West Berlin Dutschke was himself shot in the head by a young worker and did not recover his full faculties. For a while he lived in Denmark, but died of an accident in December 1979.

For a brief period in the 1960s SDS militants radicalised not only German student politics, promoting them to a front-line position, but exported overseas ugly examples of riot exploitation. At a meeting called by the Vietnam Solidarity Campaign in Grosvenor Square, London, on 17 March 1968, an SDS contingent supported Tariq Ali's International Marxist Group, organiser of the demonstration. On that occasion tactics were used in the crowd which had not been seen in Britain before, but which characterised German street politics of the period. One man died in Grosvenor Square, outside the US Embassy.

Guerilla Diffusa — GD
(Guerrilla Dispersion)

GD was first heard of in West Germany in 1981. Its members consisted for the most part of young people, many of them teenagers, who had opted into the squatting communities of the larger West German cities. They were particularly active in West Berlin and Frankfurt. GD was more a name given to an attitude of mind than an organisation. Sympathisers were characterised by an interest in ecology, opposition to the development of nuclear power, the practice of an alternative life-style and a shared hostility towards the establishment in general. They formed a pool which new Revolutionary Cells developed in the early 1980s.

Holger Meins Commando

Holger Meins (b.1941) died from the effects of a hunger strike on 9 November 1974 in Wittlich jail, West Germany, after his conviction for terrorist crimes as a member of the Baader Meinhof gang. His death caused many students to demonstrate and led to a Red Army Faction terrorist unit adopting his name.

Members exploded a number of bombs, but the most tragic event was the seizure of 12 hostages, including the Ambassador, in the West German Embassy in Stockholm in April 1975. The six terrorists demanded the release from prison of Baader, Meinhof and Ensslin. They murdered two hostages before accidentally blowing themselves up. No further hostages died, but one terrorist was killed and another died in hospital. The rest stood trial, were convicted and sentenced to imprisonment.

National Socialist Common Action Group
(Aktionsgemeinschaft Nationaler Sozialisten — ANS)

Members of the ANS seem first to have come together in 1977, carrying out a series of arms thefts and robberies. Its leader then was Michael Kühnen, a former army lieutenant, who was arrested in 1978. Thereafter Christian Worch took a leading role until his arrest on bombing charges in March 1980.

People's Socialist Movement of Germany/Workers' Party
(Volkssozialistische Bewegung Deutschlands/Partei der Arbeit — VSBD-PdA)

An ultra-rightist group with a Youth Front, the VSBD-PdA was declared illegal in January 1982. Friedhelm Busse led the party until his arrest following a shoot-out with police in Munich.

Red Army Faction
(Rote Armee Fraktion — RAF)

More popularly known after its founders as the Baader Meinhof Group, the original RAF was active in the Federal Republic between 1970 and 1972. Its roots however lay in the 1968 student revolt, which started in

Berlin, but spread quickly to other German universities in the West. The catalyst for the revolt was outrage at the Vietnam War; the first act was attempted arson at a Frankfurt department store on 2 April 1968.

Among those responsible were Andreas Baader (1943-77), son of a historian, and Gudrun Ensslin (1940-77), a clergyman's daughter and a graduate in philosophy and languages. Ulrike Meinhof (1934-76), daughter of an art historian and a graduate in philosophy and sociology, defended the attack in the left-wing journal *Konkret*, for which she wrote regularly. Horst Mahler (b. 1936) became Baader's lawyer.

The group at the time was merely a product of the anti-establishment student scene in which drugs played as great a part as politics. But the politics took the form of 'intervention in the revolutionary struggle', a struggle which was 'universal' and of which the RAF was but one 'faction'. Because of deep-seated hostility towards American action in Vietnam, Israeli obstinacy over Palestine, the nature of democratic law, education and government, their targets included US property, Israeli airlines, German magistrates, school buildings and administrative offices, and US targets in Germany.

Baader and Ensslin had been sentenced to three years imprisonment for the Frankfurt arson attack, but Baader jumped bail, was arrested in 1970 and weeks later rescued by Mahler and Meinhof. In the course of the escape a bystander was wounded. The RAF then went underground, financed itself through bank robberies (DM 1.7m) and embarked upon armed revolution. As Meinhof put it, 'we say the person in uniform is a pig, that is, not a human being, and thus we have to settle the matter with him. It is wrong to talk to these people at all, and shooting is taken for granted . . . '.

Despite the arrest of a dozen key members, the RAF could mount in May 1972 a series of 15 coordinated bomb explosions which killed a US officer in Frankfurt and seriously injured 38 people in Hamburg. For the first time an individual judge was singled out for attack, a tactic justified theoretically by Mahler, who argued that the revolutionary forces held officials personally responsible for actions 'hostile to the people'.

At the time the RAF could rely upon a network of some 60 sympa-thisers, who were prepared to further terrorist activity by providing throughout the Federal Republic cover, transport, medical aid, and com-munications. Stretching abroad were links to France and the Nether-lands; some contact was maintained with similarly minded individuals in Belgium, Switzerland, Italy and even Denmark. Yet within the Repub-lic the RAF was only ever the first, although the best known, of a number of politically violent new left groups. It numbered no more than a score of extremists.

Aside from notoriety, the RAF attracted attention through the theoret-ical writings of Ulrike Meinhof and Horst Mahler; intellectually weak though they are, they appealed to basically selfish and undisciplined dissidents, who discovered in them a justification for what in fact were faults in character and ethics.

The term 'Red Army' was known in Germany from the actions of a Japanese extremist group of the same name and adopted by Baader on his release from prison in May 1970. Meinhof explained the RAF position in a November 1971 letter to the North Korean Communist Party: 'The group did not split off from a previously unified movement, but was forced to work illegally because of reigning repression — it is not itself a party, but is organisationally, practically, and conceptually an essential component of a Communist Party worthy of the name.' She thereby clearly rejected Moscow and Peking, and yet continued to acknowledge some precepts of Marxism-Leninism. The group did not receive systematic training abroad, although Baader and other core members visited Jordan for this purpose in June 1970. Before such instruction could be given, King Hussein's troops had dislodged the Palestinian guerillas from their bases in heavy fighting.

In February 1973 Mahler was again imprisoned, this time for 12 years for bank robbery. Meinhof was sentenced in 1974 to eight years for complicity in attempted murder; she subsequently committed suicide in 1976. Holger Meins (33) died in prison from a hunger strike. Life sentences were passed in 1977 on Ensslin and Baader, who committed suicide once colleagues had failed to secure their release by holding to ransom Dr Hanns Martin Schleyer, head of the West German Industries Federation, and by hijacking an aircraft to Mogadishu (Somalia), where the German GSG-9 anti-terrorist unit successfully liberated 87 passengers on 18 October.

The arrest of RAF members by no means ended the agitation they so violently promoted. Most cleverly their trial proceedings were exploited by sympathising defence lawyers, who not only used every legal loophole to embarrass the state in its prosecution, but resorted to undercover strategems such as the smuggling of letters and even of weapons into and out of jail, practices which, on these matters, compelled the Republic to tighten its law.

Additionally the prisoners employed the hunger strike to arouse outside attention; in 1975 the defense lawyers, Klaus Croissant and Kurt Groenewald, founded in Paris and Hamburg an international committee for the defense of their clients. On it were included lawyers, scientists, doctors and writers from France, Belgium, Holland, Italy, Britain and the USA. In 1977 Croissant was arrested in France, extradited to West Germany, tried and imprisoned for two years. The court handed down a two-year suspended sentence on Groenewald.

RAF international links in the early days have been exaggerated. They did not train abroad, although it is true they tried. Their weapons and explosives were for the most part acquired in Germany. Having committed a crime they would travel abroad, particularly to Scandinavia, to recover and to recoup, and conceivably to plan future actions. Yet there was no coordinating centre, nor did the odd contact with members of foreign groups ever result in joint operations within the Federal Republic.

But in 1977 a new generation of adherents replaced the imprisoned founders, and a rash of brutality swept the country. It included the murders of Siegfried Buback (57), the chief federal prosecutor on 7 April, and of Hanns Martin Schleyer (62), head of the West German Industries Federation, in mid-October. Buback was murdered by submachine gun fire from a passing motor-cycle. He had been the chief prosecutor at the Stuttgart trial of the West German terrorists, amongst them Meinhof, who almost a year earlier had been found hanged in her Stuttgart prison cell. His murderer, Knut Folkerts, having been arrested in Utrecht in 1977, was sentenced in July 1980 to life imprisonment. In June 1979 militants failed to assassinate General Alexander Haig, NATO commander in Europe.

The second generation RAF terrorists displayed more careful planning, a wider variety of tactics, better logistics and greater brutality than their forebears. These people benefited not only from sympathy abroad, but active support, and yet it did not help them to survive, for many were arrested in 1978 and 1979, with a consequent decrease in terrorist activity in the 1980s. Some even became disillusioned with their past life, and, like Volker Speitel and Horst Mahler, urged their former comrades to surrender.

Those who persisted in their clandestine activities merged in June 1980 with the Second of June Movement. That year a car accident saved the life of Federal Prosecutor Kurt Rebmann, who was evidently the target of two heavily armed RAF terrorists killed in the crash on 25 July. In 1981 the RAF attempted to spearhead the opposition to an American military presence in the Federal Republic by persistently attacking US military targets. An RAF grenade attack on General Kroesen, US Army Commander in Europe, failed in September.

The descendants of the original RAF still believed that an 'armed campaign' was 'the highest form of class struggle', and that far from the working class leading it the vanguard should consist of an elitist 'revolutionary intelligence'. Yet their future was increasingly in doubt following the arrests in November 1982 of three prominent second generation members, Christian Klar (b. 1952), Adelheid Schulz (b. 1955) and Brigitte Mohnhaupt (b. 1949). Few more than a score remained on the run.

Red Help
(Rote Hilfe)

The first Red Help group appeared in 1970 in Berlin, whence it spread to Munich, Frankfurt, and in 1972 to Hamburg. A magazine of the same name was first published in December 1971. Sympathisers in all four centres lent help to the Red Army Faction.

Revolutionary Cells
(*Revolutionäre Zellen — RZ*)

Revolutionary cells have been active in West Germany since 1973. Their members aim to establish autonomously organised nuclei in factories and universities so as to build up 'revolutionary counter-power'. Several issues of their magazine, *Revolutionary Rage*, have appeared, in which they name as targets representatives of 'imperialism' and of 'Zionism'. Most of their actions have been explosive and arson attacks against buildings. Damage was caused in 1976 to a US military airbase near Frankfurt.

Members regarded terrorist attacks as part of an urban guerrilla campaign, which consisted of acts of revenge and punishment. As these multiplied, their destructive effect would, they thought, educate the people, laying thereby the basis for a 'mass perspective'.

Although arrests were made in the mid-1970s, new members came forward, so that throughout 1978-80 the cells claimed responsibility for isolated bomb attacks in Frankfurt, Berlin and the Ruhr region. On one occasion in April 1981 the group caused $500,000 worth of damage to a Cologne station, yet this was but one of several hundred attacks made against NATO military targets and against West German state organisations that year in a burst of destructive action. RZ militants remained apart from the RAF, which they criticised for elitism, emphasising instead a 'contact theory', according to which its own political violence built upon existing conflicts and exacerbated them. Unlike the RAF they did not adopt a clandestine existence with false identities, but continued their normal life whilst practising what they termed Guerrilla Dispersion tactics. In the early 1980s they may have numbered some 400 activists.

Second of June Movement
(*Bewegung 2. Juni*)

The Second of June Movement grew up in Berlin in 1971 as part of the new left anarchist scene in German universities. The core, consisting of no more than 20 young people, was drawn from the anarchist Black Cells and Black Help. The name commemorated the death on 2 June 1967 in Berlin of Benno Ohnesorg.

The group raided banks, stole cars, rented 'safe houses', which they were prepared to loan to Red Army Faction members. Their explosive attacks included a raid on the British Yacht Club in Berlin on 2 February 1972. By 1972 it was difficult to distinguish between the actions of the RAF and those of the Second of June Movement.

Following the death in prison in 1974 of Holger Meins, four Second of June Movement activists shot and killed West Berlin Chief Justice, Gunter von Drenkmann, on 10 November. Members were responsible in

1975 for kidnapping the Berlin Christian Democrat leader, Peter Lorenz, for whose release five convicted terrorists were flown to South Yemen. Horst Mahler, an RAF member, refused to be released in this manner and remained behind in prison until his release in August 1980. The trial of six members charged with the kidnapping opened in April 1978; others stood trial in February 1980.

They conceived of their armed struggle as part of a 'general resistance' to liberal democracy: their tactics were no more than bank raids, bomb attacks and kidnapping and murder, for which the majority were arrested, tried and imprisoned in the mid-1970s. Those who survived joined with the rump of the Red Army Faction in June 1980, leaving a group of some 25 people wanted for terrorist crimes.

Socialist Empire Party
(Sozialistische Reichspartei — SRP)

This group was set up in 1949 by members of the German Empire Party (DRP), which had a small ultra-conservative following in the north. The SRP revived the spirit and trappings of the National Socialist Party and by 1950 embraced some 10,000 members, most of whom were in Lower Saxony. Because of the party's intimidatory tactics, its *Reichsfront* was banned and in 1952 the party was finally dissolved. The court was of the opinion that the SRP had revived anti-semitism, opposed the multi-party political system, and preached the absolute supremacy of the state over the individual.

Socialist Patients' Collective
(Sozialistisches Patientenkollektiv — SPK)

This unusual group appeared in the German university town of Heidelberg, led by a psychiatrist, Dr Wolfgang Huber. He claimed that West German society was diseased and that only socio-revolutionary action could cure the ill. Three leading members, who were detained in 1971, were sentenced the following year to prison terms of three to four years. Their aim had been to overthrow society. Other sympathisers joined the Red Army Faction. The People's Red University Information Centre succeeded the SPK in the mid-1970s.

Union for the Protection of the Tyrol
(Tiroler Schutzbund)

In the German-speaking Tyrol region of Alto Adige in Italy, members of the *Tiroler Schutzbund* have exploded a number of bombs without loss of life to advertise the separatist or, more properly, the irredentist nature of their cause. Ethnically and geographically the region naturally forms a part of Austria rather than Italy. The population is particularly fearful of the influence on government of the Italian Communist Party (PCI), and there is little doubt that disturbances of a serious nature would arise were the PCI to come to power.

Wehrsportgruppe Hoffman
(Defence Sports Group Hoffman)

Karl Heinz Hoffman was jailed in 1981, after which the group ceased to exist. Interest lies in the intense anti-semitism of its leader, which led him in 1979 to take 15 of his followers to the Lebanon, where a faction of the Palestine Liberation Organisation (PLO) gave them training. In December 1980 Hoffman ordered the murder of a Jewish publisher in Erlangen; the henchman, Uwe Behrendt, fled to a Palestinian camp in the Near East, where he commited suicide in 1982. Those who had received training were arrested on their return to the Federal Republic.

France

The French state was never threatened by terrorism in the decade of the 1970s, nor did it appear in the early 1980s that the growing campaign for separatism on the island of Corsica would be likely to succeed in wresting independence from Paris. But it is the Corsican issue that today most troubles France. Surprisingly, such relative stability followed on the student protests of 1968, when Paris became once again for Europe the very nerve centre of revolution.

A high proportion of the Paris demonstrators was in fact secondary school children who had developed emotionally critical views of US military action in Vietnam. The ultra-left had been largely responsible for reducing the age limit of the traditionally politicised French student body; their base was at Nanterre, a huge adjunct to the University of Paris. Among the leaders was Daniel Cohn Bendit, who, after Jacques Roux in 1789, referred to himself and his followers as *enragés*.

Student protests in March about overcrowding (150,000 in Paris), about the French examination system, and about the syllabus turned swiftly in May to revolution. Three exceptionally talented young men, all in their early 20s, Alain Krivine, Marc Kravets and Jean Louis Peninou led the movement. Because Paris was the centre of French education and had many thousands of students, the numbers of demonstrators involved were at once high, and young, resistant, resourceful and swift of foot. Small but highly disciplined Trotskyist groups, supported by contingents from Germany, Italy, Belgium and Spain, provided some organisation to the spontaneity, but came nowhere near mastering the course of events. Amongst themselves they were bitterly divided.

From such a spark came a general strike, in which workers seized and occupied buildings and factories all over France. Broadcasting and television ceased for a brief moment, and amazingly the established order of a nation state broke down. The powerful French Communist Party did not seek to take advantage of these events, but rather to restore the order within which it had built its industrial base.

As in every period of social upheaval the causes were multifold, but from the disorder and the elation that together coursed along the banks of the Seine there arose on the left nothing but a minute fractionalisation of idealogically competitive *groupuscules*. Their followers and sympathisers sprang from such dissident communist (PCF) splinter groups as the Maoist *Parti Communiste Marxiste-Léniniste Français* (1967), which was banned in 1968. The conflicting views of these squabbling minorities can be followed in the pages of the weekly *L'Humanité Rouge*, which for a time was supported by Peking. The offices of this publication and of *Libération* were more likely in the mid- and late 1970s to be the object of attack from a rival left-wing faction than from the ultra-right.

To one side of the Maoist groups in France were the Trotskyists, the most well-known of which was Alain Krivine's *Ligue Communiste*. Although banned, his group continued to exist, and from December 1974 it was formalised as the *Ligue Communiste Révolutionnaire*, which published *Rouge*. The League was active in rowdy street demonstrations, where armed and helmeted members caused serious injuries to police. They refrained from outright terrorism, but were nonetheless activists, encouraging the idea of a general strike to bring down the government and so to reorder society. Yet at the same time Trotskyists tried to work inside constitutional channels by standing for both European and French elections: their influence made hardly a ripple on the waters of national or international politics.

Ultra-rightist activism never succeeded in bringing the same numbers onto the streets of Paris as did leftist activism. Militants confined their activities to the occasional attack on Soviet premises in the capital, against Arab and North African workers and against Jewish targets. French anti-semitism revived somewhat in the 1980s with a number of bomb attacks which caused fatal injuries.

In the late 1970s the ultra-left terrorist fringe in France produced a number of active *groupuscules*, of which the Armed Nuclei for Popular Autonomy (NAPAP) was perhaps the best known. The French scene was nowhere near as complicated, as confusing, or as violent as the Italian. Among the more bizarre groupings however were the Independent Unit against Work in Toulouse and the Inter-Urban Narcissi Intervention Group. More seriously motivated were the Workers' International Brigades, Revolutionary Action Coordination and, despite its name, the Offensive Group for the Radicalisation of Struggles. The left politicised the ecology movement, and the ultra-left attempted to attract environmentalists' support through violent actions by the Action Committee against Atomic Waste and the Anti-Nuclear Ecological Revolutionary Cell.

Bibliography

In *Gaullism* (London, 1972) Anthony Hartley wrote a perceptive, scholarly and entertaining account of the French political and social system which the events of May 1968 attempted to overthrow. The Trotskyists related their view of events in *Revolt in France May June 1968* from the Intercontinental Press and the Militant (New York, 1968). Two British journalists, Patrick Seale and Maureen McConville, described what they saw in *French Revolution 1968* (Penguin, 1968). From a North American academic viewpoint Bernard Brown analysed events in *Protest in Paris: Anatomy of a Revolt* (London, 1969).

The role of the PCF is discussed by Richard Johnson in *The French*

Communist Party versus the Students (London, 1972). But to understand the PCF more fully, Annie Kriegel's *The French Communists* (Chicago, 1968) is essential.

Outside the press and sympathetic local journals, French separatist movements are hard to follow. But see *Nations without a State* (New York, 1980) edited by Charles Foster, for the Bretons and Corsicans, and Peter Savigear's contribution to *Actes du Congrès sur la Formation Régionale* (Nice, 1981) and two articles in *The World Today*, September 1980, Autumn 1982. Yann Fouéré, the veteran Breton nationalist, wrote a brief *Histoire résumée du Mouvement Breton* (Quimper, 1977). For the OAS, see Paul Henissart *Wolves in the City* (New York, 1970) and *OAS Parle* (Paris, 1964) by Anne Loesch. For Direct Action, Xavier Raufer resumes briefly the background in part three of his *Terrorisme Maintenant, La France?* (Paris, 1982).

Action for the Rebirth of Corsica
(Action pour la Renaissance de la Corse — ARC)

ARC was the parent body of Corsican autonomist sentiment, led by the brothers Siméoni, Max and Edmond. Active throughout the first half of the 1970s, it never indulged in armed campaigns of violence. In August 1975, 50 ARC members faced hundreds of police in what became known as the Aléria siege, which followed an ARC Congress decision to raise the level of autonomist action to 'total revolution'.

The ARC militants were in fact local farmers armed with hunting rifles, who occupied a farmhouse in protest at the owner's alleged complicity in the adulteration of wine. When police rushed the building, two lost their lives and three were seriously injured. The incident radicalised the autonomist movement, for Dr Edmond Siméoni was taken to Paris to face charges carrying the death penalty before the Court of State Security. The Court sentenced him to a five-year prison term and banned the ARC.

The group was replaced in 1976 by a cluster of organisations — Corsican Revolutionary Action (ARC), Association of Corsican Patriots (APC) and the Corsican National Liberation Front (FLNC). Dr Siméoni was released in 1977, having served half his sentence.

Armed Nuclei for Popular Autonomy
(Noyaux Armés pour l'Autonomie Populaire — NAPAP)

NAPAP was an ultra-leftist terrorist group in France, which emerged in 1977 and consisted of pro-Maoist elements. It claimed responsibility for an attack upon the home of the prominent Gaullist minister, Alain Peyrefitte, in October 1977 and was active that summer in the strikes at the Citroën plant near Paris. By 1980 no further actions had been heard of and it was thought that militants, if still active, had joined Direct Action (AD).

Association of Corsican Patriots
(Associo di Patrioti Corsi — APC)

The APC, led by Marcel Bartoli, succeeded in January 1976 the banned Action for the Rebirth of Corsica. It remained in the early 1980s less militant than the separatist organisations on the island, such as the Corsican National Liberation Front. By 1978 most APC sympathisers had joined a new, legal, autonomist body led by Dr Edmond Siméoni, the Corsican People's Union *Unione di u Populu Corso* (UPC).

Basque Justice
(Euzkal Zuzentasuna)

This Basque nationalist group appeared briefly in the late 1970s, when over a period of three years it exploded 11 devices. Militants were motivated by growing unemployment and attacked the tourist industry for inhibiting industrialisation. On one occasion in 1979 shots were fired at the Paris-Madrid luxury express, *Puerta del Sol*.

Breton Fight
(Argad Breizh)

The veteran Breton nationalist figure, Jean Le Calvez, set up Breton Fight in 1979 to campaign on behalf of Breton autonomy. Previously Le Calvez had led the Fatherland Party *(Strollad ar Vro)*, which was founded in 1972. The new grouping published a monthly paper entitled *Combat Breton*. It did not in the 1980s promote political violence.

Breton Liberation Front
(Front de Libération de la Bretagne — FLB)

The FLB appeared in June 1966, and then exploded a number of bombs each year in Brittany outside government buildings. The campaign developed in 1968, when the FLB created what it termed an armed branch, known as the Breton Republican Army *(Armée Républicaine Bretonne — ARB)*. It claimed responsibility early that year for having stolen explosives locally and for having destroyed the police barracks car park in Saint Brieuc.

Yet come the events of May 1968 in France, the FLB chose to suspend its actions. When Paris offered national reform in the way of regionalisation, the FLB, wary of the designs of the 'nationalist, capitalist and imperialist' French state, rejected proposals for greater autonomy. The FLB would have no truck with 'statist, bureaucratic, authoritarian and imperialist socialism', which merely 'replaced private capitalism by an equally oppressive state capitalism.'

At this point (1969) the police intervened, arresting some 60 people and seizing a quantity of explosives and literature. Those who were charged appeared before the Court of State Security, and for bomb attacks in Nantes, Quimper and Saint Brieuc were sentenced to terms of imprisonment. Within months, however, most had been granted an amnesty and were released.

Bombing was resumed in November 1971 in Dinan, but still with a view to attacking buildings rather than killing people. Further explosions occurred in 1972 in Saint Malo and Rennes, the Breton capital. At this time an attempt was made to radicalise the ideology of the FLB and to turn it into a socialist movement rather than a nationalist Breton movement. The result was to split the organisation: the ideologists called themselves the FLB-National and Socialist Liberation (FLB-LNS). A handful was arrested in 1973 and little was heard of the FLB-LNS after 1975.

Meanwhile, the activists had continued to bomb administrative buildings, symbolic of the French state, but also targets such as local barracks and police stations and industrial concerns, which the group viewed as foreign enterprises. By this time the FLB-ARB had made contact with Corsican separatist bodies as well as Basque nationalists in Spain. Yet the FLB-ARB had not decided on whether to adopt separatism as a final political objective, or whether to opt merely for local autonomy. To this day the movement is still more autonomist than separatist.

During the mid-1970s the most prominent in the movement were Yann Fouéré, Yann Puillandre, Dr Gourves and a local priest, Father Le Breton. Imprisoned for a time, these men were supported by certain sections of nationalist opinion in Scotland, Ireland and Belgium (Flanders). The European Parliament took an interest in their fate, and in 1976 as a result of pressure they were released.

That year was a watershed, for in October the FLB-ARB issued a 'declaration of war': in reality it meant that bombing attacks were resumed. In the course of the campaign one member was killed planting a bomb near Dinault (Finistère). No longer could legal and peaceful methods be relied upon to 'break the economic and political power and the cultural dictatorship of the French state', but the FLB-ARB had not embarked on an 'armed people's struggle'. The indecision over ideology and over whether or not to embrace separatism caused the autonomist movement to split in 1977.

Fewer than 100 militants were active in the FLB-ARB in the late 1970s, but they were sufficient to place bombs on television and radio premises and near magistrates' offices and police stations. In 1977 some 25 attacks were made. It was by no means proven that such action increased the popularity of the FLB-ARB in Brittany, but there can be no doubt that general sympathy was lost in 1978, when two militants bombed one wing of the Palace of Versailles. They received jail sentences of 15 years each.

In desperation the group attempted to embrace the ecology movement by adopting an anti-nuclear power stance, but could do little more in 1979 than distribute tracts. Nor was the FLB-ARB in a position to resume militant action in the 1980s: most of its members were in jail.

Breton Nationalist Resistance Movement
(Mouvement de Résistance Nationaliste Bretonne — MRNB)

Set up in September 1977 the MRNB split from the autonomist Breton Liberation Front, which pursued relatively moderate political objectives, falling short of separatism. The MRNB aimed at 'total independence for Brittany and the emancipation of the Breton people by a socialist system'. Despite its intentions, it never succeeded in the late 1970s in launching a terrorist campaign, nor was it heard of in the early 1980s.

Charles Martel Club
(Club Charles Martel)

Named after the Frankish King who hammered the Arabs at Tours (732), the group sprang to prominence in 1978 with attacks on North African targets in France. The novelty lay in the name, for such sporadic attacks had occurred in France throughout the 1970s. In May 1980 similar attacks were made, at the same time as *Delta* struck and in the same locality, near Paris. The coincidence suggested the same individuals operated under different labels: there was certainly no structured organisation to these miniscule groups of the ultra-right.

Communist Youth Union, Marxist-Leninist
(Union des Jeunesses Communistes, Marxistes-Léninistes— UJC-ML)

This Maoist body was active on the streets of Paris in the events of May 1968.

Confrontation
(Faire Front)

Confrontation replaced New Order in 1973 as the principal activist ultra-rightist group in France. It was never a tightly organised or controlled group, and members confined their activities to the occasional bomb attack against Soviet-bloc targets in Paris or against ultra-leftist newspaper offices.

In electoral terms members were drawn firstly to a new party, the *Parti des Forces Nouvelles* (PFN) in 1974, and then to the *Front National* of Jean Marie le Pen. Both of these political groupings attracted the occasional violent attack on premises they occupied. A handful of younger members was active in the *Front National de la Jeunesse*, which bombed the Paris-Moscow express in April 1980.

Corsican National Liberation Front
(*Front de la Libération Nationale de la Corse — FLNC*)

With the radicalisation of Corsican autonomist sentiment in 1975, militants formed the FLNC in May 1976 to seek self-determination for the island, if necessary through the use of force. The movement attempted in 1977 to internationalise the Corsican separatist struggle by linking up with other groups in Europe, but the approaches were never fully realised.

Until his arrest in 1979 Jean Paul Roesch led the FLNC, which published a journal called *The Rebel* (U Ribellu). Bomb attacks escalated (379) on the island in 1978, but the separatists were careful not to cause death. They aimed their attacks at the holiday homes of mainlanders, and on one occasion blew up the spectacular early-twentieth-century mansion known as the Château de Fornali. The press were invited to watch as dinner guests were escorted under armed guard from the château minutes before its destruction.

The most serious FLNC attack, from the point of view of political ramifications, was that undertaken on the Solenzara air base on the island in January 1978. The installation allowed, in the words of the FLNC communiqué, 'Western imperialism to threaten the free peoples and progressive states of the Mediterranean'. According to the FLNC, it served as a base for aggression against the Palestine Liberation Organisation (PLO), and for French operations in Chad and in the Western Sahara, of which it disapproved. The international alignment and indeed the stance itself were new, and in 1979 hardened further.

The FLNC bombing campaign persisted (329) and was extended to Paris, where the Ministry of Finance and the Palais de Justice became targets. Banks in the capital and on the island suffered damage 'because they were the pillars of colonisation'. The FNLC warned, 'our people target the privileged political, military, and economic structures of the colonialist French state and in so doing fight for their liberation.' As FLNC members stood trial in June 1979 it was clear they came from a broad background of local trades, in age ranging from 23 to 44 years. To the FLNC the French state had chosen to destroy its people, whilst the group 'had chosen to liberate the nation by armed revolutionary struggle.'

The prison sentences imposed in Paris did nothing to alleviate FLNC

violence in Corsica. Costly damage continued to be inflicted on property
in the capital, on the island and in Nice; worse, the movement took
hostages in 1980, but without loss of life. Numerous bombs (463) were
exploded on the island in the course of 1980: targets on the mainland
included the Hôtel de Ville in Paris. In 1981 the movement called a truce
in April, when a dialogue was initiated with the new socialist administration. By 1982 a dissident FLNC faction had resorted once again to
bombing on the island and in Paris. Furthermore it resorted to demanding of the local French inhabitants sums of money with which to pursue
its terrorist campaign. It showed signs of adopting assassination as a
tactic, and appeared to be establishing links with other terrorist groups
in Europe.

Corsican Peasant Front for Liberation
(Front Paysan Corse de Libération — FPCL)

The FPCL grew in the early 1970s as a clandestine separatist organisation
in Corsica, more radical than the merely autonomist demands of the
Action for the Rebirth of Corsica (ARC). Appealing to fewer people, the
FPCL demanded the creation of a sovereign state of Corsica and the
withdrawal of recently established French mainland farmers. It claimed
to be a genuine national liberation movement fighting French imperialism, although it refrained from murder and assassination.

From 1976 however it exploded bombs in the Corsican towns of Bastia
and Ajaccio, and was active in the general strike promoted to coincide
with the trial in Paris of Dr Siméoni, the ARC autonomist leader, who
was jailed for five years. Many FPCL militants joined the Corsican
National Liberation Front, which became in the late 1970s the dominant
Corsican separatist group.

Corsican Revolutionary Action
(Action Révolutionnaire Corse — ARC)

The ARC succeeded the Action for the Rebirth of Corsica, when this
autonomist movement was banned by the French authorities in 1975.
ARC was set up in July 1976 and was intended 'to advance the cause of
the Corsican people'. It was not as revolutionary as its name implied and
never launched an armed campaign. Other autonomist movements,
which worked alongside ARC, were the Corsican People's Union and the
Association of Corsican Patriots.

Delta

Delta emerged in France in 1977 with a single attack. Another followed in

1978, when it claimed responsibility for the murder of Henri Curiel (63), the founder of the Egyptian Communist Party. Militants chose to attack a communist party (PCF) town council in January 1979 and again in 1980. The group was localised and consisted of no more than a handful of individuals who belonged to the political ultra-right.

Direct Action
(Action Directe — AD)

AD made its first appearance on 1 May 1979 in France. It was thought that its handful of members was drawn from two older terrorist groups, the International Revolutionary Action Groups (GARI) and the Armed Nuclei for Popular Autonomy (NAPAP).

AD perpetrated six attacks in 1979 and more than a dozen in 1980. The targets were varied and included obvious 'capitalist targets', such as the French employers' federation and the offices of the factory and labour inspectorate, as well as symbols of the state, such as a magistrates' court, a police station and the Ecole Militaire in Paris.

A communiqué issued in March 1980 by the group denounced French 'neo-colonial' actions aimed at preserving France's overseas economic interests, and specifically cited French interventionist policy in Tunisia, Chad, Djibouti and the Central African Republic. 'To struggle against French imperialist politics in Africa is to struggle against the French state in its world institutions. It is time to take up arms against the slave-making state.'

Police arrested over 20 people suspected of being involved with AD in March 1980, but the two principal figures, Jean Marc Rouillan, previously imprisoned for his activities in GARI, and Nathalie Menignon, were not arrested until mid-September 1980 after a shoot-out in Paris. The group operated in Paris, Marseilles and Toulouse for the most part. It seemed not to be short of cash, for £16,000 was reportedly discovered in one safe house in Toulon. The weaponry employed, which included bazookas and plastic explosives, was indicative of international links and a degree of training, albeit incomplete, not normally found in purely indigenous French terrorist groups. Members exhibited knowledge regarding computers, and chose computer companies as a target, especially in Toulouse, where Honeywell and Philips have offices. Such action suggested that the group was aware of the capital it could make out of armed action against computers, which arouse widespread fears, not only in radical fringe groups but in a wider public sympathetic to left-wing politics generally. Some arrests were made in 1981, but Rouillan was amnestied following the presidential elections that year. Direct Action atrocities in Paris in August 1982 were partly responsible for the sweeping changes in French security announced then.

Enbata
(Galerne, an Atlantic sea wind from the north-west)

When set up in 1953 *Enbata* was nothing more than a student association in Bordeaux, itself far from being a Basque city. Ten years later those belonging to this nationalist organisation proclaimed the Itxassou Charter, which declared that Basques were not only one people but a nation that had the right to seek its own unification and self-determination.

Yet a further decade passed before the 1972 Enbata Congress in Bayonne took up the struggle for national liberation against the Spanish and French states. Members saw parallels in the nationalist movements in Algeria, Ireland, Palestine, and Vietnam, and supported the violent campaign pursued by Basque Fatherland and Liberty (ETA) across the border in Spain. At this point when the first terrorist acts were committed, the government banned *Enbata* in January 1974.

Militants went underground and two years later began a campaign of violence which continued intermittently into the early 1980s. Bombs were invariably placed so as to avoid death until March 1980, when two members of the security forces died. Militants in this campaign acted within a variety of clandestine groups, the two most active being *Iparretarrak* and *Hordago*. *Enbata* itself did not act as a terrorist group.

European National Fasces
(Faisceaux Nationaux Européens — FNE)

This neo-fascist group adopted as its title the Latin *fasces*, a bundle of symbolic rods signifying the power of life or death, which were carried before the ruler, and which reappeared in modern European fascism in a number of guises. FNE succeeded the Federation for European National Action (FANE) in late 1980, when FANE was banned. It claimed responsibility for arson attacks against two Paris synagogues that year, and was at first suspected of the rue Copernic bombing, which subsequently turned out to have been a Palestinian attack. The leadership of FNE and indeed the membership were identical to those of FANE — Robert Petit (b. 1900) chaired the group. He had once been director of the Vichy regime's Centre for the Study of Jewish Questions.

Federation for European National Action
(Fédération d'Action Nationale Européenne — FANE)

FANE was led by Marc Fredricksen, whose ultra-rightist sympathies and involvement in political violence and terrorist acts provoked left-wing attacks against his home and eventually his own arrest in 1980. The group was held responsible for having sent several dozen death threats to Jewish citizens in France and for having exploded bombs at the premises of Jewish traders. In September 1980 the French government banned the organisation, which was estimated to have some 200 sympathisers. In January 1981 the former treasurer, Michel Caignet, suffered burns to his face in an ultra-leftist attack. FANE had been set up in 1966, one of a number of French fascist groups that included the *Mouvement Nationaliste du Progrès* (MNP), which, as a political party, had a wider following of a few hundred thousand.

French National Liberation Front
(Front de Libération Nationale Française — FLNF)

The FLNF is a right-wing group which surfaced in France in 1978. In 1980 it exploded a bomb at the Pompidou Centre in Paris. The group claimed it was anti-Jewish, anti-black and anti-Arab.

French Revolutionary Brigades
(Brigades Révolutionnaires Françaises — BRF)

Belonging to the ultra-right, the Brigades surfaced in 1982, when they kidnapped a left-wing writer, Jean-Edern Hallier, demanding in return for his release the dismissal from government of four communist ministers and of Gaston Deferre, the interior minister. A week later he was released unharmed: the ministers remained at their posts. A further incident occurred in July, when the group exploded a bomb at the Paris left-bank flat of Régis Debray, an adviser on Latin American affairs to President Mitterrand and former companion of Che Guevara. No one was hurt in the explosion.

High School Action Committee
(Comité d'Action Lycéen — CAL)

In May 1968 secondary or high school children in Paris played a principal role on the streets in the events which led to the revolution that year. They were organised through CAL, a politicised body, but one which reflected too the generation gap in attitudes between French middle-class parental aspirations and the hopes held by their sons and daughters.

Hordago
(Je Tiens)

The Basque nationalist group *Hordago*, first appeared in 1978, when, during the French prime minister's visit to the Basque country, a tourist centre was bombed. It has since been active four or five times a year in St Jean de Luz, Biarritz, and Bayonne, where official buildings were targets. The organisation calls for a halt to what it describes as cultural oppression and to the influx of summer tourists upon which so many Basques live. Six members were pardoned when socialist President Mitterand abolished the Court of State Security in 1981. It was inactive in the early 1980s.

Iparretarrak
(Those from the North)

Although set up originally in 1973, this French Basque nationalist terrorist group first turned to violence in 1976, when militants exploded three devices. Those who belonged had previously been active in *Enbata*, and ideologically were inclined to the left. By its own definition, *Iparretarrak* was a Basque revolutionary socialist national liberation organisation, enjoying close ties with the Spanish Basque Fatherland and Liberty (ETA). In *Iparretarrak* Basque nationalism was wedded to the class struggle through its underground broadsheet, *Ildo* (Furrow).

For the most part militants set off bombs no more than four or five times a year until 1981, when 12 devices exploded, although six of them occurred simultaneously in Bayonne. A tactical change came in 1982, when a police patrol was gunned down on 19 March at Saint Etienne de Baigorry, where two men died.

New Action Front against the Independence and Autonomy of Corsica
(Front d'Action Nouvelle contre l'Indépendence et l'Autonomie — FRANCIA)

The violent action of the separatist minority in Corsica, where terrorist bombing incidents steadily increased after 1975, provoked a reaction in 1978 with the emergence of a counter-force, FRANCIA. Since the local targets of the Corsican National Liberation Front (FLNC) included the homes of French Algerian *pieds noirs*, who had settled on the island in the wake of Algerian independence, many supposed that FRANCIA recruited among them. Some 40 attacks were perpetrated in 1979. Police arrested one of the movement's leaders, Yannick Leonelli, in August 1980. In the upsurge of violence in 1982 FRANCIA played no part.

New Order
(Ordre Nouveau)

An ultra-rightist group in France, New Order was set up in 1969, but was banned in June 1973 for its racialist attitudes, a measure taken in accordance with the law of 1 July 1972. New Order sympathisers felt particularly strongly about the number of immigrants, especially Arabs from North Africa, coming to France. Almost immediately after the demise of New Order, it was replaced by Confrontation.

Revolutionary Communist Youth
(Jeunesse Communiste Révolutionnaire — JCR)

In 1968 the JCR played a foremost part in the events in Paris. It was Trotskyist in orientation and remains so to this day.

Secret Army Organisation
(Organisation de l'Armée Secrète — OAS)

French settlers organised the OAS in Algeria to resist General de Gaulle's decision to negotiate Algerian independence with the National Liberation Front (FLN). On 22 April 1961, four French generals, Chalan, Zeller, Jouhaud and Chalel, seized Algiers, but the coup failed because the bulk of the French army remained loyal to the government.

There followed a terrorist campaign directed against the Algerian nationalist community and also against selected targets in France. For a short while Salan headed a National Council of French Resistance, but it failed to establish an area of influence which it could use as a base, and eventually negotiated its own demise.

Twenty-Second of March Movement
(Mouvement 22 mars)

A Paris-based student body crystallised on 22 March 1968, when students at Nanterre (Paris) protested at the arrest of five students allegedly responsible for causing explosions four days earlier at a number of US premises in Paris. Daniel Cohn Bendit, at home equally in Germany as in France, led it.

Cohn Bendit belonged to the German ultra-leftist Socialist Student Association and believed that a militant minority could initiate an irreversible change in the 'bourgeois order' by applying to it a series of shocks. Quite unlike the Trotskyists, who came to manipulate the May 1968 events, Cohn Bendit did not accept that his avant-garde should

control the course of revolution. Spontaneity should rather guide the
workers' enthusiasm. He reacted strongly and hostilely to 'established
communism'. Cohn Bendit never in fact spoke for the workers, but he
did lead the students. 'What is happening tonight on the streets is a
whole generation rising against a certain type of society.' Shortly after,
the French authorities refused Cohn Bendit the right of residence and he
returned to the Federal Republic, where he dropped from sight, overtaken by the more dramatic terrorism of the Red Army Faction.

Greece

Surprisingly, for the country tends towards political extremes, political violence in Greece has been minimal. Until the 1981 socialist electoral victory Greeks had not put behind them the horrors of civil war (1944-49), which provided a legacy of conservative rule, first under a monarchy, then a junta of colonels (1967-74) fearful of leftward drift and communist subversion, and finally a democratic republic under the veteran politician Karamanlis. In 1981 an overwhelming popular endorsement of Andreas Papandreou's Pan Hellenic Socialist Movement (PASOK) again made the left legitimate.

Within that political context terrorism has been the resort of disappointed and disillusioned extremists, either from within the military or from the extreme left. Incidents are few and have not claimed many lives, although property and government premises have suffered, particularly in Athens, from arson. Because the level of this sort of violence is so low, the interested reader can but turn to a chronology of events. No analysis of such a minor problem exists.

Bibliography
Edgar O'Ballance provided an account of the Greek Civil War in a book of that name published in London in 1966. Kenneth Matthews wrote *Memories of a Mountain War Greece 1944-49* (London, 1972), George Kousoulos *Revolution and Defeat* (London, 1965) and J.O. Iatrides *Revolt in Athens* (Princeton, 1972). On Greece's conflict with Turkey over the Aegean, see Andrew Wilson's Adelphi Paper, 'The Aegean Dispute' (IISS, London, 1980).

Autonomous Resistance
(Aftonomos Antistasi)

This ultra-leftist group carried out an attack upon a factory in Athens in 1981.

Blue Archer
(Galazios Toxotis)

This group emerged in 1981 on the far right of the Greek political spectrum, claiming responsibility for an outbreak of fires outside Athens.

Fourth of August
(4 Avgoustou)

Named after the date of the military takeover in 1936, this group was one of a number of ultra-rightist organisations active in Greece in the period following the demise of military rule in 1974. It found some support in the army, and in 1977 was suspected of favouring a coup. Nothing further was heard of it in the late 1970s, although with the election of a socialist government in 1981 the political climate favoured its revival.

National League of Greek Regular Officers
(Ethnikos   Syndesmos   Ellinon   Monimon   Axiomatikon — ESEMA)

ESEMA was one of a number of shadowy and insignificant organisations of the ultra-right to emerge in Greece in 1979. Whilst ESEMA had little support under the conservative government of Karamanlis, with the election in 1981 of a socialist administration, some recruits fearing left-wing policies were attracted to its banner.

October 80 Revolutionary Organisation
(Epanastatiki Organosi 80 Oktvri)

This small ultra-leftist terrorist group emerged in Greece in 1980, claiming responsibility for arson attacks on two Athens department stores.

Organisation for National Recovery
(Organismos Ethnikis Anorthosoos — OEA)

The group emerged in the late 1970s on the Greek ultra-right, in sympathy with the military rule of the junta (1967-74) after which it hankered. With no political support, its handful of members, consisting of disgruntled and displaced disciplinarians, was reduced to meddling with conspiracy. Nothing of substance came of such nostalgia: their 1978 Athens bombings claimed no lives, caused minimal damage and made little public impact.

People's Revolutionary Struggle
(Epanastatikos Laikos Agonas — ELA)

The group's acronym appeared on Athens' walls in 1979, claiming responsibility for a number of bombings, targeted mainly at official buildings. No loss of life ensued from its activities, which persisted into the early 1980s, despite the arrest and conviction for terrorist offences of a number of those involved, who in age ranged from their early-20s to mid-30s. It placed a bomb outside the American ambassador's residence in April 1982, and attacked US multinational companies.

Revolutionary Nucleus
(Epanastatikos Pyrenas)

This is an ultra-leftist group which carried out an isolated attack in 1981 on an Athens store.

Revolutionary Organisation 17 November
(Epanastatiki Organosi 17 Noemvri)

The organisation claimed responsibility in 1976 for the death of CIA station chief, Richard Welch (46), in Athens on 23 December 1975. Welch had first been publicly named by the US magazine *Counterspy*, published by Fifth Estate for Security Education, and run by defected CIA agents. Almost a year later it admitted to the murder of a former police officer, Evangelos Mallios, strongly suspected of having abused his powers of interrogation under the military rule of the junta (1967-74). In the leftist jargon of those days, the organisation defended its actions as 'armed and dynamic defence of the people's movement'. Its activities petered out before the more robust political growth of Greek socialism, although not before assassinating a senior police chief in January 1980.

Italy

Political violence on the streets of Italy in the early 1980s stemmed from the turbulence of 1968, the year of student revolutions throughout Europe. Italy, unlike France and Germany, never recovered from the shock the 1968 disturbances gave to institutions of all kinds, parliamentary, judicial, educational and even penal. Indeed throughout a decade and more of weak democratic government, which did not reflect weak democratic institutions, Italy suffered ongoing politically motivated terrorism, until 1983, when the movement, due to police successes and terrorist exhaustion, appeared to abate.

If measured in terms of incidents (2150 in 1979 although fewer in the early 1980s), or numbers of people involved, or even technical sophistication and brutality, Italy ranks in Europe as having the most debilitating of all terrorist problems — it is national in extent and generalised in its impact. Yet because the violence concentrates not upon specific nationalist demands, but upon necessarily vague ideological notions, Italian terrorism of the ultra-left differs in kind from the needle-eyed fanaticism displayed by Irish Republican Army supporters in Northern Ireland. Undoubtedly, it threatens the state. But terrorism is not the cause of Italy's political weakness, although it may take advantage of it.

Intellectually the roots of contemporary Italian violence lie inside Italy — nowhere else is debate on the ultra-left as fervent or as original, or as brilliant. No unity or orthodoxy prevails, rather a fractious, shifting sea of arrogantly pitted hostilities. Except perhaps in one respect, the political consequences are disastrous: the Italian Communist Party (PCI) is totally committed to fighting terrorism, furthermore, without its support democracy might be endangered.

Equally, on the extreme right, political violence is quintessentially an Italian phenomenon. Enjoying an indigenous history, to some people it is still attractive, for fascism in Italy is not disfigured by the holocaust, which makes neo-Nazism in Germany fundamentally unacceptable. In Italy the ultra-right has a snobbish attraction among a small circle of politically marginalised minor aristocracy. It attracts young people with a flair for cheap theatrical gesture and who disparage the common man.

What of stimuli from abroad? Much has been speculated, but little proven in this regard. It is true that on both extremes of the political spectrum violence stems from Italian and not foreign soil, but from contacts abroad it can be enlivened and grow. Over a period of time and on both sides contacts have been established and maintained, but the ultra-left has benefited more than the ultra-right from actual links with foreign extremist groups. In addition, red violence, as it is known, learned much from Uruguayan and Argentinian guerrilla exiles, who in the mid-1970s found asylum in Rome from the military regimes they themselves had provoked in Latin America.

The role of patron states is important to the ultra-left. Of greatest practical benefit are the training facilities available in the Middle East to prospective European terrorists provided, depending upon the year when training was undertaken, by Palestinian nationalists in the Lebanon, in Syria, in Iraq and in the People's Democratic Republic of the Yemen (South Yemen). Libya also played a role in providing arms.

Financially, foreign support is quite unnecessary: the ultra-left finances itself through kidnap and ransom operations and by demanding protection money from commercial concerns. Weapons and explosives too are for the most part stolen: some arrive via Libya and from the Near East.

A decision to escalate terrorism, however, perhaps using surface to air missiles, would require outside support. Indeed the PLO was the source of an SA-7 missile discovered in late 1979 in Rome. In future, 'crazy states' like Libya may provide them.

Contacts of the ultra-left with Eastern Europe, particularly Czecho-slovakia, and with the Soviet Union are hard but not impossible to document. There exists a feeling within certain circles of the PCI that Moscow, hostile to Enrico Berlinguer's leadership of a new-style 'Euro-communist' party, may well promote dissidence on the ultra-left to embarrass him. Yet it must be said that control of such fissiparous elements is beyond Moscow's reach, for they rely neither financially nor militarily upon the Soviet Union. Naturally, insofar as political violence from either side weakens the Italian democratic system, Moscow bene-fits: ultimately the USSR is constitutionally and ideologically bound to extend to Italy, as elsewhere, Soviet influence, and when possible the Leninist political system. Ministers, and indeed the President himself, have recorded their anxieties regarding Soviet manipulation of Italy's terrorist troubles. The Chinese have fostered such suspicions.

Earlier, Maoist groups in Italy contributed to disturbances. A pro-Peking Marxist-Leninist party (PCI-ML) was founded in 1966 under Fosco Dinucci, who maintained links with other Chinese communist splinter parties in West Germany and France. Their principal purpose was to oppose the Soviet Union, but by the late 1970s differences be-tween the PCI and Moscow were such that Peking became friendly to Berlinguer.

In the meantime other Maoist groups had proliferated, even if mini-scule in membership. They included the Organisation of (Marxist-Leninist) Communists of Italy, the Red Star Marxist-Leninist Revolu-tionary Front, the Marxist-Leninist Organisation of Italian Bolshevik Communists and the League of Marxist-Leninist Communists of Italy. More important in the mid-1970s was the confusingly named *Partito*

Comunista *(Marxista-Leninista) Italiano* (PC(M-L)I), under Aldo Brandirali, particularly active in the south. The role of all these groups was to exploit disaffection locally at a popular level and to undermine established institutions, for instance the trade unions, whenever possible. In demonstrations and direct action they frequently adopted a prominent position.

Mention should be made of the extraordinary role of the ultra-left autonomy *(autonomia)* movement in Italy, of which the Maoists formed but one element. With such bodies as Workers' Vanguard, which embraced Trotskyists as well as Stalinists, and Permanent Struggle *(Lotta Continua)*, the autonomy movement numbered more than 200,000 loosely affiliated activists, all under 40 years old. Sometimes willingly, at times unconsciously, this band of opinion lent support to political terrorism.

It would be wrong to consider Italian violence as principally a phenomenon of the extreme-left. In the early 1980s the ultra-left was preponderant, but this was not so a decade earlier. There had then been a real fear of a fascist resurgence, and there were those who planned for a fascist *coup d'état*. Indeed in the large cities the principal threat came from neo-fascist thugs, and not from the left. To meet it, President Leone called in 1973 for a strengthening of democratic institutions.

In 1974 two 'black' bombs were exploded at an anti-fascist gathering and on the Rome-Munich express. By 1975 the ultra-right Italian Social Movement (MSI) could describe the situation as 'an authentic state of civil war'. But then MSI meetings were characterised by violence, a black violence which embraced school children as much as students and industrial workers. To some extent the MSI acted upon the climate of right-wing opinion as the autonomy movement did on the left. It provided a national umbrella and a cloak of parliamentary respectability for fascist terrorism. The most infamous black group remains Black Order, the latest to surface is Armed Revolutionary Nucleus (NAR), thought responsible for the horrifying deaths of 84 people in a bomb explosion at Bologna railway station in August 1980.

Bibliography

The best documentary introduction to contemporary political violence is provided in the fascinating textual selection translated in *Italy: Autonomia* (Columbia University, New York, 1980) and edited by Sylvere Lotringer and Christian Marazzi. For the development of the Red Brigades, Vitorfranco Pisano contributed *The Red Brigades: A Challenge to Italian Democracy (Conflict Studies*, No. 120, July 1980, ISC, London). A fuller and most excellent account was given by Alessandro Silj *Never Again without a Rifle: The Origins of Italian Terrorism* (New York, 1979), see also Alberto Ronchy, 'Grass and Gray Matter: Terrorism in Italy' in *Foreign Affairs* Spring 1974 Vol 57, No.4. For terrorism of the right, see Thomas Sheehan 'Italy: Terror on the Right' in *New York Review of Books*, 22 January 1981. A full bibliography is contained in *Terrorism*, Vol 2, nos 3/4, 1979.

Otherwise the student must resort to Italian, where a proliferation of literature awaits the reader. On terrorism generally, the following can be recommended: Roberto Mazzetti, *Genesi e sviluppo del terrorismo in Italia* (Milan, 1979); Giorgio Bocca, *Il terrorismo italiano 1970/78* (Milan, 1978); Romano Cantore, *Dall'interno della guerriglia* (Milan, 1978) and Gabriele Martignon and Sergio Morandini *Il diritto all'odio dentro/fuori/ai bordi dell'area dell'autonomia* (Verona, 1977).

For the Red Brigades in particular, there is Rosso Soccorso's *Brigate Rosse* (Milan, 1976); *Br: imputazione banda armata* (Milan, 1977) by Vincenzo Tessandori, and Emilio Papa's *Il processo alle Brigate Rosse* (Turin, 1979). *'Mai piu senza fucile!' alle origini dei NAP e dell BR* (Florence, 1977) is an excellent work by Alessandro Silj dealing with the origins of the NAP. On the Moro kidnapping see Robert Katz, *Days of Wrath: The Ordeal of Aldo Moro* (New York, 1980).

On Italian neo-fascism, there is Petra Rosenbaum's *Il nuovo fascismo da salo ad almirante, storia del MSI* (Milan, 1975) and *Agenda Nera, Trent' anni di neofascismo in Italia* (Rome, 1976) by Daniele Barbieri. More generally, two useful essays on Italy can be found in *European Fascism* (London, 1968) edited by S.J. Woolf and in *Faschistische und neofaschistische Bewegungen* (Darmstadt, 1977) edited by Hans-Ulrich Thamer and Wolfgang Wipperman.

Armed Proletarian Nuclei
(Nuclei Armati Proletari — NAP)

The origins of the NAP can be found in the Italian prisons where jailed terrorists had politicised numerous common criminals. The politicisation took place at a time of general ferment in Italian society and after major uprisings in Turin and Milan jails in 1969. Further disturbances followed in the south, where a number of police and prisoners lost their lives in armed conflict. From inside, the 'movement of proletarian prisoners' attempted to link up with radical leftist groups outside, thus giving birth to NAP.

The first actions occurred in 1974, when prisoners were incited to riot in Milan, Rome and Naples jails. Those outside broadcast over loudspeakers to those inside and exploded devices in front of the prison gates. To finance the movement militants resorted to kidnapping, and to prove their political credentials attacked ultra-rightist political premises, notably those of the neo-fascist Italian Social Movement (MSI).

Before the following year was out, magistrates had become a target for NAP attacks, which were also launched against police stations. At this time the group's most notorious action was the abduction of the Rome Supreme Court Judge, Giuseppe di Gennaro, who was released once three prisoners had been transferred to the jails of their choice.

The group was still active in 1976, shooting a Rome judge in January and in March operating alongside the Red Brigades against police stations in Rome, Naples, Florence, Turin, Genoa and Pisa.

Many members were caught by police in 1977, after which the movement was largely absorbed into the Red Brigades. Among the principal organisers were Giovanni Gentile Schiavone and Domenico delli Veneri, who were imprisoned. Antonio Lo Muscio was killed and so too was Martino Zicchitella, who had escaped from prison. That year others who had escaped were recaptured, in particular Maria Pia Vianale and Franca Salerno.

Thereafter the NAP never recovered. The group was characterised by weak ideological motivation, poor security, incompetent weapons handling, indifferent training and lax morals. It probably never numbered as many as 100, and most members were only loosely attached to the organisation. Yet for all that, while it survived, it was dangerous.

Armed Revolutionary Nuclei
(Nuclei Armati Rivoluzionari — NAR)

The NAR emerged in the late 1970s as a new fascist group employing the panoply of terror used by the ultra-leftists in Italy. Two names have been prominently associated with NAR, those of Paolo Signorelli, who has been arrested three times in two years, and Aldo Semerari, allegedly the mastermind behind the fateful Bologna station bombing which killed 84 people and wounded 200 bystanders in August 1980.

NAR activists raided a Rome armoury for their weapons, although weapons are anyway easy to come by in Italy. Some at least of their number were drawn from the upper professional classes. Their tactics included for publicity exploding a bomb on the Capitoline hill and attacking left-wing radio stations in Rome. They bombed a PCI office in 1980, murdered two policemen, assassinated a deputy state prosecutor and killed a young Workers' Autonomy Group militant. They also kneecapped victims, a common device of the Red Brigades, and murdered informers. In October 1981 NAR militants shot dead two Rome policemen, and in December assassinated a Carabinieri officer. Further shootouts occurred in Rome in 1982, although it was impossible to determine the strategy behind what appeared to be no more than a violent rump.

Black Order
(Ordine Nero)

The immediate forerunner of Black Order was New Order, which had been banned in 1973 because the group was found guilty of attempting to set up a fascist party in Italy. The aims of Black Order were identical; its methods more bloody. Its neo-fascist activities were overtaken in the late 1970s by those of the Armed Revolutionary Nuclei.

Numerous bombings took place in 1974 against the premises and property of known left-wing supporters in Italian cities. Some were claimed specifically by right-wing extremist groups, and prominent on the scene were militants from Black Order. One such atrocity occurred on the Rome-Munich express near Bologna on 5 August. Twelve people died and 48 were injured by the bomb placed by Black Order. 'The Nazi flag did not die in Berlin in 1945. It still lives for a powerful Fascist and Nazi Italy. Nazism will return for the salvation of a renaissance Italy.'

Unlike left-wing groups in Italy, Black Order had no proper structure, nor did it have contacts abroad. It probably numbered some 300 loosely affiliated individuals. Like most of the ultra-right in Italy, they were psychologically more prepared than the left to resort to mass killing and indiscriminate terrorism. In some respects they were like mercenaries. They loved uniforms and thought of themselves as soldiers, although without the discipline. Black Order's military leader, Pierluigi Concutelli, was convicted in Florence in 1978 of the 1976 murder of Judge Vittorio Occorsio, who had been responsible for the dissolution of New Order in 1973.

Front Line
(Prima Linea — PL)

Front Line first surfaced in Italy in November 1976 with an attack upon Fiat in Turin. The group looked very much like a copy of the Red Brigades, until police the following year captured a group of militants, all of whom were students under 21 years of age. In the early days PL was weak on internal security and planned haphazardly.

Nonetheless, in 1977 PL chose the same targets as the brigadists — businessmen and Christian Democrat supporters, and with a view to general intimidation shot people in the leg. It came as no surprise to learn in 1978 that Corrado Alunni, a leading BR figure, was behind the growth of PL that year, nor to see it express its solidarity with the older group.

The organisation spread to the cities of Milan, Florence and Naples, where columns similar to the Red Brigades were established. There appeared to be no recognised leadership in PL; rather each unit or cell, when it operated, elected its own director for a specific operation. These terrorist acts were aimed at the state, 'to break up the enemy command network, to attack the military and political institutions of the State and to sabotage the regular functioning of the capitalist machinery.' The philosophy therefore is akin to that of the Red Brigades.

From the number of actions perpetrated by PL the group clearly had less members than the Red Brigades, possibly 100 people who were prepared to shoot to kill and to maim. Since they collaborated with brigadists it is hard to see the need for two organisations, other than to throw sand in the eyes of the security forces. Up to December 1978 it had claimed responsibility for some 25 operations. In 1979 PL increased this incidence, particularly with the murder in January of the Milan Assistant

Attorney General, Emilio Alessandrini, who was engaged upon the preparation of a data bank to control terrorism. Of outstanding boldness and cruelty was an attack by a dozen militants on the Turin School of Industrial Management, where staff and students were held hostage and a random selection made of ten people, who were shot in the leg. By the end of the year 131 PL members had been apprehended or identified by the police.

As the Red Brigades increased the number of assassinations in Italy, so too did Front Line in 1980. The targets remained the same, but with special emphasis upon intimidating the process of law: magistrates and juries who convicted terrorists were singled out for murder. From recent and slow beginnings PL had grown to present the second greatest terrorist threat in Italy. It deepened its local roots in society by adopting popular local causes, often becoming the champion of the underdog so as to build up the Robin Hood image of the Uruguayan Tupamaros. In this they differed from the Red Brigades. However these terrorist triumphs were short-lived. Front Line suffered from police actions in 1981 and in particular from the arrest and subsequent conviction for terrorist offences of Maurice Bignami. Several PL militants were extradited from France, and in July as many as 77 were convicted in Turin. A further 87 were convicted in August 1982: no PL terrorists acts were recorded that year, and with the capture in October of PL leader Suzanna Ronconi (b. 1954) in Milan the organisation appeared moribund.

Mussolini Action Squads
(Squadre d' Azione Mussolini — SAM)

These squads were active in Italy in the early 1970s and claimed responsibility for numerous bomb attacks against the premises of left-wing political parties, especially in the northern industrial cities. The squads were loosely organised and composed more of political bully boys than hardened terrorists. They did not receive the sort of terrorist training for which the left-wing later became famous.

Other groups which acted alongside the SAM were Phoenix (*La Fenice*), Year Zero (*Anno Zero*), National Vanguard (*Avanguardia Nazionale*) and Young Italy (*Giovine Italia*). Which group was responsible for the major terrorist outrage in May 1974, when a bomb was timed to explode during a public rally against fascism in Brescia (Lombardy), was not clear. But of all the groups, SAM was most active at the time. On that occasion eight people died and 95 were injured. Throughout 1975 it continued to be the right wing which provoked the bulk of the political violence on the streets of Italy. The ultra-right indulged less however in the spectacular political assassinations for which the ultra-left was becoming notorious. By 1976 ultra-leftist or red political violence had probably overtaken black violence, as it was known. Yet numerous attacks were made against PCI offices in Rome and Milan, and more than one magistrate responsible for trials of neo-fascists was murdered.

New Order
(Ordine Nuovo)

Right-wing extremism in Italy was more to the fore in the late 1960s than in the late 1970s, although a resurgence occurred in 1980. New Order, under the leadership of journalist Pino Rauti, was the most prominent group. Whilst the Italian Social Movement (MSI) was led by Arturo Michelini (d.1969) ultra-rightists were kept out of the party; under his successor, Giorgio Almirante, they crept in under the umbrella of the parliamentary party. Thenceforth New Order militants were present at MSI meetings and took a greater hand in the party's activities.

New Order was held responsible for an attempt to sabotage the Rome-Turin rail link in April 1973. It was accused of attempting to reform the Fascist party, for which it was promptly declared illegal. It had some 600 members coming from a dozen cities up and down the country. Thereafter militants joined other organisations, particularly Black Order, which like its predecessor held training sessions for young people in which para-military exercises were practised.

At the time a real fear existed that fascism might be restored through a *coup d'état*; certainly right-wing extremists engaged in political thuggery on the streets and contributed to a climate of general insecurity which was supposed to prepare the way for an authoritarian government of the right. New Order membership ranged from lawyers and businessmen to students and workers, mostly under 30 years old. There was no structure to the organisation, nor was it clandestine, merely politically ugly. Many of its members later associated with the Armed Revolutionary Nuclei (NAR) active in the 1980s.

For the few that attended summer camps for training, denims and berets were obligatory. Self-defence, wrestling and firearms practice were taught. Individuals carried arms, the group as a whole was not armed. By and large these firearms were purchased, although there were at the time stories of weapons being smuggled in from Greece, France and Switzerland.

October XXII Circle
(Circolo XXII Ottobre)

An Italian group which emerged in the ferment of the 1968 student revolution in Europe, the Circle principally attracted former members of the Communist Party (PCI). The reason for the defection was the pragmatic and less doctrinaire approach to politics which Enrico Berlinguer, the PCI leader, had introduced so successfully, at least in terms of PCI electoral support. Amongst the better known names were Rinaldi Fiorani, Silvio Malagoli and Mario Rossi.

Without resort to kidnapping, the Circle would have had no funds with which to launch itself in 1970. Bank robbery followed. With Partisan Action Groups (GAP), the Circle indulged in a number of joint actions in Genoa. Most members were caught and imprisoned within months, others joined the Red Brigades. Rossi became famous for having written a book about guerrilla warfare on prison lavatory paper.

Partisan Action Groups
(Gruppi d'Azione Partigiana — GAP)

The GAP were very largely the creation of the radical left-wing million-aire publisher, Giangiacomo Feltrinelli, in the late 1960s. Militants were based primarily in Milan, but recruits were also found amongst the Italian guestworkers in West Germany. Modelled on wartime partisan groups, the GAP were prepared to fight in the countryside in the event of a neo-fascist takeover, a development which Feltrinelli thought more probable than was in fact the case.

After Feltrinelli's death in 1972 the GAP dispersed and members probably joined other groups. Whilst active, although practising violence, they had stayed apart from the Red Brigades. Their principal activity was setting fire to industrial premises, as well as shipyards in northern Italy. On one or two occasions they had intervened on local television and radio stations, making an impact similar to that of the Tupamaros in Uruguay. Many of the groups' members were disgruntled Communist Party (PCI) members.

Permanent Struggle
(Lotta Continua)

Permanent Struggle is an ultra-leftist Trotskyist organisation in Italy, that held its first national congress in January 1975. It had existed for a decade with pockets of local support and had successfully drummed up considerable interest through the columns of its own publication, *Lotta Continua*. Active during the mid-1960s, *Lotta Continua* promoted wild-cat strikes, squatters' groups and street demonstrations, and was prominent in the disturbances of 1968.

At that time some of its leaders were sentenced to terms of imprison-ment for incitement to violence and subversion, among them the journal's editor, Francesco Tolin. The group's most famous member was the film director, Pier Paolo Pasolini, who also for a time edited *Lotta Continua*. In the 1960s the group may have enjoyed the support of some 25,000 sympathisers.

The fortunes of *Lotta Continua* changed in the 1970s. From promoting violence on the streets of Milan and other cities — and in 1973 Fulvio Grimaldi, another editor of the journal, was jailed for two years — the group turned to working through constitutional channels and in 1976 had one deputy elected to parliament. *Lotta Continua* thenceforth acted still more dangerously for it gave a kind of cover to what was described as the 'armed party' — the terrorist groups. 'We have roundly condemned unprovoked attacks on policemen and journalists', it claimed. 'But we consider our comrades have the right to fire back if they are shot at by police in demonstrations.' An indication of the group's support can be gauged by the attendance of 50,000 people at a Bologna rally called in September 1977. Abroad, *Lotta Continua* from the mid-1970s developed contacts with People's Democracy in Northern Ireland and with the Popular Front for the Liberation of Palestine.

Red Brigades
(Brigate Rosse — BR)

Although BR violence dominated the Italian terrorist spectrum in the 1980s, the movement's origins date back to the intellectual ferment of 1968. Ideologically astonishing and politically macabre, the BR, although few in number, presented Italian democracy with its most serious challenge. To meet it, all parties, including the powerful Communist Party (PCI), were united.

Renato Curcio (jailed 1976) and his wife, Margherita Cagol (killed in a 1975 shoot-out), were the intellectual founders of the movement and provided it with high quality leadership in the early 1970s. Around them gathered the 'historic nucleus', principally Giorgio Semeria, like Curcio a sociology graduate from Trent University, and Mario Moretti, who came from an industrial background in Milan, where he recruited Pier Luigi Zuffada, Corrado Alunni and Paolo Besuchio. Some had been practising Catholics, others were former members of the PCI, amongst whom for their prominence should be mentioned Pietro Morlacchi, Alberto Franceschini, Prospero Gallinari, Tonino Loris Paroli and Laura Azzolini.

If Curcio inspired the BR, Semeria organised the movement's logistical structure. In a pyramid of authority, he built it on the cell basis with each cell containing no more than five members, only one of whom had knowledge of and contact with the leader of a higher cell. In the larger cities of Milan, Rome, Turin and Genoa, pyramids of cells, known as columns, each independent of the other, were set up.

Contact with other groups in Italy and with foreigners, especially Uruguayans and Argentinians after 1975, was the responsibility of Mario Moretti. The Latin Americans handed on considerable skills, having fled from the military regimes which they themselves had provoked. They contributed to the painstaking constructional detail discovered in safe houses used by the BR, and to the strict attention paid to security.

Led by the historic nucleus, the earliest BR activists were largely confined to Milan, where pamphlets were scattered on the streets and damage inflicted upon the property of prominent conservatives and businessmen, as well as being directed against the ultra-right Italian Social Movement (MSI). For the most part arson was used. After a couple of years BR militants launched systematic campaigns in Turin and Genoa, transforming the industrial triangle into a terrorist triangle. Kidnappings played an increasingly important role from 1972, with Fiat, Alfa Romeo, Sit Siemens and Pirelli taking the brunt. Money was not the sole objective; publicity too was sought.

BR first challenged the state in 1974, when Mario Sossi, assistant attorney general in Genoa, who had successfully prosecuted terrorists, was held for the release of eight convicted members of the October XXII band. In the autumn of 1974 police took their first toll on the organisation with the capture of Curcio and Franceschini. BR militants responded violently. Duping the prison authorities at Casale Monferrato, Curcio's wife freed her husband in February 1975. Christian Democrat premises were specifically attacked and kneecapping began. Bank robberies were openly committed for the cause. Yet by the end of the year most of the historic nucleus had been removed from the action. Police recaptured Curcio in January 1976.

The new leaders were no less skilled technically, but lacked ideological preparation. Brutality grew, especially the practice of kneecapping and other forms of intimidation. The targets were selected carefully so as to strike and thus undermine the pillars of the establishment — magistrates and jurors to prevent conviction in court, journalists and editors to prevent exposure in the media, teachers and university professors to ensure that intellectually the left-wing climate prevailed, and finally Christian Democrat supporters so as to weaken the political opposition to terrorism. Industrialists paid protection money. By the occasional assassination, as well as by kneecapping, managers were warned to adopt conciliatory attitudes towards an infiltrated workforce.

In kidnapping Aldo Moro, former premier and architect of numerous coalition governments, in March 1978, the BR not only displayed a new ruthlessness and precision, but dealt a body blow to Italian democracy. Insofar as BR policy is defined, it sought to free Italy from an 'imperialist state of multinationals', for which Christian Democracy was held primarily responsible. The way forward, brigadists believed, was 'to mobilise, to extend and to deepen the armed initiative against the political, economic and military centres' of such a state.

Political action was pursued jointly in broadsheets and local, regularly produced publications, as well as in violent terrorist acts, both of which contributed to the 'Offensive Proletarian Resistance Movement' (MPRO), not in fact an organised body, but rather a climate of opinion favourable to the destruction of liberal democracy. A 'dialectical relationship' was supposed to exist between the MPRO and the BR, which acted as the 'vanguard' of a party yet to be formed. Much of the rhetoric was

Marxist-Leninist, harking back increasingly to Stalinism. Brigadist literature criticised the PCI, which, under Berlinguer's leadership, was accused of collaboration with the bourgeois state, as indeed had occurred in the so-called 'historic compromise' of March 1978, when the PCI supported Giulio Andreotti's minority Christian Democrat government until January 1979.

Evidence of a split within the ranks of the BR movement surfaced in 1979. It came to light in January with the murder in Genoa of a communist shop steward and electrical fitter, Guido Rossa, apparently for informing on the organisation. Confirmation of the split came in July, when a dissident group of activists accused the leadership of becoming remote from the working class. Only proletarian discontent could form, they argued, a solid basis for revolutionary action. Furthermore, the Moro murder had been misused; the crime had been exploited as a platform from which to launch assaults on society, instead of highlighting present-day conditions as the cause which drove the proletariat to desperate action.

The dissidents displayed dissatisfaction with the hard-line authoritarian Stalinist attitudes of the leadership — 'Italy of the 1980s is not Russia of 1917 and still less China of 1949'. These top men were few in number, and were concerned only with directing military-type terrorist operations from an underground headquarters in self-imposed, dictatorial isolation. Two names behind the revolt were Valerio Morucci and Adriana Faranda.

With the general elections in 1979, the BR directed its campaign at the Christian Democratic party, whose supporters did not feel safe going about their business. After stealing files, brigadists wrecked the party's headquarters in Rome. 'The showdown with the bosses of the Christian Democratic party and their hideouts will take place with arms in hand. With words, we have nothing more to say . . . The only language is that of arms.' Behind the philosophy lay the works of Herbert Marcuse, Abraham Guillén and Ulrike Meinhof.

In the 1980s the BR attack on large Italian companies continued unabated, as did the targeting of policemen and Christian Democrat spokesmen. Magistrates were so intimidated that they went on strike in July 1980, demanding better police protection. But the principal target remained big business, at which over 75 per cent of all BR attacks were aimed. The brigadists had murdered over 50 people and had undertaken more than 50 kidnappings by 1982. Losses due to BR arson were reckoned at some £65 million.

Most of the brigadists weapons were acquired locally: for instance, they used the Beretta M-4 and M-12 submachine guns, but on significant occasions they employed the Scorpion submachine gun, made in Czechoslovakia. The weapon is also available to German terrorists, with whom the BR have been in close contact. Being light and relatively small, it is favoured by women, who form a high proportion of brigadists.

Police have made inroads into the BR organisation, contrary to the general impression given by the continuity of attacks. By the close of 1979 some 360 BR terrorists had been imprisoned, indicted or identified. The historic names were behind bars. Among those sentenced in 1980 were Corrado Alunni (32) and Pier Luigi Zuffada, two of the more important leaders of more than a dozen militants who stood trial. The seizure in April 1981 of Mario Moretti (34) was a signal success for the police. Still more important was the discovery of US General Dozier, whom the brigadists had kidnapped in December 1981. From that operation stemmed many arrests and successful prosecutions the following year.

It may be that the BR had been depleted, yet it was known that their actions were supported by an outer ring of sympathisers and that brigadists who had served their time in jail reverted on release to the terrorist fold. Even so, the intellectual tide was turning against them diminishing their fortitude in 1983.

Revolutionary Action Movement
(Movimento d'Azione Rivoluzionaria — MAR)

In the ferment of ultra-rightist activity in the Italy of the early 1970s, MAR played a role in attempting to bring about a fascist coup. In the north of the country, the MAR ran para-military training camps for young men who wished to pose as soldiers. The man behind the movement was Carlo Fumagalli, who was jailed in Florence in 1978. The MAR was found guilty of political conspiracy. In addition, it had sought and gained funds through ransoms.

Revolutionary Fascist Nuclei
(Nuclei Fascisti Rivoluzionari — NFR)

NFR emerged as a right-wing terrorist group in the south of Italy in 1980, one of a number of small units which operated that year. In January militants murdered the President of the Sicilian Regional Council in Palermo.

Workers' Vanguard
(Avanguardia Operaia)

Workers' Vanguard emerged in Italy as part of the New Left in 1971. Its members were drawn from the Italian Communist Party (PCI), but more particularly from Maoist and Trotskyist groups. By the early 1970s it enjoyed a national network in Italy probably numbering some 30,000 adherents, many in the south. It did not advocate terrorism, but supported a more thorough-going revolutionary approach to politics than either the PCI or the Trotskyist Permanent Struggle group, from which it split. Workers' Vanguard contested the June 1975 local elections without much success. It was close to the Democratic Party of Proletarian Unity and elected one deputy to parliament. Although by the end of the decade Workers' Vanguard largely consisted of middle-class supporters, in its formative years it had contributed to ferment on the left as an extra-parliamentary group. It was active amongst both workers and students, mobilising street demonstrations in support of ultra-leftist causes.

Netherlands

Political violence in the Netherlands arose from the new left ferment of the mid-1960s, when dissidents from the small Communist Party of the Netherlands set up splinter groups. From those days stemmed Red Youth, then Red Help, and most recently the Red Resistance Front. Members of these organisations had contacts with West German militants, with whom they acted in sympathy. Less close was contact with the Irish Republican Army. Although the Netherlands never suffered from a serious ideological terrorist campaign, to promote one militants had been given training in South Yemen in 1976.

Quite the most dramatic terrorist incident in the Netherlands arose from the alienation of young South Moluccans from a community (40,000) which had left the islands when the Dutch gave independence to Indonesia. In December 1975 five gunmen held captive 50 people on a train. Thenceforth the Free South Moluccan Youth Organisation organised a number of bloody and desperate incidents calculated to force the Indonesian government into giving to the islands the independence which had once been promised by the colonial power. The campaign proved quite fruitless, and after 1979 little more was heard of Moluccan terrorism.

Bibliography

On the Moluccan issue see Ben van Kaam, *The South Moluccans: Background to the Train Hijackings* (London, 1980) and Ralph Barker's objective diary of events *Not Here but in Another Place* (New York, 1980). Schmid and de Graaf published an exploratory analysis of the train siege in *Insurgent Terrorism and the Western News Media* (Leyden, 1980). See also the article by Herman Valentine and Rob van der Laan Bouma 'Nationalists without a Nation: South Moluccan Terrorism in the Netherlands' in *Terrorism* Vol 4, Nos 1-4, 1980.

Free South Moluccan Youth Organisation
(Vrije Zuidmolukse Jongeren — VZJ)

In 1975 militants from this organisation broke with the moderate South Moluccan government-in-exile, and determined on using political violence to achieve the independence from Indonesia which, before withdrawing from that region, the Dutch government had once promised the islanders. Unsuccessful in a plan to kidnap Queen Juliana, they first drew the world's attention in December 1975, when five gunmen held 50 people captive on a train at Beilen. They demanded the recognition of a non-existent Republic of the South Moluccas, and an amnesty for jailed colleagues. Within a fortnight they had given in. Simultaneously another group had seized the Indonesian consulate in Amsterdam, but after 15 days' negotiations they too surrendered. In 1976 all received jail sentences.

To effect the release of these men a further group of seven held 54 passengers hostage on a train in May 1977. At the same time four colleagues held more than a hundred school children hostage in Bovensmilde. Both sieges ended in military actions, one of which caused the death of two hostages. No immediate backlash was felt in the community, although there were riots in September, when police recovered firearms.

A further hostage incident occurred in March 1978, when three youths stormed government offices in Assen, fatally wounding one victim. Again the terrorists were overcome by the military. The following year young Moluccan militants failed in an attempt to kidnap the prime minister, Andreas van Agt. Since then efforts by the Dutch government to integrate the Moluccan community appear to have met with success: yet by the very nature of the problem further isolated incidents will occur.

Red Help
(Rode Hulp — RH)

Members and sympathisers of Red Youth set up Red Help in 1973 to agitate for the release of two colleagues from jail — van Hoessel and Geert Flokstra. The principal organisers included Henk Wubben, Willem Oskam, Evert van den Berg, Roel Koopmans and Joost van Steenis. In jail, van Hoessel came into contact with Adri Eeken and his wife, who were active on behalf of the Palestinian cause. The contact was extended once van Hoessel had been released in November 1974, so that in July 1976 ten RH militants were able to visit South Yemen for three weeks' training under the auspices of the Popular Front for the Liberation of Palestine (PFLP). In return RH agreed to carry out a terrorist attack at Tel Aviv airport, but the Israelis averted a tragedy by arresting two militants, Ludwina Janssen and Marius Nieuwburg. The incident discredited RH, which was disbanded in December 1976.

Red Resistance Front
(Rood Verzetsfront — RVF)

The roots of the RVF, like so many leftist groups in Europe, go back to the events leading up to the student revolution of 1968. It was in fact set up in January 1977 by Adri Eeken and his wife, Ciska Brakenhof, both of whom had been active in the recently disbanded Red Help. The purpose of the new organisation was to lend support to the German Red Army Faction.

During the first year of its existence it indulged in little more than painting graffiti on public buildings, but in 1978 and 1979 members were active in sit-ins and even attempted to occupy the offices of Swissair. RVF pamphlets were singularly hostile to the European elections held in 1979. That year in Groningen the group made its first armed assault with the purpose of stealing blank passports. Those involved, Johannes Bolt (b. 1953) and Ferdinand Westen (b. 1958), were jailed, but others were involved in an explosion the following year and attempted to disrupt the inauguration of Queen Beatrix. Of the small numbers involved Eeken and his wife remained the leaders.

Red Youth
(Rode Jeugd — RJ)

Red Youth was the name of a Dutch newspaper printed in 1970 by dissident members of the pro-Chinese Dutch Communist Party, itself a splinter from the original Communist Party of the Netherlands. Around the production of the paper there gathered young enthusiasts attracted by libertarian ideas. Together they participated in street demonstrations and contributed to the radicalisation of protests which ended in street fights with the police. RJ never had a national organisation, although it enjoyed support outside Amsterdam.

Its members adopted the ideas of Carlos Marighella, whose *Minimanual of the Urban Guerrilla* was translated from Portuguese in 1971. Consequently RJ activists took to throwing fire and smoke bombs, and in 1972 attacked a Holiday Inn in Utrecht and the Philips corporation in Rotterdam and Eindhoven. These latter attacks, more serious in nature, were undertaken in the name of the Revolutionary People's Organisation of the Netherlands. Others were perpetrated under the name of the Red People's Resistance. Neither of these bodies had an independent existence. Following the arrest in 1973 of Lucien van Hoessel and Geert Flokstra, Red Youth dissolved itself and instead set up Red Help.

Portugal

In January 1980 a new conservative government took office in Portugal, marking the end of a six-year period of socialist political experiment, which started with a military coup in April 1974. Behind the coup was a group of officers who were convinced that no military solution could contain the rising black nationalism evident in Portugal's African possessions, a spirit which had given rise in all three territories — Angola, Mozambique and Guinea Bissau — to wars of liberation from colonial rule.

The officers concerned were middle-ranking: none sought through military ambition to impose upon Portugal military rule. Their convictions and determination encouraged the growth of a democratic common purpose, which gradually crystallised into an Armed Forces Movement (MFA). The MFA proffered itself to General António de Spínola, who accepted the leadership of the revolution and became President in May 1974.

Amongst the top military hierarchy of Salazarist Portugal General Spínola was the only man with lengthy experience in Africa who had expressed his conviction that a political solution to the African wars was required. But his vision of a Lusitanian commonwealth never came about; too much blood had been spilt for the guerrilla leaders to accept anything less than total independence, an independence furthermore that was to follow a radical course.

By foreshortening the outcome of the battlefield, the Armed Forces Movement brought independence precipitately to Portuguese Africa. But it also set in train a remarkable course of events in Portugal, a revolutionary cycle which began moderately, reacting to the stuffy intellectual and political obscurantism of Dr Salazar, but which in the capital and in the extreme south of the country quickly led to upheavals in the conventional social order. For a time the exercise of authority was so diffuse as to allow small ultra-leftist and largely unrepresentative groups a disproportionate influence over events. As in all revolutions, they exercised power on the streets.

Fearing the disorder, which had led to land seizures in the south, to factory takeovers, and to the financial collapse of the state, and fearing most of all the pretensions of the Moscow-line Portuguese Communist Party (PCP), led by a skilled and charismatic politician, Alvaro Cunhal, General Spínola lost his political nerve and resigned in September.

Thenceforth the threat to the maintenance of law and order came from two sources.

On the left were numerous groups, loosely termed Maoists, such as the Revolutionary Brigades and the Reorganisation Movement of the Party of the Proletariat. The PCP, because of its superior numbers, organisation and outside support was the principal threat on the left, challenging the establishment of liberal democracy in Portugal. On the right were members of the former establishment, who sought to reverse the revolution, and increasingly the reaction of the north, centred around Oporto, the second city, and the island archipelagos of the Azores and Madeira. In these areas the attraction of tradition and of the Church remained firm, as it had done on previous occasions when revolution had engulfed the capital in the nineteenth century.

General Spínola proved a disappointing statesman, indeed in this respect he displayed no talent at all. From September 1974 to March 1975 he attempted to lead the country's moderates, the silent majority as they were termed. Badly advised, in March 1975 he attempted to seize power in the name of moderation. The coup failed, causing Spínola to seek refuge in Spain, and finally asylum in Brazil.

For a while there was speculation that he would attempt a comeback, but the leadership of the non-Marxist officers devolved upon a group of nine men, who that summer devised a strong and moderate course, which arrested the leftward drift which Spínola's behaviour had inadvertently encouraged. Led by Major Melo Antunes and Captain Vasco Lourenço, they rejected the East European model of socialism, 'which obstinately believes that a vanguard with a very narrow social base will make the revolution in the name of the whole people'. A new government in September 1975 pledged the country to 'socialism and democratic pluralism'.

At the time the PCP formed part of the government, with one seat in the cabinet. The party was favoured by the President, General Costa Gomes, and it largely controlled the press, radio and new trade union structure. It attempted to strengthen communist support by keeping close to grass roots military opinion, expressed in the Soldiers United Will Win (SUV) movement, as well as to parallel movements in the navy and in industry. Copcon, the internal security body set up in the heady days of 1974 to ensure the survival of the revolution, actively furthered PCP designs. Led by Major Otelo Saraiva de Carvalho, Copcon had scarcely provided minimal security on the streets, and was thus responsible for the mushrooming of political vigilante groups.

The crisis came in November 1975, when the PCP launched its coup. On 13 November some 20,000 striking construction workers besieged the prime minister's residence for 36 hours. From the suburbs and from the countryside, truckloads of replacements kept up the pressure for immediate wage increases, to which the government was compelled to accede. Meanwhile the deputies were prevented from leaving the Constituent Assembly, Copcon having refused to guarantee their safety.

A week later the government suspended its own powers until the President guaranteed military protection. At this point, Alvaro Cunhal, the PCP leader, returned from Eastern Europe to find the Belém Palace besieged by his own supporters; he promptly called on the government to resign. When the President dismissed instead Saraiva de Carvalho from his post of commander of the Lisbon military region, the communists struck on 25 November.

The immediate goal was to oust the moderate Air Force members of the Supreme Military Council. Paratroops from the Tancos training school attacked three air bases, and rebel troops in the capital occupied the radio and television stations. The revolt was supported by the Communist-dominated *Intersindical* organisation and various union bodies in and around the Lisbon industrial complex.

Prompt action from the Amadora commando base put the revolt down in a matter of hours. The man to emerge as leader, and who had applied firm action on the streets, was Colonel Ramalho Eanes, subsequently elected President of Portugal. Under his guidance Portugal returned to normal democratic procedures with a socialist government until 1980.

In the late 1970s political violence in Portugal revolved around the land issue, especially in the south. Many estates had been taken over by landless workers, so that when the government authorised resumption of private ownership, rural brawls naturally ensued. By and large few lives were lost, although bitter feelings of deception engulfed the countryside, where hope of escaping from a mean rural poverty had briefly flowered. Still, the disillusion did not express itself in political violence and with the exception of isolated bombing incidents by the Popular Forces of 25 April (FP25) Portugal's towns were quiet in the early 1980s.

Bibliography

The best contemporary history of Portugal is Richard Robinson's *Contemporary Portugal* (London, 1979), but in addition António de Figueiredo, a distinguished liberal exile, provided essential reading in *Fifty Years of Dictatorship* (Penguin, 1975). Prior to these two books, Hugh Kay had written the best account in *Salazar and Modern Portugal* (New York, 1960). The book that heralded April 1974 was António de Spínola's *Portugal and the Future* (Johannesburg, 1974), a translation of the original Portuguese published in Lisbon that year. *Ao Serviço de Portugal* (Lisbon, 1976) followed, in which the General endeavoured to portray himself as a statesman. From exile, the President of Salazarist Portugal, Marcelo Caetano, excused himself in *Testimonio* (Madrid, 1975) in Spanish, as well as in Portuguese.

The Socialist leader, Mário Soares, gave an account of the conflict in *Portugal's Struggle for Liberty* (London, 1975); and Neil Bruce recounts events well and briefly in *Portugal: The Last Empire* (London, 1975). *The Sunday Times* journalists were present and contributed *Insight on Portugal* (London, 1975); a year later Michael Harsgor wrote in the Washington Papers series *Portugal in Revolution* (Sage, London, 1976). Douglas Porch analysed events in *The Portuguese Armed Forces and the Revolution* (London, 1977). The separatist challenge was considered by Tom Gallaher in 'Portugal's Atlantic Territories', *The World Today*, September 1979.

Among those who took part in events and who wrote with an interest were Jacinto Baptista, *Caminhos para uma Revolução* (Lisbon, 1975), Luis Calafate, *A Liberdade tem um Preço* (Lisbon, 1975), Otelo Saraiva de Carvalho, *Cinco Meses Mudaram Portugal* (Lisbon, 1975), Manuel Barão de Cunha, *Na 23a Hora do MFA* (Lisbon, 1975), Feio, Leitão and Pinha, *11 de Março, Autópsia de um Golpe* (Lisbon, 1975), Vasco Lourenço, *MFA, Rosto do Povo* (Lisbon, 1975), Galvão de Melo, *MFA, Movimiento Revolucionário* (Lisbon, 1975) and on the SUV *Os SUV em Luta* (Lisbon, 1976).

Armed Revolutionary Action
(Acção Revolucionária Armada — ARA)

The principal and sustained opposition to the Salazarist regime in Portugal came from the Portuguese Communist Party (PCP), which in 1970 backed a campaign aimed at sabotaging Portugal's military effort to retain its African colonial possessions. The majority of those involved were based in Paris, where a substantial body of Portuguese workers lived and were influenced by vigorous PCP activity. The campaign was formalised as a quasi-independent body, known as ARA, which never carried out more than a handful of explosions and certainly never jeopardised the Portuguese presence in Africa. But ARA served for propaganda purposes to show the ultra-left in Portugal that the PCP was also activist, for at the time Maoist influence on the left of the Moscow-line Communist parties in Europe was strong. In May 1973, the ARA central command suspended violent action, evidently in the hope that signs of liberalisation could lead to PCP legalisation. Hitherto the party had existed only in clandestinity.

For a brief period after the April 1974 Lisbon coup, the legalised PCP reactivated ARA, but this was in response to the attempted coup by General Spínola in 1975. In fact ARA consisted then of a PCP militia numbering some 2,000 people, who patrolled the streets of Lisbon. They formed the back-bone for an attempted PCP coup later that year.

Front for the Liberation of the Azores
(Frente da Libertação das Açores — FLA)

The FLA was a direct result of the leftward drift of politics in Lisbon following the April 1974 coup in Portugal. As the Armed Forces Movement (MFA), which had promoted the coup against the authoritarian government inherited from Salazar, appeared to lose power to the Portuguese Communist Party (PCP) and to ultra-leftist groups, the islanders reacted strongly against the left.

Prompted by local landowners and businessmen, they backed a call for independence rather than submit to a Lisbon-dominated left-wing government. In this they were supported in the Americas by many Azorean emigrants, who still kept in contact with their poorer families. On 10 October 1975, the FLA informed the United Nations that the islanders would have no part in any system other than a democratic one, and rejected the revolutionary course of events which culminated in the unsuccessful coup led by the PCP in November 1975.

With the resumption of law and order on the mainland and of democratic party politics under President Eanes, the FLA separatist movement receded. Most important of all, the new Portuguese constitution gave a statute of autonomy to the islands in 1976.

The separatist movement had adopted its own flag, which had flown in the eighteenth century and which sported the colours of the Holy Spirit, blue and white. Armed backing came from local military units, which called themselves Azorean Patriots in the Garrisons (PAG). A separatist newspaper, *O Milhafre* (The Kite), was printed in 1977. Behind the FLA activity two principal names were mentioned, José de Almeida and Manuel Bento. They maintained contact with FLAMA — a parallel separatist movement in the Madeira archipelago.

Front for the Liberation of the Madeira Archipelago
(Frente da Libertação do Arquipélago de Madeira —FLAMA)

FLAMA emerged in the Atlantic archipelago of Madeira in 1975 as a reaction to the left-wing politics of ultra-leftist groups and parties which sought to seize power through armed action. It was not apparently as active as the Front for the Liberation of the Azores, but would no doubt have clamoured loudly for independence had the Portuguese Communist Party (PCP) succeeded in its violent bid for power in November 1975.

The group still published in 1978 a separatist newspaper, *Jornal Insular*. Many inhabitants have successfully escaped the poverty of the islands for a life in America; they retained links with their families however, and strongly supported their independent stand *vis à vis* Lisbon's leftward political drift.

League of Union and Revolutionary Action
(Liga de União e Acção Revolucionária — LUAR)

Hermínio da Palma Inácio founded LUAR in 1966 in Paris, following the murder on the Spanish frontier of the principal Portuguese opposition figurehead, General Delgado. Never more than a small group, LUAR was the personal creation of its founder, and when in 1976 he moved towards the Socialist Party, the group lost its identity. There was no longer room in post-Salazarist Portugal for the singular stance of charismatic individuals like Palma Inácio, who, among the police of the old regime, had developed a will-o'-the-wisp reputation for his elusiveness. His followers gravitated to one or other of the historic left-wing parties, the Socialist Party and the Communist Party (PCP).

During the late 1960s the exiled radical initiated a handful of violent actions aimed at drawing attention to the lack of liberty under the Salazarist regime. But Palma Inácio achieved nothing in the way of a campaign, nor did LUAR develop a coherent policy. In 1973 Palma Inácio was arrested on one of his clandestine visits to Lisbon, having twice in the past escaped from jail in Portugal. Revolutionary events in 1974 overtook his trial, so that he was released alongside a number of his closest supporters.

There followed a brief period when LUAR was actively engaged in the street politics of 1974/75 in the capital, although it never adopted terrorist tactics. A congress was held in February 1975 when some 400 delegates agreed to define LUAR as a 'revolutionary Marxist organisation', which was committed to 'acceptance of a revolutionary grass-roots socialism springing from the class struggle of the working class, and not from a party political struggle'. They rejected democratic elections. The harder ideological line in LUAR was determined by Agostinho Pessanha Gonçalves and the brothers Pereira Marquês.

Like the members of the Revolutionary Brigades, LUAR militants were armed and may have numbered as many as 2000. For a while it published a fortnightly paper, *Fronteira*, under the direction of Fernando Pereira Marquês, who believed in a people's revolutionary government responsible in some form to new working-class organisations which encapsulated 'people's power'. Some LUAR members were in contact with ultra-leftist exiles from Uruguay and Argentina, who were at the time attempting to give body to a Latin American umbrella group known as the Revolutionary Coordinating Junta (JCR). The group cooperated with the Maoist Popular Democratic Unity (UDP) party as well as with the Revolutionary Brigades, and formed part of the United Revolutionary Front (FUR) of that time.

New Order
(*Ordem Novo*)

Ultra-rightist officers launched New Order in May 1981. The move followed the attempted coup in Spain three months earlier and was supported by the conservative newspaper, *O Dia*. Colonel Gilberto Santos e Castro, an outstanding officer in Angola, founded the group, which had links with the Spanish ultra-rightist leader, Blas Piñar, who led New Force. New Order favoured the corporatist state of Salazar and Primo de Rivera.

Popular Forces of 25 April
(Forças Populares do 25 Abril — FP-25)

FP-25 emerged in 1980 when it committed a number of bank robberies and demanded money of businessmen. One, failing to respond to the demand, was murdered in April. That same month the terrorists attempted to kidnap the Portuguese Finance Minister, but succeeded only in wounding his bodyguard.

Isolated FP-25 bomb explosions were recorded in Lisbon and Oporto in 1981, when the group acted in support of the Provisional IRA by attacking British property. Several people died from the results of its activities. In February 1982 militants not only supported a communist call for a general strike, but called for an insurrection. They carried arms and explosives, but made little or no popular impact.

Popular Unity Force
(Força de Unidade Popular — FUP)

Major Otelo Saraiva de Carvalho (44) founded the FUP in Portugal in 1980. Because of his radical politics and his admiration for Cuba's Fidel Castro, Carvalho had attracted great attention at the time of the April 1974 Lisbon coup.

After his brief moment of responsibility as military commander of the Lisbon region and commander of the revolutionary internal security force, Copcon, he was imprisoned for failing in his duties. Although the simplicity of his handsome personality never translated itself into effectual leadership, the high regard in which he was held by ultra-leftists did not fade. He remained a hero, and in 1978 headed a new radical grouping, the United Workers' Organisation (OUT). FUP was the latest embodiment in Portugal of dissident or 'original' communism, that rejected democratic centralism and put its faith in grass-root committees. Its political role was so marginal as to have no effect on the course of events.

Portuguese Liberation Army
(Exército de Libertação Português — ELP)

The ELP was little more than a phantom organisation in Madrid, the product of a number of Portuguese exiles from the April 1974 coup in Lisbon. Connections with white mercenaries and with South Africans were alleged to exist. Whoever was behind it, 'the objective was to demonstrate opposition to Marxist military power in Portugal'. It also threatened to 'liquidate any figure in the Marxist military government' in 1975. Some weight was given to the ELP after General Spínola had failed

in a March 1975 coup to capture the Portuguese revolution for the moderates and had consequently fled into exile. The right wing did eventually
prevail in Portuguese politics and indeed in the military, but the swing
owed nothing at all to the cloak and dagger activities of the ELP: it arose
from the traditionally conservative nature of the north and of the islands
of the Azores and Madeira.

Reorganisation Movement of the Party of the Proletariat
*(Movimento Reorganizativo do Partido do Proletariado —
MRPP)*

José Luis Saldanha Sanches and Arnaldo Matos led the MRPP, a Maoist
movement in Portugal at the time of the April 1974 revolution. It published a weekly newspaper, *Luta Popular*. MRPP was actually constituted
in 1973, but only emerged on the streets in the violence following the
collapse of Salazar's Portugal. It was one of the principal groups responsible for political violence in the capital, so much so that it was banned in
March 1975. Members had been active before the April coup in sabotage
operations against the African war effort; after it Sanches was jailed for a
short period for inciting soldiers to desert. Supporters were held responsible for considerable intimidation, particularly in enforcing strikes,
which inflamed an unstable situation and in fact led to loss of life in the
streets.

The government suppressed *Luta Popular* on 4 August 1974, although
for a while it continued to publish clandestinely. Later that year MRPP
supporters were involved in serious clashes with police and with conservative political supporters; Saldanha Sanches himself was hurt in a
November brawl in which iron bars, clubs and bicycle chains were used
with effect. The MRPP was virulently hostile to the pro-Soviet
Portuguese Communist Party (PCP), and against the moderate line of
President Spínola. Incidents occurred not only in the capital, but in
Oporto in January 1975 and in Figueira da Foz in February, where
members of Social Democratic rallies were intimidated. Later in the year
the MRPP was influential in the journalists' union. It dropped from sight
in the later 1970s and did not reappear in the early 1980s.

Revolutionary Brigades
(Brigadas Revolucionárias — BR)

The Brigades were the armed wing of dissident communists who looked
to Mao Tse-tung in their desire for militant action to bring down the
tottering authoritarian structures of Salazarist Portugal in the early 1970s.
Their parent body, the National Liberation Popular Front (FPLN), had

emerged in 1962 and had found a home in Algiers. But it only began in 1970 to carry out 'armed struggle' in Portugal.

To do so, FPLN militants formed themselves into revolutionary brigades, which consisted of autonomous units acting independently against the Portuguese authorities of the time. They hoped thereby to bring about a genuine Portuguese revolution, 'not modelled on other revolutions'. In this they were supported by radio broadcasts from Algiers — the Voice of Freedom, and by a news-sheet, *Frente*.

The Brigades modelled their action on the anti-Vietnam War campaign in the USA, only aimed instead at Portugal's withdrawal from Africa. They scattered pamphlets in Lisbon, worked on the student body and set off a number of explosions in or near government offices. Militants targeted a computer centre, a recruiting office, supply depots, vehicles, barracks and other buildings. No loss of life was intended, although on one occasion two people died.

Their organisation changed somewhat in 1973, when the BR September Congress decided to rename the party the Revolutionary Party of the Proletariat (PRP), which was to publish *Revolução*. It adopted a virulently anti-Portuguese Communist Party line, and opposed the PCP after the April 1974 Lisbon coup as the PRP-BR.

Thereafter the Brigades ceased their sabotage activities, but worked in the new party to set up revolutionary councils 'with the eventual aim of arming the working class'. The councils would become the nucleus, it was hoped, of a true revolutionary party, which would control industry and restructure the armed forces as a 'people's army'. The PRP-BR was close to Peking, but retained a degree of independence. Partly because of the lack of foreign back-up, but mostly thanks to the political swing away from the left, the party fell from view in the conservative reaction of the late 1970s.

In the early days the most renowned BR name was that of the poet, Manuel Alegre. But in 1975 the most prominent leaders were a woman endocrinologist, Dr Isabel do Carmo, and Manuel Crespo, a former welder from the giant Lisnave shipyard. The party's members were for the most part armed, and were very much to the fore in the street disturbances of 1975. Their weapons came from government depots and were made available in the turmoil of the time by such men as Major Otelo Saraiva de Carvalho, who controlled the internal security body, Copcon.

PRP members were active too in factories, where they set up councils prepared to seize control of industry. But their influence was brief, especially after the dismantling of the PCP-controlled *Intersindical* trade union organisation in October 1976. Some robbed banks for funds and others exploded bombs; for these crimes Isabel do Carmo and Carlos Antunes, arrested in 1978, were sentenced in 1980 to lengthy terms in jail.

Soldiers United Will Win
(Soldados Unidos Vencerão — SUV)

SUV, an ultra-left military pressure group, emerged in Portugal following the April 1974 coup in Lisbon. By 1975 it was clear to some officers
and soldiers who had participated in overthrowing the old authoritarian
regime inherited from President Salazar (retired 1968) that the change of
regime did not, at least under President Spínola, imply a socialist revolution. SUV opposed Spínola, and his successor Admiral Pinheiro in 1975,
advocating a 'unified anti-capitalist and anti-imperialist front'. It found
the Movement of the Armed Forces (MFA), which had promoted the
original April coup, less than radical, indeed it considered the MFA was
'at the service of counter-revolutionary elements'.

Whilst not actually led by Major Otelo Saraiva de Carvalho, SUV
derived support from his sympathy as head of the military internal
security force, Copcon, until this was largely replaced in November 1975.
SUV was essentially a spontaneous movement, without hierarchical
structure or proper leadership. With the restoration of military discipline
under President Eanes in 1976, SUV and movements like it disappeared
in Portugal.

United Workers' Organisation
(Organização Unida dos Trabalhadores — OUT)

OUT was set up by Otelo Saraiva de Carvalho in 1978 from two small
groups on the ultra-left of Portuguese politics, the Popular Socialist Front
and the Revolutionary Party of the Proletariat. His intent was to head a
mass movement in which the workers seize power using 'revolutionary
force and violence'. Such 'adventurist actions of leftist radicalism' hor-
rified the Portuguese Communist Party (PCP) because OUT advocated
direct rule through committees of workers, peasants and soldiers.

Some radical contacts were made with terrorist groups outside
Portugal, with the Basque separatist group ETA and the Irish Republican
Army in particular. But the links were not sustained, nor did Carvalho's
ideological interests have anything to do with Basque or Irish national-
ism. The group dropped from sight after Carvalho had founded Popular
Unity Force (FUP) in 1980.

Workers' and Peasants' Alliance
(Aliança Operária e Camponesa — AOC)

AOC was born in Portugal in the wake of the April 1974 revolution in
Lisbon. It was Maoist in orientation and led by Carlos Guisote, leader of
the Lisbon chemical trade union. Members were active on the streets of

the capital and were behind so much of the revolutionary disturbance that the new government banned the movement in 1975, thereby disqualifying AOC from participating in the elections of that year. Most of its members joined the Maoist National Democratic Front, which was set up to absorb the AOC in February 1976. It ceased to have any impact on revolutionary events after the brief hey-day of ultra-leftist activity in 1974/75. AOC published *A Voz do Trabalhador*.

Spain

The most terrifying of all forms of political violence afflicted Spain in the early 1980s — that of a vicious internal war in the northern Basque country, where a minority of the population sympathised with the separatist aspirations of hard-core Basque nationalist terrorists. With professional training taking place in the Middle East, the terrorist campaign latterly moved into a new and most dangerous phase threatening the establishment of democracy in the region. At a national level separatist violence provoked old guard militarists to attempt an unsuccessful coup in February 1981 and to plot during the run-up to the October 1982 elections.

The Basque problem had its roots in the nineteenth century, when liberal centralised government from Madrid imposed its norms upon a rural Catholic peasantry passionately attached to ancient rights, known as *fueros*. More recently, prior to General Franco's rebellion in 1936, the region achieved briefly a certain independence. But such autonomy as then existed was taken away after Franco's nationalist victory in the Civil War (1936-39), which led to the setting up of a rigidly centralist government, a policy designed to preserve the unity of historic Spain.

Alongside the Basques, the Catalans too had opposed General Franco's 'crusade', and had consequently suffered enormous cultural deprivation in the aftermath of the war. Both regions are strongly characterised by their local cultures, which differ linguistically and ethnically from those of other parts of Spain. Yet during the 1970s nationalist political violence in Catalonia never took on the proportions it adopted in Vizcaya, Guipúzcoa, Alava and Navarra. As a historic centre of anarchism, on the other hand, Barcelona suffered from the sporadic activities of a number of libertarian groups, which developed terrorist links over the border with like-minded political idealists in France.

The civil war had brought yet again to the fractured surface of Spanish political life the antagonisms which had plagued nineteenth-century Spain between progress and tradition, and between liberalism and conservatism. Violence at that time was as endemic to the right as it was to the left, but after 1939 Franco contained both sides, so that under his authoritarian rule Spain experienced a remarkable 35-year period of peace and prosperity.

Towards the end of his long life, however, pressure for reform grew, and as change became more probable an ugly reaction broke out on the right from such bully groups as the Warriors of Christ the King. Like their intelligence, their influence was minimal.

Confronted by extremist threats from the neo-fascist ultra-right, and for a time in the mid-1970s from the Maoist ultra-left, the new political parties which emerged under Franco's designated successor (1975), King Juan Carlos, united in their condemnation of political violence. The Spanish Communist Party (PCE) was as insistent upon this point as the Socialist Party (PSOE) or the ruling conservative Central Democratic alliance. Together they faced the appalling spectre of Spain's wealthiest provinces deprived of their rich cosmopolitan tourist trade, and also of essential industrial capital, on account of the terrorist campaign waged by Freedom for the Basque Homeland (ETA). In the early 1980s this small body of divided but ruthless men held Madrid to ransom for unobtainable political objectives, and was the principal cause for an attempted military coup on 23 February 1981, when Civil Guards briefly captured the Cortes building in Madrid.

Bibliography

Without going into the nineteenth-century roots and the Civil War period, for an introduction to Spain's contemporary political violence, Professor Raymond Carr and Juan Pablo Fusi provide an excellent analysis of Franco's rule in *Spain: Dictatorship to Democracy* (London, 1979).

With the exception of two essays, one in Paul Preston's *Spain in Crisis* (Brighton, 1975) and the other Peter Janke's *Spanish Separatism: ETA's Threat to Basque Democracy (Conflict Study*, No. 123, ISC, London, 1980), there is no analysis in English of Basque violence, nor indeed of any contemporary Spanish political violence. Ortzi (Letamendia) provided an outstanding account of ETA's early years, as he participated in them, in the detailed *Historia de Euskadi: el nacionalismo vasco* (Paris, 1975). See also G. Jauregui Bereciartu, *Ideología y estrategia política de ETA 1959-1968* (Madrid, 1981). The activities of the 1960s culminated in the Burgos trial, related by Gisèle Halimi in *Le Procès de Burgos* (Paris, 1971).

For the 1970s, the journalist, José María Portell, wrote two popular accounts, *Los Hombres de ETA* (Barcelona, 1974) and the somewhat better *Amnistía Arrancada* (Barcelona, 1977); presumably because he knew too much, ETA militants murdered Portell. A detailed account of the planning and murder of Admiral Carrero Blanco is provided in Julen Agirre's *Operación Ogro, cómo y porqué ejecutamos a Carrero Blanco* (Hendaya, 1974), the 'official' ETA version published in English in New York in 1975. To understand the development of ETA-VI, Angel Amigo's *Pertur ETA 71-76* is essential reading, both for its documents and for the insights into the character of ETA-VI's principal ideologist. Alejandro Muñoz Alonso recounts ETA's story in *El Terrorismo en España* (Madrid, 1982).

The background to the Catalan problem is splendidly and brilliantly portrayed in Victor Alba's *Catalonia: A Profile* (New York, 1975). Catalan regional violence however has been contained in the 1970s. But for the ideologically motivated FRAP, the student can turn to Alejandro Diz's *La Sombra del FRAP* (Barcelona, 1977), in which a former central committee member of the Maoist party relates his tale, and to the *Operación Cromo, Informe Oficial de los GRAPO* (Madrid, 1977) for details of GRAPO. The Spanish authorities shed light on this activity in *Terrorismo y Justicia en España* (Madrid, Centro Español de Documentación, 1975).

Two books serve as an introduction in English to the post-Civil War activities of anarchism in Spain, the first by the International Black Cross member, Miguel García, *Franco's Prisoner* (Hart Davis, 1972), the second a translation of Antonio Tellez's biography of an anarchist militant, *Sabate: Guerrilla Extraordinary* (Davis Poynter, London, 1974), on which Stuart Christie worked enthusiastically.

Anti-Fascist and Patriotic Revolutionary Front
(Frente Revolucionario Antifascista y Patriótico — FRAP)

FRAP was defunct in Spain in 1980, although other ultra-leftist groups like the *Grupo de Resistencia Antifascista Primero de Octubre* engaged in terrorist activity. FRAP, like GRAPO, was the result of the influence of Maoism on the orthodox Moscow-line communist parties of Europe. It was set up by the Maoist Communist Party of Spain — Marxist-Leninist (PCE-ML) in 1973, some nine years after the founding of that party.

FRAP sought to overturn the Franco regime by violence and by so doing to strike a blow at United States 'imperialism'. In its place a People's Republic would nationalise all property and industrial enterprises, withdraw from African colonial possessions, and institute agrarian reform. Because of its ideological persuasion FRAP found sympathy with like-minded Maoist groups all over Europe. Minute splinter groups though these were, they provided sufficient external support to plan abroad a campaign of terrorism inside Spain. The main centres were West Germany, Belgium, Holland, France and Italy. Switzerland also played a role.

Abroad, a central committee and executive were set up, to which regional committees in Spain were responsible. On an operational level terrorists worked in units of three members. Ideological in-fighting caused it to split in 1976, the year in which France took action against the movement. It continued in Spain to have some influence on university campuses, but its members were reported to have decided at a meeting in February 1978 in Bilbao to withdraw from armed action.

FRAP began its campaign of terror in 1975, specifically targeting the security forces. That summer three policemen were killed and another wounded in the capital, as Franco lay on his death bed. Other attacks took place in Valencia and Barcelona. Militants were frequently under 20 years of age and tended to come from working-class urban backgrounds.

The state reacted swiftly, arresting more than 100 activists before the end of that year, and uncovering that autumn at least 15 flats which had afforded the movement facilities. Thereafter FRAP was more active in crowds and demonstrations, and never again mounted a similar wave of murders. Killing had attracted to FRAP no public sympathy whatever, and from its own political point of view had undoubtedly harmed the group.

Other activities during FRAP's brief campaign included bank robberies in Madrid, Barcelona, Seville, Valencia and Zaragoza, and a number of bomb attacks against buildings, most of which took place in Madrid. Amongst the targets were foreign, particularly United States, interests.

Anti-Terrorism ETA
(Antiterrorismo ETA — ATE)

Actions by the clandestine ATE began in earnest in 1976 in the Basque country as a reaction to the left-wing separatist violence of ETA. In particular ATE has sought out Basque terrorists in France and murdered them, and has bombed dwellings and premises known to be meeting places for separatists. Several hundred such actions have been recorded since the first appearance of the group in April 1975. ATE had similar aims and methods to the Apostolic Anti-Communist Alliance (AAA) and the Spanish National Action (ANE) group. By the 1980s similar actions were claimed in the name of the Spanish Basque Battalion (BVE).

Apostolic Anti-Communist Alliance
(Alianza Apostólica Anticomunista — AAA)

The Spanish AAA was a para-military right-wing group operating principally in the Basque country against left-wing separatist violence from ETA in the early 1980s. A precedent for this type of activity was found earlier in the 1970s in Argentina, where the Triple A was an extremely ugly phenomenon.

In Spain the AAA was generally considered responsible for assassination attempts on ETA personalities in the Basque region and across the border in France. In this it was joined by overlapping organisations known as Spanish National Action (ANE) and Anti-Terrorism ETA (ATE).

But the AAA was also active against purely left-wing activities in the labour movement. Quite the most notorious of this type of activity occurred in January 1977 in Madrid. It arose shortly after the December 1976 referendum, which determined whether or not the young King Juan Carlos should pursue reform. Acting in the name of the AAA, two gunmen assassinated four leading left-wing lawyers well-known for their defence of illegal workers' organisations, in their offices in broad daylight. They were subsequently caught and a number of men behind the organisation were brought to justice.

Members of the group viewed themselves as defenders of Spanish national unity, and as such attacked not only ETA, but also bombed the Catalan centre in Madrid, and the Barcelona newspaper offices of *El Papus*.

Armed Struggle Organisation
(Organització Lluita Armada — OLla)

OLla was the armed branch of the Spanish Iberian Libertarian Movement (MIL), active mainly in Catalonia in the early 1970s. Members demonstrated under the Franco regime alongside other groups in favour of greater liberalisation, and were active in stimulating strikes. At least one policeman lost his life in an exchange of shots with an OLla activist, but the group never managed to launch a sustained urban campaign of violence favouring anarchism. OLla was not active in the Catalan separatist violence of the early 1980s.

Autonomous Anti-Capitalist Commandos
(Comandos Autónomos Anticapitalistas — CAA)

Having sprung from the Basque separatist organisation ETA, the Commandos were active in the north of Spain, where in October 1980 they claimed responsibility for the murder of Juan Manuel García Cordero, a telephone company employee. A further assassination occurred in March 1982; again the victim, Enrique Cuesta, was employed by the telephone company.

Catalan Liberation Front
(Front d'Alliberament Català — FAC)

Members of the FAC were active in 1971/72 in and around Barcelona, where they perpetrated a number of terrorist incidents. Bomb targets included television and radio stations as well as the railway station at Casteldelfels. As with the Basque separatist movement ETA, FAC attacked Civil War monuments and magistrates courts. But for the death of a civil guard in an explosion in 1971 in La Sagreda, FAC caused no deaths. Police captured a number of those involved; no further violence ensued until 1979.

Militant Catalans working for the independence of a united Catalonia, which embraced Valencia, the Balearic Islands and the French province of Roussillon, turned instead to the *Partit Socialiste d'Alliberament dels Paisos Catalans* (PSAN), which in 1975 declared its intention to link up with ETA. Some help was afforded the Basques, but neither FAC nor PSAN undertook armed action to anything like the same extent. The organisation claimed responsibility for the murder in Barcelona of two policemen in January 1979, but since then the few incidents of Catalan separatist terrorism have been claimed by Free Land (TL).

First of October Anti-Fascist Resistance Group
(Grupo de Resistencia Antifascista Primero de Octubre — GRAPO)

GRAPO was active in Spain in the early 1980s, despite the severe depletions inflicted by successful police operations in 1979. It remained an ideologically motivated terrorist group on the far left of the Marxist-Leninist spectrum, functioning as the armed branch of the Reconstituted Spanish Communist Party (PCE-R) set up in 1975. Within GRAPO there were probably not more than a few dozen members prepared to kill or engage in terrorist incidents.

GRAPO is responsible to the central committee of the PCE-R, which is linked to sister parties outside Spain, particularly in Belgium and France. They arose from the influence of Maoism on the far left during the 1960s, and declined in influence and numbers during the 1970s. At the top of the GRAPO structure is a military commission which directs all terrorist operations and maintains contact regionally in Spain through local committees. The network is national so that terrorist-related activities have occurred outside Madrid and Barcelona, the main centres, in Valencia, Cadiz, Seville, Segovia, Burgos and Valladolid, and in the north-west in Santander and Oviedo.

GRAPO emerged fully in 1976 with a number of dynamite bombings and two spectacular kidnappings. The bombings occurred simultaneously in the summer in seven different cities, thereby proving the extent of the movement's activities. That December the group kidnapped Sr Oriol y Urquijo, President of the Council of State, in Madrid, and followed up with the seizure in January 1977 of Lieutenant General Emilio Villaescusa Quilis, President of Spain's highest military tribunal. Both men were freed in February thanks to prompt police action. Arrests followed, but not sufficient to prevent continued activity from a group which may not have numbered more than 60 people. The majority of their targets were police officers, five of whom died in the first half of the year. Bombs were exploded at the French Lycée and the US Cultural Institute in Madrid, as well as Lufthansa offices in Barcelona. Militants robbed banks for funds in Barcelona, Madrid and Valencia, and stocked their arsenals from raids on military armouries in Madrid, Seville and Santiago de Compostela.

Throughout the summer and autumn of 1977 many members were detained by the police, particularly in Madrid, and safe houses discovered in the capital and Barcelona. The following year further hideouts were uncovered in Galicia. Notwithstanding, the organisation was able to assassinate a number of policemen and to shoot dead in March the

Director General of the Prison Service, Jesús Blanco. In 1979 the French embassy became a target for GRAPO bombs in Madrid, and militants murdered a further dozen people. Amongst the assassinations were a Supreme Court Judge, Miguel Cruz Cuenca, in January and Brigadier Agustín Muñóz Vásquez in March. Further killings, including that of General González de Suso, occurred in 1981.

Police action took its toll on the rank and file, as well as on GRAPO leadership. On 20 April 1979 Juan Carlos Delgado de Codex (b.1950) was killed resisting arrest — he was considered a key man in the leadership, and on 13 October José María Sánchez Casas (b.1942), the top GRAPO leader, was arrested in Valencia. By the start of 1979 as many as 52 GRAPO militants were in prison, and more were awaiting trial. In December 1979 five actually escaped from Zamora maximum security jail: one member, Fernando Hierro Chomón, was recaptured in May 1980. Further sentences were handed down in 1980 to men guilty of murder and related terrorist acts; because of police action it appeared GRAPO was unable to pursue its campaign any further that year. In September 1981 the GRAPO leader, Cerdán Calixto (b. 1950), was shot dead in Barcelona, and his successor, Juan Martín Luna (b. 1954) was killed in the same city in December 1982. In November GRAPO had announced a truce, following a spate of bomb attacks during the general election campaign that autumn.

The movement takes its name from a series of murders on 1 October 1975, when four policemen were assassinated simultaneously in Madrid. The act was to revenge the execution by General Franco's government on 27 September of several terrorists, including ultra-leftists.

Free Land
(Terra Lliure — TL)

Free Land surfaced in May 1981, when members shot a Spanish language professor in the legs in Barcelona. It was militantly pro-Catalan, and subsequently exploded a number of small devices in Barcelona, Tarragona, Valencia and Alicante. The Spanish police carried out a number of arrests in December that year, but the occasional bombing continued in 1982. Thanks to the devolution measures adopted by the Spanish government, there seemed little likelihood that Catalans would be attracted by political violence.

Freedom for the Basque Homeland
(Euskadi ta Askatasuna — ETA)

An ugly campaign of terrorism waged by ETA threatened Basque democracy in Spain in the early 1980s; furthermore, imaginative moves towards Basque autonomy, planned and even set up by the government in Madrid, were not put into effect, so that ETA appeared to increase its following. At the close of 1982 the movement had been killing for 14 years — in fact since 1968. In all some 350 people had died as a result of ETA-inspired political violence, most of them in the Basque region.

ETA sprang from the Basque Nationalist Party (PNV), which had been founded in 1894 and had continued to exist illegally under General Franco. The PNV supported a Basque government-in-exile in Paris (France) headed by Jesús María de Leizaola, who, when approached by younger party members in 1957, rejected their intention to embark upon armed struggle to promote the separatist cause. Undeterred, activists set up ETA in 1959 and three years later launched a violent campaign. This early endeavour, in which Julián de Madariaga, José María Benito del Valle, José Manuel Aguirre Bilbao, Sabino Uribe Cuadra and José Luis Alvarez Emparanza were prominent, failed completely. The police moved in and broke up the movement, causing most of those involved to seek exile across the border in France.

If violence failed in the early 1960s, the movement did not die intellectually. To ideas of national liberation, apparently made politically feasible by events in Cuba and Algeria, were added Maoist concepts. But ideology merely split ETA into quarrelsome factions, provoking arguments which continued to plague the movement throughout the 1970s and early 1980s. As a result of acrimonious discussions held by a handful of members at ETA's fifth assembly in 1966, the organisation broke into two wings known as ETA-V and ETA-VI. Fundamentally the parting was due to a clash of interests between 'nationalists' and 'ideologists' who leant towards some form of Marxism-Leninism. Before either group could make any impact on the Basque country, the police again moved in and put the principal leaders on trial at Burgos in 1969.

The Burgos trial provided ETA with widespread publicity and attracted a new generation of recruits. But the ideological divisions continued. Those nationalists who were headstrong and motivated by acute nationalism favoured action at all costs and became known as 'militarists' or ETA-M. They were led until his death in a shoot-out with police in 1973 by Eustakio Mendizábal Benito. Afterwards the organisation crumbled swiftly, many members were imprisoned, others fled.

Those Basque nationalists who had a keener eye for the science of revolution, and who considered revolution could only be brought about by a long-term political campaign aimed at mobilising the working class, adopted the label 'politico-militarists', or ETA-PM. Their principal leader was Moreno Bergareche, until rivals murdered him in 1976. A further split occurred in 1982 following an ETA-PM assembly, when the majority (ETA-PM VIII) determined to resume violent action under Jesús Abrisketa Korta, and the minority following José Aulestia Urrútia and José Miguel Goiburu Mendizábal remained close to ETA-PM's political front, Basque Left (EE).

Most of the political violence in the Spanish Basque country in the 1970s arose from the actions of ETA-M, although ETA-PM did not exclude the option of armed actions. In 1980 the violent ETA-M leadership came from men and women outside the country in France, principally Domingo Iturbe Abasolo (b.1944), Francisco Múgica Garmendía (b. 1954), Juan Angel Ochoantesana Badíola (b.1955) and Juan Lorenzo Santiago Lasa Michelena (b. 1954).

They organised a new and altogether more ruthless ETA-M in the late 1970s. It enjoyed a certain freedom of movement across the French frontier, where French Basques were sympathetic to ETA's cause. It did not lack funds, for it levied what ETA termed a 'tax' on small firms and industrialists, the majority of whom paid up through fear. It benefited from international contacts, particularly with Latin American exiles from Uruguay (former Tupamaros) and Argentina (former Montoneros), but also with Red Brigade members in Italy, where the Latin Americans had found sanctuary in the early/mid-1970s.

Such links had their impact on tactics, particularly kidnapping, and on the provision of weaponry and the construction of 'safe houses' and 'people's prisons'. But of greatest importance was the availability of training in the People's Democratic Republic of the Yemen (PDRY). At least a dozen trained recruits returned from the Middle East in 1979, a development which elevated to an altogether new level the threat posed by ETA to Spanish democracy. It meant that the sophisticated professional complex of intelligence, of experience and of long-term back-up available to the Palestinians was provided to ETA. In the past, at any rate since 1975, the group had relied upon instruction received in Algeria at the old Police Academy in Souma. Possibly 150 were trained in this manner.

In addition to the four men already mentioned, who were principally responsible for the execution of armed actions, other members of the Executive Committee included María Dolores González Catarain (b. 1954) and Eugenio Echeveste Arizguren (b. 1950), who ran the political side of the organisation. Propaganda was entrusted to Juan Ramón Aramburu Garmendía (b. 1953), logistics, armaments and explosives were the concern of Isidro María Garalde Bedilauneta (b. 1951). José Luis Ansola Larranaga (b. 1936) was responsible for information and for ETA-M's internal organisation. Lastly, three more men concerned themselves with relations abroad, Elou Uriarte Diaz de Guereno (b. 1942), José María Ganchegui Arruti (b. 1948) and Carlos Ibarburen Aguirre (b. 1939). Through them contacts with other terrorist groups were maintained.

ETA's actions had begun in the 1960s with little more than the painting of graffiti on walls and the attempts to bomb regime monuments and government buildings. The first death occurred in 1968, but the latest phase did not start until 1974, when 19 people died.

The high level of deaths began in 1978, with a sudden jump from previous years of less than a score to over 60 killings a year. Most took place in San Sebastián, Madrid and Bilbao. The victims were high-ranking military officers, senior judges and government officials, but also journalists and workers who were suspected of providing information to the police. Many ordinary policemen (Civil Guards) died in the course of their duty or were murdered at home or on their way to work.

Kidnapping did not play an important part in the build-up, although several celebrated cases occurred: the honorary German consul in San Sebastián, Eugenio Beihl (1970); Lorenzo Zabala, a local industrialist (1972); Felipe Huarte Beaumont, a wealthy businessman (1973); José Luis Arasate, a local businessman (1976); and the same year Angel Berazadi, another local entrepreneur, who was murdered by ETA-PM; Javier de Ybarra Bergé, president of Babcock and Wilcox in Spain (1977); Luis Sunyer Sanchis, reputedly the wealthiest man in Spain (1981); and José Lipperheide, a German-born Bilbao industrialist (1982).

ETA's most infamous act was to plan and execute the death of Spanish Prime Minister Admiral Carrero Blanco in 1973. He was blown up in Madrid on his way home from hearing mass. His death changed the face of Spain, for without him there was no one to continue Franco's system of authoritarian rule, so that King Juan Carlos was free to reform after the old dictator's death in 1975. The action was exceptional and did not represent at the time ETA's real strength, which was exceedingly weak.

Assassination continued to play a role in the separatist campaign: the most prominent victims were Juan Mariá Araluce Villar, Counsellor of the Realm, Member of the Cortes and President of the Diputación of Guipúzcoa (1976), General Juan Manuel Ramos Sánchez Izquierdo and Supreme Court Judge José Francisco Mateu Cánoves (1978), Lieutenant General Ortín Gil, Madrid's military governor, and Lieutenant General Gómez Hostiguela (1979), Lieutenant General Joaquin de Valenzuela (1981), and General Lago Román (1982).

A later development within ETA was the breaking away of so-called 'autonomous commandos' in November 1979. Their intention was to create 'nuclei of armed popular insurrection'. For them the 'armed struggle was an indispensable means of developing the class struggle', but then so it was for ETA-M. The autonomous commandos had existed since 1977, but they first came to the fore in 1978. They had engaged in a number of minor bombing incidents.

The arms employed by ETA include the Beretta 9mm model 4 submachine gun, the Sten gun and the French MAT-49 submachine gun. Smaller arms used are the Browning 9mm and the Firebird, Astra and Llama pistols. Shotguns stolen from local gunsmiths were also used with effect. Explosives too were stolen — for most of its bombings ETA has used dynamite. Their targets have included the nuclear facility at Lemóniz (Vizcaya), Altos Hornos in Bilbao, and the Iberduero corporation.

Both wings of ETA have political fronts, or parties, which contested elections in the post-Franco period. ETA-PM formed the Party for the Basque Revolution (*Euskal Iraultzako Alderdia* — EIA) whose principal spokesman was Mario Onaindia, a man sentenced to death at the Burgos trial. EIA joined a coalition of groups, which was known as the Basque Left (*Euskadiko Ezkerra* — EE) to contest the 1977 and 1979 elections, when it did less well than the militarists. EIA was subsequently disbanded and Onaindia joined EE, which in 1982 broke with ETA-PM over the issue of whether to pursue terrorism. EE polled 99,000 votes in the 1982 elections and sent Juan Maria Bandres to the Cortes.

ETA-M formed its own coalition with two left-wing, non-Marxist groups; it was called People's Unity (*Herri Batasuna* — HB). It elected Telesforo Monzón (d.1981), Francisco Letamendia and Pedro Solabarria to the Cortes, alongside Senator Miguel Castells in 1979, polling 172,000 votes, or 15 per cent of the vote. In 1982 HB polled 207,000 votes returning Iñaki Esnaola and Solabarria again to the Cortes.

International Revolutionary Action Groups
(Grupos de Acción Revolucionaria Internacionalista —GARI)

GARI was a Spanish anarchist group active in the early 1970s, but which largely disappeared after the death of General Franco in November 1975. The handful of people involved in GARI was mostly sympathetic to the Iberian Libertarian Movement (MIL), an anarchist organisation especially active in Catalonia. In May 1974 GARI militants kidnapped the Spanish bank manager of the Paris branch of the Banco de Bilbao. For his release they demanded the freedom of MIL militant, Santiago Solé Amigo. Police recovered the ransom paid and detained the abductors.

That summer the group exploded a number of bombs outside Spanish consulates and airline offices in Belgium and Holland. The favoured tactic was to leave a stolen vehicle with a time bomb in it outside the building. Some of these police defused, others exploded causing damage, but no loss of life.

Nearer Spain, on the frontier, GARI sabotaged high tension cables and pylons in July 1974. French police arrested half a dozen members in September 1974 and in Paris stumbled across the organiser of many of the attacks — a French Catalan, Jean Marc Rouillan. Other anarchist groups survived GARI.

Moroccan Patriotic Front
(Frente Patriótico Maroquí— FPM)

In 1979 Moroccan nationalists bombed a café in Melilla and a hotel in Ceuta, the two Spanish enclaves in North Africa. There is clearly a potential for political violence should King Hassan wish to support terrorism as a means of driving Spain from Africa. The enclaves have belonged to Spain since the sixteenth century. No further actions were reported in the early 1980s.

Movement for the Self-Determination and Independence of the Canary Islands Archipelago
(Movimiento para la Autodeterminación e Independencia del Archipiélago de las Canarias — MPAIAC)

The MPAIAC was still headed in 1983 by its founder, lawyer Antonio Cubillo (b.1930), who was based in Algiers. Ever since 1964 Cubillo had achieved a paper notoriety through his dispatches and communiqués, which were broadcast by Peking radio. The Liberation Committee of the Organisation of African Unity (OAU) declared at a meeting in Algiers in 1968 that the Canary Islands formed part of Africa, and recognised the MPAIAC. However, the Canary Islands were not on the United Nations list of non-autonomous territories as set out by the UN General Assembly. Still, there was a danger that Spain's enemies working diplomatically would embarrass her over the islands, which form an integral part of the nation.

The movement is in fact the personal creation of Cubillo, who left the islands after receiving two jail sentences for his part in labour disputes in 1962. For a decade (1964-74) nothing but written propaganda was put out from his office, but in December 1975 Algeria gave him time to transmit the Voice of the Free Canaries for one hour a day. The following year Cubillo approached Libyan President Gadaffi. In 1977 MPAIAC claimed responsibility for a number of bomb attacks in Tenerife, Las Palmas and La Laguna.

Although the devices were amateur, they caused considerable disruption — one was placed in the flower shop at Las Palmas airport and as a result traffic had to be rerouted to smaller airports. Again, in October 1977 ground control equipment was destroyed at Tenerife airport.

The first MPAIAC action on the mainland occurred in December 1977 in Madrid, at Atocha metro station. The explosion followed very swiftly on the death of a student killed in a demonstration in the Canary Islands. But the movement had no capacity to mount a campaign in the capital, and even in the islands could never count on more than a couple of dozen youthful but misguided enthusiasts. Although a policeman was killed defusing a bomb, no lives were lost in the bombings of 1978, the year when, after the personal intervention of Don Juan de Borbón, Algeria ceased to provide the movement with radio facilities. In April Cubillo was wounded in an attack in Algiers.

The incident did not prevent the explosion of further bombs in 1978 at a Las Palmas police station, at the naval headquarters and at the South African Airways office in Puerto de la Luz. That year arrests were made, but continued MPAIAC activity in 1979 suggested that behind the movement larger forces were at work, possibly North African. In the past the MPAIAC had been of use to the Algerian-backed Polisario guerrillas in the Western Sahara, where Spain had backed the Moroccan claim to the territory.

Certainly the MPAIAC adopted new tactics, similar to ETA, when it attempted to raise money from local businessmen and even took to kidnapping for ransom. Foreign companies engaged in tourism were also at risk, again a target first selected on the mainland by ETA. Yet there was no suggestion that the two separatist movements were in any way working together. Militarily the MPAIAC remained an irritant rather than a threat, mainly because the islands' one million inhabitants are all of Spanish descent, and although some speak a dialect, it has no linguistic roots in Africa. No incidents were recorded in the early 1980s.

New Force
(Fuerza Nueva — FN)

During the latter days of General Franco's life New Force was founded in Spain as an organisation on the political ultra-right. Young members engaged in clandestine para-military exercises in uniform outside Madrid. The man principally responsible for the movement's political orientation was Blas Piñar, a prominent lawyer and politician. After Franco's death in 1975, New Force supporters were increasingly involved in political violence.

The party made capital of the general fear of public disorder and the alarming growth of leftist extremist groups dedicated to political violence and terrorism. In 1977 it was able to mobilise as many as 25,000 people in Madrid for a rally against terrorism. In the course of 1978 and 1979, New Force members were themselves involved in political violence, although not in a coordinated manner. Violent behaviour and even death sometimes characterised their meetings.

New Force spokesmen undoubtedly sought support amongst members of the Civil Guard, and in the ranks of the military, where they had some success in eliciting the sympathy of the military hierarchy, which refused to turn its back upon the personalised authoritarianism of the past, a past still attractive to New Force sympathisers. The survival of this sentiment encouraged die-hard militarists to attempt a coup in February 1981.

Spanish Basque Battalion
(Batallón Vasco Español — BVE)

A right-wing para-military group, the BVE emerged in 1980 to contribute to the earlier terrorist activity of Anti-terrorism ETA (ATE) and the Apostolic Anti-Communist Alliance (AAA). It was active in Durango, Berriz and Hernani, small towns in the Spanish Basque country, where it attacked separatist bars. On occasions ETA suspects were targeted, particularly in the French Basque country, where they had sought refuge or where they planned attacks in Spain. The group was held responsible for a score of deaths.

Spanish National Action
(Acción Nacional Española — ANE)

ANE emerged in the northern Basque region of Spain as a reaction to the left-wing separatist terrorism practised by the two wings of the Freedom for the Basque Homeland movement, ETA. It used assassination tactics, with members seeking out prominent ETA terrorists across the border in France, where they sought refuge and where they planned their attacks in Spain. Members of ANE also attacked with bombs the premises of Basque separatist parties in Bilbao and San Sebastián in 1979, but such activities diminished in the early 1980s.

Warriors of Christ the King
(Guerrilleros de Cristo Rey)

The Warriors of Christ the King sprang up in Spain in the late 1960s as a reaction to liberal tendencies in the Spanish Church and in schools and universities. For the most part they were young people who indulged in vandalism against modern art and architecture, and who smashed the windows of left-wing bookshops. Their slogans and graffiti could be seen principally in Madrid and Barcelona.

As it became clearer in the early 1970s that Franco's authoritarian system of government would not survive his death (1975), an older generation of politically-minded men used the younger right-wing militants in new political organisations such as New Force (*Fuerza Nueva*), led by lawyer Blas Piñar. The Warriors of Christ the King provided these new groups with a recruiting pool of young and physically strong men and women, who were prepared to indulge in political violence. Little was heard of them in 1980, as the group, insofar as it ever was a group, had been recruited into other organisations with a neo-fascist political programme. The name most associated with the Warriors in the mid-1970s was that of Mariano Sánchez Corvisa.

United Kingdom

The early 1980s showed little respite from the seemingly intractable conflict in Northern Ireland, where political violence had required of the British army an active presence since 1969. No other country in Europe had found it necessary or appropriate to employ military force against terrorism — not even Spain, where the Basque conflict was closest to conditions in war-torn Ulster. By mid-1982, alongside some 170 policemen, 475 soldiers had died in the province. Civilian deaths amounted to three times this total.

If such problems can at all be put briefly, the nub lay in the settlement of 1920, when the Government of Ireland Act partitioned the island of Ireland into an overwhelmingly Roman Catholic Republic in the south and the predominantly Protestant British province of Northern Ireland, with its own Parliament at Stormont. Thenceforth the Protestant majority outvoted and therefore excluded from decision-making the northern Catholic minority of one third, who could not in any way participate in the proper democratic ordering of their lives. Under such a system abuses thrived, and were only remedied by a reform programme passed into law in the late 1960s.

For Stormont to undertake reform, Westminster had had to lean heavily upon the Protestant political leadership; in so doing it broke the Unionist party, whose leaders failed to carry with them the Protestant industrial workers. The reaction brought to the surface new militant spokesmen, such as the Rev. Ian Paisley and William Craig. As the old guard Unionist politicians like William Faulkner died, no one replaced them. In the Catholic community politicians were slow to emerge. When they did, with men like Gerry Fitt, they found the new Protestants spoke with a strident, intransigent and puritanical tongue, a blend of religion and politics characteristic of Irish politics for centuries.

To reinforce the new 'loyalist' political voice, there arose Protestant para-military organisations such as the Ulster Defence Association (UDA). However far from the truth, members felt that they, and not the British army, stood as the only bulwark preventing the Provisional IRA from bombing their way to the creation of a united socialist Ireland.

Towards the end of the 1960s the old Irish Republican Army (IRA) was a mere shadow of its former self — but in 1969 the turbulence surrounding reform sparked again the fire of militant nationalist republicanism. From an IRA which had turned to political theory by embracing

Marxism-Leninism (Official IRA) emerged new men who formed the Provisionals, who since the Official IRA suspended its actions in 1972 were solely responsible for the IRA terrorist campaign in the north.

The Ulster conflict had three further dimensions to it. First, the IRA used the Republic as a base and crossed the border to perpetrate terrorism. Protestant groups responded by carrying out isolated incidents south of the border. The border problem is not one which can be solved effectively by military means — other than by building a 'Berlin wall', a measure totally unacceptable to democratic government. This Irish dimension remained in the early 1980s a permanent factor, even although the IRA did not attract significant political support in the Republic.

Second, on a number of occasions in England the Provisionals had built up cells which in addition to specifically targeted individuals, killed and maimed innocent victims. Police work in England prevented the build-up of a terrorist campaign, but as the Hyde Park murders of Household Cavalrymen in July 1982 showed, the isolated incident could be successfully mounted by Irish terrorists.

Finally, the Irish conflict spread into continental European countries, where the new 'ideologists' of the north, militants of the Irish National Liberation Army (INLA), found common ground with the Dutch Red Help group and with German terrorist circles. From these contacts sprang the murder of the British Ambassador to The Hague in 1979, and the bombs planted in Brussels and Dortmund to kill British soldiers posted abroad.

Of all European countries Britain was touched least by the student revolution of 1968, perhaps because the impact of the New Left on British politics was minimal. It certainly never provoked the persistent disorders at street level, common in France, Germany and Italy. And although the Vietnam War was hotly debated, the issue never led to prolonged riots.

Race however provoked ongoing violence, and led to clashes in Notting Hill (London), Bristol, Brixton and Liverpool of a largely spontaneous and communal nature. Earlier attempts in the 1950s by Sir Oswald Mosley, the pre-war British fascist leader, to make political capital from racial antagonisms around Notting Hill had failed miserably. In the late 1970s on the other hand, the National Front and its opponent, the Anti-Nazi League, did their best to politicise race in the crudest manner and with regrettable results. Yet the outbursts of 1981 cannot be attributed to them: bad housing and unemployment were the cause.

For a brief period Celtic separatism in Wales and Scotland bred the prospects of violence in the 1970s, but the political sting was drawn from the issue by the debate on devolution, so that no conflict arose. Scotland however found itself on occasions drawn into the Irish question, for Ulster Protestantism retained its links with its Scottish forbears. Orange militancy in Glasgow fed Belfast and Londonderry.

Bibliography

An extensive literature exists on the Irish problem and excellent research published in the 1970s is available. Of especial note is the work of Professor Richard Rose, starting with *Governing without Consensus* (Faber and Faber, 1971), a scholarly discussion of fundamental government structures. A good general account can be read in John Darby's well-researched *Conflict in Northern Ireland* (Gill and Macmillan, 1976) and in Conor Cruise O'Brien's excellent general history, *State of Ireland* (Hutchinson, 1972). Essential documents have been selected and introduced by John Magee in *Northern Ireland: Crisis and Conflict, A Chronology of Events 1968* (Routledge and Kegan Paul, 1974), and Richard Deutsch and Vivien Magowan have compiled a three-volume chronology in *Northern Ireland: A Chronology of Events 1968-74* (Belfast, 1974).

The *Sunday Times* Insight Team wrote a vivid account of the early years in *Ulster* (Penguin, 1972). Paul Arthur has provided a sympathetic account of *The People's Democracy 1968-73* (Belfast, 1974) after its infiltration by ultra-leftists. Better are the books by the correspondents of *The Times* and the *Guardian*, Robert Fisk's *The Point of No Return* (Deutsch, 1975), a superb account of the 1974 UWC strike, and Simon Winchester's *In Holy Terror* (Faber, 1974), by an outstanding Ulster journalist in the early 1970s. Paddy Devlin recounted *The Fall of the Northern Ireland Executive* (Belfast, 1975) in which he participated. Lord Gardiner reported for the Government on *Measures to Deal with Terrorism in Northern Ireland* (London, HMSO, 1975).

For the background to Protestant militancy, Tony Gray's *The Orange Order* (Bodley Head, 1972) is essential. David Boulton describes the uglier side in *The UVF 1966-73* (Dublin, 1973). Reliable histories of the IRA have been written by Tim Pat Coogan, *The IRA* (Collins, 1970), and by J. Bowyer Bell, *The Secret Army* (London, 1970). Two personal accounts have been provided in Maria McGuire's *To Take Arms* (London, 1973) and Bernadette Devlin's *The Price of My Soul* (London, 1969). *Memoirs of a Revolutionary* (Edinburgh, 1975) are those of a former IRA Chief of Staff, Sean MacStiofain. The British army's role was well analysed by a former serving officer, Robin Evelegh, in *Peacekeeping in a Democratic Society* (Hurst, 1978). For a swift reference, the reader can turn to Peter Janke's *Ulster: A Decade of Violence* in the *Conflict Studies* series, No. 108 (ISC, London, 1979).

Ideologically inspired political violence is best understood by reading the authors themselves in *Student Power: Problems, Diagnosis, Action* by A. Cockburn and R. Blackburn (Penguin, 1969), and in a collection edited by Tariq Ali *New Revolutionaries and Left Opposition* (Peter Owen, 1969). From the Trotskyist point of view, Tariq Ali has written *The Coming British Revolution* (London, 1972) and *1968 and After* (London, 1978). Professor Bernard Crick and W.A. Robinson edited a good selection of left-wing opinion in *Protest and Discontent* (Pelican, 1970), whilst D.E. Apter and James Joll edited *Anarchism Today* (Macmillan, 1971), both excellent volumes. *The New Left — Six Critical Essays* (Bodley Head,

1971), edited by Professor Maurice Cranston, provides the counter-argument.

Amongst many articles, the following are of particular worth: Leo Labedz, 'Student and Revolution', *Survey*, July 1968; Max Beloff, 'University and Violence', *Survey*, October 1968; Richard Lowenthal, 'Unreason and Revolution', *Encounter*, November 1969; Edward Shils, 'Plenitude and Scarcity', *Encounter*, May 1969; and D.W. Brogan, 'The Student Revolution', *Encounter*, July 1968. Against these powerful voices of the intellectual establishment might be read 'The Politics of Terror' by Martin Jay in *Partisan Review* (London), I, 1971.

On the ultra-right, *The National Front* (Fontana, 1977) by Martin Walker analyses the movement, whilst Neill Nugent and Roger King look at it within the overall context of conservatism in *The British Right* (Saxon House, 1977). Robert Benewick wrote well in *The Fascist Movement in Britain* (London, 1972). Fascism in Britain today is analysed in brief by Peter Shipley in *The National Front: Racialism and Neo-Fascism in Britain* (*Conflict Studies*, No. 97, July 1978, ISC, London). The same author looked at the Front's opponents in *Trotskyism: 'Entryism' and Permanent Revolution* (*Conflict Studies*, No. 81, March 1977).

From the Trotskyists themselves, Tony Cliff's *The Crisis — Social Contract or Socialism* (London, 1975) argues for revolution. Gordon Carr, a BBC TV journalist, wrote the best account of *The Angry Brigade* (Gollancz, 1975). The 1968 Grosvenor Square demonstration against Vietnam was excellently analysed by Halloran, Elliot and Murdock in *Demonstrations and Communications: A Case Study*.

Scottish nationalism can perhaps be best approached in a volume of 28 essays introduced by the Rector of the University of Edinburgh, Gordon Brown, *The Red Paper on Scotland* (Nottingham, 1975). For Welsh nationalism, a good introduction is provided in *The Welsh Question* by Alan Butt Philip (Cardiff, 1975); for keen feeling, see Ned Thomas's *The Welsh Extremist* (London, 1971) and Derick Hearne's *The Rise of the Welsh Republic* (Talybont, Wales, 1975).

Angry Brigade

Closely following the 1968 disturbances in France and the development of Baader Meinhof terrorism in Germany, libertarian ideas in Britain produced the Angry Brigade. A small circle of friends emulated the activities of Daniel Cohn Bendit's *enragés* at Nanterre, influenced by the 'situationist' thought of Raoul Vaneigem and Guy Debord and by Spanish anarchists.

Most spectacularly the Brigade claimed responsibility for the explosion of two bombs in January 1971 at the home of the Secretary of State for Employment, Robert Carr. Neither this action nor any of a small series of explosions before and after that date was designed to cause loss of life, and fortunately no one was killed. The targets were symbolic — a fashionable clothes store in Kensington, the Miss World contest at the Albert Hall, a London Territorial Army centre, a police computer at Tintagel House on the Thames Embankment and the homes of the Attorney General and the London Metropolitan Police Commissioner. In all 25 bombs were planted, six of which failed to explode.

Following the arrest of what became known as the Stoke Newington Eight in August 1971, the incidents petered out: the anarchist effervescence had subsided. Those responsible, Anna Mendelson, Hilary Creek, John Barker and Jim Greenfield, all of whom were sentenced to ten years' imprisonment in 1972, were university students at Essex and Cambridge. They rejected the historic ultra-left, the Trotskyists, as too authoritarian, turning instead to a looser libertarian creed, closer to anarchism.

In particular, they made contact with Stuart Christie, who had been jailed for three years in Spain during the mid-1960s for carrying explosives in the anarchist cause, and linked up with the anarchist First of May Group. Together they used the 'alternative press' to publicise their actions, particularly the *International Times*. The link provided the Angry Brigade with some of their explosives, which came from France.

Anti-Nazi League

In November 1977 members of the Trotskyist Socialist Workers' Party combined with a sprinkling of Labour Party left-wingers, such as Peter Hain, to form the League. Their objective was to capitalise on the fear produced in the heart of Britain's immigrant black and Asian communities by the provocative marches of the National Front (NF). The League's activities acted as a foil to the NF and merely heightened tension, making ugly scenes still uglier. Members organised counter-marches to those planned by the NF, often with a view to confrontation in the streets. One of the worst examples was that of Southall (London) in April 1979, when one man died and scores of police and demonstrators were injured.

British Movement

Set up in 1968 by Colin Jordan to succeed the National Socialist Movement, the British Movement probably had less than 2000 sympathisers in 1980. Jordan resigned in 1975, and Mike McLaughlin (then 32) took over the direction of the Movement's 25-odd branches. For contravening the Race Relations Act he was jailed in August 1979 for four months. Another member, Roderick Roberts, was sentenced to seven years' imprisonment on arms charges in January 1981. Many of the Movement's political bully boys paraded in punk Nazi regalia. It published a monthly journal, *British Patriot*.

First of May Group

Although briefly active in the late 1960s in Britain, the First of May Group emerged from Spanish political circumstances and was closely connected with anarchism. It first practised terrorism in Rome on that date in 1966, when a Spanish priest seconded to the embassy at the Vatican was kidnapped for a fortnight. The group's spokesman was Octavio Alberola, son of a Spanish Republican exile in Mexico.

In August 1967 the group sprayed the US Embassy in Grosvenor Square, London, with submachine gun fire. On 3 March 1968 militants exploded devices outside the Spanish Embassy in Belgrave Square and at a US officers' club in Lancaster Gate. That attack was coordinated with explosions in Turin and The Hague; the anarchist network was the first to demonstrate its capacity in Europe to set off simultaneously a number of explosions in different countries.

In 1969 three further attacks were made on Spanish banks in London and Liverpool. Thereafter the group had contacts with the Angry Brigade in Britain, where together they disrupted Iberia Airlines at Heathrow Airport, and the Regent Street offices of the Spanish corporation. At the same time the First of May Group was active in continental Europe. In London the group used the 'alternative press' publication, *International Times*, to publish its communiqués.

Free Wales Army
(Mudiad Amddiffyn Cymru — MAC)

MAC, a Welsh nationalist group, claimed responsibility for a number of arson attacks against English holiday homes in Wales in 1980. Extremists operated only occasionally and under a variety of romantic pseudonyms.

International Marxist Group (IMG)

The IMG is the British section of the 1963 Trotskyist United Secretariat of the Fourth International (USFI), but it is in fact less numerous than the Socialist Workers' Party. Set up in 1965, its most prominent spokesman was Tariq Ali, but its best mind belonged to Robin Blackburn. IMG published *Socialist Challenge*, and was sympathetic towards the Provisional IRA.

The IMG is linked internationally through the USFI to some 26 countries, 12 of them in Western Europe (Belgium, Denmark, France, Greece, Ireland, Israel, Italy, Portugal, Spain, Sweden, Switzerland, and West Germany) and ten in Latin America (Argentina, Bolivia, Brazil, Mexico, Panama, Peru, Uruguay and Venezuela). But the main centre is Brussels, where Ernest Mandel leads the movement. In France the principal theorist was Pierre Frank, who was associated with the fortnightly bulletin, *Imprecor*, and the weekly *Intercontinental Press*. In the United States,

Joseph Hansen, leader of the Socialist Workers' Party, spoke for the USFI, internationally the largest Trotskyist grouping.

Irish National Liberation Army (INLA)

Had the Irish Republican Socialist Party (IRSP) not split from the Official IRA in December 1974, there would have been no INLA. Its aims are quite straightforward: through armed warfare it intends to compel the British to withdraw militarily from Northern Ireland, which would then unite with the south. The new republic would then withdraw from the European Economic Community and would practise 'socialist' principles. INLA members, who numbered no more than four dozen, were Marxist-Leninists, although they were fiercely critical of the pro-Soviet stance of the Officials.

The organisation is based in Dublin, where it picked up recruits expelled from the Provisionals. The quality proved poor, however, so that the leadership quickly turned to more careful screening of candidates, which led to a tighter organisation. The majority of their weapons and explosives came from communist sources via the Middle East.

Quite the most spectacular murder undertaken by the INLA was that of Airey Neave, the Conservative Party spokesman on Northern Ireland, in the forecourt of the House of Commons in March 1979. He was blown up in his car.

In Ulster the group's activities continued throughout the early 1980s, although with nothing approaching the incidence attributable to PIRA. Their targets included Protestant para-militaries as well as members of the security forces. In their misguided determination there was nothing to distinguish INLA militants from PIRA; both groups had members who died on hunger strike in 1981.

Irish Republican Army (IRA)

Today's IRA is split between the so-called Officials (IRA) and the Provisionals (PIRA), a distinction born in 1969. Prior to that, since 1956, the IRA had waged a campaign against the British authorities in Northern Ireland. Little was achieved in the border areas where militants operated, so that eventually in 1962 all activity ceased. Effectively, the IRA no longer existed as a military force.

In the mid-1960s however, under the influence of Cathal Goulding, a Marxist wing of the IRA was resurrected. It was close to the nucleus which was shortly to become the Communist Party of Ireland (1970) and to the orthodox Communist Party of Great Britain. Goulding's followers involved themselves in exploiting social issues and were not prepared for the armed struggle which emerged from the communal violence of the mid- and late 1960s in Northern Ireland.

Whilst not ruling out military actions, the Marxist wing indulged in relatively little terrorism, and in May 1972 declared a unilateral ceasefire. Since then the bulk of their activity has taken place through the political front, known as the Official *Sinn Fein*, which was registered in the Republic as a party with a national organisation. In Northern Ireland the Officials worked through the Republican Clubs. Both in the north and the south the Officials fielded candidates in all elections during the 1970s, winning the support in the north on average of less than 2½ per cent of the vote.

They argued that class politics should supercede sectarian issues, and that the violence practised by the Provincials merely entrenched reactionary attitudes. The most prominent Official leader in the late 1970s was Tomas MacGiolla, who in 1977 became leader of a new *Sinn Fein* the Workers Party (SFWP) in the Republic. By 1979 the links with *Sinn Fein* were ultimately dropped and with them all confusion between the Officials and Provisionals cleared up, so that the party contested the 1982 Ulster Assembly elections as the Workers Party (WP).

In the north the Officials, through the Republican Clubs, supported the establishment of devolved government within the United Kingdom. But in the long run they looked forward to a united socialist Ireland 'where all the people of Ireland own and control the wealth and run their own affairs'.

Irish Republican Socialist Party (IRSP)

Blood flowed between the Official IRA and the dissidents who formed the IRSP in December 1974. Six people died and several dozen received injuries following the break led by Seamus Costello. These men were Marxist-Leninists, former Officials who had come to believe that the Irish revolution could only be accomplished with militant action, including violence. For them the 'national struggle' was inseparable from the 'class struggle', and they did not condemn the terrorist campaign waged by the Provisional IRA. The IRSP journal, *The Starry Plough*, carries news of Provisional activities and the party acts as a political front for the Irish National Liberation Army (INLA).

Ideologically the new party was closer to Trotskyism than to Moscow's communist line, and it sought to establish contact abroad with like-minded groups. Prominent in these efforts was Bernadette Devlin (married name McAliskey), who quarrelled with Costello for reverting to 'the sterile nationalism of traditional Republicanism'. In late 1976 she left the party to found the Irish Socialist Party in February 1977. Costello was assassinated in Dublin in October 1977.

Keepers of Wales
(Cadwyr Cymru — CC)

Like the Free Wales Army, Cadwyr Cymru was involved in a number of arson attacks in 1980 against English holiday homes in Wales and against Conservative Party premises in Cardiff. It allegedly had links with the IRA and with ETA in Spain; if so, they had little effect. Only occasional incidents were recorded in the early 1980s; furthermore each was claimed as the work of a different organisation, among them Sons of Glendower and the Workers' Army of the Welsh Republic. A handful of militants were jailed in November 1981 for some 18 months on account of arson. In age they ranged from 51 down to 23 years.

Loyal Citizens of Ulster (LCU)

The LCU emerged in Northern Ireland in 1968 under the leadership of Ronald Bunting, a former British army officer in his 60s. He taught mathematics at Belfast College of Technology and was a member of the Ulster Protestant Volunteers in East Belfast. LCU membership was largely drawn from the Volunteers and had no formal structure of its own.

Bunting was an eccentric figure, organising, amongst other bodies, the Knights of Freedom. But he lent power to Ian Paisley's political arm in 1968, when he accompanied him to Londonderry to 'retake' the city for protestantism. Bunting's car was set alight outside the city's Guildhall, and his followers were prominent in the running clashes with marchers outside Londonderry, where clubs, bottles and stones were wielded against unarmed demonstrators. He was sentenced in 1969 to three months in jail, together with Paisley, for organising an unlawful assembly in Armagh.

Loyalist Association of Workers (LAW)

Billy Hull of Belfast, then 60 years old, was behind the setting up of LAW in 1971. The organisation drew support from the industrial workers employed at Harland and Wolff's shipyards, Short's military engineering plant, Mackie's foundry and Gallaher's tobacco factory. That year LAW was able to rally as many as 25,000 workers to an open air loyalist meeting.

As Hull put it, 'we are British to the core, but we won't hesitate to take on even the British if they attempt to sell our country down the river.' Most LAW supporters gave their political sympathy in 1972 to William Craig's Vanguard party, a new umbrella movement for traditional loyalist groupings. By 1974 nothing remained of Billy Hull's organisation, which suffered from poor leadership and was discredited following cases of embezzlement.

Yet the power of Protestant industrial workers was only too clearly displayed in the 1974 general strike, which was called by the Ulster Workers' Council (UWC) and on which LAW members Harry Murray, Hugh Petrie and Jim Smith also sat.

Militant

The Militant group is a Trotskyist tendency within the British Labour Party. Its tactics represent an alternative to the normal Trotskyist endeavours to create a tightly disciplined party of revolutionary Marxist-Leninist cadres, whose task is to exploit the divisions which exist in any society, and especially the freedoms which democracy offers, in order to take advantage of the resulting collapse of order and impose their own.

Instead, Militant Trotskyists penetrated the Labour Party, using what they termed 'entryist' tactics, after Trotsky's own instructions in the 1930s. Entryism had always been a revolutionary tactic recommended by the Trotskyist United Secretariat of the Fourth International (USFI), and before that of the International Secretariat. In particular, the Labour Party has been a target for entryism since 1947, but although younger members had been impressed, until the late 1970s little impact had been made on the party as a whole.

The group derives its name from a paper which first appeared in 1964, the product of activists from the Revolutionary Socialist League who had joined the Labour Party. By 1980 the group had a representative on the National Executive Committee, and was influential in some 60 constituency organisations. It tried to politicise the 1981 racial outbursts in London and Liverpool, but failed. In 1982 the Labour Party took steps to expel members of Militant.

National Front (NF)

In 1977 the NF was the largest racialist political group in Britain, attracting 5 per cent of the votes of Greater London's local council elections (120,000). It had been set up in 1967 from several smaller neo-Nazi groups which had made no political headway. They amounted to several thousand supporters, led by Colin Jordan, John Tyndall, Martin Webster and A.K. Chesterton, the chairman, whose politics stretched back to Oswald Mosley's pre-war British Union of Fascists.

The NF derived support from the general concern at the effects of immigration from India, Pakistan, Africa and the black Caribbean on British industrial communities, and, in particular, in 1972 from the expulsion by Idi Amin of Asians from Uganda. Attempts to establish links with Ulster loyalists at this crucial period of Northern Ireland's history failed. Yet in England the NF fielded 90 candidates in the October 1974 general elections, winning a total of 114,000 votes, or an average of 3.1 per cent of the poll in each constituency.

Chesterton, who died in 1973, was succeeded until 1980 by John Tyndall, an authoritarian and populist leader. Some resented his style and in 1975 he left to form the National Party, under John Kingsley Read, a local councillor in Blackburn. But the NF continued to expand, to provoke racial hatred, and to take on the ultra-left in street clashes in British cities, especially London, Birmingham, Leeds, Manchester and Wolverhampton.

The Front was an activist movement and overtly anti-black, anti-Asian, anti-Jewish and anti-communist. It was also anti-capitalist, in that it advocated a corporatist system of economic nationalism, in which the state would regulate all aspects of economic activity. NF policies can best be followed in its monthly magazine, *Spearhead*.

At election time the NF was regularly involved at street level in political violence, and by marching through predominantly black and Asian areas of British cities has often sought to provoke violence. Whilst being the largest of Britain's neo-fascist groups, the NF has suffered from splits and defections, and the leadership is frequently at loggerheads.

In October 1979 NF leader Martin Webster (36) was given a one-year suspended jail sentence for inciting racial hatred. In May 1980 Kenneth Matthews (44), a former NF chairman, was sentenced to six years in jail for attempting to burn down the offices of the Trotskyist publication, *Socialist Challenge*.

National Party (NP)

John Kingsley Read led this splinter group from the National Front in December 1975. NP lasted a couple of years, after which most of its few hundred members returned to the National Front. More populist in tone than the mother fascist party, it had sought to establish links with the neo-Nazi National Youth Alliance in the United States and the German National Democratic Party (NPD) in the Federal Republic.

People's Democracy (PD)

In Ireland as in other countries of Europe, 1968 was the year of revolution, and it was amongst students of Queens University, Belfast, that People's Democracy was born in October. In January 1969 PD staged a civil rights march against the inequities practised by the Protestant establishment of Northern Ireland on the Roman Catholic minority. Members infiltrated the Northern Ireland Civil Rights Association (NICRA), which had initiated the 1968/69 marches, for their own purposes, and exploited the grievances so as to foment disorder and violence in the guise of supporting a non-violent movement. By this time it had fallen rapidly under the influence of the Trotskyist Young Socialist Alliance, which broadened PD's original Irish perspective to embrace world revolution.

Thenceforth it existed as a revolutionary splinter group, sympathetic to the Provisional *Sinn Fein* and to the Irish Republican Socialist Party, with whom PD toured Europe on behalf of the Irish republican cause in 1975. That same year PD representatives attended the national congress held by *Lotta Continua* in January, when firm links were established with the Italian ultra-leftist group.

Protestant Action Force (PAF)

In the mid-1970s, when it was active as a sectarian terrorist gang, the Force drew its members from the Ulster Volunteer Force. It chose its first victim from Belfast, but later carried out sectarian murders in Armagh and East Tyrone. With the flare-up of violence in mid-1982 the group surfaced again, murdering a Sinn Fein election worker, Joseph Corrigan, in October.

Provisional Irish Republican Army (PIRA)

The IRA split in December 1969 into Provisional and Official wings, the latter being Marxist-Leninist and sympathetic to the Soviet Union. Conscious that the Officials were putting ideology before nationalism, the Provisionals parted company. The actual point at issue was whether or not to participate in elections to the parliaments in Dublin, Belfast, and London, with which the Provisionals would have no truck. They were led by John Stephenson (Sean MacStiofain), Rory O'Brady (Ruairi O Bradaigh), Leo Martin, Billy McKee, Seamus Twomey and Francis Card (Prionnsias MacAirt), who together formed the Provisional Army Council.

PIRA's goal in the 1970s was to unite the north with the south into a 32-county island of Ireland, which would be republican and socialist. Adopting a non-aligned posture, the 'New Ireland' would neither form part of the European Economic Community, nor would it belong to NATO. On the economic front, PIRA advocated the nationalisation of key industries and severe limitations on foreign investments, largely, it appeared, for nationalistic reasons. The political programme was put over by a political organisation or party — the Provisional *Sinn Fein* (Ourselves Alone), which published a newspaper, *An Phoblacht*.

PIRA is a revolutionary organisation, in that its members believe that 'a revolutionary movement does not depend on a popular mandate as a basis for action. Its mandate comes from the justice and correctness of its cause . . . '. Militants believe in revolution as a means to accomplish their ends, but deny vigorously that they are Marxists or Communists.

The present troubles in Northern Ireland began with violence in the mid-1960s from Protestant extremist groups, or para-militaries as they are called, and it was to defend the Catholic community that PIRA took up arms in 1969. Their campaign exacerbated sectarian differences and hardened loyalties into two utterly opposed blocks separated by the religious divide. Symbolic of the divide were the 'no-go areas' in Belfast in 1972, when the government's writ no longer ran. Operation Motorman removed the barricades that summer.

The tactics employed by PIRA have included petrol and nail bombs in the early days, car bombs from a few pounds of explosives to over 1000 pounds left outside public buildings, incendiary devices in shops and department stores, letter bombs, assassination, kneecapping, and tarring and feathering. Snipers have picked off individual soldiers, mortars have been employed on specific targets like barracks and airports, whilst delayed action explosive devices and booby traps have stretched the ingenuity of the security forces. In assassinating Earl Mountbatten of Burma in 1979 PIRA reached out and struck at the highest in the land.

In jail Provisionals have embarked upon hunger strikes and died, others have for months on end refused to wear clothing. In protest they have fouled their cells persistently with their own excrement — certainly the most dramatic gesture encountered in the free world. Yet the men who have so fanatically dehumanised themselves in these ways had all been found guilty of serious crimes relating to one or other of the 2269 political killings, the 7521 bombings, which had killed 608 people, or the 1000 kneecappings which had occurred between 1969 and the end of 1982. Aside from the soldiers and policemen, the murders included judges, civil servants, and prison officers, but also the random individual killing, gangster style, of anyone across the religious divide.

In order to survive, PIRA requires something in the region of £¾ million a year. Much of this money comes from across the Atlantic, where Irish Americans are touched for contributions. Some is raised voluntarily, more comes from protection money paid by large companies in the area as well as by the humblest shopkeeper. A hotelier may pay £400 a week, a taxi-driver £2 a day. Prostitution and gambling also pay a political tax. Two of those most prominent in fund-raising are Charles McGlade and Joe Cahill; both men have terrorist records. Armed robbery is also employed — at least £6 million has been stolen over a decade.

Most of the Provisionals' modern arms come from the USA and include the M1 carbine, the Garand armour-piercing rifle and latterly (1978) the M-60 machine gun. Little was done in the early 1970s to stop this traffic; security was tighter from 1975 onwards. Besides North America, three consignments have been intercepted: from Czechoslovakia in 1971, from Libya in 1973 and from the Palestine Liberation Organisation (PLO) in 1977.

Outside Northern Ireland, PIRA has been active in England. The first bombs exploded in London and Birmingham in 1973. Others followed in 1974, when a coach carrying soldiers and their families was blown up, killing 12 people. Targets that year included Heathrow Airport, the National Defence College, Westminster Hall, the Tower of London, and three public houses known to be frequented by servicemen off duty. The worst act was a revenge bombing in Birmingham in November, when 21 people were killed and 180 injured in two blasts.

With bomb attacks upon a local pub in Caterham, Surrey, and explosions at the Hilton Hotel, in Piccadilly and in three London restaurants, 1975 was no quieter. As he opened his front door, the writer Ross McWhirter was shot dead, and a car bomb killed a renowned cancer specialist in Kensington, London. When four Provisionals surrendered to police after the six-day Balcomb Street siege, the London terror ended.

Abroad, PIRA was able to establish international contacts through the loosely affiliated Trotskyist network linked to the Fourth International in Brussels. The affinity existed from early days (1970) with the development in Belfast of People's Democracy and with the interest taken in the Provisionals by Gerry Lawless from the International Marxist Group (IMG) and Ernest Mandel, the Fourth International leader. On the continent Risteard Behal became European press officer and in 1978 struck up links with the French Revolutionary Communist League and the Portuguese United Workers' Organisation (OUT).

In addition to the ideological network, which was in fact of greater importance to the Irish National Liberation Army (INLA) than to the PIRA, there were contacts with European separatist groups, particularly the Freedom for the Basque Homeland group, ETA. PIRA recognised in 1975 the similarity of aims, but contacts had been established as early as 1972, when José Echevarrieta visited Dublin. Members of the political front set up by ETA's militarists, the Party for the Basque Revolution (EIA), attended the Provisionals' annual convention in 1977, and later that year Rory O'Brady visited the Basque country. EIA representatives were again present in 1978 at the Provisionals' Dublin convention. Such contacts were important from the point of view of morale, but insignificant so far as arms and training were concerned. Of still less impact were the contacts PIRA established with Breton, Flemish and other European minority ethnic groups.

The Middle East connection has been of less use to PIRA than it has to ETA. The Provisionals support the Palestinian cause, and alongside a dozen other national liberation groups the Popular Front for the Liberation of Palestine (PFLP) signed a declaration of support for PIRA in 1972. But very little use was made of training facilities, so that the Irish element in the transnational terrorism which arose from the training provided to foreigners was minimal. The PLO attempted nonetheless to deliver £¼ million worth of arms in 1977 by sea via Antwerp and Dublin. The shipment was intercepted and Seamus McCollum who had arranged it was sentenced to ten years in jail.

Libya provided help in the early and mid-1970s. Sean Ryan and Louis Maguire visited Tripoli as guests of Gadaffi in 1972. In June the Libyan leader stated that there were arms and support for Irish revolutionaries 'who are motivated by nationalism and religion'. But the running of arms from Tripoli by a West German smuggler on board the *Claudia* in March 1973 was frustrated by the Irish navy. Joe Cahill arranged the deal, which included 250 Soviet automatic rifles. For his trouble he served a three-year term. The Irish government itself succeeded in persuading Libya to desist from its support for PIRA in 1975, although Gadaffi still regarded Northern Ireland as under British colonisation.

In the early 1980s PIRA was variously estimated to have around 400 active adherents. This number was considerably less, possibly half the activists operating in the early 1970s. But there is no lack of recruits with high unemployment, should PIRA decide to escalate the violence. Many are in their teens, trained in the Republic, and cross the border with no difficulty. They are controlled by an Army Council, under a so-called Chief of Staff. They operated in the early 1980s in small independent units set up largely by Gerry Adams, who was released from prison in January 1977 and elected to a new Ulster Assembly in 1982, and Ivor Bell, who came out in September 1978.

Radical Student Alliance (RSA)

The RSA, formed in 1966, was Britain's counterpart to West Germany's ultra-left Socialist Student Alliance. Behind it was Fergus Nicholson, a student organiser of the orthodox Communist Party of Great Britain (CPGB), who hoped the RSA might act as a radicalising ginger group on the moderate National Union of Students (NUS).

The RSA had links abroad through the Amsterdam-based Congress of European Syndicalist Students (CESE), organised by Martin Abeln. The CESE kept small groups of students in Belgium, France, Germany, Britain, Holland, Ireland, Luxembourg, Switzerland, and Canada and the United States in contact with one another.

Christopher Gilmore, a CPGB member, became secretary to the RSA, which concerned itself through David Adelstein with student protest at the London School of Economics, and through David Triesman at Essex University. RSA representatives were present in Paris during the May 1968 events and also at demonstrations in West Germany. But student protest in Britain never reached the proportions experienced in France, Germany and Italy.

Red Hand Commandos

After being forced out of the Ulster Defence Association, John McKeague set up this para-military clandestine group in Belfast in mid-1972. It consisted of the uglier elements of society, whose crimes fortunately never rooted themselves in the community. McKeague was shot dead in January 1982, reputedly by militants from the Irish National Liberation Army.

Shankhill Defence Association (SDA)

Set up in 1969, the SDA was largely the creation of its chairman, John McKeague (shot dead 1982), and his deputy, Fred Proctor. Originally a community association, the new SDA in Wilton Street, Belfast, became a Protestant armed vigilante group in one of the city's toughest areas. It swiftly boasted of a thousand members, who patrolled the upper Shankhill, and came to symbolise 'loyalist' militancy. Members wore armbands and crash helmets and carried cudgels, using them to intimidate the isolated Catholic family, so as to force it to move from a predominantly Protestant area to a Catholic one, and to encourage Protestants to leave predominantly Catholic communities.

The worst rioting where SDA men were involved took place in front of Unity Flats, a Catholic complex, near Shankhill road, on 2 August 1969. Police battled with a crowd under McKeague's direction, several thousand strong. Shops were looted, cars burned, windows broken, and a police water cannon attacked with petrol bombs and gelignite. The fighting lasted until the early hours, when fires were eventually quelled. Some 70 policemen and 200 civilians were injured. The incident put the SDA beyond the political pale; thenceforth the Rev. Ian Paisley, who came to symbolise loyalist politics, dissociated himself from the movement.

Undoubtedly, many SDA members also militated in the ranks of the Ulster Volunteer Force (UVF) and together for a short while that summer they broadcast Radio Free Shankhill. Wearing anoraks and hoods, and in defiance of the army, vigilantes threw up barricades until such time as the Catholic no-go areas were removed. In September they took on the army in street fighting; in October the Catholics of Unity Flats.

In response to increasingly ugly SDA terror tactics, the Provisional IRA was born that year in the Clonard district of Belfast, and so too were British troops first used in the present troubles. Under SDA auspices gun clubs were formed in the Shankhill, Oldpark, Crumlin and Glencairn areas of Belfast. But the armed potential of the SDA was never realised: the movement was overtaken by the Provisionals' armed offensive against the British army. In this encounter the militant loyalists took a ring-side seat only.

As an organisation, the SDA broke up in factional quarrelling; McKeague himself was prosecuted unsuccessfully in 1971 for inciting racial hatred in a Loyalist Song Book. A decade later he was murdered in Belfast.

Sinn Fein
(Ourselves Alone)

Sinn Fein was the original Irish nationalist party founded in 1905, when Ireland was still British. The party won overwhelming support in the elections of 1918 (73 out of 105 seats), but the elected MPs, instead of attending at Westminster, convened a revolutionary parliament in Ireland, the *Dail Eireann*. Their stand was supported by armed militants, who from mid-1919 until the truce in July 1921 attacked the British administration, earning for themselves the title of Irish Republican Army (IRA).

Some members of *Sinn Fein* accepted the partition of Ireland in 1921, others did not, so that a civil war was fought between June 1922 and May 1923. Those who lost became today's *Sinn Fein*, a nationalist party dedicated to reuniting Ireland. Their armed branch was the IRA. But whereas today the IRA is illegal in both Northern Ireland and the Republic, *Sinn Fein* is not. Their aims are identical, but their methods differ, although in fact members of the one more often than not pass over to become members of the other.

When the IRA split in 1969 into a Provisional and an Official wing, *Sinn Fein* split too. The Provisional *Sinn Fein* organised itself with regional committees and local branches covering all 32 counties of Ireland. It took no part in any of the elections held in the north, urging, uselessly as it turned out, a general boycott. In the Republic too it abstained from general elections, largely because of the party's minimal following. The principal personalities include Rory O'Brady, Provisional *Sinn Fein* president, Seamus Twomey and Martin McGuiness. According to its president, in 1977 Provisional *Sinn Fein* was 'a movement totally committed to revolution right across the board from top to bottom . . . .'

The Official *Sinn Fein* is led by Tomas MacGiolla in the Republic and Seamus Lynch in the north, where the party operates through the Republican Clubs, which became an integral part of a new Official party, known as *Sinn Fein* the Workers' Party (1977). By this time the Officials had renounced all links with para-military or terrorist activity, and in 1979 so as to avoid further confusion with Provisional *Sinn Fein*, even proposed dropping *Sinn Fein* from the title. Thereafter it was known simply as the Workers' Party, leaving the Provisionals' political front to contest the 1982 Northern Ireland Assembly elections as *Sinn Fein*.

Socialist Workers' Party (SWP)

The British SWP was formed in December 1976 from a group of Trotskyists who were previously known as the International Socialists, men and women who had left the Fourth International because of their conviction that the Soviet Union had become a 'state-capitalist' society. They possibly number some 5000 individuals, who are convinced that both Stalinists and those Trotskyists that remained in the Fourth International have deviated from the original Bolshevik truth. An armed revolutionary struggle is needed, and in the course of the conflict new representative bodies will emerge.

The SWP chairman in 1979 was Duncan Hallas, but better known were journalist Paul Foot, related to the British Labour Party leader, and Tony Cliff, a pseudonym for Ygael Gluckstein. Their views are published in the weekly *Socialist Worker*. They keep in close contact with the French Workers' Struggle (*Lutte Ouvrière*) and the Italian Workers' Vanguard (*Avanguardia Operaia*) movements. In Britain the SWP claims its greatest support in the north of England and in Glasgow. SWP members were prominent in the demonstrations organised by the Anti-Nazi League against the National Front in the late 1970s, when the streets of some British cities saw a resurgence of political violence.

Tartan Army

The Army for Freeing Scotland, or the Tartan Army, emerged in 1974, the fanciful product of a small group of young people out of work. In 1975 four sabotage attacks were made, twice on an oil pipe-line, on the Clyde tunnel, and on a railway line near Dunbarton East station. A further bomb scare closed the Forth Bridge for a while.

That year several arrests were made, and prison sentences followed on the conviction of six young men for conspiring to set up a clandestine military force. Two more were sentenced in January 1976 to a total of ten years in jail.

Troops Out Movement (TOM)

TOM was formed in September 1973 to lobby the trade union movement into supporting the withdrawal of British troops from Northern Ireland. Trotskyists soon penetrated the group, a development which led ultimately to a split in mid-1977 and the creation of United Troops Out Movement (UTOM). TOM ceased to exist; UTOM, although Trotskyist, drew close to the Provisional *Sinn Fein*. Most of the supporters were drawn from the International Marxist Group (IMG) and the Socialist Workers' Party (SWP).

Ulster Defence Association (UDA)

The UDA was formed in 1971 to group the various Protestant defence associations in Belfast, particularly the Shankhill, Woodvale, Ormeau, Carrick, Donnegall Pass, Hammer, Newtownabbey, Abbots Cross, Woodburn, Lisburn Road, Seymour Hill, Suffolk, Castlereagh, Beersbridge, Upper Woodstock and Dundonald areas. The initiative was taken by Charles Harding Smith in order 'to see law restored everywhere, including the "no-go" areas'. Members were to call themselves Ulster Volunteers, and to publish a *UDA Bulletin*.

From the start the UDA was faction-ridden, with the principal contestants being John McKeague, with his base in Shankhill, and Harding Smith, strongly supported in Woodvale. In 1972, with the formation of William Craig's Vanguard party, the UDA became virtually its paramilitary wing.

Most of that year Harding Smith, the UDA chairman, spent in prison, accused of negotiating an illegal purchase of arms. He was however acquitted, and in January 1973 was reinstated as joint-chairman of an organisation that had grown to 60,000 strong. Within months he was back in custody, and a glazier, Jim Anderson, then 42 years old, took over the UDA.

Anderson reorganised the UDA along military lines. Tommy Herron (34), an ex-garage mechanic, became until his death in 1973 its principal spokesman. At the top of the UDA was a 13-man Inner Council consisting of Samuel Doyle (Oldpark and Crumlin districts), David Fogel, a Londoner and ex-army NCO (Woodvale and Ardoyne), John Graham, a former SDA man (Shankhill), Ernest Willis (Rathcoole), Tom McCreary (Ballysillan), Billy Rowan (Newtownards and Dundonald), Frank Jones (Woodstock and Cregagh), Edward McCreery (Newtownards), Jack Watson (Sand Row and Lisburn Road), Ernie Elliott (Woodvale) and David Payne (Shankhill).

It was the UDA which manned the Protestants' barricades of 1972, characterised by their combat jackets and hoods. They aped the IRA purposefully, even to copying the Provisionals' funeral ceremony. Like the UVF, members were drawn from the Protestant urban working classes, and until a truce was called in October they challenged the British army in Belfast.

Afterwards the UDA took to making up explosives in Belfast and bombing south of the border. These explosions continued intermittently through the mid-1970s; the bombs were often placed in hotels and known meeting places of the IRA. Sometimes these actions were claimed by the Ulster Freedom Fighters, an off-shoot of the UDA.

In 1974 the UDA opposed political reform based upon power-sharing, and took part that year in the general strike, which the Ulster Workers' Council coordinated. Consequently, the British Government resumed direct rule of the province, and abandoned its attempts to set up a new Assembly to replace the old Stormont Parliament. The UDA maintained its place throughout the decade as the most important Protestant paramilitary grouping in Ulster. It also had strong links with Scotland, whence it derived support. It did not shrink from murder for which several members have been tried, found guilty and sentenced.

Ulster Freedom Fighters (UFF)

The UFF emerged in the summer of 1973 from the Ulster Defence Association in Northern Ireland. It was a militant para-military Protestant organisation, loosely composed of violent firebrands anxious to take the law into their own hands, more for kicks than through fear of the Provisional IRA. Members carried out assassinations across the political divide, and may have numbered several dozen regulars. Sporadic activity continued throughout the decade and into the 1980s, when fears of a political sell-out by Westminster to Dublin were sharpened. UFF activities were a constant reminder of the terrorism which might surface with a vengeance were the British army to withdraw from Ulster.

Ulster Protestant Volunteers (UPV)

Set up in early 1966 by Noel Doherty, the UPV was quickly submerged in the Ulster Constitution Defence Committee (UCDC), which formed the political nucleus of Ian Paisley's future group, the Democratic Unionist Party. Doherty was Paisley's political organiser in the early days, responsible for producing his propaganda in Ravenhill Road at the Puritan Printing Company opposite Paisley's Free Presbyterian Church, which he had joined in 1956. He became a Protestant Unionist candidate at the age of 23 (1964), and was a member of the B Specials, a police force later disbanded by the government. The UPV adopted the motto of the proscribed Ulster Volunteer Force (UVF), 'For God and Ulster'.

The UCDC was defined as the 'governing body' of the UPV, for which only 'born Protestants' were eligible. Following the descent into bloody violence by the UVF, the link was broken by Paisley himself in June 1966. He and the vice-chairman of the UCDC, James McConnell, summarily expelled Doherty from the movement he had helped found.

But with divisions all over the province, the UPV continued to exist, and was closely involved in the demonstrations against the 1968 civil rights marches. Among the organisers were Douglas Hutchinson, Frank Mallon, John McKeague and Major Ronald Bunting. The UPV remained a legal organisation after the UVF had been proscribed in 1966, and was used as a front by UVF sympathisers.

Ulster Volunteer Force (UVF)

Throughout the decade of the 1970s, the UVF was a force of militant Protestant loyalists, whose origins go back to 1912, when from the individual forces of Orange lodges Edward Carson founded such a body, which in 1929 became the Ulster Special Constabulary. In 1966 Augustus Spence set up the present organisation, which within weeks was proscribed under the Special Powers Act by the Northern Irish Government at Stormont.

Spence defined the UVF as 'a military body dedicated to upholding the constitution of Ulster by force of arms if necessary'. At its height in Belfast in the late 1960s and early 1970s, it probably claimed the allegiance of 500 members, who financed their activities largely through protection rackets.

'Gusty' Spence came from the notorious lower Shankhill area of Belfast, of tough Protestant working-class antecedents. He had served in the British army and as a military policeman in Cyprus, and in 1966 was 33 years old. Together with Ian Paisley and Noel Doherty, he reconstituted the UVF in March, at the time of the foundation of Paisley's fortnightly *Protestant Telegraph*, printed by Doherty's new Puritan Printing Company. He was a member of the Apprentice Boys and of the Royal Black Preceptory, both arch-Orange organisations.

The first recorded UVF action took place on 16 April 1966, when bullets were fired at the door of Unionist MP John McQuade, in the Shankhill area. Yet earlier in March unclaimed attacks had been made on Catholic premises in Belfast. These petrol bomb attacks continued in April and May, when through court conviction UVF responsibility was confirmed.

On 21 May 1966 the UVF declared war against the IRA. 'Known IRA men will be executed mercilessly and without hesitation. Less extreme measures will be taken against anyone sheltering or helping them, but if they persist in giving them aid then more extreme measures will be adopted. Property will not be exempted in any action taken.'

The first UVF murder occurred on 26 May, when one John Scullion was shot on his way home from the pub. A second murder attempt followed on 4 June.

Official Unionism was quick to dissociate itself from the UVF and from Paisley himself. In the words of Terence O'Neil, the Northern Irish premier, 'the contempt for established authority, the crude and unthinking intolerance; the emphasis upon monster processions and rallies; the appeal to a perverted form of patriotism; each and every one of these things has its parallel in the rise of the Nazis to power . . . History must not be allowed to repeat itself in this small corner of the Commonwealth.'

On 25 June Spence was involved with two other men in the cold-blooded murder of a Catholic barman in Belfast. Within hours he was arrested and later convicted in court and sentenced to life imprisonment. Paisley denied all contact with the UVF, and steered well clear of political violence. But the Ulster Constitution Defence Committee (UCDC), of which Paisley was chairman, remained tainted by the early association.

With Spence in Crumlin Road jail, the UVF fell apart in 1967. But in 1969 a series of blasts which damaged an electricity pylon and the control valves and supply pipes of Belfast's water supply saw the reemergence of the UVF as a sabotage unit. In all, five attacks were mounted in which Frank Mallon, Samuel Stephenson, Thomas McDowell, who blew himself up, and John McKeague were accused of being involved. Some were Ulster Protestant Volunteers (UPV), but their association overlapped with the UVF. Stephenson was found guilty and sentenced to 12 years imprisonment, but Mallon and McKeague were acquitted. Both denied membership of the UVF.

Thenceforth the potential membership of the UVF was more important than its actions. The spirit which had led to its formation was channelled in 1971 into the Ulster Defence Association, although the UVF still operated as an independent organisation in 1972, helping to establish a Protestant 'no-go' area in Londonderry that June.

When 'Gusty' Spence was briefly released on parole that year, he was kidnapped by his well-wishers and hidden from the police for some months. The UVF enjoyed a revival, with members adopting a uniform of black berets and leather jackets. A number were arrested and stood trial, but refused to recognise the court. To a man the UVF remained a working-class organisation, and without intellectual or middle-class political leadership. With Spence in jail, Kenneth Gibson was the leading personality.

The most savage killings took place in the autumn of 1974, after the murder of a judge and a magistrate in Belfast by teenage Provisional gunmen. Within a month, 16 Catholics had been shot dead in the city. But subsequently UVF gunmen settled personal scores with the rival Protestant Ulster Freedom Fighters.

There was little Protestant violence after 1976, when the UVF suspended 'military activity' in May. Eight men belonging to the UVF were sentenced to life imprisonment for murder in March 1977, and 23 others were convicted of attempted murder, armed robberies, bombing and illegal possession of arms. Further convictions followed in 1978, when one UVF member was sentenced to life-imprisonment sixteen times over, and in 1979, when the 'Shankhill butchers' (11 men) were given a total of 42 life sentences for 19 killings.

Ulster Workers' Council (UWC)

The UWC emerged in Belfast in 1973 on the same lines as the Loyalist Association of Workers, which it replaced. By 1974 the UWC covered the whole province, so that each of its seven sections held regular meetings and elected three deputies to the 21-man Council. Most prominent was Glen Barr, then 31, a former shop steward and a Vanguard Assembly member for Londonderry.

The UWC concentrated upon recruiting key workers in key industries, a policy which gave it the power in 1974 to shut down all activity in Ulster, and thus compel London to abandon its political reform programme. The elected leaders of the trade union movement condemned the strike which the UWC called in May, but, undeterred, workers brought the province to a standstill.

Central government authority was replaced by that of a 15-man Co-ordinating Committee, made up of three UWC members, William Craig, leader of the Vanguard political party, Ian Paisley, leader of the Democratic Unionist Party, Harry West, and seven representatives of the Protestant para-military groups. Barricades of vehicles, wood and sheet metal stopped public transport. Commerce ceased, with banks and offices closed. The strike committee authorised chemists to stay open; food could be sold in the mornings. Volunteers manned advice centres, and pensioners received free candles, tea and butter. Streets were swept and rubbish regularly collected: order reigned throughout. Outside Belfast, farmers cooperated by bringing in supplies of milk, butter, eggs and fuel.

The unanimity then displayed brought about the resignation of Brian Faulkner's power-sharing Executive, and the collapse therefore of Westminster's attempt to reform Ulster's political system. London assumed responsibility for government in the province, and immediately the UWC called off the strike.

Workers' Revolutionary Party (WRP)

Gerry Healy is the only name popularly associated with the WRP, known as a dogmatic and pedantic theoretician, but also as a leader who exacted the greatest discipline from his followers. He claimed the WRP was an orthodox Trotskyist party, although it had in Britain fewer adherents than either the International Marxist Group or the Socialist Workers' Party. However, in the 1960s Healy made his impact upon the Labour Party by infiltrating the Young Socialists, which Labour subsequently excised.

Abroad, the WRP had its links through the International Committee of the Fourth International (ICFI), based in London. Including Britain it had eight national sections in Australia, Canada, United States, Ireland, West Germany, Greece and Sri Lanka.

Yugoslavia

Yugoslavia was created in 1918, when former Austro-Hungarian territories were added to Serbia, an independent country since the first half of
the nineteenth century. Consequently it comprises many peoples
amongst whom are Serbs, Croats, Slovenes, Albanians, Macedonians
and Montenegrins. Not surprisingly, Yugoslavia's greatest internal
problem has been its pluri-national complexity. Croats have been particularly active in asserting national rights and under fascist sponsorship
even enjoyed a short-lived state of their own (1941-45). Since then the
original Croat nationalist or *Ustaša* (pl. *Ustaše*) movement has
spawned many terrorist groups, largely active abroad against Yugoslav
targets but from time to time in Yugoslavia itself.

Kosovo, with its predominantly Albanian population, has been a
source of sporadic violent unrest in the 1970s and early 1980s. Albanian
nationalists, spearheaded by student groups, have pressed nationalist
demands for Kosovo to be created an autonomous republic within
Yugoslavia, demands which Belgrade fears would lead to the pressing of
irredentist claims from neighbouring Albania.

That the modern Yugoslav state has functioned so well despite strong
centripetal tendencies is largely the achievement of Marshall Tito (d.
1978), who, at the end of the Second World War, emerged as the leader of
the principal resistance movement and hence of Yugoslavia. Tito's rift
with the USSR in 1948 led to the expulsion of Yugoslavia from the
Soviet-controlled Cominform organisation, and subsequently Moscow
intrigued virulently against Tito. Pro-Soviet communists have therefore
been dubbed Cominformists and rigorous police action against them,
notably in the mid-1970s, has been a feature of Yugoslav political life.

Bibliography
On the contemporary Croat problem, see Stephen Clissold's excellent
paper 'Croat Separatism: Nationalism, Dissidence and Terrorism' (ISC,
London, 1979), and for the nationality problem, Paul Lendvai 'National
Tensions in Yugoslavia' (ISC, London, 1972) in the same series.

Cominformists

Since 1948 a group of anti-Tito exiles known as 'Cominformists' has lived
in the USSR and Eastern Europe and been used by Moscow for pro-

Soviet subversion within Yugoslavia. In Autumn 1973 a group of 'Cominformists' in Kosovo-Metohija, headed by Dr Branislav Bošković, a university professor from Pristina, made contact with another group in Montenegro. The meeting paved the way for a clandestine congress held in Bar, Montenegro, in April 1974. The group was arrested shortly afterwards, and following two trials in Pec (Kosovo) and Titograd (Montenegro) 32 'Cominformists' were sentenced to jail terms ranging from one to 14 years. Subsequently, in July 1975, a group of seven, including the former head of the Bosnian secret police, was sentenced as 'Cominformists' in Tuzla, Bosnia in July 1975.

Support for 'Cominformism', with its emphasis on Soviet-style centralism and firm direction from above, has been most associated with Serbs, particularly those living outside Serbia proper. A 'Cominformist' leader, Colonel Vlado Dapčević, was kidnapped in Bucharest (Rumania) in 1975 and taken to Yugoslavia, where he was sentenced to death, later commuted to 20 years imprisonment. By early 1976 the state's campaign against the 'Cominformists' was largely over.

Croat Illegal Revolutionary Organisation
(Hrvatska Ilegalna Revolucionarna Organizacija — HIRO)

This is a front name which the Croatian Revolutionary Brotherhood (HRB) used in the mid-1970s.

Croat Liberation Movement
(Hrvatski Oslobodilački Pokret — HOP)

HOP was founded in 1956 by the *Ustaša* veteran, Pavelić, in Argentina. It was a front organisation for the still extent Rebel Croat Revolutionary Organisation (UHRO). Its purpose was to provide a more respectable front for the old fascist *Ustaša* organisation. After Pavelić's death, it was headed by one of his former ministers, Dr Stjepan Hefer, and from 1976 by the writer, Ante Bonifačić.

Croat National Congress
(Hrvatsko Narodno Vijeće — HNV)

Founded in 1974 in Toronto, the HNV attempts to serve as an umbrella organisation for the many exiled Croat groups. Officially it deprecates terrorism but the organisation includes many prominent *Ustaše* veterans and provides moral and financial support for arrested Croat terrorists. It actively promotes Croat nationalist propaganda and is believed to undertake additional illegal work.

Croat National Resistance
(Hrvatski Narodni Otpor — HNO)

This *Ustaša* organisation was founded in the aftermath of the Second World War in Spain under the direction of General Max Luberić. He had been in charge of the Croat concentration camps during the brief period of the fascist 'Independent Croat State' (1941-45). As such he had earned himself the unenviable reputation of being a 'Croatian Himmler'. The HNO ran a terrorist organisation, *Drina*, which continued to be active well into the 1970s. Luberić was murdered in 1969, but the HNO survived. It continued in Australia under the former UHRO militant, Srecko Blaž Rover, and in West Germany under Stjepan Bilandžić. It carried out several attacks in the mid-1970s on Yugoslav officials and trains. It was banned in West Germany in 1976 but maintained a clandestine existence publishing *Otpor* (Resistance). However, on 25 May 1978 the HNO chairman, Stjepan Bilandžić, was arrested in West Germany on terrorist charges.

The Croatian Revolutionary Brotherhood
(Hrvatsko Revolucionarno Bratsvo — HRB)

The HRB emerged in Australia in the 1950s, when it engaged in the training of terrorists who were infiltrated into Yugoslavia in 1963 and 1972. The HRB was held to be responsible for the murder of Stuttgart Yugoslav Consul, Sava Milovanović, in 1967. The movement was banned in West Germany in 1968, but carried out a number of bombing attacks against Yugoslav properties in Australia and allegedly planned to murder Yugoslav prime minister Bijedić during his visit to Australia. Under police pressure it disappeared for a while, but reemerged as the Croat Illegal Revolutionary Organisation before reverting to its HRB label.

The HRB has been attributed with the murder of the Yugoslav Ambassador in Stockholm, and the hijacking of a Swedish airliner, the murder of the Uruguayan Ambassador in Paraguay (mistaken for the Yugoslav Ambassador), and the seizing of hostages in West Germany's Chicago consulate.

Croatian Youth
(Hrvatska Mladež — HM)

HM serves largely as a legal support movement for the United Croats of West Germany. Several of the latters' tougher militants are known to have been inducted into full membership after activity in HM. The HM has a quasi-fascist ideology and still venerates the memory of the founder of the *Ustaša* movement, Dr Ante Pavelić.

Drina

Drina is the terrorist wing of the Croat National Resistance (HNO). It was active in terrorist attacks in the 1960s and 1970s, especially in West Germany where it was formally banned in 1976. It is named after the river Drina.

Fighters for a Free Croatia
(Borci za Slobodnu Hrvatsku — BSH)

Based in the United States, this group has been responsible for a number of attacks on the Yugoslav mission to the United Nations. In September 1976 its members hijacked a Transworld airliner on a flight between New York and Chicago and compelled it to fly to London and Paris, where the terrorists finally gave up after scattering leaflets.

Krizari
(Crusaders)

The *Križari* were small bands of anti-communist guerrillas active in Bosnia in the immediate aftermath of the Second World War.

Rebel Croat Revolutionary Organization
(Ustaša Hrvatska Revolucionarna Organizacija — UHRO)

The UHRO was founded in Italy in 1932 under the leadership of a Zagreb lawyer, Dr Ante Pavelić. Enjoying Mussolini's patronage, UHRO set up training camps near Brescia. Its initial membership was by no means entirely Croat: among its ranks UHRO also counted poor and discontented emigrant workers from Belgium and Latin America. By 1934 UHRO had some 550 terrorists acting for it.

First fascist Italy and then Nazi Germany backed the UHRO as a way of securing Axis objectives in the Balkans. Not surprisingly, the *Ustaše* adopted the ideology and trappings of fascism. Pavelić himself became *Poglavnik (Duce, Führer)*. UHRO's first spectacular achievement was the assassination of King Alexander and the French foreign minister, M. Barthou, in Marseilles on 9 October 1934.

On 10 April 1941 German troops entered Zagreb and set up an 'Independent Croat State' under *Ustaše* administration. The new Croat state comprised not only Croatia but also Bosnia-Hercegovina with its substantial Serbian population. The brief period of *Ustaše* rule was characterised by a barbarous repression of Serbs, Jews, gypsies and Croat democrats, many of whom were slaughtered. On 6 May 1945

Pavelić and many of his closest supporters fled the country and made their way to Argentina, where the UHRO maintained a shadowy existence.

In 1956 Pavelić founded the Croat Liberation Movement (HOP), but the old UHRO organisation remained intact under the control of the HOP Military Office. However by the 1970s this original *Ustaša* organisation had been eclipsed by the rise of new Croat nationalist groupings such as the Croatian Revolutionary Brotherhood and *Drina*.

United Croats of West Germany
(Ujedinjeni Hrvati Njemaske — UHNj)

UHNj specialises in the assassination of Yugoslav officials and in intimidating Yugoslav emigrés into supporting and financing its activities.

World League of Croat Youth
(Svetska Liga Hvratske Omladine — SLHO)

SLHO provides many recruits for the United Croats of West Germany organisation. Its members are required to take a traditional *Ustaša* — style oath dedicated to the destruction of Yugoslavia, reminiscent of its fascist background.

AFRICA

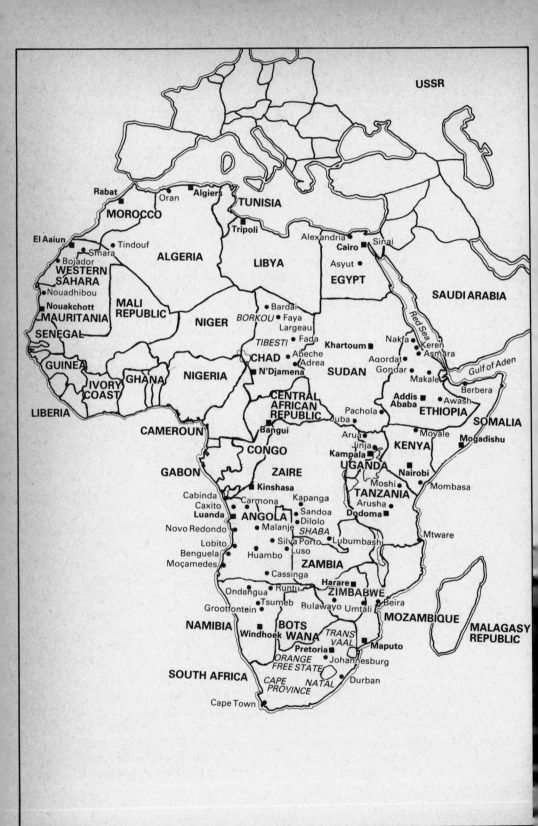

Introduction

Where Europeans had settled in Africa, they sought to protect their interests from the reemergence of black political power, a strength which the black man acquired by mastering the basic elements of the very technology and education with which the white man had first enslaved and colonised him. Elsewhere, the colonising power withdrew, thereby allowing most of Africa to recover bloodlessly its political independence.

There were exceptions. The Kikuyu in Kenya were the first blacks to rebel (Mau Mau), but having put down the revolt the British granted independence not only to Kenya, but to their other colonial territories. Here the exception was Southern Rhodesia, whose white population declared unilateral independence in 1965. White intransigence immediately transformed black nationalism into a liberation struggle: the guerrilla forces of the original Zimbabwe African People's Union (ZAPU) under Joshua Nkomo, and of Ndabaningi Sithole's more militant Zimbabwe African National Union (ZANU) began their armed incursions from Zambia and later continued from Mozambique. These movements grew in strength to the point when in December 1979 they virtually negotiated their independence at the Lancaster House Conference in London.

Until 1974 the white settlers in Rhodesia derived great advantage from Portuguese rule in Mozambique, where blacks in the Mozambique Liberation Front (Frelimo) were unable to afford their Zimbabwean colleagues a comfortable haven or base, intent as they were upon achieving their own liberation. Following the April 1974 revolution in Lisbon and the subsequent Portuguese withdrawal from Africa, the position changed. It changed not only for Rhodesia, but for that great citadel of white industrial power, the Republic of South Africa, with its four million Europeans, who had felt protected from black demands by the lax Lusitanian colonialism to the north.

With the coming to power of Frelimo and the Popular Movement for the Liberation of Angola (MPLA), the liberation movements in Namibia, a territory under South African tutelage, and in South Africa were given an immense moral boost, and in the case of the South West African People's Organisation (SWAPO) a base in territory contiguous to the struggle. In Mozambique the South African African National Congress (ANC) found a welcome in Maputo. The new proximity of hostile forces compelled South Africa to take the war outside its frontiers and to attack the guerrillas at base, in Angola and Mozambique. Undoubtedly successful in military terms, the raids did nothing to contain the keen sense of injustice felt towards a system which excluded blacks not only from participation in government but from most of the advantages of a developed economy. Nor did they contain the occasional terrorist incident inside the Republic in the early 1980s, when it seemed more than ever that the Afrikaaner would be compelled to compromise in a new constitutional deal.

French Africa, with the exception of Algeria, where the National Liberation Front (FLN) fought a campaign and lost but in 1962 inherited the territory nonetheless, received its independence without a struggle. The manner in which France divided its vast possessions into new states and incorporated them in economic and military arrangements gave rise to charges of neo-colonialism. However other than in Guinea the French presence seems not to have been resented, and was on occasions welcomed as a stabilising force in the late 1970s, when the Arabs to the north threatened the negro, as in times past they had enslaved him.

Spain withdrew from its African territories of the Western Sahara and Equitorial Guinea in a hurry, anxious to complete the exercise before General Franco's death in 1975. In doing so it left the problem of the Polisario guerrillas to fester. By the early 1980s the whole Saharan region was affected by the ambitions of Colonel Gadaffi, a man whose power derived from oil and whose motivations came from the Koran. His particular pan-Islamic interest threatened the territorial integrity of Mauritania and Chad, in addition to the Western Sahara, and further afield through his interest in the Palestinian cause, in the Middle East itself.

Hunger contributed to political violence in Africa. It drove nomadic tribes across frontiers to seek shelter in refugee camps which then became recruiting grounds for Polisario. As a root cause it contributed to a number of *coups d'états*, and most particularly to the fall of the Ethiopian Emperor Haile Selassie in 1974. In Ethiopia the struggle for power was relatively long — some three years — and singularly bloody. In 1977/78 the ultra-leftist Ethiopian People's Revolutionary Party (EPRP) was all but annihilated by a government-backed 'red terror' campaign. The terror left Colonel Mengistu in sole command, having physically eliminated his rivals, and with the help of Soviet and Cuban forces he warded off the military threat of Somali irredentism in the huge Ogaden region, and of Eritrean separatism along the Red Sea coast.

The sources of political violence in Africa are most frequently tribal in nature, and undoubtedly account for more deaths than the ethnic struggle waged either against colonialism or against white settlers. The worst and largely unrecorded instance is that of Burundi in 1972, when the ruling Tutsi elite exacted from the majority Hutu a revenge for rebellion which left 100,000 dead. In Nigeria the strong sense of ethnicity among the Ibo prompted Colonel Ojukwu to secede, which in 1967 provoked the Biafran war. Before battle commenced at least 10,000 fleeing Ibo refugees had been slaughtered by their black Islamic brothers. During the conflict further massacres occurred.

In the Sudan, ever since independence in 1956, the southerner with his tribal links stretching into Uganda and the Congo had revolted against his post-colonial Islamic northern masters. In 1963 the southern Anya Nya instigated a cruel terrorism, which in turn brought down upon their heads a repression that drove 100,000 blacks into exile. The conflict dragged on until 1972, when a degree of autonomy in the south provided the basis for a political settlement.

Finally, tribal violence marked the conflict in the Congo (Zaïre) in 1960, when several thousand people died. Moises Tshombe failed to bring Katanga (Shaba) province to birth as a state — but the revolt left the seeds of conflict, which were revived from Angola in the Shaba (Katanga) invasions of 1977 and 1978. With Cuban help, the newly independent Angolan regime had sought and had succeeded in destabilising Zaïre, in retaliation for the harassment which Holden Roberto's Front for the National Liberation of Angola (FNLA) practised from its Zaïrian haven.

In its often private barbarity, tyranny too has contributed to modern Africa's political violence. In Uganda Amin subjected high and low alike to a most brutal rule (1971-79), as in the latter days of his Empire did Bokassa in the Central African Republic (1966-79). Similarly disgusting in nature was Macia's cruelty in Equatorial Guinea (1968-79).

Bibliography

To comprehend conflict in Africa some general books dealing with the fundamental problems of African nationalism, of the role of colonialism and slavery and of military intervention in politics are essential reading. Often the protagonists themselves contributed greatly to the literature, see especially Kenneth Kaunda, *Africa's Freedom* (London, 1964) and *Zambia Shall Be Free* (London, 1962), Kwame Nkrumah, *Africa Must Unite* (London, 1963), and Julius Nyerere, *Freedom and Unity* (London, 1966) and *Freedom and Socialism* (Dar es Salaam, 1968). For Malawi and Zambia, see Robert Rothberg, *The Rise of Nationalism in Central Africa* (Cambridge, Mass., 1966); for French Africa, there are three basic books, Edward Mortimer, *France and the Africans 1944-60* (London and New York, 1969), Ruth Morgenthau, *Political Parties in French Speaking West Africa* (London, 1964) and Franz Ausprenger, *Politik im schwarzen Afrika* (Cologne, 1961). The work of Ali Mazrui, is particularly perceptive, see *Violence and Thought: Essays on Social Tensions in Africa* (London, 1969) and Robert Rothberg and Ali Mazrui, *Protest and Power in Black Africa* (London, 1970). On pan-Africanism, read Richard Cox, *PanAfricanism in Practice 1958-64* (London, 1964). On the military, see William Gutteridge, *The Military in African Politics* (London, 1969) and from an author committed to the Left, but nonetheless sincere, Ruth First, *The Barrel of a Gun, Political Power in Africa and the Coup d'Etat* (Penguin, 1970), and the essay by Edward Feit in *World Politics* Vol. 20, No. 2 (January 1968) entitled 'Military Coups and Political Development: Some Lessons from Ghana and Nigeria'.

Portuguese Africa is best approached for the first time through James Duffy's *Portugal in Africa* (Penguin, 1962), Ronald Chilcote's *Portuguese Africa* (Prentice Hall, 1967) and Malyn Newilt's *Portugal in Africa* (London, 1981). David Abshire and Michael Samuels contributed a series of essays in *Portuguese Africa: A Handbook* (New York, 1969). William Minter discussed the Western interest in the conflict in *Portuguese Africa and the West* (New York, 1972). Neil Bruce provided a brief introduction to the fighting in *Portugal's African Wars* (ISC, London, 1973).

Kenneth Grundy dealt generally with the history of the whole liberation struggle in *Guerrilla Struggle in Africa* (New York, 1971), whilst Richard Gibson chronicled the main English-speaking movements in *African Liberation Movements* (OUP, 1972). Michael Morris, a South African writer and former Special Branch officer, considered the overall problems of the area in *Southern African Terrorism* (Cape Town, 1971). Peter Janke reviewed succinctly the mid-1970s in *Southern Africa: New Horizons* (ISC, London, 1976) and *Marxist Statecraft in Africa: What Future?* (ISC, London, 1978).

Algeria

Algeria is no longer afflicted by the political violence which brought about the country's independence from France in 1962, nor internally does it suffer from violent opposition. Of all French acquisitions in Africa, Algeria had the longest history, having been first colonised in the 1830s. By the post-war period there were one and a half million Europeans, not all of them French, living in the territory and enjoying the bulk of the wealth produced.

Conditions for the indigenous Muslim population (nine million), with the exception of an elite, were poor, but deprivation and inequality did not in itself cause Algerian nationalism to assert itself. Rather it was the example of their Muslim brothers in Tunisia and Morocco, both countries which received their independence in 1956, and further afield President Nasser in Egypt, which finally stimulated nationalist feeling to revolt.

At first moderation prevailed with the establishment in 1946 by Messali Hadj of the Movement for the Triumph of Democratic Liberties (MTDL). From this body militants split to found the Secret Organisation (OS), led by Ahmed ben Bella (b.1916). And finally ben Bella established the Revolutionary Committee for Unity and Action (CRUA), which in 1954 became the National Liberation Front (FLN).

Over the next eight years French security forces in the territory were to increase from 50,000 to half a million. Of these, 12,000 died in the struggle. In addition some 3000 Europeans lost their lives. Of the Muslims, French authorities estimated a death toll of 141,000; the FLN maintained four times that number had died.

Independence at once lent an added importance to the political infighting that had characterised the FLN during the struggle. Private rivalries became public policy differences. Ben Bella and the FLN military commander Colonel Boumedienne (1927-78) triumphed, their rivals slipped one by one into exile as dictatorial tendencies in the new government hardened. An armed revolt in 1964 failed.

The following year ben Bella was deposed on 19 June by his former comrade Boumedienne, who rightly suspected ben Bella of being on the brink of seizing absolute power and of installing a Leninist-type state. The FLN accepted the coup; left-wingers went into exile. Thereafter Boumedienne presided over a military Council of the Revolution, which sought to create a 'true socialist society'.

Active opposition to Boumedienne's policies arose on the left, particularly among student circles in the late 1960s. For a time there was even sporadic guerrilla activity in the Aurès and Kabyle regions, where the original nationalist revolt had first begun 15 years earlier. Behind the violence lay the Organisation of Popular Resistance (ORP). It came to nothing. As Boumedienne consolidated his power, further violent opposition arose in 1975 from the Soldiers of the Algerian Opposition, which bombed three Algerian embassies in Europe, ironically demanding free democratic elections.

Since Boumedienne's death in December 1978, President Chadli has had to contend with disturbances caused by the growth of religious fundamentalism, which although appearing later in Algeria than elsewhere in the Arab world was a cause for concern in 1982.

Bibliography

Alistaire Horne wrote a fine account of the Algerian struggle in *A Savage War of Peace Algeria 1954-62* (London, 1977); a more detailed work is the three-volume *La Guerre d'Algérie* (Paris, 1968-70) by Yves Courrière. Edgar O'Ballance wrote reliably in *Algerian Insurrection 1954-62* (London, 1967), but useful material can also be found in earlier works by Joan Gillespie, *Algeria: Rebellion and Revolution* (London, 1960) and by Edward Behr, *The Algerian Problem* (London, 1961). William Quandt takes the Algerian story further than independence in *Revolution and Political Leadership Algeria 1954-68* (Cambridge, Mass., 1969). Martha Crenshaw contributed *Revolutionary Terrorism* (Stanford, 1978).

Roger Trinquier upheld the use of torture by the French military in *Modern Warfare — A French View of Counter-Insurgency* (New York and London, 1964). Torture was exposed by Jean Jacques Servan-Schreiber in *Lieutenant in Algeria* (London, 1958), by Henri Alleg in *The Question* (London, 1958) and by Jean Lartéquy in *The Centurions*. See also the excellently brief *Torture: Cancer of Democracy* (Penguin, 1963) by Pierre Videl Naquet. On the OAS, see Paul Hennissart, *Wolves in the City* (New York, 1970), the memoir *La Valise et le Cerceuil* (Paris,1962) and J.R. Tournoux, *L'Histoire Secrète* (Paris, 1962).

National Liberation Front
(Front de Libération Nationale — FLN)

The FLN's military arm, the National Liberation Army (ALN), first struck in rural areas in November 1954 against French colonial rule in Algeria. The Front had had forerunners led by Ahmed ben Bella who, whilst following a French military career, had been impressed by the achievements of Mao Tse-tung in China and by Marshal Tito in Yugoslavia. Largely thanks to the tactless brutality of French policing, which alienated a previously passive and illiterate population, the FLN uprising spread quickly from the Aurès region. To torture, the nationalists responded with terrorism.

From outside Algeria the FLN relied particularly upon support from Egypt, but once Morocco and Tunisia had achieved their independence in 1956, it also enjoyed sanctuaries across the border. At that time the militants in the field probably numbered no more than some 8500, but many more gave their support. Friction arose between those who directed the FLN from Cairo and those who risked their lives inside Algeria. Randane Abbane led the internal delegation and within the city of Algiers itself instituted an urban terrorist campaign. It lasted for eight months from January 1957 through to September, by which time, although at the cost of alienating the entire Muslim population, the 1200 hard core members had been roundly defeated by the systematic practice of torture.

In the countryside, however, the FLN organisation spread by setting up dual military committees, responsible for political affairs, military operations and intelligence, and civil committees, which were concerned with justice and economic problems. An alternative administration raised taxes and trained recruits clandestinely. Arms were purchased with money from Arab states and were also sent by Egypt and Syria.

Eventually the FLN established a government-in-exile in Tunis, which included Ferhat Abbas as prime minister, the imprisoned ben Bella as his deputy, and Belkacem Krim as minister of defence. Besides Arab and African countries, the USSR and the People's Republic of China recognised its legitimacy.

By 1958, the year in which General de Gaulle assumed power in France, the FLN insurrection in four years had cost the lives of 7200 French soldiers and 1500 European civilians, for a toll of 77,000 insurgents. Naturally many non-combatant Muslims died as well, conceivably over 10,000 between 1954 and 1958. Many more on both sides were to die in the course of 1959, at the end of which the French military authorities believed they had contained the insurrection. But de Gaulle thought differently and offered the FLN self-determination. It is true that French counter-insurgency prevented the FLN from fighting a conventional war, although FLN units attacked French positions on occasions in battalion strength; yet the FLN was not beaten militarily. If in 1961 there were but 5000 guerrillas inside Algeria, there were 25,000 waiting to infiltrate from Tunisia.

FLN leadership in the field was provided by men with military backgrounds; they were fervently nationalistic, frequently quarrelled, and very few owed anything at all to Marx or to Lenin. Nothing in the FLN literature of the time suggests that the movement was fighting for more than national liberation. From guerrilla bands its forces grew to number at least 25,000 by 1956, equipped furthermore with machine guns, mortars, recoilless rifles, mines and bangalore torpedoes. The military campaign lay in the hands of Colonel Houari Boumedienne, who moved the FLN towards a socialist stance. When France, recognising the post-Second World War trend of third world national liberation, withdrew in

1962, the FLN was left, not without in-fighting, to become the sole political movement in Algeria, a socialist Islamic state.

Revolutionary Committee for Unity and Action
(Comité Révolutionnaire pour l'Unité et l'Action — CRUA)

CRUA consisted of young militant Algerians, who in 1954 determined upon taking up arms against French colonial rule. They chose to lead them Ahmed ben Bella, who had escaped from French custody in 1952, and who from Cairo agreed to head the new movement. Before the first armed action was launched, it was decided to rename CRUA the National Liberation Front (FLN).

Secret Army Organisation
(Organisation de l'Armée Secrète — OAS)

Founded in 1960, the OAS consisted of European settlers in Algeria who resisted General de Gaulle's policy of self-determination. It had the active support of certain sections of the French security forces, particularly Generals Challe, Zeller, Jouhaud and Salan. These men failed in an attempt to seize power in April 1961, before which the OAS had turned to terrorism not only in Algeria but also in France. Bomb attacks and shootings were mounted in Paris and continued sporadically throughout the year.

After the Evian agreement, which paved the way for Algerian independence, had been signed in March 1962, the OAS attempted to set up a National Council of French Resistance with Salan at its head. But on 20 April he was captured, having failed to do more than destroy a number of public buildings in the Orléansville area and to intimidate selected Muslim spokesmen. Nonetheless, the leaders enjoyed the support of as many as 40,000 troops, although the air force and the navy remained loyal to the government. Some 200 officers were arrested, Salan and Jouhaud received death sentences *in absentia*, Challe and Zeller had sentences of 15 years handed down to them. For a few weeks after Salan's arrest terrorism persisted; divided leadership caused the organisation to break up with bitter recriminations.

Secret Organisation
(Organisation Secrète — OS)

A forerunner of the Algerian National Liberation Front (FLN), the OS, led by Ahmed ben Bella, was a clandestine para-military organisation which split from the essentially non-violent Movement for the Triumph of Democratic Liberties (MTDL) in 1947. It numbered some 500 members and carried out one spectacular action in 1949 against the Oran post office. Following this robbery, French police arrested ben Bella and uprooted the OS in 1950.

Angola

Unlike Mozambique, the Angolan black nationalists were split three ways on independence from the Portuguese in 1975. The first group, which had taken up arms in 1961, was the Popular Movement for the Liberation of Angola (MPLA), which with help from the Soviet bloc contested the combined opposition of the northern National Front for the Liberation of Angola (FNLA) under Holden Roberto (b. 1925) and the Ovimbundu National Union for the Total Independence of Angola (UNITA) led by Jonas Savimbi (b. 1934). Savimbi was backed by South Africa, Roberto by Zaïre, but US support never materialised, so that in the civil war of 1975/76 superior Cuban forces and *matériel* won the day.

Yet Savimbi survived in the bush, where for years he had successfully eluded capture by the Portuguese colonial forces. A talented and charismatic guerrilla, he disputed MPLA control, denying the new government the satisfaction of revenues from the Benguela railway, which he regularly sabotaged. Supplied by South Africa, Savimbi found himself in the late 1970s operating as frequently against Angolan-backed South West African People's forces (see Namibia) as against Cuban-backed MPLA units. It was clear that for all its numbers Cuban support proved inadequate in eradicating a guerrilla threat in the heart of Angola, so long at least as outside support was available.

The threat to MPLA control in the north was solved ingeniously. If President Mobuto refused to contain the activities of his brother-in-law Roberto, by denying him bases and training facilities on the border, the MPLA leadership would lend support to dissident Zaïrian factions, particularly in Kolwezi, where the Congo civil conflict had left scars unhealed (see Zaïre). From Angola two invasions of the mineral-rich Shaba province were launched in 1976 and 1977. Thereafter, by mutual interest and agreement, friendship was consolidated.

By the early 1980s the Cabindan separatists (FLEC) had failed to wrest control of the enclave from the Luandan government, although acts of terrorism were still recorded from time to time. The issue was a minor one in comparison with the conflict in the south. There the level of hostilities left the Angolan political leadership with no alternative but to retain a Cuban connection, albeit a costly and divisive factor.

Bibliography
The best introduction to the country remains Douglas Wheeler and René Pelissier's classic *Angola* (London, 1971). Readers requiring a more de-

tailed analysis of the early years should consult Pelissier's *La Colonie du Minotaure (1926-61)* (Montamets, France, 1978), but the actual organisation of colonial liberation is best read in John Marcum's *The Angolan Revolution* (Cambridge, Mass., 1969). Basil Davidson knew many of the guerrillas as a reporter, but wrote *In the Eye of the Storm* (London, 1972) with a lifetime's dedication to African history. Don Barnett and Roy Harvey provided MPLA notes in *The Revolution in Angola: MPLA Life Histories and Documents* (Bobbs Merrill, 1972). Useful insights into character were recorded by Robert Devezies, a priest close to the independence movement, in *Les Angolais* (Paris, 1965) and *La Guerre d'Angola* (Paris, 1968). The effects of the war on the economy are looked at in *The War in Angola* (Dar es Salaam, 1975), written by Mario do Andrade and Marc Ollivier. Al Venter, the South African war reporter, told the story from the other side in *The Terror Fighters* (Johannesburg, 1969) and *Portugal's Guerrilla War* (Cape Town, 1973). Journalists Arslan Humbaraci and Nicole Muchnik wrote *Portugal's African Wars* (London, 1974) from a popular third world viewpoint. Barbara Cornwell was an American journalist who, having visited the guerrillas, wrote *The Bush Rebels* (London, 1971). An Austrian journalist, Franz Sitte, provided one of the few accounts of UNITA in *Flammenherd Angola* (Vienna, 1972). John Barrat wrote a useful paper, 'The Angola Conflict' published by the South African Institute of International Affairs in 1976.

Front for the Liberation of the Enclave of Cabinda
(Frente da Libertação do Enclave de Cabinda — FLEC)

FLEC derived great benefit from the intervention of Cubans in the Angolan civil war (1975-76), for their activity in the enclave provoked the animosity of local Cabindans who resented their presence. FLEC militants still bear arms in the bush, although they would probably not long survive without the benefit of sanctuary across the border in Zaïre.

Armed struggle is new to FLEC for it never participated in the conflict which overwhelmed Angola after the withdrawal of the Portuguese in 1975. The movement based its stand on a rejection of the independence agreement made by the Portuguese with the three main contenders for Angolan sovereignty, the *Movimento Popular para a Libertação de Angola*, the *Frente Nacional da Libertação de Angola* and the *União Nacional para a Independência Total de Angola*, arguing correctly that Cabinda had never, until it was incorporated in 1958, formed part of Angola. In fact the Portuguese had signed a separate treaty in 1885 at Simulambuco with the local chiefs, so that the territory had some right to consider itself a separate entity. The argument was favourably viewed by the neighbouring states of Congo and Zaïre, and also by Guinea, the Ivory Coast and Uganda.

FLEC was largely the creation of one man, Luis Ranque Franque, who in 1959 had founded in Brazzaville a separatist movement which favoured independence *(Mouvement de Libération de l'Enclave de Cabinda* — MLEC). Although first in the field, he lost control to Telo Gérard, but reasserted his influence in 1963 by incorporating MLEC and the *Comité d'Action de l'Union Nationale des Cabindais* (CAUNC), set up in Kinshasa (Zaïre) by Nzita Henrique Tiago, with the FLEC.

FLEC was nurtured by both the Congo and Zaïre, for both countries could see their advantage in having such a strategically placed outlet to the Atlantic detached from Angola, the more so after oil had been discovered in 1966. Yet there was undoubtedly a feeling for independence based upon a Cabindan identity. In 1975 FLEC split after a quarrel between Ranque Franque and Nzita Tiago, and shortly afterwards even the rump over which Ranque Franque presided split again, with Marcelino Luemba Tubi and Luis Matos Fernandes at odds with the leadership. In 1977 they formed a *Comando Militar para a Libertação de Cabinda* (CMLC). Meanwhile Nzita Tiago seized control of FLEC in 1978 and claimed guerrilla successes against the Cubans and MPLA government troops in 1979. Although exaggerated reports appeared, sabotage attacks were indeed carried out on oil installations.

In January 1979 Luizi Ballu, FLEC member responsible for foreign affairs, announced that he had taken over the movement. No cohesive policy line emerged in 1980. Nor indeed did there appear to be very much activity reported from the Front. Yet from time to time in the early 1980s MPLA authorities spoke of Cabindan separatists being sentenced to death for terrorist outrages, for the most part sabotage operations.

National Front for the Liberation of Angola
(Frente Nacional da Libertação de Angola — *(FNLA)*

Two parties, the more important of which was the *União das Populações de Angola* (UPA), joined in 1962 to form the FNLA. The UPA, founded in 1954 and led by Holden Roberto (b.1925), had embarked upon an armed uprising in 1961 against Portuguese rule in Angola, and in the course of the rebellion pitted itself against a rival nationalist group, the Popular Movement for the Liberation of Angola (MPLA). To strengthen its hand, the UPA joined with the *Partido Democrático de Angola* (PDA) to form not only the FNLA, but a government-in-exile (GRAE).

The *Governo Revolucionário de Angola no Exílio* (GRAE) was at once recognised by a score of African countries and, when this body came into being in 1963, by the Organisation of African Unity (OAU). In this the FNLA had the edge on the MPLA, until outside recognition was withdrawn in 1971, by which time it was clear to all that the FNLA was not the sole representative of Angolans fighting for their independence. Both the MPLA and the National Union for the Total Independence of Angola (UNITA) carried support, and were effective on the ground.

The FNLA suffered its fair share of quarrels and splits. Roberto sur-

vived attempts against his leadership in 1965 and 1972 to emerge at the
independence talks with Portugal in 1975 as the legitimate representative
of a liberation movement. Like other liberation movements the FNLA set
up a youth branch and a women's section as well as a trade union.

As a military force the FNLA recruited in 1963 an Angolan National
Liberation Army (ELNA), but it was not an effective force under the
Portuguese, who had confined its activities very largely to the occasional
foray across the border from Zaïre, where the FNLA had its base in
Kinshasa. The military headquarters were at Kinkuzu Camp in Zaïre,
but in reality during the latter days of Portuguese rule very little guerrilla
activity was sponsored by the FNLA.

Despite the lack of success in guerrilla warfare, the FNLA claimed the
allegiance of the Bakongo peoples in the north, and was certainly more
popular there than the MPLA, which had its main support in the capital,
Luanda. Centred upon Carmona, the strongest support for the FNLA
came from Uige and Zaïre provinces, but the sympathy was in no way
formalised, as was the membership of the MPLA.

When hostilities with the Portuguese were suspended on 15 October
1974, the FNLA sent representatives and troops to the capital, only to
clash with the MPLA. Unable to maintain a foothold in Luanda in the
face of armed opposition and a terrorist campaign, the FNLA was forced
to withdraw in August 1975, by which time civil war had become inevitable.

The FNLA was supported in its stand by Zaïre, whose President
Mobuto was linked by marriage to Roberto. Since the Soviet Union had
all along backed the exclusive pretensions of the MPLA, China rather
obviously lent aid to Roberto, who welcomed 100 Chinese advisers in
Kinshasa in addition to medical and arms supplies in the summer and
autumn of 1974. As Angola slid into civil war, the aid was increased in
1975. The FNLA was also accused of employing Zaïrean regulars in its
ranks.

As the contest moved to the north of Angola, the FNLA was
strengthened by the advent of Daniel Chipenda's followers, who had left
the MPLA. Although a southerner, born in Lobito, Chipenda brought to
the FNLA more than 1000 supporters, most of whom had been trained by
the Chinese. They ensured that the FNLA secured for a time such towns
as Caxito, Malange, Carmona and Negage.

Roberto was unable to hold his position because his outside base
collapsed. Fearing reprisals for his support of Roberto, President Mobuto
of Zaïre signed an agreement with MPLA President Neto on 28 February
1976 whereby both countries desisted from promoting military activities
directed against the other. Many refugees (500,000) crossed the border
into Zaïre as the FNLA position collapsed, and the guerrillas again went
underground.

Thenceforth sabotage and guerrilla operations impeded the development of MPLA central government control of the area. The activity was
a factor in leading President Neto to encourage in 1977 the invasion of

Shaba province (Katanga) by Angolan-backed Katangese refugees. The FNLA still claimed in 1980 to control rural areas of the north, but such activity as occurred on the ground was hard to verify.

Principal leaders of the FNLA under Roberto and Chipenda included Dr Samuel Abrigada, Ngola Kabango, Dino Mavinga, Hendrik Vaal Neto, Pedro Ngadimpovi and Johnny Pinnock. After Chipenda, the principal military leader was Nzambio Nzenga. Most of these men had visited China in the early and mid-1970s. The movement was badly affected by the offer of an amnesty in 1978, when five senior officials returned to Angola. Heedless of ideological inconsistencies, the FNLA rump continued to seek aid across the globe from China to Uruguay. By mid-1981 Holden Roberto was reported to have been replaced by Paulo Tuba and Hendrik Vaal Neto.

National Union for the Total Independence of Angola
(União Nacional para a Independência Total de Angola —
UNITA)

Owing to differences between Holden Roberto and Dr Jonas Savimbi, the latter left the National Front for the Liberation of Angola (FNLA) in July 1964, founding UNITA in 1966. Savimbi was in every way an exceptional man, having studied medicine at Lisbon university (1957-60), before becoming involved in politics. From the Swiss university of Fribourg he was awarded a doctorate in law and politics, before undergoing guerrilla training in China in 1965.

On returning to Africa he made his base in Lusaka (Zambia), where he was well received by President Kaunda, who remained loyal to UNITA until the movement lost the civil war in Angola (1975-76) to the MPLA. Savimbi directed UNITA from within Angola, unlike the leaders of the two rival nationalist organisations, the MPLA and the FNLA.

For years he harassed the Portuguese forces from the countryside, although he never controlled a town. Savimbi's great advantage was that by remaining in the field he built up over a period of time an impressive popularity, the more so since he operated in the central and southern Ovimbundu area, where he was born in 1934. UNITA profited from the fact that the Benguela railway ran through its territory, carrying much of Central Africa's wealth to the Atlantic. Because of sabotage attacks, the railway remained closed throughout most of the late 1960s and the whole of the following decade.

Unlike the MPLA, UNITA remained a cohesive body, virtually free of faction fighting. Congresses were held in 1966, 1969 and 1973, from which were drawn a Central Committee of 24 members and a political bureau of ten. On Angolan independence in 1975, UNITA set up its centre in Nova Lisboa (Huambo) and held its fourth Congress in Silva Porto during August. There it decided to issue a formal declaration of war against the MPLA, whose troops were fighting the FNLA in the north and in Luanda. It had become clear to Savimbi that the MPLA was not interested in sharing power, as had been agreed in the Alvor Agreement signed with the Portuguese on 15 January 1975. To survive, he was forced increasingly into the hands of the South Africans, who supported him against the Soviet and Cuban-backed MPLA. In November 1975 Savimbi announced the creation of a joint political and military command with the FNLA. In fact the two organisations remained separate, fighting for the most part in different parts of the country. But when on 11 November MPLA President Neto became President of the People's Republic of Angola, UNITA, alongside the FNLA, proclaimed a Popular and Democratic Republic of Angola, with its capital at Huambo. It remained unrecognised internationally, but there was no doubting UNITA's military success, or its popularity in the centre and south.

After initial successes UNITA was forced to abandon the towns, retreating before superior weaponry employed by the MPLA. One by one Novo Redondo, Lobito, Benguela, Moçamedes and finally Huambo fell in February 1976. UNITA announced its intention to return to guerrilla warfare, fighting against the MPLA.

For a time, while UNITA reorganised, little was heard of the organisation, but it reemerged in 1977, inflicting a constant trickle of casualties on government forces. Savimbi had no problem with supplies, for they came through Namibia with the connivance of the South Africans, so that it became increasingly clear that even the presence of 15,000 Cubans in Angola would not eradicate UNITA's guerrilla threat, which survived repeated drives through the centre and south.

Furthermore, from 1979 into the early 1980s it penetrated the cities, including Luanda, to commit sabotage attacks. Those that were caught were executed. UNITA claimed to deploy in 1980 as many as 12,000 troops, although they were undoubtedly fewer in reality. Its leadership remained cohesive and disposed of a remarkable degree of talent trained in North American and European universities. Amongst those to the fore were Samuel Chiwale (b.1940), Miguel Puna (b.1940), António da Costa Fernandes, Jorge Sangumba (b. 1944), Dr José N'dele, António Dembo (b. 1942), Dr Eduardo Wanga (b. 1944), Jeremias Chitunda (b.1942) and Dr Jaka Jamba (b.1949).

UNITA's future depended upon the resolution of the conflict in Namibia, for were South Africa to trade its support for UNITA in return for Angola's support for the South West African People's Organisation (SWAPO), which is based in Angola, Savimbi would be hard pressed to survive. He can expect to benefit from Chinese diplomatic support so long as Peking contests Moscow's backing for African liberation movements. But his dream of an Ovimbundu state achieved by seceding from Angola, although geographically and economically feasible, would be resisted by the Organisation of African Unity (OAU) as well as by the might of the Soviet bloc, which supports the centralised government of the MPLA. UNITA's only chance to share power depends upon the

MPLA splitting: one faction might seek Savimbi's support and together they might achieve power.

Popular Movement for the Liberation of Angola
(Movimento Popular para a Libertação de Angola — MPLA)

Under Portuguese colonial rule in Angola, attempts were made after the Second World War to establish an Angolan Communist Party. Few people were interested; the best were motivated by a desire for independence rather than a conviction that Marxism-Leninism provided the basis for a just and healthy state. Because of their failure to attract recruits, the communists jettisoned attempts to promote an Angolan party, and, merging in December 1956 with nationalist groups, formed the MPLA.

From the beginning the MPLA was faction-ridden, torn apart by fundamental differences regarding motivation, but also by tribal divisions and personal jealousies. Yet, with all its difficulties, the MPLA finally triumphed and became the ruling party in Angola after a bitter civil war in 1975/76, when it received substantial military help from the Soviet-bloc countries, particularly Cuba and the USSR.

The first MPLA programme calling for an all-out struggle against the Portuguese was issued in 1961, when an attempt was made to release a number of political prisoners from jail in Luanda. For three years nothing came of MPLA determination to fight 'by every means', but in 1964 guerrilla action began in Cabinda. Two years later a front was opened in Eastern Angola. Desultory activity continued for the rest of the decade, but guerrilla forces were unable to escalate the conflict. Those parts of the territory where MPLA was most active in the early 1970s included Luanda, Cuanza Norte, Moxico, Lunda, Cuando-Cubango and Bie, yet it must be admitted that the level of guerrilla activity had declined in the years immediately preceding the April 1974 Lisbon coup, which brought about Portuguese withdrawal from Africa.

If one man's name is identified with the MPLA, it is not that of its first President, Mário de Andrade, but that of Agostinho Neto, who succeeded him in 1962 and remained President until his death from cancer in Moscow in 1979. Neto was born in 1922 and studied medicine in Portugal. He was a poet of some renown in Angola and played a leading part in Luandan cultural life before turning to politics, for which he was imprisoned twice in 1955 and 1960. Forbidden to return to Angola, Neto nonetheless left Portugal for Morocco, where he took over the MPLA leadership. In exile, he travelled widely in Eastern Europe and the Soviet Union, and although using to further Angolan independence the front organisations set up by the USSR, such as the World Peace Council and the Afro-Asian People's Solidarity Organisation, Neto never sold his party to Moscow. Indeed his leadership was criticised for not being sufficiently pro-Soviet, especially by Nito Alves, commander of the first military region, who unsuccessfully attempted to usurp Neto's position in July 1975.

If Alves' opposition to Neto was based upon an ideological position, Daniel Chipenda's was rooted in tribal differences. Chipenda was born in Lobito, the son of an Ovimbundu tribal chief, and had long been a member of the MPLA Central Committee. He represented the movement in Dar es Salaam (Tanzania) during the 1960s, but in 1972 and 1973 was said to be behind two assassination attempts on Neto. Chipenda was expelled from the party in December 1974, after which he joined forces with the rival FNLA in Kinshasa (Zaïre), acting as Assistant Secretary-General. His faction had been known as the Eastern Revolt Faction.

Opposition to Neto's leadership came from a third source, the Active Revolt faction, led by former MPLA President, Mário de Andrade. Around him gathered a number of party intellectuals based in Brazzaville (Congo), who in May 1974 appealed to party militants against the links which Neto was trying to develop with other nationalist groups fighting for independence in Angola. The majority of these men were reconciled with Neto as he arrived in Luanda in February 1975 with the assured support of Soviet-bloc military supplies.

Having signed a ceasefire agreement with the Portuguese on 21 October 1974, the MPLA agreed to participate in a transitional coalition government with the rival FNLA and UNITA. Such an arrangement had been encouraged by other African states which were anxious to prevent open warfare between the nationalist inheritors of colonial power. Yet, despite agreements on paper, factional fighting ensued in March and April 1975.

By May the MPLA was contesting the authority of the FNLA in street fighting in the capital and had launched a military campaign to flush the FNLA out of Cabinda and Cuanza Norte. During this period the MPLA relied upon Soviet arms shipments, without which the movement would not have succeeded in driving the FNLA from Luanda in July.

MPLA troops were not involved in fighting UNITA until August 1975, when clashes occurred in the south at the Ruacana Falls hydroelectric project. In this struggle the MPLA had to contend with South African reinforcements to UNITA in the south, and later in the year with a drive on Luanda. To withstand such support, the MPLA relied upon Cuban troops, who began arriving in October and effectively prevented UNITA making common cause with the FNLA in the north, thus reducing MPLA control to the capital. Amidst general fighting, the remaining Portuguese troops withdrew in November, and Neto became President of the People's Republic of Angola, which was at once recognised by the Eastern-bloc countries and by African socialist states.

MPLA forces wrested control of the north and the south of Angola from the FNLA and UNITA in fierce fighting throughout November and December, during which it received an estimated £55 million worth of Soviet aid. As the numbers of Cubans increased, so the MPLA regained control of the main towns, forcing the FNLA across the border into Zaïre and compelling UNITA to return to guerrilla warfare.

Once in power, the MPLA transformed itself in December 1977 into a 'vanguard' Leninist party guided by the principles of 'scientific socialism'. In the 1980s it was led by José Eduardo dos Santos (b. 1942), who had been Neto's designated successor in 1979.

Central African Republic

The territory was unfortunate in having to suffer the tyranny of a buffoon from 1966, when Colonel Jean Bokassa (b. 1921) ousted President David Dacko (b. 1930). In 1976, with French encouragement, Bokassa crowned himself Emperor in Bangui, only to be overthrown three years later by the very forces which had sustained him in power. Neither scandal nor cruelty, of which there had been evidence enough, caused his fall, but rather greed. Libyan Colonel Gadaffi bribed him with offers of security at a moment when France was fearful of Libyan influence replacing her own in neighbouring Chad. To prevent still further expansion of Libyan influence, France sent troops to the capital in September 1979 to ensure that former President Dacko was returned to power without bloodshed.

None of the opposition groups abroad played any part in the preparations for the coup; nor had they been effective in organising resistance to Bokassa's tyranny inside the country. In September 1981 Dacko was overthrown by a military coup led by General Kolingba, the Armed Forces Chief of Staff. Once again, the opposition, which had lost out to Dacko in elections held in March 1981, played no part in the proceedings.

Bibliography
An introduction to the country can be found in Pierre Kalck's *Central African Republic* (London, 1971).

Central African Movement for National Liberation
(Mouvement Centreafricain de Libération Nationale — MCLN)

The movement emerged in July 1981, when it exploded a grenade in a Bangui cinema where three people were killed. It was led by Idi Lala, who had previously worked closely with Dr Goumba's Oubanguian Patriotic Front.

Independent Reflection Group
(Groupe Indépendant pour la Réflexion — GIRA)

Having won only 5 per cent of the vote in the March 1981 elections, François Pehoua set up GIRA, whose objective was 'to struggle against all forms of domination and subjugation whether by forces inside or outside the country, to see that the rights of man are respected and to do everything within its power to promote the rebirth of the republic.'

The new movement cooperated with other groups which opposed President Dacko, but was not heard of after the military coup which deposed him.

Movement for the Liberation of the Central African People
(Mouvement pour la Libération du Peuple Centreafricain — MLPC)

Ange Patasse (b. 1937), former prime minister (September 1976 – July 1978), set up the MLPC in Paris in 1979. Later that year he returned via Libya to the Central African Republic and opposed President David Dacko, who in September 1979 had succeeded his cousin, Emperor Bokassa. In the March 1981 elections he came close with 39 per cent of the vote to beating Dacko. For a while he was held prisoner in Bangui after an unsuccessful bid to escape responsibility for political violence. He then left for France, but returned in February 1982, when he bungled a coup attempt against Dacko's military usurper, General Kolingba. He took refuge in the French embassy.

Oubanguian Liberation Front
(Front de Libération Oubanguienne — FLO)

Set up in 1979 and led by a former ambassador to France, Sylvestre Bangui, the FLO worked to overthrow the self-styled Emperor Bokassa in the Central African Empire. The FLO cooperated with Abel Goumba's Oubanguian Patriotic Front (FPO) and the Movement for the Liberation of the Central African People (MLPC) led by former premier, Ange Patasse.

Oubanguian Patriotic Front
(Front Patriotique Oubanguien — FPO)

Led by the socialist Dr Abel Goumba, who had briefly led the Central African Republic government in 1960, the FPO rejected David Dacko's presidency in 1979, when he succeeded his cousin Emperor Bokassa. The FPO was based in the Congo and called at the time for restoration of 'true democracy'. The Front was founded by Goumba in 1977. In 1980 Goumba worked in Benin for the World Health Organisation, but in 1981 returned to France, where he was close to President Mitterrand. His Front became known as the FPO-Workers' Party (FPO-PT). It contested the March 1981 elections, but did so poorly that Goumba went into hiding, fearing for his life in the political violence that succeeded them.

Chad

Since the mid-1960s factional violence has impeded political development in Chad. In 1960 the French had handed power to the Christian negroid south, wealthier and more populous than the vast northern territories, inhabited, if at all, by nomadic Muslims, but in so doing they reversed the historically dominant order wherein Arabs traded black slaves. In the Tibesti, Borkou and Ennedi regions, French law was unknown. President Tombalbaye (1960-75) had little chance therefore of imposing southern rule. When he tried, a tradition of self-defence and banditry was transformed into guerrilla war. Only the advent of French troops in the late 1960s reduced the rebellion.

The Chad Liberation Front (Frolinat), founded in 1966, gave political form to the revolt, and drew on outside support, first from Algeria and then from Libya. An attempted accommodation in 1971, whereby northerners joined the cabinet, failed to impress Frolinat, which was then receiving Libyan arms. Tombalbaye, reluctant to rely upon French neo-colonialism for security, discovered too late his own weakness. Failing to contain the civil war, he died in an army coup in April 1975.

General Malloum, (b. 1932), whom two years earlier Tombalbaye had dismissed, headed a Supreme Military Council. Malloum proved incapable of subduing the north or of contesting Libya's annexation of the Aouzou strip, territory which reputedly contained mineral deposits. Thenceforth the Libyan factor dominated Frolinat. When its founder, Dr Abba Siddick, resisted Libyan influence, he lost out to Goukouni Ouaddai, who used it to enhance his position.

By providing tanks, armoured vehicles and anti-aircraft missiles that wrested control of towns like Bardai, Faya Largeau and Fada from Malloum's government, Libya escalated the conflict. Whilst admittedly increasing the military threat, Libyan involvement still further divided the rebels, who were nothing if not proud, independent-minded and resistant to ultimate Libyan expansionism. They represented the reaction of the Islamic nomadic north to government by black southerners, a reversal of historical fortunes. This and not ideology lay at the root of rebellion in Chad, even although Frolinat variously described itself as socialist and even Marxist-Leninist. In fact, Frolinat never proposed a coherent Leninist programme. Its demands had been for redress of Muslim grievances and particularly for the introduction of Arabic to the French educational and governmental system.

In the course of time Ouaddai, whose faction became known as the

Popular Armed Forces (FAP), proved too independent for Gadaffi, who transferred his support to another Frolinat faction led by Ahmat Acyl, known as the Vulcan Force. In 1979 the Vulcan Force renamed itself the Common Action Front (FAC).

A more important faction operated in the north-east under Hissen Habré, whose followers were known as the Northern Armed Forces (FAN). For a while, throughout 1978, Habré cooperated with Malloum until in February 1979 he staged a coup in Ndjamena. Malloum was destroyed politically and the country plunged into generalised civil conflict, with black Christians slaughtering Arab Muslims in the south.

A measure of order was reestablished under Colonel Abdelkadar Kamougué, who had commanded the southern gendarmerie, which with remnants of the armed forces became known as the Chadian Armed Forces (FAT). At this point Nigeria, fearful of Libyan pretensions, backed its own party, the Chad Popular Liberation Movement (MPLT), and attempted unsuccessfully to mediate.

In November 1979 an ill-described 'government of national unity' included the main contenders for power, but quite failed in 1980 to prevent the breakdown of all semblance of order. The fighting stopped in December with the arrival in the capital's rubble of 5000 Libyan troops, supportive of Ouaddai's FAP. A merger between the two countries was proposed in January 1981.

However, Habré's forces, admittedly defeated in the capital, in the east never accepted the merger plans, nor were Libyan troops ever influential in the south, where the FAT refused to acknowledge Libyan interests. Ten months later, at the instigation of Goukouni Ouaddai and in accordance with overwhelming OAU opinion, Libya withdrew its forces. An alternative OAU peace-keeping force replaced the Libyans in 1982, but they did not stop the FAN recapturing from the withdrawing Libyans most of the east and the north, and thereby compelling Goukouni Ouaddai to negotiate. By mid-1982 Hissen Habré had replaced his rival and later compelled Kamougué to flee the south. In the absence of one dominating force, which the Libyans for almost a year had provided, the exercise of power was influenced by the competing interests of Libya, Nigeria, Sudan and France, imposed upon an ethnic competition between north and south, which in 1983 Habré had still to resolve.

Bibliography
Virginia Thompson and Richard Adloff researched the background from press reports and provided the only account in *Conflict in Chad* (London, 1981). Julian Crandall Hollick summarised events in 'Civil War in Chad', *The World Today*, July 1982.

Chad Armed Force
(Force Armée du Tchad — FAT)

The FAT represented in the late-1970s the rump of the Chadian armed forces, commanded by Colonel Abdelkadar Kamougué, former chief of the gendarmerie. The movement was based in the populous negroid south of Chad and had no representation in the capital, Ndjamena. Although included in the February 1979 government of national union, Kamougué played no part in that agreement. Furthermore, his forces took no side in the disputes which caused violent conflict between the various factions of the northern Islamic opposition group, Frolinat, which from 1977/78 had reduced Chad to civil war chaos. The FAT had even considered partition, opting for separatism rather than to continue the black south's colonial legacy of having to rule the sparsely populated northern nomadic regions of Chad.

The FAT naturally opposed Libyan interventionism throughout 1981, although Libyan troops never penetrated the southern provinces, which became virtually self-governing. Kamougué, however, failed to emerge as a political leader and in the autumn of 1982 was compelled to flee the south before the victorious northerners led by Hissen Habré.

Chad Liberation Movement
(Mouvement pour la Libération du Tchad — MPLT)

The MPLT emerged in 1978 as central authority broke down in Chad, giving way to Libyan-backed insurgency in the country's Islamic northern region. Led by Abubakar Abderaman, until his death in 1979, the MPLT represented Nigerian interests and operated from islands in Lake Chad. It influenced events in Kanem province. Nigeria felt compelled to take an interest in the conflict, fearing Libyan expansionism. Idris Adoum Mustapha led the MPLT's so-called 'Third Army in Chad' until April 1981, when his place was taken by Lool Mahamat Choua.

Chad National Liberation Front
(Front de Libération Nationale du Tchad — Frolinat)

Frolinat had disintegrated by 1980 into many warring factions, so that little was heard of its founder, Dr Abba Siddick. For a decade from 1966 he had nominally led the movement from Algiers, but real control in the mid-1970s belonged on the ground to those to whom the nomadic tribes in the vast northern area gave their allegiance. Two men emerged as guerrilla leaders of Frolinat factions, Hissen Habré and Goukouni Ouaddai.

Habré's name was first publicised in 1974, when he kidnapped a French ethnologist, Françoise Claustre, holding her and her husband captive until January 1977. Their release was negotiated by Libyan President Gadaffi, who used the good offices of the son of the Derde, the spiritual leader of the local Toubbou people, Goukouni Ouaddai. Habré proved less pliant to Libyan interests and retired with his followers to his native area of Fada, where he continued to engage central government troops in skirmishes. His force took on a separate identity and became known as the Northern Armed Forces (FAN).

Ouaddai received weaponry from Libya and engaged the central government in conventional desert warfare, laying siege to towns in the Tibesti region. Libyan convoys of armoured vehicles and broadcasts from Tripoli supported Ouaddai's military effort, which evolved from Frolinat to become the Popular Armed Forces (FAP). They based themselves at Faya Largeau, after the capture of that town in 1978. The FAP became known as the Second Army. In all there were over a dozen Frolinat factions competing for influence in the late 1970s: that which bore its name in 1982 was a group around Babiker Ismail, known as the Fundamental Frolinat.

Common Action Front
(Front d'Action Commune — FAC)

The FAC was the third principal faction in 1980 to have emerged from the northern Islamic opposition group in Chad, known as Frolinat. Prior to becoming the FAC, the group, which was led by Ahmat Acyl, was known as the Vulcan Force. It operated in Eastern Chad. The FAC derived much of its support from Libya, which transferred its favours to this movement after other Frolinat factions, FAN and FAP, under Hissen Habré and Goukouni Ouaddai respectively, had proved less than pliant towards Libyan expansionist ambitions.

The FAC formed part of the Chadian government of national unity in February 1979, and was involved in the subsequent fighting in 1980, when that agreement broke down. It supported Libyan military intervention in 1981 and was exposed when these forces withdrew in November. Never disposing of a large force, Acyl was unable to prevent the advance of Hissen Habré's FAN in mid-1982 into the Faya Largeau region. In July that year Acyl was accidentally killed in a helicopter incident.

National Patriotic Movement
(Mouvement National Patriotique — MNP)

The MNP was set up in July 1981 by Doungou Kimto, a former administrative director of Chad's defunct army, as a politico-military front to resist Libyan expansionism. Those that welcomed its formation included Mussa Medela, who had some support known as the Armed Forces of the West (FAO), Babiker Ismail, of the Fundamental Frolinat, and the Nigerian-backed MPLT. It appeared to have no reason to continue to exist in 1982, once the Libyan leader had withdrawn his troops from Chad.

Northern Armed Forces
(Forces Armées du Nord — FAN)

Under the command of Hissen Habré, the FAN emerged in 1978 in Chad as a faction of the northern Muslim opposition movement, Frolinat. Habré was known to be an ardent nationalist, favouring the Muslim north, and was well-known for a decade of desert campaigning.

The FAN agreed to take part in the government of national unity in November 1979, but fell out with its rivals in early 1980. In fierce fighting in the capital, Habré's forces were eventually beaten by those loyal to Goukouni Ouaddai, who drew upon Libyan reinforcements.

Whilst Goukouni Ouaddai governed in 1981 with the help of Libyan troops, Habré retired to the Sudan, where his forces were reequipped and trained to a high standard. Once the Libyans withdrew from Chad in November 1981, Habré reoccupied those towns previously under FAN control — Iriba, Abeche, Adrea and Guereda. In 1982 he moved on to capture Faya Largeau in the north, thereby isolating Ouaddai from his sources of support. By mid-year he had replaced his rival in the capital, Ndjamena, but had still to work out an accommodation with the negroid south. Even this he accomplished, so that by late 1982 Chad enjoyed a measure of peace under a man who had proved himself an adept guerrilla commander and who skilfully elicited support for what he saw as the nationalist cause.

Popular Armed Forces
(Forces Armées Populaires — FAP)

Goukouni Ouaddai led the FAP until 1982, when he lost power in the capital, Ndjamena, to the advancing forces of his rival, Hissen Habré, whom he had condemned to death *in absentia*. The FAP, in origin a splinter group of the northern Chadian Islamic opposition movement, Frolinat, became for a short while in 1981 the dominant faction.

Ouaddai presided over the government of national unity, set up in November 1979, until Habré's FAN attempted a coup in early 1980, after which the capital saw little respite from fighting, until Libyan troops intervened in support of Ouaddai. Thereafter he complied in January 1981 with Libya's request to bring about a merger between the two countries. Confronted by opposition within and outside the country to this proposal, he eventually negotiated the withdrawal in November 1981 of the very support which had helped him to power in 1980.

Habré, taking advantage of the withdrawal, reoccupied wide areas of the country and cut off Ouaddai from his sources of support in the north, where his father, the Derde, was the spiritual leader of the Toubbou people.

Popular Front for the Liberation of Chad
(Front Populaire pour la Libération du Tchad — FPLT)

The FPLT, led by Awad Moukhtar Nasser, represented Sudanese interests in Chad. The Front emerged in 1979, as the country underwent serious factional fighting, which raised the prospects of both secession by the black negroid southerners, and Libyan-inspired partition involving the separation and annexation of the vast Islamic, nomadic northern region. By supplying Chadian guerrilla factions with heavy weaponry, Libya had taken a keen interest in the future of the north. In response, neighbouring Sudan also felt obliged to take an interest in the conflict. By 1982 the Sudanese interest was spoken for by Hissen Habré's Armed Forces of the North (FAN), with the consequent decline of the FPLT.

Egypt

Modern Egypt emerged in the late nineteenth century from the crumbling influence of the Ottomans only to fall victim to British colonialism. Following the First World War Britain recognised national sentiment and in 1922 transformed the sultan into the constitutional King of Egypt. To protect the Empire's trade routes British troops remained in the Suez Canal zone, where hostility resulted in widespread clashes in 1952.

The disturbances provided young nationally-minded officers with their chance to topple the monarchy. King Farouk went into exile; power flowed from a Revolutionary Command Council of nine officers. The struggle for mastery that ensued between the traditionalist General Neguib and Colonel Nasser (1918-70) mirrored the conflict between Islam and nationalism, which in the 1980s still constituted the basis for political violence.

On the one hand emergent Islam produced the Muslim Brotherhood, that developed a terrorist arm to effect Islamic political change, and on the other nationalism produced in the military a determination to secularise political institutions. The antagonism between the two forces caused the Brotherhood to attempt Nasser's assassination in 1954 and again a decade later, and caused one of the organisation's many splinter groups to murder President Sadat in 1981.

Bibliography

Egyptian nationalism was analysed by J.M. Ahmed in *The Intellectual Origins of Egyptian Nationalism* (London, 1960), and the Muslim Brotherhood by Richard Mitchell in *The Society of the Muslim Brothers* (London, 1969), which although it under-rated the force of Islam at the time it was written, remains an outstanding account of the Brotherhood from its early beginnings to 1954. On later developments in Islam generally, see G.H. Jansen, *Militant Islam* (London, 1979), and Edward Mortimer, *Faith and Power: the Politics of Islam* (London, 1982).

On the nationalist revolution, see especially Nasser's *Egypt's Liberation: The Philosophy of the Revolution* (Washington, 1955); and Anwar Sadat's *Revolt on the Nile* (London, 1957). Neguib published his viewpoint in *Egypt's Destiny: A Personal Statement* (New York, 1955). For the influence of the Canal, see D.C. Watt, *Britain and the Suez Canal* (London, 1956), and on the campaign, see Edgar O' Ballance, *The Sinai Campaign 1956* (London, 1959) and K. Love's *Suez: The Twice Fought War* (London, 1970). P.J. Vatikiotis analysed military intervention in *The Egyptian Army in Politics* (Bloomington, Indiana, 1961) and wrote the reliable *Modern History of Egypt* (London, 1969). *The Road to Ramadan* (London, 1975) by Mohammed Heikal is an account by Egypt's most distinguished opposition spokesman.

Atonement and Flight
(Takfir wal Hijra)

In 1971 Shukri Mustafa founded this splinter group of the Muslim Brotherhood. He was executed in 1977. Following the arrest of several members that year, the group kidnapped a former minister of religious affairs, Dr Hussein Zahabi. The government refused to negotiate and the group carried out their threat to murder the captive. In October 1981 the organisation, which may number several hundred core members, claimed responsibility for the murder of President Sadat.

Like other fundamentalist groups in Egypt, Atonement and Flight (the name refers to the Flight of the Prophet from Medina to Mecca) flourished as a direct result of the materialism associated with President Sadat's rule. It was so baptised by the Egyptian police in 1977, Mustafa's original name being Muslim Association (*Jamaat al Musalamin*). He believed that the whole of Egyptian society, and not merely Sadat's government, was corrupt; to root out the evil 'sacred violence' was not only right, but a duty.

Believers established model communities in the desert, although the movement was strongest in Asyut, where Mustafa had first taught. In the late 1970s the movement was discovered to have had as many as 5000 followers, who found sympathy and finances in Libya and among expatriate Egyptians. The majority came from hard-working backgrounds with university education.

Coptic Societies in the Near East

First heard of in mid-1981, this organisation had a base in the Lebanon, where it issued material supportive of Copts in Egypt. It reacted in defence of a Coptic 'nationality' when Copts were involved that year in rioting with Muslims in Cairo and Alexandria.

Egyptian National Front — ENF
(Jabhat al-Wataniya al-Misriya)

Former Chief of Staff, General Saad Eddine Shazli, set up the ENF in 1981 to oppose the policies of President Sadat. The Front received money from Libya and had offices in Syria, Libya, Algeria and Lebanon. Shazli was unable to substantiate his claims to lead a significant internal opposition at the time of Sadat's assassination, and the subsequent changes in 1982 introduced by President Mubarak deprived the Front of any influence it might have had in a period of national uncertainty.

Holy War
(Al Jihad)

Holy War was one of many fundamentalist factions in Egypt which adopted the use of political violence in the latter years of President Sadat's rule to change the nature of Egyptian society from one characterised by materialistic modernity to one totally transfused by Islamic values. In 1981 the group was active in promoting attacks upon the Christian Coptic community. Five of its members were sentenced to death in April 1982 for their involvement in the death of President Sadat six months earlier.

Islamic Associations
(Jamaat Islamiya)

Inspired by Islamic fundamentalism, the Associations sprang from the ranks of the Muslim Brotherhood and were principally active among student circles in colleges and universities. Unlike the Brotherhood, the Associations are organised on a cellular basis with the aim of transforming Egyptian society into an orthodox anti-communist Muslim republic. In the latter years of President Sadat's rule, the Associations were behind much of the student disturbance.

Muslim Brotherhood
(Majallat al-Ikhwan al-Musalamin)

The Society of Muslim Brothers was founded in 1928 by Hassan al-Banna (1906-49), the son of an Egyptian imam. The primary concern of the Society was to contribute to the regeneration of Islam. It began its activities among the Suez Canal workers of Ismailia and spread to Cairo, where in the 1940s its infrastructure was established. Thanks to Banna's leadership, the society became one of the two mass parties in Egypt. Its involvement in political violence between 1946 and 1948, and particularly the murder of Prime Minister Nuqrashi Pasha, led to its official dissolution and the murder by security forces of its leader.

For a time the society remained underground as a clandestine organisation, but after the July 1952 revolution it reemerged. Some of the officers who overthrew the monarchy were Brothers, but the organisation as a whole grew to oppose the secular nature of Gamal Nasser's nationalism, which led it to attempt the new leader's assassination in

October 1954. Once again it was dissolved in Egypt, and Hudaibi, who succeeded Banna in 1949, was hanged. Until Nasser's death in 1970 the Brotherhood remained underground, although it undoubtedly retained its structure and appeal.

From the start the society had played an active role in education and industry, from which Egyptian society benefited. But it also built up a secret apparatus that practised the 'art of death', and which may in the 1940s have numbered 40,000. The society spread abroad to many countries including Morocco, Sudan, Iraq, Syria, Jordan, Yemen and Saudi Arabia.

In Egypt the society increasingly criticised the corruption and secularism which President Sadat's rule exhibited, and bitterly opposed his rapprochement with Israel and the 1977 Camp David peace treaty. Although repressed by the government, the movement had its revenge in 1981 with the murder of the President, although by that time it was hard to determine how far the Brotherhood controlled the splinter movements into which emergent Islamic fundamentalism had broken.

Ethiopia

Contemporary Ethiopia was born when the Emperor Haile Selassie fell from power in 1974. At the time no observer had forecast the precarious nature of his throne, although the unity of his African empire had long been challenged by Eritrean separatists in the coastal provinces along the Red Sea. But Eritrea was a recent acquisition. Once an Italian colony, Eritrea was administered by Britain after the Second World War until 1952, when the territory was federated to Ethiopia. A decade later, Haile Selassie abolished Eritrea's autonomous status, an act which immediately drove recruits into the Eritrean Liberation Front (ELF). In explaining his fall, some observers criticised the Emperor's rule, yet Haile Selassie was toppled not by opposition but as a result of administrative inability in a crisis. His bureaucracy proved unable to cope with the stresses the Sahel draught had laid upon it. Exposed as corrupt and inefficient, the façade of Empire crumbled, leaving a power vacuum.

In the capital, after strikes and an army mutiny had compelled the government to resign, a socialist Provisional Military Government took power in September 1974. The Emperor was deposed and some time later murdered. The new forces competing for power were far from united, so that in-fighting at once took its toll of many of those at the top. As central power collapsed new separatist forces emerged to demand independence, and had it not been for divisions on ideological grounds the Eritreans might have won their independence through a swift military victory.

The frontiers of empire were in fact saved by a ruthless military dictator, Mengistu Haile Mariam, who cut his way to the top over the bodies of his colleagues, Brigadier Teferi Bante and Colonel Atnafu Abate. In a palace revolution in February 1977, he seized power from Teferi Bante, and with Abate's assistance set up a Provisional Military Administrative Council. He had his colleague executed in November, by which time Mengistu could safely rely upon Cuban and Soviet support, both countries having applauded his bloody rise to power.

From the Soviet bloc Mengistu was to receive the prompt military backing required to put down an invasion of the Ogaden region to the south by Somali troops in July 1977. The Somalis fought for 'the unity of the Somali nation' by supplying and training their brothers across the border in the Western Somali Liberation Front (WSLF). This and other smaller movements linked to the Somali struggle were beaten in conventional warfare by Ethiopia's restructured armed forces in the early months of 1978; thereafter they returned to guerrilla warfare.

Having repelled the danger from the south, Mengistu set about regaining territory lost to the Eritrean separatists. The towns that the Eritrean People's Liberation Front (EPLF) and other groups had won for the first time in 1977 were retaken at great cost, but the countryside remained in guerrilla hands. Indeed the presence of large numbers of foreign troops in active combat quite failed to eradicate nationalist opposition to the new socialist Ethiopian imperialism. No resolution of these problems had been reached by the early 1980s, although serious in-fighting between the Eritrean separatists in 1981 left all but the EPLF a shadow of their former selves.

Bibliography

The historical background of the country is best read in A.H.M. Jones and Elizabeth Monroe, *A History of Ethiopia* (Oxford, 1960). Colin Legum, a welcome authority for keeping abreast of events in Africa, wrote a contemporary account of the fall of the Emperor. For an early look at the Eritrean problem, see John Franklin Campbell, 'Rumblings along the Red Sea: The Eritrean Question' in *Foreign Affairs* (April, 1970) and J. Bowyer Bell, 'Endemic Insurgency and International Order, the Eritrean Experience' in *Orbis* (Summer, 1974). On the legal background and the attitude officially of the US and USSR, see Alain Feret and Cao Huy Ihuan, *La Question de l'Erythrée* (Paris, 1979). David Hamilton had a long acquaintance with the country and wrote 'Ethiopia's Embattled Revolutionaries' (ISC, London, 1977). David Pool is an expert on the problem of Eritrea, having spent time there and published for the Anti-Slavery Society 'Eritrea: Africa's Longest War' in 1979. The kidnapped missionaries Karl and Debbie Dortzbach related their experiences with the ELF in *Kidnapped* (New York, 1975). On the Ogaden invasion from Somalia, consult James Mayall, 'The Battle for the Horn: Somali Irredentism and International Diplomacy' in *The World Today*, September 1978. For some concise views on the rights and nature of the Eritrean conflict, read the brief volume edited by Basil Davidson, Lionel Cliffe and Bereket Habte Selassie, *Behind the War in Eritrea* (Nottingham, 1980), which has good bibliographical references. See too Colin Legum's earlier *Conflict in the Horn of Africa* (London, 1977).

Eritrean Liberation Front (ELF)

In the early 1980s the ELF or the ELF-Revolutionary Council, as it had become, had declined to a rump of its former membership and eminence. Conflict with rival factions caused the transformation, for in the late 1970s the movement had resisted attacks by air and wide security force sweeps backed by Soviet weaponry, training and planning. Still, sometimes with and often against other groups which had split from the parent body of Eritrean nationalism, the ELF-RC fought to set up an independent nation state.

In 1958 the ELF had been set up in Cairo. During the first ten years of its life, it held to its nationalist convictions. But in 1969 the younger militants accused the leadership of being 'feudalist' and 'capitalist', beginning the shift towards a socialist commitment. Radical Arab governments in Iraq, Libya and Syria championed the new political stance, as did the Palestinian Al Fatah guerrilla movement. The following year (1970) the revolutionary faction took command of the Eritrean Liberation Army (ELA) and, using the Sudan as a base, within a period of four years, built isolated terrorist incidents into a systematic guerrilla campaign. At the time the ELF possibly numbered 2500 followers.

They won the support of large sections of the rural population, and set up an alternative administrative system, which replaced the imperial government. Eritrea was divided into five provinces, each administered by a five-man committee responsible for security and defence, information and political propaganda. Had ideology not caused the ELF to split in 1970, and again in 1975, the movement might well have been in a position to seize independence on the fall of the Emperor in 1974.

As it was, Marxist-Leninists led by Mohammed Nur broke away from the separatist movement in 1970 to form the Eritrean People's Liberation Front (EPLF). Five years later a further faction led by a founder member of the ELF, Osman Saleh Sabbe, broke away to found the ELF-Popular Liberation Forces (ELF-PLF).

Eritreans flocked to join the separatist forces as the old Empire collapsed. Estimates in 1977 put the ELF at 22,000 guerrillas, who engaged in full-scale warfare with the revolutionary forces of the new government under the control of Mengistu Haile Mariam. That year, the ELF took control of a number of towns, but was unable to hold them in 1978, when the government launched a counter-offensive backed by massive Soviet armaments. Reduced again to controlling the rural areas in 1979, the ELF sustained vigorous resistance throughout 1980, only to be worsted in battles with its rival body, the EPLF, in 1981.

Because the ELF was directed by a Revolutionary Council led by Ahmed Nasser, in the late 1970s it became customary to refer to the movement as the ELF-RC. The movement held talks with the EPLF in an endeavour to adopt a common stance in negotiations with Addis Ababa, and efforts were made to form a joint military command. Joint actions had taken place since 1977, but no lasting agreement emerged, indeed an agreement signed in Tunis in March 1981 between all four Eritrean separatist groups was followed by the fiercest in-fighting yet seen. It was said to leave the EPLF as the strongest rebel group.

From the start of the struggle, the ELF had found considerable support for its pretensions amongst Islamic countries, by whom it sought to be recognised as 'the legitimate representative of the Eritrean people'. In the early 1970s the ELF had representatives in Syria, the Lebanon and Libya, as well as in Egypt and Algeria. In 1974 Iraq offered aid. Chinese-manufactured arms reached the insurgents through Somalia, Soviet weaponry through the People's Democratic Republic of the Yemen (PDRY). The greatest debt was owed to the Sudan, which offered a haven to refugees and safety across the border.

After the revolution in 1974/75 international aid and support changed. The Soviet Union no longer saw its interest in supporting separatism, but worked instead to secure the revolutionary government of Mengistu. The Cubans too changed sides, although they declined to fight in Eritrea on behalf of the central government and against their former friends. The PDRY was less scrupulous, and actually lent pilots to bomb the people they had previously supported.

In 1982 the Chairman of the ELF Executive Committee and Revolutionary Council remained Ahmed Nasser. Three men of importance worked with him: Abdullah Suleiman, Chairman of the Foreign Affairs Bureau; Ibrahim Idris Totil, Vice-Chairman and Head of the Political Bureau; and Abdullah Idris, Chairman of the Military Bureau.

Eritrean Liberation Front — Popular Liberation Forces (ELF-PLF)

The veteran Eritrean Nationalist, Osman Saleh Sabbe, was instrumental in the setting up of a third Eritrean separatist movement in 1975. Previously prominent in the parent Eritrean Liberation Front (ELF), Sabbe drifted into the break-away Marxist-Leninist Eritrean People's Liberation Front (EPLF) around 1970. It was the smallest of the Eritrean factions, and at its height in 1977 may have numbered 5000 adherents. Under Sabbe's leadership, the ELF-PLF resisted integration until November 1980, when it allied with the ELF-Revolutionary Council. By 1982 it had lost many supporters from savage in-fighting with other factions the previous year.

Eritrean People's Liberation Front (EPLF)

Alongside other Eritrean separatist groups, the EPLF reached a maximum strength in 1977, when it may have numbered 12,000 members. At that time it seized towns, sometimes cooperating with the parent Eritrean nationalist body, the Eritrean Liberation Front (ELF). It lost control of urban areas in 1978, but continued to exist as a rural force, replacing the ELF in 1981 as the principal Eritrean guerrilla movement. throughout the early 1980s.

For some time the EPLF had existed as a faction within the ELF, consisting of the more politicised and ideologically-minded of the nationalists. It crystallised as a separate entity in 1970, and spent the decade making and breaking alliances with the parent body. On occasions its supporters even fought with ELF cadres. Abroad, the EPLF sought to minimise ELF support and maximise its own impact. Its principal spokesman was EPLF Secretary General Mohammed Nur; his deputy was Isaias Afewok.

The EPLF had not only a rural guerrilla capacity, but operated in the urban centres of Eritrea as well. Its terrorist campaign included kidnapping and assassination, as well as the explosion of bombs. It found no difficulty in penetrating the towns and attacking representatives of central government authority either before or after the 1974 revolution which brought about the deposition of the Emperor Haile Selassie.

During 1977 the EPLF captured Keren, which it had besieged in the past, but never taken. The town had symbolic importance, for the EPLF thought to establish there the capital of an independent Eritrea. Elsewhere, the EPLF mounted successful sabotage operations. Confronted by an overwhelming government offensive in 1978, the EPLF felt compelled to explore further the possibilities of forming a united front with the ELF. Talks took place in Khartoum (Sudan) in January 1979, and in March that year further agreement was announced in Kuwait. Neither these, nor discussions held in Tunis the following year, produced a long-lasting settlement. The separatists remained bitterly divided to the point of armed conflict, which by late 1981 had seriously debilitated their movement. Of the four main factions, the EPLF appeared the strongest in 1982, with an ability to field some 8000 guerrillas.

Ethiopian Democratic Union (EDU)

When the central government of Ethiopia foundered after the 1974 deposition of the Emperor Haile Selassie, democratic opinion centred upon the EDU, which consisted largely of liberals who had been exiled during the reign of the Emperor. Formed in 1975 to preserve what its supporters saw as the centre, the EDU was led by General Iyassu Mengesha, who lived in London. In July 1977 he moved his headquarters to the Sudan.

It was in 1977 that the EDU fought successfully in the north against the attempts of the government to impose by military force a Marxist-Leninist regime on Ethiopia. Indirectly, the EDU aided the Eritrean separatists by holding the roads in the North leading to Eritrea. Yet because it favoured a federal solution to the separatist issue the movement never allied with the Eritreans.

In July 1977, some of the towns which had been taken by EDU forces were recaptured by the government, which offered an amnesty in July to EDU supporters who had taken up arms. Few accepted the offer. Militarily the EDU was defeated the following year, with the advent of large Soviet-bloc reinforcements to the central government. Those who could fled to the Sudan, others were put to death. No further action was reported in 1979, although EDU members were still being brought to trial, suggesting activity in northern Gondar.

Ethiopian People's Revolutionary Party (EPRP)

As Ethiopia slid into revolution following the 1974 deposition of
Emperor Haile Selassie, the ultra-leftist EPRP emerged in the capital,
Addis Ababa, and other towns. It was principally an urban phenomenon
to which young people were attracted, and for which they fought tenaci-
ously in a bitter terrorist campaign carried out on the streets. They were
accused by government forces of being Trotskyists. The government
resorted to a 'red terror' campaign to counteract EPRP 'white terror'.
Thousands died in a matter of months, as government radio urged the
slaughter of EPRP militants.

> The red-terror campaign which is being intensified with revolutionary discipline is
> coordinated and undertaken by leaders of urban dwellers, farmers, workers, youth and
> women's organisations, members of revolutionary defence squads and by progressive
> comrades drawn from government organisations at the repeated requests of the broad
> masses . . . .

By April 1978 the government's ruthless task had been completed.

> When the power of the counter-revolutionary EPRP had increased to the extent of
> enabling them to shed the blood of struggling comrades in every square, revolutionary red
> terror was unleashed to counter their white terror. After this there was a decline in
> anti-revolutionary and threatening graffiti, which had been scrawled on every corner, a
> decline in slogans worn by individuals on their clothes, and in crypto-counter-
> revolutionaries . . .

The EPRP had successfully taken over many branches of the new trade
union organisation and was prominent in many neighbourhood associations (*kebeles*), the grass-root units on which revolutionary support was
founded. Very little EPRP activity survived into the early 1980s.

Oromo National Liberation Front (ONLF)

Like the Somali-Abo National Liberation Front (SALF), the ONLF
depended upon Somali support to resist the central government of
Ethiopia in Addis Ababa. The front emerged during the 1977 war in the
Ogaden region, which Somalia attempted to annex. At the time the
ONLF cooperated with the SALF and with the larger Western Somali
Liberation Front (WSLF). It based its appeal upon the ethnic indivi-
duality of the peoples living in Bale, Sidamo and Haraghe provinces.
Despite having an office in Mogadishu, and despite attempts to ally itself
with dissident groups in the capital, the Front was less active militarily in
the early 1980s than other separatist groups.

Somali-Abo Liberation Front (SALF)

Operating in the south of Ethiopia, the SALF is one of the Somali-backed
liberation fronts which emerged in the course of the 1977 Ogaden war.
The SALF cooperated with the more substantial Western Somali Libera-

tion Front (WSLF) against central government troops in the Sidamo region, where at least in the early 1980s it denied Colonel Mengistu's regime control of the countryside. Wako Guto led the Front in 1980.

Tigre People's Liberation Front (TPLF)

Following the deposition of Ethiopian Emperor Haile Selassie in 1974, central government authority broke down. In the province of Tigre, bordering on Eritrea, where separatist sentiment had long been expressed in terms of guerrilla warfare, local nationalist sentiment surfaced and the TPLF was founded.

At first the TPLF allied with the conservative forces of the pro-Western Ethiopian Democratic Union (EDU); later it moved left, largely as a result of its training with the Eritrean People's Liberation Front (EPLF). A new dimension of social revolution was brought to the nationalist rebellion as younger militants sought to overturn the established social order. The transformation brought them into conflict with EDU supporters in the region, whom they subsequently eliminated from Tigre province.

A greater threat emerged to the TPLF in 1977 and 1978 from the ultra-leftist forces of the Ethiopian People's Revolutionary Party (EPRP), which to defend itself from a government-backed terror campaign had formed an Ethiopian People's Revolutionary Army (EPRA). TPLF supporters found themselves attacked by EPRP-sponsored terrorism, and to get the better of this ideological fanaticism they allied with the EPLF.

Using arms captured from central government forces and from Cuban troops used in the recapture of the Ogaden region from Somali-backed insurgents, the TPLF mounted a guerrilla campaign in 1979 claiming the capture of government garrisons and the deaths of many hundreds of soldiers. By August 70 per cent of Tigre province was said to be under TPLF control. The group was most active around the Amba Alagi pass, near Makale and Maichew.

It did not seem that in the early 1980s Colonel Mengistu's government had got the measure of this ethnic revolt. Reports continued to filter out of Tigre of considerable losses to government and guerrilla forces, which apparently not only laid ambush but besieged and took small garrisons.

Western Somali Liberation Front (WSLF)

In 1980 the WSLF had recovered from massive losses inflicted by the conventional forces of the Ethiopian government, backed up by Cuban personnel. After the crossing by many thousands of refugees from the vast Ogaden region into Somalia, where they were welcomed by people of their own ethnic stock, WSLF guerrilla fighters infiltrated back across the border at night to attack the Ethiopian positions.

The Ogaden region of Ethiopia comprises almost a third of that country's territory, but it is peopled by nomadic Muslim Somalis, whose grazing lands were conquered by the Ethiopian Christian Empire in the nineteenth century. However, Ethiopian expansion southwards never reached the coast because it encountered the stronger colonising powers of Europe. Since independence in 1960 Somalia has claimed the region, as indeed it seeks to unite all Somalis living across frontiers in Djibouti and Kenya.

When in 1974 revolution overturned the Ethiopian Emperor Haile Selassie, the WSLF was set up to take advantage of the collapse of power in Addis Ababa. Abdullah Hassan Mohamoud Dubed led the movement, both as Secretary-General and Commander-in-Chief. His assistant was Abd An-Nasir Sheik Adam. The WSLF central committee consists of 15 members, who meet in the Somali capital of Mogadishu. It claims all territory east of a line running from Moyale, on the Kenyan border, through Awash, which lies 100 miles east of Addis Ababa, to the Djibouti border. Before the exodus of refugees, some two million people inhabited the desert region.

From 1975 armed clashes had occurred in the area, but in mid-1977 the WSLF was backed up by the Somali armed forces, many of whom resigned their commissions to join what they viewed as a liberation army. Many of the smaller villages in the region fell to the invaders, but the WSLF never succeeded in taking the provincial capitals of Sidamo and Bale. Greater successes attended their push to the north, but by then the full might of the Somali armed forces lay behind the WSLF, so that it was hard to distinguish the one from the other. The heavier engagements were clearly the work of the Somali professional forces, the sabotage attacks on the vital Addis Ababa-Djibouti railway the work of guerrillas.

The WSLF cause, promoted by the Somalis, foundered in 1978, as the Ethiopian government employed large numbers of Cuban troops and Soviet and East German advisers to plan a counter-strategy, which in March pushed the Somalis out of the Ogaden. Yet in the course of 1979 and 1980 it became increasingly clear that the Ethiopians were unable to close the Somali border, and consequently to prevent infiltration across it.

WSLF guerrillas filtered back into the region and found support amongst the local inhabitants in the countryside. From their rural bases, travelling at night, they carried out ambushes on Ethiopian convoys, and attacked small garrisons with some success. They received help and encouragement from smaller local liberation groups in the region particularly the Somali Abo Liberation Front (SALF) and the Oromo National Liberation Front (ONLF). Ethnically these movements are akin to the Somalis. Abroad, Egypt and Iraq favoured the WSLF in 1980.

Guinea Bissau

Since Liberation from Portuguese colonial rule in 1974, Guinea Bissau has been ruled by the African Party for the Liberation of Guinea and Cape Verde (PAIGC), which was already the sole political vehicle in the country. Indeed, prior to the April 1974 revolution in Lisbon, the PAIGC had proclaimed the state independent, a move which was formally recognised by the Soviet Union and by China, as well as by African and Arab countries.

From its inception in 1956 PAIGC had always claimed the right to liberate the Cape Verde Islands, whence the majority of the party's mulatto leadership had sprung. In fact, no campaign at all had taken place on the islands, so that the imposition by PAIGC of party rule subsequent to Portuguese withdrawal was resented by broad sections of the population, just as on the mainland the black party members grew to resent what to them appeared a somewhat alien leadership from the islands.

Although until January 1981 one party in name governed the islands and the mainland, in fact the hoped-for union did not come about, nor did it look in 1982 as if developments would move that way. On the contrary, territories which had only become yoked by colonial rule tended to revert to their more natural tribal, geographical and separate economic interests. A split in the mainland PAIGC furthered these tendencies, for in November 1980 Luis Cabral lost control of the movement to a pro-Soviet faction led by General Bernardo Vieira. Pedro Pires, who ran the island government, favoured the Front for National Unity and Development, which was faithful to the memory of Amílcar Cabral, the PAIGC founding father.

Bibliography

The PAIGC had the good fortune to be led by an outstanding intellectual, Amílcar Cabral, whose selected texts can be read in English in *Revolution in Guinea* (London, 1971) *Unity & Struggle* (London, 1980) and at greater length in *La Pratique Révolutionnaire* and *l'Arme de la Théorie* (Paris, 1975). More readily available and essential works are Basil Davidson's *The Liberation of Guinea* (Penguin, 1969) and Gérard Chaliand's *Armed Struggle in Africa* (New York and London, 1969). Lars Rudebeck visited the area as well, and wrote *Guinea Bissau: A Study of Political Mobilisation* (New York, 1975).

African Party for the Liberation of Guinea and Cape Verde
(*Partido Africano da Independência da Guiné e Cabo Verde — PAIGC*)

Of the three former Portuguese African territories, Guinea Bissau was the smallest and poorest: consequently it attracted no settlers from Europe. Amílcar Cabral (1924-73), who had graduated from Lisbon University as a hydraulic engineer five years earlier, set up PAIGC in 1956. Both as an international promoter of his country's cause and as a strategist in the field of national liberation from colonial rule, Cabral proved outstanding.

At the outset he concentrated on non-violent methods of protest with strikes and demonstrations, but when Portuguese troops fired on rioting dockers in 1959 PAIGC adopted armed struggle. Sabotage acts followed, but a more important development was the creation of a rural guerrilla force known as the Revolutionary Armed Forces of the People.

Because the determination of PAIGC recruits overcame, indeed used to advantage, the difficult nature of the terrain, the rural guerrilla struggle prospered. The party began to administer the hinterland, which had never been developed or even governed by the Portuguese administration. Under party direction, elementary schooling and political discussion for adults took place in the bush. Before long an alternative judicial and even commercial structure had begun to emerge in areas outside Portuguese control. Although the guerrilla forces could never deny the colonial army access to any part of the country by helicopter, they disputed claims to permanent Portuguese control on the ground.

All told, PAIGC was estimated by 1972 to have recruited and trained a force of some 7000 men, who inflicted upon the Portuguese army some 300 casualties a year. Towards the end of the struggle guerrilla deaths were running at more than a thousand every year, and yet it was clear to the Portuguese commander, General Antonio Spínola, that the colonial power could not win the struggle. It was this conviction that led him to support the April 1974 coup in Lisbon, which led to Portuguese withdrawal from Africa.

PAIGC received aid and support from the Organisation of African Unity (OAU) and sent its militants abroad for training, mostly to the Soviet Union and Cuba. PAIGC weaponry was largely Soviet supplied; of particular importance was the introduction in 1973 of SAM-7 ground-to-air missiles. No longer could the Portuguese fly in and out of rural areas without risk; militarily it marked the beginning of the end, although the Lisbon coup intervened and shortened the conflict. Towards the final stages, Cuban advisers played a more important role, and there were reports of their having been active on the ground; they were certainly present at the principal PAIGC training base in neighbouring Guinea at Candiafera.

Cabral organised PAIGC through a Central Commitee, his two principal colleagues being Aristides Pereira (b. 1924) and Amílcar's younger brother, Luis Cabral (b. 1931). Participation from the rank and file was ensured through a three-tier system of elections which were actually held, making of PAIGC a more democratic body than the majority of liberation movements in Portuguese Africa. Although no other movement contested PAIGC leadership within Guinea Bissau, the movement itself was not without internal quarrels, which were exploited by the Portuguese authorities.

In January 1973 Cabral was murdered in Conakry (Guinea), where PAIGC had its base, by dissident members. Pereira took over the leadership of the movement, with Luis Cabral heading the armed forces. Others prominent in PAIGC at the time were João Bernardo Vieira (b. 1939) and Francisco Mendes (b. 1939). The rift in PAIGC was largely caused by a Cape Verdean leadership at odds with mainlanders — there had been no armed action on the islands of the Cape Verde archipelago.

After the PAIGC Second Congress had confirmed the appointment of Pereira as the new Secretary General, the movement announced the creation in September 1973 of an independent state of Guinea Bissau, a ceremony witnessed by selected journalists from Sweden, the Soviet Union, East Germany and China. The new state was at once recognised by the Soviet Union and China and by African and Arab countries.

Internationally recognised and military successful, PAIGC was in a strong position to take its independence from Portugal in 1974, when Lisbon recognised a *fait accompli*. Thenceforth PAIGC became the ruling party and formed the government on the mainland territory, leaving the Cape Verde islands to set up a linked but independent government. These links were broken in 1981.

Kenya

Political violence arose early in colonial Kenya. The first of the post-war insurrections, the Mau Mau organisation, based upon the dominant Kikuyu tribe, began in the late 1940s and caused the British government to mount a major counter-insurgency campaign in defence of the lives and properties of 65,000 white settlers in the territory. The movement was nationalist, or more particularly tribalist, in nature; despite subsequent endeavours to see it as an early example of Marxist-Leninist revolution, it contained not a shred of social revolutionary content.

The fact that the emergency lasted eight years (1952-60) and that Jomo Kenyatta (d. 1978), who was suspected of being behind the Mau Mau organisation, was only finally allowed to live as a free man in 1961, itself indicates the strength of the threat and the gravity with which the authorities viewed it. Taken seriously, the revolt was put down with military measures, but the unrest contributed to an anxiety on the part of the authorities to bring forward African participation in government, so that blacks eventually formed a majority in the Legislative Council. Britain conceded independence in December 1963.

Almost immediately, the colonial boundaries imposed from Europe on African ground raised the problem of a dispute in the north-east frontier district, where ethnic Somalis found themselves governed by southern Kikuyu. Known as *shiftas*, those who took up arms were aided and abetted from Somalia, which has never renounced its claim on the area. Until 1967 the Kenyan armed forces were employed in the area to counter the threat. Despite diplomatic agreements, the problem persisted, although the threat to Kenyan territorial integrity was not cumulative. In 1982 the Northern Frontier District Liberation Front (NFDLF) represented this particular dimension of Kenyan political violence.

Bibliography

Essential to an understanding to the background of the Mau Mau rebellion are two books by LSB Leakey, *Mau Mau and the Kikuyu* (London, 1952) and *Defeating Mau Mau* (London, 1954). The official British investigation into the rebellion can be found in FD Cornfield's *Historical Survey of the Origins and Growth of Mau Mau* (HMSO, London, 1960). The Governor, Sir Philip Mitchell (1944-52) wrote his apologia in *African Afterthoughts* (London, 1954). Some of those who took part in the security force campaign left most interesting accounts, especially Ian Henderson and Philip Goodhart, *The Hunt for Kimathi* (London, 1958), Frank

Kitson's *Gangs and Countergangs* (London, 1960), and *Bunch of Five* (London, 1977).

For the organisation of the movement and the operations of the gangs, see Donald L. Barnett and Karari Njama, *Mau Mau from Within* (London and New York, 1966) and the equally excellent *State of Emergency — The Full Story of the Mau Mau* (London, 1962) by Fred Majdalaney. The former guerrilla, Waruhiu Itote, published *Mau Mau General* (Nairobi, 1967); see also *Life Histories from the Revolution Mau Mau 1-3* (Richmond, Canada, 1974).

Jomo Kenyatta studied anthropology and analysed his own people in *Facing Mount Kenya* (London, 1979). His political opponents published accounts of their part in the political developments in *Not Yet Uhuru* (London, 1967) by Oginga Odinga and *Freedom and After* (London, 1963) by Tom Mboya.

Mau Mau

British colonialism came late to Kenya (1895) and within years of the government establishing a settler population in the White Highlands region the Kikuyu protested at the way they had been dispossessed of their farmlands. From these early years (1921) dates the Kikuyu Association, the product of an educated black elite; and into this tradition the Mau Mau knitted its gangs in the late 1940s.

Jomo Kenyatta had returned from 15 years in Britain in 1946 and was generally considered to be behind the new 'evil and subversive association'. Consequently, between 1953 and 1961 he was detained. In the early years the colonial authorities had quite failed to realise what was being organised under their very noses, so that by 1952 the society was deemed to have many thousands of members, although they disposed of only some 500 firearms, which had been stolen from police posts or armouries.

At that time the Mau Mau was run from Nairobi through seven district committees, each one supporting division, location and sub-location committees. In the capital Mau Mau orders were carried out in the heart of the city, where courts sat in judgment and sentences were carried out. Food and arms were purchased with money raised by intimidation; such revenues as the organisation disposed of were also used to bribe. With their oaths lay the key to Mau Mau success in retaining the allegiance and security consciousness of their members, who were afraid to betray the movement for fear of supernatural retribution.

Mau Mau activity covered a relatively small area of the country, about one-sixth of the land area, but the terrain was suitable for guerrilla warfare, which never developed. The Mau Mau campaign was indeed a campaign of intimidation using terrorism to drive the white man from Kikuyu lands. So, in the early days of September 1952, the first crops were burned, the first cattle slaughtered and native huts burned. Fourteen people were murdered; other attacks were beaten off.

Throughout 1953 the campaign intensified — most attacks taking place at night. Possibly the worst incident occurred at the native village of Lari with a police post at Naivasha, where the policeman lost his life alongside 84 Africans. Thirty-one tribesmen were cruelly mutilated. The attack succeeded in freeing 173 prisoners and stealing 47 firearms. Yet by the end of the year some 3000 Mau Mau activists were dead, and 1000 had been captured. Only 18 Europeans had died, 11 Asians and 613 Kikuyu.

Early in 1954 Waruhiu Itote, who led some 5000 terrorists in the Mount Kenya region, was captured and from his cooperation stemmed subsequent serious losses to the Mau Mau organisation.

Thenceforth Dedan Kimathi in the Aberdare forest region caused the security forces most concern. Once massive sweep operations had proved ineffective in 1955, he was finally wounded and captured in October 1956. His death by execution effectively ended the resistance, although for a while longer desultory terrorist acts continued. In all, 11,000 Mau Mau had been killed in security force operations which had cost £55 million. The security forces lost 167 men, 101 of whom were Africans. Civilian casualties amounted to under 2000, the vast majority of whom were also blacks.

On independence in 1963 the survivors were honoured as heroes, and recognition of the part they had played in determining the British to grant independence was made. But neither their barbarous methods, nor their primitive skills were of use in modern administration; their deeds were purposefully confined to history.

Northern Frontier District Liberation Front (NFDLF)

Although set up in 1981, the origins of the NFDLF go back to the mid-1960s, when Somali irredentists caused the Kenyan army to engage in a number of actions in the district to preserve Kenyan sovereignty. Since those days the area was better known for the activities of *shiftas* (bandits), who rustled cattle and smuggled ivory across the border, but being of ethnic Somali stock Somali interests encountered little difficulty in politicising their lawlessness, which under Abd al Qadir Sheik Hussain and Ali Abdullah Sheik Abd al Rahman was transformed into the NFDLF.

Once constituted as a movement, representatives toured Arab capitals in search of funds sympathetic to their cause. To Kenyan Vice-President Kibaki they were no more than 'a bunch of Somali con men'. True or not, these ethnic differences contained the seeds of conflict.

Lesotho

Political violence in the early 1980s arose from a desire on the part of ruling Chief Jonathan to adopt a more independent stance towards the neighbouring Republic of South Africa. Unable or unwilling to stop black African nationalists from crossing into Lesotho, Chief Jonathan aroused white South African fears by establishing diplomatic relations, first with Cuba in 1979 and then with the Soviet Union in 1980. Responding to what they saw as a threat in their midst, the whites, fearful of guerrilla bases just across their border, took steps to destabilise the tiny country.

Accordingly, Chief Jonathan's political opponents were given succour, and, as the Lesotho Liberation Army (LLA), provoked attacks against the regime in power, targeting western diplomatic and commercial interests as well as the local elite. Although Lesotho attempted to police its borders more closely, conflict between black South African nationalists and South African security forces were set to continue into the mid-1980s so that Lesotho's political violence remained subject to outside manipulation.

Basotho Congress Party (BCP)

The opposition BCP has been involved in political violence in Lesotho since the late 1970s, when party members clashed with police in the northern areas around Butha Buthe. In November 1979 Chief Lepata Mou, a leading government supporter, died in an attack upon a police station. The party is led by Ntsu Mokhehle, who, because ruling Chief Jonathan had unjustly denied him power in 1970, attempted four years later to overthrow him. Since 1974 he has lived in Zambia, although there were reports of his reappearance in Lesotho in 1982 at the head of armed resistance. Such as it was, the BCP guerrilla arm was known as the Lesotho Liberation Army.

The party itself was socialist oriented and opposed to South African apartheid, the doctrine of which it fought by aligning itself with the African National Congress. An internal faction returned to legality in 1981, calling upon all members to lay down their arms in response to an amnesty, but attacks continued.

Lesotho Liberation Army (LLA)

The Basotho Congress Party controls the LLA, whose leader, Ntsu Mokhehle, claimed in December 1979 to have Libyan backing. Although at the time boasts were made of 500 fighters, in reality there was but a handful. True, its ranks swelled somewhat following the exodus from Lesotho of a number of tribesmen. Evidence pointed to the LLA finding support in South Africa, which used it to put pressure on Lesotho's ruler, Chief Jonathan, who harboured South African nationalists and appeared prepared to play the Soviet-bloc card.

From time to time, although on a diminutive scale, clashes occurred in 1980 with Lesotho police. Leribe airport in the north was attacked, but such activity as occurred did not seriously threaten the government's hold on power. Bombs exploded in September and December in Leribe, Teyateyaneng and the capital, Maseru, and a cruel murder was inflicted upon the family of a leading politician. Of greater political consequence, the capital's electricity and petroleum installations suffered attacks in March 1981, when mortars were employed. In September a worse spate followed as six bombs exploded at the airport terminal, the Hilton Hotel, the US cultural centre, a downtown bar, an electricity sub-station and on the West German Ambassador's car.

Towards the end of that year the campaign reverted to the rural north, where a number of people died. In August 1982 militants were considered responsible for the murder in the north of Jobo Rampeta, the Minister of Works. LLA activity fluctuated according to the changes registered in Lesotho-South African relations, but continued to operate from the black independent homeland of Bophuthatswana in South Africa, which adjoins Lesotho.

Liberia

In April 1980 a sergeants revolt led by Samuel Doe (b. 1952) toppled the ruling oligarchy, which since 1877 had held power through the True Whig Party. Its cohesion derived from its members' shared descendence from freed American slaves who had founded the country in 1847. Numbering fewer than 10,000 they fell an easy victim to rough military justice, which had a dozen of the country's leaders, including President William Tolbert (1971-80), shot dead publicly on the capital's beaches. The military acted independently of opposition forces, although the leaders of the Progressive Alliance of Liberia (PAL) and the Movement for Justice in Africa (MOJA) were appointed to high office after the coup.

Bibliography

For a background to Liberian political developments, see Martin Lowenkopf, *Politics in Liberia: The Conservative Road to Development* (Stanford, California, 1976) and Christopher Clapham 'Liberia' in John Dunn (ed.), *West African States — Failure and Promise: A Study in Comparative Politics* (Cambridge, 1978). Dr Julius Okolo analysed the April 1980 coup in *The World Today* April 1981, 'Liberia: The Military Coup and its Aftermath'.

Movement for Justice in Africa (MOJA)

From his post in the Faculty of Economics at the University of Liberia, Dr Togba Nah Tipoteh set up MOJA in 1973. It was a socialist movement, mass-oriented, but without particular revolutionary designs upon the old order of the True Whig Party. It sought to raise the level of political consciousness through instigating strikes, demonstrations and work-to-rule protests, a campaign attended by success. MOJA never became a political party, although its chairman was appointed Minister of Economics by Head of State Samuel Doe in 1980, until he proved too ambitious and resigned the following year. Tipoteh then left Liberia, accused by Doe of being a traitor.

Progressive Alliance of Liberia (PAL)

Liberians studying in the United States formed this radical alliance in 1974. From its inception, PAL sought to function as a legal political party inside Liberia, although it only started operating in January 1978. Behind PAL was the forceful and youthful personality of Gabriel Baccus Matthews, whose aim was to found a mass movement which would bring socialism to power in Liberia. His concept of socialism was that of an African and democratic variety, although in bringing the new order about he did not rule out the use of force. In December 1979 PAL became the Progressive People's Party, which the following year the government of President Tolbert banned. Following the *coup d'état* of April 1980 Matthews became Minister of Foreign Affairs until his dismissal in November 1981.

Malawi

In 1944 blacks established the Nyasaland African Congress to work for indigenous interests and especially to prevent association with Rhodesia. It failed to impede the 1953 Federation of Rhodesia and Nyasaland, but thereafter grew more militant at the instigation of younger men like Chipembere (d. 1975) and Kanyama Chiume. To lead the movement they chose the expatriate Dr Hastings Banda (b. 1902), who returned in 1958.

There followed a brief period of agitation and the declaration of a state of emergency in March 1959, during which 52 Africans died. Banda, who had been interned, was released in April 1960 and as leader of the Malawi Congress Party was swept to power in the 1961 elections. Independence followed in 1964.

Since then Dr Banda has ruled Malawi in an authoritarian, puritanical manner, and has met with economic success. He survived the coming to power of a radical regime in Mozambique in 1975, which has awoken little or no internal discontent. Those opposition organisations which existed in the early 1980s posed no challenge to Banda's rule, seemingly anxious merely to establish their presence before the President's death, so as the better to jockey for power after it.

Congress of Second Republic of Malawi

The Congress was led in the early 1980s by a former external affairs minister, Kanyama Chiume, who began to establish his position in the expectation of Dr Hastings Banda's death.

Malawi Freedom Movement (MAFREMO)

Former justice minister, Orton Chirwa, who was resident in Tanzania, headed MAFREMO in opposition to President Banda. He claimed in March 1981 to have started a guerrilla training programme, but no evidence had emerged by 1982 that armed conflict was pursued in Malawi.

Socialist League of Malawi (LESOMA)

Whilst opposed to the authoritarian government of President Banda, LESOMA did not promote terrorism in Malawi in the early 1980s. Led by Attati Mpakati, the movement expected to gain influence on the old president's death.

Mozambique

Political violence in Mozambique continued after the 1975 independence celebrations, largely thanks to the foreign-assisted banditry of dissident blacks who at some time had been caught up in the guerrilla struggle against the Portuguese, but who had fallen foul of the dominant guerrilla leadership of the Front for the Liberation of Mozambique (Frelimo). Gathered together in the Mozambique Resistance Movement (MRM), they tended towards an independent existence, for first the Rhodesians and then the South Africans found MRM actions difficult to control, although not hard to sustain.

Frelimo, although not winning a military victory over the Portuguese, certainly eliminated rival nationalist guerrilla movements such as the Revolutionary Committee of Mozambique (COREMO). As the sole contestants for power, when Portuguese government collapsed in the Lisbon coup of April 1974, Frelimo inherited Mozambique, becoming shortly afterwards a vanguard Leninist party.

Bibliography
The Frelimo movement had at its head Eduardo Mondlane; his biography is published by Panaf (London, 1972), and his own account exists in *The Struggle for Mozambique* (Penguin, 1969). The Portuguese commander-in-chief, Kaúlza de Arriaga, briefly summarised his views in *The Portuguese Answer* (London, 1973), and the South African reporter Al Venter wrote *The Zambesi Salient* (Cape Town, 1974). Adrian Hastings related doubtful second-hand accounts of an alleged massacre in *Wiriyamu* (London, 1974). Peter Janke traced the geographical extent of guerrilla penetration in *Southern Africa, End of Empire* (ISC, London, 1974).

Free Africa Movement
(Movimento da Africa Livre)

Said to be based in Malawi, the Free Africa Movement was first cited by the Mozambican authorities in February 1981, when they condemned to death four terrorists. They had been found guilty of killing policemen, soldiers and peasants inside Mozambique. A further 27 members received prison sentences for recruiting rebels and committing armed robbery.

Mozambique Liberation Front
(Frente da Libertação de Moçambique — Frelimo)

In Mozambique the liberation struggle against Portuguese colonial rule began with the formation of a number of movements, three of which came together in 1962 as Frelimo under the presidency of Dr Eduardo Mondlane. Thanks to his guidance, Frelimo developed into a well organised movement, which withstood a number of potentially disastrous splits, the worst being Mondlane's own murder on 3 February 1969.

Mondlane, educated in South Africa, Portugal and the United States, where for a time he lectured as an anthropologist, shaped Frelimo according to his own cosmopolitan background. He sought and gained support from East and West, resisting the temptation of relying exclusively on Soviet-bloc support and of being drawn into the Sino-Soviet conflict.

Despite Mondlane's exceptional qualities, Frelimo suffered tensions because the leadership for the most part came from the south of the country, whereas the fighting force was mainly drawn from the north, especially from the Makonde tribe. But there were serious dissensions among the Frelimo leadership too, for instance Jaime Sigauke, in charge of internal organisation, was shot dead in Lusaka (Zambia) in July 1966, and in December 1968 Samuel Kankombe, a prominent military leader, was assassinated in Tanzania.

Naturally the Portuguese promoted discord within the movement, but the authorities also succeeded in persuading the Makonde chief, Lazaro Kavandane, to leave Frelimo and surrender in April 1969. With him came a number of defectors.

Opposition to Mondlane came principally from ideologically committed militants, who felt that their leader was treading too careful a path between the capitalist and communist worlds. They wanted the full-hearted adoption of Marxist-Leninist principles, which they believed held the key to successful political organisation. For his moderation, Mondlane was murdered by a book bomb sent to his offices in Dar es Salaam in 1969.

Two men came to the fore after Mondlane's death, Samora Machel (b. 1933), Commander-in-Chief of the armed forces, and Marcelino dos Santos, who was more talented intellectually, but less practical. He had directed Frelimo's foreign contacts. At first the military activity was confined to the northern area of Mozambique, operating across the border from Tanzania, where Frelimo had its headquarters and its training camps. Because of tribal opposition Frelimo found it could make no headway southwards, and so turned its attention in 1964 to penetrating the Tete salient in the interior. Here guerrilla activities were more successful, although Frelimo never succeeded in halting the construction of the giant Cabora Bassa dam, a stated objective of the campaign.

Leaving the dam, guerrillas penetrated further south to Manica and Sofala provinces, but never operated in more than one-third of Mozambique, barely reaching south of the Pungue river. The cities were never threatened by infiltration or sabotage. During the last three years of the struggle against the Portuguese no more than 7-8000 guerrillas could have been inside Mozambique, probably a lot less. During the period May 1970 to May 1973 Portuguese sources gave the number of 3815 Frelimo guerrillas as having died in combat. It was a heavy toll, which, taking into account the reduced area in which they operated, denied to Frelimo forces the claim of having won independence militarily from the Portuguese.

The level of insurgency was always greater in the dry season, during which Frelimo mounted an average of 70 actions a month. Towards the end of the campaign these were spread over a wider area, but the number of incidents did not rise, indicating very little increase in Frelimo strength. For part of the time Frelimo was engaged in fighting a rival organisation, *Comitê Revolucionário de Moçambique* (Coremo), which it decimated in the bush in 1972.

Standing alone in 1974, Frelimo inherited Mozambique's independence from the Lisbon coup, which caused Portugal to withdraw from Africa. After independence on 25 June 1975 Frelimo, under the guidance of President Samora Machel, became a 'vanguard party' in the Leninist mould, seeking first to align the country with the Soviet-bloc, but latterly adopting a more independent third world socialist stance.

Mozambique Resistance Movement subsequently known as Mozambique National Resistance (RNM)
(Movimento da Resistência Moçambicana — MRM

Following Mozambique's independence from Portuguese rule, the MRM emerged in 1976. Its members were drawn from dissident Mozambicans trained in Rhodesia and led by former disaffected Frelimo guerrillas and seasoned Portuguese fighters.

As the white Rhodesian government came under increasing attack from Zimbabwe African National Union (ZANU) guerrillas based in Mozambique, Salisbury attacked the guerrillas in preemptive raids on their base camps, and went on in 1978 to attack Mozambique's economic infrastructure. In these operations the Rhodesians used both bombardment from the air and the infiltration of groups who established a semi-permanent presence inside Mozambique. As the MRM, they recruited dissident Mozambicans and operated against the Frelimo government.

For a while these groups fomented tribal and economic discontent in the remote rural areas, backed up by a clandestine radio station known as *Voz da Africa Livre* (Voice of Free Africa), which broadcast from Rhodesia. On the ground the MRM was led by former guerrilla commander, Andrew Matade Matsangai, who claimed to lead a force of 1000 men. In 1979 the group had established a base in the Gorongoza mountains, supplied by air from Rhodesia. These men were flushed out in October that year.

Among the names associated with the MRM in the late 1970s were Miguel Murupa, Mateus Gwengere and João Mário Tudela, but perhaps most of all Domingos Arouca, a man whose financial interests had firm roots in Portuguese colonialism. Further support came from South African interests, which with the proclamation of an independent Zimbabwe in 1980 substituted Rhodesian backing.

South Africans realised that they could use the MRM to put pressure on the Frelimo regime to desist from encouraging African National Congress (ANC) attacks on the Republic. MRM guerrillas received supplies by air on a regular basis, which led them to embark upon a successful sabotage campaign that cut the Umtali-Beira (Mutare-Sofala) railway line, sabotaged oil storage depots, cut power lines and blew up roads and bridges.

In July 1980 a camp of 500 men in Manica province was reportedly taken, but the dynamiting of power lines continued and in April 1981 an attack was mounted on the giant Cabora Bassa dam. MRM bases lay close to the Zimbabwe border and on several occasions the terrorists attacked the town of Espungabera. Many black refugees fled to Zimbabwe to escape death and mutilation. The group was particularly merciless towards anyone in any form of authority. Lengthy engagements took place in 1982 — Zimbabwe was so concerned that it set up special border units to help control the situation and to cooperate with Frelimo.

Revolutionary Committee of Mozambique
(Comitê Revolucionário de Moçambique — Coremo)

Coremo was formed in 1965 by a number of dissidents from the main Mozambique liberation organisation, Frelimo. Led by Paulo Gumane (b. 1918), who found refuge and support in Lusaka (Zambia), the majority were to receive or had already undergone guerrilla training in China. Indeed, Coremo supporters were encouraged to split from Frelimo by the Chinese, who were anxious to outwit the Soviet Union in Africa and to win for themselves the primary supporting role of African liberation movements.

Coremo guerrillas never amounted to much on the ground, and nothing more was heard of their guerrilla activities after a party of infiltrators from Zambia had been ambushed by Frelimo in February 1972. Three prominent leaders — Gabriel Machava, Bernardo Chambata and Julio Sarume — were killed.

Coremo was a nucleus, however, to which dissident Frelimo followers could adhere. They tended to be those who favoured the Chinese position in world politics. Possibly the most significant Frelimo defector was Uria Simango (b. 1933), formerly vice-president of Frelimo and acting-president after Mondlane's assassination in 1969. He was expelled from Frelimo in 1970, and joined Coremo the following year.

Although Coremo relied upon Chinese support, China was anxious to control the larger Mozambique parent movement, Frelimo, to which it continued to pay attention and increasingly backed, to the point that most of Frelimo's arms came from that source. Under such circumstances, Coremo withered, so that in 1975, when the Portuguese withdrew, it was in no position to contest Frelimo's assumption of the leadership of an independent Mozambique.

United Mozambique Front
(Frente Unida Moçambicana — FUMO)

Behind FUMO lay the financial interests of Portuguese bankers in Mozambique, principally Jorge Jardim and Domingos Arouca. They promoted FUMO as an alternative front to Frelimo, which had no administrative capability when the Lisbon coup of April 1974 handed to it the task of governing an independent Mozambique. However, FUMO never became a political party and was reduced to supporting the clandestine operations of the Rhodesian-backed *Movimento da Resistência Moçambicana* (MRM) in 1979.

Namibia

South West Africa was a German colony which with allied approval South Africa occupied in the First World War. The League of Nations approved South Africa's administration of the territory in 1920, but this authority lapsed in April 1946 after the final meeting of the League. When South Africa proposed to the United Nations Organisation, which succeeded the League, that SWA should be incorporated into South Africa, the plea was turned down. Since then protracted litigation in the International Court of Justice and discussions in the UN General Assembly have quite failed to accommodate the interests of those parties involved in the dispute.

The dominant tribal group is the Ovambo, who inhabit the north and whose people spill across the border into Angola. In 1960 Sam Nujoma founded the South West African People's Organisation (SWAPO), which in 1966 adopted armed struggle. The Herero-backed South West African National Union (SWANU) having faded out in the course of the 1970s, SWAPO remained the sole liberation movement in the 1980s.

SWAPO's military development was hampered by South African military operations as troops pursued infiltrating guerrillas back to their bases in Angola, as well as by the development inside the territory of other political parties, which, once organised, were allowed to hold elections, after which much of the territories' administration devolved into local hands. The party favoured by the South Africans until 1982 was Dirk Mudge's Democratic Turnhalle Alliance (DTA), which included black and coloured representatives. Increasingly, the policing and indeed the defence of the territory were turned over to locally recruited bodies trained by the South Africans. Yet in 1982 there were no indications that the South African military were in fact preparing to abandon these newly created forces. Indeed, in 1983 the Republic revoked the powers it had conceded to Windhoek, so that administrative control returned to Pretoria.

Bibliography

Ruth First provided an introduction to the territory, *South West Africa* (Penguin, 1963) and a more up-to-date white liberal view has been written by JHP Serfontein *Namibia* (London, 1977). Two papers by Daan Prinsloo, 'SWA: The Turnhall and Independence' and 'SWA/Namibia: Towards a Negotiated Settlement' published in 1976 and 1977 respectively by the South African government-backed Foreign Affairs Association dealt with the diplomatic tussle. For the later position, see Michael Spicer, 'Namibia — Elusive Independence' in *The World Today*, October 1980. A useful symposium was held by John Barratt at the South African Institute of International Affairs, which published in August 1977 'The Future of South West Africa/Namibia'. In Oakland, USA the Liberation Support Movement published *Namibia: SWAPO Fights for Freedom*, which puts together a selection of SWAPO's documents and aims. Randolf Vigne, a white South African spokesman for SWAPO wrote 'A Dwelling Place of Our Own' (London, 1975) published by the International Defense and Aid Fund.

South West African National Union (SWANU)

Prominent Herero tribesmen, anxious to promote the independence of Namibia from the South African mandate, founded SWANU in 1959. The union swiftly lost ground to the South West African People's Organisation (SWAPO) in the early 1960s, largely because the Ovambos who set it up were more numerous and more powerful.

SWANU nonetheless continued to exist throughout the 1960s with representatives in London, New York, Dar es Salaam and Cairo. The leadership consisted of politically-minded, post-graduate students at Oxford, Princeton, London, and Uppsala. They were courted by the Chinese, so that for a time SWANU was described as being pro-Peking. It is certainly true that SWANU was excluded from Moscow-backed gatherings and initiatives during the 1960s.

Inside Namibia a number of its followers were sentenced to terms of imprisonment, so that after 1967 little was heard of the organisation. It took no part in the launching of guerrilla warfare in Namibia in 1966. As a minority people, the Herero were drawn increasingly in the late 1970s to cooperate with other political forces bent upon wresting power from the South Africans by negotiation and in collaboration with the white population.

South West African People's Organisation (SWAPO)

Although SWAPO in 1980 was the principal liberation movement active in Namibia/South West Africa, indeed the only one engaged in guerrilla warfare, it was not the first black nationalist movement to be established in the territory. In 1960 SWAPO grew out of the Ovamboland People's Organisation under the direction of its present leader, Sam Nujoma, (b. 1930) a former Windhoek railway clerk who studied at Lincoln University in the United States.

At first SWAPO cooperated with its rival group, the predominantly Herero South West African National Union (SWANU), but quickly overtook it as Professor Mburumba Kerina argued forcefully from a SWAPO platform at the United Nations on behalf of Namibia. The case of South

West Africa, which in 1920 the League of Nations had entrusted to South Africa, was taken to the International Court at The Hague, which rejected the charge that South Africa was abusing its mandate over the territory. Following that decision SWAPO embarked in 1966 upon a course of armed struggle to achieve liberation.

Aside from Kerina, who resigned in 1962, the principal SWAPO leaders included Jacob Kuhangua (b. 1933) and Louis Nelengani, both of whom had lost influence by the end of the decade. In the 1970s Misheck Muyongo, who became acting vice-president in December 1969, Moses Garoeb, who became secretary general that year, Peter Katjavivi, who was active in Europe and Andreas Shipanga in Cairo, all contributed in a major way to SWAPO's activities.

SWAPO remains principally an Ovambo organisation, important because the Ovambos make up half of Namibia's population, but ethnic homogeneity did not save it from internal dissension. In the 1960s this took the form of those who were pro-Soviet and the moderates, who were pro-West. In the 1970s there was serious complaint over the conduct of the war, and of Nujoma's capacity to run it, for he is both president and commander-in-chief of the People's Liberation Army of Namibia (PLAN). It came to a head in 1975/76.

The division was so bad that the Zambian authorities (SWAPO was based at the time in Lusaka) arrested Shipanga and some 50 followers and had them detained in Tanzania. On his release in 1978, he formed a small group known as SWAPO-Democrats and returned to Namibia, where in the 1980s he was losing influence.

In 1980 the defection of Mishek Muyongo, vice-president of SWAPO and a man who had defended Nujoma's leadership, was a blow which undermined SWAPO's influence in Caprivi. Earlier the dismissal of Peter Katjavivi in October 1979 had weakened SWAPO abroad. Yet despite the divisions, Nujoma remained in control of the bulk of his supporters, and had set his ideological imprint on the organisation.

SWAPO is fundamentally a nationalist movement which on achieving power intends to carry out a socialist economic programme. Two formative influences on SWAPO have been the Lutheran church, strong on the ground in Namibia, and Marxism-Leninism. SWAPO has a hierarchical structure with considerable power vested in the hands of Sam Nujoma, who heads the central committee. Leninism plays a central role in the organisational structure, which is based upon democratic centralism, the principle that ensures control from the top, and not, as in democratic structures, from the general membership. As Nujoma came to rely increasingly on Cuban military instructors in Angola in 1978 SWAPO committed itself more clearly to 'scientific socialism'.

SWAPO's effective military commander in the late 1970s was Dimo Hamambo, whose headquarters at Cassinga (Angola) the South Africans raided in May 1978. From Cassinga Hamambo had organised PLAN in three sectors along the Namibian frontier. He counted some 3000 guerrillas in all, of which 400 were possibly active for short periods in Namibia ın 1979. The recruits came willingly enough from Ovamboland, but often returned disillusioned.

Training is undertaken for the most part in Angola by Cubans, and since 1978 by East Germans as well. A few recruits are sent to Cuba. Much of SWAPO's military activity took place inside Angola, where the government encouraged SWAPO to take action against guerrilla fighters from the *União Nacional para a Independência Total de Angola* (UNITA). themselves encouraged by the South Africans to attack SWAPO.

Inside Namibia SWAPO seldom penetrated very far, confining its actions for the most part to hit and run raids across the border. One of the principal targets was electricity pylons, which in repairs cost the South Africans dearly. But the military campaign is conducted at such a low level that by itself it would take many years for SWAPO actually to win power through armed action. That does not mean that SWAPO is short of support amongst its own tribesmen in the north, although many have been intimidated into actively providing help. SWAPO terror has not stopped short of murdering local headmen, or indeed the Herero Chief Kapuuo, whose people resent the prospects of an independent Namibia ruled by Ovambos. The military position suggested that in the end SWAPO will be compelled to negotiate Namibian independence, and possibly in the course of negotiations to compromise. Nujoma remained President of SWAPO, Davis Meroro was the National Chairman and Bredan Simbwaye the new Vice-President in 1980.

Somalia

Somalia took its independence bloodlessly in 1960 from Britain and Italy, the two colonising powers. That event left significant Somali communities in Kenya, Ethiopia and Djibouti outside the new national boundaries. President Siad Barre (b. 1919), who seized power in 1969, in pursuit of national reunification, has not stopped short of war.

His campaign in the Ogaden region of Ethiopia did not meet with success. Furthermore, military defeat weakened his hold on power, so that in the early 1980s he was threatened by mutiny. The greatest challenge to his authority came from the Somali Salvation Front (SOSAF), which formed part of a united Democratic Front for the Salvation of Somalia set up in October 1981.

Democratic Front for the Liberation of Somalia (DFLS)

The DFLS was led by Abd Rahman Aidid Ahmad, who brought his front into the Somali Democratic Salvation Front in October 1981, with a view to waging armed struggle against President Siad Barre.

Somali Democratic Salvation Front (SDSF)

The SDSF was established in October 1981 as an umbrella organisation grouping three movements opposed to the government of President Siad Barre. These were the Somali Salvation Front, the Democratic Front for the Liberation of Somalia and the Somali Workers Party. It had an 11-member Executive Committee under Colonel Abdullah Ysuf Ahmad (SSF leader) which was determined to make the SDSF 'the political weapon used by all Somali democratic national forces against the dictatorial regime'. The Front enjoyed the use of a dissident Radio Kulmis, which broadcast from Ethiopia.

In November 1981 five leading Somali officials defected to the front with a view to waging armed struggle against President Siad Barre. With this in mind, Ethiopia supported the Front, which claimed in July 1982 to have attacked towns and bases in Mudugh, Nujal and Hiram regions of Somalia. The Somali government accused the Soviet Union of aiding the rebels, whose forces numbered some 8-10,000 men. There was no doubting that Ethiopians fought for the group and may even have formed the majority. Libya too gave its backing. Later that year the Front announced the creation of a joint military committee with the Somali National Movement, the ultimate objective being unification.

Somali National Movement (SNM)

The SNM drew its support from the Isaaq clan, known to be conservatively inclined, in the north of the country. These tribesmen resented the dominance of southerners in President Siad Barre's government and were given military aid by Ethiopia with which to wage armed opposition. In late 1982 the movement joined the Somali Democratic Salvation Front in its attempts to engage the Somali military in limited actions. A joint military committee was formed with a view to an eventual merger.

Somali Salvation Front (SOSAF)

The SOSAF leader, Colonel Abdullah Ysuf Ahmad, became chairman of the 1981 umbrella grouping of Somali opposition factions known as the Somali Democratic Salvation Front. He had opposed President Siad Barre for some years and had found support from across the Kenyan frontier in Somali-speaking areas and in Ethiopia, which feared President Barre's irredentist claims on the Ogaden region. In January 1981 SOSAF was thought to be responsible for a bomb blast in the capital, Mogadishu. A year later the Front was responsible for incursions from Ethiopia when they actually held the town of Bototleh for a few hours. The incident caused the President to execute several officers whom he thought sympathetic to the Front. This in turn led to a more serious mutiny in the Eighth Army.

Somali Workers' Party (SWP)

The SWP was led by Sa'id Jama Husayn, who joined the Somali Democratic Salvation Front (SDSF) in October 1981 with a view to waging armed struggle against the regime of President Siad Barre.

South Africa

Contemporary political violence in the Republic of South Africa has to do with the rise of black nationalism. Two internal events are of outstanding importance in the development of black consciousness in the Republic: a tragedy which took place in 1960 at Sharpeville, where police opened fire on demonstrators killing 69 blacks, and riots which took place in Soweto, the black township outside Johannesburg, in the summer of 1976. Abroad, the collapse of Portuguese rule in Africa in 1974 and the independence of Zimbabwe in 1980 exposed the Republic directly to infiltration from black nationalists trained abroad for sabotage and guerrilla warfare.

That is not to say that black political awareness is purely a contemporary phenomenon. The first outward manifestation of these stirrings occurred in 1912, when the African National Congress (ANC) was set up by local chiefs to resist white legislation. It remained a non-violent body until the 1960s. By the end of the decade the ANC had moved close to the South African Communist Party (SACP), which supported armed struggle against not only *apartheid*, but against the democratic system as well.

The SACP is a multi-racial body; the ANC is less militantly black than its formerly important rival, the Pan Africanist Congress (PAC) which broke away in 1959. The PAC had support from China, where a handful of its militants was trained in the 1960s. The Chinese used the movement to promote rivalry in an effort to outbid the Soviet Union, which promoted the armed struggle of the ANC. Internal wrangling had reduced the PAC to a somewhat moribund organisation in 1980.

The growth of terrorist acts committed by black nationalists in the early 1980s caused the government urgent and serious concern. It was prepared to face up to a dilemma of its making by reforming the Republic's constitution, but in so doing risked not only losing support on the political right, but exposing the white community to a new terrorism from the ultra-right, which had begun to set up such groups as the White Commando, prepared to carry out physical attacks against prominent white liberals.

Yet it seemed clear that the South African military, which was engaged in a low intensity conflict on Namibia's frontier, firmly backed reform, and would if necessary support such political measures through some form of military intervention in politics. There was no doubting the will to reform, indeed in 1981 considerable changes had already been effected; the question remained whether fundamental changes could be instituted in such a way as to attract the support of politically responsible blacks.

Bibliography

The ANC has its own publications in English printed in East Germany and distributed from London and elsewhere; they include the writings of Nelson Mandela, the imprisoned father figure of black nationalism, whose biography PANAF published in London in 1980. For the background to the struggle, consult Peter Walshe, *The Rise of African Nationalism in South Africa: ANC 1912-52* (University of California, 1971). For those quite unfamiliar with the history of the struggle, Alan Paton's *Cry the Beloved Country*, originally written in 1948, started a tradition of protest. One such classic is ANC leader Albert Luthuli's *Let My People Go* (London, 1963). M. Benson reviewed the struggle in *South Africa: The Struggle for a Birthright* (Penguin, 1966), and Muriel Horrell wrote as a concerned white South African *Terrorism in Southern Africa* (Johannesburg, 1968). See also G. Mbeki, *South Africa: The Peasants Revolt* (Penguin, 1964).

Donald Woods, the South African newspaper editor who sought exile in 1977, commemorated the shocking death of a friend in *Biko* (London, 1978). The correspondent of the London *Guardian*, John Kane Berman, was a close observer when he wrote after the Soweto outburst *South Africa, the Method and the Madness* (Pluto Press, 1979). A swiftly written but challenging appraisal can be found in *How Long Will South Africa Survive?* (London, 1977) by R.W. Johnson. Edward Feit published a monograph on the cities in *Urban Revolt in South Africa 1960-64: A Case Study* (Evanston, USA, 1971). Baruch Hirson, writing as a dissident with prison experience, looked at the Soweto revolt in *Year of Fire & Year of Ash* (London, 1979).

African National Congress (ANC)

In the Republic of South Africa the ANC is the principal black African nationalist movement; in the 1980s it was infiltrating guerrillas into northern Natal from Mozambique. Inside the country it would be hard to estimate support, but the movement derives respect from being the oldest black organisation. It began life in 1912, the creation of an elite of tribal chiefs and black professional men who sought to prevent Africans from being dispossessed of their land by the Native Land Bill — a British act which subsequently became the cornerstone of the Afrikaner *apartheid* system of separate development.

Nurtured by graduates from the black university of Fort Hare, the ANC attempted in the 1940s to transform itself into a mass movement. A more radical leadership was elected in 1949, among them Nelson Mandela, who in 1982 was still imprisoned on Robben Island, and Oliver

Tambo (b.1917) the actual President. Yet throughout the 1950s the predominant influence was that of Chief Albert Luthuli (d. 1967), who kept the ANC out of violent politics.

The death in 1960 of 69 demonstrators at Sharpeville changed the climate of politics, causing the government to ban the ANC in April that year. Oliver Tambo left the country — to become the veteran leader of black nationalism. Tanzania remained his principal base, although Alfred Nzo operated the secretariat from Lusaka. The external organisation which Tambo set up was boosted after the 1976 Soweto shootings by several thousand blacks who left the Republic. Many received guerrilla training in Angola, alongside militants from liberation groups in Namibia (South West Africa) and Rhodesia (Zimbabwe).

Those that remained in South Africa began a campaign of limited violence, promoted by *Umkhonto we Sizwe* or Spear of the Nation. Telephone wires were cut and a number of bombs damaged electricity pylons. By and large the targets were government installations rather than private property or people.

The South African Communist Party (SACP), a multi-racial, orthodox Marxist-Leninist party, approved of such a course, and when the authorities cracked down in 1963 the court found a number of SACP members guilty alongside ANC militants in the April 1964 Rivonia trial (named after the town where they were apprehended). Mandela (ANC), Walter Sisulu (ANC) and Govan Mbeki (SACP) received sentences of life imprisonment.

The ANC did not recover from this setback for a decade. It lost all influence inside the country because at home the exiles had no way of making their voice heard. In 1969 the ANC formally committed itself to a policy of multi-racialism alongside the SACP. Six years later, taking advantage of Portuguese withdrawal from Africa and the consequent exposure of South African frontiers to radical influences, the ANC announced it would step up preparations for armed struggle.

In June 1977 the ANC admitted responsibility for shooting two whites in Johannesburg. A limited number of explosions followed and then in 1980 came a spectacular sabotage attack upon an oil storage depot. More recently Cuban training in Angola and Zambia has caused the level of militants infiltrated into the Republic to rise. Consequently, terrorist acts increased in the early 1980s with attacks upon military facilities, government buildings, railways, electricity supplies and the nuclear power plant near Cape Town.

Like most liberation movements, the ANC has suffered splits, but they stemmed from policy disagreements rather than conflicting tribal allegiances. A central question has been whether or not to pursue armed struggle; the relationship with the SACP, which has been very close ever since the ANC committed itself to becoming a multi-racial body in 1969, is also criticised within the movement.

The ANC is recognised by the Organisation of African Unity (OAU) Liberation Committee, and by the United Nations as 'a true (but not sole) representative of the South African people'. It maintains offices, in addition to its headquarters at Morogoro in Tanzania, in Algiers, Cairo, Dakar, Delhi, Luanda and Lusaka. Front-line African states lend it time on their radio stations and it publishes a regular journal, *Sechaba*, which is printed in East Germany and distributed from London.

In 1982 the leadership remained in the hands of the educated elder statesmen of black politics. Tambo is a graduate of Fort Hare university and practised with Mandela as an attorney. Alfred Nzo (b. 1925) is secretary general and Duma Nokwe (b. 1927) is his deputy. Others prominent in the movement include Thomas Nkobi (b. 1922), Dr Yusuf Dadoo (b. 1909 and elected SACP chairman in 1972) and Moses Kotane (b. 1905 and general secretary of SACP).

Azanian People's Organisation (AZAPO)

AZAPO was tolerated by the South African authorities until November 1981, when it declared 'total war against white supremacy, oppression and exploitation'. The Organisation took over from the Black Consciousness movement in 1977, and was led in the early 1980s by Khehlka Mtembe.

Pan Africanist Congress (PAC)

The PAC broke away from the parent body of South African black nationalism, the African National Congress, in 1959 over a disagreement on whether or not to adopt a multi-racial approach to the South African problem of how to include blacks in a political settlement.

Those who left followed Robert Sobukwe (1924-78) and set up a militantly Africanist organisation under Potlako Leballo (b. 1925) and Peter Molotsi. In 1960 they opted for a non-violent political campaign against the pass laws, and were immortalised by the police reaction to their demonstration at Sharpeville, where 69 of their supporters were shot dead.

PAC was then banned by the government, and the organisation went underground. Leballo left South Africa in 1962 and subsequently set up PAC headquarters in Tanzania. Sobukwe remained in prison, to die under house arrest 18 years later.

Supporters who remained behind set up an armed branch, known as *Poqo* (We Alone), which had a brief career as a terrorist organisation. Following a number of actions, which included the murder of a handful of whites and blacks, most members were arrested by the police and imprisoned in the 1960s. No more was heard of the campaign within South Africa.

Abroad, the leadership was persuaded to adopt a protracted revolutionary struggle along the lines advocated by the Chinese. Anxious as always to rival Soviet influence in Africa, China took up the PAC cause and provided guerrilla training facilities. Courses were run firstly in China, but later in Tanzania, once the Chinese had established a presence through the building of the Tanzara railway and the training of Frelimo guerrillas for the struggle against the Portuguese authorities in Mozambique. In 1967 Leballo issued a 'revolutionary message to the nation', asserting the primacy of armed struggle and emphasising the importance of self-reliance. Until the Portuguese withdrawal in 1975, PAC had no success in infiltrating its cadres through Mozambique into South Africa.

PAC leadership was always in dispute. In 1964 Molotsi, then in Dar es Salaam, challenged Leballo's position, but failed to oust him. Again in 1967 Raboroko, the Education Secretary, and A.B. Ngcobo, the PAC Treasurer, attempted to remove Leballo, but failed. Yet another manoeuvre in 1968, engineered by T.T. Letlaka and Z.B. Molete came to nothing. Such disruption caused Zambia to ban the movement from Lusaka altogether. During the early 1970s Leballo looked to Libya and to Uganda, but the principal encouragement continued to come from China.

Following the Soweto disturbances in 1976, many PAC militants left South Africa; some received guerrilla training, only to return and fall into the hands of the police in 1978. Possibly as a result of Leballo's overall failure to mount an effective campaign inside the country, he was finally ousted from the leadership in 1979, but was accused by his rivals of having plotted the death of his successor, David Sibeko, shortly afterwards in Dar es Salaam. The Tanzanian authorities arrested six PAC members and charged them with murder. The dissident wing called itself the Azanian People's Revolutionary Party (APRP) and looked for leadership to Templeton Mukisi Ntantala, the PAC guerrilla commander.

The new PAC chairman who took over in October 1979, was Dr Vusumzi Make, supported by Henry Isaacs, responsible for foreign affairs, and D. Mantshontsho, who was PAC administrative secretary. Elias Ntloedibe held the post of Director of Publicity and Information, E.V. Radebe was responsible for finance and E.L. Makoti for defence.

South African Communist Party (SACP)

The SACP was founded in 1921 as a white party, but moved before the end of the decade to embrace members of other races. Banned in 1950, it reformed illegally in 1953 but was largely inactive until 1960. It dropped its policy of non-violence and was associated with the political violence mounted by the African National Congress at that time.

The police effectively broke up the party in 1963, when most of its leaders went into exile. The SACP chairman, J.B. Marks, died in Moscow in 1972. He was succeeded by Dr Yusuf Dadoo (b. 1909), who had trained in medicine in Edinburgh, Scotland. A Central Committee meeting in

1970 decided to concentrate on building in South Africa 'an organisation of professional revolutionaries'. Yet the armed struggle was only one part of the organisation of the masses, so that it became policy to support the ANC's military wing in its aims 'to recruit and train guerrilla fighters, and to spread guerrilla war to the heart of the Republic.'

The SACP was accused by the South African authorities of fomenting disturbances in Soweto in 1976; true or not, the party remains close to the black nationalist movement, as it does to Moscow. Those prominent in the SACP include Moses Kotane (b. 1905), who has spent many years in Algiers and Dar es Salaam, Brian Bunting (b. 1922), a *Tass* correspondent in London, and Joe Slovo (b. 1926), who was based in Lusaka.

White Commando
(Wit Kommando)

The White Commando, before it was broken by police activity in 1981, was an example of the white racialist violence a reformist government might expect in the Republic. Although it consisted of but a handful of militant individuals who took the law into their own hands, its actions were nonetheless sinister. Members attacked the property of liberal academics and multi-racial establishments, for which they used explosives and weaponry stolen from the South African defence force. It had no formal constitution or membership.

Sudan

Government in Khartoum must be ever mindful of the dual nature of the Sudan, itself a vast hinterland to the dominant northern power of Egypt. In 1972 a conflict which had lasted 17 years came to an end with an agreement between Arab northerners and African southerners to opt for regional autonomy backed by economic development on socialist lines. The rebels, known as Anya Nya, recalled a long history of exploitation and slavery imposed by northerners, who outnumbered them by three to one.

Since that agreement peace has been maintained and the refugees who fled the fighting have returned. Estimates of those who died from starvation and disease brought on by the disruptions caused by persistent irregular warfare hover around half a million.

Bibliography

The best book on the southern conflict was written by the Principal of Khartoum University, Mohammed Omer Beshir, *The Southern Sudan — Background to Conflict* (London and New York, 1968), which should be read with Oliver Albino's *The Sudan: A Southern Viewpoint* (Oxford, 1969). A reliable account of the whole conflict can be read in *The Secret War in the Sudan 1955-72* (London, 1977) by Edgar O'Ballance. Cecile Eprile provided an excellent informed summary in *Sudan: The Long War* (ISC, London, 1972) and at greater length *War and Peace in the Sudan: 1955-1972* (Newton Abbot, UK, 1974). Background notes can be found in a Minority Rights Group publication by Godfrey Morrison, *The Southern Sudan and Eritrea* (London, 1974).

Anya Nya

Some 500 soldiers from the former Equatoria province corps provided the nucleus for the southern Sudanese rebel guerrilla force known as *Anya Nya* (A snake poison). At first they lacked firearms and scavenged for food like bandits until a semblance of military discipline was imposed in 1963 by Emilio Tafeng, a former lieutenant. It was he who adopted the name.

Thenceforth *Anya Nya* established training camps for blacks across the southern borders in Zaïre and Uganda and waged an intermittent war of sabotage and ambush against government forces. The first police posts were attacked in September 1963; by the end of the following year *Anya Nya* ranks numbered some 2000 men. Government forces pursued them across the borders to the guerrilla havens.

Southern politicians who sought refuge abroad claimed from time to time to control *Anya Nya* activities, but, although contacts were made, the guerrillas never became the armed branch of the Azania Liberation Front (ALF), which was set up in 1965, nor indeed of the longer established Sudan African National Union (SANU). The politician who came closest to *Anya Nya* in the 1960s was Aggrey Jaden, who in August 1967 set up the Southern Sudan Provisional Government to establish an administration in areas under *Anya Nya* influence. From that point on the movement became the *Anya Nya* National Armed Forces (ANAF), which in 1968 may have fielded 10,000 recruits, a quarter of whom were armed.

Tafeng lacked real control over the movement, which had no firm political doctrine. Nonetheless in 1969 he set up a revolutionary government, which Jaden joined. It was predominantly a tribal movement and was contested by half a dozen rival organisations, particularly a Zande separatist movement on the Sue river, led by Michael Tawili.

That year the guerrillas had for the first time to counter government attacks from the air on their hideouts. The flow of refugees increased but the insurgency was not eliminated, nor did the razing of villages by government troops endear the local population to northern rule. On the contrary, throughout 1970 and 1971 the government suffered greater casualties as *Anya Nya* attacked in greater numbers. The first such encounter occurred on 5 January 1971 at Pachola, where the rebels killed some 150 men.

It was thought that the rebels were receiving aid from Israel, in fact their success owed more to the character of Joseph Lagu, who captured the leadership from Tafeng, succeeded in unifying the *Anya Nya* rebels and in establishing an alternative civilian administration in areas under rebel control. In August 1971 he became military and political head of a new Southern Sudan Liberation Movement with headquarters in the Immatong Mountains.

As the fighting intensified, President Numeiry ordered a ceasefire in March 1972, when *Anya Nya* dropped its opposition in return for southern autonomy. Their numbers (12,000) were absorbed into the police and the armed forces; Lagu was appointed officer commanding in the south in 1974.

Azania Liberation Front (ALF)

A group of southern Sudanese politicians set up the ALF in 1965, when they splintered from the black Sudan African National Union (SANU). Those involved included Joseph Oduhu, Saturnino Lohure, George Kwani, Pancrasio Ocheng, Marko Rume, all of whom clashed with the personality of SANU leader, William Deng. From his exile in Uganda, Oduhu led the ALF and approached Kenya unsuccessfully for political support in July 1965.

Sudan African Liberation Front (SALF)

Aggrey Jaden set up SALF as a splinter group from the Sudan African National Union in 1965. Jaden subsequently became vice-president of the Azania Liberation Front (ALF), only to be expelled after which he set up the Southern Sudan Provincial Government, which had links with *Anya Nya*.

Sudan African National Union (SANU)

William Deng, a former Assistant District Commissioner, promoted this southern Sudanese political movement in the early 1960s, when he sought a peaceful means to establish a separate non-Muslim southern Sudan. He did so from abroad, having first worked with Joseph Oduhu, Marko Rume and Aggrey Jaden in the Sudan African V Closed Districts National Union (SACDNU) in Kinshasa (Zaïre), which in 1963 became SANU. Its new headquarters were in Kampala (Uganda). In 1965 SANU rejected federal autonomy offered by Khartoum, but Deng favoured negotiation and remained in the Sudan as head of the internal SANU.

The exiles promptly splintered, leaving Deng as sole leader of SANU, which contested elections in March 1967, when it won ten seats in Bahr el-Ghazal province. The following year Deng was assassinated.

Sudan Communist Party (SCP)

The party was set up in 1946, but only at its third congress in 1956 did it adopt the name SCP. It remains an orthodox Moscow-line Marxist-Leninist vanguard party existing in clandestinity. In the early 1980s membership was thought to be several thousand, less than half that of the early 1970s, when the party apparatus was uprooted after an attempted coup in 1971. For three days in July the communist-backed insurgents appeared to have wrested power from President Numeiry, at which point Moscow welcomed the coup. Many members, including its leader Abd al-Khaliq Mahjub, were executed for their involvement; others went into exile, whence they led the opposition to Numeiry. The party's secretary general is Muhammad Ibrahim Nuqud.

Sudanese Socialist Popular Front (SSPF)

Based in Tripoli, the front had the backing of Colonel Gadaffi, whose intent in 1982 was to overturn President Numeiry. Front members believed that true revolutionary change stemmed from popular mass bases provided by the Sudanese trade unions, which should be reformed to reflect this direct democracy, and the economy generally should be run by people's committees.

Uganda

The political violence rife in Uganda in the early 1980s owed its origins to the struggle for power between President Milton Obote (b.1924) and the followers of former leaders, Lule and Binaisa. Dr Obote had founded the socialist Ugandan People's Congress in 1960 and in 1962 became prime minister. In 1966, as President, he assumed full powers, which he exercised until Idi Amin led a military coup which deposed him in 1971.

Thereafter Uganda became increasingly renowned for a barbarism singular even in Africa. Amin's foreign policy, if it could be so dignified, led him into conflict with Tanzania, whose armed forces moved against him in 1979. The dictator had found support in Libya, and Libyan troops sustained him in his final military retreat from the capital, Kampala. After a brief sojourn in Libya, Amin settled in Saudi Arabia.

Uganda returned to civilian rule under the controlling influences of Tanzanian troops, which remained in Uganda and were instrumental in ousting Dr Yusuf Lule (b. 1913) in June 1979. It became clear that socialism as a political system would only be implanted with military assistance, accordingly Lule's successor Godfrey Binaisa (b. 1920) succumbed to the military in May 1980 when, following elections, Obote was again installed as president. Indiscipline from the armed forces caused great suffering to the population in 1981/82, and guerrilla activities by marauding gangs of dissident soldiery threatened the government even on the outskirts of the capital.

Uganda Freedom Movement (UFM)

The UFM emerged in February 1981, when it launched a series of well planned, well armed and well executed attacks upon a number of police posts in and around Kampala. In March that year it threatened to stop the passage of all goods on roads into the capital; only on occasions did it carry out this threat. The movement was led by a former minister of internal affairs, Andrew Kayiira, and was one of three anti-Obote groups to come together in January 1982 in a joint Uganda Popular Front.

Uganda National Liberation Front (UNLF)

In March 1979 at Moshi in Tanzania 18 Ugandan exile groups set up the UNLF under the chairmanship of Dr Yusuf Lule (b. 1913), former vice-chancellor of Makerere University. The UNLF was very largely a creature of Tanzanian political intentions, although its overt purpose was 'to restore the democratic way of life for all Ugandans and as soon as conditions permit, arrange for free elections.' In fact it developed into a vehicle which pressed for the return of ex-President Obote, backed by Tanzania.

The UNLF was never in a position to carry out independent aims, since the Ugandan dictator, Idi Amin, was toppled in April 1979 by the Tanzanian armed forces, who remained in Uganda until 1981. Dr Lule became head of a provisional government, but there developed within the UNLF a power struggle between his supporters and those in Dr Obote, a socialist. Lule was ousted in June 1979 in favour of left-of-centre Godfrey Binaisa (b. 1920), a former attorney general, who transformed the UNLF into Uganda's sole political movement 'committed to unity, democracy, defence of freedom and the social advancement of Ugandans'.

As the UNLF turned itself into a single party under the influence of ex-President Obote in the course of 1980, exiled Ugandans in Zambia and Kenya accused the movement of 'dictatorship'. Army officers favouring Obote ousted Binaisa in May, when their candidate returned from exile, and ruled through a Military Commission of the UNLF.

Uganda National Rescue Front (UNRF)

Brigadier Moses Ali, one-time finance minister under Idi Amin, announced in the autumn of 1980 that he was chairman of the UNRF. He was joined by a former Obote minister, Felix Onama, and together they disposed of a force of several thousand men in the West Nile district. In January 1982 the UNRF joined the umbrella movement set up in London by former leaders, Lule and Binaisa, the Uganda Popular Front.

Uganda National Resistance Movement (UNRM)

The UNRM was one of three principal anti-Obote movements in the early 1980s that staged guerrilla attacks inside the country. It was led from his London exile by Dr Yusuf Lule, former provisional head of government. Lule helped set up the joint Uganda Popular Front in January 1982.

Uganda Popular Front (UPF)

The UPF was set up in January 1982 by former leaders, Lule and Binaisa, in London. It grouped the three principal anti-Obote movements in Uganda, the National Resistance Movement, the Freedom Movement and the National Rescue Front, all of which determined to overthrow President Obote by force and to hold democratic elections.

Ugandan People's Movement (UPM), Sometimes quoted as Ugandan Patriotic Movement

The UPM was led by Yoweri Museveni, who carried out guerrilla attacks against the government of President Obote in the early 1980s. His followers, known as a People's Revolutionary Army were encamped around the capital, Kampala, and numbered a thousand or more. Museveni learnt his guerrilla warfare tactics with the Frelimo fighters in Mozambique and had then engaged in sabotage attacks against the regime of Idi Amin. The aim of the UPM, which joined the Uganda Popular Front in 1982, was to topple Obote and hold free and fair elections 'under neutral supervision agreed on by all'. Early in 1981 he had set up a political front, known as the Movement for the Struggle of Political Rights (MOSPOR).

Western Sahara/ Morocco

The disputed territory of the Western Sahara was a Spanish colony until 1975, when Spain hurriedly withdrew, handing its rights to Morocco and Mauritania, whose frontiers adjoined the colony. The arrangement did not suit Algeria, to whose safety a number of tribesmen had fled. Based at Tindouf alongside drought refugees from all over the Sahara, an incipient liberation movement, Polisario, was given succour and built up into a credible guerrilla force. Behind the growth lay firstly an Algerian interest in an outlet to the Atlantic for its vast hinterland, and later an old Libyan ambition to create a greater Saharan political entity in the Maghreb.

While Moroccan King Hassan could galvanise national sentiment with such an expansionist enterprise, Mauritania to the south was too weak in 1977 to withstand Polisario guerrilla attacks against its mining interests and against its very capital. The conflict contributed to violent changes of power in Nouakchott, and finally caused the country in August 1979 to renounce its hold on its portion of the Western Sahara, whereupon King Hassan declared the whole territory Moroccan and occupied Dakhla.

For two years the conflict between Moroccan armed forces and Polisario continued, with the guerrillas making important strikes into southern Morocco, where considerable losses were inflicted. Then in mid-1981 at a meeting of the OAU a lull was imposed upon the conflict by talk of a referendum imposed over the heads of Polisario leaders, by Morocco and Libya. Nothing emerged from this political initiative, so that fighting continued throughout 1982 with the Moroccans intent upon preserving control of the El Aaiun, Smara, Bojador triangle that contains the Bou Craa phosphates deposits.

Bibliography

The first general introduction to the disputed Saharan territory was John Mercer's *Spanish Sahara* (London, 1976), but the actual conflict is best approached through two studies by David Lynn Price, 'Morocco and the Saharan Conflict and Development' and 'Conflict in the Maghreb: The Western Sahara' (ISC, London, 1977 and 1981). See also Price's *The Western Sahara* (Sage, 1979). Robert Rezette's *The Western Sahara and the Frontiers of Morocco* (Nouvelles Editions Latines, Paris, 1975) is available in French and English; the rather longer *La Dossier du Sahara Occidental* by Attilio Gaudio and published by the same house in 1978 contains useful documentation supportive of the Moroccan cause. From the

Polisario standpoint, see Ahmed-Baba Miské, *Front Polisario: l'Ame d'un Peuple* (Paris, 1978). Virginia Thompson and Richard Adloff wrote a thorough background account including the war in *The Western Saharans* (London, 1980). Polisario put out considerable propaganda for the press via Algeria, where it is based. But the communiqués are even less trustworthy than the Moroccan versions. The Polisario case is put sympathetically by John Gretton in a 1976 Anti-Slavery Society Report published in Birmingham, UK, entitled 'Western Sahara: The Fight for Self-Determination'. See also his article in *The World Today*, September 1980. The most exhaustive study of the region was made by Tony Hodges, *Historical Dictionary of Western Sahara* (Scarecrow Press, New Jersey, 1982) with an excellent bibliography. For diplomatic documentation of the dispute, see Ursel Clausen, *Der Konflikt um die Westsahara* (Hamburg, 1978).

Association of People from Sahara (AOSARIO)

A Moroccan-backed organisation in the Western Sahara, the Association was set up to counteract Algerian-backed Polisario military operations in the former Spanish Sahara. It was active in 1980, but failed in succeeding years to make any local impact militarily or any international impact diplomatically.

People's Front for the Liberation of Saguiat al Hamra and Rio de Oro (Polisario)

In the early 1980s Polisario was fighting a guerrilla war in the Western Sahara against Moroccan armed forces. It disputed Morocco's control of the territory formerly known as Spanish Sahara, territory which General Franco on his Madrid death bed in 1975 had agreed to divide between Morocco and Mauritania, the neighbouring countries.

The first mention of a Saharan Liberation Front was made in 1967 by an organisation based in Morocco, but Polisario was not founded until May 1973 in Nouakchott (Mauritania). That month Polisario claimed actions against the Spanish colonial authorities, but until the Spaniards actually withdrew from the territory the movement had no following. When the Spanish settlement with Mauritania and Morocco was made public, Algeria proceeded to arm, train and give succour in Tindouf to large numbers of Saharans, some of whom had come from the former Spanish territory.

Within months the Algerian military had organised infiltration of the territory in columns, but these forces lost a pitched battle with the Moroccans at Angala in January 1976. Thereafter, the Polisario flying columns turned their attention upon the weaker inheritor, Mauritania, whose capital was attacked by 500 guerrillas in 100 vehicles in June 1976.

In 1977 Polisario attacked the Zouerate mining complex, upon which the Mauritanian economy depended, and kidnapped six French technicians working there, a move the organisation was to regret for it brought French support to Mauritania in the form of air strikes aimed at the motorised columns of guerrillas. But before they intervened Polisario shelled the Presidential Palace in Nouakchott. Further attacks on the Zouerate-Nouadibou railway, which brought iron ore to the coast for export, showed how easily guerrilla forces could disrupt the whole economy of a poor third world state (per capita $240). The toll on the armed forces was heavy too, for in 1977 some 500 Mauritanians were killed as a result of Polisario activity.

Similar attacks occurred in 1978 until a bloodless military coup overthrew the President in July, and Polisario announced a ceasefire in that area, hoping to persuade Mauritania to renounce its claim to its portion of the Western Sahara. Whether or not Mauritania was inclined to give it up, Morocco, the stronger and more determined partner in the struggle, refused to accept such an outcome. As Mauritania renounced its portion of the territory in August 1979, Morocco moved in and occupied the towns. That year heavy clashes occurred with Moroccan troops, not only in the Western Sahara, but in southern Morocco as well. Losses ran into hundreds on both sides.

The nucleus of the Polisario guerrilla force is made up of about 1000 Spanish trained nomadic troops, who fled the territory when Morocco took over. They found shelter in Algeria at Tindouf, where refugees from all over the Sahara had gathered to avoid the worst ravages of the drought which had destroyed their flocks and their livelihood. Of the territory's 74,000 inhabitants (1974 Spanish census) possibly 5000 fled to Tindouf; some returned. Those that stayed mingled with an many as 100,000 men, women and children.

Training in Tindouf was undertaken by the Algerians and given to a force which in 1980 was estimated to number some 10,000, although fewer than half of these were committed to the struggle inside the territory. They controlled no towns, but were able to mount attacks from time to time from a distance. Their most significant impact has been on the phosphate mining operations at Bou Craa, which for the past few years, if at all, has been operating at minimal capacity. The conveyor belt which transports the phosphates to the coast was kept out of action by the guerrillas, who compelled the authorities to send it in convoys by road. The trucks were escorted by military vehicles and helicopters, to protect them from Polisario attack.

In February 1976 Polisario announced the creation of a Saharan Arab Democratic Republic (SADR), which North Korea immediately recognised. Leninist states in Africa, such as Angola and Mozambique, followed the lead, as did others which inclined towards an independent socialism, such as Algeria, Benin, Madagascar, Guinea Bissau and Congo. By 1979 it was clear that wider support was coming from the Organisation of African Unity, and indeed more widely still, for world opinion was favourably impressed by democratic Spain's rejection of the 1975 Saharan agreement. With Cuba's recognition in January 1980, the SADR could count upon the backing of 36 countries, and two years later it was admitted to membership of the OAU.

The issue is unlikely to be resolved by force of arms, for although Morocco and Algeria have come perilously close to open and conventional war with one another, both countries have held back from the final step of embarking upon a war which neither wants. King Hassan has sunk too much of his reputation in the acquisition of the Spanish Sahara to withdraw, and his determination has been backed by Moroccan political opinion of all shades. In Algeria, the death of President Boumedienne in December 1978 did not weaken Algerian support for Polisario, nor its use of that movement to acquire an Atlantic outlet for the future mineral production of the Tindouf area. Polisario, armed with Soviet manufactured AK-47s, anti-tank rockets and mortars, continued throughout the early 1980s to attack Moroccan outposts.

The movement exhibited a remarkably stable leadership, since the setting up in 1976 of the Saharan Arab Democratic Republic and the adoption of a constitution in February that year. The Revolutionary Command Council was still headed in 1982 by the movement's Secretary-General, Mohamed Abdelaziz, who relied upon Ibrahim Hakim to deal with foreign affairs and Ibrahim Ghamli for defence matters. The Prime Minister of the exiled administration was Mohamed Lamine Ould Ahmed until his replacement in November 1982 by Malifoud Ali Beiba, formerly responsible for internal matters. The constitution favoured Maghreb unity as a step towards pan-Arab unity and made Islam the state religion and socialism the ultimate goal. There was no commitment to Marxism-Leninism.

Zaïre

In the early 1980s the improbable personalised style of government set by President Mobuto (b. 1930) was not in any overt manner threatened by political violence. Yet the huge territory gave every appearance of being the weakest and most vulnerable of African states.

Zaïre's independence from Belgium in 1960 was accompanied by bloodshed, a conflict in which several thousand people died. The principal problem lay in the attempted secession of the province of Katanga, a movement led by Moïses Tshombe (d. 1969), who accused his rival, Patrice Lumumba (d. 1961), of wishing to sell out to the Soviet Union. It was indeed the first time the USSR had displayed an active disposition to influence events in the continent.

Lumumba appealed for assistance to the United Nations, which made haste to fly in a combined force of African and Swedish troops. That very year Lumumba succumbed to a military coup, led by the Congolese Army Chief of Staff, Mobuto. Tshombe survived somewhat longer.

In Katanga (now Shaba province), Tshombe could rely upon the backing of the Belgian capitalists who exploited the mineral deposits of copper and cobalt. To preserve their interests and his own, he was protected by mercenaries flown in to support the secession, and by a new gendarmerie numbering some 10,000 men. The remnants of this force fought for the Portuguese in Angola until 1974, when they joined the MPLA and then formed the basis for the Shaba incursions of 1976 and 1977, which were supposedly controlled politically by the Congo National Liberation Front (FLNC).

Since 1965, when Mobuto seized absolute power, Zaïre has been ruled weakly; it is the absence of any effective opposition rather than the presence of governmental talent that has ensured continuity of rule in a territory so vast that it contains more than 200 ethnic groups.

Bibliography

Quite the best introduction to Zaïre is Crawford Young's *Politics in the Congo* (Princeton, 1965), but the raw facts of the Congo rebellion can be found in *Revolt in the Congo* (New York, 1965), a Facts on File publication. Patrice Lumumba told his story in *Congo My Country* (London, 1969) and Conor Cruise O'Brian, who was involved with the UN intervention, related his version in *To Katanga and Back* (London, 1962). Kwame Nkrumah published his views as an influential onlooker in *Challenge of the Congo* (London, 1967); Thomas Kanza was closer to the scene and wrote first *Conflict in the Congo* (Penguin, 1972) and then *The Rise and Fall of Patrice Lumumba* (London, 1978). Lumumba's most important speeches were published posthumously in *Lumumba Speaks* (London, 1972).

For the later Angolan incursions into Katanga, Jean François Chauvel, the correspondent of *Le Figaro*, wrote *Kolwezi* (Paris, 1978), whilst Crawford Young wrote an excellent article in *Foreign Affairs* the same year.

Council for the Liberation of Congo-Kinshasa
(Conseil pour la Libération du Congo-Kinshasa — CLC)

In May 1980 Mungul Diaka, who had served President Mobuto as minister for many years, accepted the chairmanship of a new umbrella movement of Zaïrian exiles in Brussels. Diaka worked closely with Mobuto's former foreign minister, Nguza Karl-i-Bond. The groups which the CLC gathered within its fold included the People's Revolutionary Party, the Congolese Socialist Party, the Progressive Congolese Students and the National Movement for Union and Reconciliation in Zaïre (MNUR). None of these had any following inside Zaïre.

Congo National Liberation Front
(Front de Libération Nationale du Congo — FLNC)

Former gendarmes from Katanga set up the FNLC in Paris in 1963. Exiles gathered around Mutombo Cartier, who ran the office, but the front was one of many factions in France and Belgium, none of which had much impact on the security of Zaïre until in 1977 the FNLC claimed responsibility for invading Zaïre from Angola.

The force, estimated at some 2000 men, consisted of a core of Katangese gendarmes, who had fled from Zaïre as Mobuto assumed control of Moïses Tshombe's secessionist province in 1965. The gendarmes (5000) had then fought for the Portuguese colonial authorities in Angola, and after independence had been employed in the 1975/76 Angolan civil war by the *Movimento Popular para a Libertação de Angola* (MPLA), which subsequently formed the new government in Luanda.

The FNLC became the vehicle by which Angolan President Neto controlled President Mobuto's support for the dissident *Frente Nacional de Libertação de Angola* (FNLA), based in Kinshasa (Zaïre). Troubled by FNLA activity across his border, Neto launched the Katangese exiles into Shaba (Katanga) province in March 1977. The invasion touched the nerve centre of Mobuto's rule, for the government depended upon the earnings of the copper mines in the province. The invaders were led by Nathaniel Mbumba, one-time commander of the Katangese gendarmes, whose purpose was not merely to reawaken separatist sympathy, but 'to create a government of national unity'.

The rebels, employing long-range missiles and 122 mm rockets, met with little resistance. Within days they had occupied Dilolo, Kapanga, Kisengi and Sandoa, but they never took Kolwezi. The operation provoked international support for Mobuto, causing FNLC troops to retreat in May 1977.

However, the following year the FNLC again invaded. The first attack had not damaged the mining installations. The second was more professional and appeared to have had Cuban back-up.Mbumba infiltrated Shaba from Zambia, having prepared for a rising beforehand. Dressed as civilians, his men assembled near Kolwezi and using previously cached weapons seized the mining town, its airport and the railroad town of Mutshatsha. Europeans were held hostage. Once again, international help forced the FNLC to withdraw in May 1978.

No subsequent guerrilla action occurred in 1979 or 1980, because Zaïre signed an agreement with Angola, whereby both countries undertook not to promote disaffection on their common border. Yet in July 1980 the FNLC was reported to have joined with four other exiled groups, none of which had engaged in guerrilla activities, the Council for Liberation of the Congo, led by Mungul Diaka, a former education minister.

National Movement for Union and Reconciliation in Zaïre
(Mouvement National pour l'Union et la Réconciliation — MNUR)

Mbeka Makosso, a former minister who in 1978 resigned as Ambassador to Iran, set up the MNUR that year. It was based in Brussels and was not thought to have any influence within Zaïre. In 1980 it joined the opposition Council for the Liberation of Congo-Kinshasa (CLC).

Zimbabwe

Amazingly, the integration of two rival guerrilla forces and then the scaling down of this unwieldy body to the proportions of a more professional army were accomplished in newly independent Zimbabwe without great conflict. By 1982 the antagonisms which for 20 years had riven the black nationalist movement had subsided temporarily, with Robert Mugabe (b. 1925) clearly the victor. His rival, Joshua Nkomo (b. 1917), still retained firm tribal loyalty in Matabeleland to the south-west, but for the time being accepted Mugabe's triumph.

It had been Nkomo who first lit the contemporary flame of rebellion in 1961 with the foundation of the Zimbabwe African People's Union (ZAPU). Two years later Ndabaningi Sithole (b. 1920) broke with the older movement to found a more militant Zimbabwe African National Union (ZANU), dedicated to armed warfare. He was to lose control of ZANU, which had always been faction ridden, to Mugabe in 1975.

Attempts on all sides were made to draw the two movements together, and for the purpose of independence negotiations in 1976 they acted under the joint titles of the Patriotic Front (PF). Nkomo was to retain this label for ZAPU when he contested the February 1980 elections, which gave his rival so resounding a victory. A further contestant was Bishop Abel Muzorewa (b. 1925), a high-minded nationalist who proved a disastrous politician. He led the African National Council (ANC), which had been set up in 1971 to resist the limited constitutional settlement, which was then being proposed. Although in origin a non-violent body of opinion rather than a party, it developed a political life for a short period when, following the internal elections of April 1979, the Bishop joined Ian Smith's government. It played no part in the post-independence politics of Zimbabwe.

Bibliography

Robert Blake, Provost of Queen's College, Oxford, wrote the fine *History of Rhodesia* (London, 1977). The UDI period was well analysed by James Barber in *Rhodesia: The Road to Rebellion* (London, 1967). A former editor of the *Yorkshire Post*, Kenneth Young, wrote *Rhodesia and Independence* (London, 1969), which takes the story into the late 1960s. Lawrence Vambe describes the African background in *From Rhodesia to Zimbabwe* (London, 1976). It is worth reading too his earlier book, *An Ill-Fated People* (London, 1972). In the same vein, see *Rhodesia: Struggle for a Birthright* (London, 1972) by E. Mlambo. The measure of some of the protagonists can be gathered from their writing: see especially *African Nationalism* (OUP, 1968) and *Roots of a Revolution* (OUP, 1977) by Ndabaningi Sithole and *Rise up and Walk* (London, 1978) by Abel Muzorewa. For a popular biography of Mugabe, see that of David Smith and Colin Simpson (London, 1981), who interviewed many who know him. Martin Meredith, who worked for *The Observer* and *The Sunday Times*, wrote a detailed yet readable account in *The Past is Another Country: Rhodesia UDI to Zimbabwe* (London, 1980). Anthony Wilkinson analysed the early insurgency in an Adelphi Paper (IISS, London, 1973) *Insurgency and Counter-Insurgency in Rhodesia 1957-73* and contributed to Basil Davidson, Joe Slovo and A.R. Wilkinson *Southern Africa: The New Politics of Revolution* (London, 1976).

African National Council (ANC)

The ANC, led by Bishop Abel Muzorewa (b. 1925) joined Ian Smith's government in Rhodesia (Zimbabwe) after winning internal elections in April 1979. But as international recognition did not follow and the war in the bush did not stop, further talks were held in London leading to new elections in which the Patriotic Front (PF) participated and decimated the Bishop's organisation. The ANC was reduced to a parliamentary rump in Salisbury, referred to inappropriately as the United ANC (UANC).

The ANC had been founded in December 1971 as a temporary body to lead the African opposition to the constitutional settlement terms then being proposed. Although a non-violent body, the Bishop united under his banner prominent members of the banned nationalist parties — the Zimbabwe African People's Union (ZAPU) and the Zimbabwe African National Union (ZANU).

Once the original aim had been achieved, and the Bishop's standing in the countryside established, the ANC declared itself a permanent body pledged to the goal of universal adult suffrage in Rhodesia. It set up a national structure with a central committee and acted as an outlet for black opinion in the absence of the nationalist parties which had been banned in 1964. In 1974 it held its inaugural conference, by which time it had become a vehicle for the Bishop and for Dr Edson Sithole. The ANC contested several constituencies in the elections of 1974, winning seven out of eight possible seats, which they then resigned in protest.

During the course of the war the ANC did not participate in the fighting and had no guerrilla force of its own. For a brief period it became again an umbrella movement under which the militant nationalists agreed to unite, but in September 1975 disunity again came to the fore splitting the movement along the old ZAPU/ZANU lines. The Bishop retained his prestige as a leader, however, almost above party politics, and the movement became known as the United African National Council, although in fact it only represented Muzorewa's supporters.

After the Bishop had agreed to participate in an internal settlement in

1979, he lost influence and depended increasingly upon a private army of supporters who were drilled and sent out into the rural areas to drum up support for his cause. There was in this militia a strong element of self-defence, since law and order could not be guaranteed on account of the escalating rural war.

Patriotic Front (PF)

The two Rhodesian liberation movements, the Zimbabwe African People's Union (ZAPU) and the Zimbabwe African National Union (ZANU) agreed in 1976 to attend talks with the Rhodesian government in Geneva, sponsored by Britain and the United States. They attended as the Patriotic Front.

From the mid-1960s the liberation struggle in Rhodesia had been plagued by the fundamental division in the nationalist forces, a division which Zambia and Tanzania had worked strenuously to overcome. They were joined in this endeavour in the 1970s by Botswana and later, as they became independent (1975), by Angola and Mozambique. They never succeeded.

But from 1976 the two movements acted together on the diplomatic front as the Patriotic Front, although retaining their separate identities and military forces. For a brief moment in 1979 it seemed as if military cooperation might emerge from an agreement signed in May to set up a joint command in Ethiopia. But before this could take form, the nationalists were negotiating in London at Lancaster House, where they agreed to participate in the elections of February 1980, which heralded the independence of Zimbabwe.

Once a ceasefire had been agreed upon, and actually established in December 1979, the two movements drifted apart to fight the elections as separate parties. Nkomo, the ZAPU leader, retained the label of the Patriotic Front, but it had ceased to include the other wing, ZANU, which went on to win the elections.

Zimbabwe African National Union (ZANU)

ZANU became the ruling party in an independent Zimbabwe, following the elections of February 1980. It began life, however, not under the leadership of Robert Mugabe (b. 1935), who was elected prime minister, but under the Congressional minister, Ndabaningi Sithole (b. 1920). It was he who led the breakaway faction from the Zimbabwe African People's Union in July 1963, alongside Leopold Takawira (d. 1970), Herbert Chitepo (murdered 1975) and Mugabe.

ZANU at first attracted mainly intellectual support, but of a dynamic and militant kind. It opted early for guerrilla warfare against the white state and found sympathy in China, which supplied military training and aid. For the most part, the training took place in Tanzania and after the independence of that country in 1975, in Mozambique.

The Salisbury government outlawed ZANU in August 1964, at the same time that ZAPU was made illegal. Military training followed and the first incursions occurred two years later. At that time the movement was based in Lusaka, so that infiltration of Rhodesia came from Zambia. The tactics failed in the late 1960s; further action only began in December 1972, and continued right up to the Lancaster House settlement of December 1979.

Like most African liberation movements, ZANU was riven by internal factions, often based upon tribal animosity. Although the split with ZAPU was not caused by tribal in-fighting, serious quarrels emerged in 1974 between Manyika and Karanga ZANU supporters. They culminated in the loss of over 400 lives in Zambia and the murder on 18 March 1975 of Chitepo, allegedly by Josiah Tongogara, the ZANU military chief, who himself died in a suspicious car crash in Mozambique in December 1979. The 1975 quarrel led eventually to a split between Mugabe and Sithole, who that year was released for talks with the Salisbury government.

The Chitepo murder in Lusaka provoked President Kaunda to hold at least 50 ZANU nationalists for questioning. Zambian enquiries subsequently found the Tongogara faction responsible for the murder and closed the ZANU offices. Mugabe was compelled to find refuge in Mozambique, where he maintained his headquarters until 1980.

ZANU pursued guerrilla war through the actions of its Zimbabwe African National Liberation Army (ZANLA), which first penetrated Rhodesia in the north-east. Later the guerrillas were able to use Mozambique freely, and were even provided by Frelimo with transport, camping and training facilities close to the border.

Their initial actions were aimed at white farms, but the important agricultural sector of the economy was never seriously disrupted. Of Rhodesia's 6000 farmers, not more than 2000 had abandoned their estates by 1979. Later targets included hotels, which shut down the tourist industry; road traffic, which compelled drivers to travel in convoys; trains, although railways continued to function throughout the conflict; fuel depots, which were replenished by South African supplies, but the dramatic destruction of which did much to raise ZANU guerrilla morale, and finally urban targets in Salisbury and Bulawayo suburbs.

Throughout the war, ZANU intimidated local blacks into providing facilities for the guerrillas. Often where disinterest or hostility was displayed, the guerrillas inflicted the most horrendous torture. They deprived a large percentage of children of education, as mission schools closed following guerrilla attacks. Cattle died from disease as dipping tanks were destroyed and the tsetse fly reappeared.

The numbers of ZANU guerrillas operating inside Rhodesia increased steadily to a total of some 10,000 by 1979; at any time they were always more numerous than ZAPU guerrillas on the ground. Throughout the war the two guerrilla movements functioned independently, from different bases, in different countries but with the same objectives of winning power through armed struggle. ZANU was less disciplined than ZAPU, a fact which caused Frelimo concern and led the Mozambicans to take a hand in controlling dissident elements.

On independence in 1980, Mugabe was thought to be able to rely upon a force of some 20,000 ZANLA cadres, under the command of Dumiso Dabengwa. These had been integrated into a new national army alongside ZIPRA recruits, to whom they were generally hostile, by 1982.

Zimbabwe African People's Union (ZAPU)

ZAPU, led by Joshua Nkomo, (b. 1917), formed one wing of the Patriotic Front (PF) in the Rhodesian liberation struggle (1972-80). In the February 1980 elections the party lost out heavily to Robert Mugabe's Zimbabwe African National Union (ZANU) and so played little part in the reorganisation of life in an independent Zimbabwe. For a time, fears were generally entertained that Nkomo might seek Soviet-bloc backing to mount a come-back in Zimbabwe politics, but nothing of this nature transpired.

In many ways Nkomo was not only the founder of ZAPU in 1961, but the father figure of Zimbabwe nationalism, for in the late 1950s he had built up in his home town of Bulawayo the first nationalist organisation in Rhodesia, the African National Congress. Like the ANC, ZAPU was swiftly banned by the authorities, an act which forced its sympathisers to operate from abroad, firstly in Dar es Salaam and from 1964 in Lusaka. (Zambia).

Besides Nkomo, those prominent in ZAPU in the late 1960s included James Chikerema, who had been detained (1959-63) and who took over the leadership of ZAPU whilst Nkomo was in prison (1964-74), George Nyandoro, Jason Moyo, Edward Ndlovu and George Silundika. These men visited China in 1964, but the following year the relationship was broken off in favour of the Soviet Union, which provided guerrilla training for ZAPU militants as well as arms and ammunition.

Thus equipped for an armed struggle, ZAPU launched against Rhodesia in 1967 a joint military offensive with members of the South African ANC. These incursions from Zambia failed. In fact, the more militant nationalists had already broken away from ZAPU in August 1963 to form the Zimbabwe African National Union (ZANU) under Ndabaningi Sithole (b. 1921) and Robert Mugabe.

At the time of the split fierce factional fighting between the two movements broke out in most towns. ZAPU survived, only to be torn apart by tribal animosities in 1969-70, when Zambian President Kaunda was compelled to intervene. Although Nkomo had carefully balanced his ten-man central committee between Shona from Mashonaland (Salisbury) and Ndebele from Matabeleland (Bulawayo), jealousy arose between Chikerema (Shona) and Moyo (Ndebele), who led their respective factions until Chikerema left ZAPU in October 1971 to form a new organisation, the Front for the Liberation of Zimbabwe (Frolizi).

After the first wave of ZAPU incursions across the Zambezi, a lull occurred whilst new cadres were trained in Zambia and Tanzania. In December 1972 ZANU elements began renewed penetration, to which ZAPU only contributed in 1976. The reason was that Nkomo was negotiating with the Smith government in an attempt to come to power over the head of ZANU. The talks failed and led directly to the reentry into the guerrilla war of ZAPU guerrillas infiltrating Rhodesia from the southwest, through Botswana.

Over the next three years ZAPU activity increased in Matabeleland; the guerrillas were said to be better trained than ZANU cadres operating from Mozambique in the west. In the final year of the conflict ZAPU men were fighting for territory in the south in areas of ZANU influence, where guerrilla met guerrilla in combat.

Recruits into the ZAPU force were drawn principally from Ndebele-speaking peoples in the west and were personally loyal to Nkomo. They began penetrating from Botswana, and within a year had some 300 guerrillas operating in the region. By 1978 this figure had risen to around 1250, and in the last year of the conflict it probably stood at around 3000 men.

ZAPU organised its guerrillas as an army, known as the Zimbabwe People's Revolutionary Army (ZIPRA), members of which in the early days were trained in the Soviet Union. They attended special schools at Simferopol and Odessa, where military engineering and radio operations were taught as part of a guerrilla course. The course also included instruction in weapons training, the manufacture and use of explosives, grenades and bombs, and sabotage and demolition. Guerrilla tactics included ambushes against vehicles and personnel, camouflage, spoor covering and map reading.

Intelligence training was undertaken in Moscow. Here guerrillas learned how American, French and British intelligence organisations are run. Instructors taught them how to deal with codes and cyphers and gave them a basic understanding of counter-intelligence operations.

From 1976 this type of training was made available in Africa, by Cubans working in Angola and Zambia on behalf of the Russians but attached permanently to ZAPU. Some ZAPU cadres even went to Cuba for training. Yet there was never any question of Nkomo's overall authority being challenged by outside influences: he remained very much his own man.

Nkomo never committed the bulk of his trained ZIPRA force to the conflict, holding them in reserve in large camps in Zambia, ready for the outbreak of civil war in Rhodesia once white power had collapsed. In the event they were never called on; some remained in Zambia in 1980, to return, armed, in October. Housed in separate camps outside Salisbury, and still commanded by their leader, Rex Njongo, these Soviet-trained troops (5000) formed a private army loyal to Nkomo, until they were integrated in a new national army in 1981. Some found the transition impossible and from their detention camps returned to the bush as dissident ZAPU guerrillas. It was not clear if Nkomo retained any control over their actions, which reverted to terrorism of the crudest kind and included murder and kidnapping.

MIDDLE EAST

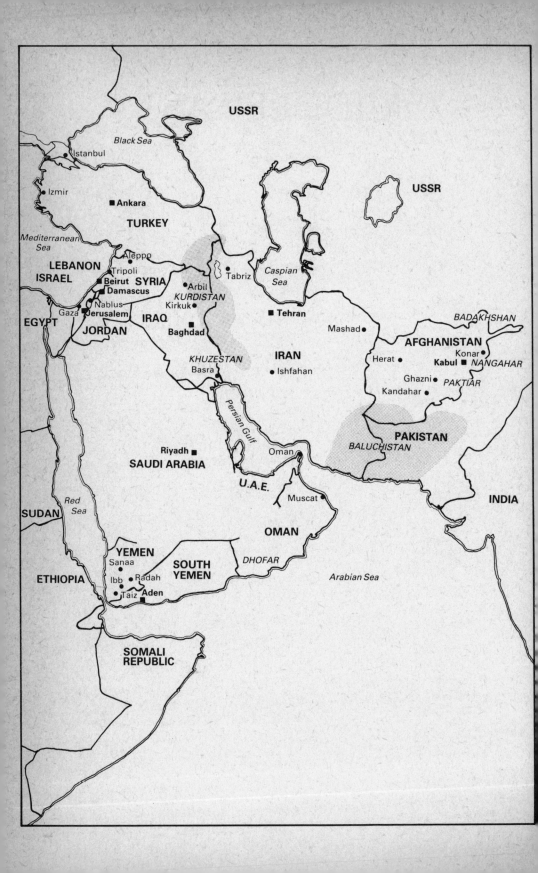

Introduction

Of any region of the world the Middle East has presented the most complex pattern of political violence since the Second World War. It is a crucible of ethnic, religious and big power interests compounded by colonial legacies, oil dependency and the economic problems arising from the petrodollar.

With the exception of Aden no Middle Eastern country was compelled to fight for its independence from France and Britain, the nineteenth and twentieth century colonising powers, although it is true both nations resorted to arms in 1956 in a fruitless gesture to preserve the Suez Canal from nationalisation. In Aden the nationalist revolt of 1963 led to victory four years later for the National Liberation Front. South Yemen subsequently fell under Marxist influence (1970) and turned increasingly towards the Soviet Union, which gave support in Dhofar to rebels who challenged the power of the pro-British Sultan of Oman.

The establishment in 1948 of the state of Israel, itself partly the fruit of a terrorist campaign waged by Zionists against the British mandate to rule in Palestine, interjected an element that could not but cause bitter conflict. Military confrontation saw the Arabs worsted in 1948, in 1956, when Israel invaded Sinai on behalf of Britain and France, and again in the preemptive attacks on Egypt, Jordan, Syria and Iraq in June 1967.

This six-day war deeply wounded Arab pride, leaving Israel in possession of the Golan Heights, taken from Syria, of Jerusalem, and the West Bank, taken from Jordan, and of Sinai, taken from Egypt. It was left to Egypt's President Sadat (1970-81) to exact revenge in 1973, when he organised the Yom Kippur offensive in which Arabs acquitted themselves well, although both sides suffered heavy losses in conventional engagements.

Beneath the level of this warfare, displaced Palestinians organised themselves in 1959 to pursue a terrorist campaign against Israeli interests. From the original *al Fatah* organisation and then the Palestinian Liberation Organisation (PLO — 1964) stemmed the various violent factions set up after the 1967 six-day war. A decade and more of terrorist incidents followed, when the Middle East became the training ground for the revolutionary flotsam and jetsam of the first world.

From Japan to Ireland the odd revolutionary turned up in search of training and arms in pursuit of vague notions of world revolution, which somehow or other the Palestinian guerrillas, in pursuing their own nationalist terrorist campaign, were seen conveniently to embody. Arab states interested in having a hand in the Palestinian outcome — Iraq, Syria, South Yemen and, perforce, the Lebanon — at one time or another provided facilities. As the weapons used and supplied had been manufactured in the Soviet bloc and were purchased by foreign revolutionaries, the development gave rise to the idea of a terror network, a concept attractive to journalists as good copy.

The terrorist sub-world indeed extended across frontiers, and even in some instances across continents, much as crime does. From this no deduction should be drawn that such a network is controlled or even to any great extent influenced by the Soviet bloc. Suspicions will abound, and it is true active participation in destabilisation is fostered, but, essentially, political violence, and within that spectrum acts of terrorism, is by nature a complex of local phenomena, sometimes exploited by outside interests, but often with little success and even with a contrary outcome to that intended.

The Palestinian issue spilled into Lebanese territory and contributed to the civil conflict that shattered the Lebanon's unity in 1975-76, when Christian Phalangists fought with radical Muslim political forces, both indigenous and foreign. Because PLO units were based in southern Lebanon, and in 1977 continued to threaten Israel, from 1978 onwards that country supported a Christian militia that came to control a belt of territory south of the Litani river. For the most part, the rest of the country was dominated by Syria, which since 1976 had had up to 40,000 troops there, deployed originally to control the Palestinians rather than to threaten Israel. In 1978 a United Nations Interim Force for Southern Lebanon (UNIFIL) attempted ineffectually to keep the peace. It failed to prevent the Israeli invasion of June 1982, when the PLO's conventional war capacity was destroyed.

Contemporary hostility between Syria and Iraq had its origins in the rival attractions to Syrians of Egypt and of Iraq, for, in wooing Syrian interests, both countries found supporters. For three years Syria was united with Egypt in the 1958 United Arab Republic, which enjoyed the support of the Baath socialists. That union was overthrown by a Syrian military coup in September 1961. There followed the revolution of 1963, which brought to power the Baath supporters, who enacted sweeping nationalisation and land reform. Reacting to change, conservative elements, backed by the Muslim Brotherhood, opposed modernisation. The Syrian Baath party soon divided into two factions, the one more doctrinaire and Marxist, the other more nationalistic, led by Hafiz al-Assad, who in 1971 became president. Still greater hostility existed towards the rival wing of the Baath party in Baghdad, which in 1963 had come to power through a military coup.

Iraq found its greatest internal problem lay in the Kurdish minority, which, under Mustafa Barzani's leadership, fought more or less continuously for autonomy or independence throughout the 1960s and 1970s. Kurdish dependence on Iranian support brought Iraq into conflict with Iran. It was the 1975 Algiers agreement, which had led Iraq to sign away rights in the Shatt al-Arab waterway in return for the Shah's betraying the Kurds, that partly explained the Iraqi invasion of Iranian Khuzestan in 1980.

Just as modernisation had caused the growth in the Arab world of branches of the Muslim Brotherhood, so the Shah's land reform and industrialisation provoked the rise of militant Shii fundamentalism in Iran, symbolised by the Ayatollah Khomeini. Ineffectively, the Shah had been opposed by a number of leftist groups that had practised terrorism in the 1970s; his downfall was due to religious reaction that in 1979 triumphed with the establishment of an Islamic Republic.

Yet that very republic proved unable to prevent the reemergence of separatist forces in the Iranian provinces peripheral to the Persian heartland. These forces, tribally and ethnically motivated, and acting alongside the armed opposition of *Mujahideen and Fedayeen* guerrillas in the cities, battled in 1980/82 against clerical rule upheld by Revolutionary Guards in Tehran. Ultimate success eluded them in 1982, when thousands were murdered.

Afghanistan, long regarded as the gateway to the Indian subcontinent, resisted colonialism until December 1979, when it fell victim to Soviet invasion. Since that date the country has seethed with insurgency. The rebels, divided ethnically, tribally, geographically and by religion, fight within a plethora of organisations, which continued in the early 1980s to harass occupation forces. Afghan resistance finds support in both Iran and Pakistan, and many of its peoples straddle at least one frontier.

Bibliography

Bernard Lewis provided a classic introduction, *The Middle East and the West* (London, 1964). Fundamental to a deeper understanding of conflict in the region are Walter Laqueur's *Communism and Nationalism in the Middle East* (London, 1956), Hisham Sharabi's *Nationalism and Revolution in the Arab World* (Princeton, 1966) and J.B. Kelly's *Arabia, the Gulf and the West* (London, 1980). Covering each coup methodically is George Haddad's three-volume *Revolutions and Military Rule in the Middle East* (New York, 1971). A more stimulating work is *Cohesive Force* (Oxford, 1975) by Jacob Black-Michaud, who examines feud in the area. Professor P.J. Vatikiotis wrote an authoritative survey in *Conflict in the Middle East* (London, 1971), and edited a distinguished collection of essays in *Revolution in the Middle East* (London, 1972). Britain's experienced ambassador, Lord Trevelyan, published *The Middle East in Revolution* (London, 1970), whilst Sir Richard Allen contributed *Imperialism and Nationalism in the Fertile Crescent* (Oxford, 1974); both men were highly astute observers. For an excellent corrective to the imperial tradition, see Fred Halliday's *Arabia without Sultans* (Penguin, 1974). For the best brief and contemporary discussion of the Palestinian problem, see Avi Plascov's Adelphi Paper, 'A Palestinian State? Examining the Alternatives' (IISS, London, 1981).

Afghanistan

Afghanistan has long been prey to tribal fighting and foreign intrigue stemming from the geo-strategic interest great powers have taken in the country. Tribes and provincial *sarders* (Chieftains) are as quick to resist any form of centralised government as foreign domination.

Monarchy imposed a loose unity until 1973, when King Zahir Shah was overthrown by Prime Minister Daoud. Since then government has been unstable. Between 1973 and 1978 there were at least two attempts to overthrow Daoud. Finally, after he had initiated a purge of communist elements, Daoud was overthrown on 27 April 1978 by a communist coup which installed Nur Mohammed Tarakki as president. Within weeks of the coup the army was encountering stubborn resistance from tribal sources. Two small fundamentalist factions of the Islamic Party, the Islamic Afghan Association, and the Movement for the Islamic Revolution, had already been fighting for the establishment of an Islamic state; their fortunes changed dramatically after April 1978, when resistance to the pro-Soviet regime in Kabul became a general civil war. Numerous guerrilla factions, rooted in ethnic and tribal differences, emerged to fight central government. Two loose fronts — the National Liberation Front and the National Islamic Front for Afghanistan, both largely representing Pukhtoons, were created in an attempt to improve rebel unity.

The leaders of the four fundamentalist parties claimed to be leading a holy war (*Jihad*) against communism and Soviet domination. Yet their real appeal to tribal groupings was not so much their championing of strict Islamic practices as arms deliveries and promises of continued arms supplies.

The great advantage over the fundamentalists of the two Afghan Fronts has been the status of their traditional hereditary leaders. Pir Seghbatullah Mojaddedi and Pir Sayed Ahmed Gailani have devoted followings among the Pukhtoon tribes. The Mojaddedi family, in particular, has long been an important conservative influence in the country, enjoying close links with the royal family, exiled since 1973.

As the war went badly from Kabul's point of view, Tarakki was murdered in September 1979 by Prime Minister Hafizullah Amin, who replaced him. His regime fared no better, and in the face of imminent defeat the USSR invaded Afghanistan in December 1979. Amin was summarily executed and replaced by a loyal Soviet lieutenant, Babrak Karmal. By the end of January 1980 Soviet combat troops in the country numbered an estimated 85,000, a figure that rose steadily in 1981 to over 100,000.

Muslim rebel groups intensified the fight against the Soviet-backed Afghan army, and in January and February 1980 underground organisations instigated anti-Soviet strikes in several towns. Since then Soviet forces have tended to occupy the cities, but have not prosecuted the war too vigorously in the provinces other than in the strategically vital Panjshir valley, which links the country to the Soviet Union.

Muslim rebels, collectively known as *mujahideen* maintained a steady level of attacks on Soviet and government forces, particularly in the mountainous regions to the north and east of Kabul, but also around Kandahar, Herat, Nangarthar and Konar. Total guerrilla fighting strength was estimated at about 100,000, but the guerrilla organisations suffered from chronic feuding, although some rival groups succeeded in coordinating tactics in limited areas.

Bibliography

There are few good up-to-date accounts of conflict in Afghanistan; one of the best is Anthony Hyman's *Afghanistan under Soviet Domination* (London, 1982). Another recent and well-researched work is *The Struggle for Afghanistan* (New York, 1981) by N.P. Newell and R.S. Newell.

Afghan Nation
(Afghan Mellat)

The group was founded in the early 1960s and formerly enjoyed the reputation of being an extreme nationalist party, particularly strong in the army and civil service. It enjoyed wide support among the Pukhtoons before the Marxist-Leninist coup of April 1978, but its activities were severely circumscribed in subsequent months. In the early 1980s Afghan Nation still ran several small guerrilla bands along the Waziristan borders. Its headquarters were based in New Delhi, General Zia having ejected the group from Pakistan.

Afghan National Liberation Front

Imam Seghbatullah Mojaddedi set up the Front in December 1978, when he promised in a political programme to pursue material and social progress but in accordance with the tenets of Islamic socialism. Its manifesto rejected one man and one party dictatorship, supported Islamic social justice, the right to personal property, a neutralist foreign policy, and above all rejected atheism and foreign domination.

Alliance of Islamic Fighters
(Hedadia Mujahideen Islami Afghanistan)

Under the leadership of Wali Beg, the Alliance was formed in May 1979, among the Hazara tribes in central Afghanistan. It disposed of about 5000 guerrillas. The headquarters are in Quetta, Pakistan.

Islamic Afghan Association
(Jamaat-i-Islami Afghanistan)

The association was founded in the early 1970s by a religious scholar, Ustad Burhanuddin Rabbani, a former professor of Muslim law at Kabul University. From 1974 onwards Rabbani travelled widely in the Middle East in search of patrons for an armed struggle to create an Islamic state. Its strength only began to grow markedly after the April 1978 Marxist Leninist coup.

Unlike most resistance movements the *Jamaat-i-Islami* is mainly non-Pukhtoon in membership. Its main strength is in the Tajik (Persian-speaking) Afghan community of distant Badakhshan and the north-east, but it is also active on fronts close to the Peshawar border. It currently maintains two centres in Iran and in Peshawar, Pakistan, where the party of the same name supports it. Rabbani's purpose is to establish a government based on a liberal reading of Islamic law, but accommodating political competition.

Islamic Alliance for the Liberation of Afghanistan (IALA)

An umbrella organisation of doubtful effectiveness, the IALA was formed by the merger of six rebel movements on 27 January 1980 at the Islamic Conference of Foreign Ministers held in Islamabad. The new organisation comprised the Islamic Afghan Association, led by Professor Burhanuddin Rabbani; the National Liberation Front, led by the Imam Seghbatullah Mojaddedi; two factions of the Islamic Party, one led by Gulbuddin Hekmatyar and the other by Maulavi Mohammad Yunus Khales; the National Islamic Front for Afghanistan, led by Sayed Ahmed Gailani; and the Movement for the Islamic Revolution.

Islamic Party
(Hizb-i-Islami)

One of the most important fundamentalist groupings, the party was set up in the early 1970s by Gulbuddin Hekmatyar, a former engineering student at Kabul University who fled to Pakistan after an abortive coup against the Daoud regime. It was in effect an off-shoot of the Muslim Brotherhood in Afghanistan. It rose to prominence after the April 1978 Marxist-Leninist coup.

In 1979 the party split into two factions: one led by Hekmatyar, another by Maulavi Mohammad Yunus Khales. Hekmatyar's group is the larger and receives aid from Iran. Of all resistance groups it enjoyed the most widespread support in the early 1980s. It was totally opposed to Marxism-Leninism, vowing to overthrow the 'atheist, communist and pro-Soviet government in Kabul'. In its place it would set up a funda-mentalist political system with no opposition. It remains sceptical of western values and is opposed to the return of the monarchy. Its sup-porters organised a highly effective general strike in Kabul in February 1980 in protest at the Soviet invasion, but enjoyed a following in town and country.

Yunus Khales's group, although small (7000), is one of the best armed and most effective, possibly due to Libyan backing. It is strongest in the southern provinces of Nanghar and Paktiar, but its military units extend even to the north of Kabul; it has made lightning raids on the capital.

Movement for the Islamic Revolution
(Harakat-i-Inkalab-i-Islami)

The movement is one of the largest Afghan resistance factions, number-ing perhaps 20,000 guerrillas in 1982. Led by Muhammed Nabi Muhammedi, it is essentially fundamentalist in character, with a strong following in the south between Kandahar and Ghazni. As a member of the Islamic Alliance for the Liberation of Afghanistan, it is linked to the still larger National Liberation Front, led by Mojaddedi, and the National Islamic Front for Afghanistan, led by Gailani.

Muslim Brotherhood
(Ikhwan-i-Musalamin)

During the mid-1970s members of the Brotherhood, led by Muhammad Niazi, attacked Daoud's regime, accusing it of being anti-Islamic and atheistic. Niazi was imprisoned and subsequently disappeared, after which members of the Brotherhood went still more deeply underground and adopted violent tactics. Following the Soviet invasion of December 1979, the Brotherhood launched sporadic attacks against the Russians, and claimed credit for instigating tribal resistance. Many members were subsequently arrested and shot; some found safety in exile.

National Islamic Front for Afghanistan
(Makaz-i-Milli)

The front is led by Pir Sayed Ahmed Gailani, a traditional leader, who is supported financially by the Gulf States. It emerged in 1979 in opposition to the newly installed Marxist-Leninist regime and subsequently opposed the Soviet occupation. Gailani had intended to overcome the differences in the numerous Afghan guerrilla factions, but his own front developed factions. In July 1980 Gailani's nephew, Sayed Hassan, formed a splinter group. The family came originally from Baghdad and earned for itself a distinguished reputation in religious scholarship, which afforded its members great influence.

The movement is strongest in the south-east on the Pakistan border. It is fortunate to enjoy strong backing from abroad and to employ for its armaments the workshops of Darra Adam Khel, south-west of Peshawar, which serve the entire area as they have done for generations.

People's Democratic Party of Afghanistan (PDPA)

The PDPA is a Marxist-Leninist party which was founded by Nur Mohammed Tarakki in 1965. It split into the Khalq (people) faction under Tarakki and the Parcham (flag) faction under Agbar Qabir in 1968. Generally, the Parchams were a Persian-speaking urban minority more responsive to rigid Soviet-style communism than the Khalq, which was a more independent grouping based on the Pushtu-speaking rural majority.

The PDPA, working clandestinely, was particularly effective in the armed services during the 1970s. Initially the USSR encouraged a build-up of the Parcham wing, but changed its policy in 1976, when it began to work for a reunification of the two factions. In 1977 this bore fruit as Babrak Karmal's pro-Soviet Parcham began to cooperate more closely with the Khalq faction headed by Hafizullah Amin.

On 27 April 1978 the PDPA, strong in the army and civil service, carried out a successful coup. From the start there was intense personal and ideological hostility between Tarakki and Amin. On 16 September 1979 Tarakki was murdered. The Khalq faction under Amin then assumed power. Unable to contain country-wide rebellion, Amin was dropped by his Soviet backers. On 26 December 1979, two days after the massive Soviet invasion of Afghanistan, Amin was killed. Babrak Karmal, head of the intensely pro-Soviet Parcham faction, returned from Eastern European exile, to assume the puppet leadership.

In the early 1980s the Parcham faction conducted a purge against Khalq supporters. Parcham also attempted to change the social basis of the PDPA by recruiting more workers. Previously the working class had been conspicuously poorly represented. However, even with the coercive powers of the state at its command, the PDPA probably numbered no more than 15,000 members by 1982, and to sustain its position depended upon the Soviet army.

Teiman Atahad-Islami

Teiman Atahad-Islami (Those who have sworn to fight for Islam) was formed in Peshawar (north-west Pakistan) on 11 August 1979 by a merger of four groups: the National Liberation Front, led by Imam Seghbatullah Mojaddedi; the Movement for the Islamic Revolution led by Maulavi Mohammadi; the Islamic Afghan Association led by Professor Burhanuddin Rabbani; and the splinter of the Islamic Party led by Maulavi Mohammad Yunus Khales. Its ultimate aim was the establishment of an Islamic Republic. The group was overtaken by the formation of the Islamic Alliance for the Liberation of Afghanistan (IALA) the following year.

Iran

Since the fall of the Shah in January 1979, Iran has been plagued by fighting and political violence stemming from competing nationalist, ideological and political ambitions. Surrounding the Persian heartlands are ethnic minorities, Kurds in the north-west, Arabs in the south-west (Khuzestan), and Baluchs in the south-east, all of whom to a greater or lesser degree nurse the potential for separatist revolt.

Most troubling to Tehran have proved the Kurds, whose Kurdish Democratic Party of Iran (KDPI) fought to bring down the Shah and then to topple the theocratic rule of the Islamic Republic in the early 1980s. Baluch resistance to Tehran had been encouraged by Iraq, and persisted in a fitful manner in rural areas in 1982. Weakest of the national resistance groups were the Arabs, who failed to rise and to welcome the Iraqis in 1980, when that country attempted to seize the province of Khuzestan (or Arabistan). More effective in their opposition were the Quashai, Naqshbandi, Baban and Jaaf tribes. The Turkic minority was represented by the Party of National Equality.

Under the Shah the communist Tudeh party lost the role of revolutionary vanguard to two guerrilla groups, the *Fedayeen* and the *Mujahideen*, which, numbering several hundred, waged a terrorist campaign in the cities during the 1970s. Yet it was not this violent opposition that caused the Shah's downfall, but the resurgence of Islamic feeling led by the clergy. The Islamic Revolutionary Guards outnumbered the guerrillas and contributed not merely to the establishment and preservation of the Islamic Republic, but to the 1982 military victories over Iraqi troops which two years earlier had occupied parts of Khuzestan.

The defeat of a longstanding and powerful imperial regime in 1979 produced many exiles, whilst the uncompromising character of the Islamic Republic which succeeded it caused still more Iranians to flee. Most of these political exiles organised themselves abroad in bodies such as the Guards of the Monarchical Regime, the Free Iran Movement, the Iranian Liberation Army and the National Resistance Front. Individually none had any great impact upon events inside the country, nor collectively had the National Resistance Council, set up in the fall of 1981, made any impression by 1983.

Bibliography

The best general introduction to Iran is that of Fred Halliday, *Iran: Dictatorship and Development* (Penguin, 1979), in which the violent opposition to the Shah is well analysed. Biographies of two terrorists were published in English, *The Life of Hamid Ashraf* (London, 1977) and *Biography of Said Mohsin* (London, 1976) by the Liberation Movement of Iran Abroad. For guerrilla strategy, see Amir Parviz Pouyan, *On the Necessity of Armed Struggle and a Refutation of the Theory of 'Survival'* (New York, 1975), Massaoud Ahmadzadeh *Armed Struggle: A Strategy and a Tactic* (New York, 1976), Ali Akbar Safayi Farahani, *What a Revolutionary Must Know* (London, 1973) and Bijan Jazani, *Armed Struggle: The Road to the Mobilisation of the Masses* (London, 1976), all of which Halliday discusses. For the Kurdish opposition, see Richard Sim's Conflict Study No. 124 *Kurdistan: The Search for Recognition* (London, 1980), and Gérard Chaliand *People without a Country* (London, 1980), which deals generally with Kurdish affairs. There exists, too, a Minority Rights Group pamphlet by Short and McDermott, *The Kurds* (London, 1977). On Islamic fundamentalism, see the introductory *Militant Islam* (London, 1979) by *The Economist* correspondent, G.H. Jansen. For resistance under the Shah, see Paul Vieille, *Pétrole et Violence; Terreur Blanche et Résistance en Iran sous la Direction de Paul Vieille et Abol Hassan Banisadre* (Paris, 1974). The veteran Egyptian journalist, Mohammed Heikal, recounted the course of the revolution with a first-hand acquaintance of many of the participants in *The Return of the Ayatollah* (London, 1982). J.D. Stempel was an American hostage and wrote *Inside the Iranian Revolution* (Indiana University Press, 1981). Robert Graham reported for *The Financial Times* and wrote *The Illusion of Power* (London, 1978), whilst Michael Fischer analysed developments in *Iran from Religion to Revolution* (1981). V.S. Naipaul conveyed a sure feeling for the country in his novel, *Among the Believers*. Based on interviews with exiles, *In Afghanistan's Shadow* (New York, 1981) by Selig Harrison is excellent on Baluch nationalism.

Baluchistan Liberation Front (BLF)

Working from Dubai, Jumma Khan, a graduate of Karachi university, set up the BLF in 1964. The following year Mir Abdi Khan (b. 1908) of the Sardarzai tribe joined the Front and from the Gulf States mobilised support among Baluch exiles for an armed struggle against the Shah's regime in Iran. Attacks were made on Iranian army units, although these tended to be the work of local nationalists who acted in the Front's name, rather than the result of a planned campaign launched from abroad. Mir Mauladad was behind these armed confrontations.

The Front received financial contributions from local chieftains and radical Arab sources, the more so since it favoured Iraq's claims to the Shatt-al-Arab waterway and backed the Palestinian cause. Indeed,

Jumma Khan became a member of the PLO's central advisory committee. The Front later opened offices in Syria and Egypt.

From 1968 Jumma Khan worked from Baghdad, where for five years Baluch were trained for their armed struggle. Arms were shipped from Gulf coast ports to Rahim Zardkoui, whose strongholds lay in the Ahuran mountains to the south. In making his peace with the Shah in 1973, the influential Mir Abdi Khan severely weakened Baluch resistance. The final blow came two years later, when Baghdad ceased to aid the Baluch in return for Tehran's agreement not to aid Iraqi Kurds. After the Shah's fall Jumma Khan returned to Iraq, whilst Zardkhoui was killed in a clash with Khomeini's revolutionary guards. In the early 1980s a rump continued to espouse independence.

Baluchistan Peoples' Democratic Organisation (BPDO)

The Organisation was founded by Baluch adherents of the *Fedayeen-e-Khalq* and *Peykar* factions to contest the Ayatollah Khomeini's post-Shah regime in Iran. It attacked the new constitution, but did not seek to secede from Iran. One of those who backed the Organisation financially was Khalidad Arya, an elderly Baluch intellectual. In the early 1980s the group claimed some 200 clandestine members and several thousand sympathisers.

Baluch Pesh Merga
(Baluch Volunteer Force)

Organised by Amanullah Barakzai (b. 1924), this guerrilla group opposed the Khomeini regime in Iran, fighting for Baluch freedom in the early 1980s. It worked alongside the *Vahdat Baluch* (United Baluch) seeking to unite tribal resistance with urban nationalists against Tehran. Its links with Pakistani Baluch were tenuous.

Forghan
(Koran)

A small but fanatical group, *Forghan* militants were responsible for the murder of a number of clergy in 1981 on the grounds that the clergy interfered with man's relationship with God.

Hezbollah
(Party of God)

This fundamentalist group actively supported the Islamic Republic on the streets of Tehran and other cities, where militants clashed with leftist opposition elements in 1981/82.

Iran Liberation Army (ILA)

Led by exiled General Aryana in Paris, the ILA was responsible in August 1981 for hijacking a French-built Iranian gunboat off the Spanish coast.

Iran Liberation Movement (ILM)

This group was founded by Mehdi Bazargan in 1961 as a splinter group of the National Front. From it split a number of militants, who, impressed by the arguments of Mao Tse-tung, formed the guerrilla group, People's *Mujahideen*, in 1965. Dr Bazargan later became prime minister under the Ayatollah Khomeini's Islamic Republic, until his fall in November 1979.

Islamic Arab Front for the Liberation of Baluchistan (IAFLB)

In 1980 Sheikh Mohammed Bin Hassan Al-Mohammed (b. 1952) set up the Front in Bahrein, where he sought to unite the 350,000 Baluch living in the Gulf States behind an independent Baluchistan. He was particularly influential among Baluch whose families had lived in the Gulf for some 200 years, having fled from former Persian persecution. The Front received little attention from Arab sources, although some contacts existed between it and Pakistani Baluch.

Kurdish Democratic Party of Iran (KDPI)

Founded in 1945, the KDPI went underground the following year as Iranian armed forces occupied the autonomous republic of Kurdistan. A decade later the KDPI established links with Mustapha Barzani's Kurdish Democratic Party in Iraq; for political reasons warm relations never flourished. In 1965 a revolutionary tendency broke away to start a guerrilla campaign against the Shah two years later. For a brief period guerrillas were active in the mountains between Mahabad and Sar Dasht, where they were crushed by Iranian counter-insurgency operations.

　　In 1973 the KDPI broke with its Iraqi counterpart and turned towards the Soviet Union. It sought 'democracy for Iran and autonomy for Kurdistan'. The guerrilla force of *Pesh Mergas*, or partisans, was nominally under the control of Prague-educated Dr Abdel Rahman Qasemlu in Paris, although local leaders took the initiative in rising against the Shah in 1978, when they wrested control of the cities from Tehran. They won limited autonomy in 1979 but opposed the establishment of the Islamic Republic so that fighting continued with the deaths of many hundreds of people that year. By September central government troops had retaken Mahabad and KDPI members were offered an amnesty. Armed opposition continued in the mountains, and the following year the guerrillas faced major counter-insurgency strikes from the air. Despite heavy deaths, fighting continued throughout 1981 as power slipped from the hands of government. The KDPI joined the National Resistance Council in September 1981 and continued its armed revolt in 1982.

National Front (NF)

The Front was a parliamentary coalition of four factions which followed Dr Mossadeq (d. 1967) in the mid-1940s. It came to power in the nationalist government of 1951-53, after which the Shah's regime suppressed its activities. In exile some followers remained politically active and in 1977 resurrected the Front.

National Front of the Iranian People (NFIP)

The Front was sponsored in Baghdad by the Iranian Communist Tudeh party during the Shah's rule. It broadcast and published in Arabic, Kurdish, Persian, Turkish and Baluchi and was led by a former Iranian army general, Mahmoud Panahiyan. In the late 1960s the Front worked with difficulty alongside the Baluchistan Liberation Front.

People's Fedayeen
(Fedayeen-e-Khalq)

The Iranian *Fedayeen* guerrillas split from the pro-Soviet Tudeh communist party in 1963 under the leadership of Bijan Jazani (1937-75). Some received training abroad from the Palestinians and returned in 1971 to the Caspian province of Siakhal, where they launched a campaign against police posts, banks, government buildings and army barracks. Led by Hamid Ashraf (1946-76), most were students and that year lost their lives.

But other groups, particularly those led by Massoud Ahmadzadeh, joined them so that the organisation grew. It assassinated two of the Shah's supporters, General Farsiu in April 1971 and the industrialist Mustapha Fateh in August 1974. Like the *Mujahideen*, the *Fedayeen* drew their support from student circles and were active in the cities, principally Tehran, Mashad, Isfahan and Tabriz. On the Shah's fall in 1979, the *Fedayeen*, who played a crucial role in the street fighting, cooperated with the Islamic Republic supporters. They numbered some 5000 activists and advocated an Iranian form of scientific socialism defended by a people's militia and people's committees. They were decimated by the Islamic Republic's Revolutionary Guards in 1982.

People's Mujahideen
(Mujahideen-e-Khalq)

A militant splinter group of the Iran Liberation Movement, the *Mujahideen* guerrillas launched their armed struggle in 1971 after five years of debate and preparation. Undoubtedly inspired by Islamic thinking, and particulary that of Dr Ali Shariati (d. 1975), the *Mujahideen* fought against what they saw as the Shah's tyranny. In 1975 the *Mujahideen* veered ideologically towards a secular stance, embracing, at least theoretically, Marxism-Leninism.

They were responsible for the deaths of General Teheri in August 1972, US Colonel Hawkins in June 1973, US air force Colonels Turner and Sheafer in May 1975, and three American technicians working on defence-related projects in August 1976.

It seems that in the mid-1970s the *Mujahideen* numbered no more than several hundred, although they had little trouble in recruiting new members for hazardous enterprises as several hundred militants died in clashes with the security forces, or, following their capture, were executed. Like the *Fedayeen*, the *Mujahideen* had higher education backgrounds and were drawn from the towns uniquely. Following the fall of the Shah, the *Mujahideen* supporters, estimated in tens of thousands, opposed the pretensions of the ruling Islamic Republican Party and under their exiled leader, Massoud Rajavi, joined other groups in a resistance council.

Peykar
(Struggle)

This Maoist group was active on the streets of Tehran in 1981, when it opposed the authoritarian and Islamic nature of the Ayatollah Khomeini's Republic.

Popular Front for the Liberation of Ahvaz (PFLA)
(Jabhat Tahrir Ahvaz)

Two decades before Iraqi forces invaded Iran in 1980, Iraq had displayed an interest in supporting Arab separatism in the Iranian oil-producing province of Khuzestan. In 1975 the PFLA became known as the Ahvaz National Front. That year Iraq withdrew most of its support when the Algiers agreement with Iran was signed. On occasions the Front had launched armed actions against the Shah's government. A Marxist--Leninist splinter group known as the Revolutionary Democratic Movement for the Liberation of Arabistan broke away in the mid-1970s. With the fall of the Shah and the crumbling of central authority under the Islamic Republic, Iraq again supported Ahvaz separatism, which proved a weak movement when it came to supporting the Iraqi invasion of Iran in 1980. Nevertheless, an Arab Front for the Liberation of Ahvaz continued to have the support of Baghdad in late 1981, before the Iranian advances of 1982 caused the Iraqis to retreat.

Razmandegan
(Fighters)

This is an activist group of the ultra-left, whose supporters contributed to the political violence on Iranian city streets in 1981-82.

Tudeh
(Party of the Masses)

Founded after the Allied invasion of Persia in 1941, the *Tudeh* party remains the orthodox pro-Soviet communist party of Iran. Based upon unionised urban workers and led by middle-class intellectuals, the *Tudeh* in the 1940s was a predominantly Persian party. Banned in 1949 and again by the Shah in 1953, its members suffered persecution under the Shah's authoritarian rule, during which time it operated from East Germany. By and large the party consistently opposed political violence as a means to achieving power; it returned under the Islamic Republic in 1979, when it again functioned legally. On the ultra-left the *Tudeh* was overtaken by the violence-prone *Fedayeen* and the establishment of the Trotskyist Socialist Workers' Party.

Iraq

Political violence in Iraq stems principally from the problem of a Kurdish minority of three million people in the mountainous north-east of the republic. Despite the defeat in battle of Mustafa Barzani's Kurdish Democratic Party (KDP) in 1975, resistance under his sons and from the Patriotic Union of Kurdistan (PUK) continued in the early 1980s as Kurds took advantage of war between Iran and Iraq to pursue their nationalist ambitions. In addition to the two main parties, splinter groups such as the Kurdish Revolutionary Party and the Unified Kurdistan Socialist Party also pursued political violence.

The 1979 collapse of the Shah's regime in Iran and the emergence of a militant Shia political interest in the Islamic Republic stimulated Shia opposition to Iraq's ruling Sunni elite. Comprising over half of Iraq's 13 million people, Shia followers were a matter for considerable concern to the regime of Saddam Hussein, the more so since unrest had taken a violent form promoted by the *Al Daawa* party and the Islamic Liberation Movement. In its own interests the Syrian leadership supported the dissidents and helped promote in 1980 a National Front for the Liberation of Iraq.

Bibliography

Dr Abbas Kelidar wrote an excellent introduction to Iraqi internal problems in Conflict Study 59, *Iraq: The Search for Stability* (ISC, London, 1975). The nature of military rule and the conflicting trends among civilian groupings are dealt with in greater depth by M. Khadduri in *Republican Iraq: A Study in Iraqi Politics since the Revolution of 1958* (London, 1969). For Kurdish separatist activities, see Richard Sim, *Kurdistan: The Search for Recognition* (Conflict Study 124, ISC, London, 1980) and Andrew Whitley, 'The Kurds: Pressures and Prospects' in *The Round Table*, July 1980. For the earlier years, see Edgar O'Ballance, *The Kurdish Revolt 1961-70* (London, 1973), which is based upon personal observation, and René Mauries, *Le Kurdistan ou le Mort* (Robert Laffont, 1967). The fundamental reference work on Iraq was written by Hanna Batatu, *The Old Social Classes and the Revolutionary Movements of Iraq* (Princeton, 1978). For an Iraqi defence of its war with Iran (1980-82), see Tareq Azis, *The Iran-Iraq Conflict* (London, 1981).

Al Daawa
(The Call)

The *Al Daawa* party is a militant Shia organisation which reflects in Iraq the powerful Shia sentiments that provided the basis for the Ayatollah Khomeini's Islamic Republic in Iran. It opposed the ruling Baath regime in Baghdad by waging a guerrilla struggle in the south of the country in 1981, and was prepared to operate in conjunction with Kurdish groups in a National Front for the Liberation of Iraq (NFLI), which in November 1980 had been set up in London. *Al Daawa* tactics included the assassination of Sunni Baathists in Baghdad and the sabotage of rail links and ammunition depots near Basra. Behind *Al Daawa* lay the spiritual inspiration of Ayatollah Sayyid Muhammed Baqir al-Sadr, whom the government arrested in April 1980, after which he was secretly tried and executed.

Kurdish Democratic Party (KDP)

Following the collapse of the autonomous Kurdish Republic of Mahabad in 1946 and with the support of the legendary Kurdish national leader, Mustafa Barzani, Ibrahim Ahmed set up the KDP. Organised as a clandestine cellular movement in 1953 the KDP adopted Marxist-Leninism with the aim of achieving national liberation.

For a while Kurdish leaders collaborated with the republic that in 1958 succeeded the Iraqi monarchy, but national antagonisms and political incompatibilities soon led to armed clashes and in 1961 to outright military offensives in which KDP forces *(Pesh Mergas)* were estimated at 20,000 in the 1960s and 50,000 in the 1970s. A peace agreement of 1970 was not honoured to the Kurds' satisfaction so that after a brief lull clashes continued. Wide areas of Kurdistan remained beyond the control of Baghdad and in 1974 general hostilities again broke out.

At great cost Pesh Merga guerrillas were driven into the mountains and across the Iranian border. Baghdad committed 120,000 men to the offensive, taking the KDP headquarters at Galala in April 1975. Barzani fled to Iran before emigrating to the United States, where in 1979 he died. Meanwhile his sons, Idris and Massoud, inherited the KDP leadership and reverted to traditional guerrilla warfare tactics. The party was known as the KDP (Provisional Leadership) and counted on 7000 armed men.

National Front for the Liberation of Iraq (NFLI)

Set up in November 1980, the NFLI consisted of dissident Baath party factions brought together by Syria, which had an interest in toppling Iraqi President Saddam Hussein. Other factions, including the two major Kurdish parties and the Iraqi Communist Party, were also involved in Front activities.

Patriotic Union of Kurdistan (PUK)

In the aftermath of the Kurdish military defeat of 1975, Jallal Talabani set up the PUK as an alternative Kurdish national resistance movement. Fierce clashes with Iraqi forces followed in the late 1970s, some help being received from Kurdish interests in Iran. Talabani's main support, however, lies in Syria, whose government is bent upon embarrassing Iraq. For many years Talabani lived there after he had lost control of the Kurdish Democratic Party in 1964 to Mustafa Barzani. The PUK acts as a nationalist umbrella movement for a number of ideologically motivated Kurdish groups such as the Trotskyist Kurdistan Socialist Movement and the League of Toilers of Iraqi Kurdistan. In 1981 the PUK followed the tactics of the Unified Kurdistan Socialist Party (UKSP) by kidnapping a group of West German technicians working on a government project in Kurdistan. They were released in August that year.

Unified Kurdistan Socialist Party (UKSP)

An ideologically motivated splinter group of the Kurdish nationalist movement, the UKSP found support from Syria when it emerged in 1979. The group sprang to prominence in January 1981, when it kidnapped a number of foreign technicians, including a Briton, Michael Powell, who was working on a government water supply project in Kurdistan. Until he lost control in August 1981, Dr Mahmoud Osman led the UKSP.

Israel-Palestine

The present conflict between Jew and Arab derives from the establishment in 1948 of the state of Israel. Such an extraordinary event came about as a result of anti-semitic pogroms in late nineteenth-century Russia, where the Zionist movement was born. Under the leadership of Theodor Herzl it strove 'to create for the Jewish people a home in Palestine secured by public law' (1897).

As Turkish rule in Palestine crumbled and was finally dismantled by the allies after the First World War, new opportunities opened up for Zionists. First they secured the Balfour Declaration (1917), which committed Britain to favouring a Jewish national home in Palestine, and then, as Britain was given by the League of Nations a mandate over Palestine (1922), they secured the inclusion in the terms that a Jewish agency be established to advise on the creation of a national home.

Thenceforth Arabs intermittently clashed not only with politically militant Jews, but with the British authorities, particularly in 1922 and 1929, and again between 1936 and 1939, a period known as the Arab rebellion. But when the horrifying dimensions of German anti-semitism became apparent, the British policy of restricting Jewish immigration into Palestine became increasingly unrealistic, if not absurdly cruel. Under the chairmanship of David Ben Gurion in the United States, Zionists rejected such restrictions (Biltmore Conference, 1942); by the end of the war in 1945 the Jewish population of Palestine numbered over half a million, compared with only 56,000 in 1922.

To protect themselves from Arab hostility, first the *Hashomer* and *Haganah* were set up. And then, to goad the British into allowing immigration and approving of Jewish land purchases, militant Zionists in Palestine turned to terrorism. The *Irgun Zvai Leumi* (IZL) and later the Stern gang (LHI) were formed. Backed up by more conventional forces in the *Haganah*, the policy of armed struggle succeeded in making British rule untenable. The problem of the mandate was referred to the United Nations in 1947, and amidst the greatest disorders the following year Britain withdrew.

Arabs objected violently to the division of Palestine into two ethnically based states, and in the disturbances some 1700 people died. The Jews seized their chance. Driving 400,000 Arabs from Palestine, Jewish forces declared the existence of the state of Israel, to which the USA and the Soviet Union at once accorded recognition.

The exodus of Palestinians fostered a new sense of Palestinian nationhood, which stimulated conflict; what had begun as communal violence was transformed into a national liberation movement. Encouraged by Syria, the Palestinians formed their own guerrilla organisation, *Fatah*, in 1959. Later, in 1964, Egypt supported the foundation of a more structured force, the Palestine Liberation Army (PLA), as the conventional armed forces of the Palestine Liberation Organisation (PLO) set up that year.

For a while the two organisations rivalled one another, but when in 1966, acting together from the Lebanon and Jordan they raised the guerrilla threat to Israel, they provoked war. In 1967 Israel occupied in lightning strikes Jordan's West Bank, Syria's Golan Heights, and Egypt's Sinai and Gaza strip.

In the wake of the six-day war a number of terrorist bodies splintered from the original movement, depending upon individual Arab patron states. So Syria sponsored *Sa'iqa* and Iraq the Arab Liberation Front (ALF).

But it was not merely rival nationalist interests that split the Palestinian exile movement; ideology too played its part. From the establishment in 1967 of the Marxist-Leninist Popular Front for the Liberation of Palestine (PFLP), which conceived of the Palestinian struggle in terms of an internationalist and a socialist context, rather than in that of a nationalist cause, sprang other groups such as the Democratic Front for the Liberation of Palestine (DFLP).

As the Palestinians took to international terrorist incidents, hijacking aircraft, slaughtering bystanders, seizing hostages and mailing letter bombs, but particularly in response to the Olympic massacre in Munich, the Israeli secret services replied in kind. PLO members were singled out and killed or wounded in retaliatory attacks. By mid-1973 five Arabs and five Israeli agents had been murdered, mostly in Europe.

Egypt had not forgotten the humiliating loss of Sinai in 1967, and prepared for war with Israel. Saudi Arabia paid for the arms which the Soviet Union supplied. Syria and Jordan agreed to hostilities, the purpose being to regain the occupied territories. The Arabs struck on 6 October 1973, on the Jewish festival of Yom Kippur, when on two fronts they broke across the Suez Canal through Israeli defences, and regained most of the Golan Heights. The Israelis counter-attacked, driving the Syrians back to within 20 miles of Damascus; in Sinai they all but encircled the Egyptian Third Army, before a ceasefire was imposed. Israel lost 3000 dead and was compelled to recognise a new military efficiency and political determination in the Arab world. Egypt regained its stature as the leading Arab state.

After the war the Arabs recognised the PLO as the 'sole representative of the Palestinian people' (November 1974). The movement had fallen under the influence of *Fatah*, and progressively turned to achieving diplomatic recognition by setting up offices abroad and by becoming accepted on numerous bodies and councils as representative of Palestinian interests.

The high tide of Palestinian terrorism (1968-70) receded swiftly in the

1970s, so that by the end of the decade incidents were running at around 150 a year, which included airport-related attacks, explosions, small arms incidents, letter bombs, hostage taking and arson. The fear remained in Israel that guerrilla encampments in Lebanon, although restrained by a belt of Israeli-controlled territory south of the Litani river in the hands of a Christian militia led by Major Haddad, would at some time succeed in infiltrating the occupied territories and turning an unsuccessful terrorist campaign into a national uprising.

Responding partly to this fear and knowing that the PLO had stashed large quantities of weapons in bunkers, Israel invaded Lebanon in June 1982. Palestinian forces suffered high casualities: death and misery inflicted upon the civilian population was still worse. Yet the Israelis held back from their final assault on Beirut, whence the majority of guerrillas were evacuated in August and September that year.

Bibliography

Political violence surrounding the birth of the state of Israel is described by Netanel Lorch, *The Edge of the Sword: Israel's War of Independence 1947-49* (New York, 1961), by Christopher Sykes, *Cross Roads to Israel* (London, 1965) and by Arthur Koestler, *Promise and Fulfilment: Palestine 1917-49* (London, 1949). The most revealing book on Jewish terrorism is Menachem Begin's *The Revolt* (London, 1947). His predecessor in the IZL, Yaacor Meridor, wrote *Long is the Road to Freedom* (Johannesburg, 1955), but *Days of Fire: The Secret History of IZL* (London, 1968) by Samuel Katz is of greater interest. Burgo Partridge translated *Memoirs of an Assassin* (New York, 1959) by 'Avner', an IZL terrorist. Aside from the official histories in Hebrew of the *Haganah*, the IZL, the Palmach and the LHI, on the *Haganah*, see Munya Mardor, *Haganah* (New York, 1966), Yonah Goldberg, *Haganah or Terror* (New York, 1947), Ephraim Dekel, *Shai: Historical Exploits of Haganah Intelligence* (New York, 1959), Thierry Nolin, *La Haganah: L'Armée Secrète d'Israel* (Paris, 1971) and Leonard Slater's *The Pledge* (New York, 1970). On the LHI, see Y.S. Breener's article 'The Stern Gang 1948' in *Middle Eastern Studies*, October 1965, and specifically on Lord Moyne's assassination *The Deed* (New York, 1963) by Gerald Frank. Cohen Guela was a member and wrote *Women of Violence: Memoirs of a Young Terrorist* (New York, 1966). Two contemporary accounts were written by J. Borisov, *Palestine Underground: The Story of Jewish Resistance* (New York, 1947) and M. Davis, *Jews Fight Too* (New York, 1945), but a modern synthesis was provided by J. Bowyer Bell, *Terror out of Zion* (New York, 1977). For an excellent analysis of extra-parliamentary protest movements of 1970s, see *Radical Dissent in Contemporary Israeli Politics* by David Schall (New York, 1979).

Two Arab journalists, Riad El-Rayyes and Dunia Nahas, provided one of the best introductions to Palestinian guerrilla organisation in *Guerrillas for Palestine* (New York, 1976), but see also Gérard Chaliand's characteristically personal and sympathetic approach to the Palestinian struggle in *The Palestinian Resistance* (Penguin, 1972). Thomas Kiernan wrote a hostile biography of the PLO leader, *Arafat, the Man and the Myth* (New York, 1976). The facts of Palestinian terrorism are recorded in Lester Sobel's Facts on File volume *Palestinian Impasse: Arab Guerrillas and International Terror* (New York and Oxford, 1977). The revolutionary texts can be found in Leila Kadi's *Basic Political Documents of the Armed Palestinian Movement* (Beirut, 1969). Reliable British accounts of developments in the 1960s are found in Edgar O'Ballance, *Arab Guerrilla Power 1967-72* (London, 1974) and the more pro-Israeli John Laffin, *Fedayeen: The Arab Israeli Dilemma* (London, 1973). Y. Harkabi provided one of the first analyses of guerrilla developments in *Fedayeen Action and Arab Strategy* (IISS, London, 1968). For later developments, see D.L. Price's *Since Jordan: The Palestinian Fedayeen* (ISC, London, 1973) and the same author's *Jordan and the Palestinians: The PLO's Prospects* (ISC, London, 1975). For the role of Palestinian guerrillas in the Lebanon, see Kamal Salibi's *Cross Roads to Civil War: Lebanon 1958-76* (New York and London, 1976), and more generally Mehmoud Hussain,*The Palestine Liberation Organisation a Study in Ideology, Strategy, and Tactics* (Delhi, 1975). Galia Golan dealt with the Soviet interest in *The Soviet Union and the PLO* (IISS, London, 1976). See also the American Bard E. O'Neill's later study *Armed Struggle in Palestine: A Political Military Analysis* (Boulder, Colorado, 1978). For Palestinian guerrilla and terrorist strikes up to 1978, see the analysis of Israeli defence force statistics in Hanon Alon's most useful summary *Countering Palestinian Terrorism in Israel: Toward a Policy Analysis of Countermeasures* (Rand, Santa Monica, 1980). Aryeh Yodfat and Yuval Arnon Ohanna took the story up to 1980 in *PLO Strategy and Tactics* (London, 1981), which also deals with the diplomatic side. Better is David Schiller's *Palästinenser zwizchen Terrorismus und Diplomatie*. Brief, but stimulating is Avi Plascov's *A Palestinian State? Examining the Alternatives* (IISS, London, 1981). Journalistic accounts include the two Israelis, Zeer Schiff and Raphael Rothstein, *Fedayeen: The Story of the Palestinian Guerrillas* (London, 1972), John Cooley, the *Christian Science Monitor* correspondent, *Green March, Black September* (London, 1973) and the *Daily Telegraph*'s Christopher Dobson, *Black September* (London, 1974). On the 1972 Olympic Games outrage, see Serge Groussard, *The Blood of Israel: The Massacre of the Israeli Athletes* (New York, 1975) and for an account of the Israeli revenge, David Tinnin, *Hit Team* (London, 1976). Peter Snow and David Phillips recounted *Leila's Hijack War* (London, 1970) and Leila Khaled retorted with *My People Shall Live* (London, 1973). On the Entebbe raid, see Yehuda Ofer, *Operation Thunder: The Entebbe Raid* (Penguin, 1976), which uses Israeli sources, as more authoritatively does *Entebbe Rescue* (New York, 1977) by Yeshayahu Ben Porat and others. See also Tony Williamson's *Counter Strike Entebbe* (London, 1976) and the London *Evening Standard*'s Max Hastings', *Yoni, Hero of Entebbe* (London, 1979). On the Vienna OPEC kidnapping, see Colin Smith's *Carlos: Portrait of a Terrorist* (London, 1976).

Arab Liberation Front — ALF
(Jabhat al-Jahrir al-Arabiya)

Jealous of Syrian influence in the Palestinian movement, Iraq set up the ALF in 1969 to represent its interests. The 500 or so ALF militants were closely integrated with the political and military structures of the Iraqi Baath party, which funded the organisation. In 1981 it was led by Abd-al-Rahim Ahmed, who also sat on the Executive Committee of the PLO. Although not the most active of groups, the ALF undertook guerrilla raids into Israel from the Lebanon, where it kept Iraqi interests alive. As a supporter of the Rejection Front it opposed *Fatah*. When the Israelis invaded Lebanon in June 1982 ALF members found a natural sanctuary in Iraq.

Black June Organisation
(Munadamat Huzairan al-Aswad)

Sabri al-Banna (Abu Nidal), one-time member of *Fatah*, founded Black June in 1976 with Iraqi backing to counteract Syrian influence in the Lebanon, where Syrian troops were imposing some form of order during the civil war period. An attempt upon the life of the Syrian foreign minister failed in 1977, but the United Arab Emirate's minister of state for foreign affairs was killed in the attack.

Black June opposed the PLO's conciliatory line, and was responsible for a series of assassinations in 1978, when the PLO representatives in London (Said Hammami), Kuwait (Ali Yassin), and Paris (Izz ad-Din Qalaq) were murdered, and in Istanbul, four people died in an attack upon the PLO office in August. After that spate of killings, a truce was drawn with *Fatah*. Black June again resorted to terrorism in Europe in the early 1980s, when it indiscriminately attacked the congregation of a Vienna synagogue, having first murdered a city counsellor prominent in the Austrian Israeli lobby. In 1982 its attack upon the Israeli ambassador in London was taken by Prime Minister Begin as the token excuse to invade Lebanon. There followed further attacks in Paris, Karachi and Madrid, where the hand of the organisation was seen. It was believed to number some 500 members; it was not affiliated to the PLO. As before, so after the Lebanese 1982 debacle, Black June was centred on Baghdad.

Black September Organisation
(Munadamat Aylul al-Aswad)

Black September derived its name from the September 1970 conflict between Palestinian forces in Jordan and King Hussein's army, which routed and later expelled the PLO guerrillas from Jordanian territory. It was set up in December that year under Salah Khalaf (Abu Jyad), Arafat's deputy in the PLO, and Hassan Salameh. In November 1971 Black September murdered Jordanian Prime Minister Wasfi Tal in Cairo.

In 1972 the group struck in Hamburg, sabotaging an electronics plant which traded with Israel. But the worst outrage, and the one that caused Western nations to devise new response mechanisms to deal with terrorist attacks, occurred during the Olympic Games at Munich. On 5 September eight terrorists seized the dormitory which housed the Israeli team and in a tragic attempt to rescue the hostages 11 athletes were killed. Five terrorists died; three were captured but subsequently released in October when the West German government gave in to demands made by the hijackers of a Lufthansa aircraft. Later that year in December four Black September terrorists occupied the Israeli embassy in Bangkok. In March 1973 the Saudi embassy in Khartoum was attacked and in 1974 a plot laid against the Arab summit in Rabat, where the Moroccans aborted the attack.

To some extent, Black September rivalled the PFLP terrorist strikes abroad, but essentially the movement was born from the anger and frustration of defeat at the hands of King Hussein. Salah Khalaf retained his position in the PLO long after Black September operations had ceased in December 1974 as a result of a *Fatah* decision to suspend terrorist operations.

Democratic Front for the Liberation of Palestine — DFLP
(Jabhat al-Dimuqratiya li Jahrir Falistin)

When first formed in 1969 the DFLP was known as the Popular Democratic Front for the Liberation of Palestine and was composed of Marxist-Leninist dissidents from the Popular Front for the Liberation of Palestine (PFLP) and the Movement of Arab Nationalists (MAN). The split caused fighting in the streets of Amman (Jordan) to which *Fatah* put an end. The DFLP was led in 1982 by Naif Hawatmeh who depended upon three close advisers, Yasser Abd Rabbu, responsible for information, Qais Samarra'i (Abu Leila), who enjoyed a reputation as an ideologist, and Abd-al-Karim Hammad (Abu Adnan), a member of the Front's political bureau.

The stance adopted by the DFLP was internationalist, placing the Palestinian struggle within a general world context of liberation in Africa, Asia and Latin America. It probably numbered no more than 1000 members, some of whom established contact with equally internationalist Marxist-Leninist Israelis who rejected the Zionist cause in Israel. The Front's principal supporter was South Yemen, where it had an office, but contact with Libya was also maintained. It enjoyed warm relations with the Soviet Union, but also with China, where some members had trained.

Ideologically the Front opposed international terrorist acts and in this differed from the PFLP in its early years. Inside Israel terrorism was another matter: it claimed responsibility for the May 1974 Ma'alot school massacre. Externally it allied itself with the Popular Front for the Liberation of Oman (PFLO) and with the Lebanese Organisation of Communist Action (OCA). Putting politics above the role of armed action, the DFLP plays a part within the PLO, on whose Executive Committee Yasser Abd Rabbu sat in 1981. DFLP members sought refuge in Tunisia, Sudan, Iraq and Syria on leaving Beirut in mid-1982.

Haganah
(Defence Organisation)

Active before the Arab rebellion of 1936-39, the *Haganah* was an underground Jewish defence organisation in Palestine. During the Second World War the British military used the men involved for unconventional warfare in Syria, where the units were known as *Palmach*. They numbered some 32,000 and in 1944 became the Jewish Brigade Group.

After the war these men were disbanded, whereupon the *Haganah* revived as a clandestine body of men and women with remarkable fighting experience. The *Haganah* did not support the campaign of terror launched by the *Irgun Zvai Leumi* and the Stern Gang in 1944 against British rule. Indeed, at first it contributed to countering that threat.

Later the movement actively smuggled European Jews into Israel against British immigration restrictions, and in 1945 reinforced the guerrilla sabotage operations against railway installations and the Haifa oil refinery. Attacks increased in 1946 and included the destruction of 22 aircraft at one airfield. The worst attack was against the King David Hotel in Jerusalem, where 91 lives were lost. At the time the *Haganah* could count upon a wide network of supporters, numbering as many as 40,000 and operated a clandestine radio station, Kol Israel.

Favouring the establishment of the state of Israel, the *Haganah* took an increasingly prominent role in military activity in 1947 and 1948, when the British withdrew from Palestine leaving the Israelis to fight the Arabs in the first Arab Jewish war. In this war the *Haganah* formed the backbone of the Israeli army.

Hashomer
(Watchman)

The Watchmen were Jewish vigilante groups who protected the property of Jews that had emigrated to Palestine in the early part of the twentieth century. They have been described as 'a kind of Hebrew cowboy'; in time their tradition formed the basis of the Jewish underground *Haganah*.

Heroes of the Return
(Abtal al-Anda)

The PLO set up Heroes of the Return in the Lebanon, where it recruited guerrilla fighters from the refugee camps in the mid-1960s. It rivalled *Fatah* for a time, until it merged in December 1967 with the Popular Front for the Liberation of Palestine (PFLP).

Irgun Zvai Leumi — IZL
(National Military Organisation)

David Raziel, a militant Zionist and brilliant, unusually learned activist, who was determined through armed action to wrest a Jewish state from the British authorities in Palestine, founded the IZL in 1937. The IZL not only responded to Arab attacks upon Jews with offensive actions, but started a general terrorist campaign against the Arab population. Led well, and exceptionally highly motivated, the IZL fought with singular ferocity. Raziel's closest colleague and rival was Abraham Stern, who in 1940 broke away to form *Lohame Herut Israel* (Fighters for the Freedom of Israel) or Stern Gang. The IZL was led after 1941 by Menachem Begin, (b. 1913) who succeeded Raziel after the latter's death in Iraq whilst helping the British to quell a pro-German revolt.

In 1944 Begin operated alongside the Stern Gang in attacking British rule in Palestine by launching raids on government offices aimed at eroding British prestige. His campaign found support from the US Hebrew Committee of National Liberation. Actions were stepped up through 1945 and 1946, by which time Jewish terrorism had cost the lives of 373 people in Palestine. The IZL responded to British counter-terrorist measures intelligently, and effectively tied down 100,000 troops at a cost of £40 million per year. Many members subsequently joined the Israeli army in 1948, and its supporters established the right-wing Herut party.

Lohame Herut Israel — LHI
(Fighters for the Freedom of Israel, or *Stern Gang)*

In 1940 Abraham Stern (1907-42) led a breakaway faction from the *Irgun Zvai Leumi* that became known as the Stern Gang. The point at issue was the truce drawn between the IZL and the British on the outbreak of war with Germany, which Stern would not observe. To his fanatical temperament he owed the strong antipathies displayed by colleague and foe alike, and eventually in 1942 his death. But for a while he inspired and led terrorist attacks against the British in Palestine, and against more moderate Jews who opposed the use of terrorism to gain political objectives.

Stern was succeeded by David Friedman Yellin. Up to 1943 no more than a handful of Jews, Arabs and British policemen died at the hands of the gang. But thereafter isolated attacks were escalated into a campaign of murder — in 1944 at least 15 Jews were killed and several police stations attacked. That year in Cairo the gang assassinated Lord Moyne, the British minister for Middle Eastern affairs. The gang never had more than a few hundred members. Many were rounded up and deported, but some escaped detention and remained to work alongside the *Haganah* in a Jewish Resistance Movement in 1945.

Movement of Arab Nationalists — MAN
(Harakat al-Qaumiyyin al-Arab)

On the establishment of the state of Israel in 1948, MAN attracted the support of Palestinian exiles. The Egyptian nationalist leader Nasser, supported its growth, and among the founding members were future Palestinian guerrilla activists such as Naif Hawatmeh and George Habbash. Essentially MAN was a pan-Arab movement; it split up after the 1967 Arab defeat with members founding local liberation groups in South Yemen, Oman and the Lebanon.

MAN played an active role in the Yemen after the September 1962 revolution, when it organised labour in Taiz. With unionised support MAN members broke with their Nasserite tradition and adopted a more radical line forming themselves into a people's militia to defend the Yemen Arab Republic. In the countryside MAN set up peasant leagues *(Lejan Fellahia)* around Taiz, Ibb and Radah. Eventually the MAN network in Yemen broke with headquarters in Beirut to become the Marxist-Leninist Revolutionary Democratic Party *(Hizb al-Thawri al-Dimuqrati)*, which in December 1968 was banned.

Further south in Aden the MAN formed the nucleus in 1963 for the establishment of the National Liberation Front, to which the British handed power in November 1967.

Palestine Armed Struggle Command — PASC
(Qiyadat al-Kifah al-Mussalah)

As Palestinian factions engaged increasingly in terrorist and guerrilla attacks, the PLO set up the PASC in 1969 to act as a joint military coordinating body. For a time it appeared to perform this task, unlike the Palestine Coordinating Council, which it effectively replaced. By 1980, however, the PASC had been reduced to acting as an arbiter in factional disputes, and to keeping the peace between rival Palestinian factions in the refugee camps and guerrilla bases in the Lebanon. In 1981 its commander was Mustafa Dib Khalil (Abu Ta'an).

Palestine Liberation Army — PLA
(Jaish Tahrir Falistin)

The PLA was set up in 1964 as the armed forces of the Palestine Liberation Organisation (PLO). It was conceived as a conventional force and was trained originally in Egypt as a counterweight to the unconventional guerrilla and sabotage operations carried out by *Fatah*, and which the Egyptian leader Gamal Abdal Nasser, strongly criticised.

As the PLO fell under *Fatah* influence, so did the PLA; in principle, its commander-in-chief is the PLO Chairman, Yasser Arafat. In fact, PLA contingents are naturally dependent upon the good will of their host countries: the bulk of PLA forces were in Syria in 1980, having acted alongside the Syrian armed forces in the Lebanese civil war of 1975-76. The rest were in Jordan. In all they amounted to some 4500 men. The organisation's chief of staff in 1981 was Brigadier General Tariq Khadra. According to the revised PLO Constitution of 1968, the PLA's national duty was to become the vanguard in the battle for the liberation of Palestine. Having fought against the Israelis in the 1982 Lebanese conflict, PLA contingents remained under the control of their sponsors, Syria and Jordan, with whose troops they were largely integrated.

Palestine Liberation Front — PLF
(Jabhat Tahrir Falistin)

Led by Tala'at Yaqub, the PLF split from the PFLP-General Command in 1977, over the issue of Syrian influence, which it sought to escape. In fact, Iraqi interests lay behind the faction, which staunchly supported the Rejection Front. Based in the Lebanon, the PLF kept the Iraqi interest alive, despite opposition from *Fatah*. It numbered no more than 250 members, but undertook the occasional guerrilla raid on Israeli settlements, for instance, on the coastal town of Nahariya in April 1979, when four Israelis lost their lives. Despite daring and imaginative attempts by air and sea to infiltrate into Israel, PLF guerrillas have had no greater success than other Palestinian factions intent upon terrorist attacks. Its members would have found a welcome in Baghdad after the 1982 Israeli siege of Beirut broke the Palestinian presence in Lebanon.

Palestine Liberation Organisation — PLO
(Munadamat Tahrir Falistin)

The 1964 Arab Summit Conference decided to create a Palestinian entity, which was subsequently set up at a meeting in Jerusalem, where a Palestine National Charter and a Constitution were approved by participants in a Palestine Congress. Four years later the Charter was amended, but it remained in 1983 the basic definition of Palestinian objectives.

These objectives included a commitment to struggle and to national action, an agreement to defer to majority opinion, to support armed revolution 'so that the impetus of the masses towards liberation may take its course until victory is achieved'. All Palestinians were considered natural members of the PLO, so that the PLO had as its base the Palestinian people. Dues, or taxes were regularly paid to the organisation.

The supreme authority of the PLO, according to the Constitution, was the National Assembly or the Palestine National Council (PNC), elected every three years by direct ballot and convened every six months in a suitable town. Two-thirds constituted a quorum. In practice, the PNC had by 1981 met only 15 times. Members elected the 11-man executive committee, which then elected its own chairman, who since 1969 has been Yasser Arafat (b. 1929). This body was the highest PLO authority, responsible collectively and individually to the PNC. In practice, the PNC is dominated by the various guerrilla factions, of which *Fatah* is the most powerful.

In 1973 a Central Council of 55 members was created to link the PNC and the Executive Committee; its chairman in 1981 was Khaled al Fahoum. The Council met several times a year.

All efforts to integrate the PLO since 1969 have failed, so that it remains an umbrella organisation that shelters politically violent factions, but at the same time operates internationally as a diplomatic front for Palestinian interests, which in 1974 the United Nations recognised the PLO exclusively represented. It obtained observer status in the UN, and the following year was made a member of the non-aligned movement. In January 1976 the Group of 77 developing countries admitted the PLO, and it also became a member of the Arab League that year. Attempts have been made to gain observer status at the International Monetary Fund, but by 1981 the PLO had not succeeded, although in many international forums Yasser Arafat was received with head of state protocol. After the 1982 Israeli siege of Beirut Arafat left Lebanon for Tunisia, where he established PLO headquarters.

The PLO had offices or representatives in all Arab states but Oman; in Africa, in Burundi, Chad, Congo, Guinea, Mali, Senegal, Tanzania, and Uganda; in the Americas, in Cuba and Mexico; in Asia, in Bangladesh, Cambodia, China, India, Japan, Laos, Malaysia, North Korea, Pakistan, Sri Lanka and Vietnam; in Europe, in Belgium, Cyprus, France, West Germany, Italy, Netherlands, Spain, Sweden, the United Kingdom and Yugoslavia; and in all Soviet-bloc states.

Palestine National Front in Occupied Territories — PNF
(Jabhat al-Wataniya al-Falistiniya fi al-Aradi al-Muhtala)

The PNF was set up in 1973 by the Jordanian Communist Party to operate clandestinely in the communities of the West Bank. Its purpose was first to put an end to Israeli occupation, and then to establish a Marxist-Leninist social and political system in the territory. Three members sat on the PLO Executive Commitee in 1981 — Muhammad Abd al-Mohsen (Abu Maizer), Dr Walid Qamhawi and Abd al-Jawad Saleh. The PNF did not play a notably active role in the late 1970s: it appeared to have been contained by Israeli surveillance.

Palestine National Liberation Movement

(Al-Fatah)
Harakat al-Tahrir al-Watani al-Filistini — the reverse acronym spells *Fatah*, or Conquest)

Fatah was the first Palestinian commando organisation to emerge in the mid-1950s, although only publicly in 1959. It was a nationalist movement set up to liberate Palestine from Israeli occupation by waging low intensity warfare. In this it enjoyed Syrian support, so that *Fatah*'s headquarters were established in Damascus, where weapons, money and training facilities were provided.

Thus equipped, and under the command of Yasser Arafat (b. 1929), *Fatah* attacked Israeli settlements and quickly grew in organisational capacity. With the formation of the Palestine Liberation Organisation (PLO) in 1964, *Fatah* was confronted by a rival, which after a period of enmity, it ended by dominating when Arafat became chairman of the PLO in 1969. Throughout the 1970s and in the early 1980s *Fatah* was the dominant Palestinian guerrilla group, whose three most important leaders were Yasser Arafat, the Central Committee chairman, Salah Khalaf (Abu Iyad), the deputy chairman, and Khalil al Wazir (Abu Jihad), commander of *Fatah* forces. Arafat, Faruq Qaddumi (Abu Lutf), head of the PLO political department, and Mahmud Abbas (Abu Mazen) an Executive Committee member, served as elected members of the PLO Executive Committee.

In June 1980 at its fourth congress *Fatah* emphasised the role of armed struggle, together with all other means to achieve national liberation for the Palestinians. To wage such a struggle it disposed of an estimated 9000 guerrilla fighters, most of whom were based in the Lebanon, where to defend themselves from Israeli ground and air strikes they had constructed underground bunkers. Their weapons arrived by sea at the ports of Sidon and Tyre, which were largely controlled by the Palestinian interest. *Fatah*'s problem was to infiltrate men into Israel, an obstacle which, they seemed unable to overcome.

The movement called for Israeli withdrawal from the occupied territories of the West Bank and Gaza, and implementation of the United Nations resolutions recognising the Palestinians' right to repatriation and the formation of an independent state. It was particularly concerned that Jordan should not repossess the West Bank, a claim King Hussein had ceded to the PLO. Furthermore *Fatah* has not forsworn to liberate the rest of Palestine from Israeli rule, a development that would entail the demise of the state of Israel.

Having been created as a non-conventional armed force, *Fatah*'s military strength grew until it threatened King Hussein's rule in Jordan. A confrontation ensued in 1970, when the Jordanian armed forces defeated *Fatah*, whose forces retired to Syria and Lebanon. For a time, through Black September, *Fatah* engaged in terrorist actions abroad, but these activities were suspended in December 1974. During the civil war in the Lebanon (1975-76) *Fatah* played an important role, especially in the negotiations which brought an end to the fighting, but it emerged from the conflict more closely involved with Syria.

In March 1978, because of the incursions it made into Israel and particularly because of a bloody incident surrounding the hijacking of a bus by 11 terrorists who, using grenades and firearms, killed 32 Israelis, *Fatah* provoked an Israeli invasion of southern Lebanon. Fierce encounters saw 200 guerrillas killed and ended with Israeli occupation of territory south of the Litani river. A form of order was restored by a United Nations peacekeeping force and an Israeli-backed Christian militia under Major Haddad, which replaced the Israeli presence. But a ceasefire agreed in September 1979 did not bring about a cessation of *Fatah* guerrilla attacks on the border, where encounters were relatively frequent in the early 1980s. In particular, sabotage operations inflicted damage upon Israeli farming enterprises. Such attacks provided the Israelis with an excuse to invade the Lebanon in June 1982, when Palestinian guerrillas took refuge in Beirut. Most were evacuated in August and September. Yasser Arafat sought to establish his headquarters in Tunisia: his *Fatah* guerrillas went to Syria and Iraq as well as Tunisia.

Palestine Popular Struggle Front — PPSF
(Jabhat al-Kifah al-Shaabi al-Falistini)

Emerging in Jordan in 1968, the PPSF had its origins in the commando force of the Palestine Liberation Army (PLA). It was essentially a hardline nationalist organisation in 1981, supporting the Rejection Front and led by Bahjat Abu Garbiyya and Dr Samir Ghusha. The 200 or so members of the PPSF looked to Iraq for their support, but appeared to engage in very little activity. Baghdad provided a haven after the Israelis had invaded Lebanon in June 1982.

Popular Front for the Liberation of Palestine — PFLP
(Jabhat al-Shaabiya li Tahrir Falistin)

From merging four organisations — the Movement of Arab Nationalists (MAN), the Palestine Liberation Front (PLF), Heroes of the Return and

Vengeance Youth — Dr George Habbash created the PFLP in December 1967. His motives were personal and ideological: not only did he seek to rival Arafat's position in *Fatah*, but he sought to inject a Marxist-Leninist content into the Palestinian nationalist movement. Being essentially an ideologically motivated organisation, the PFLP suffered from internal intellectual disputes that gave rise to factions. Among the most prominent were the PFLP-General Command, the Organisation of Arab Palestine (OAP) and the Popular Democratic Front for the Liberation of Palestine (PDFLP).

From its inception Dr Habbash retained control of his organisation. His deputy in 1981 was the editor of *al-Hadaf* (Aim), Bassam Abu Sherif, but the PFLP was represented on the Executive Committee of the PLO, which it had left in 1974 but rejoined in 1981, by Ahmed Yamani (Abu Maher). They rejected all forms of political compromise with Israel, and headed what became known as the Rejection Front. Nothing but the elimination of the state of Israel was acceptable to the PFLP, which accused the PLO of cooperating with 'capitulationist Arab regimes'. It was vigorously anti-Western, on grounds of being 'anti-imperialist' and 'anti-capitalist'. Support came from Libya, Algeria, and South Yemen (PDRY); relations with the Soviet bloc have been strained, largely due to the organisation's uncompromising political stance.

From the start the PFLP gained notoriety for its international terrorist compaign, which Habbash had begun in July 1968 with the hijacking of an El Al aircraft en route from Rome to Lod. 'To kill a Jew far from the battlefield had more effect than killing hundreds of Jews in battle.' The effect in bringing to the attention of the world the Palestinian issue was electric.

Two further El Al aircraft were attacked by PFLP terrorists in Zürich and Rome in February and September 1969, but the most dramatic incident took place the following September. Three aircraft with 400 passengers on board were hijacked and at Dawson's Field in Jordan two were blown up, the incident caused King Hussein to expel the Palestinian guerrillas. The third was exploded in Egypt. Worse was to follow in May 1972, when at Lod (Tel Aviv) airport the PFLP organised the slaughter by a handful of militants from the Japanese Red Army of as many as 27 innocent bystanders. A further joint terrorist operation occurred in July 1973, when a Japanese aircraft was hijacked to Libya and blown up. In 1975 PFLP terrorists fired rockets at an Israeli aircraft in Orly (Paris) airport and in August 1976 four passengers were killed in an attack in Istanbul on an El Al flight. Such actions were condemned alike by East-bloc nations and Western countries.

Partly as a result of condemnation, and partly because terrorism had achieved the desired publicity, Habbash renounced its use, although his former colleague, Wadi Haddad, continued to carry out such operations until his death from cancer in March 1978. Among the more sensational of these operations were those at Entebbe in June 1976 and at Mogadishu in 1977. Haddad's faction, based in Baghdad, was known as the PFLP Special Commando; it remained active in terrorism under the command of Salim Abu Salim. The main PFLP guerrillas sought refuge in South Yemen.

Popular Front for the Liberation of Palestine-General Command — PFLP-GC
(Jabhat al-Shaabiya li Tahrir Falistin al-Qiyada al-Ama)

Ahmed Jibril (Abu Jihad), one-time leader of the Palestine Liberation Front, a group associated with the Movement of Arab Nationalists broke away from the PFLP in October 1968 to form the PFLP-GC. His was an activist group, keener on fighting than on politics. Talal Naji (Abu Jihad Talal) was thought to be the deputy leader in 1981, when he represented the PFLP-GC on the Executive Committee of the PLO. It had no more than 250 members, but all were dedicated to ruthless terrorist action: the group thought nothing of firing on a school bus in May 1970 near the Lebanese border, nor of undertaking suicide attacks on Israeli villages. Although condemned for these activities by other Palestinian groups, Jibril rationalised the action as a 'new struggle based on the highest degree of revolutionary violence'. He found a measure of support in Libya and Syria.

Rejection Front
(Jabhat al-Rafud)

In June 1974 the Palestine Liberation Organisation (PLO) drew up a ten-point Phased Political Programme that accepted the principle that the PLO should set up some form of national Palestinian authority as soon as possible on any corner of territory liberated from Israeli occupation. This was a compromise decision, but it rejected negotiations based on UN resolution 242. At the time, the Programme received wide endorsement, but later certain more extreme sections of Palestinian opinion formed a Front Rejecting Capitulationist Solutions, which became known as the Rejection Front. Those behind it included the Popular Front for the Liberation of Palestine (PFLP), the Popular Front for the Liberation of Palestine — General Command, (PFLP-GC), and the Arab Liberation Front (ALF). They were later joined by the Palestine Popular Struggle Front (PPSF) and the Palestine Liberation Front (PLF). In 1977 the PFLP-GC was expelled from the Front, but the group continued to espouse rejectionist policies. Libya particularly favoured the Rejection Front; so too did Iraq and Syria.

Sa'iqa
(Thunderbolt)

In 1968 Syrian interest in the Palestinian problem led that country's Baath party to set up *Sa'iqa*, which was closely linked to the Syrian army. In fact the group began life as the military wing of the Vanguards of the Popular War for the Liberation of Palestine, which consisted of members of the Palestinian branch of Syria's Baath party and the Syrian army's Palestinian battalion. Originally therefore a rival to *Fatah*, in the early 1980s *Sa'iqa* cooperated with the larger movement and opposed the Rejection Front groups. It was militantly nationalistic, but compromised on territorial ambitions in backing the establishment of a Palestinian state confined to the West Bank.

Leading *Sa'iqa* in 1982 was Dr Issam al-Qadi, the group's secretary general, Sami al-Attari, Muhammed Khalifah and Majed Mohsen. As a policy, *Sa'iqa* opposed the use of terrorism: an attack in Septembr 1971 on a train in Austria carrying Soviet Jews to Israel and the occupation of the Egyptian embassy in Ankara in July 1979 were uncharacteristic. On both occasions *Sa'iqa* members admitted responsibility under the title of Eagles of the Palestinian Revolution. For the most part, the estimated 2000 supporters operated as a military body undertaking low intensity guerrilla strikes. Like other bodies within the PLO, *Sa'iqa* suffered from internal tensions and from the hostility of rival Palestinian organisations. In 1979 the group's leader, Zuheir Mohsen, was assassinated on the French riviera.

Lebanon

Unable to bear for longer the rising tensions between Maronite Christian and Muslim interests, which had grown disproportionately since the original constitution had attempted to accommodate them, the Lebanese state collapsed in civil conflict in 1975-76. The Phalangists defended Christian enclaves, alongside National Liberal militiamen. From these two organisations sprang a number of para-military organisations such as the Guardians of the Cedars of Lebanon.

On the Muslim side, the gunmen of the Progressive Socialist Party found themselves developing links with the Palestinian factions that had grown up since the 1967 war with Israel, and which had their territorial and party bases in the Lebanon. Other groups supportive of the PLO included Irahim Quleilat's Nasserite Morabitoun militia in Tarik Jdedeh, and the Shia *Amal* militia with a base in Nabaa and which fought alongside the PLO at Khalde in June 1982. To prevent the growth of Palestinian influence in the country Syria intervened in the civil war in 1976, subsequently turning her forces into an Arab Deterrent Force (30,000), which at the outset had contingents from other countries. True, the move contained the Palestinians, the intervention however brought Syrian forces into conflict with Christians in and around Beirut.

The civil war hardly affected the south, but in 1977 PLO hostilities across the Lebanese frontier provoked Israeli retaliatory raids and military occupation of the south. In 1978 a United Nations force (UNIFIL) replaced the Israelis. In fact a more real guarantee for Israel turned out to be an Israeli-backed Christian militia, the Free Lebanese Army, under Major Haddad, who carved out a personal fief south of the Litani river, where he threatened to hold elections. Thus, in five years a prosperous and peaceful country had been reduced to regional rule by Syrian troops, Palestinian guerrillas and an Israeli-backed Christian militia. From a guerrilla force, the Palestinians adopted the profile of a conventional armed force, which intimidated the Lebanese, antagonised the Christians and ultimately in June 1982 provoked Israel to invade the Lebanon, driving the Palestinian fighters from the south and then from West Beirut.

Bibliography

The complex development of Lebanese political parties is well analysed by Michael Suleiman in *Political Parties in the Lebanon* (Cornell University

Press, 1967), but for a competent listing of the terrorist factions and groups with their various leaders, see Marius Deeb, *The Lebanese Civil War* (Praeger, 1980). Abbas Kelidar and Michael Burrell dealt succinctly with the civil war in *Lebanon: The Collapse of a State* (ISC, London, 1976). At greater length see Harold Vocke, *The Lebanese War, Its Origins and Political Dimensions* (London, 1978), John Bulloch's journalistic *Death of a Country: The Civil War in Lebanon* (London, 1977) and D.Th. Schiller, *Der Bürgerkrieg in Libanon Entstehung, Verlauf, Hintergründe* (Munich, 1979). For the complications which resulted from the Palestinian presence in Lebanon, see Walid Khalidi, *Conflict and Violence in the Lebanon* (Harvard, 1979) and a collection of essays in *Lebanon in Crisis* (Syracuse University, 1979) edited by Edward Haley and Lewis Snider, particularly that by John Cooley. For the view of one who suffered see *Crise au Liban* (Beirut, 1977) by Camille Chamoun.

Arab Revolutionary Brigades — ARB
(Wahdat al-Thawra al-Arabiya)

Based in Beirut, the ARB claimed responsibility in April 1982 for the murder of an Israeli diplomat in Paris. The Brigades described themselves as 'a world pan-Arab movement, whose objective is to free Arabs and to restore their dignity, and to fight in association with their friends in all organisations throughout the world.'

Arab Socialist Action Party — ASAP
(Hizb al-Amal al-Ishtiraki al-Arabi)

George Habbash formed the party in July 1972, after which it played a principal role in the Lebanese civil war of 1975-76 in the towns of Beirut, Tripoli and Tyre. It was the Lebanese counterpart of the Popular Front for the Liberation of Palestine (PFLP). The party formed a component of the National Movement.

Conservative Lebanese Front, or Kufur Front

During the Lebanese civil war of 1975-76, the CLF consisted of five principal organisations: the Lebanese Phalangist Party, the National Liberal Party, Al Tanzim, Guardians of the Cedars of Lebanon, Zghartan Liberation Army and the Permanent Congress of the Lebanese Order of Monks. Other militias allied to the CLF were the Zahla Bloc, Mountain Brigade, Akkar Brigade, Al-Muqaddamin Brigade, Lebanese Youth Movement, the Fayadiya army units and Lebanon's army.

Free Lebanese Army — FLA
(Jaish Lubnan al-Hur)

In May 1980 Major Saad Haddad (b. 1938) forged his Free Lebanese Army out of Christian militia groups, which, with Israeli support, had for some years been active in southern Lebanon. In an attempt to control as much territory as possible, Haddad's forces clashed not only with Palestinian guerrilla units, but with United Nations forces that had been stationed in the south since 1976.

In effect, Haddad's men, who consisted of several thousand hardened Phalangists and National Liberals, took control of territory previously occupied by the Israelis, who had initially agreed to have their presence replaced by UN forces. In doing so the FLA formed a buffer zone that extended north to the Litani river between Israel and that part of the Lebanon under Syrian military influence. The need for such a zone disappeared with the Israeli invasion of the Lebanon in June 1982, when the Palestinians were driven from the south with appalling losses.

Front for the Liberation of Lebanon — FLL
(Jabhat Tahrir Lubnan)

The front emerged in West Beirut in 1980. In 1981 it claimed responsibility for an attempt on the life of Greek Orthodox Archbishop Maximum Hakim and for a shooting incident at Rome airport that year. The FLL was an example of the reactionary terrorism provoked by the occupation of the Lebanon by Palestinians and Syrians.

Guardians of the Cedars of Lebanon
(Hurras al-Arz)

The Guardians were prominent in the Lebanese civil conflict of 1975-76, when they upheld the Christian interest through a campaign of murderous revenge. Their intention was to liquidate the Palestinian presence in the Lebanon. It was led by Etienne Saqr, although the group's intellectual leader was the poet and writer, Said Aql, who inclined towards a fascist anti-capitalism. Militants allied with the Phalangists during the fighting. The Guardians were again active in the conflict of 1982, during and after the Israeli invasion of Lebanon.

Independent Nasserite Movement — INM
(Harakat al-Nasiriyin al-Mustaqallin)

The INM was an essential component of the National Movement in Lebanon during the civil war period of the mid-1970s. Its militia was known as the *Morabitoun*, who were recruited from the lower-class, urban Sunni community. The militia was commanded by Ibrahim Qulailat in Beirut and fought on several fronts. Law and order in western Beirut depended upon its presence.

Lebanese Communist Party — LCP
(Hizb al-Shuyu'i al-Lubnani)

The pro-Soviet LCP consisted of only a couple of thousand members until the civil war of 1975, when its ranks swelled to several thousand. Having been primarily a Christian party, the LCP was transformed into a predominantly Muslim organisation actively engaged in promoting Palestinian resistance and anti-Israeli and anti-US actions. George Hawi was elected secretary general in the 1979 Fourth Congress.

During the fighting of the mid-1970s the LCP possibly had 1000 militiamen, 200 of whom died in the conflict, mostly in Beirut. At the time Niqula al-Shwi led the party.

Lebanese Youth Movement — LYM
(Harakat al-Shabiba al-Lubnaniya)

The movement comprised a local militia in the Dikwana suburb of Beirut during the civil conflict of 1975-76. It was led by Marun al-Khuri.

Marada Brigade
(Liwa al-Marada)

This was a local militia in the Zgharta region which fought with the Conservative Lebanese Front in the civil conflict of 1975-76.

Movement of the Disinherited
(Harakat al-Mahrumin)

A faction of the Syrian Social Nationalist Party, and led by Musa al-Sadr, the Movement formed the Nationalist Movement in late 1975 with the Organisation of the Baath Party. Imam Musa al-Sadr was the spiritual leader of the Shiites in Beirut, where many had taken refuge from Israeli raids in the south. The title referred to the newly disinherited rural worker separated from his traditional leader. Its militia, *Amal*, fought with the National Movement until early 1976, when it adopted a pro-Syrian stance.

Muslim Brotherhood
(Majallat al-Ikhwan al-Musalamin)

As in other Near Eastern countries, the Brotherhood existed in the Lebanon, and was active in the civil conflict that afflicted Lebanese society in the late 1970s. For the birth of the Brotherhood, see under Egypt.

National Liberation Militia — NLM
(Numur al-Ahrar)

Known as the Tigers and led by Nihad Shalhat, NLM militants represented the interests of Camille Chamoun's National Liberal Party in the Lebanese civil conflict of 1975-76. As leader of the Lebanese rightist bloc, Chamoun (b. 1900) was soon reliant upon Israeli military aid and French diplomatic support as the conflict continued throughout the late 1970s. Very little control could be exercised over the militiamen, who found themselves fighting in pockets defending local communities, some in the south, some in and around Beirut. In 1980 National Liberal militiamen contended with the Phalangists for control of the Lebanese Christians. The outcome left the National Liberals stripped of their military wing. Destroyed as an organisation, NLM militants nonetheless survived, active in pockets of violence in a leaderless and war-torn society.

National Movement
(Harakat al-Wataniya)

The movement was a leftist coalition set up in 1972 and led by Kamal Jumblat, the traditional Lebanese Druze leader. In addition to several minor groups, it comprised six organisations: Jumblat's own Progressive Socialist Party, the Independent Nasserites Movement, the Lebanese Communist Party, the Organisation of Communist Action, the Syrian Social Nationalist Party and the two Baath parties, Organisation of the Baath Party and Arab Socialist Baath Party. The smaller groups included the Union of the Forces of the Working People — Corrective Movement, October 24 Democratic Socialist Movement, National Christians' Front and the Populist Nasserite Organisation.

Nationalist Front
(Jabhat al-Qaumia)

This group was formed by the Organisation of the Baath Party in November 1975, together with the Movement of the Disinherited and other pro-Syrian factions such as the Union of the Forces of the Working People, the Syrian Social Nationalist Party and the Progressive Vanguards.

Organisation of the Baath Party — OBP
(Munazzamat Hizb al-Baath)

Asim Qansu led the leftist OBP in the Lebanese civil conflict of 1975-76, when it supported first Kamal Jumblat in the National Movement and later the Nationalist Front.

Organisation of Communist Action — OCA
(Munazzamat al-Amal al-Shuyu'i)

Formed in 1970 under Muhsin Ibrahim, formerly of the Arab Nationalist Movement, OCA found support among workers and students in Beirut, in the Bekaa valley and in the south. Its militia fought in the civil war of 1975-76, losing some 75 men. Maronites, Catholics and Sunnis joined OCA.

Permanent Congress of the Lebanese Order of Monks

Led by the head of the Maronite Order of Monks, Father Sharbal Qassis, the Congress formed part of the Conservative Lebanese Front during the civil conflict of 1975-76 and to which it lent strong political support. Qassis played a leading role in political discussions and was instrumental with others in founding the Front.

Phalange, or Lebanese Phalangist Party
(Hizb al-Kataib al-Lubnaniya)

The Lebanese Phalange had its origins in the 1930s, when young Maronite Christians sought to preserve the independence of their country, which was threatened by Syrian expansionist ambitions. The vehicle inside the Lebanon for the expression of greater Syria sentiment was the Syria National Social Party, whose Muslim supporters also favourably viewed the violent activities of exiled Palestinian groups in the Lebanon.

Seeing their interests threatened by such an armed presence, Phalangists opposed this development, and in April 1975 clashed with the PLO in street confrontations that left over 100 dead. Thenceforth the country was seized by civil war in which the Phalangist militia battled to maintain control of the Christian sectors of Beirut. The Phalangist leader at the time was Sheikh Pierre Gemayel (b. 1905), who was the political head of the movement. His son, Bachir, later became the Phalangist military commander in the south. In 1980 the Phalangists struggled with the National Liberals for control of the Christian community and formed a Christian army to protect that part of the Lebanon that remained to them. The Syrian military restricted this activity in December 1980. Eighteen months later the Phalangists welcomed the Israeli invasion of Lebanon, although they fought shy of appearing accomplices. The fact remained that by shattering PLO power and restricting the influence of the Progressive Socialist Party militias, the Israelis had immeasurably strengthened the position of the Phalange, whose military commander, Bachir, was elected president in 1982. Before he could take office a bomb at his Beirut headquarters killed him in September that year. His brother, Amin, succeeded him.

Populist Nasserite Organisation — PNO
(Tanzim al-Nasari al-Jamahiri)

Led by Mustafa Saad, the Organisation was based in southern Saida and fought as part of the National Movement during the 1975-76 conflict, first in Damur, and later in Jizzin and Mount Lebanon.

Progressive Socialist Party — PSP
(Hizb al-Taqqadami al-Ishtiraki)

The leftist Muslim PSP had close links with the Palestinian guerrilla groups active in the Lebanon, and in 1975 found itself in armed conflict with the Christian Phalangist militia. Kamal Jumblatt (1917-77) led the party at that time, which was allied with the Syrian interest through the Syrian National Social Party, with the orthodox Marxist-Leninist left through the Lebanese Communist Party and also with the Arab socialists, whose connections lay with both the Iraqi and the Syrian wings of the Baath movement. He was succeeded by his son after his assassination, the work it was thought of Syrians who opposed his support for the Palestinians.

Progressive Vanguards
(Tali'a Taqqadamiya)

Led by Muhammad Zakariya, the Vanguards were in fact pro-Syrian militiamen fighting within the Nationalist Front during the 1975-76 Lebanese civil war.

Revolutionary Islamic Organisation
(Tanzim al-Islami al-Thawri)

This group was active in 1980 in Beirut, where it claimed responsibility for the assassination of the Lebanese Shia leader, Hassan Shirazi. Militants were anti-Iranian and were backed by Iraqi elements. Its activities sparked off a number of retaliatory actions against Iraqi interests in the Lebanon.

Syrian Social Nationalist Party — SSNP
(Hizb al-Suri al-Qaumi al-Ijtimi)

The party attempted an unsuccessful coup in 1961, from which it only recovered a decade later, when it supported the Palestinian interest in Lebanon. Kamal Jumblat legalised the SSNP in 1970, when it adopted a nationalist, secular and reformist line, attracting Greek Orthodox, Shiite, Druze, Maronite and Sunni support. Its militias fought in the 1975-76 civil war in Beirut and the Matn mountains.

Tanzim
(Organisation)

Active in the Lebanese civil war of 1975-76, this militia formed part of the Conservative Lebanese Front and was thought to be financed by the Maronite League. Fuaad Shamali set it up; it enjoyed a reputation for discipline.

Union of the Forces of the Working People — Corrective Movement
(Itihad Qawa al-Shaab al-Amal al-Harakat al-Tashihiya)

The original Nasserite Union, from which the Corrective Movement split in 1974, had been founded in 1965. During the course of the Lebanese civil war of 1975-76 the movement created a militia, *Quwwat Nasir*, led by Isam al-Arab. It formed part of the leftist National Movement and was Nasserite in tendency. During the fighting this faction was active in Beirut and Mount Lebanon, where its main support lay.

Zahla Bloc
(Tajammu al-Zahli)

A regional organisation led by Ilyas al-Harawi, the Maronite deputy for Zahla, the bloc had its own militia in the Lebanese civil war of 1975-76.

Zghartan Liberation Army — ZLA
(Jaish al-Tahrir al-Zghartawi)

The Zgharta region of Lebanon included five clans which joined together to fight as a militia for the Conservative Lebanese Front in the 1975-76 civil war. It formed the principal opposition to the Palestinians in and around Tripoli and was loyal to Sulayman Franjiya, leader of his clan.

Oman

The sultanate was afflicted in the 1960s and 1970s by an insurgent movement in the western mountains of Dhofar, where in 1963 rebellious tribesmen revolted. When Britain withdrew from Aden in 1967 the newly independent government of South Yemen aided the Dhofar Liberation Front (DFL) and in doing so politicised the rebellion.

The DLF became in 1971 a Marxist-Leninist Popular Front for the Liberation of Oman and the Arabian Gulf (PFLOAG) with wider subversive pretensions. When these more extensive ambitions proved hard to realise, the PFLOAG became the Popular Front for the Liberation of Oman (PFLO) in 1974. As an insurgent movement, the PFLO collapsed in 1975, although the latter years of the decade continued to see the occasional cross-border raid from South Yemen. Friendlier relations existed between the two ideologically opposed states in the early 1980s, when no Front activity was recorded.

Bibliography

The best summary of the Dhofar rebellion is contained in D.L. Price's *Oman: Insurgency and Development* (ISC, London, 1975). The most detailed account of ideological developments can be found in Fred Halliday's excellent *Arabia without Sultans* (Penguin, 1979). For the effect of the insurgency on the economy, see the Sultan's advisor, John Townsend, *Oman: The Making of a Modern State* (London, 1977). The PFLO publishes, intermittently, in English; see the translation of a Danish pamphlet 'The Revolution is Alive: The Liberation Struggle in Oman' (KROAG, 1979).

Dhofar Liberation Front — DLF
(Jabhat al-Tahrir al-Dhofar)

The DLF was originally a tribally-based opposition group which from 1963 contested the repressive rule of the Sultan of Oman. In seeking autonomy for Dhofar, it was supported by the newly independent government in South Yemen (1967), which promptly politicised the rebellion. In 1971 the DLF was incorporated in the Popular Front for the Liberation of Oman and the Arabian Gulf (PFLOAG).

Popular Front for the Liberation of Oman — PFLO
(Jabhat Tahrir Janub Oman)

The PFLO was the name adopted in August 1974 by the Marxist-Leninist Popular Front for the Liberation of Oman and the Arabian Gulf (PFLOAG). It retained that organisation's structure and remained firmly in the hands of a political directorate known as the People's Revolutionary Movement (PRM). The PRM was based in Aden, where it enjoyed international communist sponsorship and access to press and radio.

Despite the change in title, the wider subversive designs of the PFLOAG were not dropped — rather a shift in emphasis occurred with effort being concentrated on the military overthrow of the Sultan of Oman. The campaign failed. By sending troops in 1974-75 the Shah of Iran greatly contributed to the elimination of the rebels in the Dhofar mountains and to forcing PFLO guerrillas back into South Yemen. British counter-insurgency training and leadership of the Sultan's forces had provided the basis for military victory over the insurgents, who since 1976 ceased to exist as an insurgent threat. Occasional cross-border raids continued.

More widely, the PFLO retained its contacts in the Gulf and enjoyed close relations with the Popular Front for the Liberation of Palestine (PFLP). Together the two organisations developed a regional network for smuggling arms and exchanging information, and for training. PFLO influence, although never extensive like that of the PLO, was present in the United Arab Emirates and in Bahrain. Financially the Front was dependent upon radical Arab states such as Libya and Iraq, and indirectly on the Soviet Union.

Certainly some training of PFLO guerrillas took place there, and South Yemen is heavily dependent upon the USSR. Even so, the PFLO probably derived more benefit in the long run from weapons, clothing and medicine supplied by Iraq and Libya, where the PFLOAG had had an office since 1973.

Following military defeat, the PFLO fell victim to internal disputes, although it continued to exist in the early 1980s, when it appeared unable to take advantage of the political ferment affecting the Gulf area in the wake of the Iranian revolution.

Popular Front for the Liberation of Oman and the Arabian Gulf — PFLOAG
(Jabhat Tahrir Janub Oman wa al-Khalif al-Arabi)

The PFLOAG was set up in 1971 in Aden with the support of the newly independent and Marxist-Leninist government in South Yemen. The central committee was based in Aden, but subordinate committees were established in Dhofar, the United Arab Emirates, Bahrain, Qatar and

Kuwait. These were clandestine bodies intent upon promoting subversion against the traditional rulers of Arabia.

Only in Dhofar did the PFLOAG direct a force of trained guerrilla fighters, that at its peak in 1972 numbered some 800 men, with an additional 1000 militia. They were well armed with Soviet supplies, well trained by Soviet and Cuban advisors, and thanks to intensive doctrinal education were highly motivated politically. Since they fought on their own ground and enjoyed the benefits of short communication lines to their supplies in South Yemen, they proved a match for the Sultan's force in Dhofar. Yet on three occasions the PFLOAG attempted unsuccessfully to extend its campaign to northern Oman — in June 1970, December 1972 and October 1974. In August 1974 the Front became the Popular Front for the Liberation of Oman (PFLO). In time British training and leadership of a counter-insurgent force and Iranian troops eliminated guerrilla actions, whilst reformist government on the part of the new and young Sultan Qaboos eliminated the cause for rebellion.

South Yemen

The old order in southern Arabia began to change in September 1962 when revolution broke out in Sanaa (Yemen). It was led by Colonel Sallal, whose army colleagues were influenced by the republican and national-ist ideals of the Egyptian leader Gamal Nasser (1954-70). Some were members of the pan-Arab and Nasserite Movement of Arab Nationalists (MAN). They were successful in the towns, but failed to carry the coun-tryside, where royalist support rallied sufficiently for civil war (1962-70) to account for the deaths of 200,000 people. Outside intervention on both sides, principally from Egypt on behalf of the republicans and from Saudi Arabia for the royalists, contributed to the toll and lengthened the conflict. It also contributed to the launching in October 1963 of a cam-paign against the British in Aden.

After the High Commissioner in Aden had escaped an assassination attempt in December 1963, the British declared a state of emergency and arrested many activists. Despite security force operations, over the next three years terrorist acts accounted for the death of 60 people. Various nationalist organisations were responsible, but it was the National Liberation Front (NLF) that emerged victorious and to whom power was transferred by Britain in November 1967, when the NLF proclaimed the People's Republic of Southern Yemen, which three years later became the People's Democratic Republic of Yemen (PDRY), or South Yemen. That regime, increasingly inclined towards the Soviet bloc, had to con-tend with the subversive activities of two rival political movements in exile supported by Saudi Arabia — the South Arabian League and the Front for the Liberation of Occupied South Yemen (FLOSY).

Bibliography

The most comprehensive and painstaking work on revolution in southern Arabia has been undertaken by Fred Halliday in *Arabia without Sultans* (Penguin, 1979), an indispensable book, but see also Tom Little, *South Arabia* (London, 1968). For a British account of military operations, see Julian Paget, *Last Post: Aden 1964-67* (London, 1969) and for a diplomatic memoir, Sir Humphrey Trevelyan, *The Middle East in Revolu-tion* (London, 1970). Dana Adams Schmidt, the *New York Times* corres-pondent, covered the Yemeni civil war in the north and subsequently wrote *Yemen: The Unknown War* (London, 1968), whilst Edgar O' Ballance summarised the course of events in *The War in the Yemen* (London, 1971).

Front for the Liberation of Occupied South Yemen — FLOSY
(Jabhat al-Tahrir al-Janubi al-Yaman)

FLOSY was created in January 1966, when two Yemeni movements opposed to the British presence in Aden, the Organisation for the Liberation of the Occupied South and the National Front for the Liberation of the Occupied South, fused. Prominent in FLOSY were the exiled notables Abd al-Qawi Makkawi, a former Chief Minister in Aden, and Abdallah al-Asnag, leader of the People's Socialist Party, both of whom operated from Yemen.

FLOSY militated in favour of a nationalist government which would supercede the traditional authority of the local chieftains in south Arabia. It received Egyptian backing, but had few armed militants so that its influence paled before the military successes of the National Liberation Front (NLF) in 1967. FLOSY was nonetheless involved in political violence, being held responsible for the murder in 1966 of a leading communist trade unionist and for the sabotage in January 1967 of a communist press. Clashes between the two nationalist movements occurred in Aden in January, June, September and November 1967, when FLOSY militants were soundly thrashed. Their leaders took no part in the independence talks held in Geneva that year.

Nevertheless, after independence FLOSY claimed the credit for disturbances in South Yemen when in July 1968 the NLF government was threatened by an uprising. Although FLOSY was no longer backed by Egypt, it remained in existence in northern Yemen thanks to Saudi aid. The movement represented traditionalist Arab interests and criticised the pro-Soviet inclinations of the NLF government in the PDRY.

National Democratic Front — NDF
(Jabhat al-Wataniya al-Dimukratiya)

The NDF consisted of opposition elements in North Yemen who were backed by Marxist-inclined South Yemen (PDRY) in its bid to destabilise the north. By so doing, the PDRY sought to further the unification of the traditionalist Yemen Arab Republic with the southern People's Democratic Republic. In early 1979 the Front engaged in military activities on the border of the two Yemens, but after the flare-up it continued to promote the southern interest in the north through clandestine activities and subversive actions in 1980.

National Liberation Front (NLF)
(*Jabhat al-Tahrir al-Qaumia*)

In 1968 the British government handed power to the NLF in Aden, where in 1970 the movement established the People's Democratic Republic of the Yemen (PDRY). Superceding the traditional authority of the sheiks, the NLF was formed as a nationalist front in June 1963 and did not develop until after independence a Marxist-Leninist orientation. Two men played key roles at this stage — Qahtan ash-Shaabi and his cousin, Feisal ash-Shaabi, who published *The Revolutionary* in Aden. From the start, the NLF was determined upon armed struggle and upon mobilising support in the hinterland. The British did not ban the organisation until June 1965.

The first NLF attacks occurred in October 1963 in the mountains of Radfan, and were directed by Ali Antar. They spread to adh-Dhali, to Haushabi and to Dathina-Audhali-Fadhli, where the Front took four years to undermine the authority of the local sheiks and to substitute its own.

The urban campaign was initiated in August 1964, when attacks began on British military installations and officials. Thenceforth NLF actions grew from 36 in 1964, to 286 in 1965, to 510 in 1966 and to some 3000 in 1967. For arms the NLF employed those which the British had previously distributed to the sheiks. Militants lived off the land, closely interwoven with the local population, and easily penetrated the local army and police, whom the authorities soon realised could not be trusted.

In developing the armed struggle NLF leaders read the works of Mao Tse-tung and were influenced by the experience of the Vietnamese. In 1967 NLF members visited China. More important were NLF contacts with Palestinian exiles, particularly George Habbash, through the Movement of Arab Nationalists (MAN) in Beirut.

Organisation for the Liberation of the Occupied South — OLOS
(*Munadamat Tahrir al-Janub al-Arabi al-Mutal*)

The Organisation was set up in May 1965 in Yemen from a fusion of the People's Socialist Party, the South Arabian League and the Committee for the Liberation of Occupied South Yemen. In January 1966 it united with the National Front for the Liberation of the Occupied South (which became the NLF) to form the Front for the Liberation of Occupied South Yemen (FLOSY).

South Arabian League
(Ussbatt al-Janub al-Arabi)

A nationalist movement of the mid-1960s, the South Arabian League disapproved of terrorism, opposed Egyptian influence in the Yemen, opposed continued British presence in Aden and proposed a united state of South Arabia embracing Aden, Yemen and the principalities of the East Aden Protectorate. For a short time League members supported the Front for the Liberation of Occupied South Yemen (FLOSY), when this body was set up in January 1966, but later in the year it withdrew.

League members were not represented at the independence talks in Geneva in 1967, and took no part in the formation of the National Liberation Front (NLF) government, which in 1970 eventually proclaimed the People's Democratic Republic of the Yemen (PDRY).

The League remained in existence in northern Yemen, where armed militants threatened the NLF government in Aden. They relied upon Saudi aid and promoted a moderate social ideology at odds with the overt socialism and Eastern-bloc alignment of the PDRY.

Syria

Political violence in Syria stemmed throughout the 1970s and increasingly in the 1980s from two sources: Islamic fundamentalism and opposition factions of the Baath party supported by Iraq. As in Egypt, the principal fundamentalist drive was provided by a movement known as the Muslim Brotherhood. The Iraqi regime of Saddam Hussein sponsored the National Front for the Liberation of Arab Syria.

Bibliography
A Dutch foreign office researcher, Nikolaos van Dam, wrote an excellently brief although detailed analysis of contemporary Syrian violence in *The Struggle for Power in Syria* (London, 1981).

Muslim Brotherhood
(Majallat al-Ikhwan al-Musalamin)

The Brotherhood, a fundamentalist movement identical to that which operated in Egypt, presented in the early 1980s the principal opposition threat to the Syrian regime of President Assad. Although its characteristics were similar to its Egyptian counterpart, it was an autonomous body led and nurtured locally, and particularly in Hama and Aleppo. There was no established leadership or even membership, but many prominent spokesmen existed, some of whom had fled to Europe. The political violence practised by the movement's supporters included a terrorist campaign of bombings and assassinations against the ruling Alawite community, which undermined confidence generally in the Syrian regime. The Brotherhood's influence lay behind the considerable disturbances experienced in early 1982.

National Front for the Liberation of Arab Syria
(Jabhat Tahrir Suria al-Arabiya)

Just as Syria backed dissident Baathists in Iraq against the government of Saddam Hussein, so Saddam Hussein sponsored dissident Syrian Baathists against the government of the ruling Alawite regime of President Assad. Exiled Akram al-Hourani led the Iraqi-backed Front, but others prominent in the group were the former Syrian president who had been ousted in 1966, General Amin al-Hafiz, a former chief of staff, General Hamud Suwaidani, Shibli al-Aysami and Mahmud al-Shufi.

Turkey

Twice during the decade of the 1970s democratic Turkey was afflicted by political violence serious enough to provoke the Turkish military into restoring order by intervening in the political process. On the first occasion it was sufficient to place some provinces under martial law (1971-73) so that civilian government was never actually replaced, but merely operated in the shadow of military power. On the second occasion (1980) the death toll was so high and the threat to national unity sufficiently apparent that the military suspended all political activity.

The growth of ultra-leftist political violence had much to do with the influence of the May 1968 events in Paris, which electrified Turkish university circles. At the time teaching was undergoing a transformation in the hands of a new Marxist intelligentsia active politically in the Turkish Workers' Party, which from 1965 was represented in the Turkish Assembly. The Revolutionary Youth Federation (*Dev Genç*) provided the network on which organisations like the Turkish People's Liberation Army (TPLA) recruited.

On the right the Idealist clubs motivated some to resist capitalism (Islamic fundamentalism) and others to resist Marxism (populist neo-fascism). The National Salvation Party and the Nationalist Action Party were both reformed at that time to become the political channels for the two currents on the ultra-right.

Towards the end of the decade ideological extremism was killing 1000 people a year, many of them, it is true, murdered by their own fraternity. But, in addition, the Kurdish nationalist movement (8 million) was boosted by events in Iran, where Kurds had succeeded in obtaining a measure of *de facto* independence.

To the Kurdish problem were added the appalling communal clashes in south-eastern Turkey between Sunni and Alevi (Shia) Islamic believers, whose differences had been studiously politicised so that rightist Sunni fought leftist Alevi. Responding to the death of 100 people in Kahramanmaras, the government declared martial law in December 1978. The measure was insufficient to quieten the country — the death toll mounted and national unity was seriously threatened, not least by evidence of support for political violence from abroad. To stem the tide, the military banished all parties when they seized power in September 1980, on the understanding that military rule was temporary and that fresh elections would be held.

Bibliography

A good introduction to modern Turkey was provided by Feroz Ahmed in *The Turkish Experiment in Democracy 1950-75* (London, 1977). More specifically on political violence, see that author's article 'The Turkish Guerrillas: Symptoms of a Deeper Malaise' (*New Middle East*, 55, 1973) and Jacob Landau's fundamental book *Radical Politics in Modern Turkey* (Leiden, 1974). Kenneth Mackenzie wrote two well considered papers, *Turkey after the Storm* and *Turkey under the Generals* (ISC, London, 1974 and 1981), but see also Aydin Yalcin, 'New Trends in Communism in Europe: The Case in Turkey', *Foreign Policy* (Ankara) 7, 1/2 July 1978. On the Kurdish problem, see Richard Sim's *Kurdistan: The Search for Recognition* (ISC, London, 1980). On Turkish terrorism in the early 1970s, see the excellently researched paper by Margaret Krahenbuhl, 'Political Kidnappings in Turkey 1971-72' (Rand Corporation, Santa Monica 1977), which contains an authoritative and succinct introduction. For an analysis of student activism, see J. Szyliowicz, *A Political Analysis of Student Activism: The Turkish Case* (Beverley Hills, California, 1972). The government published its account in Turkish in the *White Book: Turkish Realities and Terrorism* (Ankara, 1973). For the 1970s the student is indebted to Clement Dodd, *Democracy and Development in Turkey* (Beverley, N. Humberside, for Hull University, 1979), which is particularly good for the ultra-right.

Armenian Secret Army for the Liberation of Armenia (ASALA)

ASALA was founded in Beirut in December 1975. It is a clandestine Marxist-Leninist terrorist organisation structured on a cellular basis. The organisation seeks revenge for the one and a half million Armenians massacred in Turkish Armenia in 1915/16 and to have Turkey admit responsibility for the killings. More specifically, ASALA wants an end to what it considers is Turkish discrimination against Armenians by winning official Turkish recognition of the Armenian language and by revenging both the careless and wilful destruction of Armenian architecture and culture. In the long term ASALA seeks to create an independent Armenian state.

ASALA has often adopted a pro-Soviet stance. It describes Soviet Armenia as 'free', and it is conceivable that the USSR favours ASALA so as to destabilise Turkey and weaken NATO. ASALA has certainly received support from ultra-leftist radicals in Western Europe.

Tactically, ASALA chooses to murder Turkish diplomats in Western Europe and North America; by mid-1982 it had murdered 24 Turkish officials abroad and carried out over 100 bombings against Turkish targets in most major European capitals. ASALA was not known to have carried out any attacks in Turkey, until August 1982, but it seemed unlikely that it had many members inside the country.

ASALA's outlook is deeply permeated by vengeance. Not only does it act to avenge the earlier massacre of Armenians, but arrests of its militants by third countries usually spark revenge. When, in October 1980 and June 1981, ASALA militants were arrested by Swiss authorities, ASALA retaliated by carrying out attacks on Swiss targets, using the front names October Movement and 9 June. Other ASALA front names are Justice Commandos for Armenian Genocide and New Armenian Resistance, neither of which appeared to have any independent organisation in the early 1980s.

Federation of Turkish Revolutionary Youth
(Türkiye Devrimci Gençlik Federasyonu — Dev Genç)

Atillâ, an Ankara University student, set up *Dev Genç* in 1969, when the events of May 1968 in Paris had spread like wildfire in Turkish university circles. *Dev Genç* was never much of a formal body, but from its ranks of several hundred thousand youthful idealists sprang recruits to the ultra-leftist urban terrorist groups, such as the Turkish People's Liberation Army. Many *Dev Genç* militants were supporters of the Turkish Workers' Party, which in 1971 was banned for involvement in acts of terrorism.

Under Ertuğrul Kürkçü, Sarp's successor, *Dev Genç* veered towards violent action, and endless ideological debate on the merits of whether to pursue urban or rural actions split the movement into violent and often warring factions. Nevertheless, its influence embraced most Turkish universities, although the ties between one group and another were loose. Still it provided a network of similarly minded activists, who within their own group were often highly disciplined. In principle, members attempted to influence and to lead the industrial working class and the peasants, but with no success. Nor, later on, were they any more successful at penetrating the military, although their attempts probably added weight to the military decision to intervene with martial law in March 1971.

Grey Wolves
(Bozkurtlar)

Colonel Alparslan Türkes, in 1976 Deputy Prime Minister of Turkey, supported the Grey Wolves youth movement, which attracted several thousand enthusiasts, all of whom were dedicated to eradicating Marxist-Leninist influences. Militants adopted a high profile and antagonised the left with bully-boy tactics, heightening tension in university circles, where in 1977 the worst violence occurred. The Grey Wolves operated under the aegis of the Nationalist Action Party until the military intervention in September 1980 put a stop to political terrorism.

They had been set up originally in the late 1960s to counter leftist influence in the universities, embarking upon their first violent action in December 1968 at Ankara University. Whilst adopting the tactics of para-military fascist groups, the training of these commando-style groups included little ideological content beyond an emphasis upon nationalism. In charge of the training camps near Ankara and Izmir were two of Türkes' closest colleagues, Dundar Taser and Rifat Baykal.

Idealist Clubs
(Fikir Kulupler Federasyonu)

The clubs existed in Turkey in the mid-1960s; a loose network of politically concerned students belonged to them.

Marxist-Leninist Armed Propaganda Unit — MLAPU
(Marksist Leninist Propaganda Silahli Birliği)

Turkish students who fled from the military crackdown on terrorism in 1971-73 formed this ultra-leftist group in Paris. Among those prominent was the widow of Mahir Cayan, who had founded the Turkish People's Liberation Front. Trained in the Middle East by Palestinian guerrillas, militants who returned to Turkey in 1979 claimed responsibility for the death of two US servicemen. Subsequently a dozen suspects were arrested. Before the military intervention of September 1980 the MLAPU operated primarily in Istanbul, Izmir and Ankara, where conservative Turkish businessmen were at risk from abduction.

Because of its origins, the MLAPU had contacts with European terrorist groups in Germany and Italy, and because of its training it was hostile towards Israel.

National Salvation Party — NSP
(Milli Selamet Partisi)

On the back of the National Order Party and as an ultra-rightist party that stood for the revival of Islamic values against the corruption of Western materialism, Nacmettin Erbaken founded the NSP in 1972. He had split from the middle-of-the-road Justice Party, calling for 'revolutionary religion'. In 1973 it won 50 seats in the Assembly, in 1977 only 24. The party leader, a former university professor and chairman of the Chamber of Commerce, was held responsible in 1980 by the military for provoking political violence and under martial law faced serious charges in 1981. Less obscurantist than some fundamentalist movements, the NSP tended towards Islamic socialism.

Nationalist Action Party — NAP
(Milliyetçi Hareket Partisi)

An ultra-rightist Turkish party, the NAP acted as a political umbrella for commando-style para-military groups that pursued violent politics in the mid-to-late-1970s. It was founded in 1969 from the Republican Peasants' Nation Party and led by the former Deputy Prime Minister, Alparslan Türkes (b. 1917), an authoritarian colonel who had played a prominent role in bringing about the military revolution of 1960, and whom the military government of 1980 jailed for his part in promoting disturbances. NAP units were involved in the murder of several prominent leftists in 1979 in the larger towns, and in turn were the targets of ultra-leftists. Because of its dislike of communism, the NAP favoured NATO, but was critical of foreign capitalism and indeed banking in general as being destructive of a truly national economy.

Revolutionary Left
(Devrimci Sol — Dev Sol)

This Turkish radical group split in 1978 from Revolutionary Road. Its members attempted to embark upon a campaign of armed action across the country. In the capital it waged a war of assassination on the Nationalist Action Party, and attempted to politicise inhabitants on the city's outskirts.

Revolutionary Road
(Devrimci Yol — Dev Yol)

The group split in 1975 from the Turkish People's Liberation Army (TPLA) over loyalty to the Soviet bloc. For a time the group existed merely as an intellectual splinter until some members, tired of inactivity, set up a further faction known as Revolutionary Left (Dev Sol) in 1978.

Socialist Enlightenment
(Sosyalist Aydinlik)

Socialist Enlightenment was active in the late 1960s in Turkey and particularly in Ankara, where the group published a monthly intellectual magazine of that name. Among those who wrote for it were Mihri Belli, who had been sentenced to prison for his membership of the Communist Party and who preached in favour of a 'national democratic revolution'. Of many ultra-leftist thinkers, Belli had a greater effect than most on radicalising the Turkish left. The group looked forward to bringing about a Marxist-Leninist order with the aid of revolutionary-minded officers. Some followers split in June 1970 to form a still more extreme circle, Revolutionary Proletarian Enlightenment (*Proleter Devrimci Aydinlik*), under Doğu Perinçek, who favoured rural guerrilla activity.

Turkish People's Liberation Army — TPLA
(Türk Halk Kurtuluş Ordusu)

Led by Deniz Gezmiş, former leader of the Union of Revolutionary Students, the TPLA nucleus came from the Middle East Technical University in Ankara, where from the wider *Dev Genç* movement it emerged as a tightly knit clandestine body. Once bent upon armed robbery, the group swiftly progressed in 1969 to professing broader revolutionary ambitions. The Palestinian revolutionary movement provided the TPLA with facilities for training, and with arms.

They were afforded little time to employ them. In February and March 1971 Gezmiş caused an immediate impact internationally by abducting four American servicemen attached to NATO bases, crimes which provoked the military to proclaim martial law. Gezmiş (24) and 17 colleagues were arrested and sentenced to death in October. He was executed the following year.

A political amnesty in 1974 provided the TPLA with the chance to re-emerge in 1975, when it again became active in Ankara and Istanbul in ultra-leftist student circles. By 1976 militants were sufficiently audacious to risk clashes with the military, who to their cost discovered that the TPLA had been armed and trained abroad with the support of the Soviet bloc. They attacked police posts, banks, right-wing newspaper offices and the premises of conservative political parties. By mid-1977, a year in which the death toll from political violence climbed to 260, police announced the arrest of 50 TPLA members.

But the group remained actively involved in the spiralling violence of 1978 and 1979, when as many as 2000 people died from conflict purposefully provoked by the TPLA with Moscow's connivance. It engaged in calculated political assassination, and was particularly hostile to the US, targeting American military personnel. In 1980 military intervention in the political process reduced TPLA activity sharply.

Members of the TPLA came from privileged intellectual backgrounds, normally from Ankara, Izmir or Istanbul and were for the most part in their mid-20s. Women played as prominent a role as men: together they shared an anti-Americanism to which their nationalism rather than doctrinaire leftist politics pricked them, although in later years and with a second generation of recruits the movement practised a more orthodox Marxist-Leninist belief.

Turkish People's Liberation Front — TPLF
(Türk Halk Kurtuluş Cephesi)

Mahir Çayan set up the front to appeal specifically to young people to overturn Turkey's democracy in favour of a Marxist-Leninist order under which Turk and Kurd would oppose imperialism and particularly the US. It was closely linked to the Turkish People's Liberation Party. Their organ was *Liberation: The Magazine of Workers and Peasants*. Çayan's followers were seized by his argument that Turkey had been duped by the West and NATO into fighting a war against the Soviet bloc, in which third world countries like Turkey had no part. Like the Turkish People's Liberation Army, the TPLF received training abroad in Syria, where they adopted the cause of the Palestinians against Israel. In May 1971 they kidnapped and murdered the Israeli Consul General in Istanbul. Çayan was caught, but escaped from jail in November.

Hoping to secure the release of TPLA leader Gezniş, Çayan kidnapped a Canadian and two British NATO technicians in March 1972. But the military, having discovered the terrorists' Black Sea hideout, launched an attack in which Çayan and nine colleagues died. A former president of *Dev Genç*, Ertuğrul Kürkçü, was captured. The hostages had been killed before the shoot-out.

A second action in May — the hijacking to Sofia (Bulgaria) of a Turkish airliner on an internal flight — failed to move the Turkish government to free jailed terrorists. The hijackers released their hostages in return for asylum in Bulgaria. An identical outcome arose from a further hijacking in October.

Afer Çayan's death, the TPLF remained pro-Soviet, and yet originally the group had no central committee, nor indeed was the TPLF a classical Marxist-Leninist party. Structures, it was thought, would emerge in the course of the struggle, as would the leadership. It survived thanks to foreign backing and recidivism: those imprisoned for politically motivated crimes returned on release to the terrorist underground. Most were under 30, some had served in the army, others belonged to the professions. Together they composed an educated middle-class elite motivated by the ideological conviction of the need to pursue urban and rural terrorist actions against the Turkish state.

Like all ideologically motivated terrorist groups, the TPLF suffered from splits, but it survived nonetheless as a vigorous violent faction in the late 1970s. Its activities were curtailed by the military intervention of September 1980.

Turkish Workers' Party — TWP
(Türkiye Işçi Partisi)

Professing socialism, in fact the TWP is a Marxist-Leninist party founded in 1961. In 1965 it was the first such organisation to be represented in the

Turkish Assembly, where it had 14 members. In 1969, following a change in the election law and a split in the party, it was reduced to holding only two seats; in 1971 the government banned the TWP for its part in political violence.

In 1975 it was again legalised, but suffered from the general penalties laid upon all political parties by the military intervention of September 1980. The TWP enjoyed close links in the 1960s with the Federation of Revolutionary Youth, and was led (1962-69) by Mehmet Ali Aybar (b. 1910), who attracted students and young lecturers to join. At the time it supported the establishment of a new Revolutionary Workers' Trade Union (DISK). Mrs Behice Boran (b. 1910), an Ankara University sociology lecturer, later led the TWP into a more determined adoption of Marxist-Leninism until its proscription in 1971. Others close to her included journalist Çetin Altan and economics professor Sadun Aren.

Turkish Workers' Peasant Party — TWPP
(Türkiye Işçi Köylü Partisi)

Backed by China, the party was legally established in 1978 to counter the growing influence of the Soviet Union on the Turkish Marxist-Leninist left.

Union of Turkish Nationalists
(Türkiye Milliyetciler Birliği)

Established in Ankara in 1964 under Nejdet Sançar and Hikmet Tanyu, the Union opened branches, known as hearths or homes, in dozens of towns and villages throughout Turkey. Their purpose was to promote a militant pan-Turkish nationalism. It was not the first, nor indeed the only such organisation, but it was probably the largest. Islam was emphasised as being fundamental to Turkish national militancy; small-town patriotism and hostility towards communism were basic tenets.

SOUTH ASIA

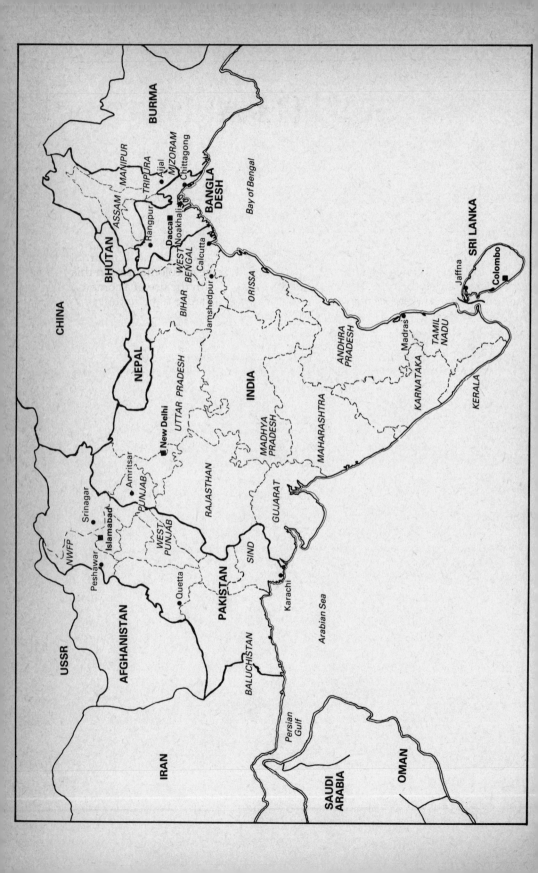

Introduction

The countries of South Asia — Pakistan in the north-west, Bangladesh to the north-east, and India and Sri Lanka to the south, as indeed the smaller Himalayan kingdoms such as Nepal, which do not suffer from political violence, all share the mutilated heritage of colonialism, in this case, largely British. The experience left them with the use of a common language and access to European thought. None had to fight for independence (1947), nor did the introduction of western political philosophy or constitutional models cause political violence. Yet emergence from the colonial era saw the bitterest fighting between Indian Hindus and Muslims, and caused the partition of British India into Muslim Pakistan and predominantly Hindu India.

Many Muslims remained in India but those inhabiting the north-west (Sind, West Punjab, Baluchistan and North West Frontier Province) and the north-east (East Bengal) were fashioned into the state of Pakistan. Fully 1500 miles separated the two parts of the country, which had very different economic and social features. Indeed the only common link was Islam, which proved insufficient to prevent the development of sharp divergences and ultimately separation.

The East Pakistan Bengalis rebelled in 1971 against the artificial capital of Islamabad in the west and, after bitter fighting and thanks to the intervention of the Indian army, won independence as Bangladesh. Conflict left a scar upon the new country, which was unique in the region to suffer as a result of its violent birth from politically violent organisations. Most of these derived from Marxism-Leninism, such as the People's Revolutionary Army, the armed wing of the National Socialist Party.

Since independence in 1971 Bangladesh has maintained a dependence upon its larger southern neighbour, whose political interests are reflected in the outcome of Bangladeshi political turmoil. Twice political leaders have fallen victim to the assassin's bullet. In August 1975 Sheik Mujibar Rahman was murdered with his family in an army coup. Having restored order some months later in a third coup that year, General Ziaur Rahman ruled until he was killed in an attempted coup in 1981, although his own period of power was punctuated by a bloody mutiny (1977) put down at considerable cost in lives, and an attempted coup in June 1980.

Pakistan, since its creation in 1947, has existed in potential and actual conflict with India, which never accepted the partition of a natural geographical and historical entity. Consequently there was war in 1965 and again in 1971 over Bangladesh.

After military defeat in 1971 Zulfikar Ali Bhutto (1928-79) restored the hurt pride of his people and did much to reestablish the country in the eyes of the international community. A military coup in July 1977 overthrew him on charges of corruption and the Chief of Army Staff, General Zia ul Haq, has ruled since in an authoritarian and Islamic manner. Opposition to this state of affairs organised itself around Bhutto's family, who after Bhutto's execution became the centre for opposition through the more liberal Movement for the Restoration of Democracy and the terrorist Al Zulfikar Movement.

India suffers from communal rather than political conflict. Based on the values of caste, language and religion, intercommunal differences often flared into violence in the 1970s and the 1980s, but only rarely entailed political consequences, and even then never at a national level. To an exceptionally high degree, political movement is contained within the political system and even within the ruling Congress party itself. No major terrorist or guerrilla group has emerged, although secessionist ambitions are harboured in Assam and Tripura giving rise to small organisations like the Mizo National Front and the Tripura Sena.

Sri Lanka too is affected by traditional communal tensions. Tamils, originally from the Madras area of India, today form an important ethnic minority on the island, trading, or working on tea plantations. Relations between these Hindu immigrants and native Sinhalese Buddhists are frequently tense. In recent years the notion of separatism has grown in the Tamil community, giving rise to political terrorism from the Liberation Tigers, whose activities exacerbated communal relations.

Bibliography

Overviews of the region are to be found in M. Ayoob, *India, Pakistan and Bangladesh* (New Delhi, 1975) and in two fundamental books by Hugh Tinker, *India and Pakistan, A Political Analysis* (London, 1967) and *South Asia: A Short History* (London, 1966).

Contemporary international conflicts are examined in W.J. Barnds, *India, Pakistan and the Great Powers* (New York, 1972); R. Brines, *The Indo-Pakistan Conflicts* (New York, 1968); G.W. Choudhury, *India, Pakistan, Bangladesh and the Major Powers* (London, 1975); R. Jackson, *South Asia Crisis* (London, 1975); and A. Lamb, *Asian Frontiers: Studies in a Continuing Problem* (London, 1968).

Bangladesh

In 1947, when the British were preparing to give independence to India, a bitter civil war between Hindus and Muslims led to the partition of the Raj. Most Muslims lived in the north-east or in East Bengal, two vast areas which then became the new state of Pakistan. Apart from a shared religion, West and East Pakistan had little in common. Discontent, largely articulated through Mujibur Rahman's Awami League, simmered in East Bengal for many years. Finally, after the League's efforts at negotiations had failed, despite winning an absolute majority in Pakistan's national assembly, the Pakistani military authorities launched a campaign of repression in East Bengal in March 1971. It signalled a national uprising. Freedom Fighters (*Mukti Bahini*) fought the Pakistanis in conventional and guerrilla warfare before winning Bangladeshi independence, thanks to the decisive intervention of Indian armed forces. The province of East Bengal became the new state of Bangladesh.

The war mobilised vast numbers of people and left few parts of Bangladesh unaffected. Powerful populist sentiment led to the emergence of strong left-wing movements which influenced the new Bangladeshi army. Bengali officers and men, who had hitherto spent much of their time repressing tribal and peasant malcontents, found themselves forced to fight alongside such people in the *Mukti Bahini*. They came into contact with members of small Marxist groups seeking not merely independence, but socialist revolution.

The immediate post-independence period proved deeply disillusioning for many leftists, who found Mujibur Rahman's regime (1972-75) corrupt and too pliant to US and Indian interests. Increasingly, leftist groups, spearheaded by the Sharbohara party, took up arms against the government. In 1974, the year of the left, dreadful famine exacerbated the discontent. That year even the ruling Awami League admitted that over 3000 of its officials had been killed by leftist agitators. Meanwhile, the ultra-leftist National Socialist Party (JSD), active in the armed forces since 1971, continued its subversive activity, a process which culminated in the mutiny of 7 November 1975 and the presentation of twelve revolutionary demands. To prevent these being met, General Ziaur Rahman staged a successful coup on 23 November 1975, the third that year. In the following months he presided over a purge which essentially broke the far left for the rest of the decade, although some clandestine activity continued. He himself was murdered in 1981. Since then the military has excluded left-wing factions from government, but has still had to contend with tribal resistance in the Chittagong Hill Tracts.

Bibliography

General introductions to Bangladesh include M. Ayoob, *Bangla Desh. A Struggle for Nationhood* (Delhi, 1971) and A.M. Muhith, *Bangla Desh: Emergence of a Nation* (Dacca, 1978). A partisan background on Bangladeshi nationalism is to be found in Jyoti Sen Gupta, *History of the Freedom Movement in Bangladesh 1943-47* (New Delhi, 1973). The founder of the nation, Sheikh Mujibar Rahman, has published his own account of the country in *Bangladesh My Bangladesh* (New Delhi, 1972). A Pakistani view of the break up of Pakistan is available by A.M.K. Maswami, *Subversion in East Pakistan* (Lahore, 1979), while a good left-wing view of what happened afterwards is to be found in L. Lifschultz, *Bangladesh: The Unfinished Revolution* (London, 1979). Lachman Singh, an Indian general who fought in the 1971 campaign, recounts his experiences in *Victory in Bangladesh* (Dehra Dun, 1981). See also T. Mani Ruzzanan, *The Bangladesh Revolution* (Dacca).

Communist Party of Bangladesh (CPB)

The party sprang from the Communist Party of Pakistan (CPP). After the CPP was banned in 1954, most of its members joined the left-wing National Awami Party (NAP). In 1957 the NAP split into pro-Soviet and pro-Chinese factions. The pro-Soviet faction in East Pakistan (later Bangladesh) fell under the leadership of Muzaffar Ahmed and became NAP (M). The pro-Chinese faction, led by Maulana Bhashani, known as the NAP(B), later split into several Maoist groups.

NAP(M) supported the Awami League during the struggle for independence. It deployed armed units which fought alongside the *Mukti Bahini* against the Pakistani army, but restricted its activities to guerrilla warfare and the disruption of supplies. At the end of the war the NAP (M) became the Communist Party of Bangladesh (CPB).

Although the CPB was represented in the first government of Bangladesh, the party's programme was not easily distinguishable from that of the Awami League and consequently it fared badly in elections. Along with other parties it was banned in 1975, but reemerged in 1977 as a small party without an armed wing. It was banned again in 1977, but resurfaced in 1979.

East Bengal Communist Party (EBCP)

A pro-Chinese party formed in the 1960s under the leadership of Abdul Matin and Alauddin Ahmed, it advocated the independence of East Bengal (later Bangladesh) under the leadership of a worker-peasant alliance. In the event, the leaders hesitated to fight because of Peking's non-committed stand over Bangladesh's war of independence. Regardless, local sections of the EBCP played an important role in the fighting. Ohidul Rahman, the EBCP local head in Rajshahi, recruited over 1000 guerrillas and worked closely with the *Mukti Bahini* (Freedom Fighters). In Pabna too the EBCP was in the forefront of armed resistance. The party was dismantled during General Ziaur Rahman's anti-communist repression of the mid-seventies.

East Bengal Communist Party, Marxist-Leninist (EBCP-ML)

The EBCP (M-L) was formed in 1971 as a result of a split in the East Pakistan Communist Party (Marxist-Leninist). One faction, which retained the old name, led by Abdul Huq, advocated limited collaboration with Pakistan in order to defeat Soviet and Indian expansionism. However, Mohammed Toaha and many of his colleagues found this an untenable position in the context of civil war and broke away to form the EBCP(M-L). It based itself in the Noakhali-Chittagong region and fought against both *Mukti Bahini* and Pakistani armed forces. The party continued a clandestine existence in the early 1980s.

East Bengal Proletarian Party, or East Bengal Workers' Movement
(Purba Bangla Sharbohara — PBSP)

The Sharbohara Party originated as a small group of Marxists in the 1960s, but rose to prominence in the fight for independence in 1971. After independence it reorganised its guerrilla bands and identified the Mujibar Rahman government (1972-75) as its new enemy. Led by Siraj Sikdar, the Sharbohara built up a campaign of attacks on police posts throughout the land. The movement reached its peak during the famine of 1974, when it sometimes broke open government warehouses to distribute food to the hungry. In the spring of that year it won its most distinguished recruit when Lieutenant Colonel M. Ziauddin, the former commander of the important Dacca garrison and a distinguished *Mukti Bahini* senior officer, joined. He had become disillusioned by the corruption and lack of idealism in the independent Bangladesh. In the face of stern repression, the Sharbohara faded in the late 1970s. It was also sometimes known as the East Bengal Workers' Movement.

East Bengal Workers' Movement see East Bengal Proletarian Party

East Pakistan Communist Party, Marxist-Leninist (EPCP-ML)

The party was the main pro-Peking group in East Pakistan prior to the 1971 Bangladeshi war of independence. It split into two wings during the war when Mohammed Toaha broke away to form the East Bengal Communist Party (Marxist-Leninist), which fought against Pakistan. The remaining members of the EPCP-ML, under Abdul Huq, viewed the war as the product of Indian and Soviet expansionism. Accordingly Huq made contact with the Pakistani martial law authorities in East Pakistan, offering support provided the Pakistani army would cease its brutal repression. In the early 1980s the EPCP-ML, still using the name of East Pakistan, continued as an underground urban subversive group.

Mukti Bahini
(Freedom Fighters)

The *Mukti Bahini* was the armed movement which fought for Bangladeshi independence from Pakistan in 1971, when in March the Pakistani crackdown on East Bengal nationalists sparked the rising. *Mukti Bahini* resistance took three forms. First, conventional warfare with Bengali officers was waged by General M.A.G. Osmany, who created two brigades based in the Indian border territories of Assam and Tripura. Second was that of guerrilla resistance exemplified by the commanders Taher and Ziaddin. This group, bitterly opposed to Indian intervention, was furthest to the left. Lastly, a loosely organised guerrilla resistance embracing thousands of civilians operated without a formal command structure, and initiated hundreds of guerrilla attacks on Pakistani forces.

National Socialist Party
(Jatyo Samajtantrik Dal — JSD)

The Maoist JSD grew out of the activities of a small group of intellectuals at Dacca University in the early 1960s who formed the Revolutionary Centre of Bangladesh (*Bangladesh Biplopi Kendra*). The group believed not only in socialism as the solution to East Bengal's problems, but also that a revolutionary war was an essential precondition for achieving socialism. They held that a war of national liberation, involving millions in the struggle for democracy against an authoritarian military regime, would mobilise the masses for socialism. Its members infiltrated the Awami League, hiding their true Maoist identity. Indeed, many of the League's more vociferous members were in fact JSD militants so that when the *Mukti Bahini* took up arms in 1971 the JSD was in the forefront of the liberation struggle.

After independence the JSD founded a committee in October 1972 to prepare for the next stage of socialist agitation. Leading members included Major M.A. Jalil, Bidan Krishna Sen, Shajahan Siraj, Nur Alam Ziku, Abdur Rab, and Sultan Uddin Ahmed. In April 1974 the JSD began publication of *Samyabad* (Communism) and *Larai* (Struggle). In July it founded its armed wing, the People's Revolutionary Army, and at about the same time a clandestine organisation within the army, the Revolutionary Soldiers' Organisation.

Following the right-wing pro-Indian coup of 3 November 1975, the JSD initiated massive agitation against the government, and in the wake of the soldiers' mutiny of 7 November 1975 the JSD's Revolutionary Soldiers' Organisation took over many army barracks. This was to prove the JSD's high tide, for General Ziaur Rahman's counter-coup of 23 November 1975 led to a thorough purge of the army and the banning of the JSD. Thousands were arrested; Major J.A. Jalil, JSD president, was imprisoned, while Colonel Abu Taher, head of the JSD's People's Revolutionary Army, was executed.

People's Revolutionary Army
(Biplopi Gono Bahini — BGB)

As agitation against the Mujib government grew, the National Socialist Party (JSD) secretly formed its armed wing, the BGB, in July 1974. It concentrated upon building up a peasant para-military force to challenge the police and army. At its head was Colonel Abu Taher, a renowned *Mukti Bahini* commander. When General Ziaur Rahman struck against the left after the coup of 23 November 1975, he repressed the BGB and largely dismantled its organisation. Taher himself was arrested, tried and executed at Dacca central jail on 21 July 1976. Taher's death seriously weakened the movement.

Revolutionary Soldiers' Organisation
(Biplopi Shainik Sangstha — BSS)

The Maoist National Socialist Party (JSD) penetrated the Bangladesh Army by infiltrating members of the BSS, which it set up in 1974. Working on the ranks, the organisation radicalised broad sections of the armed forces and so contributed to the Maoist revolution planned by the JSD. It chose to surface two days after the right-wing coup of Brigadier Khaled Musharraf on 3 November 1975, when it issued 12 revolutionary demands. These included the foundation of a people's revolutionary army, whose officers would be selected from the ranks, and the establishment of revolutionary soldiers' councils.

On 7 November 1975 BSS supporters mutinied and found some following in Dacca, Rangpur and Chittagong. It might have succeeded entirely, at least for a while, had not General Ziaur Rahman struck a counter-coup on 23 November. He then carried out a thorough-going purge of the BSS, and had thousands executed. Afterwards, little or nothing was known of its existence.

Shanti Bahini
(Peace Fighters)

Shanti Bahini is a loose collective name for the rebel groups which have operated in the Chittagong Hill Tracts since 1974. Rebel activity centres on the Chakma tribe and the total number of rebels is probably about 2000. One of the *Shanti Bahini*'s better known leaders is a former schoolteacher, Manabendra Lama, whose followers are determined to restore the autonomy of the tribal regions, previously enjoyed under British rule.

The insurgency was partly sparked by the government's development and resettlement drive, which although beneficial has aroused fears among the hill people. *Shanti Bahini* units have accordingly attacked Bangladesh army patrols, police and border security units. The fighting was at its worst in the mid-1970s, when as many as 30 Bangladeshi soldiers might be killed in an ambush.

India

Political violence in contemporary India is largely communal in nature: despite the presence of widespread poverty and unemployment, ideologically motivated violence was comparatively rare in the early 1980s. Yet it was not always so, for India suffered from ultra-leftist terrorism in the late 1960s. Secessionist movements were active, but posed no fundamental threat to the unity of the state.

The Maoist groups, collectively known as Naxalites, which sponsored rural violence in the late 1960s and early 1970s signally failed to win support. Because of the peculiar religious and social context of modern India, no tradition of peasant rebellion existed on which to build. It was the survival of the caste system that ensured that revolutionary solidarity made no headway, whilst Hindu and Buddhist traditions sustained and reinforced stoicism and acceptance of adversity. Faced with failure in the countryside, the Naxalites attempted a terror campaign in Calcutta before being broken by the police (1970-72). Since then factious Naxalite groups such as the Communist Party of India — Marxist-Leninist, the Unity Centre of the Communist Revolution and the Central Organisation Committee, have proliferated, but no longer pose a serious threat.

True, in the remote north-eastern territories where Chinese influence was felt significant guerrilla bands emerged, yet their impact was negligible; only the tiny People's Liberation Army (PLA) took its terror campaign to the capital. Banditry in the northern states remains a problem, but unlike other parts of Asia it never adopted political overtones.

By the late 1970s India's traditional communal violence, springing from the competing values of caste, and from religious or linguistic differences, was increasingly exploited by extremist factions. Groups like the Dalit Panthers encouraged low-caste members to unite and fight for their rights in Gujarat, while *Rashtriya Swayamsevak Sangh* and the *Dal Khalsa* respectively encouraged Hindu violence against Muslims and Sikh violence against Hindus.

Bibliography

P. Spear's *A History of India* (London, 1970) is excellently concise. The hand-over of power and the attendant problems of partition are examined in *Freedom at Midnight* (London, 1975) by L. Collins and D. Lapierre, and in E.W. Lumby, *The Transfer of Power in India* (London, 1954).

Scholarly analyses of the rise of Indian nationalism are available in V.

Mehta, *Mahatma Gandhi and his Apostles* (London, 1977); A. Seal, *The Emergence of Indian Nationalism* (Cambridge, 1967); and B.R. Tomlinson, *The Indian National Congress and the Raj 1929-1942* (London, 1976).

Useful introductions to contemporary Indian political problems can be found in K.P. Karunakaran, *Continuity and Change in Indian Politics: A Study of the Indian National Congress* (New Delhi, 1964), and in the biographies by Z. Masani, *Indira Gandhi: A Biography* (London, 1974) and B. Pandey, *Nehru* (London, 1976). More germane to political violence are two books by A. Shourie published in New Delhi and Bombay *Symptoms of Fascism* and *Institutions of the Janata Phase*, in 1978 and 1980 respectively.

The roots of communal problems are looked at in J.A. Curran's *Militant Hinduism in Indian Politics; A Story of the R.S.S.* (New York, 1951) and Kushwant Singh's *A History of the Sikhs* (London, 1966).

T.J. Nossiter provides an account of communism in a south-Indian state in *Communism in Kerala: A Study in Political Adaptation* (London, 1980). An historical overview of India's leftist movements is found in Satyabrata Rai Chowdhuri's *Leftist Movements in India 1917-1947* (Calcutta, 1976). B. Dasgupta analysed the Naxalites in 'Naxalite Armed Struggles and the Annihilation Campaign in Rural Areas', *Economic and Political Weekly*, 4-6, Bombay, 1973. For contemporary considerations see James Manor's article: 'Party decay and political crisis in India, *Washington Quarterly* Summer 1981, and the papers he edited with W.H. Moris Jones in *Perspectives on Political Violence* (Institute of Commonwealth Studies, London).

Amra Bengali
(We Bengalis)

Linked with the *Anand Marg* sect, *Amra Bengali* was particularly active in communal violence during 1978/79 in Tripura. Immigrant Bengalis had begun to outnumber the local people by the late 1970s, and when the left front took office in the state in January 1978 it sought to restore to the local tribesmen land taken by Bengali immigrants. The immigrants, spearheaded by *Amra Bengali*, fiercely resisted the moves. Many were killed and hundreds of homes burnt.

Anand Marg
(Path of Bliss)

Anand Marg is a quasi-political sect founded in India by Prabhat Ranjan Sarkar, alias Anand Murtiji. Its 1000-odd members seek a new world order, combining with more authoritarian ideas worship of the Hindu goddess of destruction, Kali. It was banned during the Emergency (1975-77), but otherwise operates legally, principally in West Bengal, where the sect's abductions have led to serious clashes with police. The sect has supporters within Indian communities abroad.

Anand Marg's involvement in terrorism began as a result of the life imprisonment of its founder, who had been convicted of murder. Sarkar's followers, intending to secure his release, carried out a series of bombings in 1977 against Indian interests abroad. In February 1978 the Sydney Hilton Hotel (Australia) was bombed and three people killed during a meeting of the Commonwealth Heads of Government. Since then the movement has been relatively inactive in terrorism.

Dal Khalsa

Based in the Punjab, *Dal Khalsa* is a militant Sikh body seeking secession and the establishment of independent Khalistan. It numbers about 200 and was founded in 1979 by Dr Jagjit Singh, former finance minister of the Punjab. As it played a prominent part in serious Sikh-Hindu rioting in April 1982, the government banned it. Trouble had erupted when in a gesture of calculated insult *Dal Khalsa* members deposited cows' heads outside Hindu Temples in Amritsar. The aim had been to incite Hindus to attack Sikhs, in the hope that the Sikhs would thus be driven into the militants' camp. Trouble followed in 20 Punjab towns where Sikhs fought Hindus.

Yet *Dal Khalsa* had first come to international attention in September 1981, when five of its members, armed with knives, seized an Indian Airlines Boeing 737 carrying 111 passengers and six crew on a flight between New Delhi and Srinagar. The hijackers ordered the crew to land at Lahore (Pakistan), where they freed 66 passengers. For the release of the others they demanded freedom for sect leader Jarnail Singh Bhindranwale and all those who had been jailed for agitating on behalf of an independent state of Khalistan. They also demanded $500,000 in cash. The following day the hijackers were overpowered by Pakistani soldiers.

Dalit Panthers

The panthers were a militant lower-caste organisation, which emerged in Gujarat during the 1980 inter-caste rioting. It was partly influenced by the American Black Panther Movement. Members encouraged low-caste harijans to resist attacks from high-caste members, and even fomented violence against them. By encouraging a refusal by the lower castes to accept traditional constraints, panther activity threatens to upset traditional Indian social structures.

Mizo National Front (MNF)

Formed in March 1966, the MNF is a Mizo separatist organisation engaging in fitful guerrilla activity in Mizoram, but also periodically extending

its operations to neighbouring Tripura. Various attempts to arrange
ceasefires have largely failed. The MNF attempts to impose its own levies
on the local population. Those who refuse to pay are raided. Even
policemen have been compelled to pay protection money.

The assassination of three senior police officers in Aijal in January 1975
led to a major security force drive against the MNF. It was partly successful: Lal Mian, an MNF leader, was arrested, along with over 100
colleagues. With more arrests that year, the MNF moved its headquarters
from Southern Mizoram to Chittagong in Bangladesh. At the time the
MNF numbered about 850 guerrillas.

In 1976 the MNF held talks with the government and agreed to work
within the framework of the Indian constitution. Many laid down their
arms. The MNF never recovered its former strength, although it
remained sporadically active attacking police stations and radio trans-
mission centres. The government attempted to renew negotiations, and
on 30 July 1980 the MNF offered to suspend underground activities in
return for a suspension of all military activities against it. In mid-1982 Lal
Denga headed the front.

Naga Federal Army (NFA)

The NFA is a clandestine separatist organisation active in the extreme
north-east of India since the early 1970s. In 1974 a 300-strong NFA
contingent was reported to have crossed to China for training. It has
harassed Assamese settlers in Nagaland, which borders on the Burmese
frontier.

Naga Nationalist Council (NNC)

An illegal but large Naga secessionist movement, the NNC was headed
by Hthungalin Muiva during its most active period in the late 1970s. It
was principally active in attacks on Assamese villages on Naga territory,
which borders on Burma in the extreme north-east of India.

Nagaland Federal Government (NFG)

The NFG was one of several separatist guerrilla movements operating in
Nagaland during the 1970s. It was however seriously damaged in 1975
when a determined counter-insurgency campaign led to the arrest of
Lieutenant Colonel Yonga, an NFG leader, and the location of an NFG
headquarters. Subsequent NFG attacks were carried out under Isaac
Swu. It was one of the larger Naga organisations.

Naxalites

Naxalites is a collective term for extremist Marxist-Leninist factions in India which emerged in the late 1960s and continued actively into the 1980s, although practising a much reduced level of violence.

The Naxalites stemmed from the far left of the Communist movement. The original Communist Party of India had split in 1964, giving rise to the Communist Party — Marxist. When this party participated in government in West Bengal and Kerala in the late 1960s, militants split from it.

Most of these radicals, opposed to parliamentary democracy and admirers of the Maoist model, turned their attention to rural guerrilla warfare. One of the first incidents was in Naxalbari, West Bengal, where ultra-leftists instigated a brief peasant revolt in 1967. From this incident the general term 'Naxalite' was coined to identify all Maoist groups. Of these factions the best known was the Communist Party of India — Marxist-Leninist (CPML) founded in 1969.

In February 1969 most Naxalites declared support for the so-called 'annihilation tactic' and began organising squads to attack the larger landlords. At bottom the Naxalites lacked peasant support, so that police found roving bands of urban terrorists easy to identify and destroy in rural areas.

CPML leader, Charu Mazumdar, unleashed a 'Red Terror' in Calcutta in 1970, murdering policemen, military personnel and 'capitalists'. It proved to be the height of the Naxalite campaign, for police response in 1970-72 decimated the urban movement, which never recovered. In December 1973 the CPML decided to abandon armed revolution in favour of united front tactics. It did not save them. Thousands of Naxalites were detained during the 1975-77 Emergency.

In March 1977 the Janata government Home Minister, Charan Singh, struck a deal with Naxalite leader, Satyanarain Singh, from Bihar. He recommended to state governments that Naxalites who renounced violence should be released. Accordingly, the left-wing governments of Kerala and West Bengal responded quickly by releasing several hundred Naxalites, many of whom had been held for six years without trial.

Within a year Naxalite actions recommenced: eighteen police stations were attacked in April 1978 and two bombs thrown at the Soviet Trade Mission in Calcutta. The occasional terrorist action was committed in the early 1980s by these groups, but they never again constituted an insurgent threat. Their organisations proliferate, although their membership falls. Activity is restricted to West Bengal, Andhra Pradesh, Bihar, Kerala, Tamil Nadu and Assam.

People's Liberation Army (PLA)

Led by Bisawar Singh, the People's Liberation Army conducted a small secessionist guerrilla war in the early 1980s. It was behind much of the student agitation which afflicted Manipur, particuarly in the 1980s, demanding the expulsion of Bangladeshis, Nepalis and Bengalis. Allegedly it enjoyed Chinese support.

In May 1982 the PLA was responsible for planting a number of dyna-mite sticks in a shopping centre in New Delhi, a new tactic which won them increased police attention.

Rashtriya Swayamsevak Sangh — RSS
(National Self-Service Organisation)

A militant Hindu organisation, the RSS was banned during the Emergency in 1975 but reemerged in 1977. Although the RSS briefly sought a more respectable image, it was widely held responsible for fomenting serious Hindu-Muslim clashes in the summer of 1979 in Aligarh and Jamshedpur. It is an adjunct of the Hindu nationalist party, Jan Sangh.

Revolutionary Army of Kuneipak (RAK)

The RAK is a small secessionist guerrilla movement active in Manipur in shootings and ambushes in the early 1980s. It is alleged to have received support from the Chinese in Tibet, but most of its money has been raised by bank robberies, the proceeds of which have been used to purchase arms and ammunition in Thailand.

Revolutionary Government of Manipur (RGM)

The RGM, a miniscule ultra-leftist group, was held responsible for attacks in July and November 1978, in which police were shot dead, weapons stolen, a bank robbed and a police station set ablaze in Manipur.

Revolutionary Youth and Students' Federation

The Federation was a small revolutionary youth movement, influenced by the Naxalites and active in Uttar Pradesh in the late 1970s. It was held responsible for a number of attacks on police stations in 1978. Police action in rural areas uprooted the group.

Pakistan

Ethnic differences form the essential component of most political violence in Pakistan, yet during the 1960s East Bengal (Bangladesh) posed the greatest problem until in 1971 that province, led by the Awami League, won its independence after a bloody civil war. Bangladesh's independence did not end Pakistan's nationality problem. In February 1973 Prime Minister Bhutto, encouraged by the Shah of Iran, who had his own difficulties with Baluch separatists, dismissed the locally elected administration in Baluchistan and imposed centralised rule. A tribal uprising resulted, which continued until 1977; the fighting claimed the lives of at least 3300 soldiers and a further 5300 Baluch guerrillas. A tense peace prevails.

Lacking a deeply rooted national party, Pakistan still faces enormous difficulties that impede the development of national characteristics which might unify the country. On independence from the British Raj in 1947, the original concept had been that Islam alone would unify the disparate peoples and cultures of the new state: Baluch, Bengali, Pathan, Punjabi, Sindhi and others. In practice, it has proved difficult defining the precise role Islam should play in the nation's political life and it is the army which has been the principal unifying force.

Ideologically-motivated terrorist groups are not a problem, but the constant requirement for military regimes to hold the country together has fuelled anti-authoritarian opposition in recent years. In particular, the repressive character of General Zia's regime caused the formation of the Pakistan Liberation Army in 1979 and its successor in 1981, the Al-Zulfikar Movement, which was led by the son of former Prime Minister Bhutto, whom Zia had executed in 1979.

Bibliography

A reliable biography of the founder of the state can be found in H. Bolitho, *Jinnah: Creator of Pakistan* (London, 1954).

The problems and circumstances of partition are amply examined in G.W. Choudhury, *The Last Days of Pakistan* (London, 1974) and K. Dissiqui, *Conflict, Crisis, and War in Pakistan* (London, 1972).

For an insight into contemporary political problems, a consideration of former Prime Minister Bhutto's writings is advisable. These include *The Myth of Independence* (London, 1969); *The Great Tragedy* (Karachi, 1971); *New Directions* (London, 1977). For the break-up see L.F.R. Williams, *Pakistan under Challenge* (London, 1975); several aspects of modern

Pakistan's problems are dealt with most competently in L. Ziring, R. Braibanti and H. Wriggins, *Pakistan: The Long View* (Durham, 1977). For Bhutto's trial, see Victoria Schofield, *Bhutto: Trial and Execution* (London, 1979). On the Baluch problem, see a most excellent account *In Afghanistan's Shadow* (New York, 1981) by Selig Harrison, who interviewed refugees.

Al-Zulfikar Movement

The Al-Zulfikar Movement emerged in early 1981, and is dedicated to the violent overthrow of the regime of General Zia ul-Haq. It was called after the former prime minister, Zulfikar Ali Bhutto, who was executed on 4 April 1979 in Rawalpindi prison (but his name also means 'sword'). His elder son, Murtaza, headed the organisation.

The Al-Zulfikar Movement first claimed responsibility for a bomb attack on 17 February 1981 at Karachi's National stadium as Pope John Paul II was due to say Mass. A fortnight later members hijacked a Pakistani airliner, flying it to Damascus, where over ten days they successfully bargained for the release of 55 detainees back home. The hijacking, which involved a stop-over in Kabul (Afghanistan), suggested support for the Al-Zulfikar Movement from the pro-Soviet Afghan authorities.

Baluch People's Liberation Front — BPLF
(Baluch Awami Azadi Mahaiz)

The Front was set up in 1976 as the *Parari* guerrilla organisation retreated over the Pakistan border into Afghanistan. During the early 1980s it was led by Mir Hazar Ramkhani, who had actively prosecuted the guerrilla insurgency of the mid-1970s in Baluchistan. In essence the Front was socialist-oriented but in tone strongly nationalist, indeed it was through nationalism, the founders believed, that the left would come to power in Pakistan. At that time the Front envisaged either secession or a loosely federated socialist Pakistan. The leaders were scions of wealthy and well-connected leading families, some of whom were not even Baluchs although they had been attracted to armed struggle as a means of effecting revolutionary change. The Front received support from the Kabul government for every member, totalling something in the order of $875,000 a year. Previously, two score Baluchs had received training from the Popular Front for the Liberation of Palestine in Beirut.

By creating the Front the *Pararis* set up an organisation that could more happily accommodate nationalist and ideological motivation, although it still acts more as an umbrella grouping than a unified front. It received encouragement from Afghanistan, where the Front had set up its camps once the security forces in Pakistan had got the measure of the insurgency inside the country. At most no more than 3000 guerrillas were present in Afghanistan during the early 1980s, whilst less than 2000 maintained an armed presence in Baluchistan. A further 3000 members were active in Karachi and elsewhere in Sind. Whilst claiming to be able to mobilise thousands, the leaders admitted to a shortage of weaponry.

The Front is not organised along orthodox Marxist-Leninist lines, but rather follows Régis Debray's model, where combat units serve as the party organisation. By the early 1980s the front had fairly explicitly adopted independence as its goal, and even contemplated a Greater Baluchistan, comprising in addition Baluch regions of Iran and Afghanistan.

Baluch Students' Organisation (BSO)

From the BSO the Baluch People's Liberation Front draws its recruits. It was established in 1967 and grew considerably during the 1973-77 insurgency. By the early 1980s some 25,000 young Baluch had received their political formation through the BSO. The organisation then claimed a membership of some 4,300 students active in 46 chapters, 13 of which were in Sind. A 200-member national council met twice a year and saw to the publication of a monthly newsletter *Girukh* (Lightning), a doctrinal journal *Sangat* (Truth) and a literary magazine *Bam* (Morning Star).

In 1978 the BSO took a firm stand against compromise with the central authorities, and under Razik Bukti (b. 1951) and Habib Jalib (b. 1959) adopted a more radical and pro-Soviet stance. Yet it maintained an ideological independence and distanced itself from the Baluch People's Liberation Front, although Khair Jan Baluch, then BSO president, had organised his own guerrilla group during the 1973-77 insurgency. In the early 1980s, following General Zia's 1979 ban on political activity, small groups were training for guerrilla warfare in the hills.

Baluch Students' Organisation-Awami (BSO-Awami)

The BSO-Awami is a militant dissident faction which in 1972 split from the original BSO, and was reckoned in the early 1980s to enjoy a membership of 2,000 in all major Baluch teaching establishments. It published a newsletter *Pajjar* (Awakening) and a literary journal *Labzank* (Treasure of Language). It unambiguously supported the armed struggle waged by the Baluch People's Liberation Front, although it remained a separate organisation. 'We accept the relevance of armed struggle for the Baluch, but what the Liberation Front is doing is only part of the struggle at this stage. If we find we cannot win our rights in Pakistan, we shall go to the hills and fight for independence.'

Movement for the Restoration of Democracy (MRD)

The MRD was formed in early 1981, following agreement between nine political parties of differing outlook, all of whom agreed on the need to lift martial law, to secure President Zia's resignation, to hold fair and free elections to national and provincial assemblies and to restore the 1973 constitution, which General Zia had suspended in 1977. The component parties included the Pakistan People's Party, the Tehrik-i-Istiqlal, the National Democratic Party, the Jamiat-i-Ulema-Pakistan, the Muslim League, the Kashmir Muslim Conference, the National Liberal Front and the Labourers' and Farmers' Party.

The movement is not in itself a violent faction, but given the limits imposed on political activity by President Zia its pronouncements strongly influence discontented student elements, which incline towards direct action.

Pakistan Liberation Army (PLA)

Murtaza Bhutto, son of the former prime minister who was executed in April 1979, founded the PLA that year, to overthrow President Zia. Its headquarters are in Kabul. The political wing was led by Raja Anwar, a former adviser to Bhutto on student affairs; the military wing was composed largely of former students who received military training from Pakistani army defectors. It began operations inside Pakistan in December 1979, and in the course of 1980 claimed responsibility for numerous acts of terrorism and sabotage.

The PLA passed through a crisis in late 1980 when several of its members were arrested and tried. Furthermore, members were bitterly divided among themselves: Raja Anwar was accused of being a government agent and sentenced to death at a secret trial in Afghanistan in February 1981. At his mother's request, Murtaza Bhutto dissolved the PLA shortly afterwards. However, following talks with Libya's Colonel Gadaffi, he reorganised opposition in the form of *Al-Zulfikar* Movement.

Parari

(A Baluch word meaning a person or a group with grievances that cannot be solved through discussion)

Behind the emergence of the *Parari* lay the initiative of a prominent Baluch leader, Sher Mohammed Marri, who through the admixture of Marxism-Leninism to separatist revolt endeavoured to give Baluch tribal resistance continuity and cohesion. For models his followers looked to China, Algeria, Cuba, and Vietnam.

By mid-1963 the *Pararis* had established a score of camps from

Jhalawan in the south to well north of the Karachi-Quetta railway. Each camp called on the services of local part-time volunteers, who ambushed convoys, sabotaged trains and raided Pakistani military encampments. On rare occasions in the mid-1960s they inflicted losses of up to 200 on the military, for which the local population was severely castigated by General Tikka Khan. Fighting continued sporadically up to 1969, when a ceasefire was negotiated.

Regardless, the *Parari* organisation continued to recruit under Sher Mohammed's deputy, Mir Hazar Ramkhani (b. 1936), whose power was particularly strong in the Marri areas of the north. This force formed the nucleus of the Baluch People's Liberation Front, but not before a further period of intense fighting, during which 178 major recorded encounters with the army took place.

Popular Front for Armed Resistance (PFAR)

PFAR was a Baluch separatist organisation active in the early 1970s. Its support came mainly from the Mengal and Marri tribes. At its height in 1974 it probably disposed of as many as 7000 armed men. Although essentially a tribal movement, some evidence suggested that PFAR members were being politicised by socialist students from college in Quetta and Karachi. PFAR carried out bomb attacks in the cities, including an attack on 2 August 1974 on a meeting addressed by Prime Minister Bhutto.

The authorities steadily gained the upper hand in 1974 and in December felt confident enough to declare an amnesty, which elicited a positive response from hundreds of tribesmen. In 1975 the rebels mounted only one major guerrilla offensive.

World Baluch Organisation (WBO)

Two prominent Baluch tribal leaders cooperated in the establishment of the WBO in February 1981 in London. Both Khair Bux Marri and Ataullah Mengal were determined to unite emigré circles with a view to raising funds in support of Baluch nationalist activity in Pakistan and Iran. The two men had been arrested in 1973 for their anti-state activities, and were only released in 1977.

Sri Lanka (Ceylon)

Sri Lanka, situated off India's southern coast, has always been strongly influenced by India. The island, British in the eighteenth century after a period as a Portuguese and then a Dutch possession, became independent in 1948. Relations between the native Sinhalese Buddhists, who comprise 70 per cent of the population, and the Tamil Hindu community, who live mainly in the north-east, are tense, especially since many Tamils harbour separatist ideas. Violence resulting from these tensions usually takes the form of intercommunal strife, but in the 1970s there was a growing political sentiment among the Tamils favouring the creation of an independent State of Eelam, in the north-east. The Liberation Tigers, a small but dedicated terrorist group, emerged in 1977 to promote this goal.

Politically, much of Sri Lanka's life since independence has been dominated by two families, the Bandaranaikes and the Jayewardenes. Nonetheless, left-wing extremist groups have shown a capacity to recruit, especially in Colombo, where the problems of the urban poor press more heavily. However, even here there seems little prospect of overcoming the fundamental racial divisions of the island. The Liberation Tigers, though Marxist, have no connections with the Sinhalese Marxist groups. Conversely, the Sinhalese Marxist groups, such as the People's Liberation Front (JVP), have made no appeal to the Tamils, whom they regard less as an exploited class than as visible proof of Indian expansionism.

Ideologically motivated groups of the far left have concentrated on urban and industrial agitation since the collapse of the JVP's insurrection of April 1971, which, though briefly successful, was unable to attract wide support and was quickly repressed.

Bibliography

A general introduction is to be found in K.M. De Silva (ed.), *Sri Lanka, A Survey* (London, 1977). Another useful work is E.F.C. Ludowyk, *The Story of Ceylon* (London, 1962).

In looking at the communal problems facing Sri Lanka, the following books are helpful: R.N. Kearney, *Communalism and Language in the Politics of Ceylon* (Durham, USA, 1967); M.D. Raghaven, *Tamil Culture in Ceylon* (Princeton, 1962). See also R. Kearney, 'Language and the Rise of Tamil Separatism' *Asian Survey*, May 1978. On the 1971 revolt see A.C. Alles, *Insurgency* (Trade Exchange, Ceylon, Colombo, 1976).

Liberation Tigers

The Liberation Tigers first emerged in August 1977, when, after attempting to assassinate a moderate Tamil politician regarded as a collaborator with the Sinhalese authorities, they murdered a number of policemen. They are campaigning for an independent state of Eelam in the north of Sri Lanka, where the bulk of the Tamil population lives. Their motivation derives from both a feeling of nationalism and Marxist convictions. They are organised in four groups, based around Jaffna, with a membership of around 100. Recruits come mainly from the student body; members are often well armed and reputed to be well trained. They began their campaign in 1977 by mounting assassination attacks on moderate Tamil politicians regarded as traitors, but latterly they have also robbed banks and shot members of the security forces.

They enjoy safe havens in the predominantly Tamil Indian state of Tamil Nadu, which lies close to Sri Lanka. Generally the Tigers desisted from violence in India itself, but in June 1982 five leading Tigers were arrested in Madras for engaging in gunfights.

People's Liberation Front
(Janatha Vimukthi Peramuna — JVP)

The JVP was founded in 1965 by Rohan Wijerwee, a former student at Moscow's Patrice Lumumba University. Although nominally a Trotskyist party, most JVP members were disaffected former members of the pro-Chinese Communist Party who had come to believe the party leadership was more interested in talk than action. Although the JVP maintained in public that it was committed to achieving socialism through peaceful means, it began in the late 1960s making preparations for an armed insurrection. The JVP sought to appeal to the peasantry, but in fact most of its recruits came from among former students whose career expectations had not been fulfilled.

The insurgency broke out on 5-6 April 1971, when JVP squads of 25-30 militants attacked some 90 police stations, capturing a substantial number of arms and ammunition. The rising, strongest in the south and centre of the island, succeeded in briefly holding two towns and in badly disrupting communications. The security services, initially taken by surprise, recaptured the initiative and by the close of April had broken the insurrection.

The JVP was banned, but after its imprisoned leaders had made assurances that the use of force would henceforth be renounced, it was again legalised in 1977. Its leaders, although sentenced to long terms of imprisonment, were released in October 1977. Since then the JVP has not generally resorted to force, concentrating instead on building an urban structure based largely on the trade unions. True, members of its youth movement were held responsible for bomb attacks on the opposition leader, Mrs Bandaranaike, on 12 August 1981. By 1982 the party had become a marginal factor in Sri Lankan politics, with little trade union support and was generally ostracised, even by the far left, which accused it of nurturing contacts with Moscow.

FAR EAST

(including Oceania)

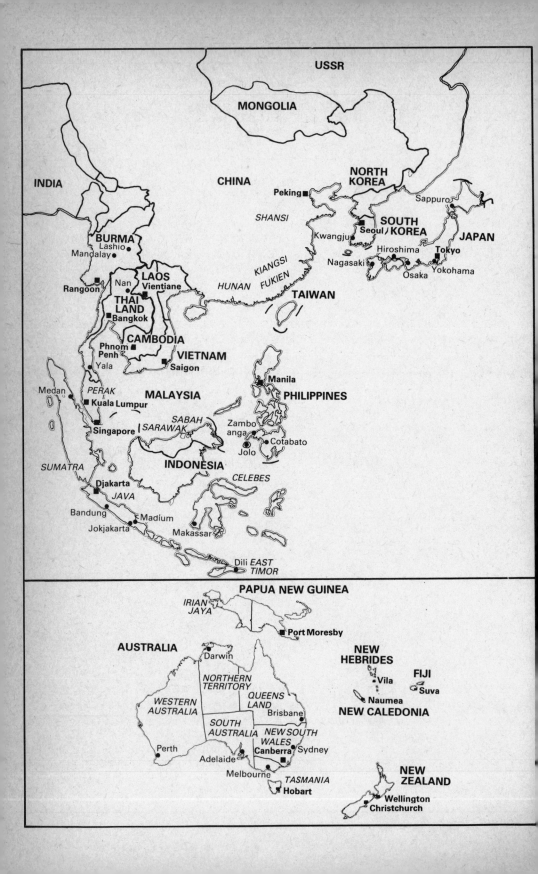

Introduction

Few parts of the globe have been as conflict ridden in modern times as South-East Asia. Firstly, native peoples fought to displace colonial rule, building upon a resurgence of nationalism. Only Thailand in South-East Asia preserved itself from European domination. Elsewhere the French dominated Vietnam, Laos and Cambodia in Indo-China, while the British ruled in Burma, Malaya and North Borneo. European sea power also caused the thousands of islands which form the archipelagos to the south and east of the South China Sea to be dominated by western nations. The Dutch ruled Indonesia from the seventeenth century until the Japanese invasion of 1942. From the sixteenth century Spain ruled the Philippines until displaced by the United States in 1898. After a brief period of Japanese occupation, the Philippines became an independent state in 1946.

The political development of these colonised countries in the early twentieth century was dominated by three factors. The first was the fundamental opposition of the great majority of the region's population to changes which the western economic and administrative strucures were bringing about. The opposition, although largely passive, was marked by occasional outbreaks of revolt. Secondly, the economic conditions of the indigenous peoples deteriorated, a process to some degree caused by the system imposed on them. Lastly, there emerged an intelligentsia educated in the western mould, some of whom absorbed revolutionary ideas deriving from western thought which convinced them that the colonising powers had no intention of granting independence. So it was that the region's nationalists found it easy to identify the European powers with capitalism; and Marxism-Leninism became the most satisfactory revolutionary doctrine for liberation.

This led to the emergence of a strong communist element in the nationalist guerrilla armies. In Vietnam they became paramount. In all these struggles the Soviet Union provided vital moral and logistic support. Paradoxically, in defending itself from the West, South-East Asia and even China opened themselves to Soviet influence.

The destruction of western colonialism in the region also paved the way to a new struggle for power between competing Chinese and Soviet interests. This conflict, brought to the fore in the wake of South Vietnam's collapse in April 1975, was largely fought between China and the USSR's client state, Vietnam. This took the form both of outright war as well as the use of small guerrilla movements. Following Vietnam's

December 1978 invasion of Kampuchea, formerly Cambodia, guerrilla warfare assumed a particularly bitter form, with the Vietnamese troops in the unfamiliar role of garrisoning lands beset by guerrilla activity. The Chinese armed and abetted not only the *Khmer Rouge* in Kampuchea, but mountain tribesmen in Laos and even in Vietnam. The non-communist nations of ASEAN attempted to sustain their interest in the conflict by backing the small anti-communist *Khmer Serei* units in Kampuchea.

Elsewhere, too, the Chinese and Vietnamese vied for control of communist movements. The Chinese, largely because of their strong ethnic presence in most countries of the region, have retained control of the main communist parties in Burma, Thailand and Malaysia. Yet the Vietnamese control a splinter group in Thailand and have made overtures to the Burma Communist Party.

Other problems stem from the region's diversity. Minority Muslim groups in Thailand and the Philippines, such as the Moro National Liberation Front, continue to struggle for increased autonomy as they have since the demands of the modern state first made their impact. The threat they pose is sharpened by an injection of pan-Islamic funds from Libya. Ethnic rebellions remain problems for Indonesia and Burma. Hill tribesmen in Laos and Vietnam and Stone-Age peoples in Irian Jaya (Indonesia) resist government pressures and have repeatedly resorted to armed insurrection.

North-East Asian countries — Japan, Korea and China — with their more homogeneous populations and stable national traditions have been largely free in the post-Second World War period of guerrilla war. China's civil war entered its final period in the late 1940s, ending with the proclamation of a communist state in 1949. Since then the Communist Party's close control of the life of the nation has eliminated violent dissent. Korea, divided in 1945 between a communist north and a pro-western south, nurtured no insurgent or terrorist groups. Outbreaks of violence have occurred, for instance the Kwangju student uprising of May 1980, which, although serious, proved short-lived in the face of massive security force deployment and government restrictions.

Japan has succeeded in preserving social discipline and containing political violence. Opposition to US policies led to the emergence of a small terrorist band, the Red Army, which enjoyed a brief notoriety in the late 1960s before police action uprooted it. Subsequently, extremist political activity has been restricted to exploiting mass campaigns to do with environmental and nuclear issues.

Bibliography

The most authoritative work on the development of communism is J.H. Brimmell's, *Communism in South East Asia*, (London, 1959). M.A. Kennedy's *A History of Communism in East Asia* (New York, 1957) still merits attention. A fascinating account of the transmutation of Marxism in Asian conditions is provided by Hélène d'Encausse and S.R. Schram, *Marxism and Asia* (London, 1969). Ruth McVey examined the role of the

1948 communist conference at Calcutta in fomenting the communist insurrections which swamped South-East Asia shortly afterwards in *The Calcutta Conference and the South East Asian Uprising* (New York, 1958). For rural insurgency in its early stages see E.H. Jacoby, *Agrarian Unrest in Southeast Asia* (New York, 1949). Robert Shaplen wrote a stimulating history of the revolutionary process in Asia in *A Turning Wheel: Three Decades of the Asian Revolution* (New York, 1979). Michael Leifer incisively analysed South-East Asia's conflicts following Vietnam's invasion of Kampuchea in an Adelphi Paper, 'Conflict and Regional Order in South-East Asia,' (IISS, London, 1980).

Burma

On attaining independence from Britain in 1948, Burma adopted the title of Union of Burma, more a matter of form than of substance, for the country was faced with a series of secessionist demands from ethnic minorities. The most important are the Karens, Kachins, Shans, Mons, Chins and Arakanese, although the majority of the population are Burmans. Almost every ethnic minority has taken up arms; some sponsor competing liberation fronts, many engage in banditry and drug trafficking. Behind them loom the forces of the pro-Chinese White Flags — a communist guerrilla force only some 10,000 strong, but which ties down 120,000 government troops in the north-east of the country. The plains, peopled by the Burmans themselves, are relatively quiet.

On the ethnic insurgencies, it is the Karens who present the most formidable challenge. They occupy the long mountainous strip between Burma and Thailand. Shan state harbours numerous rival armed bands, of which the most destructive may be the Shan United Army, in fact more interested in promoting the drug trade than Shan nationalism. Divided, and under pressure from the Burmese Army, the Shans are threatened by the communist White Flag insurgents.

The White Flag pro-Chinese forces are in effective control of the state of Wa, and have concluded alliances with the Kachin Independence Army (KIA) and the Shan States Army (SSA). The White Flag units, with their bases close to the Chinese frontier, whence they draw vital supplies, appear almost indestructible. Yet it is true they have discovered difficulties in reestablishing their power west of the Salween river, an area from which they were ejected in 1975. Following this success, President Ne Win made overtures to the Chinese and in 1977 twice visited Peking. In January 1978, on his first visit abroad since his rehabilitation, Vice-Premier Deng Hsiaoping visited Rangoon. But support for the insurgents continued. The White Flags mounted increasingly effective attacks in 1978/79. One reason was Chinese fear that the Burmese Communist Party would, if rejected, turn for aid to the Vietnamese and thereby fall under the Soviet influence. Rangoon is scarcely in a position to challenge Peking's policies: the proximity of China demands an Asian prudence.

Thailand's attitude to Burma's multifarious insurgencies is ambivalent. Providing the rebels are not communists, Bangkok offers no serious opposition to their use of Thai territory. Karens, Shans, Mons and so-called expatriate supporters of ousted premier U Nu have all found refuge. At the heart of the minority problem lie fears of Burmanisation, with the attendant loss of cultural identity.

The sources of division are historical. A hurried independence in 1948 forced several minorities into a union which they had not sought. During the Second World War the Japanese occupation had provoked the formation of a broad-based resistance — the Anti-Fascist People's Freedom League (AFPFL), which refused to cooperate with the British after the war. Buttressed by its para-military guerrilla units, the AFPFL demanded immediate independence, and was at once brought in to participate in an accelerated programme for the transference of power. But during the negotiations AFPFL leader, Aung San, together with members of the ruling Executive Council, were assassinated. Burmese nationalism had lost its natural leader, but the AFPFL still inherited political power.

Opposed to it was the Burmese Communist Party (BCP), which with White Flag guerrillas initiated a rebellion, which still persists, in March 1948. Shortly afterwards, the AFPFL's military arm, the People's Volunteer Organisation (PVO) split, the dissidents joining the BCP. Next to join the revolt were the Karens, who formed the Karen National Defence Organisation (KNDO), which encouraged a number of Union army soldiers to desert. In 1952 a further complication arose when remnants of Chiang Kai-Shek's Nationalist Chinese Army, fleeing the victorious communist forces, took refuge in Burma.

In dealing with its rebels, the government used a combination of military and civil methods. Numerous amnesties were proclaimed and indeed some demoralised rebels laid down their arms. But territory under insurgent influence nonetheless grew; in 1959 the Shans and Kachins took up arms in pursuit of greater autonomy. The new combined threat forced Prime Minister Nu to turn to General Ne Win, the army chief, to lead a caretaker administration. His methods were often severe and were directed at reducing the influence of the smaller nationalities.

Elections in 1960 brought a reforming faction of the AFPFL under U Nu to power. He hoped to build confidence among the minorities by giving some of their leaders cabinet posts. But in March 1962 General Ne Win seized power, overthrew parliament and arrested the minority leaders. The coup was swift and efficient. The military created its own party, the Burma Socialist Programme Party (BSPP), which still rules the country. The past 20 years have seen an endeavour to transform Burma into a socialist society ruled by a popularly supported but authoritarian government. U Nu initiated a terrorist campaign in Rangoon in 1969.

At first the military rulers exerted real efforts to strengthen ties between the Burmans and the minorities, but to little avail. The threat diminished after 1967, following a major military offensive and a split in the BCP. But neither offensive nor amnesty has settled the problem of insurgency.

Bibliography

Hugh Tinker's *The Union of Burma* (London, 1956) is perhaps the best general survey of politics, economics and society in Burma, covering the period of early independence. Richard Butwell gives an interesting account of an early nationalist in his biography *U Nu of Burma* (Stanford, 1963). In *Burma in the Crucible* (Rangoon, 1951) Maung Maung gives a journalistic account of the rise of the nationalist movement.

Josef Silverstein in *Burma: Military Rule and the Politics of Stagnation* (New York, 1977) provided an excellent account of the course of military government and the fundamental problems which need to be resolved. His *The Dilemma of National Unity* (New York, 1980) is a fascinating study of Burma's problematic diversity. Other useful studies on this question include Hugh Tinker's 'Burma's Northeast Borderland Problems', *Pacific Affairs*, December 1956, and Josef Silverstein, 'Politics in the Shan State: The Question of Secession from the Union of Burma', *Journal of Asian Studies*, November 1958. Sao Saimong Mangrai in *The Shan States and the British Annexation* (New York, 1965) provides a historical context for Shan separatist agitation, while John Badgley in 'Burma's Radical Left: A Study in Failure', *Problems of Communism*, January, 1961 gives an account of the early splits in the communist movement.

Arakan Liberation Front (ALF)

Periodically the Muslim Arakanese have revolted against Rangoon, but in the past never succeeded in forming a cohesive movement which could stand up to the power of the Burmese. It was with this in mind that in 1974 Khaing Mo Lin formed the ALF. His hopes came to nothing: confronted by Burmese security forces, his followers suffered serious losses in the mid-1970s and he himself was killed in June 1977. The movement did not appear to recover, so that nothing was heard of their activities in the 1980s.

Burma Communist Party (BCP)

Founded on 15 August 1939, the BCP joined the nationalist coalition agitating for independence from colonial rule. Following independence, it split from the nationalists in March 1948, whereupon the government outlawed the movement. Since that date the Burmese communists have been in perpetual insurrection. Their guerrilla forces are known as the White Flags, and were estimated in the early 1980s to number some 10,000 men, a figure which made them the most potent insurgent force in Burma.

For more than 20 years the BCP followed Moscow, but in 1962 the pro-Chinese H.N. Ghosthal replaced the Soviet-line Thakin Than Tun as party leader; since then the BCP has remained Peking-oriented. Indeed, in 1982 the party chairman, Thakin Ba Thein Tin, resided in Peking. Other members of the BCP central committee were not publicly known. As befits a party committed to guerrilla warfare, the BCP is organised in military-administrative districts, the most extensive of which is in northern Shan state. BCP forces operate east of the Salween river in the mountainous area bordering China's Yunnan province.

The BCP has made tactical alliances with three non-communist guerrilla groups: the Shan States National Liberation Organisation (SSNLO), the larger Shan States Army (SSA) and the Kachin Independence Organisation (KIO). Despite the nationalist backgrounds of these organisations, the BCP has never acknowledged separatist pretensions.

Guerrilla operations in the mid- to late 1970s reached serious proportions with heavy casualties on both sides from engagements that included battles at Hopong and Kunlong. Since then actions have reverted to ambushes and to traditional raids on police and army posts and the mining of roads. In the early 1980s BCP units were attempting to infiltrate the Burmese lowlands, but without significant success.

Although Peking is seeking to improve its relations with Rangoon, the BCP continues to receive arms from across the border, whence a supply of 120mm mortars, recoilless rifles, assault rifles and mines come. It could prove dangerous for the Chinese to drop their sponsorship of the White Flags, who might turn to the Vietnamese for supplies and change their allegiance to the Soviets. BCP talks with the government in March 1981 failed to produce any accommodation: nor could they, for the aims of the two sides remained diametrically opposed.

Chin National Organisation (CNO)

This small guerrilla group, campaigning in the 1960s and 1970s for Chin autonomy, lacked the advantages of topography and remoteness which helped the Karens and Shans mount more successful campaigns.

Kachin Independence Organisation (KIO)

The most radical of the Kachin separatist groups, the KIO signed an alliance with the Burmese Communist Party (BCP) in 1976. Initially the move was regarded purely as a marriage of convenience because the BCP's long-term objectives do not include secession. Yet in October 1980 it seemed that ideology triumphed over separatism for the KIO forswore independence, committing itself instead to national revolution. In this manner the KIO's guerrilla force, estimated at 1500 men, lay at the disposal of the BCP.

Karen National Liberation Army (KNLA)

South of the Shan states, the KNLA's estimated 4000-strong army controls much of the countryside of seven provinces along the rugged and forested Burma-Thai border. It is relatively well armed, despite the absence of external backers, thanks to an illegal arms market and theft from the Burmese Army, sources which furnish it with rifles, machine guns, mortars and artillery pieces. The movement's ageing leadership, headed by Bo Mya, is largely composed of men who fought with the British against the Japanese occupation.

The KNLA operates an effective tax system: a 5 per cent customs levy is imposed on consumer goods passing through 'liberated' territory. This can be lucrative on the border paths, where daily up to 1000 people pass with rice, cloth, candles, shoes, and kitchen goods, bought at well-provisioned Thai border villages.

The KNLA is dedicated to setting up an autonomous Karen republic. In practice, the KNLA administered a significant area in the 1980s and claimed to have largely eradicated gambling, prostitution, corruption and petty crime. It engaged in traditional guerrilla tactics, but in October 1980 and January 1981 was known to have deployed larger units.

Karen National Union (KNU)

The KNU first became active in 1949 following Burma's independence. Its purpose was to fight for greater autonomy for the Karens. Initially the union cooperated with the New Mon State Party and the Karenni National Progressive Party in an illegal umbrella organisation known as the National Democratic United Front (NDUF). In 1963 the NDUF negotiated with the authorities. The talks collapsed, after which the three factions again drifted apart. Ever since, the KNU has maintained a dogged resistance in the east but without making a substantial impact.

Karenni National Progressive Party (KNPP)

The KNPP was active in the 1950s against the Rangoon government. It was a member of the National Democratic United Front, which also comprises the Karen National Union (KNU) and the New Mon State Party.

National Democratic United Front (NDUF)

Set up in 1949, the NDUF was an illegal coalition of minority guerrilla movements seeking greater autonomy from Rangoon. Its components were the Karen National Union (KNU), the New Mon State Party, and the Karenni National Progressive Party. This coalition allied itself to the Burma Communist Party. Later in the 1950s the NDUF cooperated with the Kachin Independence Army and the Shan State Independence Army. The NDUF negotiated with the Rangoon military government in 1963, but following the collapse of the talks the NDUF fell apart with each unit seeking to achieve its goal independently.

New Mon State Party (MNSP)

The party crystallised in the late 1940s from Mon resistance to the newly-independent Union of Burma. The NMSP had as its goal the winning of greater Mon autonomy from Rangoon. It was a member in the 1950s of the National Democratic United Front (NDUF), which additionally consisted of the Karen National Union and the Karenni National Progressive Party, a coalition loosely allied to the Burma Communist Party. The NMSP fought a fitful guerrilla war during the 1950s and 1960s, but had largely disappeared by the end of the next decade.

Parliamentary Democratic Party (PDP)

Former Prime Minister U Nu set up the party after the establishment of military rule on 2 March 1962. It conducted small-scale guerrilla raids into Burma in the 1960s and for a while even held territory along the Thai border. However the party was increasingly obliged to work from abroad, especially Bangkok, so that it earned the appelation 'expatriate'. It was responsible for some small bomb attacks in Rangoon in 1976 and 1977.

Shan State Army (SSA)

The SSA is Burma's largest ethnic rebel group, deploying some 8000 guerrillas, some 3500 of them well armed. It dates from the 1957 Shan rebellion, in which many groups were active. Most notable was the Shan National Army (SNA), from which a nucleus of 90 joined 140 Shan deserters from the Burmese Army to form the Shan State Independence Army (SSIA) in 1959. Until his death in 1964, this army was headed by Pi Sai Luang, when it changed its name to the SSA.

It consists of four brigades of three battalions. Its forces are principally concentrated on the Thai border east of the river Salween, but they are known to patrol as far north as the government-held towns of Mong Pan and Nam Sang. It also has units well to the east towards Keng Tung, where the Burmese Communist Party is active; and north of the Mandalay-Lashio line, where its most distant units draw on support from the Wa population.

Their presence in this area caused strained relations with the BCP, upon which it has depended for weapons since the war in Vietnam ended. The equipment includes drum-fed Chinese light machine guns, AK47 automatic rifles, B40 rocket grenades and Chinese-made recoilless rifles. To maintain this supply, the SSA, although not communist, co-operated increasingly with the BCP, particularly in the east.

By the mid-1970s the BCP had attained a degree of influence in the SSA controlled area in southern Wa state on the Chinese border, an enclave approximately 30 miles wide and about 50 miles long. Resenting this interference the SSA broke its links with the BCP in 1977, but finding itself short of arms settled for a compromise whereby the BCP was permitted to use the enclave as a staging post in exchange for continued supplies. The seeds of future discord are present, for while the SSA fights a nationalist struggle, the BCP fights for the conquest of power in Rangoon.

Shan United Army (SUA)

The name is misleading. Most of the 2000 SUA members are not Shans, but ethnic Chinese, who follow a notorious narcotics warlord, Chan Shee-fu, alias Khun Sa. The SUA's sole function in the 1980s was smuggling narcotics and jade out of Burma and smuggling in consumer goods.

Since 1973 the SUA controlled a stretch of north-west Thailand, where Bangkok tolerated its presence because it served to counter Thai communist influence in the area. However in January 1982 the Thai Border Patrol Police reinforced army units and launched an offensive against the SUA near Chiang Rai. The SUA was dislodged from most of its base areas; the government renamed the town of Ban Hi Taek, Ban Therd Thai to mark its recapture.

It was hoped the attack would disrupt the opium trade, of great concern to the United States, which had prompted the offensive. However, militarily the SUA remained largely intact and was believed to have withdrawn across the Thai border.

Shan United Revolutionary Army (SURA)

A small ethnic-based rebel group, the SURA is active along the Thai border in Burma and is involved in the opium trade. Its operations have more in common with banditry than with genuine secessionist aspirations of a political nature.

United Pa-O Organisation

A small ethnic rebel movement, the United Pa-O Organisation operates on the borders of the Shan and Karen states, west of Mong Mah. It claims 300 regular soldiers and an armed militia of 500 men. It is pro-communist and operates alongside the BCP, particularly with the BCP's 683rd Brigade.

China

Today political violence is comparatively rare in China and there are no active violent factions. That this is so is largely due to the Chinese Communist Party (CCP), which since coming to power in 1949 has succeeded in controlling the population to the point of monopolising all political and social movement.

A tradition of peasant unrest, crumbling monarchical authority, and persistent foreign encroachments gave rise to a period of profound social dislocation in the wake of the downfall of the Manchus in 1911. Central power had rarely been so weak in China's history so that effective power passed to provincial military generals, who, because of their persistent feuds, were better known as warlords. Pillaging warlords, rising rents, and natural disaster contributed to growing misery and restlessness in the countryside. Young peasants took to banditry or to the formation of secret societies to defend their local interests. Revolutionary groups proliferated.

In 1921 the CCP was founded and its influence quickly spread to the cities, attracting support from students. After a long period of civil war (1927 49), compounded by the Sino-Japanese War and occupation of 1936-45, the CCP emerged triumphant over the Nationalist (*Kuomintang*) government. On 1 October 1949 the communists proclaimed the People's Republic of China and the Nationalists, under Chiang Kai-Shek, withdrew to Taiwan (Formosa).

On its victory, the CCP rapidly effected its political programme, which was aimed at mobilising and controlling the entire population. The emphasis on rural control established peace in the countryside. So far as is known, and very little news came out of the Chinese interior until the late 1970s, the only disorders were those actually sponsored by Mao Tse-tung in the 1960s, when the CCP Chairman mobilised young people as Red Guards to purge officials hostile to his policies.

Bibliography

Lucien Bianco's *Origins of the Chinese Revolution 1915-1949* (Stanford, 1972) provides an introduction to contemporary China. *Mao and the Chinese Revolution* (London, 1965) by J. Chen is an account of the revolutionary progress up to the Cultural Revolution. That period is examined in Jurgen Domes, *China after the Cultural Revolution* (London, 1977) and in the left-wing analysis offered by K.H.Fan, *The Chinese Cultural Revolution* (London, 1967). Roxane Witke in *Comrade Chiang Ching* (Boston, 1977) analyses the more radical implications of the cultural revolution in a biography of one of the most important personalities. J.B. Starr, *Continuing the Revolution: The Political Thought of Mao* (Princeton, 1979) looks at Mao's more challenging concepts. Paul J. Hiniker studies the opposition to the application of those ideas in *Revolutionary Ideology and Chinese Reality: Dissonance under Mao* (Beverly Hills, 1977). P.R. Moody's *Opposition and Dissent in Contemporary China* (Stanford, 1977) provides instructive reading.

Chinese Communist Party (CCP)

The CCP, founded in 1921, spread quickly in the cities and among students. Initially it placed its faith in urban insurrection, but when this was put down in 1927 it turned its attention to the peasantry. Mao Tse-tung (1893-1976), head of the CCP's peasant department, was foremost in urging rural struggle. From August 1927 to October 1934 Mao and his chief military commanders, Chu-Teh and Peng Teh-Huai, organised the first communist revolutionary bases in the Hunan-Kiangsi-Fukien area. In January 1935 Mao was elected chairman of the Military Affairs Committee, thereby effectively becoming head of the party. During this time the communists gradually developed guerrilla warfare in the Kiangsi area.

Short of arms, supplies and recruits, Mao made use of ideology to inspire a younger generation. In the early days communist experience of guerrilla warfare was frequently negative so that many commanders regarded it as a defeatist strategy. Only after the Red Army's massive defeat at Kuangch'ang in April 1934 were guerrilla tactics widely used, but preference to guerrilla warfare was only given after the Japanese invasion of September 1937. Thenceforth Mao sought the establishment of Red Areas in the countryside in which the Red Army could be nurtured and the cities ultimately encircled.

The years of hardship and military defeat became legendary. On 16 October 1934 some 100,000 men and women set out on what became known as the Long March. For twelve months the communists were pursued and harassed by enemy troops and bombing aircraft; they crossed 18 mountain ranges, 24 rivers and took 62 cities. They covered a distance of 6000 miles before arriving in Shansi. The epic nature of the Long March has tended to obscure the fact that it was not a victory but a massive retreat. Nonetheless, during the March the communists steeled themselves to face hardships. Yenan became the distant capital of communism, where the Red Army reorganised and consolidated its political base. The *Kuomintang* (Nationalists), having lost most major cities and lines of communication, and bearing the brunt of Japanese attacks, was reduced to restricting communist activities in areas under its control.

Mao, with 40,000 troops, then brought his guerrilla theory to bear on the occupying Japanese. He distinguished between 'zone' and 'base' areas. A guerrilla zone became a base area only after the enemy had been routed, the masses involved in political activity and control established. The base area served to launch further attacks on other areas. Geographical factors were held to be important in the selection of base areas, mountains being preferred to plains. However, Japanese forces were so stretched it was even possible to utilise the plains. In fact, although the communists subsequently stressed their military activity against the Japanese, their military impact was marginal. Japanese troops in China were not defeated by the communists: the events which led to the Japanese surrender in 1945 occurred at home, in the holocausts of Nagasaki and Hiroshima.

Yet in undermining *Kuomintang* influence, Japanese occupation paved the way for the communists' ultimate success. The CCP rallied the peasantry in a patriotic war and in contrast to the *Kuomintang* presented itself as a party of the poor. From 1945, in holding out regeneration, the CCP simply offered more.

CCP negotiations with the *Kuomintang* continued until 1947, when civil war erupted. The fighting largely consisted of conventional warfare. By the end of 1948 the CCP's Red Army had inflicted serious defeats on the *Kuomintang*. A year later, on 1 October 1949, Mao proclaimed the People's Republic of China. Thenceforth the party cooperated with the Communist Party of the Soviet Union until the Sino-Soviet split, after which around the world it promoted splinter communist movements hostile to Moscow and militantly subversive of local non-communist governments.

Kuomintang
(Nationalists)

Sun Yat-Sen (1866-1925) founded the Nationalist movement towards the end of the nineteenth century and contributed greatly towards the growth of Republican sentiment in China. For years he worked upon the Chinese community abroad, particularly in Japan, organising a party that infiltrated the young officer class in the new model army. The party played an important role in the turbulence of the early twentieth century but never dominated events. Its centre of power was Canton, Sun's home town.

After Sun's death the Nationalists were led by their army commander, Chiang Kai-Shek (1887-1975), who, using Canton as a base, conquered the middle Yangtze region in 1926-27 from the southern warlords. In Shanghai he massacred the communists, with whom he had previously allied to fight the warlords. Military success against the warlords brought international recognition of Chang's *Kuomintang* government in 1929. Thenceforth the *Kuomintang* fought on two fronts — against Japanese encroachments, which culminated in invasion in 1937, and against communist subversion.

The *Kuomintang* armies failed to stop the Japanese, who withdrew in 1945 leaving Chiang Kai-Shek to fight the communists, who had set up an administration in the north. A three-year civil war followed in which the *Kuomintang* were beaten, largely as a result of their own indiscipline and corruption. In 1949 the remnants of this force retreated to Formosa (Taiwan), where, under US protection, they set up a government.

Red Guards

The Red Guards was the collective name for young leftist radicals who participated in the violent upheavals accompanying the Cultural Revolution (1966-67) in China. The Chinese Communist Party Chairman, Mao Tse-tung, risked losing control to rightist elements in the party, most notably Head of State, Lin Shao-chi and CCP Secretary General Teng Hsiao-ping. To reestablish his authority Mao declared that the Communist Party itself had become counter-revolutionary. Working through the armed forces and young people, he overturned the party bureaucracy and remained in control until his death in 1976. In their intimidation of rightist elements, the Red Guards operated independently and outside the constraints of law and order, as Mao's instrument to purge the party.

They came mainly from the high-school fraternity, aged 14 to 18 years, and were directed by one of three national organisations — the Communist Party's Youth League, the armed forces, especially the General Political Department, and the newly constituted Cultural Revolution Group. With free travel, young people from the provinces flocked to Peking for mass meetings in Tien An-Men Square. Before summer ended in 1966 11 million young people had visited the capital. These 'Red Guards' were instructed on their return to break the power of the local party apparatus, and to stimulate support for the changes among the rest of the population. Excesses were committed. Attacks on the Rector of Wuhan University, one of the CCP founding members, led to his death. In Canton Red Guards are believed to have caused the death of 100 people and the injuring of 1000. At the airport the security head-quarters was blown up killing those within.

In January 1967 Lin Piao, defence minister, described China as in a state of civil war. Such disorders continued throughout 1968, but once they had served their purpose, which was to lay the basis for the holding of the party's Ninth Congress in 1969, they were disbanded. The Red Guards served as a revolutionary model for many young leftists throughout the world.

Indonesia

Political terrorism afflicts Indonesia only marginally. Ever since the 1965 left-wing coup attempt by the Thirty September Movement President Suharto's New Order, with the backing of the military, has prevented the reemergence of significant leftist armed groups. Comparative stability was disturbed only by residual conflict arising from the disparate nature of the country's regions.

Comprising over 13,000 islands, which vary in size and character, it is hardly surprising that the new nation finds it hard to weld different traditions into a single loyalty. Rather naturally, political violence has arisen more markedly in those territories seized after independence by the Indonesians themselves. Irian Jaya — West New Guinea, although administered by the Dutch, was always characteristically distinguished from the Malay islands. Ethnically largely Melanesian, and often Stone-Age in culture, the people of Irian Jaya have not all adapted to the Indonesian administration established in 1963. For many years the Free Papua Movement has managed to sustain a small guerrilla campaign.

Similarly, East Timor, for centuries a Portuguese possession, is strikingly different. Fearful of Marxist influence in the archipelago, the Indonesians annexed the territory in December 1975. But Fretilin guerrillas have persisted in waging a low-level campaign.

Elsewhere, older regional traditions remain potential sources of unrest. Aceh, the northernmost tip of Sumatra, has always displayed an Islamic intensity coupled with a propensity to revolt. The Dutch fought a long war to conquer the area, declaring it annexed in 1874, but until 1912 Acehenese resistance continued. Further disturbances broke out in the early 1950s; in the 1980s the Free Aceh Movement carried the torch of rebellion.

Because of their large Christian community, the Moluccas enjoy a distinct homogeneity. Their people played an important role in the Dutch colonial army so that even today to the Indonesian authorities their allegiance is suspect. Furthermore, in the Ambonese community Dutch is widely spoken. An expatriate Moluccan Nationalist Movement (RMS) cherishes the vision of Moluccan independence, but on the islands themselves there have been no reports of attacks.

The government frequently cites the Indonesian Communist Party (PKI) as a dangerous source of political violence, but it seems to be a spent force. Since the party's involvement in the so-called Gestapu coup attempt of 30 September 1965, when General Suharto cracked the party apparatus, it has not recovered. Complete figures are not known, but it seems as if as many as half a million people lost their lives in the blood-bath. Hard-core communists were simply eliminated. True, in 1968 the South Blitar area of East Java witnessed a desultory PKI attempt to renew armed struggle, but the military soon scotched it. The PKI then split into a Moscow oriented PKI — Marxist-Leninist, and a Peking-oriented Delegation of the Central Committee (PKI-D).

Fitful guerrilla insurgency has affected Kalimantan since then, but the communists never succeeded in establishing a wide network. The government blamed PKI activity for many of the troubles arising from economic grievances. Some involvement there was. Train accidents in Jogjakarta were attributed to PKI saboteurs, incidents of arson in Jakarta's commercial quarter were highly suspect, and in 1972 in Makassar, south Celebes, the main power station was sabotaged.

Whilst the communist movement itself might not have posed a substantial threat to the government during the 1970s, the question of detainees remained highly controversial. In the wake of the Gestapu coup attempt, as many as 150,000 people were detained, and tens of thousands still awaited trial in 1979. Most had been released by 1982, but the wholesale response to insurgency left wounds in Indonesian society.

In recent years, particularly since the overthrow of the Shah of Iran (1979), concern has centred on the activities of Islamic fundamentalists. Indonesia is 90 per cent Muslim, yet only small groups of fundamentalists bent upon violence have surfaced.

Bibliography

General introductions to Indonesia can be found in M. Caldwell, *Indonesia* (Oxford, 1968), B. Grant, *Indonesia* (London, 1967), and B. Dahm, *History of Indonesia in the Twentieth Century* (London, 1971). *Sukarno — A Political Biography* (London, 1972) by J.D. Legge is probably the most objective biography of Sukarno. Harold Crouch's *The Army and Politics in Indonesia* (New York, 1978) is a masterly account of the army's role since independence.

The fullest account of Indonesia's fight for independence is George Kahin's *Nationalism and Revolution in Indonesia* (New York, 1952). Also worth consulting is B. Dahm's *Sukarno and the Struggle for Indonesian Independence* (New York, 1969). From these experiences the Indonesian Defence Minister, General Abdul Haris Nasution, wrote *Fundamentals of Guerrilla Warfare* (London, 1965). A close look at the Indonesian independence struggle in Java is provided by B.R. Anderson, *Java in a time of Revolution: Occupation and Reistance 1944-46* (New York, 1972).

The events of the 1965 coup are examined in B.R. Anderson and R.T. McVey, *A Preliminary Analysis of the October 1 Coup in Indonesia* (New York, 1971) and in D. Hinday, 'Indonesian Politics 1965-67: The September 30 Movement and the fall of Sukarno', *The World Today*, August 1968, pp. 345-50. A somewhat left-wing but well argued interpretation is provided by Brian May, *The Indonesian Tragedy* (London, 1978).

The two best works on Indonesian communism are probably in J.M. van den Kroef's, *The Communist Party of Indonesia* (Vancouver, 1965) and Arnold C. Brackman's *Indonesian Communism* (New York, 1963).

Few books are available on Indonesia's regional problems, but two which are worthwhile are B. Nicol, *The Stillborn Nation* (1979) and the left-wing *West Irian and Jakarta Imperialism* (London, 1979) by K. Lagerberg. For the problem of East Timor see *An Art of Genocide: Indonesia's Invasion of East Timor* (London, 1979) by Arnold Kohen and John Taylor and published by Tapol, which campaigns on behalf of Indonesian political prisoners. See also Helen Hill's *The Timor Story* (Melbourne, 1976), Jill Jolliffe's *East Timor, Nationalism and Colonialism* (University of Queensland Press, 1978) and J.S. Dunn, *Notes on the Current Situation in East Timor* (Parliament of Australia Legislative Research Service, March, 1979).

Communist Party of Indonesia
(Partai Komunis Indonesia — PKI)

Although Dutch Marxist-Leninists founded the PKI in 1920, making it the oldest Asian communist party, Indonesians soon assumed the leadership. Party activity was directed against the colonial regime, and in 1926/27 militants attempted to stage uprisings in west Java and West Sumatra. The Dutch authorities imprisoned several hundred party cadres and banned the organisation.

With liberation from the Japanese in 1945, the PKI was legalised. Initially it was well represented in the country's parliament and even held positions in several cabinets. Yet it persisted in non-democratic practices, established a number of armed groups, and in September 1948 for the second time attempted to seize power. Again the rising, in Madium, East Java, was put down.

Dutch recognition of Indonesia's independence in December 1949 afforded the party an opportunity to rebuild its structures. In the first parliamentary elections held in 1955 the PKI won 16 per cent of the vote, but in a short while became the most numerous communist party outside the communist bloc. It boasted three million members and enjoyed additional support from tens of thousands of trade unionists, peasants, and supporters in youth and women's fronts. Still more beneficial to it was the sympathy of the President, who sought and found support in the party for his ultra-nationalist policies against Western business interests. The party's mistake was to ignore the fierce anti-communist sentiment of the armed forces.

Yet again leading PKI personalities associated themselves with a third coup plot, the Thirtieth September Movement, better known as Gestapu (*Gerakan September Tiga Puluh*). Fears of an impending army coup, concern over President Sukarno's poor health, and Chinese communist encouragements were all factors which helped determine the party's role, when on the evening of 30 September 1965 dissident left-wing military officers attempted to seize power in Jakarta. The initial stages of the coup went well for the rebels (six army generals were murdered), but within two days loyal army units under the command of the comparatively unknown General Suharto retook the capital. For several weeks rebellious units and the PKI fought on in central Java. But in rural areas anti-communist bands of Muslim youths conducted a savage counter-revolutionary retribution, killing hundreds of thousands of communists and suspected sympathisers. Having restored order, Generals Suharto and Nasution banned the PKI in March 1966. In July the propagation and discussion of Marxism-Leninism was prohibited. The following year Suharto assumed the remaining vestiges of authority still nominally attaching to the discredited President Sukarno. Since then a visceral anti-communism has remained a constant featuer of Suharto's New Order.

The party split into two factions, the dominant one led from Peking by Jusuf Adjitorop, one politburo member who escaped the 1965 holocaust. Known as the Delegation of the Central Committee of the PKI, the group may have 200 members, yet were the political context in which it operates to change, the party would doubtless reemerge. The pro-Moscow faction is still smaller and resides in Eastern Europe.

Delegation of the Central Committee of the PKI

Following the Indonesian Communist Party's disastrous involvement in the attempted coup of September 1965, the PKI split into Soviet- and Chinese-oriented factions. The larger grouping was led by Jusuf Adjitorop who followed the Peking line: it was known as the PKI — Delegation. When this rump came to reassess its position, it blamed its failure on over-reliance on President Sukarno and determined in the future to place emphasis on armed struggle in the countryside. In practice it had no impact inside Indonesia. By the late 1970s the party had reverted to calling itself the PKI.

Democratic Union of Timor
(União Democrática de Timor — UDT)

The UDT emerged in 1974 as the Portuguese colonial government in Lisbon collapsed. Led by López da Cruz and Costa Mousinho, the mayor of Dili, Timor's capital, the UDT envisaged eventual independence but hoped to retain Timor's historic links with Porgugal. Essentially it represented those professional, merchant and tribal interests that lived well under Portuguese rule.

Fearful of the new influence which sprang to life in the wake of the Lisbon revolution, the UDT, which had worked with leftist forces in the rival Fretilin movement, staged a coup in August 1975. Its forces seized the police headquarters, the radio station and the airport. Thus strengthened, the UDT demanded immediate independence from Portugal. This action was undoubtedly determined by the earlier and unsuccessful preparations in March, when Fretilin had planned to take over the government in the absence of the Portuguese governor.

Fighting ensued between the UDT, allied with APODETI, and the Marxist supporters of Fretilin. Despite evidence of Indonesian backing for the UDT, Fretilin proved the stronger force on the streets, so much so that to preempt Fretilin's coming to power Indonesia invaded in December 1975.

Free Aceh Movement
(Gerakin Aceh Merdeka)

Based on the historic centre of Muslim resistance to Dutch colonial rule, the Free Aceh Movement, founded in 1976, feeds off a deep-rooted tradition of rebellion. The movement waged a small-scale secessionist terrorist campaign. Its most notable action was an attack in August 1978 on the Arun natural gas field, which caused the death of an American construction worker. In fact, the area around Mount Trusex was held to be its main centre of operations. In 1980 the security services claimed to have killed the movement's leader, Hasan de Toro; since then there have been few reports of rebel activity.

Free Papua Movement
(Organisasi Papua Merdek — OPM)

In 1975 the state of Papua New Guinea was set up, allowing the OPM separatists on the Indonesian side of the island of Papua a haven. Thenceforth they were free to launch raids over the border into Irian Jaya. Although claiming more, the OPM probably disposed of some 500 poorly equipped men, moved by a fairly elementary Melanesian nationalism with an admixture of socialism. Internationally it sought to identify its cause with the advancement of negroid peoples generally. Under the name of the Republic of West Papua, it established an information office in Senegal, and found a sympathetic ear in Ghana and Upper Volta.

As the movement grew it split in two. Yacob Prai's group proved the more ideological, maintaining that 'without socialism there could be no independence'. His rival, Zeth Rumkoren, accused Prai of favouring Marxism-Leninism and alleged he enjoyed links with the Australian Communist Party. In fact, Prai enjoyed the advantage of coming from a family of traditional tribal leaders. This enabled him to draw support from the border villges, particularly Hufi, Holomba, Iafar, Kambriap, Nugguf, Pigi, Sekotiau, Sram and Tagos.

On 16 May 1978 the OPM seized seven prominent Indonesian hostages, including two local military commanders and the chairman of the

Irian Jaya Provincial Parliament. All were later released unharmed.

Thanks to pressure from Indonesia, in April 1978 both Prai and Rumkoren were called to Port Moresby, Papua New Guinea's capital, to
discuss with the country's political leaders the question of havens. The
Indonesian separatists were warned that unless OPM bases were dismantled they would be razed. Prai was subsequently imprisoned as an
illegal immigrant. But in February 1979 he and his colleague Otto On-
dawame, together with two other senior OPM representatives were
deported to Sweden, where they were given political asylum.

Subsequently much of the OPM impetus was lost. Yet the movement
did not die. In mid-October 1981 militants attacked a lumber firm and
abducted 50 employees, and the Abepura prison in the provincial capital
of Jayapura. The OPM is also known to have carried out attacks on
aircraft at Sentani airport some 28 miles north of Jayapura. It is unlikely
however that OPM will ever be more than an irritant to the Indonesian
government.

Holy War Commando
(Komando Jihad)

As its name implies, Holy War is a militant Indonesian Muslim grouping
that emerged in 1976, when activists exploded a series of bombs in
Medan, northern Sumatra. It was believed to have approached Libya's
leader, Colonel Gadaffi, for support; the evidence was strong enough to
lead President Suharto to break diplomatic relations.

In April 1979 the security forces arrested the group's leader, Warman,
and charged him with murder. Subsequently Holy War was held responsible for the hijacking on 28 March 1981 of an Indonesian DC9 airliner
with 45 passengers and crew to Bangkok. It was also believed to have
been behind an attack on Cicendo police station, near Bandung, West
Java, on 11 June 1981, when three policemen lost their lives. Since then its
name has been associated with a number of small incidents involving
violence.

Popular Democratic Association of Timorese
(Associação Popular Democrática dos Timorenses —APODETI)

APODETI originated in 1974 in East Timor, the smallest of three political
associations to emerge after the Lisbon coup. The movement favoured
making East Timor an autonomous province of Indonesia, once it had
become clear that the Portuguese colonial regime was collapsing in
Lisbon. Furthermore it drew its support from the area bordering on the
Indonesian province of West Timor. When the Democratic Union of
Timor (UDT) staged a coup on 10 August 1975, APODETI allied itself

with the UDT in the subsequent fighting against leftist Fretilin forces. The movement enjoyed Indonesian backing.

Revolutionary Front for the Independence of Timor
(Frente Revolucionária Timorense de Libertação e Independência — Fretilin)

The April 1974 left-wing coup in Lisbon suddenly raised the prospect of independence for Portugal's far-eastern territory of East Timor. Left and right-wing forces began to organise, but from the outset it was plain that Indonesia coveted what amounted to a natural geographical extension of its territory. Furthermore, Jakarta, always concerned about a possible communist threat, was especially anxious to avoid the leftist Fretilin coming to power.

In March 1975 Fretilin leaders decided that in the absence of the Portuguese governor they might seize power. Non-communist forces proved stronger at that stage, but after the moderate Democratic Union of Timor (UDT) had played its hand in a coup in August, when the capital was taken, it quickly found itself worsted in the street battles. Fretilin gained the upper hand and declared East Timor independent on 28 November 1975. Indonesia countered by invading the territory on 7 December.

The initial fighting with Fretilin was over by February 1976, when Indonesia claimed it controlled Timor. Yet despite the formal incorporation of East Timor as Indonesia's 27th province, small bands of Fretilin guerrillas sustained themselves in the jungle. Vietnam and Peking lent some support. With a ban on visits by foreign journalists, it nonetheless emerged that Fretilin was indeed posing insurgency problems in its fight to establish a Democratic Republic of East Timor. Exiled leaders, including the founder, Francisco Xavier do Amaral, lost control of the movement to local commanders, and Nicolau Lobato took charge. Moderates were purged. Violent opposition was sustained for a year or more with as many as 600 active insurgents pitted against 20,000 Indonesian troops.

In September 1978 the former head, Amaral, and a senior colleague, Arsenio Horta, were arrested. The two men confirmed that Fretilin activists were demoralised and short of food. On 31 December 1978 Lobato was killed in an ambush. To break the insurgency the government resorted to the drastic use of defoliants, napalm and heavy bombing. Fretilin survivors were driven back into the mountains, where efforts were made to starve them out. The process inflicted heavy suffering on civilians.

By the early 1980s Fretilin was a spent force, thought to number less than 200 in the field, but still pursuing a stubborn campaign. In October 1981 the authorities launched a further major drive to break the last resistance. Yet the movement continued to find at least moral support in

Mozambique, which afforded Fretilin radio time, and in some leftist quarters in Lisbon.

Thirtieth of September Movement
(Geraken September Tigapulah — Gestapu)

The movement consisted of junior officers who carried out a short-lived coup in Jakarta on 30 September 1965. It was headed by Lieutenant Colonel Untung, a battalion commander in the Cakrabirawa palace guard. It claimed to be working in accordance with the principles of the Indonesian revolution and to be supporting President Sukarno. The coup leaders arrested six leading generals and took them to Halim air base, where they brutally murdered them. The Defence Minister, General Nasution, escaped arrest; no attempt was made to capture General Suharto, the commander of the Army Strategic Reserve Command. The movement enjoyed a significant measure of Communist Party (PKI) support, but its precise involvement in the actual planning and execution of the coup was never conclusively determined.

In a statement issued on 1 October, the movement claimed to have arrested members of a Council of Generals, which was alleged to have been sponsored by the United States CIA and to have been actively preparing a right-wing coup since President Sukarno fell ill in August 1965. The Thirtieth of September Movement's plan was to arrest the seven generals and then enlist President Sukarno's support. Presidential endorsement was expected to win over the army. It never came about.

In Jakarta General Suharto, on hearing of the arrest of senior generals, had swiftly assumed the leadership of the army. Nasution quickly supported him. The rebel troops in Jakarta, tired, hungry and thirsty, surrendered to Suharto at 4 p.m. on 1 October. The elite Army Paracommando Regiment took the Thirtieth of September Movement's headquarters at Malim shortly afterwards. The attack met with only a brief resistance.

The Army asserted that the PKI had masterminded the plot and used discontented officers to carry it out. Though conclusive evidence was not forthcoming, the failure of the coup led to sweeping anti-communist purges and the emergence of the army as the dominant political force.

Japan

Terrorism in Japan, by invoking the martial traditions of *Bushido*, has been able to enjoy a limited measure of legitimacy. When in the 1920s the ultra-right used terror to intimidate the court into more aggressive nationalist policies, politicians found it impossible to show any lack of respect for the terrorists' concept of the historical mission of the Japanese.

In contemporary Japan, small but active revolutionary groups were largely spawned from the National Union of Autonomous Committees of Japanese Students *(Zengakuren)*, which was in the vanguard of opposition to Japan's security treaty with the USA and US involvement in the Vietnam War. Most important of the groups concerned was the Red Army, which emerged as an urban terrorist movement committed to worldwide revolution. In 1972 it underwent a remarkable internal purge which caused the organisation to torture to death a dozen of its own members. As police measures bit into the group, members fled abroad where they achieved a brief but bloody notoriety. By the late 1970s the Red Army was largely a spent force; a danger remained in the example it had set for a younger generation. By the early 1980s most ultra-left terrorist activity was restricted to student factions. Their main preoccupation remained the US-Japan security treaty, to which they added environmentalist opposition to Tokyo's new Narita airport.

In contrast to the ultra-left's attempts to turn mass demonstrations into violent confrontations, the ultra-right has preferred the tactic of selective assassination. In the summer of 1960 the Socialist leaders, Kawakami Jotaro and Kishi Nobusake, were victims of vicious stabbing attacks. The same year the Japan Socialist Party Chairman, Asanuma Inejiro, was spectacularly assassinated in front of television cameras by a young right-wing militant. Plans for such attacks, including a plot to kill the entire Cabinet, continued to be exposed until the late 1960s, by which time rightist terrorist planning had been much reduced. In the early 1980s the ultra-right had restricted itself to legal, albeit noisy, activity. Most active in recent years had been the Showa Restoration League, which still defies the Emperor, and the Defence Youth League, a small grouping inspired by the patriotic ideals of the poet, Yukio Mishima.

Bibliography
Richard Storrey's *A History of Modern Japan* (London, 1970) is brief, but to the point. In *The Japanese Communist Movement 1920-66* (Berkeley, USA,

1967) R.A. Scalapino provided the background to the modern Japanese ultra-left. The crisis which precipitated the formation of the Red Army is examined in detail by George Packard III in *Protest in Tokyo: the Security Treaty Crisis of 1960* (Princeton, 1966). On the ultra-left and the genesis of the Red Army see Bernard Béraud, *La Gauche Révolutionnaire au Japan* (Paris, 1970).

Aso Unified Red Army

Named after a nearby volcano, this group hijacked a bus at Nagasaki in 1977 in a bid to secure one million dollars ransom. Police successfully stormed it, killing one of the gunmen.

Central Core
(Chukaku)

Central Core is a revolutionary Marxist movement which grew from the radical student fraternity in the early 1970s. It emerged out of a shared feeling of hostility towards Japan's defence treaty with the United States. Primarily a university-based group, it has carried out bombings in Tokyo, Osaka and Hiroshima, where targets included the Imperial Palace and defence facilities. For the most part these were arson attacks; they seemed set to continue into the mid-1980s.

East Asia Anti-Japanese Action Front (EAAJAF)

The Front promoted a short-lived terror campaign in 1974. An urban leftist terrorist group, it announced its existence on 28 February 1974, when it bombed the Tokyo headquarters of a large industrial organisation. Later, on 14 August, it destroyed three police boxes with explosives. On 2 March 1975 the Front bombed a government office in Sappuro, killing two people. Police arrests largely broke this group.

League of Communists
(Kyosando — known as *Bundo)*

The *Bundo* split from the *Zengakuren* in 1958, when they rejected peaceful coexistence in favour of the seizure of power by the proletariat and the destruction of bourgeois society, which was to be replaced by a classroom order. This movement, the founders felt, would form part of a new world revolution. It was active as a Trotskyist group in student circles, particularly throughout the 1960s, in Japan. From it splintered the Red Army *(Sekigun)* in 1969.

League of Revolutionary Communists
(*Kakkyōdō*)

In 1958, under the influence of Kanichi Kuroda, the *Kakkyōdō* took up the causes of mine workers and railwaymen. A number of serious strikes resulted. Later *Kakkyōdō* played a principal role in militating against the Japanese-American military alliance, an issue which through its demonstrations it brought to the attention of the Japanese people generally. The *Kakkyōdō* also set up the League of Marxist Students *(Marugakudō)*, which promptly captured the leadership of the *Zengakuren*.

In 1962 a split occurred in *Kakkyōdō*, giving birth to the League of Revolutionary Communists — Marxist Revolutionary Group (*Kakkyōdō* — *Kakumaru*) and the League of Revolutionary Communists— National Committee (*Kakkyōdō* — *Chukaku*). Both the original group and the factions were Trotskyists, and probably numbered in 1969 no more than 6000 militants.

Red Army
(*Sekigun*)

The Red Army split in September 1969 from the Trotskyist League of Revolutionary Communists, and made its first impact with the hijacking of a Japan Airways airliner in April 1970. The nine members used swords to enforce their demands to be flown to North Korea. The event was important in revolutionary mythology as proof that the vanguard party was not essential before proceeding with revolutionary tactics. In fact, the hijacking failed.

In the cities of modern Japan it was the Red Army's intention to found a revolutionary army bent on urban guerrilla warfare. This stand was envisaged as part of a world revolutionary struggle, which it would help provoke and to which it would contribute. The group proceeded to explode a number of bombs and to rob banks in 1971, but suffered the following year from extreme internal faction fighting, which caused the death of 14 members, executed by their erstwhile comrades.

The Red Army had made contact in North Korea with the extremist sections of the Palestinian movement (PFLP) in 1970, and thenceforth acted sometimes on behalf of and always with the sympathy of militant Palestinians. At Lod airport in 1972 three terrorists killed indiscriminately 25 innocent bystanders and wounded some 70.

Subsequently the Red Army achieved notoriety through a number of spectacular and bloody encounters abroad. In August 1975 five armed members seized 52 hostages in the US consulate in Kuala Lumpur (Malaysia) in return for whose release the Japanese government freed five jailed colleagues, who were flown to Libya. Two years later, in September, a Japan Airways aircraft was hijacked to Dacca (Bangladesh). Again the demand was to free colleagues and again the Japanese government conceded the release of five terrorists together with a ransom of six million dollars. On this occasion Algeria offered a haven.

The movement has subsequently led a shadowy existence, occasionally issuing communiqués from North Korea, India or the Middle East, but not undertaking any significant actions. The milieu which produced the Red Army changed, so that the group's recruiting possibilities diminished.

Revolutionary Workers' Association
(Kakumaru)

The association emerged in the early 1970s from the radical student movement. Its stronghold is in Kanagawa University, Yokohama. In the early 1980s it was particularly active in the campaign against Narita airport, Tokyo.

Zengakuren
(National Union of Autonomous Committees of Japanese Students)

Founded in September 1948 by 400 delegates from 138 universities, the *Zengakuren* grew from a student demand for grants to substitute their need to take part-time jobs. It quickly obtained the support of the Japanese Communist Party, especially in the promotion of student strikes; subsequently the party controlled the movement. By 1952 the *Zengakuren* adhered to the ideological line of armed struggle, an issue which caused the movement to split. The new line was accompanied by acts of violence and sabotage, culminating on May Day in 1953.

Following that major confrontation, the *Zengakuren* was not active until 1956, when it demonstrated against nuclear tests and against US bases in Japan. From this movement stemmed the beginnings of a Japanese New Left in 1958, when the movement split into the League of Communists and the League of Revolutionary Communists. A minority continued under a splinter group from the Communist Party. Together they demonstrated against the US-Japanese alliance in 1960, when on 15 June many hundreds were injured in clashes with police in Tokyo.

The student movement continued to exist, only in an ideologically fissiparous form. This did not prevent it from taking the lead in political violence throughout the 1960s, demonstrating in particular against the US interest and the Vietnam war. On these occasions highways were blocked and airport buildings occupied.

Although *Zengakuren* militants were wounded and inflicted wounds on police, it was rare for a student to die in the disturbances. In 1968 it played a prominent role in bringing students from all over Japan to demonstrate together against the US treaty. To the American issue was subsequently joined that of Narita airport, due to be constructed outside Tokyo, where students joined peasant farmers in protests at the requisitioning of land.

Kampuchea (Cambodia)

Kampuchea stood at the centre of a tragedy in the early 1980s, its people and culture savaged by a bitter civil war. The country had formed part of the French empire since 1864, when Siamese (Thai) suzerainty was replaced, although the Khmer monarchy retained its independence internally. Political activity was cocooned by French administration but the seeds of conflict grew in the late 1930s, when Son Ngoc Thanh began to influence groups of Khmer intellectuals who particularly resented French preferment of Vietnamese. Their vehicle was the first Cambodian language paper, *Nagaravatta* (Angkor Wat — ancient Khmer ruins), which propagated anti-colonial ideas. The Japanese occupied Cambodia in 1941, but left the French-appointed Prince Norodam Sihanouk and the Vichy French in nominal control until 1945, when they encouraged Sihanouk to declare independence. At Japanese insistence, Thanh was appointed first foreign minister and then prime minister. When Japan surrendered, Thanh attempted to declare a republic but was arrested by the French.

Small bands of pro-communist *Khmer Issarak* (Free Khmer) allied themselves with the Viet Minh, then harassing the French in Vietnam. In 1954 at the Geneva Peace Conference, Cambodia emerged as an independent neutral country under the leadership of Prince Sihanouk. Some Khmer Communists stayed in the jungle, others withdrew to North Vietnam with the Viet Minh forces, thereby dividing the Cambodian communist government.

Prince Sihanouk formed the *Sangkun Reastr Niyum* (People's Socialist Community) which gathered strength by appealing to popular themes such as Nation, Buddhism and Monarchy. The *Sangkun* swept the elections of 1955. For 15 years Sihanouk maintained his ascendancy through a brilliant combination of charismatic appeal and authoritarianism.

A few could not abide Sihanouk's authoritarian style and joined either the handful of communists who had remained in the jungle since 1954 or Son Ngoc Thanh's *Khmer Serei* (Free Khmers), which he had founded in exile in Thailand.

By 1963, convinced that Hanoi would win the war in South Vietnam, Sihanouk grew suspicious of the internal political consequences of accepting US economic and military aid, which he renounced. At the same time he cracked down on the tiny number of *Khmer Rouge* communist guerrillas operating in the countryside.

As the war in neighbouring South Vietnam intensified, more and more North Vietnamese and Viet Cong forces moved westwards and from 1965 onwards enjoyed semi-permanent bases in the east of Cambodia. They were supplied through the Cambodian port of Sihanoukville. In time US and South Vietnamese units began to raid communist bases in Cambodia. To add to Sihanouk's problems, a major peasant revolt broke out in 1967 in Battambang province. It was bloodily repressed in an episode which turned out to be a turning point in modern Cambodian history as thousands fled to join the *Khmer Rouge*. Finally, frustrated by Prince Sihanouk's compliance with communist armed presence in the east, the US encouraged General Lon Nol to stage a successful coup in March 1970.

In exile Sihanouk forged an alliance in Peking with his former enemies, the *Khmer Rouge*, whose political standing he strengthened beyond measure. Popular armed resistance to Lon Nol grew.

Backed by the Americans, Lon Nol launched several offensives against the communists, but by 1973 the *Khmer Rouge* were in control of much of the country. All direct US military involvement in Cambodia ended that year and by the beginning of 1974 Lon Nol controlled little more than the capital, Phnom Penh.

On 17 April 1975 the *Khmer Rouge* took Phnom Penh and immediately instigated a programme aimed at reducing the country to a primitive communism, the rationale of which was to create a strong, economically self-sufficient country. The cities were forcibly evacuated, peasant communities forcibly resettled and a savage terror conducted against all those deemed unsuitable for the new society. Up to two million people may have been killed in these purges.

From 1976 onwards the *Khmer Rouge's* Democratic Kampuchea (as Cambodia had been renamed) was involved in increasingly bloody encounters with Vietnamese forces. Hanoi sponsored a coup attempt in Phnom Penh in April 1977 and then an uprising in May 1978, but was unable to dislodge a barbarous regime. Finally on 25 December 1978 the Vietnamese launched an all-out invasion and took the capital on 7 January 1979. The *Khmer Rouge* forces, fairly steady at about 30,000 strong, have since waged guerrilla war in the west along Thailand's frontier, across which it derives Chinese logistic support. Efforts to unify the *Khmer Rouge* with anti-communist *Khmer Serei* (Free Khmer) forces largely failed, but in June 1982 the outlines of an agreement between the *Khmer Rouge*, Prince Sihanouk's *Moulinaka* movement and Son Sann's Khmer People's National Liberation Front (KPNLF) had been reached. Under this agreement, Prince Sihanouk was to head a new government embracing all three movements, which would however retain their individual organisations, political identity and freedom of action. The fighting is bitter and has involved the cynical manipulation of rice supplies by contending factions to secure rural support. By mid-1982 some 200,000 Vietnamese remained garrisoned in Vietnam and the prospects for peace looked bleak.

Bibliography

On the modern period, M.E. Osborne's two books provide satisfactory guides: *The French Presence in Cochinchina and Cambodia: Rule and Response 1859-1905* (New York, 1969) and *Politics and Power in Cambodia* (London, 1967) is an excellent study of Cambodia's efforts to preserve neutrality during the Vietnamese War.

William Shawcross provided a controversial but fascinating account of Cambodia's forced entrance into the second Indo-Chinese war and the rise of the *Khmer Rouge* in *Sideshow: Kissinger, Nixon and the Destruction of Cambodia* (London, 1979). V.M. Reddi in *A History of the Cambodian Independence Movement 1863-1955* (Tirupati, India, 1971) provides the most comprehensive account of Khmer nationalism available.

Prince Norodom Sihanouk in *My War with the CIA* (New York, 1973) gives a personal but important account of US efforts to draw Cambodia into the war. The period under *Khmer Rouge* rule is dealt with in a critical way by most observers. Two of the best are John Barron, *Murder of a Gentle Land* (New York, 1977) and François Ponchaud, *Cambodge, Année Zéro* (Paris, 1977), translated the following year with English and published by Allen Lane in London.

Kampuchea National United Front for National Salvation (KNUFNS)

In December 1978, shortly after signing a friendship treaty with the Soviet Union, the Kampuchea National United Front for National Salvation (KNUFNS) was set up in which pro-Vietnamese Khmers were paramount. On Christmas Day 1978 Vietnam launched an invasion of Kampuchea, took Phnom Penh on 7 January 1979, and two days later Hanoi announced the victory of its forces. The KNUFNS group, led by Heng Samrin, Chea Sim, and Pen Sovan, arrived in the baggage train of the Vietnamese army and set up a regime which Vietnam and a number of Soviet-bloc countries promptly recognised.

The KNUFNS ran the pro-Vietnamese government of the People's Republic of Kampuchea (PRK). Subsequently, small PRK forces fought alongside Vietnamese units against the *Khmer Rouge* and *Khmer Serei* resistance.

Khmer Issarak
(Free Khmer)

Khmer Issarak dates from 1945, when members fought for Cambodian independence from the French. The body is closely associated with Son Hgoc Thanh, once the protégé of the Japanese and who became Foreign Minister of Cambodia in March 1945. Five months later, on the eve of

Japan's defeat, he became Prime Minister. However on 15 September 1945 Thanh himself was arrested and taken by the French to Saigon. His followers fled to the jungle to set up the *Khmer Issarak* guerrilla forces. Thanh himself, released by the French in November 1951, joined the small *Khmer Issarak* bands in March 1952.

Khmer Issarak forces rose to a strength of about 3500 and allied themselves to the Viet Minh forces then harassing the French in Vietnam. Small Viet Minh forces were then engaging the French in Cambodia itself but withdrew after the 1954 Geneva conference. Despite strenuous efforts to win recognition the *Khmer Issarak* were successfully excluded from the independent Cambodian regime which emerged in 1954 under Prince Sihanouk. Thanh and the *Khmer Issarak* were successfully excluded from the independent Cambodian regime which emerged in 1954 under Prince Sihanouk. Thanh and the *Khmer Issarak* remnants fled to Thailand, where they continued to plot against Sihanouk, but were unable to revive their military challenge.

Khmer People's National Liberation Armed Forces (KPNLAF)

Formed in March 1979 by General Dien Del, a former officer in Cambodian leader Lon Nol's army, the KPNLAF is the strongest of the *Khmer Serei* (Free Khmer) forces, disposing of some 3000 men, although it claims 10,000. It operates close to the Thai border, north of Highway Five. The KPNLAF is the military wing of Sonn Sann's Khmer People's National Liberation Front (KPNLF). It receives arms from Singapore.

Khmer People's National Liberation Front (KPNLF)

The KPNLF is the main *Khmer Serie* (Free Khmer) political movement and disposes of an armed wing, the KPNLAF, under General Dien Del operating in the west close to the Thai border. The front was formed on 9 October 1979 and is led by Son Sann, a former prime minister under Prince Sihanouk in 1967. Son Sann pursued the possibility of forming a coalition with the *Khmer Rouge* and Prince Sihanouk's *Moulinaka* movement, and reached tentative agreement in June 1982 to form a coalition government in exile.

The KPNLF was set up by Sann and 14 other Khmers exiled in Paris. Its initial object was to rescue Khmer culture and people from the devastation of the *Khmer Rouge*, but it quickly found its main adversary to be the invading Vietnamese army. The KPNLF claims to control 100,000 civilians in Kampuchea and, in addition to its guerrilla force, to enjoy the support of a further 10,000 partisans harassing the Vietnamese occupying forces.

The KPNLF's main bases in Kampuchea had been the villages of Sokh

San, until a Vietnamese offensive of March 1982 drove them out. Such a defeat crippled the KPNLF's efforts to pose as a credible force which justified international diplomatic and military support in its struggle for supremacy over the *Khmer Rouge*. The front operated in a coalition of resistance groups.

Khmer Rouge
(Red Khmer)

Khmer Rouge was originally a pejorative term coined by Prince Sihanouk to describe the forces of the Khmer Communist Party (KCP), but it soon found popular currency. The KCP's official history claims the party was founded in 1961, a date which conveniently distances the *Khmer Rouge* from its Vietnamese origins. In fact it originated as the clandestine Revolutionary Cambodian People's Party formed in 1951 under a Central Committee of figures wedded to the Vietnamese Viet Minh. The party encouraged the formation of a legal political body, the Pracheachon group, which duly appeared after the 1954 Geneva accords that finalised the first Indo-Chinese war.

In clandestinity the KCP made little headway in the 1950s and 1960s: it was largely confined to the jungles and hills of the north-east and the Cardamon Mountains of the South-West. After 1960, when Prince Sihanouk became more authoritarian, the real core of the *Khmer Rouge* began to crystallise. The leading KCP cadres, Saloth Sar (better known by the pseudonym Pol Pot), Ieng Sarry and Son Sen, took to the jungle in 1962. All had been educated in France. Th other KCP leaders, Khieu Samphan, Hu Nim and Hou Yuon, fleeing Prince Sihanouk's bloody repression of the Battambang peasant rising, joined them in 1965. Although the KCP exploited peasant grievances with some success, it failed to enhance its position significantly and probably numbered no more than 4000 men.

After the Lon Nol coup of 1970 the *Khmer Rouge* entered into a coalition with Prince Sihanouk known as the National United Front of Kampuchea. This move increased *Khmer Rouge* support and accordingly communist controlled areas expanded. From 1973 onwards the *Khmer Rouge* became a powerful force in the land and began implementing its collectivist policies. This climaxed in military victory and the seizure of the capital, Phnom Penh, in April 1975. The party then embarked on a wholesale social revolution which necessitated wide-scale displacement of the population: the abolition of religion and culture; an emphasis on rural work; and the massacre of all deemed unsuitable for the new society. Probably two million people were killed by the *Khmer Rouge* government.

Following Vietnam's Christmas day invasion of 1978 the *Khmer Rouge* again took to guerrilla warfare against the new authorities. Khieu Samphan replaced Pol Pot as president of the movement in 1980 and the

KCP was formally dissolved in December 1981 in an attempt to attract international favour.

The *Khmer Rouge* largely operated in the west near the Thai border. The Chinese promised 'full armed support' and by 1980 aid was clearly forthcoming in the form of uniforms, medical equipment, radios, light weapons and ammunition.

By 1982 *Khmer Rouge* troops numbered about 35,000 men, of whom about 15,000 were operating in the western provinces of Battambang, Putsat and Koh Kong, in the area between Highway Five and the Cardamon Mountains. The remainder were scattered over the rest of the country in small guerrilla bands. *Khmer Rouge* activity was greatly facilitated by the Thai army, which allowed the *Khmer Rouge* to cross the frontier when pursued, to operate from bases inside Thailand, to use Khmer refugee camps in Thailand as recruiting grounds, and diverted food and medicine supplied by international relief organisations to *Khmer Rouge* forces operating in Kampuchea.

The *Khmer Rouge*'s government of 'Democratic Kampuchea' was still recognised by the United Nations in 1983 as the legitimate government of Kampuchea.

Khmer Serei
(Free Khmer)

Khmer Serei is a collective name applied to right-wing guerrillas who operated on the Thai frontier in the 1960s, later supported the Lon Nol regime in the early 1970s and resumed their guerrilla activities following the establishment of a *Khmer Rouge* government in April 1975. Several *Khmer Serei* groups, opposed to both the Vietnamese and the *Khmer Rouge*, emerged in 1979 after the Vietnamese invasion. The principal ones were the Khmer People's National Liberation Front (KPNLF) and the National Liberation Movement of Kampuchea.

Although *Khmer Serei* forces claimed strong support, it is unlikely that their total following exceeded 10,000 men. Generally the *Khmer Serei* observed an informal truce with the *Khmer Rouge* following the Vietnamese conquest of Kampuchea, but mutual distrust hindered the formation of an outright alliance. The *Khmer Serei* were concentrated north of Highway Five, the *Khmer Rouge* to the south. Fighting between them broke out from time to time, usually over the distribution of relief supplies or over recruitment, although there was less chance of this in 1983, following agreements to work together in a coalition.

National Liberation Government of Kampuchea (NLAK)

The government is in fact a small *Khmer Serei* guerrilla force operating to the west on the Thai border and north of Highway Five. It was formed on 3 October 1979 under the leadership of Van Saren.

National Liberation Movement (NLM)

This group emerged in 1979 as a *Khmer Serei* force operating along the Thai border and led by In Sakhan.

National Liberation Movement of Kampuchea
(Moulinaka)

The movement is a *Khmer Serei* (Free Khmer) force owing allegiance to Prince Sinhanouk and operating in the west close to the Thai frontier. It was formed in August 1979 by Kong Sileah, a supporter of Prince Sihanouk, after he had disagreed with General Gien Del of the KPNLAF over the role of the Prince in seeking a solution to the Kampuchean problem. In June 1982 the movement came to an agreement with Sonn Sann's Khmer People's National Liberation Front (KPNLF) and the *Khmer Rouge* to work together in a new coalition government-in-exile under Prince Sihanouk.

National United Front of Kampuchea (NUFK)

This group was formed in March 1970 under the nominal leadership of Prince Sihanouk to fight against the recently installed pro-US regime of General Lon Nol. The *Khmer Rouge* dominated the organisation. In May 1970 the coalition formed the Royal National Union Government of Kampuchea, which was immediately recognised by China and North Vietnam. It formally came to power in April 1975, but was progressively discarded by the *Khmer Rouge*, the real rulers of the country.

Laos

Political violence in contemporary Laos accords with the past history of the mountainous plateau region, which, having had no predominant ethno-linguistic character of its own, never developed a strong political identity and so fell under the influence of neighbouring peoples in Cambodia (Khmer empire), Thailand, Vietnam (Annam) and even Burma and China. In the late nineteenth century the French colonised the area, established a capital, Vientiane, from which suzerainty was established over the royal house of Luang Prabang. Even so, little national unity emerged and hill tribes continued to do battle with one another, just as they did in the early 1980s against the communist regime.

Japanese domination in the Second World War encouraged the local dynasty to declare independence from France, so that in 1946 new local political aspirations met the returning colonial power. The Free Laos (*Lao Issara*) movement went into exile. At this time the communist Vietnamese Viet Minh movement expanded is activities into Laos, using the substantial Vietnamese minority as a conductor. They formed the nucleus of the *Pathet Lao* (State of Laos) in 1953. In that year France recognised the independence of the Kingdom of Laos.

The 1954 Geneva Conference which brought the Franco-Vietnamese conflict to a close left the communist *Pathet Lao* movement active in the north of Laos. It subsequently played a political role as the Lao Patriotic Front (*Neo Lao Haksat — NLH*) and came to dominate the government in 1957.

A reaction to what was clearly North Vietnamese political influence set in, culminating with the detention in 1959/60 of NLH leaders. Political weight attached itself increasingly to the armed forces, which in August 1960 launched a coup that led to the temporary exile in Cambodia of Prime Minister Prince Souvanna Phouma, (b. 1901) and the assumption of power by what could then for the first time be termed right-wing politicians, who came to power after bloody fighting in the capital's streets.

Laotian politics were internationalised by Western support given to the right, led by Phoumi Nosavan, who controlled the troops, and Prince Boun Oum of Champassak (1911-80), and Eastern-bloc support given to Souvanna Phouma, who established a neutralist government in the north close to the *Pathet Lao*, led by Prince Souphanouvong (b. 1902). Civil war ensued. A further Geneva conference in 1961-62 led to the establishment of a government of national union under Prince Souvanna

Phouma. He failed to create political harmony, and in a coup in April 1964 nearly lost power to the army. He was saved by western support, which also preserved him from subsequent attempts to seize power made in 1965 by General Phoumi Nosovan.

As conflict in neighbouring Vietnam increased, so Laos was drawn in to the struggle, with the North Vietnamese supplying the *Pathet Lao* and the USA supporting Souvanna Phouma. Indeed, Laotian territory was crucial to the Viet Cong, which used mountainous paths as causeways for penetrating and supplying their forces in the south. The Vietnamese government signed a ceasefire in 1973 with the *Pathet Lao*. As a result Prince Souvannah Phouma remained prime minister and Souphanouvong became his deputy and minister of foreign affairs.

Peace provided the *Pathet Lao* with an opportunity to increase its political weight at the expense of the military, so that in 1975 power tilted in its favour and, following on a communist victory in Vietnam, a Democratic Republic of Laos was formed in December.

Resistance to this state of affairs continued for years, causing Vietnam to exercise greater influence over Laotian affairs. Armed opposition came not only from elements of the former regime but from Mao tribesmen in the north. To these desperate forces were added in 1978 deserting *Pathet Lao* fighters, critical of Vietnam's overweening influence in Laos. China provided support for this opposition, which persisted in mountainous areas in the north and in the southern Mekong region, where the Lao National Liberation Front operated. At least 50,000 Vietnamese troops with Soviet advisers operated in Laos in the early 1980s to contain this guerrilla threat.

Bibliography

Probably the best general introduction is F.M. Le Bar and A. Suddard, *Laos, Its People, Its Society, Its Culture* (New Haven, 1960). On communism in Laos, see J.J. Zasloff, *The Pathet Lao: Leadership and Organization* (Lexington, 1973). J.J. Zasloff and M. Brown in *Communism in Indochina* (London, 1975) have an interesting section on Laos (pp. 259-83). Early books on the war in Laos are A.J. Dommen, *Conflict in Laos* (New York, 1964) and S.N. Champassak, *Storm over Laos* (New York, 1961). The final period is covered by Prince Mangkra Souvannaphouma, *L'Agonie du Laos* (Paris, 1976). For the geo-strategic importance of Laos see Joseph Mendenhall's considerations in 'Laos: Vietnam's Stepping-Stone to Thailand' in *Conflict* Vol 2, No 2, 1980.

Lao Issara
(Free Lao)

During the Second World War the French encouraged Lao nationalists to set up a 'Young Lao' movement as a counter to the pan-Thai propaganda emanating from Bangkok. In 1945 this became the Free Lao (*Lao Issara*) movement, with independence as its main objective. After the Japanese defeat that year, the Chinese Nationalist (*Kuomintang*) forces who entered the country encouraged the *Lao Issara*. Their leader, Prince Phetsarath, proclaimed the independence of Laos on 1 September 1945. A few weeks later they deposed the pro-French King Sisavang Vong. In spring 1946 the French fought their way back, restored the King, and made Boun Oum Prime Minister. The *Lao Issara* government fled to Thailand, where it soon split. Most *Lao Issara* leaders were aristocrats and included Prince Souphanouvong, Prince Phetsarath and Phaya Khammao Vilay. The exiles organised small bands of guerrillas to harass the French but the level of violence was very low. In 1949 the more moderate *Lao Issara* leaders accepted French offers of a limited form of independence and returned to Laos. Prince Souphanouvong however would not accept such compromises and instead openly sided with the Viet Minh, who were then vigorously prosecuting the war against the French in Vietnam. He fled to the north-east, where he helped organise communist resistance, which the following year became known as the *Pathet Lao*.

Lao National Liberation Front (LNLF)

Mainly composed of soldiers and officials of the royal government deposed in 1975, the LNLF emerged in the later 1970s. It is particularly active in Champassak and Savannakhet provinces, and enjoyed success in recruiting among rural militiamen. The organisational structure is weak and LNLF units, varying in size from ten to 50, operate independently with little coordination. This reflects its origins in disparate groups of resistance fighters. It is largely armed by supplies captured from government and Vietnamese forces. LNLF activities have particularly disrupted traffic in Champassak. The communist authorities allege the LNLF uses Thai territory as a safe haven; and in the 1980s there was some evidence of *Khmer Rouge* support. The 50,000-strong Vietnamese presence and the communist system of organising village militia make it difficult for the LNLF to organise grass-roots support.

Pathet Lao
(State of Laos)

In August 1950 a conference of Laotian communist exiles was convened in North Vietnam under the direction of Prince Souphannouvong, a former *Lao Issara* leader. It proclaimed a liberation government of the *Pathet Lao* and made Souphanouvong prime minister. A People's Liberation Army was set up. In April 1953 the Viet Minh army wrested control of two northern Lao provinces, Sam Neue and Phong Saly, from the royal Laotian government and handed them to the *Pathet Lao* administration. *Pathet Lao* cells were set up in villages throughout Laos. They distributed anti-government propaganda and recruited villagers for in-doctrination. By 1958 *Pathet Lao* forces had risen to 6000.

Following the breakdown of the Geneva agreement in 1962, which brought Prince Souvana Phouma to power, the *Pathet Lao* reverted to armed struggle. It was vigorously backed by Hanoi, and by 1966 the USA estimated there were as many as 70,000 North Vietnamese fighting alongside the *Pathet Lao*. In December 1967 major communist offensives resulted in the seizure of Nam Bac on 20 January 1968, a victory which brought the forces within 35 miles of the royal capital of Luang Prabang. Fighting continued sporadically in the following years, with the *Pathet Lao* receiving substantial assistance from North Vietnam, including the use of aircraft. Gradually the *Pathet Loa* came to dominate most of the country and a ceasefire was negotiated on 21 February 1973, which paved the way to fresh negotiations for a new government of national union, involving communist participation, which was finally formed on 5 April 1974.

By this stage four-fifths of Laos and half the population were under *Pathet Lao* control. The final stages of the *Pathet Lao* takeover were virtually bloodless. On 10 May 1975 the right-wing coalition members resigned and in August the *Pathet Lao* celebrated the 'liberation' of Vientiane. On 3 December 1975 the monarchy was abolished and re-placed by a fully communist regime.

For the geo-strategic importance of Laos see Joseph Mendenhall's con-siderations in 'Laos: Vietnam's Stepping-Stone to Thailand' in *Conflict* Vol 2, No 2, 1980.

Malaysia

A relatively peaceful country in a turbulent area, Malaysia is afflicted by one of the longest running insurgencies in South-East Asia. It began with the implantation of an alien Marxism-Leninism within the immigrant Chinese community in accordance with the policy of the Soviet Comintern's Far Eastern Bureau and then of the Chinese Communist Party. But communist organisations in the Federation developed separately in the different territories which Britain linked in 1963.

In North Borneo (Sarawak and Sabah) the North Kalimantan Communist Party (NKCP) carried the Marxist-Leninist torch, while in west Malaysia the Communist Party of Malaya (CPM) and its splinter groups have waged a lengthy guerrilla campaign. The communists first took up arms during the Japanese occupation in the Second World War. The communist Malayan Peoples' Anti-Japanese Army (MPAJA), though little more than an irritant to the Japanese, nonetheless constituted the main resistance and the British actively encouraged its activities. A brief period of legality followed the declaration of peace, but in 1948 the MPAJA launched its armed insurrection under the banner of the Malayan Races' Liberation Army (MRLA).

According to the classical model of rural guerrilla warfare characterised by Mao Tse-tung, guerrillas were to harass the British in the hinterland, forcing them to withdraw to the towns. Once surrounded, the lines of supply would be attacked and as further withdrawals took place so liberated areas would fall under communist control. True, early communist successes were spectacular. The British were caught unprepared both for the scale and the violence of the attack. Moreover, when the emergency was declared in June 1948 there was little prospect of inde-pendence, so that the CPM was able to offer something of political substance to the Malayan Chinese, who had felt excluded from politics, as well as to the Malays, who were disinclined to act vigorously on behalf of the British.

All told, the insurrection (1948-60) caused the death of 11,000 people, including 2500 civilians. Thanks to a judicious mix of political incentives and security force measures, the back of the insurgency was broken. Essentially, the terrorists were deprived of contact with the population through protected villages, whilst plans for independence were accelerated. Elections were held in July 1955 and full independence followed two years later. CPM units, which once had stood at 14,000 men, were reduced to some 500 militants dependent upon bases in the Betong salient across the border in Thailand. Since 1969 these remnants have been engaged in an unsuccessful campaign to infiltrate the peninsula.

The insurgent movement developed differently in East Malaysia. During the 1950s sundry communist organisations were active in Sarawak, working through a variety of infiltrated organisations known collectively as the Sarawak Communist Organisation. From the start this SCO opposed Sarawak's joining the Malaysian Federation, opting for the creation of an independent communist state. The two principal Marxist-Leninist organisations, the North Kalimantan People's Force (PARAKU) and the Sarawak People's Guerrilla Movement (PGRS) took up arms. Indonesia supported their pretensions as it too was bitterly opposed to the creation of a powerful neighbouring state. By the late 1960s this campaign had also failed and the guerrillas were driven back to operate only in the remotest jungle areas.

Bibliography

An historical account of Malaysia is to be found in H. Miller, *The Story of Malaysia* (London, 1967). Other useful assessments include T.E. Smith and J. Bastin, *Malaysia* (London, 1967) and L.A. Mills, *British Malaya* (London, 1968).

The best history of the emergency period, scholarly and painstakingly researched, is Anthony Short's *The Communist Insurrection in Malaya 1948-1963* (London, 1975). A reliable account is contained in Richard Clutterbuck's *The Long Long War* (London, 1967) and in his *Riot and Revolution in Singapore and Malaya 1945-63* (London, 1973). A more racy but fascinating history of the emergency is Noel Barber's *The War of the Running Dogs* (London, 1971).

Justus van der Kroef's *Communism in Malaysia and Singapore* (Rotterdam, 1967) is still the best account available on the development of communism in the area.

Communist Party of Malaya (CPM)

The CPM was founded in 1930 and adopted its first constitution in 1934. It has always been primarily based on the Chinese community and has had little appeal for the Malays. Loi Tak, a Vietnamese Comintern agent, held the party together during the 1930s and under the Japanese occupation during the Second World War. Under his successor, Chin Peng, the party launched an insurrection which led to the declaration of a State of Emergency (1948-60). He remains the head of the party and is thought to reside in Peking.

After the defeat of the communist insurgency, the remnants, numbering no more than 500, fell back across the border to bases in the Betong salient in southern Thailand. There, the military wing, the Malayan Races' Liberation Army (MRLA), was renamed the Malayan National Liberation Army (MNLA), and a support unit, the Malayan National

Liberation League (MNLL), was established in Jakarta in 1965.

Since 1969 guerrilla units have attempted to infiltrate the peninsula. Small engagements take place in the 360 miles of mountainous jungle in the border area, where the Thais cooperate with Malaysian security forces in containing the threat. CPM tactical difficulties were compounded by ideological splits in 1970, when dissidents formed the CPM — Revolutionary Front and the CPM — Marxist-Leninist.

In the 1980s the CPM may have had 2500 militants operating in the border area. Infiltrators were restricted to Perak and Pahang. Yet even these numbers were able to tie down relatively large numbers of troops. Up to 12 army brigades were deployed on the border and manoeuvres were a constant feature in the early 1980s. When compared to the level of activity in the mid-1970s it was clear that the rebels had suffered from rural counter-insurgency measures.

A Central Committee of some 50 members directs the CPM. Policy is translated into practice through the North Malayan Bureau and a South Line Organisation, which operates in Negri Sembilan, Malacca, Johore and Singapore. In every state local committees direct local underground work. Money comes largely from intimidation, a primitive system of extortion or tax raising in areas where CPM control is relatively constant in the border area, and from sympathetic businessmen in some towns.

The MNLA consists of three units: the Eighth, the Twelfth, and the predominantly Malay Tenth Regiments. Each is organised in districts, while small assault units are detached for special duties. Recruits come mainly from the border villages, where a system akin to the press gang operates. A few join from the town networks. Armed groups based in the jungle have links to the outside world through cells (*Min Yuen*) in the towns. Supplies and sometimes intelligence is afforded by the nomadic aborigine population (*Orang Asli*).

Within the Malay community the CPM operates through the Malayan Islamic Brotherhood Party (*Parti Persaudaraan Islam*), whose membership often overlaps with another CPM front, the Malayan Peasants' Front (*Barisan Tani Malaya*). Its main demand is for land reform, and it tries to accommodate Islamic feeling to collectivist policy.

Communist Party of Malaya Marxist-Leninist (CPM-ML)

The CPM(ML), a pro-Chinese splinter group of the Communist Party of Malaya, dates back to 1970. It was formed partly as a result of an internal quarrel. CPM Secretary General Chin Peng suspected that his party had been infiltrated by police agents and, to counter the threat, the CPM North Malayan Bureau ordered a purge in which some 200 members were executed and 70 detained. Elements of the CPM's Eighth Regiment and the second district of the Twelfth Regiment resisted the measures.

Those in the Eighth Regiment who resisted subsequently formed the CPM Revolutionary Faction and were shortly joined by those of the

Twelfth Regiment, who set up the CPM(ML). The latter group organised in the Thai salient of Betong, but did not until 1974 become known as an organisation.

Local rural commanders had resented the distant control of the CPM's Central Committee. Moreover the 500 or so young guerrillas of the CPM(ML) soon displayed their disenchantment with Chin Peng's commitment to a lengthy rural guerrilla campaign. The new organisation concentrated instead on Malaysia's mushrooming urban areas. Urban cells were recruited and contact made with the criminal underworld. The CPM(ML)'s own support unit, the Malayan People's Liberation League (MPLL), consisted almost entirely at first of former CPM members.

In a brief mid-1970s campaign of lightening attacks in the cities, the CPM(ML) demoralised the population and undermined foreign investment. In particular the CPM(ML) targeted Special Branch officers from January 1973. Murders included the Inspector General of Police, Tan Sri Abdul Rahman Hashim, arguably the country's second most powerful man. In 1975 a record number of police agents were murdered in Johore, Perak, Kuala Lumpur, Negri Sembilan and Malacca.

In the event that year proved to be the terrorist high water mark. By opting for urban struggle the CPM(ML) paid the price for not having a secure rural sanctuary. Police infiltration and skilful use of informers took their toll on the urban network. In this way the movement was reduced to a relatively insignificant rural unit operating in the distant Betong salient. Even there it suffered from Malaysian army sweeps in the summer of 1977, when security forces captured the headquarters.

Most CPM(ML) units then turned to extortion in the Betong salient. These actions often brought it into contact with the parent CPM body. Despite its relative weakness it was still in the early 1980s estimated to dispose of some 500 members.

Communist Party of Malaysia — Revolutionary Faction (CPM-RF)

The CPM-RF emerged in 1970 following a three-way split in the parent CPM. Elements of the Eighth Regiment resisted a purge and broke away to form the new faction. Its operating ground was the Sadao district of Thailand on Malaysia's north-west frontier. Like its two sister organisations the CPM-RF set up an underground support unit, the Malayan People's Liberation Front (MPLF), but it had very little effect.

When it was set up doubts were expressed as to whether in fact the Revolutionary Faction had an organisation distinct from the CPM (Marxist-Leninist), for like the other groupings it was pro-Chinese. At the outset it numbered no more than some 500, but security force action had reduced even this figure to less than 150 by 1982.

Malayan Peoples' Army (MPA)

The MPA is the armed branch of the Communist Party of Malaya (see CPM), and was known as the Malayan National Liberation Army prior to 1983.

National Revolutionary Front
(Barisan Revolusi Nasional — BRN)

The BRN emerged in the late 1970s as a little-known splinter group of the parent Communist Party of Malaysia (CPM). It was committed to Marxism-Leninism, but largely devoted its activities to an attempt to wrest control of the lucrative extortion racket in the Betong salient, where the CPM enjoyed a monopoly. BRN-CPM clashes were first reported in 1978 and have since continued sporadically.

North Kalimantan Communist Party (NKCP)

Bong Kee Chok formed the NKCP in March 1970 from the remnants of defeated communist units in Sarawak. Its guerrilla strength was estimated at 700, but because it operated in such remote territory the party entertained hopes of speedy recruitment to its guerrilla wing, the North Kalimantan People's Guerrilla Forces (NKPGF).

Clashes occurred in the early 1970s, but a political settlement in 1974 reduced the guerrilla threat to insignificance for the rest of the decade. The initiative stemmed from Sarawak's Chief Minister, Rahman Yaakub, who acted against the advice of the federal government and made contact with the guerrilla organisation. He met Bong in March 1974, when Lasting Peace (*Sri Aman*) was agreed to. In return for a free pardon Bong and his men surrendered their arms and their pretensions. In all, 570 men came in from the jungle and settled down to farming.

A few diehards refused the settlement and they continued to pose a small insurgent threat in the early 1980s. They were thought to number about 130 and were restricted to the area near Kuching, where they maintained cordial relations with the Communist Party of Malaya (CPM).

North Kalimantan People's Guerrilla Forces (NKPGF)

The NKPGF is the armed branch of the North Kalimantan Communist Party (see NKCP).

—

Philippines

Contemporary political violence in the Philippines arises on two distinct fronts, a northern communist insurgency and a Muslim insurrection in the south.

The Philippine Communist Party-sponsored *Hukbalahap* (Huk) movement among the peasants of Luzon was developed from an anti-Japanese resistance movement into a post-war communist underground. It was succeeded in the 1960s by the similarly Marxist-Leninist New People's Army (NPA).

Yet it was in the Muslim south that the more formidable challenge to authority grew. To the festering rural problems of Mindanao were added the grievances of a Muslim minority against a majority Christian government. For many years discrimination had afforded Muslim separatist leaders with popular support against Manila. So it had been until 1898 under Spanish colonial rule, and so it was under American rule until the Japanese occupation of December 1941. Contemporary governments have sought to assuage moderate Muslim sentiment but have resisted separatist demands put forward in the early 1980s by the Moro National Liberation Movement (MNLF).

The present Marxist-Leninist insurgency owes its origins directly to the anti-Japanese resistance movement promoted by the pro-Soviet Philippine Communist Party (PKP). The party turned to its own advantage the nationalist sentiment aroused by Japanese occupation and built upon the resistance network in the post-war period. Against a background of corruption and diminishing foreign assets which followed the Second World War, the Huks continued their war. Luis Taruc, the communist leader, called for the forcible overthrow of the Quirino regime in Manila and indicated the changed nature of the war by changing the name of the *Hukbalahap* to *Hukbong Mapagpalayang Bayan* (People's Liberation Army — HMB), although they continued to be known as Huks. In no time they had gained control not only of the rice-bowl areas but even of the provincial capitals in Luzon.

Yet by 1951 the tide had turned, and two years later Huk military power was broken. On 17 September 1954 the communist leader, Luis Taruc himself surrendered. The government's counter-insurgency success was largely the work of Ramon Magsaysay, who was appointed Minister of Defence in September 1950. Under the banner of 'All-out force and all-out friendship', Magsaysay promoted rural rehabilitation schemes for Huks who surrendered. Provided they were not guilty of specific types of crime, they were given land and afforded loans. Magsaysay attacked corruption and defended peasants against vindictive landlords, with whose ways he was familiar, coming himself from a peasant background. In 1953 he was elected President, but died in March 1957.

In the mid-1960s the communists revived their challenge. But their strength failed as defections and demoralisation helped to promote internal rivalry. In 1969 the PKP split, following the great Sino-Soviet schism. In the early days both wings put their trust in armed insurrection but the pro-Soviet faction was soon in trouble. Faustino del Mundo, alias 'Commander Sumalong', was captured on 16 October. By 1974 the pro-Soviet faction had been knocked out of the insurgency and turned its energies to building up an organisation with a view to legal activity.

The larger and more significant Communist Party of the Philippines — Marxist-Leninist (PKP — M-L) remained oriented towards Peking. Its insurrection was spearheaded by the New People's Army (NPA). President Marcos attempted to stem its growth by the offer of an amnesty in April 1972, which, because of strong internal discipline within the NPA, proved unattractive.

In the south massive immigration of Christian settlers incited accusations of land-grabbing from aggrieved Muslims. In 1971 Muslims on Mindanao spontaneously rioted. The army restored order, but communal relations deteriorated still further so that by May 1972 the government had reported 111 Muslim clashes that year, resulting in 121 Muslim and 123 Christian deaths.

To contain these disorders and to counter growing communist activity in the north, President Marcos introduced martial law on 21 September 1972. Thousands were arrested; parliament was suspended; radio, television and the press were taken over; firearms were registered and a curfew imposed. Nothing so sweeping had been tried before. Within a few months some 500,000 weapons, ranging from hand guns to field guns, had been surrendered. Law and order improved. Moreover martial law halted the communist movement in its tracks. During 1973 many local NPA leaders laid down their arms and announced support for President Marcos' New Society, which promoted reform alongside martial law measures. Throughout 1974 and 1975 a combination of amnesties and military pressure brought their rewards, political reform combined with improvements in army conditions to cause serious NPA setbacks, including the arrest of its principal leaders, Bernabe Buscayno and Victor Corpus in 1976, and Jose Maria Sison in 1977.

In the south the 1972 introduction of martial law provoked civil war. Muslim insurgents, numbering some 50,000 seized control of large areas of Zamboanga and the Sulu chain, including the largest islands, Basilan and Jolo. The army sustained heavy casualties, ran short of equipment and found it difficult to procure replacements from a US administration sceptical of supporting an illiberal President Marcos. Still, by 1974 the situation had been largely retrieved, although foreign backing, particularly from Libya, continued. Towards the end of 1974 Marcos contacted Saudi Arabia and Egypt. Two years later he approached Libya.

Madame Marcos visited Tripoli and the two countries opened diplomatic relations. A breakthrough followed when talks in Tripoli between a Philippine delegation and MNLF head, Nur Misauri, concluded a ceasefire agreement on 23 December 1976. It was proposed to set up an autonomous region of 13 southern provinces with its own legislative assembly, an executive council and special Islamic Shariah courts. A mixed security force under central command was envisaged. In return the MNLF agreed to drop their demands for an independent Islamic State and to lay down their arms.

Initially, the accord was remarkably successful but disagreement arose over the holding of a referendum. President Marcos asked the inhabitants of the proposed region whether or not they wanted a virtually separate state under MNLF control or the government's own version of autonomy. The resulting referendum, held on 17 April 1977, categorically rejected the idea of MNLF rule. Furthermore, the MNLF, which had called for a boycott of the referendum, was ignored by the 75 per cent of the population which voted. It was clear to all that three million Muslims could not dominate six and half million Christians in the region. Yet, far from taking note of the referendum results, the MNLF presented new demands for a provisional MNLF government, and an army paid, armed and equipped by Manila, but under MNLF command. Peace negotiations broke down in May 1977 and MNLF leader, Nur Misauri, returned to his original demand for total independence. After this rupture minor clashes between the MNLF's *Bangsamoro Army* and regular forces continued fitfully into the 1980s.

More generally, martial law restrictions alienated young people and contributed towards radicalising sectors of the Roman Catholic Church. A new generation of urban dissidents arose; most notable of these groups was the April 6 Liberation Movement. By the early 1980s it had become clear that government restrictions had closed for too long the normal channels of political expression and that political movement of some form would have to be accommodated if the framework of the so-called New Society were to survive unchallenged.

Bibliography

Two introductions to the Philippines are T.M. Burley's *The Philippines* (London, 1973) and *The Philippines: Nation of Islands* by A. Cutshall (Princeton, 1964). Reliable books on the history of guerrilla warfare in the Philippines include D.R. Sturtevant's excellent *Agrarian Unrest in the Philippines* (Ohio, 1969) and his comprehensive *Popular Uprisings in the Philippines 1840-1940* (New York, 1976). Major R.T. Yap-Diangco has written a good study in *The Filipino Guerrilla Tradition* (Manila, 1971). N.D. Valeriano and C.T.C. Bohanan, men who fought the Huks, wrote *Counter-Guerrilla Operations: The Philippine Experience* (New York, 1962). On the communist campaigns in the Philippines see two books by the communist leader, Luis Taruc, *Born of the People* (New York 1953) and *He Who Rides the Tiger* (New York and London, 1967). From the other vantage point, two useful works include A.M. Saulo, *Communism in the Philippines* (Manila, 1969) and U.S. Baclagon, *The Huk Campaign in the Philippines* (Manila, 1960). A contemporary overview is available in A. Turpin, *New Society's Challenges in the Philippines* (Conflict Studies No. 122, London, 1980), and in the memoirs of Eugenio López, *Two Terrorists Meet* (San Fransisco, 1981).

The best work on the MNLF rising and its Islamic roots is T.J.S. George, *Revolt in Mindanao: The Rise of Islam in Philippine Politics* (Oxford, 1980).

April 6 Liberation Movement

During the period August-October 1980 in Manila, a series of bomb explosions occurred, the majority of which were claimed by the April 6 Liberation Movement. Some 70 people were injured, 33 of them in a supermarket explosion. The group took its name from a large anti--government demonstration held on 6 April 1980. By 1982 no recrudescence had occurred.

Bangsa Moro Liberation Organisation (BMLO)

Following a feud between Nur Misauri and Hashim Salamat in the Central Committee of the Moro National Liberation Front, Salamat set up the BMLO in 1977. It stood for a negotiated settlement with the Manila government in contrast to Misauri's hard line.

Mindanao Independence Movement (MIM)

Datu Matalam founded the Muslim Independence Movement in Pagalongan in May 1968. It was later renamed the Mindanao Independence Movement. MIM's original goal was the creation of an Islamic republic in the south, although this demand was subsequently modified to the recognition of statehood within a federal system. Although not strictly a violent group, the MIM lent respectability to gangs of Muslim gunmen. Many MIM members were prominent in the Moro National Liberation Front, which emerged as the armed branch of the MIM in 1972 to become the driving force of Muslim separatism.

Moro National Liberation Front (MNLF)

The movement emerged as a more disciplined successor to the Mindanao Independence Movement (MIM). Nur Misuari, a young Muslim academic and leftist thinker, assumed the leadership in 1972 and established the Bangsa Moro Army. The MNLF was left-wing and early on dissociated itself from the *Datus* (local chiefs), whose assistance had been essential for its birth. In time the ideological stance became untenable when it was appreciated that the armed Muslim groups which had gone underground in 1972 had done so in the belief that they were fighting for the preservation of their faith.

The distinctive feature of MNLF insurgency, which began in late 1972, was that it was not confined to one centre or to a limited objective. Large areas of Zamboanga and the Sulu chain, including the largest islands, Basilan and Jolo, fell under its influence. In March 1973 a well organised and equipped MNLF force of at least 6000 men took most of the towns of Cotabato province. Sulu, home of the fierce Tausug people, as well as of Nur Misuari and several of his close associates in the MNLF high command, was the core of the insurgency. It lay close to the Malaysian province of Sabah, whose chief minister provided support.

By 1973 MNLF forces numbered some 15,000, and government positions defended by over 500 men were regularly over-run. However, initial activity was not sustained. The next major engagement came in February 1974, when some 800 MNLF rebels over-ran the air force headquarters at Jolo Town and occupied Notre Dame College. Three warships bombarded the rebel positions; air force jets joined the attack. Ground forces shelled the town. Fires spread rapidly. Buildings believed to contain rebels were raided. When the main rebel forces started withdrawing on the third day, snipers stayed behind to pick off advancing soldiers before returning naval fire destroyed the few remaining structures.

The timing of these two offensives after the introduction of martial law in September 1972 revealed a strategy. The 1973 Cotabato offensive occurred on the eve of the Islamic Foreign Ministers' Conference in Benghazi; the 1974 Jolo battle coincided with the Islamic summit meeting in Lahore. Since the Benghazi conference, Libyan leader Colonel Gadaffi had been urging a diplomatic-economic boycott of the Philippines. The Jolo offensive reinforced the impression gained by Arabs of a full-scale Muslim liberation war. Since then the issue has been on the agenda of the Islamic Foreign Ministers' Conference.

In domestic terms, the internationalisation of the dispute proved counter-productive. It steeled the government's resolve to fight, and caused many Muslim intellectuals who had joined the campaign so as to ensure justice for Muslims to question the leadership of the separatist movement. Libya claimed it had channelled arms and money to the Muslim rebels, possibly via the Malaysian province of Sabah. Although the Malaysian government denied any role, it did not enjoy full control over the activities of its Chief Minister, Tun Mustapha, whose family came from Sulu. Tun Mustapha may have nourished ambitions of his own for a state comprising Sabah, Sulu and Mindanao. Libyan support enabled MNLF leadership to control rebel commanders like Usman Sali and Al Caluang, who otherwise might have operated independently. Without foreign aid the fighting could not have continued. By 1974 Misuari had established an MNLF Central Commitee, also known as the Committee of Thirteen, most of whose members lived in Tripoli.

In 1976 the MNLF agreed to a 16-point accord with President Marcos. Although this established a ceasefire and a substantial degree of autonomy for the south, a referendum conducted in the south in April 1977 rejected MNLF rule. The results were hardly surprising for Christians formed the majority in eight of the 13 provinces. Such a resounding defeat for the MNLF was all the more impressive for the peaceful conduct of the referendum, observed officially by foreign visitors. The MNLF never recovered from the set-back.

Sporadic terrorist actions broke the ceasefire. In February 1977 the MNLF murdered Brigadier General Bautista and 34 unarmed soldiers. But such incidents fell short of a campaign or a rural insurgency. To recapture attention the MNLF resorted to kidnapping foreigners, a tactic which reduced MNLF standing to the level of the gang leaders it had displaced in 1972.

Dissension within the MNLF leadership proved no less disastrous. In 1977 Misuari attempted to purge his rivals from the central committee; Alonto and Salamat, princely scions of the Muslim aristocracy, were the main targets. But at a meeting in Mecca, Salamat challenged Misuari and defeated him in an election to the MNLF chairmanship. Misuari rejected the result and left for Tripoli; Salamat set up his base in Cairo. Misuari continued to advocate armed resistance, while Salamat urged conciliation. Enjoying the support of the Islamic Conference, Misuari continued in the early 1980s to engage his supporters in small-scale actions against soft targets such as undefended boats and villages, police stations, government offices and power pylons.

New People's Army (NPA)

As active radicals from student organisations entered the Communist Party of the Philippines (PKP) in the mid-1960s an ideological division developed which ultimately led, in 1967-68, to the formation of a rival to the pro-Soviet PKP, and Maoist Communist Party of the Philippines — Marxist-Leninist (CPP — M-L). In March 1969 it founded an armed wing, the New People's Army (NPA), which persisted in rural guerrilla activities in the early 1970s. The NPA sees 'US imperialism, feudalism and bureaucratic capitalism' as the broad enemies, with the 'fascist' government of President Marcos as the principal butt. Protracted armed struggle is seen as the way to establish a 'people's democratic state'.

The NPA originally concentrated its attention on the central Luzon province of Tarlac, the traditional centre of agrarian unrest and communist rural insurgency. Yet NPA forces were soon compelled to divert their main attention to the remote north-eastern province of

Isabela. By the close of 1971 the NPA claimed to have 2000 men under the command of a former Huk, Bernabe Buscayno. He was joined by an army defector, Lieutenant Victor Corpus, who had become a hero for Manila's radical students when, as a 26-year-old graduate of the Philippine Military Academy, he had seized the Academy's arsenal on 29 December 1970, taking arms and ammunition.

In the early 1970s NPA activities were reported from the mountainous province of Nueva Vizcaya, but it was only in Isabela province that the NPA established a substantial base. In fact Maoist influence was strongest in Manila, particularly in the early 1970s, when front associations linked with the CPP (M-L) were foremost in promoting strikes and demonstrations, many of which were violent and led to fatalities.

On 9 July 1972 the security forces launched a major drive against 200 regular and 800 irregular NPA members around Digoyo Bay in north-eastern Luzon. A police unit came under heavy fire as it attempted to board the *Karagatan*, a small vessel suspected of landing weapons and Chinese-trained guerrillas for the NPA. Military patrols had frequently seized arms caches on the Digoyo Bay coast and the *Karagatan* incident seemed proof of allegations of Chinese backing for the NPA. To check the insurgency, martial law was imposed. Aggressive patrolling by the security forces combined with amnesties induced defections. Most striking was the surrender in May 1973 of Benjamin Sanguyo — alias Commander Pusa — a senior NPA figure. As in the Huk insurgency before, the attraction of the NPA's call for land redistribution was eroded by the government's own programme of land reform.

Forced onto the defensive, the first reports of internal divisions began to appear. Following disputes over strategy in January 1975 it carried out a purge which involved executions. All in all it seemed doubtful whether NPA recruiting was keeping pace with losses sustained by defection, capture and shootings.

By the end of 1976 practically the entire leadership of the NPA was behind bars. For this security force efficiency was no doubt largely responsible, but the NPA position had been weakened by the withdrawal of Chinese support, a fact which forced NPA guerrillas to rely on arms seizures. Both Bernabe Buscayno, and his chief military strategist, Victor Corpus, had been captured.

Yet the NPA continued its struggle in 1977 with strenuous efforts to ally with the southern Muslim rebels in the Moro National Liberation Front (MNLF). Cooperation proved successful, at least so far as survival of the insurgency was concerned, for in 1979 on the island of Samar the NPA claimed control of 85 per cent of the east, 60 per cent of the west and nine out of 23 towns in the north. Cooperation with the MNLF enabled the guerrillas to field over 100 men in a single engagement.

In the early 1980s the NPA was more than ever committed to years of uphill struggle in the rural hinterlands. Priority was given to target groups of about ten villages at a time until local support had been built up. The most difficult phase was the initial contact with villagers, who often reported NPA presence to the army. Once propaganda and intimidation had secured a rural area a local militia squad was established, and so the pattern was repeated to form a patchwork of insurgency. Of the estimated 4000 guerrillas, the NPA was rarely willing to mobilise large numbers for particular actions. By 1982 the NPA insurgency, while not constituting a serious threat to the government, was nonetheless growing.

Patriotic Youth
(Kabataang Makabayang — KM)

The KM was a youth front operated by the Maoist faction of the Communist Party of the Philippines in the late 1960s. It was active in street disturbances and in the early 1970s numbered over 100,000 supporters. Despite Maoist ideology its activities were largely restricted to the cities. It was crushed by the introduction of martial law in 1972. Some KM militants fled to Mindanao and offered the Moro National Liberation Front (MNLF) collaboration. KM viewed the problem of the south as essentially one of class conflict and discounted the Islamic factor. The MNLF leadership felt it would lose support by associating with Maoists and turned down collaboration.

People's Anti-Japanese Resistance Army (Huks)
(Hukbong Bayan Laban Sa Hapon — Hukbalahap)

The Communist Party of the Philippines (PKP) founded the Huk resistance movement in March 1942 to fight against the Japanese occupation during the Second World War. In central Luzon it set up a training school under Chinese instructors from Mao Tse-tung's Eighth Route Army for Huk guerrillas. Operating under the command of Luis Taruc, the Huks recruited among the peasantry, who knew little of Marxism-Leninism but held grievances against money lenders and absentee landlords. The Huks fought comparatively little against the Japanese, but with bolder attacks harassed them towards the close of 1944. After the Japanese withdrawal the Huks attempted to set up a 'People's Democratic Government'. The US commanding officer, General MacArthur, intervened, disbanded the organisation and had Taruc arrested.

After the war the movement was reactivated under a new banner, that of the People's Liberation Army (HMB).

People's Liberation Army
(Hukbong Mapagpalaya ng Bayan — HMB)

The People's Liberation Army (HMB) was set up at the instigation of the

Philippine Communist Party after the Second World War. Recruits consisted of former Huks who had cached their weapons in the countryside; their objective was to overthrow the Manila government by waging rural guerrilla warfare. Its organisation was based on the previous Huk village network, its appeal on the slogan 'land for the landless'. The movement spread quickly in central Luzon and soon dominated not only much of the rice-bowl areas of the island, but also the provincial capitals. There can be no doubt that its success lay in the popular identification of the HMB's cause with nationalism — in fact the HMB continued to be known as the Huks, and in the espousal of a just social cause.

As before, Huk guerrillas attacked police stations and military posts with relative impunity. Guerrilla movement was facilitated by blunt government counter-measures that did more to alienate the peasantry than crush the insurgency. At night Huks would penetrate villages and taught the inhabitants to resist government security measures and to deny the security forces information.

The area infiltrated in the late 1940s supported some two million people, on most of whom the Huks had made some impression. They numbered no more than 10,000 fighters at the time. Active support may have been given by as many as 200,000 local sympathisers. Huk intimidation kept many passive.

The HMB never became an army in the conventional sense. Recruits lacked weaponry, their training was rudimentary, they had no outside contacts, poor logistics, and no central command system. Actions were planned autonomously by local field commanders, who practised terrorism, the most well-known incident being the ambush and murder of President Quezon's widow in April 1949.

The turning point in HMB fortunes came in 1950 with the appointment of Ramon Magsaysay to the Ministry of Defence. He transformed counter-insurgency operations, which won back for the government peasant loyalty. Within 18 months the guerrillas had been brought under control. Luis Taruc, who commanded the Huks during and after the Second World War, surrendered in September 1954.

Thailand

Thailand never suffered colonisation, which meant that insurgents could never tap the nationalist sentiment that elsewhere in South-East Asia drove men to rebel. Support for traditional order of monarchy and Buddhism is strongly sustained. Yet like most countries in the region a persistent communist insurgency troubles Thailand: it was still active in the early 1980s in the mountains and on the border.

As in Malaysia the insurgency fed off minority ethnic groups, but to this motivation were added in the north-east economic grievances and government neglect. In the far south bordering Malaysia Malay separatism is a disruptive force. Economically the region has suffered neglect for geographical and racial reasons, so that Malay Muslims, conscious of their identity, have begun to support separatist movements.

Following the withdrawal of the military from formal power in 1973 (they enjoyed a traditional role in modern Thai government), left-wing urban groups, spearheaded by students, attempted to politicise a wider audience of labourers and peasants. The political right, convinced that monarchy itself was being undermined, grew alarmed, and promoted armed groups such as the Red Gaur and *Nawapol*. Their often repeated attacks on left-wingers even found favour among the bulk of the populace, dismayed at the lawlessness which had accompanied the military's fall from power.

Such political violence culminated in a bloody coup in October 1976, when many students died. Subsequently, the severity of the new authoritarian government alienated many former supporters of military rule, so that for the first time ethnic Thais felt attracted by communism, which posed the principal insurgent threat.

The Communist Party of Thailand (CPT), wedded to the Maoist principles of rural guerrilla struggle, had begun its insurgency in 1965, and ever since has constituted the kingdom's most persistent source of instability. Backed by China and North Vietnam at the outset, the CPT's guerrilla wing, the Thai People's Liberation Armed Forces (TPLAF) quickly spread through the north, the north-east and the far south. True, logistic support came from over the frontier, but the insurgency was fuelled by indigenous discontent.

In the north support came predominantly from the animist hill tribes, and in the south largely from Malay Muslims. Yet the more serious challenge came in the north-east, where the backers were Thai-Isan, ethnically related to the Lao, but in language and culture essentially Thai.

Government organised a Communist Suppression Operation Command, which emphasised the importance of winning the villagers' loyalty through rural development. To cope with security the government set up village defence units and withdrew from South Vietnam a 12,000-man force known as the Black Leopards to form a new counter-insurgency division.

Yet, despite security force successes, it was the growth of Sino-Vietnamese rivalry and particularly Vietnam's 1978 invasion of Kampuchea which caused the CPT's position to deteriorate fundamentally. Critical of Vietnamese policy and actions, the party's Chinese leadership found its cadres thrown out of their safe havens in Laos and Kampuchea. Policy in Bangkok further weakened the insurgent cause. Amnesties encouraged Thai communists to return to their homes, and defectors continued to surrender in the early 1980s. But at the same time clashes continued, although they involved smaller numbers and bore little comparison with former actions. Most counter-insurgency actions were conducted by the police, a para-military force, while the army had at no time committed more than 20 per cent of its forces to counter-insurgency efforts.

Bibliography
D. Elliot furnished a Marxist account of Thailand's propensity towards military rule in *Thailand: Origins of Military Rule* (London, 1978), balanced by D. Wilson, *Politics in Thailand* (New York, 1962). *Thailand and the Struggle for Southeast Asia* (New York, 1965) by D.E. Nuechterlein sets the Thai insurgency in the international political background of the mid-sixties. The best work on the communist insurgency is G.K. Tanham's *Trial in Thailand* (New York, 1974) written by one who helped devise the response. For the details see the 1977 University of Denver publication by Thomas Lobe entitled *United States National Security Policy and Aid to the Thai Police*. For the later years see R. Sean Randolph, 'The Thai Insurgency in the later 1970s' *Conflict* Vol 1 No.2 1980.

Asia 88

The group first emerged in June 1982, when it was believed to be backed by Laos and to have its headquarters and training centre in Laos' Pak Se province. It was thought to have originated from the Communist Party of Thailand (CPT) split of 1979, when pro-Soviet communists had fled to Laos. The Moscow-leaning group, *Phak Mai* (New Party), subsequently developed its own splinter, Asia 88.

Asia 88 despatched infiltrators to work in the north-east of Thailand, particularly in Yasothon and Ubon Ratchathani provinces. Membership was unknown, but certainly small.

Committee for Coordinating Patriotic and Democracy-Loving Forces (CCPDF)

The Communist Party of Thailand (CPT) set up the CCPDF in September 1977 as a front organisation which would embrace all opposition movements to the Bangkok authorities. For a while it successfully recruited ethnic Thai, but the attraction declined once communist control had become apparent. Thoetphun Chaidi, a Thai trade union official active in the committee's founding, later led a CCPDF splinter to form a pro-Vietnamese communist party in 1979 based in Laos.

Communist Party of Thailand (CPT)
(Phak Communist Haeng Pratesthai)

Although communism had been banned in Thailand since 1933, the CPT is of more recent origin. True, small groups of communists were active in Thailand during the 1930s, but the CPT proper originated as the Thai section of the Chinese Communist Party in 1942. Ten years later it was formally constituted.

From the outset therefore, the CPT has followed a pro-Chinese line and has consistently pledged itself to a Maoist strategy of people's war in the rural areas. In the late 1950s Thais began guerrilla training in China, North Vietnam and Laos. The Third Party Congress (1961) passed a formal resolution advocating armed struggle and subsequently a guerrilla infrastructure was established. The first clash between CPT guerrillas and government forces occurred in the north-east in late 1965. Four years later it set up a military wing — Thai People's Liberation Armed Force (TPLAF). The CPT's strength grew, based primarily on the support of ethnic minorities and the Chinese community. The bloody military coup of 1976, however, drove many Thai students to join CPT guerrilla ranks, thereby adding a new dimension of support to the party. In 1978 Vietnam's invasion of Kampuchea and growing Sino-Vietnamese rivalry caused a deterioration in the CPT's position. The party's Chinese leadership was critical of Vietnamese actions and as a result the CPT was thrown out of its safe havens in Laos and Kampuchea. A splinter group broke to form a rival party based in Laos.

In an attempt to strengthen its position, the CPT held its clandestine fourth congress in March 1982, the first to take place since 1962. Udom Sismuan was elected the new secretary general. He replaced Mit Sananan.

Free Thai Army (FTA)

This right-wing pressure group was active in 1973-76, practising strong-arm measures against left-wing and labour activists. Members disrupted left-wing rallies and intimidated sympathisers by bullying.

National Revolutionary Front
(Barisan Revolusi Nasional — BRN)

Founded in 1961, the BRN was led by Abdul Karim Hassam. The Front is only about 100 strong, but seeks the establishment of an independent Islamic and socialist state in Thailand's four southern provinces of Pattani, Narathiwat, Yala and Satan.

Nawapol or *Nawaphon*
(New Force)

Nawapol was a right-wing movement active in 1973-76; the group's name was adopted from legends associated with the ruling Chakkri dynasty. In its time it constituted one of a number of ultra-rightist groupings mobilised to counter leftist gatherings. Front members participated in the assault on Thammasat University in October 1976, when a number of students were lynched. It was said to be particularly strong in the provincial bureaucracy.

Pattani Islamic Nationalities' Revolutionary Party
(Phak Patiwat Phaochon Islam Pattani — PPPIP)

The PPPIP is headed by Amin Tomina. It is believed to enjoy contacts with some Arab countries. In common with other southern Muslim groups in Thailand, it seeks the secession of the five southern provinces of Yala, Songkhala, Pattani, Narathiwat and Sata. Many of its activists defected from the National Revolutionary Front (BRN). Typically, it deployed armed units of about 15-20 men, specialising in assassinating Muslim leaders who cooperated with the Thai government.

Pattani National Liberation Front
(Barisan Nasional Pembebasan Pattani — BNPP)

Founded in 1947, the BNPP is the oldest of the Thai Muslim separatist organisations. Largely Malay in composition, in the past it has enjoyed support from Malay nationalists across the border in the Malaysian state of Kelantan. When in power in Malaysia, the intensely religious Party Islam (PI) was strikingly active in its support for the BNPP. PI's electoral defeat in the 1979 Kalantan state elections and an improvement in Thai-Malaysian border cooperation diminished this effort. Badri Hamdan headed the BNPP in the early 1980s.

Pattani United Liberation Organisation (PULO)

Of Muslim separatist organisations in southern Thailand, PULO is the most active. Tunku Bira Kotanila is in political control, but possibly the more influential is the military leader, Sama-eh Thanam. Libya supports the organisation, which has an estimated following of 300 activists.

Typical PULO targets are Thai state symbols in the south, but the movement also attacks ethnic Thai in the capital. Without being a guerrilla organisation, PULO practises crude terrorism. Among its activities in the southern provinces of Yala, Pattani and Narathiwat are included bombings, arson attacks and kidnappings. In Bangkok it claimed responsibility for four bombings in public places on 30 June 1980, when 47 people were injured, and three bombings the following year in June, when 50 people in a shopping area were injured.

PULO issued threats to bomb Thai embassies and consulates abroad and to hijack Thai aircraft, but no attacks had occurred in the early 1980s.

Phak Mai
(New Party)

Phak Mai resulted from the 1979 split in the Communist Party of Thailand (CPT), following Vietnam's invasion of Kampuchea. The small pro-Vietnamese group broke away from the majority pro-Chinese party and fled to Laos, where it became known as the *Phak Mai*.

Originally based in the Laotian capital, Vientiane, *Phak Mai* moved its headquarters to Pakkading, near Thailand's north-eastern borders, in early 1982. *Phak Mai* is believed to have set up several training schools in which the Thai government alleges Soviet, Vietnamese and Lao military instructors are present. In mid-1982 *Phak Mai* still concentrated on propaganda and other political activities in the north-east border area. No guerrilla actions had been reported.

Red Gaur
(Krathing Daeng)

Red Gaur was one of several right-wing vigilante groups that emerged in 1973 to counter the growth of left-wing activism, which sprang up during Thailand's brief experiment with parliamentary democracy. Red Gaurs are buffalo found in Thailand, which, when disturbed, become violent: by adopting such a symbol militants displayed their uncompromising Thai nationalism.

Red Gaur membership exceeds 10,000 militants. Their violence is supportive of the government authorities, although members have carried out many assaults on left-wing activists. They practise widespread intimidation, and have even murdered peasant and labour leaders. More legitimately, some units provided security for development projects in communist infiltrated areas. They sought to project an image of themselves as defenders of the homeland.

Sabil-Illah
(Way of God)

This fanatical Muslim fundamentalist sect operated in the far south of Thailand. Although there would appear to be few members and no overt political apparatus, members have engaged in terrorist acts in some towns.

Thai People's Liberation Armed Force (TPLAF)

Set up in late 1969, the TPLAF is the military wing of the Communist Party of Thailand. Its membership rose swiftly, so that by 1971 it was believed to have an armed strength of 5000 men.

Not until 1971 was the first widespread offensive against the TPLAF taken in the north-eastern provinces of Makhon Phanom, Sakon Nakhon and Kalasin. In September, with the discovery of guerrilla camps in Surat Thani district, evidence emerged of CPT activity in southern Thailand. In October security forces surprised a guerrilla camp in north-east Thailand staffed by North Vietnamese and Chinese instructors.

The following year TPLAF operations increased both in number and in scale. The problem of under-security remained acute throughout 1972 in the north, around Chiang Rai, in the provinces of Phitsanulok, Loei and Phetchabun, and in the east along the Thai-Laos border in the vicinity of Makhon Phanom. A critical factor in the improvement of TPLAF technical ability in the north-east was the deployment of Vietnamese and Laotian communist guerrillas. For the first time foreign guerrillas had been found in Thailand in a combat role.

TPLAF assaults on government camps and road construction workers increased and evidence of communist success in winning the loyalty of ethnic minorities emerged; Meo tribesmen spearheaded many guerrilla assaults. In central Thailand the communists succeeded in establishing bases in the Phitsanulok vicinity. Yet it was in the north and north-east that the situation remained most critical for the government. Seven areas had been declared 'off-limits' zones because of the intensified guerrilla offensive. Owing to the shortage of manpower needed to patrol it, an attempt to close the Thai-Laos border proved ineffectual.

Despite set-backs the security forces scored some noteworthy successes. A CPT-controlled drugs network, which had been an important communist fund-raising organisation, was broken by the Bangkok police. Arms, including rockets, rifles, ammunition and rocket launchers coming in from Laos were seized.

While the communist headquarters remained in Pak Beng in north-west Laos the growth of the insurgency within Thailand was clear, with TPLAF strength rising to about 7700 in 1973, mainly grouped in the north and north east. Towards the close of that year guerrilla activity was reported in 43 out of 71 provinces.

Guerrilla tactics concentrated on selective assassination. Government officials and provincial chiefs were particularly singled out for attack. Road construction and timber workers also suffered heavily. Yet, although the TPLAF used certain general techniques in all regions of Thailand, it took pains to adopt them to local conditions. The TPLAF made much of alleged corruption and the indifference of local officials, inadequate justice and educational and health services deficiencies. TPLAF terror was seldom used systematically but it did intimidate people into not reporting communist activities and compelled peasants to work for the TPLAF, thereby involving them in the insurgency.

In 1974 the rebels set up village militia, which, though not initially armed, helped the TPLAF in matters of intelligence, logistics and supplies. Whilst carrying on irregular guerrilla activities, militants placed their emphasis on mass mobilisation, on developing and improving the organisation, and on propaganda. In 1975, taking advantage of weak central government and communist success in Laos, a sizeable TPLAF column infiltrated Chiang Rai. On 10 April 1974 some 200 TPLAF guerrillas attacked a military post in Nan province killing 19 soldiers.

TPLAF activities expanded in 1976, with an estimated 10,000 communist guerrillas in action in north and north-east Thailand. In the south a further 1500 communist guerrillas operated, often alongside Malaysian Chinese Communist and local Muslim separatists.

The anti-communist coup of October 1976 caused TPLAF insurgents to coalesce with dissident urban-based students, many of whom took to the jungle. Thoughout November the clandestine 'Voice of the People of Thailand' carried messages from former National Student Council leaders calling for insurrection. For two years TPLAF activity posed a serious threat to government so that the monarchy itself appeared in jeopardy.

There followed Vietnam's invasion of Kampuchea in December 1978, after which the dispute between China and Vietnam worsened. It became difficult for the CPT, the TPLAF ruling body, not to take sides, so that in 1979 the party sharply criticised Hanoi's actions. Consequently the TPLAF lost its safe havens in Laos and Kampuchea.

Bangkok policy further weakened TPLAF activity. Amnesties encouraged Thai communists to return to Bangkok, and defectors to surrender. Still, clashes continued, although they involved comparatively small numbers. By the early 1980s TPLAF strength was reckoned at an overall 13,000: 5000 in the north-east, 3000 in the south, and 5000 in the north. The TPLAF probably controlled about 450 villages in 1982.

Thailand Patriotic Front (TPF)

A front organisation for the Communist Party of Thailand (CPT), the TPF was active in the early 1970s. It had been intended to attract other opposition elements into a united front, but the communist affiliation was too apparent. The leadership decided to supercede the Front, and in its place set up the Committee for Coordinating Patriotic and Democracy-Loving Forces.

Vietnam

Vietnam constituted the most important part of the late-nineteenth century French empire of Indo-China; the other parts being Laos and Cambodia. The struggle for independence began in 1945 but had been prepared since 1941 under Japanese suzerainty. It ended in 1954. An early and important feature of the independence movement was the fusion of Marxist-Leninist ideology with nationalism, a process which had begun in the 1930s under colonial rule.

Ho Chi Minh (1890-1968), the founder of the Indo-Chinese Communist Party (1930), called a conference of Vietnamese nationalists in May 1941 in south China. From this congress emerged the legendary Viet Minh, or League for the Independence of Vietnam. Vo Nguyen Giap (b. 1912) was made responsible for setting up a clandestine military organisation.

Giap had spent some of his time with Mao Tse-tung's Chinese communists and came to the job as one of the most outstanding practitioners of guerrilla warfare. By the time the Japanese capitulated, Giap had some 10,000 men under arms. Ho Chi Minh set up a Vietnamese People's Liberation Committee, which, in the name of nationalism, appealed to the newly independent Bao Dai, Emperor of Annam (Central Vietnam) to abdicate. He handed over the Imperial Seals but on 28 August Ho Chi Minh dissolved the Committee and set up a provisional government with the key posts in communist hands. Nonetheless, on 2 September he proclaimed independence in a document redolent of the American Declaration of Independence and France's Declaration of the Rights of Man. Communist rhetoric played no role: independence to all appearances was a nationalist victory.

Disregarding these events, but in accordance with the decisions taken at Potsdam by the victorious allies, the departing Japanese handed power to the Chinese in the north and to the British in the south. Both subsequently withdrew, leaving power to the French, whose troops started arriving in October 1945, when the Viet Minh activated its guerrilla network.

A series of negotiations between the French and the Viet Minh collapsed in September 1946. In launching a general offensive against French forces in Tonking (northern Vietnam) in December Giap began the first Indo-Chinese war. Men he had (60,000), guns he lacked. His initial drive failed and the Viet Minh army was driven northwards into the hills on the Chinese frontier, where they languished for three years.

Then in November 1949 Mao Tse-tung's Chinese communist forces reached the Tonking border, providing the Viet Minh with a sanctuary and logistic support. In the south Viet Minh terrorism extended its hold over village communities, whose headmen if sympathetic to the French were murdered. The French appeared confident that Giap had been defeated and that the string of French fortresses on the Chinese border guaranteed security. In fact Giap's men infiltrated the countryside lying behind the border fortresses and cut them off from the main French army further south. It took 17 days in October 1950 for the Viet Minh to capture the border forts.

In January 1951 the Viet Minh began a drive towards Hanoi and mistakenly chose to fight a set-piece battle against the French at Vinh Yen. Here they were heavily defeated, losing 6000 killed and 500 captured.

A period of guerrilla warfare and relatively small-scale clashes ensued. Concerned by Viet Minh penetration of Laos, which had begun in April 1953, the French commander picked Dien Bien Phu, a few miles from the Laotian border to confront the enemy. The Viet Minh attacked in earnest in March 1954. By 6 May the garrison had fallen.

A Geneva peace conference followed that divided Vietnam along the 17th parallel. The French withdrew from North Vietnam, the Viet Minh from the south. The final agreement included a clause calling for 'free elections' throughout Vietnam in July 1956, which implied unification.

The settlement disappointed the United States, which, having poured money into the French war effort, was reluctant to see the communists triumph in the north. President Eisenhower offered aid to the south to resist aggression. A US advisory mission took over military training from the French.

The second Indo-Chinese War began with terrorist acts in 1958, when the communists attacked Ngo Dinh Diem's government by murdering provincial officials loyal to Saigon. Yet it was not until January 1961 that the communists set up the 'National Front for the Liberation of South Vietnam', better known as the Viet Cong. In October 1961 US President Kennedy, alarmed at guerrilla infiltrations, sent to Saigon a mission which recommended massive US aid. In months the number of US military advisers grew to some 15,000 men. Albeit with instructions to fire only when fired upon, US servicemen became increasingly involved. American relations with the Diem regime grew increasingly strained. Diem, with notable reforms to his credit, was nonetheless an authoritarian figure and his family corrupt. All members of the upper echelons of government were related to the ruling family. Nepotism on such a scale proved unacceptable to Congress and Washington accordingly disassociated itself from Diem. On 1 November 1963 a group of army officers, under General Duong Van Minh, overthrew Diem. Minh in turn was replaced by General Khanh, and finally a new constitution saw General Thieu elected president with a parliamentary legislative system in 1967.

The war went on. By the beginning of 1965 the Viet Cong were within sight of victory. President Johnson announced his readiness to begin 'unconditional discussions', but Hanoi responded with an uncompromising demand for US withdrawal and unification of Vietnam. In June 1965 Johnson authorised the use of US troops for combat duties.

A rapid build-up of US forces in South Vietnam followed. By the autumn of 1966 there were about 330,000 troops fighting in Vietnam. By the spring of 1967 there were 445,000 and by 1968 the figure was approaching 600,000. Nor was foreign intervention restricted to the USA. Alongside the Americans were 45,000 South Koreans, 8000 Australians, 2000 Filipinos, 540 New Zealanders and some 5000 Thais.

Despite losses it seemed to Americans in 1967 that they were winning the war. American air control and the ability to shuttle large numbers of troops quickly, backed up by massive firepower, undoubtedly gave the US advantages. Americans claimed massive body counts of communist dead. Facile assumptions were shattered by the developments of January 1968, when, during the Tet (New Year) celebrations, Viet Cong forces infilitrated Saigon, Danang, Hue and a number of other cities. They attacked a variety of military and civilian targets with devastating effect. In Hue they took the imperial palace and surrendered only after a 26-day siege.

The United States stepped up its bombing of North Vietnam, begun in 1966, inflicting enormous damage, especially to communications. Yet despite the bombs (more were dropped than in the Second World War) infiltration from the north actually increased. It proved a war of endurance with American public opinion becoming the Achilles heel of the US war effort. It forced first President Johnson's resignation and then led to the election of President Richard Nixon, a Republican candidate committed to US withdrawal from Vietnam 'with honour'.

Negotiations in Paris in 1973 produced a ceasefire agreement which left North Vietnamese units in the south. Meanwhile the US had completed its own withdrawal of ground combat forces by 1972, although air and naval power continued to be deployed. It did not save President Thieu (1967-75).

North Vietnam began a build-up in 1974 for a huge offensive the following year. It received overwhelming logistic support from the USSR. When the offensive came it was a conventional military assault. Although some South Vietnamese units put up a creditable resistance, the issue was not long in doubt. On 30 April 1975 North Vietnamese forces took Saigon and accepted the unconditional surrender of South Vietnam. There followed a most dreadful imposition of tyranny which caused many Catholic, French-oriented Vietnamese to flee their country by sea under dangerous conditions that exposed them to rape, piracy and murder.

Bibliography

J. Buttinger, *Vietnam: A Political History* (London, 1969) is good on politics and history. The background to the post-Second World War insurgencies is covered in J.T. McAlister, *Viet-Nam: The Origins of the Revolution* (London, 1970) and in D.G. Marr, *Vietnamese Anticolonialism 1885-1925* (Berkeley, 1971). An interesting Vietnamese viewpoint is supplied by Truong Buu Lam in *Patterns of Vietnamese Response to Foreign Intervention 1858-1900* (Yale, 1967).

Two excellent accounts of the fight against the French are to be found in B. Fall's *Hell is a Very Small Place: The Siege of Dien Bien Phu* (London, 1967) and D. Lancaster's *The Emancipation of French Indochina* (London, 1961).

The literature on the second Indo-Chinese War is immense. Some of the most important works are: D. Pike, *Vietcong: The Organization and Techniques of the National Liberation Front of South Vietnam* (Cambridge, Mass., 1968); D. Pike, *War, Peace and the Viet Cong* (Cambridge, Mass., (1969); G.K. Tanham, *Communist Revolutionary Warfare: From Vietminh to the Viet Cong* (New York, 1961); Dennis Duncanson, *Government and Revolution in Vietnam* (Oxford, 1968). Several works are available on the latter stages of the war, including Alan Dawson, *55 Days: The Fall of South Vietnam* (New York, 1977); Sir Robert Thompson, *Peace is Not at Hand* (London, 1974); and S. Homer, *The Fall of South Vietnam* (New York, 1980).

From the purely military viewpoint, the victor of the final campaign, General Van Tien Dung has written a riveting account in *Our Great Spring Victory: An Account of the Liberation of South Vietnam* (New York, 1977), while the US commanding officer, General W.C. Westmorland, gives the US military's view in his memoirs *A Soldier Reports* (New York, 1976). Important theoretical guerrilla books to emerge from the conflict were those of General Vo Giap which included *People's War, People's Army* (New York, 1962), and *The Military Art of People's War* (New York, 1970).

The two best works on the development of communism in Vietnam are Douglas Pike, *History of Vietnamese Communism, 1925-1976* (Stanford, 1978) and Robert F. Turner, *Vietnamese Communism: Its Origins and Development* (Stanford, 1975).

League for the Independence of Vietnam (Viet Minh)
(Vietnam Doc Lap Dong Minh Hoi)

Better known by the shortened title Viet Minh, the movement first emerged in 1941 under the direction of Ho Chi Minh (1890-1968), following an Indo-China Communist Party (ICP)-sponsored conference of Vietnamese nationalists held that year. Accordingly the Viet Minh put forward a short three-point political programme: defeat of the Japanese, close alliance with China and the United States against fascism, and the eventual establishment of a 'Democratic Republic of Vietnam'. The last point included concrete promises of extensive civil liberties, unlike other Vietnamese nationalist organisations, which merely sought independence from the French. Most telling was the omission from Viet Minh promises of former Indo-China Communist Party (ICP) pledges to confiscate private land. The ICP adopted a low profile in the apparently broader nationalist image of the Viet Minh. Yet it never forfeited control of Viet Minh activities. The ICP's existence became a still greater liability to the Viet Cong in 1945, when the Allies sent anti-communist Chinese *Kuomintang* soldiers to North Vietnam to disarm the Japanese. Ho Chi Minh announced its dissolution in November 1945, but in reality it went underground, and continued to lead the struggle for independence, albeit masking its ultimate Marxist-Leninist intentions.

As Japan surrendered on 13 August 1945, the ICP-controlled Viet Minh called for an insurrection. On 19 August 1945, without significant opposition, the Viet Minh seized control of Hanoi. In the south, however, various non-communist anti-French organisations held the initiative. But the Viet Minh pressed ahead to form their own government in Hanoi on 29 August 1945. The August Revolution was a bloody affair in which ICP influence predominated. Ideological opponents and rivals such as Trotskyists were liquidated. In Hanoi alone some 10,000 people died. Although the Viet Minh set up its own government it felt compelled to negotiate in 1946 with the returning French authorities.

As French control was reestablished and with the departure of the Chinese *Kuomintang* forces from the north, the Viet Minh turned its attention to destroying rival Vietnamese nationalist movements, a task left uncompleted the previous August. Vo Nguyen Giap, assisted in the south by Tran Van Gian, conducted this struggle against 'counter-revolutionaries' such as the *Viet Nam Quoc Dan Dang, Dong Minh Hoi*, Trotskyists and other anti-French elements which had resisted Viet Minh domination.

By December 1946 these elements had been defeated and removed from all influence. Talks failed to persuade the French colonial authorities to go home again, so that the Viet Minh embarked upon the first Indo-Chinese War. By the beginning of 1951 most of the reasons which dictated the 'temporary dissolution' of the ICP in 1945 were gone. Indeed on 1 May 1950 the Viet Minh had acknowledged for the first time that the Democratic Republic of Vietnam belonged to the 'democratic front headed by the Soviet Union'.

The Viet Minh organisation was formally dissolved on 3 March 1951. The ICP had already publicly resurfaced with the holding of its Second National Congress in February 1951. Yet the term 'Viet-Minh' continued to describe the communist-led anti-French forces which finally triumphed at Dien Bien Phu in March 1954.

National Front for the Liberation of South Vietnam (Viet Cong)
(Mat Tran Dan Toc Giai Phong Mien Nam Viet Nam)

The Viet Cong, established in January 1961, was formed as a result of a decision taken in September 1960 by the ruling party in North Vietnam, the Vietnam Workers' *(Lao Dong)* Party. It represented the communists more openly than the earlier Communist front, the Viet Minh. A year later a Marxist-Leninist party, the People's Revolutionary Party (PRP), was set up to provide political leadership to the Viet Cong.

The front's first secretary-general was Nguyen Van Hieu, who presided over the first Congress in early 1962. It envisaged forming a 'broad national democratic administration', which, once power had been won, would 'release political prisoners, guarantee freedom of all parties, accept aid from all countries, proclaim peaceful neutrality and advance the cause of peaceful reunification.' Nevertheless, Le Duan, the former commander of the Viet Minh forces in the south, played a key role in the organisation of the Viet Cong, which was always a creature of the ruling communist party in North Vietnam, the Vietnam Workers' Party (VWP) (formerly the Indo-Chinese Communist Party, which went underground in 1950 and resurfaced the next year under this name).

Prior to 1960 the VWP had openly acknowledged its leadership of communist insurgents in the south, but found that there were many benefits in the pretence that the Viet Cong was an autonomous organisation. Several Western observers were deceived and concluded that the shift to armed struggle in the south had not only been indigenously inspired but was even in conflict with North Vietnamese policy.

Like its predecessor, the Viet Minh, the Viet Cong was in theory a coalition of parties but communist dominance was still harder to hide, yet so as the better to appeal to South Vietnamese, the Viet Cong deliberately played down ideological commitments and emphasised patriotism. Initially the Viet Cong numbered some 6000 guerrillas, but by 1966 recruitment had raised this figure to 50,000 with some 100,000 part-time soldiers. At first the Viet Cong used guerrilla tactics to destroy communications, and ambush patrols. With the Tet (New Year) offensive in early 1968 that led to the occupation of Hue and parts of Saigon, the Viet Cong made the transition from guerrilla to regular warfare, although it subsequently reverted to the former. The influx of North Vietnamese regulars from the mid-sixties onwards greatly added to Viet Cong fighting power. Despite the fact that the Viet Cong were wedded to the notion of a general uprising (_Khoi Nghia) which was supposed to follow from the intensification of guerrilla fighting and acts of terrorism, no rising occurred. The southern army did not dissolve with soldiers joining the people. Northern victory, when it came in April 1975, came thanks to overwhelming conventional attacks by the North Vietnamese army working with the Viet Cong.

Viet Minh
See **League for the Independence of Vietnam**

Viet Cong
See **National Front for the Liberation of South Vietnam**

Oceania

This immense area embraces thousands of mainly tiny islands clustered in hundreds of groups, as well as the principal states of Australia and New Zealand. Since the defeat of Japan in the Second World War, most of these islands have been US overseas territories or protectorates. British colonial possessions have largely been given their independence; the transition involved no political violence except in the New Hebrides.

Apart from New Caledonia, where the French have sought to perpetuate their rule, no significant armed factions have emerged. Australia and New Zealand from time to time encounter problems with their aggrieved aboriginal and Maori minorities, which sometimes lead to outbreaks of violence. No terrorist problem has surfaced.

In the Fiji islands the colonising power, Britain, imported Indians to work the sugar plantations. Today they make up half the population and the resulting ethnic divisions dominate political life, but so far have not been expressed violently. Papua New Guinea, the eastern half of the island of Papua (the west is part of Indonesia), has problems coming to grips with the modern world. Tribes in the mountainous interior have scarcely seen white men and feud among themselves, but without causing broader political ramifications. Samoa, the Solomon Islands and French Polynesia remain politically quiet, although French nuclear tests disturbed local political opinion. Vanuatu, formerly New Hebrides, entered a difficult period of independence in 1980, with a short-lived rebellion and a separatist movement on the island of Espiritu Santo. The troubles proved ephemeral and no political movement committed to political violence remained.

In New Caledonia, a French overseas territory enjoying a measure of autonomy since 1976, violence arises between native Melanesians, known locally as Kanaks, and the European settlers over disputed land rights. In the late 1970s, the Kanak Liberation Party, a Melanesian nationalist body dedicated to the winning of independence, emerged.

Kanak Liberation Party
(Parti de Libération Kanak — Palika)

Palika emerged in the late 1970s as a small Melanesian extremist group demanding independence for New Caledonia and land redistribution in favour of natives.

It established a presence in the expatriate Kanak community in France, and in October 1981 carried out two bomb attacks on nightspots in Paris. Two waiters were injured in an attack on a restaurant. The movement commands only limited support from the Kanak community and is led by Nidouish Naisseline. The term 'Kanak' is local and was used in a derogatory manner by Europeans to denote their superiority over natives.

NORTH AMERICA

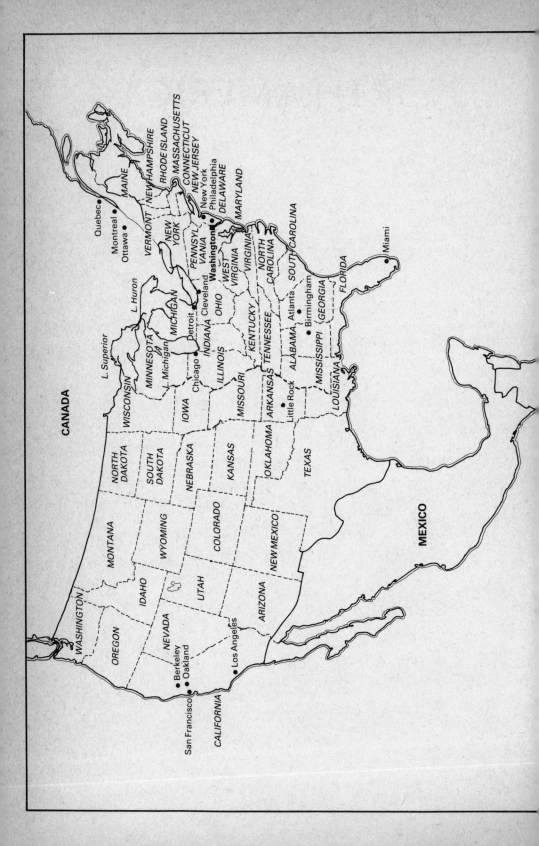

Canada

Canada avoided the traumatic political experiences which shook the confidence of the United States in the 1960s and the 1970s. There was no cause for a black power movement; student radicalism remained untouched by the Vietnam War.

Separatism in Quebec, the French-speaking, Roman Catholic province of Canada, raised the only political violence, which burst briefly in the late 1960s. It was nonetheless a fundamental issue, which in political terms still required a long-term solution, or at least an accommodation, in the 1980s. From abroad, be it from the Americas, from Europe or from the Middle East, Canada remained almost untouched by terrorist incidents.

Bibliography

Dominating Canadian politics of the late 1960s and early 1970s was the issue of Quebec separatism. To understand it Pierre Vallière's *White Niggers of America* (London, 1971) is essential. G. Morf's short book *Terror in Quebec* (Toronto, 1970) is exceptionally useful for its interviews with jailed FLQ members, whose views the author analysed. For a succinct analysis see M. Levine and C. Sylvester, *Crisis in Quebec* (Ontario, 1973). Brian Moore wrote a gripping account of the Laporte murder and the Cross kidnapping in *The Revolution Script* (London, 1972), whilst Denis Smith criticised the Canadian government's response in *Bleeding Hearts . . . Bleeding Country: Canada and the Quebec Crisis* (Edmonton, 1971). A full analysis of the Canadian response can be found in Baudoin, Fortin and Szabo, *Terrorisme et Justice — Entre la Liberté et l'Ordre — le Crime Politique* (Montreal, 1970). Malcolm Reid's *The Shouting Signpainters* (New York and London, 1972) describes the Leftist background of the 1960s in which FLQ flourished. A sketchy 'new' history was written by Jean Claude Robert, *Du Canada Français au Québec Libre* (Paris, 1975), in which the 1960s are covered in the last third of the volume. More useful is John Saywell's *Quebec 70: A Documentary Narrative* (Toronto, 1971). J. Gellner focused on the 1970 crisis in *Bayonets in the Streets —Urban Guerrilla at Home and Abroad* (Ontario, 1974). In *Quebec in Question* (Toronto, 1971) Marcel Rioux writes as a separatist and Professor of Sociology at the University of Montreal. Nicholas Regush reviewed events in *Pierre Vallière's The Revolutionary Process in Quebec* (New York, 1973). For a view from the dogmatic left on revolutionary potential, see the Trotskyist *Prospects for a Socialist Canada*

(Toronto and New York, 1977) edited by John Riddell and Art Young. Pierre Vallière criticised the middle road of the Parti Québécois in *The Impossible Quebec* (Montreal, 1980). For René Lévesque's ideas see *An Option for Quebec* (Toronto, 1968).

Quebec Liberation Front
(*Front de Libération du Québec* — FLQ)

The FLQ leapt to prominence in 1970, although members had engaged in sporadic, violent acts for at least seven years. In 1980 the movement had been moribund for a decade, partly because the early protagonists were caught, tried and imprisoned, partly because separatist aspirations were channelled into legitimate political paths — namely through the *Parti Québécois*, which won power in the province in 1976.

In February 1963 the FLQ was formed by a breakaway group from the *Réseau de Résistance*, which had begun to stockpile arms for an eventual campaign. The first FLQ actions were no more than Molotov cocktails hurled at military establishments. The group set out to attack the police and military, English-language companies and businesses. It was no less antagonistic towards US influence and connections.

In fact, the bomb targets included the National Revenue building in Montreal and Quebec City, a television transmitting tower on Mount Royal, and a dozen post boxes and telephone kiosks. Responsible were Georges Schoeters, Gabriel Hudon and Raymond Villeneuve, who led no more than a score of sympathisers, most of whom were under 24 years old. Most served sentences and had been released by 1967. Schoeters returned to his native Belgium, Villeneuve left for Cuba and Hudon went to prison again.

The 1963 arrests did not stop separatist violence. For a short while an FLQ offshoot, the *Armée de Libération du Québec* (ALQ), robbed banks; Gabriel Hudon's younger brother led the gang of six, all of whom were under 23. They too were arrested and in turn were succeeded in 1964 by the *Armée Révolutionnaire du Québec* (ARQ) led by François Schirm. He was sentenced to life imprisonment for murder in 1965, alongside four colleagues whom the FLQ sought to exchange for James Cross, the British trade commissioner, and Pierre Laporte, the labour minister, in 1970.

By the mid-1960s FLQ sympathisers were meeting up with Black Power followers in the USA. Their journal, *La Cognée*, preached in favour of a workers' revolution, and it encouraged readers to make bombs and generally practise violence for political ends. Members stole dynamite, arms and ammunition and resumed with sporadic incidents the separatist campaign in 1966.

Arrests followed, but Pierre Vallières, the FLQ's most celebrated theorist, was not immediately caught. Neither was his colleague, Charles Gagnon, a sociologist from Montreal. The two men fled south and began a hunger strike outside the United Nations in New York. It was at this time that Vallières wrote what became the classic separatist tome, *White*

Niggers of America. They were deported and imprisoned, having been found guilty of conspiracy to commit robbery and to explode bombs.

A lull in the violence lasted until the autumn of 1968, when further bombs were exploded in Montreal and Ottawa. By 1969 the authorities were convinced they faced an organised subversive movement which planned eventual armed insurrection. Indeed, Minister of Justice Remi Paul went so far as to estimate that 3000 people were involved, although by no means all were FLQ members. Furthermore, he asserted that the separatist movement was guided and partially financed by foreign countries, including Cuba. It is certainly true that Gagnon and others felt the Quebec cause was part of a world-wide liberation process which included the Palestinians, the Vietnamese and Black Americans. Such a position was considered 'internationalist' and 'anti-imperialist'.

The year 1970 saw the peak of FLQ terrorist activity. 'I do not believe in individual terrorism', wrote Vallières at the time, 'but I believe in revolutionary violence of all kinds, integrated into a very precise strategy.' In effect, the strategy turned out to be kidnapping — an aborted abduction of the US consul in Montreal, of Cross, the British trade commissioner, and of Laporte, the labour minister in October 1970. The purpose was primarily publicity, but also to demonstrate solidarity with the Cuban revolution.

The Canadian government reacted by proclaiming the War Measures Act, never before employed in peace time, and arrested some 250 suspects who could be detained without charge for 21 days. The kidnappers reacted by murdering Laporte — four men were involved: Paul and Jacques Rose, Francis Simard and Bernard Lortie. Cross was released unharmed in return for a passage to Cuba for his abductors.

Thereafter the FLQ was dormant in Canada, although politically the cause of separatism flourished when in 1976 the secessionist leader, René Lévesque, won a comfortable majority in the provincial legislature for his *Parti Québécois*. In a climate of peaceful and legitimate reform the FLQ held no attraction.

United States

Political violence in the US surrounded two issues during the 1960s — the black civil rights problem in the south and the Vietnam War. Demonstrations favouring both causes were sufficiently widespread to have national importance.

Behind the southern problem lay decades of anti-black violence promoted by the Ku Klux Klan (KKK), which reemerged right across the southern states after the Second World War. Partly in response to provocation, and partly because of the long-standing injustices practised by whites against the negro, there arose in the mid-1950s the civil rights movement led by Dr Martin Luther King.

The immediate issues were racially segregated transport and schooling. The specific instances best remembered are the cases of Mrs Rosa Parks (1955) who, refusing to give up her seat on a city bus, was arrested and fined ten dollars. Two years later riots at Little Rock, Arkansas, prevented black children attending school without the daily protection of regular federal troops.

By 1960 blacks were participating in sit-in demonstrations against racial segregation in shops and stores. Such passive action provoked an appallingly ugly white reaction, which caused, although at first without loss of life, persistent and widespread bloody incidents, frequently of a barbarous nature. Bombings and killings followed in 1962. Violence in Birmingham, Alabama, in 1963 was particularly vicious and drew the attention of the world; Martin Luther King was at the centre of the protests, before and after a bomb blast in a black church had killed four little girls that September. In all, throughout the year, 13 people died in black/white confrontation.

After the assassination of President John Kennedy in November 1963, white violence grew worse with bombings, arson and beatings, occurrances which merely consolidated black feeling and determined the Federal Government to pursue integration still more thoroughly. In Mississippi alone, more than a score of black churches were burned during the summer of 1964. That year rioting spread to the north with spontaneous racial violence in Cleveland, New York, Philadelphia and elsewhere. The appearance of television crews on the streets was seen to exacerbate the tensions.

An apparent culmination to the violence came in 1965 with the Watts riots. That year 17 people died in the south, 14 of whom were blacks and civil rights workers killed by whites, for the most part in Alabama and

Mississippi. But in the Watts district of Los Angeles in August 34 lives were lost. A minor incident in a black area erupted into six days of rioting involving as many as 10,000 blacks, and the destruction of property valued at over $20 million.

If that seemed bad, 1966 was worse. Los Angeles experienced further massive disorders, but other cities badly affected by the communal violence were Chicago, Cleveland, New York, San Francisco and Atlanta. Less serious rioting occurred in two dozen other cities, but disturbances spread in 1967, when 83 people died in 75 urban riots. Martin Luther King described American cities as 'powder kegs'. The worst hit was Detroit, where in one week in July 43 people died.

At this point consideration was given to the part played by inflammatory speeches pronounced by prominent radicals and particularly by Stokeley Carmichael, who said in Havana that the American negro was fighting a guerrilla war to establish his rights and that a 'revolutionary movement' would be initiated to help him. To Che Guevara he said, 'we eagerly await your writings in order to read them, digest them and plan our tactics based upon them.'

Hitherto, the black struggle in the south had been largely led by such bodies as the National Association for the Advancement of Coloured People (NAACP — 1909), the Congress on Racial Equality (CORE — 1942) and, more recently, Martin Luther King's Southern Christian Leadership Conference (SCLC) set up in 1957. Different in kind was the 1960 Student Non-Violent Coordinating Committee (SNCC), although it too subscribed to King's non-violent ideology until 1965, when the Watts riots convinced many members of the need for Black Power. The change came in May 1966, when Stokeley Carmichael became SNCC president. Thereafter, it was SNCC's aim to be black staffed, black controlled and black financed. Members emphasised too the right of self-defence.

A further important change came about with Carmichael's arrival — his own commitment against the Vietnam War linked SNCC to the direct action campaign of anti-Vietnam protesters. Yet within a year SNCC had lost its influence, partly because its funds dried up, but also because in 1967 Carmichael was under indictment. Meanwhile, others had taken up the radicalisation of black politics with the founding in California of the Black Panther Party, which absorbed SNCC in 1968.

Side by side SNCC in the early days was Students for a Democratic Society (SDS), founded the same year and shortly to set up its headquarters in the same city — Atlanta. SDS did for blacks in the north what SNCC did in the south, but from the start it was more politicised in that members were distrustful of representative democratic forms and looked to the formation of a new Left. Prominent in the movement was Tom Hayden, who drafted the SDS Port Huron Statement of 1962, when unilateral disarmament measures were called for alongside the gradual elimination of NATO. By 1965 SDS had moved from a reformist position to a revolutionary stance, embracing Marxism-Leninism. SDS became increasingly involved in anti-Vietnam War activity and broader Third World issues, and in doing so transformed itself into a major component of the North American New Left.

It enjoyed an active membership of some 6000 students in 200 chapters in the mid-1960s, but without either discipline or intellectual rigour SDS very quickly disintegrated. Its main inspiration had been Herbert Marcuse's *One Dimensional Man*, and from that publication freshmen and sophomores moved rapidly into the Californian hippie world.

Those who remained in politics in 1968/69 turned to quarrelling over tactics, philosophy and issues. From the factions emerged the Weatherman, with former SDS leaders like Bernardine Dohrn to the fore. These people turned to isolated acts of terrorism.

The hippie movement itself was to some extent politicised with the creation in February 1968 of The Youth International Party (Yippies), an attempt by the Free Speech Movement and the Vietnam Day Committee to widen their support. Behind this extraordinary confusion, the names of Jerry Rubin, Abbie Hoffman and Paul Krassner stood out. But it was not to last. Rubin and Hoffman changed their identities and took up normal lives, before coming out into the open a decade later.

The fractionalisation of SDS gave rise, in addition to Weatherman, to all sorts of splinter groups — the October League, the Revolutionary Union, the New American Movement, and from these in turn developed the New Year's Gang, the Red Guerrilla Family, *Venceremos*, the Symbionese Liberation Army and dozens more of still less significance.

In the mid-1970s militant Puerto Rican separatists moved to the forefront of American political violence. Active on the mainland, they lacked popular support on the island, to which they extended their intermittent bombing in the late 1970s. At this time, fearful for Israel's survival, some minority sections of the North American Jewish community took to harassment and even to terrorism through the Jewish Defence League and the Jewish Action Movement. Exiled Cubans operating through Omega 7 provided another dimension to political violence as they attacked official Cuban premises in the late 1970s. From time to time, exiled Croats from Yugoslavia were active. However, although North Americans abroad were the special targets of terrorist groups, international terrorism did not affect them at home in the early 1980s.

Bibliography
In the United States an enormous body of books exists on every facet of American violence, although much of it makes tedious reading and often consists of poor analysis. For the facts on political violence, one can start with the Facts on File series published in New York in 1974 *Violence in the United States 1956-71* (2 vols) and *Political Terrorism 1971-78* (2 vols), distributed in Europe by Clio Press, Oxford.

The black problem requires some reading of the black protest literature of the period — a selection is contained in the 25 essays presented by Richard Young in *Roots of Rebellion: The Evolution of Black Politics and*

Protest since World War II (New York and London, 1970). A documentary record of the Black Panthers is provided by Philip Foner, *The Black Panthers Speak* (Lippincott, New York, 1970); at greater length by Panther leaders are Bobby Seale's *Seize the Time, the Story of the Black Panther Party and Huey P. Newton* (New York, Random House, 1970), Earl Anthony's *Picking up the Gun* (Dial Press, New York, 1970), and Stokeley Carmichael's and Charles Hamilton's *Black Power, the Politics of Liberation in America* (Vintage Books, New York, 1967). George Jackson's *Soledad Brother* and *Blood in My Eye*, published by Jonathan Cape in 1971 and 1972 respectively, were influential, so too was the volume edited by Angela Davis, *If They Come in the Morning* (Orbach and Chambers, London, 1971). She wrote *An Autobiography* (New York, 1974). Eldridge Cleaver wrote a slim but important volume, *Soul on Ice* (Jonathan Cape, 1969), whilst Huey P. Newton contributed *Revolutionary Suicide* (Wildwood House, London, 1974), after Cleaver's defection from revolution. Malcom X's story can be read in Alex Haley's *The Autobiography of Malcolm X* (Grove Press, New York, 1964). Eric Lincoln researched and wrote *Black Muslims in America* (Beacon Press, 1961 and 1973), a model sociological analysis. *Why We Can't Wait, Strength to Love* and *Stride toward Freedom* (Harper Row, New York and London, 1964) by Martin Luther King influenced moderate black opinion.

Student protest merged with the violence surrounding the black issue. Seymour Martin Lipset analysed the upsurge in *Rebellion in the University* (Routledge Kegan Paul, London, 1972), but an earlier book he edited draws interesting cross-national comparisons in a series of essays published by Basic Books (New York and London) in 1967, entitled *Student Politics*. A more popular but nonetheless excellent account is John Searle's *The Campus War* (Penguin, 1972). More detailed accounts come in *Crisis at Colombia* (Random House, New York, 1970) by J. Eszterhas and M.D. Roberts; James Michener's *Kent State, What Happened and Why* (London, 1971); and *The Berkeley Student Revolt: Facts and Interpretations* (Doubleday, Anchor, New York, 1965) edited by Seymour Martin Lipset and Sheldon Wolin. A general summary by the US establishment is provided in a staff report to the National Commission on the Causes and Prevention of Violence entitled *The Politics of Protest: Violent Aspects of Protest and Confrontation* (1969) by Jerome Skolnick, and available through the US Government Printing Office.

To grasp some of the ideas behind the protest movement, Massimo Teodori edited a useful selection in *The New Left: A Documentary History* (Bobbs Merrill, New York, 1969), and Roderick Aya and Norman Miller edited *The New American Revolution* (New York, 1971). More specifically, Harold Jacobs edited *Weatherman* (Ramparts Press, New York, 1970) and Susan Stern wrote an account of her experiences *With the Weathermen* (New York, 1975). For the playboy terrorism of the San Francisco Bay area, read David Boulton's *The Making of Tania Hearst* (London, 1975) and the splendid introduction to the complete documentary, *The Symbionese Liberation Army* (Editions Rodopi NV, Amsterdam, 1974).

For a brief contemporary overview see Brian Jenkins, *Terrorism in the United States* (Rand Corporation, Santa Monica, 1980). *Hooded Americanism* (New York, 1965) by David Chalmers is the best modern account of the Ku Klux Klan, but the earlier fundamental work of C. Lester and D. L. Wilson, *Ku Klux Klan: Its Origin, Growth and Disbandment* (New York, 1905) edited by Walter Fleming deserves recognition. A contemporary account is provided by Stetson Kennedy, *I Rode with the Ku Klux Klan* (London, 1954), and see 'The Resurrection of the Klan' in *American Journal of Sociology* 65, 1960, pp 456-62. On Puerto Rican Terrorism see William Sater's *Puerto Rican Terrorists: A Possible Threat to US Energy Installations* for the Rand Corporation (Santa Monica, 1981).

More generally on the problems of terrorism, the following findings are useful: *Political Kidnappings*, Committee on Internal Security, House of Representatives (Washington, 1973); *Terrorism*, Parts 1-4, Committee on Internal Security, House of Representatives (Washington, 1974) and *Terrorist Activity*, Parts 1-8, Committee of the Judiciary, House of Representatives (Washington 1974/75). In addition to these reports, there exists a Staff Study for the Committee on Internal Security entitled simply *Terrorism* (Washington, 1974). On statistics of incidents, the Central Intelligence Agency (CIA) publishes a yearly report for general distribution, although the criteria used for selection are somewhat unsatisfactory.

Armed Forces of National Liberation
(*Fuerzas Armadas de Liberación Nacional — FALN*)

The FALN is a Spanish-speaking Puerto Rican separatist group active for the most part on the United States mainland in New York and Chicago. It surfaced in 1974 but sprang to prominence the following year with the dramatic explosion of a bomb in New York's Fraunces Tavern. 'The Yanki government is trying to terrorise and kill our people to intimidate us from seeking our rightful independence from colonialism.'

In fact, Puerto Rico enjoys an associated status with the United States and is self-governing. Although the island abides by US federal law, it neither pays federal taxes nor votes for the President or Congress, since Puerto Ricans have their own elected legislature in San Juan. Only the minority Puerto Rican Socialist Party (PSP) favours full independence and is sympathetic towards FALN ambitions.

Since the first bomb, which killed four people and wounded 54, others have followed. Stores in New York were targeted for incendiary attacks in the summer of 1976 and by the end of the year FALN had claimed over 50 bomb attacks. They involved little loss of life, although passers-by were accidentally injured by the explosions.

Alongside the FBI, multinational companies such as Chrysler and Gulf and Western became targets. In 1978 banks and department stores were hit in Puerto Rico itself — a new development. That year the group exploded its one hundredth bomb, a campaign which was pursued throughout 1979 and 1980 without making any significant political impact. It was thought to have no more than 50 members, ten of whom were convicted for terrorist offences in December 1980. Incidents continued however with the US military becoming special targets on the island in the early 1980s.

Black Panther Party (BPP)

In October 1966 Huey Newton (b. 1942) and Bobby Seale (b. 1937) founded the BPP in Oakland, California. Newton was a southern black who had participated in the Watts riots (1965) and was later convicted of manslaughter, a conviction quashed on appeal in 1970. Earlier he had introduced Seale to the fundamental elements of Marxism-Leninism and together they set up an Afro-American party, which subsequently became the Black Panthers.

Both men attracted devotion, Seale particularly. He had once served in the US Air Force and then worked as an industrial labourer. In Chicago he was charged and sentenced for killing a policeman, but he escaped from jail. On rearrest he had his original sentence quashed, but was imprisoned on another count. All the while he remained chairman of the BPP. Other leading members of the organisation were Eldridge Cleaver, David Hilliard, Stokeley Carmichael, Rap Brown, James Forman and Emory Douglas.

The BPP was an all-black organisation; its members were fundamentally motivated by black nationalism. The party label was not original: it was employed by a number of local groups at the time. For the first three years of its existence, the BPP was little more than a West Coast group — an offshoot of Los Angeles. Attempting to harness ghetto violence to black politics, the BPP recruited from disaffected young people in poor black districts. Most had petty criminal backgrounds, so that Panther membership did not imply any great change in their life-style.

The BPP programme, such as it was, included comprehensive welfare benefits for black people, amnesty for all black prisoners, exemption from military service, and a demand that blacks should have a distinct national identity. Newton was influenced by the political thought of Mao Tse-tung and adopted the Leninist concept of 'democratic centralism' as the basis for party decisions. Yet in reality the BPP never developed a Leninist cohesion, nor indeed applied rigorous Marxist analysis. It remained eclectic and ideologically weak. The strongest influences on the movement were Frantz Fanon, Fidel Castro, Kwame Nkrumah, and Malcolm X.

The Black Panthers shot to national prominence because the media reported an incident in 1967, when 26 Panthers dramatically walked into the Californian State Legislature in Sacramento to read a political statement. They held loaded guns. The bearing of arms is not illegal in the

USA, but the encouragement given by the party to all blacks to arm themselves bordered on incitement to revolt. And once armed, Panthers provoked armed confrontations with the police.

In February 1968 the BPP allied with the Student Non-Violent Co-ordinating Committee (SNCC), bringing into the party Stokeley Carmichael, James Forman and Hubert Geroid (Rap) Brown. Disagreeing on the coalition, some SNCC members left later that year, but thereafter SNCC ceased to exist as a separate entity. In addition, the BPP received support from the ultra-leftist Students for a Democratic Society (SDS).

Eldridge Cleaver (b. 1936) was at the time of great influence on the party. With a prison background for rape and assault, he was nonetheless lionised by the new left at Berkeley, where he was invited by the students to lecture on racism. It became fashionable among the radical chic to take up the Panthers' cause. In November 1968 Cleaver fled the US, forfeiting bail, for Cuba. After a few months it was suggested he should leave for Algeria, where he openly set up an office overseas. In 1970 he led a BPP delegation to North Korea.

Although it is true that the BPP epitomised black militancy in the USA in the late 1960s, it is also true that it never directed or controlled the communal violence, which had divers local causes. Nonetheless, at its peak the party probably enjoyed a membership of 2000 in at least 61 cities in 26 different states, mostly outside the south. A typical chapter had a hard core of a score and most of the leaders had criminal records. They ranged in age between 18 and 23, one-quarter of whom were women. Those with college backgrounds seldom stayed in the party long.

In 1969 21 BPP members were indicted in New York on charges of conspiring to set off bombs at fashionable stores and to sabotage the railway. In Sacramento, California, a gunfight raged around the party's headquarters in June, when 13 policemen were wounded before the offices were evacuated. FBI Director, Edgar Hoover, claimed after the confrontation that the BPP represented 'the greatest threat to the internal security of the country'. Further gunfights took place that year at BPP offices in nine cities including Chicago and Los Angeles, where 300 police besieged the building.

Some observers felt strongly that the BPP was deliberately provoked by police action, but there could be no denying that the BPP had turned to violence at a time of nationwide radicalisation of political issues, especially of black politics following the murder in April 1968 of Martin Luther King. The Congress Internal Security Committee reported in August 1971 that the BPP 'through its deliberately inflammatory rhetoric and through the actual arming and military training of its members, had contributed to an increase in acts of violence and constitutes a threat to the internal security of the United States.'

By then, however, the original leadership was no longer around to direct the party. Cleaver was in Algeria; Rap Brown had disappeared in May 1970 and was only recaptured in October 1971, after which he was convicted for armed robbery; Bobby Seale was in jail for contempt of court. Newton renounced violence in May 1971. In addition, serious disagreement had arisen between Cleaver in exile and those that had remained in the US, so that by 1972 the party was in steady decline.

Boricua Popular Army, or Machete Wielders
(Ejército Popular de Boricua — EPB, or Los Macheteros)

The EPB emerged in Puerto Rico in 1978 as a small separatist group practising terrorism specifically targeted at the police and the military, which for its members represented US foreign domination. The EPB's most spectacular raid took place on 12 January 1981, when militants damaged nine aircraft at a base near Isla Verde international airport. The EPB has operated on the US mainland, particularly in Chicago.

Boricua refers to the rural inland islander in Puerto Rico. The EPB is supported by the minority (6000 voters) Marxist-Leninist Puerto Rican Socialist Party (PSP), led by José Mari Bras, a close political colleague of Cuba's Fidel Castro.

Coordination of United Revolutionary Organisations
(Coordinación de Organizaciones Revolucionarias Unidas — CORU)

CORU was founded in June 1976 by Orlando Bosch Avila as an umbrella group for right-wing Cuban exiles in the USA. Among the groups supposedly represented were Cuban Action, Cuban National Liberation Front, the Bay of Pigs Veterans' Association and the National Cuban Movement. For the most part based in Florida, members attacked Cuban government interests in Miami, Washington, New York and Puerto Rico.

The worst incident was the explosion of a bomb on a Cuban airliner in mid-flight in October 1976, for which Bosch was held in jail in Venezuela. His colleagues carried out a number of attacks on Venezuelan property in the US in retaliation for the course of justice taking place. Seventy-three people had died in the aircraft explosion. Mexican government property too has suffered from CORU attacks.

DuBois Clubs

The clubs were front organisations of the Communist Party USA, and were used in the 1960s, amongst other purposes, to subvert Students for a Democratic Society.

George Jackson Brigade

The Brigade was named after a black drop-out from Chicago and Los Angeles who was killed in August 1971, during a prison riot in San Quentin jail. Whilst in prison for robbery he had been charged with the murder in a riot of a white guard. Jackson is known principally for a series of letters he wrote from jail entitled *Soledad Brothers*, which were published in 1970 with an introduction by the French author, Jean Genet.

The Brigade which took his name was active in the mid-1970s in bank robberies and bombings in the states of Oregon and Washington on the west coast of the United States. The few members were typical at the time of superficially politicised criminals who sought personal gain using political excuses.

Jewish Defence League

Led by New York Rabbi Meir Kahane, the League was founded in 1968 to defend Jews from anti-semitic acts, particularly by blacks, perpetrated in Brooklyn. In foreign policy it sought the release of Jews from the Soviet Union and was militantly pro-Israeli. Demonstrations were held outside the Soviet embassy where pickets and mass sitdowns were organised. But League members went further than most protest groups in forcibly entering Soviet diplomatic premises, chaining themselves to buildings, disrupting Soviet theatre productions and burning the Soviet flag.

On occasions there has been harassment of individuals, sometimes of Jews whom the League considered too liberal. The League numbered several thousand members in the mid-1970s. It splintered in 1978/79, with a Jewish Armed Resistance, a Jewish Action Movement and a New Jewish Defence League emerging. A handful of members was jailed on bomb charges in 1979 and 1980. Most of the devices were incendiary in nature and were thrown or left outside commercial premises considered to favour the Soviet Union or Arab political power. The League opposed the US sale of fighter aircraft to Arab States, and in January 1981 bombed an Iranian bank in San Francisco, presumably in retaliation for Iran's treatment of Jews.

Ku Klux Klan (KKK)

The Klan originated after the American Civil War, when defeated southerners found it necessary to organise a clandestine network of vigilantes to protect their womenfolk and their interests generally in times of social disorganisation and lawlessness following the collapse of traditional southern order. Night-time attacks were mounted against selected black and republican targets, during which as many as a thousand individuals were murdered. In 1869 Nathan Beford Forrest dissolved the Klan, although actions continued intermittently for a further two years.

The Klan's resurrection in the 1920s was a short-lived but national phenomenon, albeit based on Georgia, in particular in Atlanta. At that time the KKK had considerable impact upon local politics, in which Klan supporters voted for militant white Anglo-Saxon Protestant interests, yet the organisation never developed a centralised coordinating body.

Private greed and an in-built proclivity to violence reduced its attraction, causing support to shrink in the 1930s and 1940s, when it added anti-communism and anti-semitism to its tenets. The issue of integrated black-white schooling following the 1954 Supreme Court ruling, provoked the Klan into renewed action. Animated by night-time dramas of burning crosses, militants provoked violent demonstrations and sidewalk punch-ups. Arson and bomb attacks destroyed selected schools, churches, synagogues and private houses. Nor did members shrink from the murder of blacks or from fire-arms attacks. In general, however, conservative southern opposition to liberalism and to human rights regarded the Klan with suspicion and even abhorrence.

In 1966 the House Un-American Activities Committee denounced Klan members as terrorists, who were active in more than a dozen organisations in 15 states. Together they amounted to some 15,000 activists. A celebrated trial in 1967 found Sam Holloway Bowers (43), Imperial Wizard of the White Knights of the KKK, guilty of conspiracy in the 1964 murder of three civil rights workers near Philadelphia. Throughout the decade of the 1970s, Klan activities subsided, although the nature of North American society has not allowed the Klan to die completely.

May 2 Movement

This movement was the youth branch of the pro-Peking Progressive Labor Party. When the PLP disbanded it in February 1966, the party ordered the branch's members to join Students for a Democratic Society, which it actively subverted.

National Socialist White People's Party (NSWPP)

Originally founded by George Lincoln Rockwell as the American Nazi Party, the NSWPP numbered in the late 1970s several hundred activists. Rockwell was murdered by a member of his own group, but the party retained the identity it had discovered during the 1960s civil rights clashes.

In the 1970s it exploited racial tensions in Washington, Chicago Philadelphia, Detroit and Los Angeles, from its headquarters in Arlington, Virginia. The NSWPP publication, *White Power*, holds up a White

America as a political ideal, indeed it advocates a 'new faith based on race'. It uses the swastika as a symbol, and overtly insults blacks and Jews. Gatherings are predominantly male, and often seek to venerate the memory of Adolf Hitler. It was active in high schools in depressed, racially mixed areas, and instigated violence through distributing pamphlets and holding provocative meetings in extravagant political costume.

New American Movement (NAM)

A meeting of 75 people in Chicago in October 1971 founded NAM. They came from 25 cities to debate and subsequently approve the idea that the transition to socialism required struggle by the working people, particularly blacks and women, so as to oust an American ruling class which ran the US according to its own interests. Chapters were developed in places of work to further these ends.

Among the most prominent activists was Jeremy Rifkin, largely responsible for the growth too of the People's Bicentennial Commission, an 'alternative' celebration of the bicentenary of the USA.

New World Liberation Front (NWLF)

Set up in 1973 in the San Francisco Bay area, the NWLF claimed 16 out of 28 bombings in California in 1974. Targets were big business corporations such as General Motors and Standard Oil, which were allegedly hit 'on behalf of poor people who see their lives drained daily by parasitic corporations . . . Through our demands we seek relief for poor people and a chance to demonstrate that, in unity through armed struggle poor people can and will win.'

To start with, the group consisted of no more than a score of militants, largely the product of the Californian life-style. With its origins in the radicalism of the late 1960s, the NWLF was never a serious revolutionary threat, although it presented a challenge to law and order. Police uncovered a number of bomb factories in the mid-1970s and made several arrests; the explosive had been stolen from local quarries.

The NWLF supported Puerto Rican 'nationalists' in 1977 and exploded a pipe bomb outside a nuclear power plant in Oregon. Other targets were the Pacific Gas and Electric Company and the Union Oil Company, where sabotage was inflicted. Such attacks continued throughout the late 1970s, but confined largely to California. With an eye to publicity, the NWLF has adopted the habit of the press conference, which is given on behalf of the organisation by the Peoples Information Relay No. 1 (PIR-1).

October League

The League emerged from the June 1969 break up of Students for a Democratic Society, with Michael Klonsky as its chairman. Active at first in Los Angeles, it influenced other organisations, especially the labour movement. It instigated wild-cat strikes and held regional 'labour conferences'.

Ideologically the League adopted a pro-Chinese Marxist-Leninist stance, but did not indulge in terrorist acts. It published *The Call*. Klonsky later moved on to lead the official Communist Party (Marxist-Leninist), which was recognised by Peking, and which incorporated the League's journal. The new party had several thousand members, and in 1980 was one of the two most important pro-Chinese parties in the USA, the other being the Revolutionary Communist Party (RCP).

Omega 7

Omega 7 is a pseudonym used by exiled Cubans in the USA. Outrages were committed from 1978 in the name of this clandestine group, including two minor firebomb attacks on the Cuban mission to the United Nations. Other targets included radio stations, publishing houses and newspaper offices considered too favourable to the Castro regime, and on occasions commercial companies trading with Cuba. In 1980 Omega 7 showed it was prepared to kill by placing a bomb under the car of the Cuban Ambassador to the UN.

Organisation of Afro-American Unity

Malcolm X (Malcolm Little) built up the Organisation before black rivals assassinated him in February 1965. Having served time in prison, where he was converted to the Nation of Islam and took the name Al Hajj Malik Shabazz, he travelled widely, promoting the idea that black Americans should identify with the Third World's coloured minorities. Furthermore, through the Organisation he opposed US policy in Vietnam and spoke on his theme in many developing countries, where he had been invited to lecture.

At home, the Organisation advocated a right for blacks of 'retaliatory violence', or 'armed self-defense'. In some respects the Organisation was a forerunner of the Black Panther Party, whose leaders revered the memory of Malcolm X.

Polar Bear Party

The party was a Californian hybrid group which sprang up in the late 1960s. It originated as a white racist group committed to neo-Nazi notions of Aryan purity. The party described itself as politically oriented and dedicated not only to prison reform but to the abandonment of prison entirely. Despite its racism, members moved ideologically towards Maoism, before splitting and dividing their attention between a multitude of transient issues.

Revolutionary Action Movement
(Movimiento de Acción Revolucionaria — MAR)

The MAR is a separatist group which operated intermittently during the late 1970s in Puerto Rico, especially in the San Juan area. Its activities bore no comparison with the damage inflicted by the Armed Forces of National Liberation (FALN) or even the Boricua Popular Army (EPB). Other such minor groups included the so-called Revolutionary Commandos of the People (CRP) and the Organisation of Volunteers for the Puerto Rican Revolution (OVRP).

Revolutionary Communist Party (RCP)

With no more than a few thousand members, the RCP is nonetheless with the Communist Party (Marxist-Leninist) one of the two most prominent Maoist organisations in the USA. In 1979 the RCP defended the 'gang of four' from Chinese government condemnation, and demonstrated vigorously in New York against US-China rapprochement. It also threw red paint at the Soviet Ambassador to the United Nations.

The RCP had been active on certain university campuses, especially after the Kent State killings in 1970 of four white students, and among black prisoners in jail. Its strongest support lies in Chicago, but it has never actually engaged in terrorism.

Students for a Democratic Society (SDS)

By mid-1969 SDS was dead, but from it had sprung a number of violent factions such as the Weatherman. SDS had its roots in an earlier organisation, the Socialist League for Industrial Democracy, which, before the Second World War, had spoken for socialism in student circles. Its pacifist stance during the war had lost it popularity, and eventually in 1959 it changed its name to Students for a Democratic Society.

SDS was the start of a new left in North American university life, a left which rejected orthodox communism as practised by Moscow, but which was not altogether averse to Marxism. The movement's founding political text was provided in 1962 by Tom Hayden's Port Huron Statement, which called for the 'progressive realignment of the Democratic Party'.

The way to achieve such a change was through 'participatory democracy'. Sympathisers were against 'racism, militarism, nationalism, oppression of mind and spirit, unrestrained capitalism, provincialism of various kinds, and the Bomb.' The 'military industrial complex' was responsible for an illiberal foreign policy and for excessive defence spending. Such a posture, SDS argued, was illogical when the USSR did not have a first-strike capacity. The American military response had been more effective in deterring the growth of democracy than in deterring communism, and furthermore, in Hayden's estimation, the risk that the USSR would achieve nuclear preponderance was remote. For this reason, SDS urged unilateral disarmament, discontinuing the Polaris submarine programme and dismantling the bases contiguous to the Soviet Union. Lastly, NATO, it thought, should be gradually eliminated.

At first SDS concerned itself with the civil rights protests on behalf of blacks, but by the mid-1960s it was increasingly concerned with opposing the Vietnam War. The turning point was President Johnson's heavy bombing of North Vietnam in February 1965, and within a year the draft was a national issue for students across America. The tactics used however were no more than demonstrations, meetings and pickets.

By 1968 SDS had turned in its solidarity compaigns to embracing so many issues that it lacked any coherent philosophy. Amongst the causes it championed were American Indians, Puerto Ricans, Women's Liberation, homosexuals, in addition to blacks and anti-war groups. In all, SDS had some 40,000 supporters at that time.

SDS President, Carl Davidson, described his supporters as 'morally outraged about the war, cops, racism, poverty, parents, the middle class and authority figures in general. They have a sense that all those things are connected somehow, and that money has something to do with it. They long for community, and feel their own isolation acutely, which is probably why they stick with SDS.'

Within the movement, some — the Progressive Labour faction — turned to a stricter Marxism. These people were disciplined and looked for leadership to Peking. They aimed to organise revolution by infiltrating and taking over the protest vote which SDS represented. There were others too, such as the Trotskyists and the pro-Moscow members of the Communist Party of the USA, who sought to exploit SDS in their own interests.

In April 1968 SDS members turned to direct action, most memorably at Columbia University, where for six days they occupied buildings in defiance of the police. Mark Rudd, the future Weatherman, came to the fore as a leader. The activities had a direct parallel in the 1968 May events in Paris. Yet the SDS core probably never numbered more than 6000 paid-up members.

That year SDS — never a united body — moved further to the left when Bernardine Dohrn and Michael Klonsky were elected to the leadership. They called themselves 'revolutionary communists' and vied with the Progessive Labour faction for overall ideological control of the movement. Acrimonious debate became the order of the day, and as the presidential candidacies of George Wallace and Eugene McCarthy, campaigning on an anti-Vietnam War ticket, stole the SDS programme, the movement broke up into factions

The most notable faction was the Revolutionary Youth Movement (RYM), in fact the rump of the SDS national office, which refused to be dragooned into Marxist-Leninist organisation. RYM supporters, like Bernadine Dohrn, later formed the violent Weatherman faction. Other factions to emerge from the splintering of SDS in 1969 were the October League, Revolutionary Union and the New American Movement. In turn, other groups emerged from these during the 1970s, such as the New Year's Gang, the Red Guerrilla Family and the *Venceremos* Brigades.

Symbionese Liberation Army (SLA)

The product of the San Francisco Bay area of California, the SLA enjoyed a brief notoriety for the 1974 kidnapping of Patricia Hearst, the daughter of a fabulously rich and self-made business executive and newspaper proprietor. Under stress, the girl subsequently disowned her family, broke her engagement and formed a liaison with a member of the group, until his death and her capture.

Of no importance in political terms, the SLA was a classic example of criminal theatre, playing to a mass media which responded with enthusiasm. In their public performance, SLA writers displayed an unusual grasp of the sensational, and by requiring the Hearst family to distribute food to the poor the group absurdly aped the earlier actions of the Tupamaros in Uruguay.

Donald DeFreeze, a black from a respectable family, bright and literate, but with a criminal record, formed the group's nucleus in July 1973. In all, there were fewer than 20 members, aged between 22 and 30, mostly from wealthy white backgrounds. Some were militant feminists, a number were attracted to crime and sexually to criminals, and especially black criminals, through undertaking prison social work.

The SLA defined itself as a 'body of dissimilar bodies and organisms living in deep and loving harmony and partnership in the best interests of all within the body'. The title chosen by this one-time fashionable group implied that oppressed blacks and other minorities could make the 'revolution' only in symbiotic relationship with each other, united in the SLA, just as insects and birds depend for survival upon one another. The SLA never pretended to be Marxist, although it claimed to represent the 'poor', and especially 'Asian, Black, Brown, Indian, White, Grey and Gay' — the last two categories meaning the old and the homosexual.

On 6 November 1973 the SLA killed Dr Marcus Foster, a black school superintendent. In January 1974 the group's headquarters was discovered and the murderers arrested. On 4 February the SLA kidnapped Patricia Hearst (19) and by April she had adopted the name of Che Guevara's girlfriend, Tania. Later in the month she participated in a San Francisco bank raid. On 17 May the police raided the group's hide-

out, and in the ensuing gunbattle six members died, including
DeFreeze. The group never survived: Patricia Hearst stood trial in
January 1976, charged as an accomplice and was sentenced in September
to a prison term of seven years. Two other SLA members were sentenced
to life imprisonment on 10 June 1976.

Venceremos
(We Shall Overcome)

A Californian ultra-leftist group of the late 1960s, *Venceremos* originally
was little more than a campus solidarity movement for the Cuba of Fidel
Castro. By 1971 the group's politics had veered towards Maoism, but
ideological disputes eventually fractionalised the movement so that by
the mid-1970s it had broken up.

Weatherman

The Weatherman faction arose from the Revolutionary Youth Movement, the name adopted in 1969 by the unorthodox leftist core of
Students for a Democratic Society. Bernardine Dohrn and Mark Rudd led
the faction after the public announcement of their stance in a paper called
'You Don't Need a Weatherman to Know Which Way the Wind Blows'. In
it they argued that the prime purpose of revolution was to defeat US
imperialism by world communism — but a new world communism
stemming from the Third World, and not from the Soviet Union. To
achieve the new order, alliances with national liberation groups had to
be built across the globe.

Within the US, Weatherman set out to attract young people from all
classes and to form 'self-defense' groups. The police were special targets
for abuse, for they acted as 'glue', holding the neighbourhood together,
and were symbols of the state itself. Such a revolutionary youth movement was supposed to move on to train a national leadership in preparation for its role 'as a division in the international liberation army'. In
the meantime, it was hoped, 'armed struggle' against the state would
stimulate revolutionary consciousness among the American masses.

Armed struggle meant, in practice, what emerged during the October
'days of rage' in Chicago, or hurling missiles and paint at the US Department of Justice in Washington in November 1969, for these and other
demonstrations Weathermen turned up in special riot clothing. In May
1970 Bernardine Dohrn, the group's leader, declared 'war' on the
establishment, threatening terrorist acts. 'This is the way we celebrate
the example of Eldridge Cleaver and Rap Brown and all black revolutionaries who first inspired us.' She claimed, 'in every tribe,
commune, dormitory, farmhouse, barrack and town house where kids
are making love, smoking dope and loading guns — fugitives from

Amerikan (sic) justice are free to go.' The group was 'adopting the classic guerrilla strategy of the Vietcong and the urban guerrilla strategy of the Tupamaros to our situation here in the most technically advanced country in the world.' At that point, once crimes had been committed, members had to avoid arrest and took to calling themselves Weather Underground.

In July 1970 charges of conspiring to commit bombings through a nationwide network of cells, or 'focals' of three to four people directed by a central committee, were laid before Mark Rudd (23), Bernardine Dohrn (28), and William Ayres (25), among others. For many years they remained underground, until the pressure of a clandestine existence persuaded them, one by one, to give themselves up. In 1977 Mark Rudd surrendered, was fined $3,000 and placed on probation for his part in the 'days of rage'. Three years later Bernadine Dohrn and William Ayres surfaced in Manhattan, having lived and worked together for years as a normal family.

The principal publication to come from Weather Underground was *Prairie Fire* (1974), subtitled *The Politics of Revolutionary Anti-Imperialism*, which described socialism as the violent overthrow of the bourgeoisie and the establishment of the dictatorship of the proletariat. 'Revolution is a dialectical process of destruction and creation. Active combat against the empire is the only foundation for socialist revolution in the oppressor nation and revolutionaries in the US have as our main enemy US imperialism. Defeating this enemy . . . is the unique contribution we can make to the world revolution.'

In the book the group claimed the credit for 17 bombings, and cited enthusiastically the violent incidents committed by the Symbionese Liberation Army and the Black Liberation Army. It saw Puerto Rico as a focal point of world struggle and supported terrorist action favouring an independent island republic.

Weather Underground petered out in the mid-1970s, but claimed responsibility for a bomb explosion at the State Department in Washington in January 1975. Although there were no injuries, considerable damage was inflicted.

LATIN AMERICA

Introduction

In times past local politics were violent because landowners patronised banditry, and gun law prevailed in the vast rural hinterland. So it was still in many regions of Latin America in the early 1980s. The city equivalent was the death squad, hired to bully and to exact compliance with faction, party, company or union interests. At national level the military traditionally intervened in politics: often the *coup d'état* accommodated quite subtle changes in the balance of competing interests.

In some countries, most obviously Bolivia, the coup still prevails. Indeed the old order, characterised by military strongmen such as Stroessner in Paraguay, survived into the 1980s. New caudillos, like Panama's Omar Torrijos, who embodied national resistance to Yankee dominance, proved that personalised, authoritarian order could survive as a system. Furthermore, as events in Uruguay, Argentina and Chile showed, the Latin insurgencies of the past 25 years did much to reinforce that tradition. The military governments which consequently took power were not synonymous with fascism, elements of which were present only in the Argentine Peronist movement.

Despite resistance to change, which often implied the use of violence by the state, two insurgencies separated by 20 years were successful — Cuba in 1959 and Nicaragua in 1979. After Castro's victory Cuba's fate was to fall swiftly under Marxist-Leninist influence, and for economic reasons the country allied itself with the Soviet bloc. That position, by giving potential insurgents a base, and later a haven, improved the prospects in Latin America for revolution. On occasions arms and training were provided, but never in sufficient quantities in the 1960s to decide the victory. Nor in 1979 were Cuban arms the decisive factor in bringing to power the Sandinist regime in Nicaragua.

More especially Castro internationalised the struggle by offering on radio and in the press a new dimension for insurgent pretensions. For the most part programmes were couched in Marxist-Leninist terms, in their way as dated and pompous but as characteristic of their time as earlier liberal political rhetoric; they were also as far removed from reality.

The insurgencies of the 1960s, promoted by Cuba, formed the first of three complexes of revolutionary activity in Latin America. They failed outright in Paraguay, Argentina, and the Dominican Republic (1959), in Venezuela and Colombia (1961), in Guatemala, Ecuador and Brazil

(1962), in Peru (1963) and in Bolivia (1967). Often a second and third attempt was mounted until the list of dead guerrilla leaders, ending with Che Guevara, was long enough to convince the revolutionary faithful that on its own the rural guerrilla nucleus could not effect fundamental change in the established order.

These men died because their preparation was inadequte, their message was ignored and their tactics impracticable. The guerrillas, for the most part from wealthy university backgrounds, played out a romantic and dangerous role, but cut little ice with ignorant and illiterate peasants of Indian stock, whose lives were and continued to be burdened by the sole and limiting requirement of nourishing themselves and their families.

The second complex of revolutionary violence was not a product of Cuban export. It came about as a result of the determination of a handful of people to take advantage of the social, political, and economic misfortunes of rich states — particularly Uruguay (Tupamaros) and Argentina (Montoneros). Their leaders promoted violence in the cities, rather than in the countryside, and, once again, were motivated by ideological conviction. But on this occasion their rationale sprang from adverse national circumstances and local tradition. Abandoning the ideological obsolescence of Soviet propaganda, although still Marxist, they attracted greater support and so proved more difficult to overcome. In common with Che Guevara, the leaders of this second complex all held a belief that the armed struggle was more important than the vanguard party in bringing about the revolution. In this, like him, they were communist heretics. Nationalism played little part in their motivation, although by attempting to identify the ruling orders with US imperialism they sought to stimulate national resentment.

The most influential thought at a tactical level Carlos Marigella provided in *The Minimanual of the Urban Guerrilla*, closely followed by the writings of the Spanish revolutionary, Abraham Guillén. The new war waged in the cities proved ugly and destructive: it transformed traditionally liberal societies into closed ones, as the military took over government in defence of the state, and usually with the support of the overwhelming majority of the population. The loss of liberties affected every aspect of life — as officers, fearful of an internal war essentially new to them, struggled to devise governmental and even constitutional alternatives robust enough to resist what they wrongly interpreted as subversion promoted by Moscow in a clandestine third world war. In seizing power they were eventually confronted with the problem all military rulers face — a need to sustain their support and to provide for succession and continuity.

The third complex, somewhat different in nature, was played out in Central America. The Sandinist revolution succeeded because it was seen, possibly incorrectly, to embody Nicaraguan revolutionary nationalism. True, its chances were improved because, thanks to the discovery of immense oil wealth in Mexico and to the growth of a theology of revolution within the Church, the realities of power had changed. To some extent US foreign policy under President Carter (1976-81) took account of this. These factors quickened the course of change, of political movement, in a region hitherto largely ignored as a political and investment backwater. In the final analysis, had it not been for the late conversion to change of the professional and business classes, the Sandinist revolution might never have come about.

Once in power, the Sandinists provided tangible evidence that real change would come to pass and could survive. Inside, the country underwent a literary campaign that astonished the world and which history will recall as its first achievement. Second thoughts may dwell upon the violence done to dissenting ethnic minorities on the coast and to the resurgence of guerrilla warfare under Eden Pastora. Be that as it may, beyond Nicaragua's frontiers not only Cuba took heart at what it undoubtedly saw as an opportunity, but so too did progressive forces within the Church and society generally. Further afield, France took steps to underwrite the survival of the revolution by selling it military hardware, and thereby contradicted US foreign policy. French socialist policy had it in mind to outwit the long-term designs of Marxist-Leninist Cuba and of its paymaster, the USSR.

Nicaragua did not immediately have a domino effect in the isthmus. But the Sandinists stimulated guerrilla efforts in El Salvador and Guatemala, where the insurgents displayed a more hard-nosed dogmatic quality, which seemed likely to impede their riding the crest of revolutionary nationalism in the early 1980s. In El Salvador a mass revolutionary coordinating committee was set up in January 1980. Archbishop Romero saw it as the first step towards unity among the people's organisations, and for this encouragement he was murdered. His death made it impossible to view progressive change in El Salvador, or indeed in Central America, as anything short of inevitable; the timing, character and leadership were still in question in 1982.

Bibliography

Stephen Clissold wrote a reliable and readable introduction to the area in *Late America. New World, Third World* (London, 1972), which might be followed by Gerrit Huizer's *Peasant Rebellion in Latin America* (Penguin, 1973). For further bibliography on the background to violent change, consult Ronald H. Chilcote's magisterial *Revolution and Structural Change in Latin America (1930-65)* (2 vols, Stanford, 1970).

For Che Guevara's writings, see *Guerrilla Warfare* (London, 1969) and John Gerassi (ed.), *Venceremos, the Writings of Che Guevara* (New York and London, 1968), and in Spanish *Obra Revolucionaria* (Ediciones Era, Mexico, 1967). Fidel Castro can be read in *Selected Works*, Vol. 1, *Revolutionary Struggle* (Cambridge, Mass., 1971); Régis Debray in *Revolution in the Revolution* (Penguin, 1972), *Strategy for Revolution* (Penguin, 1973) and *A Critique of Arms*, Vol. 1, and *The Revolution on Trial*, Vol. 2 (Penguin, 1977). Debray's position is criticised in an interesting series of essays edited by Leo Huberman and Paul Sweezy, *Régis Debray and the Latin American Revolution* (New York, 1968) and evaluated by Jack Woddis in *New Theories of Revolution* (New York, 1972).

The other principal texts on revolution are of course Carlos Marighella's *Minimanual of the Urban Guerrilla*, reprinted in numerous editions, but most conveniently in *For the Liberation of Brazil* (Penguin, 1971), and Abraham Guillén's writings translated from the Spanish in *Philosophy of the Urban Guerrilla* (New York, 1973). Beyond these texts, the best selection of guerrilla writing is found in Vania Bambirra, *Diez Años de Insurrección en América Latina* (Santiago, Chile, 1971). The Trotskyist influence on contemporary political violence cannot be understood without first reading R. J. Alexander, *Trotskyism in Latin America* (Stanford, 1973).

Of great philosophical importance is the growth of Catholic influence over revolutionary ideology. Among the most important writings are Gustavo Gutiérrez, *A Theology of Revolution* (New York, 1973), Enrique Dussel, *History and the Theology of Liberation* (New York, 1976) and José Miguel Bonino, *Revolutionary Theology Comes of Age* (London, 1975). Conveniently summarised in one volume, *Frontiers of Theology in Latin America* (New York, 1975), and edited by Rosino Gibellini, are 13 of the most important contributors to the theology of revolution.

Naturally, the Cuban revolution is central to an understanding of contemporary political ferment in Latin America. The basic text on Cuba must be Hugh Thomas's monumental *Cuba or the Pursuit of Freedom* (New York and London, 1971). Herbert Matthews wrote a sympathetic biography, *Castro* (Penguin, 1969). Che Guevara wrote of the Cuban campaign in *Reminiscences of the Cuban Revolutionary War* (Penguin, 1969). Two others who took part were Ramón Bonachea and Marta San Martín, who wrote *The Cuban Insurrection 1952-59* (New Brunswick, 1974). The first years in power were well analysed by Andrés Suárez in *Cuba: Castroism and Communism 1959-66* (MIT, Cambridge, Mass., 1967). Most important for an understanding of the philosophical and practical legacy of the Cuban victory is the essential documentary volume edited by Donald Hodges, *The Legacy of Che Guevara* (London, 1977).

Commentators on guerrilla warfare and terrorism in Latin America are legion. Quite the best start on rural movements is still *Guardian* correspondent Richard Gott's sympathetic *Guerrilla Movements in Latin America* (London, 1970, and New York, 1971), which provides the best general introduction to guerrilla movements in Guatemala, Venezuela, Colombia, Peru and Bolivia. It also contains useful photographs and a bibliography. *Urban Guerrilla Warfare in Latin America* (London and Cambridge, Mass., 1974) by James Kohl and John Litt covers in useful brevity Brazil, Uruguay and Argentina, and includes a select bibliography. Luis Mercier Vega wrote *Guerrillas in Latin America* (New York, 1969), which was first published in French and Spanish. Also recommended are the concise volume by Lewis H. Gann, *Guerrillas in History*

(Stanford, 1971), Robert Moss, *Urban Guerrilla Warfare* (Adelphi Paper No. 79, IISS, London, 1971), Jack Davis's Adelphi Paper *Political Violence in Latin America* (IISS, London, 1972) and Samuel Huntingdon, *Civil Violence and the Process of Development* (Adelphi Paper No. 89, IISS, London, 1972). Robert Moss published the very readable *War for the Cities* (New York, 1972), an American edition of *Urban Guerrillas* (London, 1972). Robert Lamberg's article in *Foro Internacional* (Mexico, 1971), 'La Guerrilla Urbana: Condiciones y Perspectivas de la "Segunda Ola" Guerrillera', describes well the violence in Uruguay, Argentina and Brazil. See also his longer *Die Guerilla in Lateinamerika* (Stuttgart, 1972). Another excellent short general analysis was written by Ernest Halperin, *Terrorism in Latin America* (CSIS, Georgetown, Sage, 1976) and, from a different viewpoint, see Donald Hodges, *The Latin American Revolution* (New York, 1974). Juan Linz and Alfred Stepan edited an excellent series, *The Breakdown of Democratic Regimes* (London, 1978) of which Volume three deals with Latin America. For the guerrilla threat in Central America see Thomas Anderson, *Politics in Central America: Guatemala, El Salvador, Honduras, and Nicaragua* (New York, 1982).

Argentina

From 1946 to this day the name of Juan Domingo Perón (1895-1974) has hypnotised Argentinian politics. He became president that year having assiduously built a power base within the industrial proletariat, which he came to manipulate through a powerful Peronist trade union bureaucracy, which, in the short term, served labour's interests. By his side, his talented wife, María Eva Duarte de Perón, or Evita, captured through ostentatious charity the hearts of the bare-backed multitude — the *descamisados*, who had nothing to hope for but the illusion of truth and beauty which she so outrageously proffered.

Evita died of cancer in 1952; three years later her husband was forced into exile, where for 18 years he plotted a return which he finally accomplished in the triumphant presidential electoral victory of 1973. But within nine months the old dictator was dead, leaving his third wife, a foolish woman, as president.

In the early 1970s Perón had paid lip service to the younger generation of political activists who sought to transform Argentina through social revolution. For their part they responded to the Peronist cause, and in return were encouraged to pursue political violence. Therein lay the origins of the Armed Peronist Forces (FAP), but in adopting such a course Peronists found themselves in league with two competing revolutionary currents — Castroism and Trotskyism.

As elsewhere in Latin America, Castro's 1959 victory in Cuba stimulated revolutionary activity in Argentina — Che Guevara after all was Argentinian. But the Argentinian National Liberation Army (ELN) barely got off the ground in 1967. More successful was the Armed Revolutionary Forces (FAR) under Roberto Quieto (captured 1975), who eventually in 1974 brought his Havana-backed movement into the left-wing Peronist fold, which had come to be dominated by the Montoneros, and led by Mario Firmenich. Castroism and left-wing Peronism had become one force, and remained united in exile after 1976, when the military cracked down upon the appalling violence the left had deliberately and consistently provoked, actually in the hope of causing such a reaction.

Trotskyism, the third revolutionary current, was, in military terms, the greater threat, although it never embraced the urban masses in the way Peronism touched their hearts. Trotskyist analysis appeared coldly intellectual. The People's Revolutionary Army (ERP) was indeed an army, whose members submitted to military and political discipline and achieved hideous successes in terrorist warfare. Until his death in July 1976, Roberto Santucho was its guiding light.

None of these terrorist groups survived the military government of President Videla, which deposed President María Estela (Isabel) Martínez de Perón on 24 March 1976. Military intervention in politics came as a relief to a country which had fallen prey to a particularly vicious form of internal warfare, and which had inherited a government unfit for public office at any time, least of all during a period of crisis. Accused of financial irregularities, the President was placed under house arrest, where she stayed until 1981, after which she was allowed to go into exile in Spain.

For a year before the coup the country's administration had been dominated more and more by the military. Having taken complete control of the counter-insurgency campaign in February 1975, the military later in the year approved the creation of a Council of Security, placing the police under its authority. Within the year the capital and seven entire provinces had been put under military control. In these areas special war councils were empowered to hand down indefinite prison sentences, and, for persons over the age of 16 found guilty of attacking the military, the death sentence. After the March coup the military suspended all political activity and trade union rights. The press, furthermore, was forbidden to report on political violence.

General Videla clearly expressed the object of military intervention as being the establishment of a 'democratic, representative, republican and federal system'. Five years later it lay with his successor, General Viola, to return Argentina to civilian rule. He failed and was succeeded by General Galtieri, who took his country to war over the Falkland Islands.

In the meantime right-wing para-military activity, responsible for many horrifying murders and the disappearance of anything up to 10,000 people, had besmirched the honour of the military. Whether or not it had ever been within the government's capacity to control these excesses in terrorist warfare, which were not of their making, the uncomfortable truth left open the question of responsibility and the possibility of an investigation. To pursue individual responsibility within the ranks of the security forces raised the spectre of division, even conflict, within the armed forces, a proposition unacceptable to the officer corps. That issue more than any other, certainly more than the exiled rump of Mario Firmenich's Montonero Peronist Movement (MPM), complicated Argentina's desperate wish for a return to responsible civilian rule.

Bibliography

A grasp of Peronism, although an intellectually weak movement, is essential to understanding political violence in modern Argentina. Perón defined it in *Filosofía Peronista* (Editorial Freeland, Buenos Aires,

1974) and in *El Pueblo Quiere Saber de qué se Trata* published by the same firm a year earlier. An excellent short analysis by Peter Waldmann was published in *Aportes* (No. 19, January 1971) entitled 'Las Cuatro Fases del Gobierno Peronista'. Of greater length and to be recommended is his *El Peronismo* (Buenos Aires, 1981) and *La Naturaleza del Peronismo* by Carlos S. Fayt (Buenos Aires, 1967). A series of articles in *Aportes* (No. 1, July 1966) of the same title most succinctly summarises the sociological and political circumstances within which Peronism grew. Jeanne Revers provided a cursory introduction in 'Le Péronisme' ('*Revue de Défense Nationale*, December 1972). The sources of Peronism are discussed by Alberto Ciria in 'La Doctrina Peronista y Sus Fuentes' (*Mundo Nuevo*, No. 47, May 1970). François Gèze and Alain Labrousse provide good insights into the Peronist period in their *Argentine: Révolution et Contre-Révolution* (Editions du Seuil, Paris, 1975). In English, but for the earlier period, Jeanne Kirkpatrick wrote the excellent *Leader and Vanguard in Mass Society: A Study of Peronist Argentina* (MIT, Cambridge, Mass., 1971). John Barnes's popular biography of *Eva Perón* was published in 1978 by Fontana in London. The facts of the period are recorded in *Argentina and Perón 1970-75* (Facts on File, Inc., New York, 1975).

For the violence of the 1970s, the student should begin with the invaluable bibliographical article 'Urban Guerrillas in Argentina: A Select Bibliography' by Charles Russell, James Schenkel and James Miller in *Latin American Research Review* (Vol. 9, No. 1, fall issue). For all principal Argentine guerrilla groups it covers the essential newspaper sources in Spanish and English up to 1974, and for the years 1969-74 provides a chronology. Equally essential is the Argentine government publication *Terrorism in Argentina* (Buenos Aires, 1980), which lists the major guerrilla actions and includes the reproduction of newspaper reports as well as providing an analysis of terrorist assassinations. Four excellent articles by Héctor Víctor Suárez in the English-language version of the Cuban newspaper, *Granma*, provide the best short introduction to the Montoneros (13 December 1970), the FAL (27 December 1970), the FAP (3 January 1971) and the FAR (17 January 1971). For the ERP, see James Petras's equally good article in the *New Left Review* (January-February 1972) 'Building a Popular Army in Argentina'. These articles were reprinted in *Urban Guerrilla Warfare in Latin America* (MIT, Cambridge, Mass. and London, 1974) by James Kohl and John Litt. Pierre F. de Villemarest provided a detailed account of the insurgency in *The Strategists of Fear: Twenty Years of Revolutionary War in Argentina* (Geneva, 1981).

The right-wing reaction which terrorism from the ultra-left provoked has not been analysed, although numerous denunciations exist. In this vein, see 'Death and Violence in Argentina', compiled by a group of priests and published by the Catholic Institute for International Relations (London, 1976), and reports by Amnesty International.

Argentine Anti-Communist Alliance
(Alianza Anticomunista Argentina — AAA)

The AAA first claimed responsibility for terrorist crimes in October 1973. The victims were leftists in all walks of life — journalists, academics, trade union officials and students, lawyers, priests, doctors, engineers, politicians. Some were members of the pro-Soviet Argentine Communist Party (PCA), others were members of the Peronist left wing, but many were merely considered leftist from the point of view of an ignorant, anti-intellectual, blunt but also fearful right wing.

The perpetrators of these crimes were considered on good authority to be police or security force agents. There appeared to be no organisation nationwide, nor even within a city. It was uncontrolled and largely uncontrollable. Once begun, the series of murders escalated at an alarming rate and continued throughout 1974 and 1975. They coincided with a spate of anti-semitism, although Jews as such do not appear to have been selected as murder victims.

In 1974, under the acronym AAA, death lists were published in the press. A period was suggested within which the individuals might seek refuge abroad. Some did so, among them Dr Puigros, a prominent communist and rector-designate of the University of Buenos Aires. In early December such a threat caused the London *Times* correspondent to leave Argentina. By 1976 the worst of the intimidation was over, although such crimes continued sporadically without necessarily bearing the hallmark AAA.

Armed Forces of Liberation
(Fuerzas Armadas de Liberación — FAL)

Set up in 1969, the FAL operated out of Buenos Aires, intent upon amassing weapons and obtaining money so as to oust the military government. Members raided banks and attacked military posts that year, but also targeted foreign firms operating in Argentina. The FAL was typical at the time of a rash of new urban terrorist groups, whose political affiliation was variously described as Trotskyist, Castroite, Maoist and Peronist. The truth was that the FAL drew upon all these sources, but were backed by no one in particular. In time they and people like them joined the neo-Trotskyist People's Revolutionary Army (ERP), which began to supercede the FAL around 1970. By 1973 no more was heard of the FAL.

Armed Peronist Forces
(*Fuerzas Armadas Peronistas — FAP*)

The FAP eventually became a constituent of the left-wing Peronist Montonero group, but it began to operate in 1969 in a series of urban crimes in the capital, Buenos Aires. FAP members found sympathy for their cause in Havana, but drew their inspiration from the revolutionary content in Peronism — a vague and highly personalised ideology, which grew out of the weak intellectual writings of Juan Perón and admiration for his wife, Evita.

Members operated in 1969/70 as a group alongside the Armed Forces of Liberation (FAL), with whom they discussed unification. Later on FAP militants consulted and planned with the Armed Revolutionary Forces (FAR) and the Montoneros. Their target was the military government of General Lanusse, but the FAP also attacked with a vengeance the interests of multinational companies, some of which withdrew altogether from Argentina. The death in Córdoba, for instance, of John Swint, a Ford executive, decided the company to evacuate its foreign management in November 1973.

Intermittently the group continued to explode bombs throughout 1974 and in August that year claimed responsibility for the murder of IKA Renault's personnel manager, Ricardo Golla. However, by that time the attention of the group was directed principally within the Peronist movement itself, which was split into left- and right-wing factions. By 1975 nothing more was heard of FAP; those members still active in violent politics had joined forces with the Montoneros, although no formal announcement appears to have been made.

Armed Revolutionary Forces
(*Fuerzas Armadas Revolucionarias — FAR*)

The FAR was originally a rural guerrilla movement set up in Argentina to aid Che Guevara in Bolivia, but as such it was barely active in the late 1960s. Few people were involved, and by 1970 they were discussing linking up with left-wing Peronists. For a while the FAR was grouped alongside the Montoneros and the Armed Peronist Forces (FAP) in an umbrella organisation known as the Armed Peronist Organisations (OAP), encouraged by Cuba. From this emerged an agreement on 12 October 1973 to join the Montoneros. The FAR leader was Roberto Quieto, who was aided by Fernando Vaca Narvaja, both of whom subsequently held important Montonero posts.

Like other guerrilla groups at the time FAR members committed crimes for the most part in the towns, and especially in the capital, where lay the bulk of its support. It accumulated arms through theft and by attacking military and police posts; money was raised through bank raids. Its first spectacularly publicised operation occurred on 30 July 1970, when 36 members occupied for 11 minutes the small township of Garin outside Buenos Aires.

The FAR claimed responsibility for the murder on 28 December 1972 of Admiral Emilio Berisso, chief of naval intelligence. He was selected as a target because he held overall responsibility for Trelew base in Patagonia, where in August that year 16 former guerrillas were killed, allegedly whilst attempting to escape from custody. At the time the FAR undoubtedly had the tacit support of ex-President Perón, who from his Spanish exile encouraged terrorism.

After the general elections of March 1973, in which the Peronist candidate, Dr Héctor Cámpora, was returned, FAR guerrilla activity slackened; it ceased altogether for a time after Perón himself had returned as President in October. But the old leader rejected the young leftists, causing them to revert to guerrilla activities in September 1974, by which time the FAR was fully integrated with the Montoneros.

Montoneros

Of all the Argentinian terrorist groups operating in the 1970s the most well-known and numerous were the Montoneros. They sprang from the ranks of Peronism, originally a popular movement of the right and akin to national socialism, the Argentinian version of which developed in the 1970s a left and a right wing. They were not the first Peronists to resort to terrorism, but the old dictator, Juan Perón (1895-1974), living out his life in exile in Madrid, encouraged them, as he did other Peronist groups.

It was by kidnapping on 29 May 1970 former President Pedro Aramburu, who when in power had been responsible for putting down an attempt to restore Perón in 1956, that the Montoneros first hit the news. No more than a dozen people took part in the crime, which was master-minded by Mario Firmenich. After a gruesome period of captivity, Aramburu was shot dead by Fernando Abal Medina, having first been subjected to the façade of a 'people's trial'.

Thenceforth Montonero activists infiltrated the Peronist political apparatus, and together with the Armed Revolutionary Forces (FAR) recruited younger members for the left wing of the movement. Havana paid them attention, allowing them to publicise their views, which were socialist, without necessarily being Marxist-Leninist, and which did not preclude abandoning Perón, if he could not be persuaded into supporting the left wing of his own movement. They undoubtedly had contacts with the Third World Priests movement, whose supporters believed in assisting the 'socialist revolutionary process'. Thanks to their own daring and their willingness to work with other groups, the Montoneros grew in criminal stature throughout 1971/72. Short of money, they turned to kidnapping foreign business executives, whose companies paid large ransoms.

In 1973 they were active within the Peronist movement, which was returned to power through elections in May. They campaigned for Perón's return, and ultimately for his reelection that year in October. But it was a period when the left- and right-wing Peronist union officials slugged it out — the generally younger socialists attacking those powerful union bosses who had profited through collaborating with the previous military regime. Amongst many who died was the CGT trade union leader José Rucci, the foremost Peronist in Argentina, who, alongside his driver and one of four body guards, was gunned down in September. Both wings resorted to gangsterism, which was by no means new in the traditional fight to control union elections.

The biggest internecine clash took place in public at Ezeiza airport on 20 June, when Perón was due to return from exile. Shooting broke out between the two factions, killing 13 people, wounding over a hundred, and forcing the cancellation of elaborate homecoming celebrations.

During 1973 under the Cámpora administration (May–September) the Montoneros enjoyed what amounted to official protection. They were part of the young Peronist movement, which won increasing support in some of the smaller unions and in student and high-school circles.

After Perón himself was returned to power in October, in the nine months remaining to him before he died on 1 July 1974, he moved towards supporting the right. The final break with the Montoneros came at an emotional May Day rally, when he charged them with being treacherous and mercenary, upon which they marched out of the square. Thenceforth the Montoneros resorted to militant political violence. Furthermore, as they had increased their membership and widened their contacts during the period of quasi-legitimacy, they emerged as the dominant influence on the left.

On 6 September 1976 Mario Firmenich announced the group would return to clandestinity, using arson, sabotage, assassination and bombings to promote a 'popular war'. Other Peronist groups did not follow suit, and yet they acknowledged Montonero leadership. Such deliberate confusion of legality with illegality provided an excellent defence against attempts to outlaw the movement, as well as providing the widespread support network so essential to guerrilla warfare. Thenceforth the Armed Revolutionary Forces (FAR) and the Montoneros acted as one body.

There followed the most savage onslaught on government known in recent years. It began with the assassination of former Foreign Minister Arturo Mor Roig on 15 July 1974, and continued that September with the successful kidnapping of the Born brothers. Some 50 terrorists participated in that abduction, which netted US $60 million, the largest ransom known to have been paid in Latin America. The proceeds left the country with the leaders, and according to Firmenich contributed to the 1979 Sandinist victory in Nicaragua.

Other Montonero assassinations included the blowing up of the

Federal Police Chief, Alberto Villar, and his wife whilst out sailing on 1 November 1974, the abduction and murder of the US consul, John Egan, on 26 February 1975, the murder of General Jorge Cáceres Monié on 3 November 1975, of General Cesareo Cardozo on 18 June 1976, and, finally, an unsuccessful attempt upon the life of Vice-Admiral Armando Lambruschini on 1 August 1978.

In addition to murder, the Montoneros sabotaged a Hercules C130 transport aircraft in Tucumán, killing four people and injuring a further 25 on 28 August 1975. Still more spectacular was the attack two months later on the garrison of Formosa, which coincided with the hijacking of a Boeing 737 aircraft from Buenos Aires. The aircraft landed at Formosa, where guerrillas had secured the airport, and was supposed to take off with colleagues rescued from the local jail, but that part of the plan failed. Some of the attackers escaped, 15 died in the attempt, 11 soldiers were killed.

Such a military operation raised the level of the Montonero threat to that simultaneously posed by the People's Revolutionary Army, with which the Montoneros sometimes collaborated. But on the whole the Montoneros confined themselves to assassination and sabotage: they never transformed themselves into a guerrilla army. Their strength lay in penetrating the Peronist movement and thereby subverting the state.

Shocking as the toll was, the Montoneros were beaten at the terrorist game they had started by the military, which in February 1975 took control of security force operations. In December 1975 Roberto Quieto (42), the twin head with Firmenich of the terrorist activity, was captured. In 1976 some 1600 followers died, a further 500 died in the first six months of 1977, the year in which the Montoneros went into exile.

By June 1975 Firmenich was casting around for an alliance to oust Perón's wife, Isabel, who succeeded her husband as president. He spoke of a National Liberation Front, which might have included the People's Revolutionary Army and the pro-Soviet Argentinian Communist Party. It never came about, however; more interestingly and certainly more successfully, the Montoneros set out to inherit the Peronist cause by becoming first the armed branch of the Authentic Peronist Party (1975), and as that weakened in 1976 by setting up a substitute Montonero Peronist Movement (MPM). Defeated on the ground, the Montonero leadership — Mario Firmenich, Rodolfo Galimberti, Fernando Vaca Narvaja and Juan Gelman — found refuge in Rome in October 1977.

In Europe they sought to obscure the immediate past, namely, that elections in 1973 had not indicated popular support for the left, and that the 1976 military intervention in politics was widely welcomed as the only solution to the ravages of terrorism. The Montoneros presented themselves to the Third World and to European socialist parties as the victims of military repression, although they were in fact the very instigators of terror, and most ably exploited the appalling, reactionary rash of terrorism of the right into which Argentina sank in 1976/77, and which unhappily confused the Argentinian experience with crude military rule elsewhere on the continent.

With the money they had extracted from kidnapping, they set up offices in Rome, Paris and Havana, and sought to convince democrats that the Montoneros represented the proper alternative to military rule. Yet at the same time the fiction of an armed front under the leadership of Horacio Mendizábal (36) was maintained. Indeed the responsibility for occasional terrorist incidents was claimed by the MPM in 1979, until in September Mendizábal was killed in a clash. No further activity was recorded, and in December 1981 Firmenich publicly called on the movement to abandon all attempts to pursue armed struggle so as to concentrate on political action. He appeared to have Cuba's backing, and was well placed to take advantage in the long term of Argentinian instability.

National Liberation Army
(Ejército de Liberación Nacional — ELN)

The Argentine ELN was a short-lived body that arose directly out of the setting up in Havana of the Latin American Solidarity Organisation (OLAS) in July 1967. It was intended to promote guerrilla warfare in the north of the country, but was disbanded after Che Guevara had met his death in Bolivia that same year in October.

National Liberation Movement
(Movimiento de Liberación Nacional — MLN)

Unlike the Cuban-sponsored rural guerrilla groups, the MLN in Argentina sprang from the Peronist ranks and operated briefly in Tucumán province in the late 1960s. A dozen members were arrested in September 1968, after which nothing more was heard of the movement.

People's Guerrilla Army
(Ejército Guerrillero del Pueblo — EGP)

The EGP was a Cuban-backed organisation, the first of its kind in Argentina to attempt to launch rural guerrilla warfare. Che Guevara approved of the operation from Havana, where the plans had been drawn up.

In September 1963 Jorge Masetti, a journalist from Argentina who had headed Fidel Castro's press agency in Cuba, led two guerrilla columns from Bolivia into the Salta Province. They were met with utter indifference by the local population, made no military or political impact, and seven months later were captured by the Argentine armed forces. Two

Cubans were killed, Masetti most probably died, others were jailed, a handful escaped to reappear on future occasions in different circumstances.

People's Revolutionary Army
(Ejército Revolucionario del Pueblo — ERP)

Although consisting at the time of various hostile factions, the Argentine Trotskyist Workers' Revolutionary Party (PRT) set up an armed branch— the ERP — in May 1969. Eighteen months passed before the ERP had established a terrorist network capable of effective action. It began operations in late 1970 around the industrial city of Rosario, where two policemen were killed in a raid on a police station.

From the start the ERP had a clear notion of linking urban terrorist tactics with a working-class movement, although in fact such a relationship quite failed to materialise. The ERP was expected to become the 'army of the masses', to embody a so-called 'national liberation organisation'. This concept, and the relationship between the army and the party derived from Mao and Giap, but to ERP thinking Trotsky's work on permanent revolution and the Soviet bureaucracy was also important. Fundamental to it was the thought of Lenin on the role of the party, and of Marx. Yet the determination to proceed at all undoubtedly came from the example of Che Guevara, from whose concern and sincerity the ERP drew its belief in the need to create a 'new man' in the struggle for socialism.

In structure the ERP was organised on a celular basis, but adapted to military circumstances — it was an army, where other Argentinian terrorist groups were not. Throughout its hierarchy political commissars were active, in theory at least, at every level, so that the PRT, formally aligned with the Trotskyist Fourth International, controlled the military cadres. Every three years a National Congress was supposed to meet, from which was drawn a Central Committee of 28 full members and 11 supplementary members, who were supposed to meet every six months. An Executive Committee drawn from the Central Committee, consisting of six members of a political bureau and five members of a national military directorate, met once a month. The army had an operational structure responsible to a General Staff and which consisted of battalions, companies, platoons and squads, organised on a regional basis.

The structure functioned best in and around Buenos Aires, in Córdoba, in Santa Fé and in Tucumán. But at its height in 1975, the ERP had active units independent of the regional structures in Missiones, Corrientes, Formosa, Chaco, Salta, Jujuy, Catamarca, Mendoza, Bahía Blanca and Neuquen. By October 1977, but for Córdoba, the ERP had been eradicated from all its provincial bases; it retained a presence in greater Buenos Aires.

Like the Peronist left, the ERP had contacts with Cuba, some members had actually met Che Guevara and Castro in the mid-1960s, and had supported the Latin American Solidarity Organisation which Havana promoted in 1967. A decade later the leaders fled to Europe, where they had contacts in the Trotskyist network — the principal members included Arnald Juan Kremer, Enrique Gorriaran Merlo, Luis Mattini, Jorge Alfredo Oropel, Carlos Emilio All, Manuel Justo Gaggero, Juan Carlos Ledesma and Roberto Eduardo Coppo, all of whom were in their middle to late 30s.

Almost as soon as the ERP was formed it displayed the characteristic factions of the dogmatic ultra-left; a Red Faction was the closest to orthodox Trotskyist thought, an ERP-22 August emerged, which soon joined the left-wing Peronists, but the virulent mainstream terrorist ERP was that led by Roberto Santucho, as charismatic a figure as any Latin American guerrilla.

In 1971 ERP activities were stepped up. In February it carried out in Córdoba the largest bank raid in the history of Argentina (US $300,000), and succeeded in arousing sympathy by seizing food trucks and clothing vans, and distributing the loads among the slum dwellers of Buenos Aires. On 20 March a score of militants occupied a television station in Córdoba and spoke to the public for ten minutes. In May a US meat-packing company in Rosario was compelled to distribute food whilst the ERP held Stanley Sylvester, the local manager, for a week. The model for such actions was clearly the Tupamaros in neighbouring Uruguay, some of whose members may have joined the ERP after the security clamp-down in their own country.

In 1972 the ERP began to show its teeth, and swiftly developed into the most daring and notorious of Latin American guerrilla organisations. On 10 April militants murdered in Buenos Aires Dr Oberdan Sallustro, president of the Fiat Company in Argentina, and on the same day in Rosario General Juan Carlos Sánchez was gunned down in the street. Sallustro had been kidnapped three weeks earlier; Santucho master-minded the crime. Behind the attacks and those that followed lay the intent to create civic chaos so as to deflect the military regime of General Lanusse from holding elections in 1973 and returning power thereby to the civilians. In this strategy foreign business and the military became principal ERP targets.

Kidnapping netted the movement yields far in excess of anything previously considered imaginable from bank raids. For instance, Ford's of Detroit agreed on 23 May to distribute some US $800,000 worth of supplies and ambulances, following an attempt to kidnap an executive, who later died of his wounds. In December ESSO agreed to pay for its manager, Victor Samuelson, a ransom of US $12 million. Where the ERP claimed responsibility for kidnapping, as often as not it demanded the distribution of goods or cash for a specific purpose.

Military officers were singled out for attack. Among those who died were Rear Admiral Hermes Quijada, who was gunned down from a passing motorcycle on 30 April. The ERP was capable in 1973 of larger actions. A group of 30 guerrillas kept 90 soldiers at bay whilst they stole arms in Córdoba on 18 February. On 21 April a carefully coordinated assault was made on a small township 30 miles south of Buenos Aires. Of longer-term importance was the opening of a rural front in 1974 in the Tucumán area, personally under the direction of Santucho. The idea was to set up a zone in the mountains, where the ERP would establish contact with the peasantry and persuade them to transfer their allegiance from the state to the party.

Parallel with rural activity went a growth in urban actions. On 20 January some 70 guerrillas attacked the Azul garrison, 150 miles south of Buenos Aires, with the intention of kidnapping senior officers. The commanding officer was killed. On a second occasion an attack in August on barracks in Catamarca was intercepted. Nineteen guerrillas were killed, 15 were captured and 50 were pursued into the countryside.

The most spectacular assault the ERP ever mounted occurred a year later on 23 December 1975, when at night at least 150 men cooperated in a series of attacks, the main target being the barracks and arsenal at Monte Chingolo. To distract attention from the barracks, diversionary attacks were carried out on police stations and three bridges. This proved to be the height of ERP activity; in 1976 Santucho and his deputy, José Urteaga, were killed in Buenos Aires on 19 July. Heavy casualties followed in town and country throughout that year and into 1977, by which time the back of what had become an insurgency was broken. Many fled into exile, some were hired as assassins. Calling themselves Red Action, an ERP hit team comprising Hugo Alfredo Irurzún, who was killed, and Enrique Gorriarán Merlo, murdered the exiled Nicaraguan dictator, Somoza, in Paraguay in September 1980. Irurzún had directed the Monte Chingolo attack and led the ERP rural guerrillas (120) in Tucumán, who were known as the Compañía de Monte Ramón Rosa Giménez. Red Action undertook a kidnapping operation in Mexico the following year, but without success; the brothers of both Che Guevara and Roberto Santucho were captured.

Red Brigades of Worker Power
(Brigadas Rojas del Poder Obrero — BRPO)

The Brigades were the answer Trostkyists gave to the assassination squads which operated under the acronym AAA. They emerged in 1976 and were said to consist of former militants from the Armed Forces of Liberation. They never survived the uprooting of leftist terrorist groups that year by the Argentine military government.

Bolivia

Ever since Bolivia won independence from Spain in 1825 the country has been a prey to persistent military intervention in politics — almost 200 coups have failed to make any impact upon government efficiency or justice. The peasantry remain ignorant and poor, the tin miners underpaid and politically restless, the student body radical but marginalised from power.

In theory Bolivia should have been ripe for revolutionary leadership in the 1960s, but in practice Che Guevara's National Liberation Army (ELN) failed in 1967, thanks to peasant indifference and US counter-insurgency force instruction. No similar episode or movement occurred in the 1970s, with the exception of a brief reappearance in 1971, for which the Bolivians blamed the backing of the Soviet Union. The decade was, for the most part, a period of comparative calm under General Hugo Banzer's military rule (1971-78). Thereafter government returned to its old pattern of coup and counter-coup, reflecting the divisions within the armed forces and financed outside the revenue system through the huge profits of cocaine smuggling.

Bibliography

The best account of the Guevara insurgency is found in *The Complete Bolivian Diaries of Che Guevara and Other Captured Documents* (Stein and Day, New York, 1968 and Allen and Unwin, London, 1968) edited by Daniel James, but see also Gustavo Sánchez, *The Great Rebel, Che Guevara in Bolivia* (Grove Press, New York, 1969). José Luis Alcázar, a Bolivian journalist on the staff of the Catholic newspaper, *Presencia*, wrote a useful account in *Nancahuazu la Guerrilla del Che en Bolivia* (Ediciones Era, Mexico, 1969). Rubén Vásquez Diaz provided another eye-witness account entitled *Bolivia a la Hora del Che* (Sigo XXI, Mexico, 1968). The French Marxist writer and theorist, Régis Debray, who accompanied Guevara part of the time and was captured, wrote *La Guerrilla du Che* (Editions du Seuil, Paris, 1974).

A good general account, entitled *Les Guérrilleros,* by Jean Larteguy was published in Paris in 1967 and two years later in Spanish by Editorial Diana, Mexico. A concise account in English by Robert Lamberg was published in *Problems of Communism* (April 1970) 'Che in Bolivia: The Revolution That Failed'.

For a short biography of Guevara's second in command, see *Guerrillero*

Inti Peredo by Jesús Lara (Editorial Diogenes, Mexico, 1972). On Guevara's mistress and companion who accompanied him to her death, see *Tania* by M. Rojas and M. R. Calderón (Ocean Books, London, 1973).

Alistaire Horne wrote well on the second Bolivian guerrilla episode in *Encounter* (June 1971), 'Guerrillas of Teoponte'. Fuller, and of inestimable value, is *Teoponte, una Experiencia Guerrillera* (CEDI, Oruro, Bolivia, 1971) by Hugo Assman, a Brazilian priest and theologian who brought together valuable documents including the diaries of ELN leader 'Chato' Peredo, his companion Gustavo Ruíz Paz and the writings of Nestor Paz and others who joined the enterprise.

The Latin American Bureau published a special brief on the 1980 coup entitled *Bolivia: Coup d'Etat* (London, 1980) by James Dunkerley, who provided an account of the 1952 revolution and the Banzer years in the 1970s as background.

Bolivian Revolutionary Workers' Party
(Partido Revolucionario de Trabajadores Bolivianos — PRTB)

The PRTB was set up in June 1975 by the ELN political network. It described itself as part of the 'continental and world revolution', but concentrated its efforts not on guerrilla warfare but on the factory floor, where in 1976 it organised illegal strikes. Behind the PRTB was Chato Peredo's brother, Antonio. In the late 1970s party sympathisers exploded the occasional urban bomb, having in 1978 announced the intention of opposing military rule through a 'wide resistance movement combining legal, semi-legal and clandestine organisations'.

Movement of the Revolutionary Left
(Movimiento de la Izquierda Revolucionaria — MIR)

The MIR emerged in August 1971 as a student fighting force on the San Andrés University campus in La Paz. Its stated aim was 'to work seriously and silently on the construction of a political organisation capable of organising the people both politically and militarily'. It never developed a military or terrorist capacity, concentrating rather upon radicalising Christian opinion within the powerful Catholic Church.

Although some Miristas were Marxists, the majority in the 1970s were not; they saw themselves as Christian Democrats, and in 1978 under Jaime Paz Zamora joined an electoral front known as the Democratic and Popular Unity Front (FUDP) led by the veteran politician, Siles Zuazo. When these elections were annulled by military intervention, some Miristas took to political violence in 1979, and arrests followed. Occasional violence continued into the 1980s, with the death of eight militants recorded in January 1981.

National Liberation Army
(*Ejército de Liberación Nacional — ELN*)

Behind the ELN was the most charismatic of all Latin America's guerrilla leaders, Ernesto 'Che' Guevara, who deliberately set out to start in rural Bolivia a revolution which would sweep through South America. Ingloriously, he met his death there in October 1967, and became for a generation throughout the western world a cult figure.

The idea of a rural guerrilla campaign was conceived in Cuba, at the time of the Tricontinental Conference in 1966, by Guevara, who contacted and subsequently received help from the Bolivian Communist Party (PCB). It had not at first been his intention to launch the campaign in Bolivia, rather he thought to infiltrate from Bolivia into Argentina. Further consideration however convinced him that the objective conditions for revolution existed there, and not in his more bourgeois homeland to the south.

The hierarchy of the PCB did not agree, but individual members, principally the brothers Coco and Inti Peredo, gave their full backing. So too did Régis Debray (b. 1940), the French Marxist author who for a time accompanied the guerrilla band before his capture in April 1967.

The initial training, such as it was, was undertaken at Ñancahuazu on a primitive farm bought expressly for the purpose by Coco Peredo. The whole project involved no more than two score of men, a handful of whom were Cubans. After a couple of months they set off to make contact with the local population, but found firstly that they were unfit to operate in jungle conditions, and secondly that the peasantry had no time for revolution. In fact they betrayed the guerrillas. The first real contact with the Bolivian armed forces, who set out to search for the band, took place on 23 March, when in an ambush seven soldiers were killed. Days later Guevara's leadership was public knowledge.

On 4 April the guerrillas abandoned their principal camp, taking with them their supplies, which they cached in new caves, specifically dynamited for the purpose. A further clash took place on 10 April, when near Iripiti ten more Bolivian soldiers died. By June the military had the guerrillas on the run, and the occasional brushes occurred.

More significant clashes occurred on 27 and 30 July, when four more soldiers died. Guerrilla losses totalled four at that time. In August their caves were discovered, and their supplies removed. Thenceforth the guerrillas were compelled to pass through townships and pick up medicines, food and ammunition. It was the beginning of the end, for in most villages the military had placed agents disguised as peasants.

On 31 August ten guerrillas, including Tamara Bunke, (Tania) Che's mistress, were shot dead in an ambush. On 26 September Coco Peredo was killed in a clash. On 8 October Guevara was wounded, captured and died. The Bolivian version of events claimed he died of his injuries, in fact he was shot on orders. The body was disposed of, how or where is not publicly known. On 14 October four more guerrillas were killed, leaving active only six, led by Inti Peredo. Five of them, including Peredo, escaped with their lives. The three Cubans returned to Havana in 1968; Inti Peredo remained amongst his own people.

Thanks to his and others' efforts, the spirit of the ELN did not entirely die. Attempts were made to resuscitate it as an urban group in 1969, when it committed a number of terrorist acts, in one of which Peredo was killed. In July 1970 the group claimed it had returned to the mountains, where some 70 members raided a gold mine in Teoponte and seized two West German engineers as hostages against the release of ten imprisoned colleagues, subsequently flown to Chile. However, the new ELN leader, Oswaldo 'Chato' Peredo, the third brother, was captured in October that year, after which the rural base collapsed.

There was evidence of foreign support for this phase of ELN activity. Not only did Havana provide radio time and newspaper space for the ELN to publicise its aims, but in Uruguay the Tupamaros, according to the ELN, helped to accelerate the return to the mountains. The co-operation marked the start of 'integration at an international level'.

After 1970 the ELN continued to exist in La Paz and Cochabamba as a small urban nucleus. The model for this can only have been the Tupamaros, who were the forerunners in Latin America in constructing 'safe houses' and hides, in amassing equipment to print, to forge, to operate on and care for the wounded, to hold captives for lengthy periods and to manufacture and refashion weapons. All this the ELN achieved, according to the government, with the support of the Soviet embassy, most of whose officials were expelled in March 1972.

Peredo, who had been exiled to Chile for his former activity in 1970, appears to have returned in mid-1971 and directed these activities. Close links were established with individual priests and nuns, whose support widened ELN appeal. Much of the network then established was discovered in 1972, before it had been put to use. Thereafter Peredo lived in Cuba until a general amnesty in January 1978 allowed him to return to Bolivia.

As a result of discoveries the ELN was very largely inactive throughout the entire period President Banzer held office (1971-78) despite the announcement in February 1974 of the creation of a revolutionary coordinating committee consisting of the ELN, the Argentinian ERP, the Chilean MIR and the Uruguayan MLN (Tupamaros). In August 1978 Chato Peredo was arrested in La Paz: no further developments occurred over the next two years.

Brazil

Terrorist tactics practised by armed bands of political activists whose object was to overturn the state began after the armed forces overthrew the populist President Goulart in April 1964. The Brazilian military had always fulfilled a 'corrective' role in politics, and 1964 was a continuation of that tradition, not a new departure. Furthermore the coup was undertaken with the support, indeed almost at the bidding, of the business sector, which was alarmed by the frankly dictatorial ambitions of President Goulart, a man who had risen to power under the dictator Getulio Vargas (suicide 1954) and who understood how to manipulate the power of organised labour.

Aware of the growing possibility of a coup, President Goulart and his brother-in-law, Leonel Brizola, a prominent deputy and one-time governor of Rio do Sul state, accelerated preparations to resist a takeover by alerting the Peasant Leagues, Groups of Eleven, and organised labour, but come the moment, the support failed to materialise and Goulart fled to Uruguay.

The coup was the work of a military elite schooled in the War College, which united behind General Humberto Castelo Branco as president and backed a tough regime of technocrats to tackle inflation, running at nearly 100 per cent, to promote foreign investment, and to stimulate private enterprise by denationalising Brazilian minerals and industry.

Such a policy hit the wage-earner badly and caused intense suffering at the lower income level. The economic course pursued by the military government undoubtedly contributed to radicalising elements within the Church, but it would be going too far to say that it was a cause of the rash of urban and rural terrorism which broke out in the mid-1960s. Those activists were not peasants or industrial workers, but middle-class, politically-minded individuals.

The Cuban example, on the other hand, and the development from 1966 of the Havana-based Organisation for Latin American Solidarity (OLAS), which actively backed revolution, was a potent contributing factor to political violence. In part, the violence stemmed from Moscow's losing control over the Marxist-Leninist movement in Brazil, so that activists formed splinter groups, the most notable of which was National Liberating Action (ALN), led by the communist urban guerrilla theorist, Carlos Marighella, who was killed in 1969. Other groups included the Revolutionary Popular Vanguard (VPR) and the National Revolutionary

Movement (MNR). Neither these, nor the miniscule Maoist Communist Party of Brazil (PCdoB) survived the mass arrests and torture which uprooted the subversive groups in the principal cities. The most startling tactic used in their brief period of action was the abduction of foreign diplomats to secure the release of jailed colleagues.

Militancy on the left produced its counter-part on the right. The Death Squad, which had first appeared in 1958 as a police response to particularly vicious criminal violence, was resurrected as a politically oriented assassination squad. In effect, serving police officers who had taken the law into their own hands acted in the mid- and late 1960s alongside new right-wing assassination squads such as the Commando for Hunting Communists (CCC) and the Anti-Communist Movement (MAC). Although the membership had undoubtedly changed, such movements were resurrected in 1980 as the military-backed regime attempted to move towards civilianisation.

Bibliography

For an analysis of Brazilian political violence between 1966 and 1970 no better book exists than João Quartim's *Dictatorship and Armed Struggle in Brazil* (New York and London (New Left Books), 1971). But the nub of Brazilian guerrilla warfare naturally lies in the writings of Carlos Marighella, conveniently found in *For the Liberation of Brazil* (Penguin, 1971), which includes the *Minimanual of the Urban Guerrilla*. For articles, see Charles Russell, James Miller and Robert Hildner's bibliography in 'Latin American Research Review' Vol. 9, No. 1, 1974, and for a good summary of the Brazilian guerrilla phenomenon, consult Kohn and Litt's *Urban Guerrilla Warfare in Latin America* (MIT, Cambridge, Mass., and London, 1974). A brief, objective overview from an experienced observer of the whole Brazilian terrorist episode is found in *Brazil: The Road back from Terrorism* (ISC, London, 1974) by Robert Dervel Evans, also published in Montreal by McGill Queen's University Press the following year.

For the background to the Brazil of the 1960s and the problems which encouraged some activists to adopt political violence, Paulo Freire's *Pedagogy of the Oppressed* (Penguin, 1970) is an invaluable classic. Miguel Arraes, from his Algerian exile, provided an excellent introduction to the 1964 military takeover in *Brazil, the People and the Power* (Penguin, 1972). But for a cool appraisal based on sound research, see Phyllis Parker, *Brazil and the Quiet Intervention* (Austin, London, 1979). Emanuel de Kadt explored the radicalisation of the Church in *Catholic Radicals in Brazil* (OUP, London, 1972), and Alfred Stepan analaysed military intervention in *The Military in Politics: Changing Patterns in Brazil* (Princeton University Press, 1971).

Armed Revolutionary Vanguard
(*Vanguarda Armada Revolucionária — VAR*)

The VAR was created from a merger in April 1969 of the National Liberation Commando (COLINA) and the Revolutionary Popular Vanguard (VPR). Militants split in September on the question of whether to pursue armed struggle or whether to concentrate upon building a mass party. The former reverted to calling themselves the VPR, the latter became the VAR-Palmares, responsible for hijacking an aircraft to Cuba in January 1970. A further split occurred in September 1970 on ideological grounds. Thereafter the VAR was no longer active as a violent faction.

Brazilian Revolutionary Communist Party
(*Partido Comunista Brasileiro Revolucionário — PCBR*)

Under the leadership of Mário Alves and Apolonio de Carvalho, the PCBR broke away from the Moscow-line Brazilian Communist Party (PCB) in 1967. Alves died under torture in prison in 1970, but Carvalho was exchanged for the kidnapped Federal German Ambassador in June 1970 and flown to Algeria. The PCBR pursued politically violent tactics alongside other dissident communists in National Liberating Action (ALN), and was Maoist in orientation. After 1969 it hardly survived. For a brief while members cooperated with another short-lived splinter group, the Revolutionary Movement 26 July (MR-26), which took its date from Fidel Castro's attack on the Moncada barracks in Havana in 1953.

Communist Party of Brazil
(*Partido Comunista do Brasil — PCdoB*)

The PCdoB broke away from the main Moscow-line Brazilian Communist Party (PCB) in 1961 to follow Peking, a product of the Sino-Soviet split in world communism. The principal leaders, João Amazonas, Mauricio Grabois and Pedro Pomar, were all veteran Marxist-Leninists who were seized by the idea of organising the peasantry into a revolutionary force. They went into exile in 1968.

After the death of Mao Tse-tung and the subsequent reform in China, the PCdoB associated with the only remaining Maoist party in office — that of Albania. In the early 1960s the party had openly advocated armed struggle in Brazil, alongside the unorthodox Marxist guerrilla groups. In the early 1980s it was not in a position to practise political violence.

Groups of Eleven
(Grupos de Onze — G-11)

During the Goulart presidency in the early 1960s the G-11 grew up under the patronage of the leftist deputy and former governor of Rio Grande do Sul state, Leonel Brizola. In effect they were 11-man cells, which were expected to act in concert in defence of the left-wing political process, which at the time was overtaking Brazil, or, in the event of a right-wing government, to seize power by occupying key installations.

In fact the G-11 never responded when the military seized power in April 1964; Brizola fled to Uruguay. Yet it was in his native state of Rio Grande do Sul that the second wave of Brazilian political violence in the late 1960s found support, presumably due to the seeds sown earlier.

National Liberating Action
(Ação Libertadora Nacional — ALN)

Because he advocated armed struggle the Moscow-line Brazilian Communist Party (PCB) expelled Carlos Marighella from the Executive Committee in October 1967, a break which led to the independent establishment of the ALN, and its involvement in urban guerrilla warfare.

Believing that action creates organisation, ALN militants set about robbing banks in the towns, as one of a number of disaffected communist groups intent upon pursuing armed struggle. ALN's most infamous act was perpetrated in September 1969, when in conjunction with the Revolutionary Movement of 8 October (MR-8) militants successfully abducted the US Ambassador, Charles Burke Eldbrick. In return for his release the government agreed to fly 15 prisoners to Cuba. Two further abductions were made in June 1970. The ALN and the VPR took the West German Ambassador, von Holleben, whose freedom was secured in return for the release of 40 prisoners, and in December that year the Swiss Ambassador, Giovanni Bucher, was held until 70 prisoners had been released.

Marighella received warm support from Cuba and attended the first conference in Havana of the Organisation of Latin American Solidarity (OLAS) in August 1967. Some ALN militants received training in Cuba, where the widest publicity was given to Marighella's writings, and particularly to his *Minimanual of the Urban Guerrilla*, written in June 1969.

In the *Minimanual* Marighella advocated the demoralising of government by persistent terrorist actions in the cities and a concentrated attack upon the economy by targeting foreign and national businesses. Five months later he died in a gun battle with police in São Paulo. His place was briefly taken by Joaquim Camara Ferreira, who having been betrayed, died in October 1970 in prison.

The ALN never properly recovered from Marighella's death. Within a little more than a year, the security forces had uncovered the movement's links; many were jailed, others fled into exile.

National Liberation Commando
(Comando da Libertação Nacional — COLINA)

COLINA was a Brazilian Marxist-Leninist faction which formed after the Organisation of Latin American Solidarity (OLAS) Conference in Havana in August 1967. It supported armed revolution, alongside the Revolutionary Popular Vanguard (VPR), and in April 1969 united at the Monguagua Conference with the VPR to form the Armed Revolutionary Vanguard (VAR).

National Revolutionary Movement
(Movimento Nacionalista Revolucionário — MNR)

Leonel Brizola, a deputy and brother-in-law of President Goulart, was not only prominent in the setting up of Groups of Eleven but took a keen interest in the MNR, which had in its ranks a nucleus of former members of the armed services. The MNR was the first group in Brazil to set up a rural guerrilla nucleus in early 1967, and was joined by the pro-Chinese Communist Party of Brazil (PCdoB) and Popular Action (AP).

Peasant Leagues
(Ligas Camponesas)

The Peasant Leagues were originally rural cooperatives started in Pernambuco in the mid-1950s, and under the guidance of the Socialist Party deputy, Francisco Julião, they became in the north-east of Brazil a political force. By carrying out sporadic acts of violence on sugar plantations, they focused political attention on land reform. They may have numbered as many as 12,000 members in 1964, when they were disbanded following the military coup against leftist President Goulart. Julião was at first imprisoned, but then allowed to leave for exile in Mexico, where he renounced armed struggle in favour of popular front tactics.

Popular Action
(Ação Popular — AP)

AP emerged in Brazil under the military regime which seized power from President Goulart in April 1964. It was composed of young and radical

Church-minded people, who saw the resort to armed struggle as the only means of achieving social justice. They became Marxists, whilst retaining their connections with the Roman Catholic Church.

Revolutionary Movement 8 October
(Movimento Revolucionário do Outubre 8 — MR-8)

The date chosen by this Brazilian terrorist group in 1968 commemorated the 1967 death of Che Guevara in Bolivia. Miniscule in all respects, MR-8 was nonetheless responsible for projecting Brazilian terrorism on to the world stage by suggesting to National Liberating Action (ALN) the abduction of the US Ambassador, Burke Elbrick. He was taken on 4 September 1969 and released in exchange for 15 prisoners.

In the subsequent wave of arrests, however, not only was MR-8 uprooted, but the ALN as well. MR-8 had operated in Paraná, and had links with radical student circles in the Federal University of Rio de Janeiro. Like other groups of its time, MR-8 consisted of dissident Marxist-Leninists who broke with the orthodox communist movement.

Revolutionary Popular Vanguard
(Vanguarda Popular Revolucionária — VPR)

With backing from Cuba, the VPR emerged from Workers' Politics (POLOP) in March 1968 to promote armed struggle in Brazil. Prominent in the group were João Quartim and later Carlos Lamarca. The VPR made its first attack on military installations in June 1968. Lamarca had attempted to promote disaffection in the armed forces, where he served as an infantry captain in São Paulo province. Uncovered, he deserted in January 1969, and joined forces with the National Liberation Commando (COLINA) to form the Armed Revolutionary Vanguard — Palmares (VAR-Palmares), Palmares being the name of a seventeenth-century commune set up by escaped slaves.

Before the year was up Lamarca had taken VPR out of VAR-Palmares and determined to concentrate upon the countryside, where he had visions of leading a people's army. But in April 1970 their training camp in the Ribeira Valley was discovered and their supplies seized. About 100 militants were arrested, leaving no more than 50 sympathisers at large in 1971, when the struggle was abandoned.

Among the most notorious of VPR actions was the murder in October 1968 of US Captain Chandler in São Paulo, the abduction of the Japanese Consul General in São Paulo, Nobuo Okuchi, in March 1970, and in conjunction with National Liberating Action (ALN) the abduction of the West German Ambassador, von Holleben, in June 1970. The following year a number of VPR leaders were killed, including Lamarca on 18 September in Salvador, Bahía. The group never recovered from his loss.

Workers' Politics
(Política Operária — POLOP)

POLOP was a 1961 Trotskyist-inclined splinter group of the Brazilian Communist Party (PCB). Members worked ideologically among students and the industrial proletariat spreading propaganda, but did not practise violence. In 1967 POLOP split over the issue of armed struggle and some members who favoured it joined the Revolutionary Popular Vanguard (VPR). Those who remained, especially in Minas Gerais and Guanabara, set up the National Liberation Commando (COLINA).

Chile

The remarkable Chilean tradition of continuity, homogeneity and stability was broken in 1970 with a government of the left under the Marxist President Allende, a man who proved unable to cope with economic circumstances, unwilling to curb the growth of political violence from extremist pressure groups, and seemingly impervious to the damage such disruption caused to the body politic.

Yet it was not the socialist policies pursued by Allende's Popular Unity Government which provoked the outrage of the middle sector of society or caused the tragic intervention of the military. The nationalisation of copper merely built upon the Chileanisation undertaken by former President Frei, and was approved by Congress. Furthermore, the agrarian reform had been written by the Christian Democrats: Allende merely applied the law. Even the opening up to Eastern-bloc countries conformed to norms traditionally practised by Chilean foreign policy, which had always recognised the fact of established power, regardless of whether or not Chile approved of that Government.

What caused the disaffection that prompted the military to take power in 1973 was a new and irremovable element of government inefficiency caused by the introduction of a political quota system for senior government appointments, which were allotted in such a manner that no party had control of any branch of the public service. Not only did political appointees represent a threat to the established bureaucracy by trying to replace them, but inter-party rivalry in the leftist government alliance inhibited agreement on the most day-to-day practices, let alone the introduction of reformist measures. Consequently public life was seized by institutional paralysis.

Still more obviously distressing, and particularly to the military who saw in them a threat, was the development of para-military militias bearing arms in the streets, a sight never before seen in Chile. The most intimidating body was the Movement of the Revolutionary Left (MIR), which through the allegiance of close members of Allende's family not only escaped censure, but appeared to have presidential approval. They took the law into their own hands — particularly over land seizures.

Lastly, the rather dour Chilean bureaucratic tradition, a product of Spanish monarchical government and Chile's insularity, was broken by a flamboyant and shocking display of unconventional presidential behaviour, smacking not only of the parvenu, but of gangsterism. Bereft of respect, Allende lost the support of that third of the electorate which had supported him in 1970 and paved the way for the savage reaction which the *Miristas* had encouraged.

The National Party opposed the President's reformist policies, and fearful of the country's increasingly close ties with Cuba advocated civil disobedience in April 1973. Also on the right the Fatherland and Liberty movement posed a violent threat to government. In June members of the group were fighting running battles in the streets of Santiago. Amid increasing right-wing terrorism and the dislocation caused by a truck drivers' strike in July the country moved to the brink of civil war.

Congress passed a motion of censure on the government on 22 August and appealed to the armed forces to 'reestablish the Constitution and the law'. In September professional workers in schools, hospitals and transport struck with the objective of bringing down the government, and the armed forces took over on 11 September. Under bombardment, President Allende committed suicide in the presidential palace.

Resistance to the coup was remarkably weak: probably less than a thousand people died throughout the country. The reaction which set in under General Augusto Pinochet Ugarte began with the dissolution of the Congress, the suspension of all political parties and of all trade union activity. The ugly aspect was the detention of thousands of people, the use of torture and the abolition of liberties responsibly exercised by Chileans for decades. A decade later Pinochet exercised supreme power in Chile, having long since relegated the navy and airforce chiefs to secondary positions. Not until the early 1980s was there any sign of violent opposition to his rule, which he had attempted to legitimise through holding national referenda that endorsed his power.

Bibliography

Brian Loveman wrote an excellent general introduction to modern Chile in *Chile: The Legacy of Hispanic Capitalism* (Oxford, 1979). The raw facts of the Allende period can be found in a Facts on File publication, *Chile and Allende* (New York, 1974). Robert Moss provided a punchy conservative account in *Chile's Marxist Experiment* (London, 1973), but see also Robert Alexander's better grasp in *The Tragedy of Chile* (London and Westport, Conn., 1978), whilst Alain Labrousse looked at events from the left in *L'Expérience Chilienne: Réformisme ou Révolution* (Editions du Seuil, Paris, 1972). The economic background is analysed by Stefan de Vylder in *Allende's Chile* (Cambridge University Press, 1974) and the labour movement by Alan Angell in *Politics and the Labour Movement in Chile* (OUP, London, 1972). Kenneth Medhurst edited an excellent collection of nine essays by prominent Chileans entitled *Allende's Chile*. The Trotskyist view can be found in *Revolution and Counter-Revolution in Chile* by Michel Raptis (Allison and Busby, London, 1974). The French Marxist writer, Régis Debray, contributed on the theoretical level *Conversations with Allende* (New Left Books, London, 1971), whilst on the practical level Sheila Cassidy, who was arrested for tending medically a prominent guerrilla and tortured, wrote the moving *Audacity to Believe*

(Collins, London, 1974). The most detailed and sound appraisal can be found by Valenzuela in volume 3 of *The Breakdown of Democratic Regimes* (London, 1978), edited by Juan Linz and Alfred Stepan.

Fatherland and Liberty
(Patria y Libertad)

Shortly after Allende was elected to the Chilean presidency in 1970, Fatherland and Liberty was set up in the capital, Santiago. It represented the Chilean ultra-right, and was led by Dr Pablo Rodríguez Grez and Walter Roberto Thieme. It set out to combat on the streets the armed threat presented by the Movement of the Revolutionary Left (MIR) and itself indulged in anti-state arson and sabotage attacks. Grez fled to Ecuador, Thieme to Argentina in mid-1973 as the government cracked down on Fatherland and Liberty centres throughout the country, following an attack upon the life of General Prats González. Months before the Pinochet coup in September the organisation was calling for Allende's overthrow.

Movement of the Revolutionary Left
(Movimiento de la Izquierda Revolucionaria — MIR)

The original members of the Chilean MIR were radical socialist students reading for degrees in 1965 at the University of Concepción. They belonged to the fashionable ultra-left, until in 1967 some broke the law by raiding banks, which committed them to a life of clandestinity.

With money from these raids the *Miristas* infiltrated the poorer squatter quarters outside the capital, Santiago, and began thereby a process of politicisation. Some went to Cuba for training. The MIR secretary general, Miguel Enríquez, presided over the transformation of a student body into a Castroite pressure group employing violence, murder and intimidation for political ends. He, alongside Luciano Cruz and Andrés Pascal Allende, won control of the MIR central executive in 1967 and was responsible for the direct action which followed — armed thefts, bank robberies and the illegal seizure of building sites.

Come victory at the polls for Salvador Allende in 1970, the MIR remained outside government, convinced that a civil war was inevitable, and that the proper role for the left was to prepare for armed revolution. *Miristas* were also agreed that by seizing control of factories and farms smaller than the legal minimum laid down under the Agrarian Reform Law they should endeavour to force the government beyond 'bourgeois legality'. On occasions their actions were abetted by like-minded government representatives, so that the MIR became responsible for setting the pace of radical reform. The most spectacular seizures occurred in the south, particularly in Cautín province.

Some of the farms taken over were used as camps for the stocking of arms and for training. Weaponry was either stolen from police or military supplies, or came in small quantities from Argentina, where sympathetic groups traded them. Within a year *Mirista* enclaves had been established, in which the movement effectively acted as an alternative power to the state.

Outside Santiago similar camps, run by *Miristas,* were established. They bore names such as New Havana, Che Guevara and the Lenin Camp. Sited on land seized by *Mirista* commandos, squatters had been given legal titles to their plots and provided with basic amenities. Political control, however, lay with unofficial *Mirista* commissars, who ran the encampments.

To promote their armed struggle the MIR formed a series of front movements — the Revolutionary Workers' Front (FTR), the Revolutionary Peasants' Committees (MCR) and the Revolutionary Squatters' Committees (JPR). These lobbies pressurised the government and contributed to the formation of a para-military militia in readiness for civil war.

Yet when the military seized power in September 1973 the MIR was not strong enough to wage a terrorist campaign against the junta, despite the possession of large quantities of weapons and explosives. The attempt was made, and in February 1974 the MIR announced a pact with the Argentinian People's Revolutionary Army (ERP), but nothing came of this link, nor of contacts with Cuba. In fact events revealed the MIR for what it was — a small, middle-class intellectual band capable only of skirmishing with the police.

In October 1974 its leader, Miguel Enríquez, was killed in Santiago; his place was taken by the late president's nephew, Andrés Pascal Allende. But a year later he sought refuge in the Costa Rican embassy with his mistress and fellow guerrilla, Mary Ann Beausire. Nelson Gutiérrez, the MIR second in command, took refuge in the Papal Nunciature, after being treated for his wounds by the British doctor, Sheila Cassidy, who was subsequently tortured by the Chilean authorities. Both men were allowed to leave Chile in 1976.

Thenceforth the MIR was responsible for the occasional terrorist incident in the capital — mostly bombings. Arrests were made periodically of people thought to be involved; a few died resisting arrest. Essentially the movement failed to reorganise its tactics; the great majority of those actively opposed to President Pinochet had sought exile abroad following the 1973 coup. Those who did not seek exile went underground.

In 1978 it was discovered that the MIR had planned to sabotage power stations throughout the country. In the event only one attack, in Valparaiso, succeeded. Those involved came typically from the middle class with a humanistic training in law, economics, or liberal arts. Occasionally an older person was detained, but seldom from a labouring or artisan background. The MIR published a clandestine paper, *El Rebelde,* but never succeeded in disturbing the firm course plotted by President Pinochet for Chile's political future.

Throughout its life the MIR was distinguished by a hot-headed desire for action, which the Moscow-line Chilean Communist Party (PCCh) classed as mere adventurism. *Miristas* were not orthodox Marxist-Leninists, refusing as they put it 'to wait for the contradictions within the bourgeoisie to sharpen before encouraging the popular masses to resist'. In PCCh eyes the MIR had always followed a mistaken political line and, especially among young people, represented a threat to orthodox communist influence. Nonetheless, the MIR survived into the 1980s, when from time to time the occasional terrorist incident was committed in its name.

People's Organised Vanguard
(Vanguardia Organizada del Pueblo — VOP)

The VOP was set up on the Chilean ultra-left by Ismael Villegas, a former *Mirista* in 1968/69. The group was miniscule, one of a number of splintered MIR factions. Its principal claim to notoriety was the responsibility for the murder in July 1971 of the Christian Democratic leader, Pérez Zujovic. For this crime President Allende ordered the security forces to move against the VOP, and little more was heard of the organisation.

White Guard
(Guardia Blanca)

The White Guard was set up in rural Chile by landowners to protect themselves in the early 1970s from the illegal land seizures organised forcefully by the Movement of the Revolutionary Left (MIR).

Colombia

Of all Latin American countries, not excluding one, Colombia's contemporary record of political violence has been the most cruel, the most bloody and the longest lasting, indeed it seems to have had neither a real beginning nor yet sight of an end. From the civil horrors of 1948-53, the height of *La Violencia*, the country was torn apart into independent zones, where the writ of national law no longer ran. Some were supervised by the Colombian Communist Party (PCC), such as Marquetalia in southern Tolima, where Manuel Marulanda inherited a territory which became a homeland in 1966 for his own Armed Revolutionary Forces of Colombia (FARC). With the support of the local peasant population, his and a dozen other guerrilla groups flourished in the late 1950s in total isolation, lacking all contact with the cities, let alone the wider world.

Some amelioration in the violence was brought about by the military coup of 1953, which General Rojas Pinilla instigated. Many guerrillas took up his offer of an amnesty, possibly as many as 8000, but he ultimately failed to pacify the country, and was outmanoeuvred by the traditional Conservative and Liberal politicians, who manipulated in their own interest the institutions of the state. In May 1958 a mere 2,500,000 people elected to the presidency Alberto Lleras Camargo, as National Front candidate (1958-62).

Within eight months Fidel Castro had toppled a corrupt dictatorship in Cuba, establishing by guerrilla force alone a revolutionary socialist government for which in Colombia guerrillas had fought for a decade. The impact gave rise first to minor movements such as the Workers', Students' and Peasants' Movement (MOEC) and the United Front of Revolutionary Action (FUAR), and then in 1964 to the more substantial National Liberation Army (ELN), set up by Fabio Vásquez.

Fearful of this rival authority, the Moscow-line PCC established the FARC, using what base of rural influence was left to it. On its left the Chinese at once supported the creation of a Maoist People's Liberation Army (EPL) in 1967. None of these movements shook the established form of government, weak and under-representative though it was during the 1960s. The reason lay partly in their own weakness, partly in the profoundly unvigorous nature of the average Colombian, particularly in the capital, Bogotá, and partly in the training and aid given to the Colombian security forces by the United States.

Yet because of the nature of the countryside, the persistence of general injustice, poverty, and inadequate government, and the willingness of outside forces to foster the ambitions of would-be guerrilla leaders, the threat of guerrilla violence was never eradicated. It persisted throughout the decade of the 1970s, with the addition of a new hybrid group, April 19 Movement (M-19), which in 1983 seemed set upon contesting traditional politics through casting itself in a new Colombian socialist guise, akin to that successfully developed by the Sandinists in Nicaragua.

Bibliography

The background to Colombian political violence is best approached through Vernon Lee Fluharty's *Dance of the Millions: Military Rule and the Social Revolution in Colombia 1930-56* (University of Pittsburg Press, 1957) and *La Violencia en Colombia* (Bogotá, 1962 — ninth edition 1980) by Germán Guzmán Campos and others, who also wrote a biographical study of Camilo Torres which contains useful extracts from his writings, *El Padre Camilo Torres* (Siglo XXI, Madrid, Mexico and Buenos Aires). In English there is Walter Broderick's *Camilo Torres* (Doubleday, New York, 1975). An excellent book which covers the background is Robert Die's *Colombia: The Political Dimensions of Change* (Yale University Press, New Haven and London, 1971). Ulíses Casas' *Origen Desarrollo del Movimiento Revolucionario Colombiano* (Bogotá, 1980) is a slight work. Some useful interviews with Jaime Arenas and Jaime Bateman are reprinted in Germán Castro Caycedo's *Del ELN al M-19 Once Años de Lucha Guerrillera* (Bogotá, 1980). For insurgency during the 1960s, see Richard Maullin's good summary and use of statistics in *Soldiers, Guerrillas and Politics in Colombia* (Rand Corporation, Santa Monica, 1973). Jacobo Arenas wrote from the FARC point of view *Colombie: Guérillas du Peuple* (Editions Sociales, Paris, 1969). For further reading on both rural and urban guerrilla activity in Colombia, Russell Ramsay provided an excellent critical commentary on the available bibliography in *Latin American Research Review* Vol. 8, No. 1, 1973. For additional material, see Charles Russell, James Miller and Robert Hildner, 'The Urban Guerrilla in Latin America: A Select Bibliography' in *Latin American Research Review* Vol. 9, No. 1, 1974. For contemporary insurgency, see the FARC guerrilla leader, Manuel Marulanda Vélez, *Cuadernos de Campaña* (Ediciones Abejo Mono, Colombia, 1973) and on M-19, *Siembra Vientos y Recogerás Tempestades* (Bogotá, 1982) by Patricia Lara, who summarises the lives of the principal M-19 leaders usefully and includes a chronology and documentary material.

April 19 Movement
(Movimiento 19 Abril — M-19)

The origins of M-19 go back to 1973, when a dissatisfied nucleus of revolutionaries first raided banks to finance their assault upon Colombian society. Behind the initiative lay the determination of two men, Carlos Toledo Plata and Jaime Bateman Cayón. Toledo Plata was a prominent medical doctor who had represented in Congress the National Popular Alliance (ANAPO), a populist party founded in 1961 by the former dictator, Rojas Pinilla (died 1975), and led in the 1980s by his daughter, María Eugenia.

On 17 January 1974 dissident ANAPO left-wing elements stole Simón Bolívar's sword and spurs, which were exhibited in the Colombian liberator's nineteenth-century Bogotá villa. The symbolism of such daring was not lost on the common people, yet the ANAPO leadership rejected all responsibility for the act. The party fared badly in the elections of 19 April 1970, from which M-19 took its name; accordingly, the dissidents urged the party to adopt armed struggle as the path to power. But they failed to persuade the party bureaucracy, and so instead of developing as an armed branch of ANAPO, M-19 attempted to attract former populist support by claiming that its thinking was *Anapista*. A further important element in M-19 political mythology is its endeavour to inherit the equally nationalistic tradition of Jorge Eliécer Gaitán (assassinated 1948), the Liberal leader whose death set off the *Bogotazo*, three days of popular uprising that left much of the capital in ruins. Carlos Toledo Plata remained active until his capture in 1981.

Jaime Bateman remained the principal military commander, with ambitions as a potential presidential candidate for 1982. From a humble background, he never attended university, travelling instead to the USSR, Czechoslovakia and France, returning with a thorough grounding in Marxist-Leninist political philosophy. His attitudes at once prompted him to commit minor infractions, for which he was twice imprisoned between 1962 and 1964. In 1966, until he left in 1970, Bateman ran with the FARC, and came to know intimately Manuel Marulanda, Jacobo Arenas (Luis Morantes) and Ciro Trujillo, who provided a model on how to run a long-standing active communist rural guerrilla group. Others prominent in the founding of M-19 were Andrés Almarales, Iván Marino Ospina, Carlos Pizarro León, Luis Otero, Alvaro Fayad and Gustavo Arias.

The organisation was built upon the pattern of the Tupamaros in Uruguay, with columns in the principal cities of Bogotá, Cali, Medellín, and Bucaramanga. Each column, which consists of several cells, operated independently from other columns, but under Bateman's overall command. From arrests in 1979 it was clear that M-19 had benefited from the experience of former Tupamaro guerrillas, as well as from Argentinian terrorists. Evidence emerged in March 1981 that M-19 had enjoyed facilities in, and derived logistic support from, Cuba.

The terrorist network was not put into operation until 1976, when in February M-19 kidnapped José Raquel Mercado, a trade union official, who, accused of having links with the Central Intelligence Agency, was held for three months and then murdered. The following year M-19 took to sabotaging petroleum pipelines, and in 1978 extended its activities into a whole range of attacks against business, government and police installations. Still more sensational were the kidnappings of the

Nicaraguan Ambassador, Barquero Montiel, and of the Texaco manager, Nicolás Escobar Soto, who died on 4 January 1979 as police stormed the hideout. The motive behind the first abduction was to give political support to the Sandinist revolution in Nicaragua; money lay behind the second. Bateman believed multinational business enterprises should pay for the Colombian revolution as he saw it. Sears and Texaco Petroleum Company were among chosen targets. Colombian business, on the other hand, did not attract terrorist attention, for Bateman favoured national capitalism, and even, on account of its patriotism, had a good word for the army.

Two further M-19 incidents caught the attention of the world's media. In January 1979 the large sums of money raised from kidnap operations were partly used to float a company which purchased a house from which an 80-metre tunnel was dug underneath the suburban military arsenal known as Cantón Norte. As many as 120 people were allegedly involved in the operation, which netted more than 5000 arms. Yet within the month all had been recaptured.

In 1980 an M-19 group led by Rosemberg Pabón Pabón held captive 15 diplomats in the Dominican embassy in Bogotá, a siege which lasted 61 days. At the end of it an undisclosed ransom was paid, but the demand to free colleagues from jail was refused. The terrorists sought and found refuge in Cuba. Subsequently, it was in Cuba that the nucleus of a group of 100 guerrillas who penetrated across the border from Ecuador in March 1981 had received their instruction and training. That enterprise failed miserably, but in the towns M-19 terrorist attacks continued, and included a mortar attack upon the presidential palace. Attempts were made to set up a united front of guerrilla groups but little sign of coordination was apparent in 1982. For a while there was speculation that M-19 would accept the offer of an amnesty made by President Betancur, although by 1983 most members had decided to reject it. In any event terrorist acts continued.

Armed Revolutionary Forces of Colombia
(Fuerzas Armadas Revolucionarias de Colombia — FARC)

The pro-Soviet Colombian Communist Party (PCC) adopted FARC in April 1966 to act as its armed branch. It was an exceptional decision, for at that time other Latin American Moscow-line Communist Parties did not openly support armed struggle. In fact the PCC merely recognised reality, that armed peasants needed political direction if the Communist Party were to retain its leadership of the revolutionary movement. The FARC leader, Manuel Marulanda Vélez, or Dead Shot, as he was known, had for years been leading rural peasants in guerrilla warfare activities and was a PCC central committee member. In those days the movement operated in the southern departments of Tolima, Huila and Valle del Cauca.

The FARC determined to link insurgency to the establishment of a 'people's government'; in this it differed from other bandit groups, whose actions merely reflected the desperation arising from local grievances and sufferings. The Colombian political system, FARC argued, reflected the interests of North American imperialists; to oust it FARC adopted guerrilla action as the principal form of mass action, organised under one command to attack the nerve centres of the country. The new movement also embraced labour strikes and student demonstrations as part of the struggle of the masses.

In fact strategic targets such as major highways in remote areas or oil pipe lines were never sabotaged, despite their vulnerability. And before long FARC suffered from US-backed counter-insurgency operations, which deprived the group of its urban support networks and in the countryside kept the guerrillas on the move. Prevented as they were from settling into an area, very little activity — at its height seldom more than four incidents a month — was recorded by the 100-odd members.

In mid-1968 the group reemerged with urban links and succeeded in mounting the occasional ambush of military trucks. The immediate growth of FARC terrorism however was cut short by the death on 5 October 1968 of Ciro Trujillo Castaño, who was killed in a clash with the military. A year later FARC reemerged in Huila department, where nine peasants were killed and a number abducted. Part of the problem for the activists was the ambivalent attitude of the PCC, which, whenever elections were held, rather than fight in the wilderness, felt it should participate in the poll.

Nonetheless, Marulanda remained in charge of the band, which by 1971/72 numbered some 150 activists. They occupied a number of small and remote villages and clashed occasionally with the army. Contrary to terrorist groups in other countries they did not move into the cities, although they followed a trend in 1972 in financing themselves by kidnapping.

By 1973 FARC could field as many as 50 guerrillas in the occupation of a village and had made some impact on the local peasant population in Huila and Tolima. But actions were spasmodic and never really amounted to a campaign, indeed they were often confused with the common crimes of rural banditry, which is endemic to the outlying regions.

One action succeeded in putting FARC back on the guerrilla map — the kidnapping of the Dutch consul in Cali in January 1975, for whom the movement demanded a ransom of US $1 million. He was freed in October 1976. In the countryside a resurgence of activity was noted as a result of similar extortions raised from wealthy cattlemen. As they occupied townships FARC units stole food, medicines and arms. In 1977 they expanded their operations through cooperation with the Army of National Liberation (ELN). Marulanda announced in February 'a single front of popular struggle to seize power'. Nonetheless there remained ideological differences between the two groups.

Actions were still more closely coordinated after August 1978, when they spoke of a merger. The agreement was for FARC to operate in the countryside, where it claimed five fronts, two in the Amazon Andean region of Caqueta, and the others in the central mountain range, middle Magdalena and Antioquia department.

The cooperation turned out well for Marulanda, who in the late 1970s undoubtedly directed the largest guerrilla group. On one occasion in March 1978, FARC was reported to have fielded as many as 150 guerrillas in the temporary occupation of a small town, although this was exceptional.

With growing requirements, FARC relied for funds on kidnapping, which by 1980 had reached frequent and extremely ugly proportions. It became commonplace for peasants who informed on guerrilla activities to be shot dead as FARC units occupied small townships for hours at a time whilst they restocked with food, arms and medicines. Clashes persisted throughout 1981, despite the announcement of an electoral truce. There seemed no prospect in the 1980s that men inured to rural guerrilla existence would desist from either their crimes or their way of life. Scant notice was taken of President Betancur's offer of an amnesty in 1982.

Communist Party of Colombia Marxist-Leninist
(Partido Comunista de Colombia Marxista-Leninista —PCC-ML)

The party split from the Soviet-line Colombian Communist Party (PCC) in July 1965, as a direct result of the Sino-Soviet schism in the communist world. It advocated prolonged revolutionary war according to the doctrine of Mao, and supported Castro's Cuba, which was proof in the party's view that revolutionary seizure of power was possible. Later, as the Cuban leadership slipped into Moscow's hands, the PCC-ML took to criticising Castro's policies.

At home the party believed circumstances in Colombia were ripe for revolution, at a point of 'incipient insurrection'; such convictions caused the party to set up the Patriotic Liberation Front (FPL), and later the People's Liberation Army (EPL), which as a guerrilla group was active in the early 1980s. The party's general secretary, Pedro León Arboleda, died in a shoot-out with police in Cali in July 1975. It probably attracted fewer than a thousand members in the early 1980s, and although it could have sought to operate legally, as did the Moscow party, it chose to remain 'undercover', although there was nothing illegal in its status. Its organ, *Revolución*, can be bought in the capital's numerous bookstalls.

Independent Revolutionary Workers' Movement
(Movimiento Obrero Independiente y Revolucionario — MOIR)

MOIR's origins go back to the second Congress of the Workers', Students' and Peasants' Movement (MOEC) in 1965, when a split occurred. Most of those who went on to form the MOIR were students who rejected the dogmatism of hard-line Marxist-Leninists. The movement was actually constituted in Medellín in September 1969, with the purpose of promoting a national democratic revolution rather than a specifically socialist revolution. As the movement was penetrated by Maoists, the ideological line changed in the course of the 1970s, to becoming a mass-based Maoist party, but independent of the PCC-ML. Few voted for it in the 1978 elections. The movement's general secretary in 1980 was Francisco Mosquera.

National Liberation Army
(Ejército de Liberación Nacional — ELN)

The ELN was set up on 4 July 1964 in Colombia as a politico-military organisation whose principal aim was to 'seize power for the people'. It fought for a 'democratic revolutionary front of workers, peasants, intellectuals, students and progressive sectors of the middle class affected by the present system and ready to fight to change it'.

Behind the ELN lay the organising capacity and leadership of a student intellectual, Fabio Vásquez Castaño (b. 1937) whose motivation derived from Castro's 1959 victory in Cuba and who had previously supported MOEC. Indeed the first ELN action on 7 January 1965 commemorated the founding of that movement six years earlier. From the start ELN relations with the Colombian Communist Party (CCP) and the armed Revolutionary Forces of Colombia (FARC) were distant and strained, despite overtures by Vásquez to the CCP, which saw in the ELN a rival to its own leadership of the guerrilla movement. Havana, however, lent it support by providing arms, money and training facilities on a small scale; it became very much a Castroite movement.

The ELN area of operations was restricted in the 1960s to the northern departments of Santander, Antioquia and Bolívar, where many ELN members had received their higher education. Their primary concern was the plight of the rural peasantry, but they found recruitment hard. The core remained radical students, but aside from the Vásquez brothers the ELN will be remembered because Father Camilo Torres, a Louvain-educated priest from Colombia's upper classes, joined the movement in October 1965. He exchanged his role as a professor in the National University's department of sociology for that of guerrilla extraordinary;

in a clash with the army he died four months later. His spectacular commitment to the revolutionary cause was quite secular, and in no way derived from the new theology of liberation, which was about to emerge in Latin America.

The ELN made no impression militarily or politically in the mid-1960s in the rural areas. Nor did members resort to urban terrorism as they might have done by capitalising upon their urban origins. Fewer and fewer incidents were recorded in the late 1960s, and it is doubtful if the group numbered more than 80 by the end of the decade. The Colombian armed forces had successfully reduced the insurgent threat to a minimum level, although it is also true that Cuban aid was less forthcoming in the late 1960s, partly due to pressure from Moscow to reduce support. There were, too, rivalries and even splits in the movement.

The deputy leader, Víctor Medina, was accused of treason and shot dead. Juan de Diós Aguilera led a dissident 'Simón Bolívar' front in January 1968 after murdering José Ayala, the previous leader. Jaime Arenas, who joined the ELN in October 1967, left the movement in February 1969 under sentence of death for falling asleep on sentry duty; he was shot dead on 28 March 1971.

The resurgence in 1969 of ELN activity was financed by ransom money obtained from kidnaps. By and large the targets were wealthy local businessmen, but in October the international community was disturbed by the abduction of the Swiss consul in Cali. Sums of $100,000 were paid to what amounted to a very small group of people. Once guerrilla actions became profitable, recruiting became easier. By 1972 bands of up to 150 guerrillas were attacking rural communities in Bolivia and Antioquia departments, stealing food, medicine and money. Leading them were Fabio Vásquez and Ricardo Lara Parada. They failed that year to capitalise on their move into the cities, where dynamite, arms, radio equipment and propaganda in large quantities were discovered.

In 1973 Manuel and Antonio Vásquez, brothers of the leader, were killed in clashes and Ricardo Lara Parada, who had fallen out with Vásquez, was captured and remained in prison until January 1978. Despite these losses kidnappings continued, although the ransoms demanded were less than those in Argentina. Throughout the mid-1970s, bands of 50 to 100 ELN guerrillas would occupy small towns for a few hours, robbing banks and haranguing the populace. Such actions did not seriously threaten the institutional structure of the state, although due to the combined effect of guerrilla groups a state of siege was declared over the country in June 1975. It was reimposed almost continuously in the late 1970s.

In addition to rural actions the ELN turned to the cities, encouraged by the destruction wrought by the rival Popular Liberation Army (EPL) and the M-19 in 1976. Indeed in 1977 the ELN came to a measure of agreement with the Armed Revolutionary Forces of Colombia (FARC) to leave rural operations altogether to the Communist-backed movement and to concentrate on the towns, thereby creating 'a single front of popular struggle to seize power'. But such a division of labour was never strictly observed.

At the same time the remnants of the ELN were wooed by M-19, which called for unity of action; in May 1979 a joint guerrilla front was announced. In fact the ELN continued to operate in rural areas, but intermittently and without strong leadership. Vásquez was thought to be in Cuba, and to have lost control of the movement. Among those mentioned to the fore of the ELN in the late 1970s were Manuel Pérez Martinez, a priest, and Gabriel Vera Bernal, who was captured in August 1979. Occasional terrorist acts were committed in the early 1980s, but of Colombia's guerrilla groups ELN was the least active.

Popular Liberation Army
(Ejército Popular de Liberación — EPL)

The EPL emerged in late 1967 as a result of Chinese influence in Marxist-Leninist circles; it was in fact the armed branch of the miniscule pro-Peking Colombian Communist Party — Marxist-Leninist (PCC —M-L). For the EPL the war of liberation was not only directed at the Colombian bourgeoisie but also at what it termed the revisionist Moscow-line PCC and the Armed Revolutionary Forces of Colombia (FARC). The first EPL guerrillas were drawn from dissident FARC members, just as in 1965 the PCC — M-L had split from the PCC. Throughout the 1970s the EPL, although small in comparison with other active Colombian groups, retained its ideological link with Peking.

Behind the EPL were Bernardo Ferreira Grandet and Pedro Vásquez Rendón; the first died in a clash with the army, the second was disposed of by Pedro León Arboleda, who succeeded him until his own death in 1975. Riven by dissent and harassed by the Colombian armed forces on the borders of Antioquia and Córdoba departments, the EPL hardly survived in the countryside. Even with the 1971 resurgence of guerrilla activity little was heard of EPL actions, although propaganda from China was freely distributed in the towns, and some success attended the establishment of Maoist cells in high schools and universities. Among prominent members who were captured or died were Gonzalo González Mantilla and Libardo Mora Toro, a once prominent athlete. Francisco Carvallo replaced them, until he lost control in 1977.

During the late 1970s the EPL was responsible for the occasional sabotage attack, the odd kidnap, bank robbery or bomb attack, but it never developed an effective rural campaign. Its ideological stand contributed to EPL isolation from other Colombian guerrilla groups, until 1978, after which it tended to work alongside, if not actually together with, the National Liberation Army and M-19. The collaboration contributed to ideological dissension, however, and almost certainly led to independent action by the so-called Pedro León Arboleda group in 1979 and 1980.

Greater success attended EPL efforts in the towns, where eventually

EPL militants contributed to the creation of a separate Maoist movement — the workers' Self Defence Movement (MAO) in 1978. The following year the EPL cell called after Pedro León Arboleda was active in Bogotá. In 1980 the pro-Chinese ideological stance continued to appeal to a small circle of university-based intellectuals who succoured the terrorist movement, which despite arrests remained active. Towns where they retain influence include Bogotá, Convención, Medellín, Cali, Popayan, Pereira and Tierra Alta.

Revolutionary Liberal Movement
(Movimiento Revolucionario Liberal – MRL)

The MRL was founded in the wake of the Cuban revolution, which it encouraged and supported in Colombia. As a political movement the MRL won the backing of several hundred thousand supporters, led by Alfonso López Michelson, who subsequently became leader of the Liberal Party and President (1974-78).

The MRL programme was contained in the 'January Plan', which aimed to secure for the Colombian people health, education, a home and land, a slogan known in Spanish by its acronym SETT. MRL pursued its aim through encouraging political strikes, which the government declared illegal. A number of militants were imprisoned. From the younger elements came a revolutionary nucleus, which, joining with dissident communists, became the National Liberation Army (ELN).

United Front for Revolutionary Action
(Frente Unido de Acción Revolucionaria – FUAR)

The intellectuals who set up FUAR in 1960 did so as a direct consequence of Castro's victory the preceding year in Cuba. Yet they grouped around the daughter and son-in-law of Jorge Eliécer Gaitán, the populist Liberal leader assassinated in 1948, but whose name still attracted political support. Gloria Gaitán and her husband, Luis Emiro Valencia, supported the concept of guerrilla war but were not in the ideological sense 'Castroite'; their influence lay in Bogotá, at the time Colombian political violence occurred in the countryside, and they never succeeded in developing any direction of or control over it. FUAR speeches and pamphlets were swiftly overtaken by the action of the Armed Revolutionary Forces of Colombia (FARC).

Workers' Self-Defence Movement
(Movimiento de Autodefensa Obrera — MAO)

The MAO first emerged in Bogotá as an urban branch of the pro-Chinese

People's Liberation Army in September 1978, when it claimed responsibility for the murder of a former interior minister, Rafael Pardo Buelvas. Those responsible allegedly included Hector Fabio Abadía Rey, Juan Bautista González and Armando López Suárez (arrested May 1980). The assassination was an act of revenge for the death of 12 people on 14 September 1977 during a strike when Pardo Buelvas had been responsible for internal security.

In Autumn 1978 MAO members briefly took over several radio stations in Bogotá, but before any pattern emerged the authorities made a number of arrests in early 1979, which inhibited the movement's development that year. It remained active in a small way in the early 1980s.

Workers', Students' and Peasants' Movement
(Movimiento de Obreros, Estudiantes y Campesinos — MOEC)

Student leader Antonio Larotta founded MOEC in Bogotá in January 1960, when Castro's victory in Cuba was vividly in the mind. It pursued guerrilla warfare briefly and ingloriously in the Valle de Cauca region, until Larotta was killed in May 1961. Federico Arango maintained MOEC's footing for a while, until he too was killed. MOEC followed an ultra-leftist political line, independent of the Colombian Communist Party.

Dominican Republic

The Cuban revolution had its repercussions in the Dominican Republic, where in 1961 the dictator, Trujillo, was murdered after 30 years of misrule. Following shortly, a military coup ousted socialist President Juan Bosch (1961-63) in 1963. A period of extreme instability began, culminating in a bloody uprising in support of Bosch, in which the US government saw fit to intervene in 1965 to prevent the military triumph of leftist political forces under the leadership of Colonel Francisco Caamaño Deño.

Elections were held in 1966, when Joaquín Balaguer won. Until 1978 he remained president, winning two successive elections in 1970 and 1974, albeit in contests in which the left refused to participate. Under his rule the Republic suffered relatively little political violence, although he maintained control only at the expense of democratic government. Balaguer reduced to a minimum Cuban influence, which was primarily exercised through the Revolutionary Movement of 14 June (MR-14J), but also through the rival Dominican Popular Movement (MPD). Neither of these movements was able to promote sustained political violence, but they acted as nuclei for a revolutionary political alternative, as it turned out without success.

In 1978 Balaguer was persuaded to stand down, and power devolved upon Antonio Guzmán Fernández, whose Dominican Revolutionary Party (PRD) carried forward a responsible democratic reformist programme, which contributed to the political isolation of the revolutionary left. Still more important he confined the military to barracks. If Guzmán's party, which was returned in May 1982 under Salvador Jorge Blanco, can retain its unity and persist in the application of moderate socialist principles, the ultra-left may continue to lack appeal. In the early 1980s it remained fragmented in some 15 Marxist groups including the Dominican Liberation Party (PLD), led by former President Bosch; the Nucleus of Communist Workers, led by Rafael Taveras; the Patriotic Anti-Imperialist Union, under Franklin Franco; the Camilo Torres Revolutionary Committee and the Trinitarian National Liberation Movement (MLNT), which appeared to be the only faction sporadically active in political violence in 1980. Together the entire ultra-left spectrum was not thought to number more than 5000 sympathisers.

Bibliography

Two introductions exist, the latest by a retired diplomat, Ian Bell, *The Dominican Republic* (London, 1981) the earlier by Howard Wiarda, *The Dominican Republic* (London, 1969), whilst Abraham Lowenthal ably analysed the 1965 US intervention in *The Dominican Intervention* (Cambridge, Mass., 1972). See also Carlos María Gutiérrez, *The Dominican Republic: Rebellion and Repression* (New York, 1972) for some interesting journalistic impressions from the left. Based upon systematic use of Dominican archives, the best account of the conflict with good analysis of the post-1961 factions is found in Piero Gleijeses, *The Dominican Crisis: The 1965 Constitutionalist Revolt and American Intervention* (Baltimore and London, 1979). The Trujillo era is dealt with by Robert Crassweller in *Trujillo the Life and Times of a Caribbean Dictator* (London, 1966), and for his assassination see *Time* correspondent Bernard Diederich's *Trujillo: The Death of the Goat* (London, 1978). The Balaguer period of the 1970s was studied by Pope Atkins in *Arms and Politics in the Dominican Republic* (Westview, USA, 1981). The early views of Juan Bosch can be read in his *The Unfinished Experiment: Democracy in the Dominican Republic* (New York, 1965, London, 1966) and on American overseas intervention, about which he naturally had strong feelings, see *Le Pentagonisme* (Paris, 1969), a translation from the Spanish published a year earlier.

Dominican Popular Movement
(*Movimiento Popular Dominicano* — MPD)

Had it not been for Castro's 1959 victory in Cuba there would have been no MPD, for even before the revolution had triumphed the group had had its origins in Cuba. Yet both before and after that victory, the MPD was more important outside the country as a focus for exiles than inside the Republic as a revolutionary nucleus. Its relationship with the similarly Castroite Revolutionary Movement 14 June (MR-14J) was more often antagonistic than complementary.

In March 1970 the MPD claimed responsibility for kidnapping Lieutenant Colonel Crowley, US air attaché, in return for whose release the government freed 20 imprisoned members, including MPD secretary general Maximiliano Gómez. They found refuge in Cuba. Those that remained in the Republic involved themselves in ideological disputes with rival ultra-leftists, especially with members of the pro-Chinese Communist Party of the Dominican Republic (PACOREDO). In January 1971 the hostility actually provoked the deaths of as many as 40 extremists.

The MPD continued to exist throughout the decade of the 1970s, and was held responsible by the government of President Joaquín Balaguer

(1966-78) in 1975 for attempting to foment rebellion with Cuban backing. Among those who participated in the plot were Claudio Caamaño, a nephew of the dead Colonel Francisco Caamaño, who had held Santo Domingo in the 1965 revolution, and Toribio Peña Jáquez, both of whom were captured in early October 1975 in the mountains of San Cristóbal.

Movement of the Revolutionary Left
(Movimiento de la Izquierda Revolucionaria — MIR)

Led by Fernando Paniagua and Enrique Vásquez, the Dominican MIR announced its formation in 1979. It claimed that a previously unknown group, the Armed Forces of National Liberation, had joined it, but nothing further was heard of it in the early 1980s.

Revolutionary Movement 14 June
(Movimiento Revolucionario 14 de Junio — MR-14J)

The MR-14J took its name from June 1959, the month that a small band of Dominican exiles landed from Cuba with the ambition of overthrowing President Trujillo (murdered 1961). Nothing came of that attempt, nor indeed of the November 1963 insurrection against the *coup d'état* which had ousted his revolutionary successor, Juan Bosch, when the MR-14J was born. Its base lay on the university campus, where it controlled the Dominican Students' Federation; its inspiration was Castroite.

In April 1965 Amaury Germán Aristy, who led the Movement, was behind an uprising led by Colonel Francisco Caamaño Deño, who for a time held the capital, Santo Domingo, before US intervention quelled the rebellion. Caamaño was subsequently posted to diplomatic exile in London. The Movement enjoyed Cuban backing, but because of its social composition split into numerous factions.

Caamaño vanished from London in 1967 to reappear in Cuba. Six years later in February 1973 he landed with ten men on Caracoles beach, only to die in his first clash with the military in the mountains of San José de Oca. In January 1972 Germán Aristy had already been killed in a street gunfight in the capital.

By the early 1970s MR-14J had splintered irrevocably into mini-fractions, which in themselves presented no threat to the security of the state. Of these factions at least one, the Red Line of 14 June Movement, retained something of the original nomenclature. Members were responsible for kidnapping Barbara Hutchinson, US Information Service Director, in September 1974 and for seizing the Venezuelan consulate. Hostages were taken and in return for their release the terrorists accepted a safe passage to Panama.

Trinitarian National Liberation Movement
(Movimiento de Liberación Nacional de los Trinitarios —
MLNT)

The Trinitarians operated in the latter half of the 1970s in the Dominican Republic as an urban terrorist group, led by Juan Bautista Castillo Pujols. From time to time members clashed with police in Santo Domingo, causing the occasional death of a policeman. They formed one of the many factions of the Dominican ultra-left — in political terms of no significance, as disturbers of the peace — an irritant only. Panama granted political asylum in 1981 to Trinitarian leader, Lorenzo Mejía Frías.

El Salvador

Revolutionary inspiration in El Salvador draws upon the myth of the 1932 peasant insurrection, in which Communist Party leader Farabundo Martí played a legendary role. It was put down, but at the cost only of many thousands of lives. Military intervention resulted in unrelieved military rule until 1944, when for a further six years the military dictated politics through engineering a series of coups.

In 1950 Major Osorio was elected to the presidency, and for a decade he channelled the political ambitions of the military through a newly created party, which in 1960 succumbed to further coups. Yet as an instrument of power the idea of a military party retained its appeal and in 1962 the army created the Party of National Conciliation (PNC), which survived until 1979.

For a while it seemed as if the PNC might become the means by which controlled change could take place in El Salvador. But the party degenerated, and increasingly elections were fraudulently staged. Two events reawakened opposition to such fundamentally corrupt circumstances: elections to the Legislative Assembly in March 1978, and the growth of revolutionary resistance to dictatorship in Nicaragua.

But the conviction that revolution was the only means to effect change and with it bring dignity and decency to private and public life had seized the imagination of a group of men around René Cruz, who set up the People's Revolutionary Army (ERP). With Cuban support, radicated in the patent injustices of the Salvadoran establishment, where a dozen families were said to own nine tenths of the land, the ERP set out to politicise the masses through terrorist incidents and eventually a guerrilla campaign.

Ideological differences caused a split in 1975, when the Armed Forces of National Resistance (FARN) cut themselves from the parent body and took to financing themselves through kidnapping ventures, particularly directed at holding foreign enterprises to ransom through the abduction of their personnel. Other smaller groups, such as the People's Armed Revolutionary Forces (FRAP), also had their origins in the mid-1970s.

The greatest national impact attended the coordinated guerrilla activities of the Farabundo Martí Popular Forces of Liberation (FPL), which, although founded earlier, appeared for the first time in 1976, moved to the fore in 1977 and became the most active group in 1978. It was the FPL which, backed by Cuba, set up first the Coordinating Committee for the Movement of Popular Unity in January 1980, and then the Farabundo

Martí National Liberation Front (FMLN), which unsuccessfully spearheaded the civil war in 1980/82.

The turning point in Salvadoran politics came in October 1979, when the order of conflict had reached a level which provoked a coup from the established orders to oust President Romero. The bloodless affair was headed by two colonels, Arnaldo Majano and Jaime Abdul Gutiérrez, who promised free elections and a general amnesty. An interim government was formed with civilian participation, but within months the civilians had either resigned or been removed, and Majano himself had become an outlaw.

In desperation the Christian Democrats, who, before the military annulled the results, had won the 1972 elections, were brought into government. Their successful 1972 candidate, José Napoleon Duarte, returned from exile and was appointed President in 1980. To this rump the US provided financial aid and military advisers in 1981 in an attempt to shore up the defences of the West in what it saw as a confrontation with international communism. Elections were held in 1982, when, despite the rebels' call to abstain large numbers voted, the majority for conservative groups which appeared to out-flank the reformist intentions of the Christian Democrats.

The government under President Romero had been disfigured by the most appalling abuses of power in the form of death squad activities carried out by such bodies as ORDEN and the White Fighting Union (UGB). This form of murder persisted after the 1979 coup; among the victims was the reformist Archbishop of San Salvador, Oscar Romero (no relation of the President), in March 1980. After that incident the government lost all credibility and the mass organisations such as the Popular Revolutionary Bloc (BPR) and the Popular Leagues of 28 February (LP-28) found themselves acting increasingly with the support of the country's highest spiritual authority. These organisations effectively backed up guerrilla actions with demands for radical political change — demands which were reinforced by direct action, even if largely passive in nature.

Bibliography

Contemporary political violence in El Salvador is of such recent date that there is little literature beyond the press. Two books to have appeared are Tommie Sue Montgomery, *The Salvadoran Revolution: Origins and Evolution* (Boulder, USA, 1982) and James Dunkerley, *The Long War: Dictatorship and Revolution in El Salvador* (London, Junction Books, 1982). Among articles that have appeared are 'El Salvador: Another Domino?' in *The World Today*, August 1980 by James John Guy, and 'El Salvador: Background to the Struggle' in *Race and Class*, summer 1980. Plácido Endozain's *Archbishop Romero: Martyr of Salvador* (Lutterworth Press, Guildford, 1981) lacks analysis, better is Dermot Keagh's *Romero, El Salvador's Martyr* (Dublin, 1981). For the FPL line, see the Tricontinental publications from Cuba, often translated into French by Maspero in Paris.

Armed Forces of National Resistance
(*Fuerzas Armadas de Resistencia Nacional — FARN*)

In 1982 the reputation of the Salvadoran terrorist group FARN lay primarily in an ugly record of kidnapping. But its origins lay in the pro-Cuban People's Revolutionary Army (ERP), from which it split in 1975. Its principal founder would appear to have been a former ERP member, the poet Roque Dalton García, who was subsequently murdered in May for opposing ERP.

The FARN considered itself a 'Marxist-Leninist proletarian army', but while supporting the 'world socialist camp' it was critical of Moscow, which in turn was scathing in its rejection of FARN terrorism. The group drew support from left-wing student elements. As its goal the FARN looked to the founding of a 'vanguard party' and the building up of a revolutionary armed force on the base of a guerrilla army. To this end it intended infiltrating the armed forces.

Throughout 1976 the FARN concentrated upon building up its resources, in particular, an attack upon a military arsenal in Sansonate provided the group with arms. In August 1977 it carried out its first kidnap operation in the capital, to be swiftly followed by a second — that of Elena Lima de Chiorato, cousin of a former vice-president of El Salvador. There followed in 1978 an outright campaign against foreign businessmen, in particular Japanese, Dutch and British, under the guise of attacking 'international imperialism'. Multinational corporations, the FARN felt, should return to the country what they had taken from it.

The money raised from ransoms financed the FARN beyond its wildest expectations, leading it to mount more and more operations. The group became practised in gathering intelligence, sensitive to the need for exceptionally tight security, and efficient in training and back-up. Some of their victims were held in hide-outs for singularly long periods — for instance, two British bank employees, Ian Massey and Michael Chatterton, were confined for eight months in 1979, when a sum reputedly of £5 million was paid for their release. The FARN did not shrink from murder — such a fate awaited the honorary Israeli Consul, Ernest Liebes, a Salvadoran coffee millionaire, in March 1979.

In October 1979 the FARN welcomed the coup which ousted President Romero, and for a brief moment it seemed possible that the group would suspend its terrorist activities in favour of participating in reform. In January 1980 it joined with the ultra-left forces to form the Coordinating Committee for the Movement of Popular Unity, but as El Salvador slid into civil war the FARN reverted to the practice of terror and guerrilla warfare. To counter the rapid increase of right-wing terror, in June the group issued a death list — on it were more than 200 names. In 1982 the FARN operated as part of the unified guerrilla grouping, the Farabundo Martí National Liberation Front (FMLN).

Communist Party of El Salvador
(Partido Comunista de El Salvador — PCES)

The PCES was set up in 1930 under Farabundo Martí, who was shot dead in the 1932 insurrection, which was put down by the military. His name was subsequently adopted by Cayetano Carpio, when Carpio resigned as PCES secretary general in 1970 over the issue of armed struggle and set up the Popular Forces of Liberation (FPL).

The PCES remained a miniscule party for a decade, persisting in electoral tactics until 1979, when at its seventh Congress the party agreed to embrace armed struggle. Despite the decision the CPES supported the October 1979 coup which ousted President Romero, but withdrew its support from the new government in January 1980.

Thereafter the party played a revolutionary role alongside guerrilla groups and the new mass movements which they had set up in the course of the struggle during the 1970s. Under its secretary general, Schafik Handal, the party rationalised its stand by arguing that the Latin American communist movement had no monopoly of the revolutionary vanguard, and that this would have to emerge from an eventual unity of all the revolutionary organisations. 'A single revolutionary leadership can be expected in the near future and a creation of a single party in the medium term.'

Farabundo Martí Popular Forces of Liberation
(Fuerzas Populares de Liberación Farabundo Martí — FPL)

From militants who had split over the issue of armed struggle from the well established but miniscule Communist Party of El Salvador (PCES), Salvador Cayetano Carpio, former PCES secretary general, set up the FPL in 1972. The FPL adopted the name of the former PCES secretary general, Farabundo Martí, who had died at the onset of a peasant insurrection (1932), which the PCES had promoted. The new movement aligned itself with the Sandinists in Nicaragua and adopted a clear revolutionary stance towards the established order throughout Central America. It took Cuba as a model, opposed US influence in the area, and to bring about the new order of affairs advocated guerrilla warfare.

Only in 1977 did the group move to the foreground of political violence. From isolated incidents the FPL developed a sustained campaign which included setting fire to the sugar cane crops in rural areas. Militants occupied radio stations calling for a 'prolonged revolutionary struggle' and kidnapped the Foreign Minister, Mauricio Borgonovo Pohl, who, after the government had refused to meet FPL demands for the release of jailed colleagues, was murdered in May. In September 1977 the FPL murdered Carlos Alfaro Castillo, chancellor of San Salvador's National University. A year later to the day — 16 September 1978 — militants gunned down Rubén Alfonso Rodríguez, a former president of the National Congress.

It was in 1978 that the FPL emerged as the most active of guerrilla groups in El Salvador. In part this was due to a vigorous campaign of violence against the March municipal elections. Some politicians had explosive devices placed outside their homes. In rural areas telephone lines and electricity sub-stations were sabotaged. Roads, too, suffered as the surfaces were broken up, and bottles, stones and pipes were strewn so as to impede traffic. In places militants tried to burn the ballot boxes.

Over the 12-month period the group claimed responsibility for a dozen crude murders, most of which took place in the capital. Submachine guns were used. The incidence of bomb attacks increased, with targeting particularly of US interests, including the embassy. Several local industrialists were kidnapped for ransom.

Similar violent activities were pursued throughout 1979, but still more intensively. Evidence emerged of cooperation with the People's Revolutionary Army (ERP), and it seemed clear that recruits which had previously been drawn from radical elements in the universities had been joined by new working-class members coming from trade union circles.

The FPL continued to emphasise its own role as part of a global struggle and to this end kidnapped and subsequently murdered the South African Ambassador, Archibald Dunn, in November 1979. By so doing they expressed their solidarity with the black cause in southern Africa and warned specifically against the development of a South Atlantic Pact between the Southern Cone and South Africa. Israel, too, became a target for having sold arms to the Salvadoran government.

In 1980 the FPL played a prominent role in coordinating the activities of the revolutionary forces. In January, alongside the Armed Forces of National Resistance (FARN), the pro-Moscow Communist Party (PCES), the United Popular Action Front (FAPU) and the two mass movements, the Popular Revolutionary Bloc (BPR) and the Popular Leagues of 28 February (LP-28), it set up the Coordinating Committee for the Movement of Popular Unity. From this body stemmed the organisation which became the unifying umbrella for the principal Marxist-Leninist revolutionary forces — the Farabundo Martí National Liberation Front (FMLN), which was controlled by a Unified Revolutionary Directorate (DRU) led by the FPL founder, Cayetano Carpio, an experienced man of 64 years. The DRU was the principal force behind the national civil conflict which gradually engulfed El Salvador following the murder in March 1980 by the ultra-right of the liberal Archbishop Oscar Romero. Although the FPL preserved its own structure in 1981, it acted increasingly as part of the FMLN.

National Democratic Organisation
(Organización Democrática Nacional — ORDEN)

ORDEN was officially disbanded by the Salvadoran government in November 1979, shortly after the reformist junta took power after President Romero had been ousted. In the rural areas especially, the organisation had had many thousands of members, for its origins went back to 1968 when it had been set up as a part-time militia. By the late 1970s it had degenerated into a murderous organisation, responsible for indiscriminate killing of left-wing suspects in town and country. To counter these activities, the Farabundo Martí Popular Forces of Liberation (FPL) began in 1978 to take revenge specifically on known ORDEN members, a number of whom were murdered. The feuding continued throughout 1979, until general conflict broke out in 1980, when that particular feud was subsumed in guerrilla warfare.

People's Armed Revolutionary Forces
(Fuerzas Revolucionarias Armadas del Pueblo — FRAP)

The FRAP was formed as the armed branch of the Workers' Revolutionary Organisation (ORT), a body active in Salvadoran political violence in the mid-1970s. The ORT was Marxist-Leninist and committed to revolutionary violence. As a group active in terrorism the FRAP first emerged in 1977, with two murders, one of them an unsuccessful attempt to kidnap an industrialist.

Two further kidnaps followed in 1978, when Gustavo Cartagena, chairman of a construction firm, was kidnapped in December and released in January 1979 on payment of a ransom. When compared with the main Salvadoran guerrilla groups FRAP activity was insignificant. It did not join the Coordinating Committee for the Movement of Popular Unity in January 1980, nor did it become part of the guerrilla umbrella organisation, Farabundo Martí National Liberation Front (FMLN), in 1981. Indeed, by 1981 little was heard of either the FRAP or the ORT.

People's Revolutionary Army
(Ejército Revolucionario del Pueblo — ERP)

As its name implies the ERP is an army, with militaristic discipline imposed by a ranking hierarchy. It took part in the Salvadoran civil war 1980/82, but its origins stretched back to 1971, although it first surfaced with a number of bomb attacks on government and business premises in 1973. A raid on the Bank of London and Montreal provided the guerrillas with funds, and an attack upon a gunsmith stocked it initially with firearms.

The ERP was set up by Joaquín Villalobos, who subsequently formed the Salvadoran Revolutionary Party (PRS) in 1977. Among prominent members were Sebastián Urquilla and Octavio Ponce, and later René Cruz. At the top was a five-man central directorate; in the east, the west and the centre of El Salvador were regional committees. Ideologically the ERP was Marxist-Leninist, had contacts in Cuba and was hostile to the USA. During the Nicaraguan civil war of 1979 it strongly supported the Sandinists.'We regard all the revolutionary forces of Latin America, especially in the Central American area, and most especially the Cuban revolution as fundamental strategic allies of the Salvadoran revolution . . . In defining ourselves as enemies of US imperialism we also identify with the Non-aligned Movement, with the struggle of the Palestinian people and with the liberation movements of the African peoples.' In 1974 the ERP disrupted the March election campaign by occupying radio stations in the capital, and calling upon the people to rise up in arms. In response to mid-year bomb attacks in a number of towns the military were called in to contain the terrorist campaign. All was quiet for six months until after Christmas, when suddenly a spate of bombing occurred in San Salvador and in seven other towns. The damage was considerable, but no one died.

During 1975 the ERP expanded its terrorist activities to include guerrilla attacks upon small towns, all the while stocking up with stolen weapons, police uniforms, medicines and other requirements for a campaign. By the end of the year their activities were well-known through the persistent and dramatic interruption of radio emissions.

Even as the movement grew in strength and audacity its leadership fell to quarrelling; in May 1975 the cold-blooded murder took place of Roque Dalton García, a founding member who criticised ERP discipline. The divide became a split, and the deserters founded the Armed Forces of National Resistance (FARN).

Throughout 1976 the ERP continued to present a security threat, although acts of terrorism made no impression upon the course of politics; yet it is true the ERP presence was felt over a wider area. In 1977 it expanded its operations to include the murder of policemen and soldiers, the bombing of political premises and of government and business installations.

In 1978 the ERP attempted to assassinate the Chancellor of the National University, Professor Manuel Antonio Ramírez. That year in November the ERP was capable of exploding 40 bombs simultaneously in six state capitals. It claimed a similar feat in March 1979, but by then El Salvador was feeling the effect of the civil war in neighbouring Nicaragua, and ERP activity was but one element in widespread guerrilla actions carried out by larger groups. Reacting to the October 1979 coup which deposed President Romero, the ERP announced a suspension of armed struggle. In practice the group continued terrorist activities, for it kidnapped an industrialist the very same month, and in January 1980 seized a score of radio stations so as to announce the opening of its own clandestine *Radio*

Revolucionaria del Pueblo. More than any other group the ERP had placed greater emphasis on radio use.

Alongside the publicity, the ERP carried out terrorist assassinations, as well as mounting small-scale guerrilla operations against police posts and small towns. In March 1980 the world was informed of ERP aspirations when prominent newspapers in Europe and the United States published a manifesto as part of the demand for the release of industrialist Jaime Hill Arguello, whom ERP militants had kidnapped in October 1979.

For the rest of the year the ERP's campaign consisted principally of mounting damaging bomb attacks in the capital and of improving its guerrilla capacity so that the movement was able to field as many as 300 men in one provincial operation. Alongside other groups, the ERP contributed to the January 1981 offensive which failed to topple the ruling junta. It formed part of the Farabundo Martí National Liberation Front (FMLN).

Popular Leagues of 28 February
(Ligas Populares 28 de Febrero — LP-28)

LP-28 was set up as a mass organisation by the People's Revolutionary Army (ERP) as part of the generalised conflict in El Salvador in 1979. The date commemorated a mass confrontation with the military in 1977 following fraudulent elections. It was not a guerrilla group, nor was it involved in terrorist acts. Its members occupied the Cathedral in San Salvador and in San Miguel; following the October 1979 coup, the Leagues were actively engaged in mobilising revolutionary support.

They erected barricades, were prominent during strikes, occupied buildings and even seized hostages in support of their demands. It was not long after the New Year before LP-28 members were involved in clashes with the security forces in much the same way as the armed terrorist groups, which in 1980 were beginning to act in unison under the Farabundo Martí National Liberation Front (FMLN). In this way LP-28 spokesmen and organisers became the targets for the security forces, and especially the ultra-rightist para-military murder squads. But in essence, although close to the ERP, the Leagues remained a mass organisation dedicated to direct action in pursuit of revolutionary demands.

Popular Revolutionary Bloc
(Bloque Popular Revolucionario — BPR)

The Salvadoran BPR was set up in 1975 by the Farabundo Martí Popular Liberation Forces (FPL), led by Juan Chacón and Facundo Guardado Guardado, Marxist-Leninists who sought to provide one body which could unite the various peasant, labour and student organisations of the left. Illegal though it was in the late 1970s, nonetheless the BPR existed openly, in defiance of the government. It acted as a mass movement favourable to the terrorist and guerrilla campaigns waged by El Salvador's violent factions, thereby constituting a powerful lobby. One reason for its success lay in the support given by Archbishop Romero, before his murder in March 1980.

The BPR staged a number of demonstrations in the Cathedral, as well as in other churches, embassies and factories. Comfort and support were given to strikers, as BPR members joined the workforce in solidarity, frequently taking over the buildings for days and even weeks. It became an 'organisation of the masses engaged in political action'. But what started peacefully ended bloodily.

On 9 May 1979 BPR supporters gathered on the steps of the Cathedral were fired upon by the security forces, who killed 23 civilians and injured still more. The event signalled the start of the generalised conflict that caused the overthrow of President Romero in October. Yet the new government failed to convince the BPR leaders of its reformist intent, and on 24 October members occupied a ministry demanding the release of political prisoners in return for several hundred civil servants, including three ministers, held within the building.

Identical actions took place in 1980 in the Foreign Trade Institute, the Labour Ministry and the Cathedral, whilst in May all of 24 churches in the capital were simultaneously taken over by BPR supporters. In the conflict which followed Archbishop Romero's death, the BPR was overshadowed by the guerrilla warfare waged by the Farabundo Martí National Liberation Front (FMLN). Theoretically the FPL viewed the BPR as a 'revolutionary mass organisation made up of popular organisations representing the various social sectors of the Salvadoran people in strategic unity revolving around the worker-peasant alliance with proletarian hegemony . . . '.

United Popular Action Front
(*Frente de Acción Popular Unificada* — *FAPU*)

The Salvadoran FAPU emerged in 1978 as a mass movement, an alternative to the Popular Revolutionary Bloc (BPR), and was reportedly close to the Armed Forces of National Resistance (FARN). That year it carried out a number of explosives attacks, but its members were more prominent in the occupation of buildings than in terrorism. The idea of setting up the FAPU was first conceived at the time the FARN split from the People's Revolutionary Army (ERP) in 1975.

For two weeks in April 1978 FAPU occupied the International Red Cross headquarters in San Salvador, and in June the UN and Organisation of American States (OAS) premises in the capital. Most of those involved were high-school and university students, who through the Salvador Allende Revolutionary Students' University Front (FUERSA) and the Revolutionary Association of Secondary Students (ARDES) had taken to direct action.

More spectacularly in 1979 some 30 armed FAPU militants took over the Mexican embassy in January and held the staff hostage. In return for their release some members sought and obtained refuge in Mexico for themselves and for jailed colleagues. Similar demonstrations were held at the UN, the OAS, and the IRC buildings. Later that year FAPU members occupied the Cathedral and stoned the US embassy. Identical activities, especially in churches, were promoted in 1980.

The movement attracted much support from young people in the capital as a direct action pressure group, to which several thousand claimed affiliation. In January 1980 FAPU announced its participation in the Coordinating Committee for the Movement of Popular Unity. Other organisations affiliated to FAPU included the Revolutionary Peasants' Movement (MRC) and Proletarian Vanguard (VP).

White Fighting Union
(Unión Guerrera Blanca — UGB)

Part of the para-military right-wing reaction to revolutionary ferment in El Salvador, the UGB emerged in 1976. Members were particularly hostile to the Jesuits, whom they felt had betrayed the ruling class and Catholic values. In 1977 the UGP claimed responsibility for the death of at least two priests in the capital, and carried out an explosives attack on the home of a trade union leader. Teachers were assassinated by UGB members in 1979 in an attempt to intimidate the profession. Despite murder and death threats, UGB attempts to intimidate the Church generally, and especially the Jesuits, failed.

Workers' Revolutionary Party of Central America
(Partido Revolucionario de Trabajadores Centroamericanos — PRTC)

The PRTC only emerged in El Salvador in 1979 with the kidnapping of two US businessmen in September. They were released in November. It appeared to have connections with Honduras and Guatemala, and was active in a small way in 1980 in the occasional occupation of a radio station, the machine gunning of the Guatemalan embassy, and an arson attack upon a night club.

Guatemala

Contemporary political violence in Guatemala began in 1960 with a nationalist military revolt which failed. Among the protagonists were Yon Sosa (1938-70) and Turcios Lima (1941-66), who, first through the Revolutionary Movement Alejandro de León 13 November (MR-13) and then through the Rebel Armed Forces (FAR), set about organising guerrilla warfare.

But the roots of dissatisfaction extended back to 1954, the year in which the essentially reformist government of President Jacobo Arbenz (1951-54) was overthrown by US-supported Colonel Castillo Armas, who was fearful of Marxist-Leninist influence in Guatemala. In a thoroughly retrograde programme, he reversed the land expropriations, disenfranchised the illiterate population and abolished labour organisations. Three years passed before he was assassinated and succeeded by Miguel Ydígoras Fuentes (1957-63).

Faced by guerrilla insurgency, Ydígoras would have opened the political system once again to political movement by inviting back from his Mexican exile the father-figure of Guatemalan reform, former President Juan José Arévalo (1945-51). Such a move the military refused to contemplate, and so they imposed upon the country their own choice as president, substituting Enrique Peralta Azurdía (1963-66) for Ydígoras, who was ousted in March 1963.

As it turned out, Peralta Azurdía returned Guatemala to civilian rule in 1966 through elections, which were won by Julio César Méndez Montenegro, one-time rector of San Carlos University and leader of the Revolutionary Party. He proved unable to return peace to the streets, so that in 1970 the hard-line counter-insurgent chief, Colonel Carlos Arana Osorio, was elected president, an event which was tantamount to institutionalising right-wing terror in the form of White Hand and other groups.

The guerrilla threat in the 1960s began in the countryside, but quickly spread to the cities in 1963, by which time the communist Gautemalan Labour Party (PGT) was involved in clandestine armed warfare alongside the guerrillas of MR-13 and FAR. Ideological reasons lay behind the different courses adopted by MR-13 (Trotskyist) and FAR (Castroite), and both depended heavily upon their leaders, Yon Sosa (d.1970) and Turcios Lima (d.1966). Neither group survived the counter-insurgency operations led by Colonel Arana in the late 1960s.

César Montes provides the link between the guerrilla activities of the earlier period and the resurgence of the late 1970s. He was an intellectual leader of the FAR, with a PGT background. Following the defeat of the FAR in 1970, he reemerged in 1975 as leader of the Guerrilla Army of the Poor (EGP), which in 1981 presented the Guatemalan military regime with its greatest threat. The level of insurgency increased towards the end of the year with evidence of greater cooperation between the four major guerrilla groups. Indeed in February 1982 EGP, PGT, FAR and the Revolutionary Organisation of the People under Arms (ORPA) announced a unified command structure — the Guatemalan National Revolutionary Union (URNG). Not many militants took advantage of the amnesty offered by the new President, General Ríos Montt, after he had seized power in March. Consequently the military prosecuted a tough counter-insurgency campaign in 1983.

Bibliography

For the 1960s a succinct introduction to Guatemalan political violence is provided by Kenneth Johnson's *Guatemala: From Terrorism to Terror* (ISC, London, 1972), or see Chapter VII by Vincente Collazo Dávila in *Political Violence and Insurgency* (Phoenix, Arizona, 1974) edited by Bard E. O'Neill, Donald J. Alberts and Stephen J. Rossetti. At greater length and from a Marxist standpoint, Jaime Diaz Rozzotto analysed the earlier struggles in *La Révolution au Guatémala 1944-54* (Editions Sociales, Paris, 1971), a translation of the Spanish text. The violence of the 1960s was treated sympathetically by two former US missionaries, Thomas and Marjorie Melville, in *Guatemala Another Vietnam* (Penguin, 1971).

Closer to the scene are the *Lettres du Front Guatémaltèque* (Maspero, Paris, 1970) by Ricardo Ramírez, in fact a translation of a number of articles from Turcios Lima, whose biography was published in 1970 by Ediciones Tricontinental in Havana. For MR-13, see the article by Yon Sosa in *Pensamiento Crítico* (Havana) No. 15, April 1968, entitled 'Breves Apuntes Históricos del Movimiento Revolucionario 13 de Noviembre'. The same issue has relevant articles by Julio del Valle and Luís Turcios Lima. Eduardo Galeano, editor and journalist, wrote from the revolutionary viewpoint *Guatemala Clave de Latinoamérica* (Ediciones de la Banda Oriental, Montevideo, 1967), and in English *Guatemala: Occupied Country* (New York, 1969). He also contributed an essay, 'With the Guerrillas in Guatemala', in *Latin America: Reform or Revolution?* edited by the Trotskyist James Petras and Maurice Zeitlin (Fawcett Books, New York, 1968). For information on right-wing death squads, see the Committee for the Defence of Human Rights publication *La Violencia en Guatemala* (Mexico, D.F., 1969). Important articles on the Guatemalan insurgency are found in the bibliography selected by Charles Russell, James Miller and Robert Hildner in *Latin American Research Review*, Vol. 9, No. 1 spring 1974. Régis Debray analysed the Guatemalan guerrilla failure in *The Revolution on Trial* (Penguin, 1978).

Guatemalan Labour Party
(*Partido Guatemalteco del Trabajo — PGT*)

The PGT is an orthodox Marxist-Leninist Moscow-line communist party, which has been illegal in Guatemala since the overthrow of President Jacobo Arbenz in 1954. Fewer than a thousand members are thought to belong to it.

The party involved itself with guerrilla activities in the 1960s, when it attempted to control the Rebel Armed Forces (FAR), and was in some degree associated in the late 1970s with the Guerrilla Army of the Poor (EGP), whose leader, César Montes, was once a member of the PGT's central committee. Some of its members are said to be active in the EGP, certainly some EGP activists are sympathetic to the PGT. The Revolutionary Armed Forces (FAR), which the party set up in the late 1960s as an armed branch, never successfully functioned.

To some extent the PGT was dragged into political violence in an attempt to keep its influence over the communist left, but also to preserve its leadership from assassination by right-wing death squad activity. Two secretary generals have been murdered, the last in 1975. At the top of the hierarchy in 1980 was Isías de León. The party is active among students through its youth branch, but through its trade union organisation has only a slight impact upon Guatemalan labour.

Guerrilla Army of the Poor
(*Ejército Guerrillero de los Pobres — EGP*)

The Guatemalan EGP emerged in 1975, when it claimed responsibility for the murder of 19 military commissioners in Chiquimula, in the north-east of the country. One of its leaders, Valentín Ramos, was killed in January 1976, but the real initiative behind the EGP came from César Montes, who attempted to resurrect rural actions under the guise of the EGP following the earlier defeat of the Rebel Armed Forces (FAR). The EGP acted in the capital as well as in the countryside and specifically targeted politicians, thereby provoking an outbreak of political assassinations in late 1975.

The disastrous earthquake which struck Guatemala in February 1976 so stretched the slender resources of government that it was unable to control lawlessness, and of these circumstances the EGP took advantage. In April EGP gunmen assassinated Colonel Elías Ramírez, who headed the relief operations, but who previously had been active in counter-insurgency operations under President Arana Osorio.

The EGP raised its funds from kidnapping industrialists, some of whom were active in politics and were subsequently murdered. Its most spectacular action was to abduct the Salvadoran Ambassador in mid-

1977, in return for whose release a poltical manifesto was read to delegates attending an international banking conference in Guatemala City. Militants followed this action with the abduction in December of the Guatemalan Foreign Minister, Roberto Herrera Ibarguen. In 1978 the Nicaraguan Ambassador was attacked in October, an act of solidarity with neighbouring Sandinist guerrillas. A further victim was the Army Chief of Staff, General David Barrios, who was murdered in June 1979.

In rural areas the EGP burned sugar cane plantations under the pretext of disrupting 'the economy of the people's enemies'. Such sabotage was meant as a warning 'to estate owners who oppress and subjugate the peasants'. In Concepción, El Salto, La Unión, Mirandilla, Magdalena and Tulula the sugar refineries became a target in a 'war of attrition against the agro-exporting oligarchy'. Two further pockets of rural political violence opened in the mid-1970s in the mountains north of the capital and in the traditional guerrilla region of Zacapa. These three fronts were supposed to operate independently of one another and also of the urban front in the capital.

Despite the fact that both groups were welcome in Cuba in the late 1970s and that both practised political violence, the EGP maintained a distance in its relationship with the Guatemalan Labour Party (PGT). Yet a damaging attack on 15 June 1978 in Guatemala City, where a truck was blown up killing 17 military police, was claimed by both organisations, indicating identity of intent at least.

With the 1979 victory in Nicaragua of the Sandinist revolutionary forces, the EGP became still more daring in its 'people's war against the government and state institutions'. Rural villages around Quiche, Huehuetenango and Ixcoy were briefly occupied by guerrilla bands of up to 100 militants, and in return for the release of the President's nephew in October the EGP had its philosophy and political aims advertised in leading newspapers throughout the western world. By the end of the year there was talk of linking up with other active groups, specifically the reactivated Rebel Armed Forces (FAR) and the Revolutionary Organisation of the People under Arms (ORPA). An agreement was in fact announced in February 1982, when the Guatemalan National Revolutionary Union (UNRG) was set up. Despite its undoubted virulence, the EGP had not by 1982 developed the capacity to threaten the government's hold on power, although it could claim to be the most active poltically violent group, and may have numbered as many as 750 adherents.

Rebel Armed Forces
(Fuerzas Armadas Rebeldes — FAR)

Set up in December 1962, the FAR was formed by an alliance of rebellious young military officers led by Yon Sosa (1938-70) and Turcios Lima (1941-66) with the ideologically motivated communists of the Moscow-backed Guatemalan Labour Party (PGT), particularly César Montes (b.1942), a law student. The political direction came from a new United Resistance Front (FUR) dominated by the communists, but including other groups. Yon Sosa fell under Trotskyist influence in 1964/65, leaving the leadership of the FAR in the hands of Turcios Lima, who adopted an independent stance towards the PGT. His purpose was to lead a nationalist movement independent of Moscow, Peking and Havana, and with this in mind he planned for a long struggle, which, when successful, would introduce land reform and increase production through voluntary cooperation and collectivisation.

In early May 1966 the FAR abducted the Supreme Court Chief Justice, Romeo Augusto de León and the presidential press secretary, demanding to know the fate of 28 leftists who had disappeared in March. A further abduction followed, of Héctor Méndez de la Riva, vice-president of Congress, before the truth of their deaths was made public by a new president, Méndez Montenegro (1966 70).

In October 1966 Turcios Lima was killed in a car accident: his place was taken by his second in command, César Montes, a PGT central committee member, who operated in Zacapa province. He rejected the charge that the FAR had become the armed branch of the PGT and certainly encouraged an FAR alignment with progressive elements in the Catholic Church.

The FAR was kept on the move in the countryside throughout 1967 by army operations, planned and aided by US Green Berets. Worsted in clashes, the rural guerrilla movement was largely broken. The remnant sought to unite with M-13, so that Yon Sosa finally became the FAR leader in March 1968, with Montes agreeing to take second place. Since the start of the struggle the guerrillas reckoned they had lost 300 of their number. At this point the link with the communist PGT was broken.

In August 1968 the FAR attempted to kidnap the US Ambassador, John Gordon Mein, who was shot dead as he resisted an ambush in Guatemala City. The action was a presage of the move from the countryside into the cities, which happened in 1969. But the change to urban warfare split the FAR.

On 27 February 1970 FAR guerrillas kidnapped the Foreign Minister, Fuentes Mohr, and exchanged him for the release of an imprisoned colleague. They followed this action only days later by abducting the US Labour Attaché, Sean Holly, whose freedom was also secured in return for the release of three FAR guerrillas. In March they murdered the West German Ambassador, Count Karl von Spreti. Ransom money from local citizens provided the new FAR with its funds, which it used to purchase contraband arms from across the mountainous eastern frontier with Mexico in San Marcos province.

Yet the FAR had been beaten and did not recover from counter-insurgency exercises until 1975, when rural estates were again threatened in Zacapa. Because activity was only sporadic, FAR's re-emergence essentially dates from mid-1978. 'With a communist spirit and a high degree of combat preparedness, the bourgeois state and its repressive forces can be destroyed in the immediate future.' The FAR aimed at 'the transference of power to the working classes and the country's exploited masses' so as 'to build socialism, the first step on the path to communism'. To begin with it was active in Petén province, but in 1979 expanded its activities to the occasional attack in the capital. In the early 1980s FAR activity remained secondary to that of the EGP.

Revolutionary Armed Forces
(Fuerzas Armadas Revolucionarias — FAR)

Not to be confused with Rebel Armed Forces (FAR), this Guatemalan group was set up by the communist Guatemalan Labour Party (PGT) after the existing guerrillas (M-13 and FAR) had decided to break with the PGT in 1968. It was conceived as the armed branch of the PGT, an orthodox Marxist-Leninist party loyal to Moscow.

Revolutionary Movement Alejandro de León 13 November
(Movimiento Revolucionario Alejandro de León 13 Noviembre — MR-13)

Set up in February this Guatemalan guerrilla group was led by Yon Sosa (b. 1938) and Turcios Lima (b. 1941), who joined forces with the Guatemalan Labour Party (PGT) in December that year to form the united Rebel Armed Forces (FAR). MR-13 was a military grouping of young nationally-minded officers who targeted the US owned United Fruit Company as being representative of foreign economic domination and attacked a number of army posts. The group's name commemorated a colleague who died in 1961 and the date of an abortive military uprising against President Ydígoras in 1960, in which Sosa and Turcios Lima had participated.

Through the participation of Francisco Armado Granados, MR-13 fell under Trotskyist influence in 1964 and dropped the appellation Alejandro de León from its title. Yon Sosa welcomed the ideological accretion, Turcios Lima was alienated by it, and it led to his adopting an independent stance with the FAR, which he came to direct. Much of MR-13's work in 1965 consisted of 'armed propaganda' exercises, in which guerrillas entered isolated villages in Izábal province and explained to an illiterate peasantry the aims of the revolution. But it also raised money from kidnapping wealthy Guatemalans and struck an international chord in February 1965 by murdering Colonel Harold Houser, the US military attaché.

MR-13 suffered badly from the counter-insurgency operations led by Colonel Arana Osorio in 1967, and for a time linked up again with the

Rebel Armed Forces (FAR). But the alignment did not survive, and after the death in a clash with a Mexican army border patrol in May 1970 of Yon Sosa, MR-13 ceased its activities.

Revolutionary Organisation of the People under Arms
(Organización Revolucionaria del Pueblo en Armas — ORPA)

ORPA announced its formation in September 1979 'after several years of preparation in which our organisation has been set up in total secrecy'. It began as a small rural group in Sololá department, where militants were active in armed propaganda operations amongst the peasantry. A number of clashes occurred with the security forces. In November 1979 the group was reported to have joined the more substantial Guerrilla Army of the Poor (EGP), but it remained active under its own name in 1981. In addition to joint actions with EGP in the north and the west of the country, ORPA cooperated with the Rebel Armed Forces (FAR) in the capital, and contributed to an overall raising of the level of insurgency towards the end of the year. ORPA joined the Guatemalan National Revolutionary Union (UNRG) in February 1982.

Secret Anti-Communist Army
(Ejército Secreto Anticomunista — ESA)

The ESA emerged in Guatemala in 1977 as the left-wing guerrilla rump reformed under the leadership of César Montes in the Guerrilla Army of the Poor (EGP). Like its forebears in the 1960s, the ESA was aligned politically with the extreme right in defence of a privileged capitalist economic elite and a numerically diminishing, almost ultramontane body of opinion within the Catholic Church.

The ESA was involved in assaults on, and even the murder of, selected students active on the campus of San Carlos University and published death lists of prominent leftist intellectuals and labour leaders. Some left-wing politicians, with good reason, left Guatemala, fearing for their lives. Those who committed ESA murders included members of the security forces.

Twelfth of April Revolutionary Movement
(Movimiento Revolucionario 12 Abril)

This Guatemalan movement arose in 1962 among students demonstrating against the government of President Ydígoras Fuentes (1958-63). It became one of the three principal groups to join the Rebel Armed Forces (FAR) and to engage in armed resistance to the military government of Colonel Peralta Azurdía (1963-66). It withdrew from the FAR in 1965.

Twentieth of October Front
(Frente 20 Octubre)

The date of this Guatemalan guerrilla front commemorated the 1944 revolution which had overthrown the dictator Ubico, and installed the progressive Juan José Arévalo. Lieutenant Colonel Paz Tejada, who had led the revolt in 1960 against President Ydígoras, set it up in March 1962 as a means of seizing power in Guatemala. In the event troops saturated the capital, and Paz Tejada retreated to the countryside. The Front was not revived.

White Hand
(Movimiento de Acción Nacionalista Organizada — MANO, hence *Mano Blanca)*

The para-military White Hand in Guatemala had its origins in the government counter-insurgency campaign of 1966, when anti-communist vigilante groups were set up in Izabal and Zacapa provinces. Other similar bodies included the New Anti-Communist Organisation (NOA) and the Anti-Communist Council of Guatemala (CODEG) and Eye for an Eye. They degenerated into assassination squads of the most arbitrary and murderous kind, selected their targets from the progressive ranks of the professional classes, as well as from representatives of the trade union movement. In 1968 White Hand went so far as to abduct the Archbishop of Guatemala, Monsignor Mario Casariego Acevedo. Raúl Estuardo Lorenzana, who was shot dead in April 1968, was allegedly responsible. Others named as prominent in MANO were Noe Delgado Villegas and Oliverio Castañeda Paíz, vice-president of Congress, who was shot dead in a restaurant in Guatemala City in mid-1972.

Honduras

Honduras lay in danger of being sucked into a vortex of revolutionary nationalism in Central America in the early 1980s. Until the return to civilian government in 1982, the country had been under military rule for a decade, which ill-prepared it to withstand the strong ideological currents generated abroad. Honduras was too poor a country in a region known for its poverty to be in the vanguard of change: instead it followed suit.

From the illegal communist party split the People's Revolutionary Union (UPR), which quickly announced its intention to pursue armed struggle. Smaller groups such as the People's Revolutionary Movement (MPR) also announced their formation in 1979. The basis for revolutionary growth lay in the plight of the rural population, whose sense of deprivation and consequent awakening of a desire to effect improvement grew through the mobilisation by peasant organisations, such as the Peasant Alliance of National Organisations of Honduras and the National Association of Honduran Peasants. They did not in themselves promote political violence but rather contributed to a growing demand for justice, that led to incidents in which peasants took the law into their own hands by seizing land on which to grow their food.

By 1982 a number of terrorist groups had announced their formation, and a number of terrorist acts been committed, including a spectacular hijack the previous year by the Cinchonero Popular Liberation Movement (MPL). The activities of this group, of the People's Guerrilla Command (CGP), of the Juan Ray Commando (CJR), named after the founder of the Honduran Communist Party, and of the Honduran Popular Liberation Front (FHLP), all of which surfaced in the early 1980s, provoked a savage terrorist reaction from the right in the form of vigilante groups like the Honduran Anti-Communist Movement (MACHO) and the National Organised Action Movement (MANO), which abducted and murdered individuals thought to be actively associated with the left.

Cinchonero Popular Liberation Movement
(Movimiento de Liberación Popular — Cinchonero — MPL)

The movement appeared for the first time in January 1981, using the nickname given to a peasant hero, Serapio Romero, who was executed in

1865 for refusing to pay tax to the Church. The MLN appeared to act as the terrorist front for the People's Revolutionary Union (URP). Its first spectacular action occurred in March 1981, when it hijacked a Honduran airliner to Managua and then to Panama to secure the release of a dozen leftists in jail. The government gave in to the demands. The following year in September the group again made world headlines when they held hostage 105 people in the Chamber of Commerce building in San Pedro Sula. On both occasions MPL acted to secure the release of Salvadoran guerrillas held in Honduras.

People's Revolutionary Movement
(Movimiento Revolucionario del Pueblo — MRP)

The MRP announced its formation in November 1979, but nothing further was heard of its activities in the early 1980s.

People's Revolutionary Union
(Unión Revolucionaria del Pueblo — URP)

The URP had some base in rural peasant organisations after it announced its formation in September 1979. The following year it turned to armed struggle and occupied the offices of the OAS in Tegucigalpa. Until their deaths in June 1981, the URP was led by Tomás Nativi and Fidel Martínez, who died when gunmen attacked their office.

Workers' Revolutionary Party
(Partido Revolucionario de Trabajadores de América Central — PRTC)

As political movement awoke in Honduras in the aftermath of the Sandinist victory of 1979, so the Trotskyist network emerged from clandestinity. In 1980 the PRTC was supposedly responsible for the kidnapping of an executive working for the US multinational Texaco and was certainly active in student circles. It opposed the presence of foreign, especially US, capital in the country as well as the military agreements with Washington.

Mexico

Rather than Fidel Castro's victory in Cuba, the student revolution of 1968 caused the greater impact upon Mexican society, and at the time contributed more to political violence. In comparison with other states in Latin America, these demonstrations and disturbances were short-lived. In part the reason for the difference lies in the earlier violence of the Mexican revolution (1910-20), in which widespread fighting and the deaths of millions of people eventually led to the formation of the multi-factional Institutional Revolutionary Party, which ever since has been the single channel for the practice of politics and, at least in the past, for achieving important reform.

Yet despite the good fortune of enjoying reformist government in the 1950s, Mexican labour movements were infiltrated by orthodox Marxist-Leninists from the Communist Party, and political violence ensued. The disorders never threatened the state, but throughout the 1960s the ultra-leftist argument in favour of direct action gathered momentum and culminated in a student clash with the military in 1968. During this period Soviet involvement in promoting urban violence became apparent through the terrorism of the Revolutionary Action Movement (MAR). Some MAR members, in addition to having pursued guerrilla courses in Moscow and Pyongyang (North Korea), had established close links on their return with the student movement, particularly the Revolutionary Student Front (FER) in Guadalajara. Here the student body wildly acclaimed the guerrilla activities of Genaro Vásquez Rojas (d. 1972) and Lucio Cabañas (d. 1974).

The early 1970s saw a rash of miniscule urban terrorist groups like the Zapatista Urban Front (FUZ), which leapt to prominence thanks to the media coverage given to kidnapping, an activity which afforded the terrorists both funds and publicity. All, however, were short-lived. Of longer duration were the urban activities of the 23 September Communist League, although this too depended upon the fierce drive and personal motivation of individuals, rather than the conviction of a thorough-going revolutionary creed.

In rural areas, particularly in Guerrero state, the National Revolutionary Civic Association (ACNR) and later the Party of the Poor raised security problems for the government in the late 1960s and early 1970s. But here there were good social causes for radical peasant discontent. It was easy to argue persuasively that the struggle for land, machinery, cheap loans, education and medical care began with the elimination of the rich, and of the army and police force which carried out their bidding. In Guerrero the Party of the Poor became a household name, but its activities never escalated into a major insurgency.

Still, the persistence of injustice, recognised by senior members of the Church hierarchy as ranging from the unequal distribution of wealth inherent in the economic system to corruption at all levels of the judicial branch, remained, but more particularly was present in the urban slums. To combat rural guerrilla activity the government had set about providing roads into the mountains, and supplied basic services which included agricultural credit, telephone links, and even electricity and access to schooling. The military played a role in establishing the new infrastructure. Whilst banditry remained, organised political violence played no part in the problems which Mexico faced in the early 1980s.

Bibliography

Howard Cline wrote an excellent introduction to contemporary Mexico entitled *Mexico Revolution to Evolution 1940-1960* (Oxford University Press, 1962). For the revolution itself, the student might begin with John Womack's *Zapata and the Mexican Revolution* (Penguin, 1972), but John Reed's contemporary account *Insurgent Mexico* (New York, 1978) is a classic. Contemporary political violence, as distinct from banditry, began in 1968, which is described by Elena Poniatowska in *La Noche de Tlatelcolco* (Ediciones Era, Mexico, 1971). The student movement is analysed at greater length by Ramón Ramírez in *El Movimiento Estudiantil de México* (Ediciones Era, Mexico, 1969). Orlando Ortíz edited sympathetically the Marxist writings of Genaro Vásquez, who founded the National Revolutionary Civic Association (ACNR), published in 1972 by Editorial Diógenes, Mexico.

Armed Communist League
(*Liga Comunista Armada* — *LCA*)

The League operated briefly in Mexico in 1972, when police captured six members in a November bank raid in Monterrey. Colleagues hijacked an aircraft the following day, demanding the release and a ransom of US $320,000. A deal was struck, and the terrorists were flown to Cuba, where, on the grounds that their crimes were political in nature, Fidel Castro allowed them to stay. No more was heard of the League.

Los Lacandones

The *Lacandones* formed a small Mexican urban terrorist group based in the universities in the early 1970s, when they undertook a series of robberies, part of the proceeds of which went to support the rural activities of the Party of the Poor. Rigoberto Lorence, a journalist and founder-member of the Zapatista Urban Front (FUZ), was at the time reported to have led the *Lacandones*, whose title recalled a Mayan tribe. It was one of many ultra-leftist cells and did not survive police action.

National Revolutionary Civic Association
(Asociación Cívica Nacional Revolucionaria — ACNR)

Genaro Vásquez Rojas, who was killed in a car crash while trying to avoid arrest on 3 March 1971, founded the ACNR in Mexico in 1968. In composition the association was largely middle-class, consisting of professional people who attempted to set up a rural guerrilla base among peasants in the Atoyac mountains of Guerrero state in south-west Mexico.

Rafael Palomares, an industrial chemical engineer, and Vásquez's colleague, was arrested along with other principal members later in 1971, when he confessed to having received training in China in 1969. Nothing further was heard of the group, although the area in which it had operated continued to be troubled by peasant unrest, as it had been before the ACNR and other groups attempted to politicise the local misery and to nurse it into effective social rebellion.

Party of the Poor
(Partido de los Pobres)

A former school teacher and Communist Party member, Lucio Cabañas, was behind the foundation of the Party of the Poor in 1967. He lived and worked among the isolated rural peasantry in the Guerrero mountains, a fugitive from the law and, because of his belief in armed struggle, an outcast from his party. Cabañas's ideological stand and his political programme were but vaguely defined, proposing nationalisation and collectivisation as measures required to 'destroy private property as the basis of the bourgeois state'. His brother, Pablo, was active in Sonora until arrested in January 1972.

For a while Cabañas's name enjoyed the kind of aura of romantic and idealised heroism attached to the Robin Hood legend. But his stated aim, however unrealistic, was to seize power through armed struggle. To this end the group kidnapped a number of local landowners for ransom, and on occasions murdered them. In June and August 1972 his men ambushed two army patrols engaged on civilian tasks, killing as many as 30 soldiers. In 1973 a hotel in Acapulco was bombed.

In May 1974 guerrillas seized Senator Rubén Figueroa, who had set out to parly with Cabañas, but the government refused to negotiate. Four months later during massive search operations the military located his hideout and liberated the captive. In December of the same year a clash with the army cost Cabañas his life.

As with so many guerrilla groups in Latin America, the Party of the Poor did not survive the death of its leader. For a while his place was taken by Carmelo Cortes Castro, another school master turned guerrilla, but throughout 1975 he was on the run from the security forces and never reestablished the initiative. During the late 1970s nothing further was heard of the group.

People's Revolutionary Armed Forces
(Fuerzas Revolucionarias Armadas del Pueblo — FRAP)

The Mexican FRAP first surfaced in May 1973, when it claimed responsibility for kidnapping the US Consul General in Guadalajara, Terrance Leonhardy, the first foreign diplomat to be abducted in Mexico. The demands were that 30 terrorists should be freed, among them members of the Revolutionary Action Movement (MAR), the National Revolutionary Civic Association (ACNR) and the Zapatista Urban Front (FUZ), who in the event were flown to Cuba. On payment of an additional ransom, Leonhardy was released unharmed.

Three of the freed terrorists participated in the abduction of President Echeverria's 83-year-old father-in-law in August 1974. Their purpose was to extract from the old General a restatement of his belief in revolution, hardly difficult as in the original Mexican revolution he had played a prominent role. That year the FRAP was responsible for a serious outbreak of urban explosive attacks in Mexico City, Guadalajara and Oaxaca, where government and party buildings were the target. Little activity was recorded in 1975 and in 1976 police captured Ramón Campana López, whom they considered a principal organiser. On 30 July 13 FRAP militants were sentenced to prison terms ranging from six to 28 years.

Despite police successes in arresting FRAP rank and file, the group survived and in August 1977 members hijacked a long-distance bus with 40 passengers on board. During a shoot-out with police a handgrenade exploded accidentally, killing ten people and wounding 15. The terrorists' objective had been to demand the release of Campana López. In September the FRAP joined the 23 September Communist League in urban bombing incidents, but did not survive into 1978 as an active terrorist group.

People's Union
(Unión del Pueblo)

The People's Union was typical of a number of small terrorist cells which arose out of the revolutionary ferment in 1968 in Mexico, and which outside interests exploited. Behind its foundation was a Guatemalan,

José María Ortiz Vides, who had previously been trained in Cuba before joining Yon Sosa's Revolutionary Movement (MR-13), which he left after Sosa's death in 1970. The group was responsible for the explosion of a number of bombs in the capital before most members were arrested in October 1972.

The rump, which retained its separate identity, joined forces with the 23 September Communist League in 1975, claiming responsibility for bombings against banks, government offices and private businesses in Mexico City, San Luis (Potosí) and Oaxaca. The damage was calculated 'to cause material damage to the bourgeois economy and harass the government, besides creating awareness among the people to prepare for the popular struggle and overthrow of the regime'.

There followed a lull in Union violence, but it resurfaced in 1977 in Oaxaca, where it sought to 'make every place of work a revolutionary trench, under the banner of the universities for the people, factories for the workers and land for those who work it'. Militants cooperated with the League and with the People's Armed Revolutionary Forces (FRAP). The Union remained in being, although markedly less active in 1978. By 1982 little or nothing had been heard of it for four years.

Revolutionary Action Movement
(Movimiento de Acción Revolucionaria — MAR)

The MAR was a short-lived urban guerrilla group set up in Mexico City in 1970. It had its origins in the Soviet training of a group of some 40 Mexicans recruited by Fabricio Gómez Sousa in the mid-1960s. They received training in the Patrice Lumumba University outside Moscow and in Pyongyang (North Korea) in 1968. Having returned, they joined forces with a similar number and organised a bank raid in December 1970. A campaign of sabotage was prevented by police action, which uncovered the network and resulted in the expulsion of five Soviet embassy staff in March 1971 and the recalling of the Mexican Ambassador from Moscow.

During the time it was active MAR set up training establishments in Mexico City and established centres in the north and north-west of the country, where a series of coordinated raids took place in January 1972. The MAR had links with radical student protest groups in the universities, particularly the Revolutionary Student Front (FER).

Twenty-Third of September Communist League
(Liga Comunista 23 Septiembre)

The League started urban terrorist activities in Mexico in 1974, following the destruction of the Revolutionary Action Movement (MAR) in 1972. Some of its members had belonged to the earlier group. The date commemorated the League's first clash with the military; it was thought to have been set up initially by José Luis Guzmán Villa.

In December 1974 two banks were robbed in the capital; in the course of the attack five policemen were killed. There followed in January 1975 a wave of explosives attacks directed at government buildings and banks. League raids were characterised by a quite ruthless use of firearms — one member captured in June 1975, Demetrio Torralva Alvarez, was allegedly involved in the deaths of 15 policemen.

On 12 August 1975 David Jiménez Sarmiento murdered six policemen at breakfast in a cafeteria in revenge for the shooting of his wife by police on 15 June. He later attacked a naval medical centre, leaving dead two infantrymen and a policeman. In the course of 1976 a number of policemen were assassinated in cold blood. Most ferocious was an incident on 4 June, when terrorists opened fire with submachine guns from passing vehicles on ten policemen lined up for morning roll-call on the kerb opposite a small police substation in a Mexico City suburb. On 13 August Jiménez Sarmiento was killed during an attempted attack upon President López Portillo's sister.

It was to his brother, Carlos, that the League owed its survival, when it linked up with the People's Armed Revolutionary Forces (FRAP). Together the two groups were responsible for 18 bomb blasts on 14 September 1977. They damaged the High Court in Mexico City, the Chamber of Commerce and the Pepsi Cola building in Oaxaca and a six-floor department store in Guadalajara, which was gutted by fire. In telephone kiosks, banks, and public buildings in all three cities police discovered unexploded devices.

By shooting dead an important member, Antonio Solís Rodríguez, together with two colleagues, Sergio López and Pedro Cortes, in the capital, police crippled the League the following January. Eight months later Carlos Jiménez Sarmiento died in a similar clash. Incidents continued throughout 1979, although at a greatly diminished level, only to peter out in 1980.

During its four years of violence the League established for itself a reputation for ruthless murder, robbery and kidnap operations. Its recruits came largely from a middle-class university milieu and at the start at least the armed nucleus benefited from hard-nosed communist guerrilla training given previously to the MAR. Later the League exhibited the reckless dash of hooligans, as youths drove at high speed through towns to distract the attention of the police, while accomplices attacked shops, stores and banks.

Although by distributing leaflets militants attempted to influence factory workers, no impact was made, so that the League was reduced to little more than criminal polit-violence. It had never published a comprehensive political programme beyond manifesting a general intent to 'establish a Marxist-Leninist society through the nationalisation of all property and targeting business premises and company personnel'. It appeared to radiate from Guadalajara with operational cells in the capital, Oaxaca, Mérida and Monterrey. In the late 1970s one heard of the occasional incident until police claimed to have broken the last remnant in February 1981.

Zapatista Urban Front
(Frente Urbano Zapatista — FUZ)

Named after the historic revolutionary hero, Emiliano Zapata (1877-1919), the FUZ was an urban terrorist group which operated briefly in Mexico City around 1971/72. Its leader, Francisco Urango López, who was arrested in January 1972, planned to abduct prominent Mexican politicians and indeed financed the group from the ransom of US $250,000 paid for the release of Julio Hirschfeld, director of Civil Aviation Services, in September 1971.

The group operated independently, but members had received firearms training in Chiapas state in the south, alongside other radical Marxist-Leninist splinter groups in 1968/69. The training was undertaken by individuals who had received instruction either in North Korea or in China.

Nicaragua

From the Nicaraguan civil war (1978-79) and the subsequent Sandinist victory of 1979 stemmed the Central American violence of the early 1980s, most obviously apparent in El Salvador, but also present in Guatemala and even in Honduras and Costa Rica. In Honduras the People's Revolutionary Union (*Unión Revolucionaria del Pueblo* — URP) announced the start of armed struggle in October 1980 and found support among trade union and peasant circles. Other groups entered the fray in 1981. In Costa Rica labour disturbances grew, and in March 1981 the Carlos Agüero Echeverría Commando, named after a fallen hero in the 1979 Nicaraguan civil war, perpetrated the first contemporary terrorist attacks in that country.

The ousting of military dictatorship in Nicaragua caused groups of exiles to spring up abroad. Somozist forces regrouped across the borders from Nicaragua, and launched from Honduras and Guatemala attacks upon the Sandinist government. Some of those involved were the Armed Democratic Forces (*Fuerzas Armadas Democráticas* — FAD), whose leader, Carlos García Solorzano, was jailed in August 1980, the National Liberation Army (*Ejército Nacional de Liberación* — ELN) and the Nicaraguan Armed Revolutionary Forces (FARN). Only the FARN could claim any pretence to include among its members people who had not been closely associated with the Somozist regime. Unjust as the Somozist dictatorship had been, the regime which replaced it was tough on those elements, ethnic or economic, that did not conform to its collectivist dogma. The freedom of the press suffered, the coastal Miskito Indians suffered, democrats suffered, to the point when Edén Pastora, the former guerrilla commander, announced his intention in April 1982 to resume the struggle for liberty which he had first taken up against Somoza. By September he had set up a Democratic Revolutionary Alliance that grouped all the important democratic Nicaraguans in exile and which he led.

Bibliography

To understand the Nicaraguan national uprising of 1978/79 it is essential to read as background the work of its contemporary spiritual father, Ernesto Cardenal, who, although politically naïve, spoke the truth in terms which were understood. *The Gospel in Solentiname* (London, 1977) is fundamental. Carlos Fonseca helped establish the modern Sandinist myth by writing the biography *Sandino, Guerrillero Proletario* (Managua, 1980) published posthumously. Victor Tirado in *El Pensamiento Político de Carlos Fonseca Amador* (Managua, 1980) provided a further hagiographic link in what purported to be a chain of revolutionary progess. In English, the beginnings are best read in Gregorio Selser's *Sandino* (London and New York, 1981), a translation from the Spanish. For the contemporary contradictions, see Jorge Castañeda, *Nicaragua: Contradicciones en la Revolución* (Mexico City, 1980). As a sympathetic but perceptive observer, Henri Weber analaysed events well in *Nicaragua: The Sandinist Revolution* (London, 1981), a translation from French published in Paris the same year, but see also George Black's detailed account in *Triumph of the People: The Sandinista Revolution in Nicaragua* (London, 1981). For an idea as to how the left in Latin America viewed Sandinism, see the Colombian novelist, Gabriel García Márquez, *Los Sandinistas* (Bogotá, 1979). The Sandinist leader, Humberto Ortega, published his own short history of nationalist struggle in *Cincuenta Años de Lucha Sandinista* (Medellín, Colombia, 1979), but of greater interest is Jaime Wheelock Román's *Imperialismo y Dictadura: Crísis de una Formación Social* (Mexico City, 1975) for the insight into the theoretical formation of a Sandinist. Richard Millett analysed the Somozist National Guard in *Guardians of the Dynasty* (Orbis, New York, 1979), whilst the Argentine journalist, Eduardo Crawley, wrote *Dictators Never Die* (London, 1979), an account of Somozist rule. A further journalistic account can be found in Bernard Diedrich's *Somoza and the Legacy of US Involvement in Central America* (London, 1982). For life under the new order, see John Booth's *The End and the Beginning: The Nicaraguan Revolution* (Boulder, USA, 1981).

Nicaraguan Armed Revolutionary Forces
(Fuerzas Armadas Revolucionarias de Nicaragua — FARN)

The FARN consisted in 1981 of exiled Nicaraguans who had sought refuge abroad from what they considered a Marxist-Leninist government dominated by Sandinists. At first the nucleus consisted largely of national guardsmen who had fled following the collapse of the Somoza dictatorship in 1979. But these elements were joined in 1980 by compatriots, who, although active in the fight against Somoza, soon discovered that their own hopes and ideals had been defrauded. Some found a haven in Miami, others preferred to work for a change in the order of affairs from Honduras and Costa Rica, whence they planned and put into effect raids on their homeland.

Sandinist National Liberation Front
(*Frente Sandinista de Liberación Nacional — FSLN*)

The FSLN was named after a Nicaraguan patriot, General Augusto César Sandino, who, having opposed US rule for six years, was treacherously murdered in 1934 by supporters of the Somoza family, which ruled Nicaragua until the flight in July 1979 of the dictator Anastasio Somoza Debayle to the US and then to Paraguay, where in September 1980 he was assassinated. The front was set up in 1958 by Carlos Fonseca Amador, who led it until his death in a clash with security forces in November 1976.

Fonseca had for years led a band of militants in the hills, activity which posed no greater problem to the dictatorship than the occasional skirmish. Despite persistent contact with Cuba during the 1960s their stand made no impression militarily, and from the rural population awakened no echo. Their haven even then lay in Costa Rica, where, in 1969 Fonseca was arrested. Guerrillas under Carlos Agüero Echeverria secured his freedom by hijacking a Costa Rican airliner in October 1970, when in exchange for the release of the hijacked passengers he was flown to Havana.

During the early 1970s guerrilla actions were sporadic, for the most part in the north near Matagalpa. In these encounters no more than a score of national guardsmen lost their lives. But in December 1974 a daring raid on a party thrown by a former agricultural minister, José María Castillo, enabled the Sandinists to hold hostage the cream of Nicaraguan society, including the foreign minister and two ambassadors, the capital's mayor and prominent businessmen. The Papal Nuncio and the Archbishop of Managua conducted the negotiations which led to the release from prison of 14 Sandinist colleagues, who were flown to Cuba, the broadcasting of a communiqué and a ransom of US $1 million.

Notwithstanding the success of that action, which undoubtedly drew the attention of the world to a hitherto unknown group, guerrilla activity throughout 1975 and 1976 was an unmitigated disaster. Mauricio Duarte Alvarez, who had planned the Managua raid, died in a clash in Jinotepe in January 1975, Eduardo Contreras Escóbar, who had led the attack, was killed in November 1976, the day before FSLN leader Fonseca was shot dead in the northern hills. Among those arrested was a future Sandinist leader, Tomás Jorge Martínez, in February 1976.

During this unsuccessful period of operations the FSLN were led in two columns by Carlos Agüero and Victor Manuel Tirado López, with between them no more than 50 militants. Each column operated in units of six and with the purpose of deepening and extending their contacts with the local peasantry. Although undoubtedly strongly influenced by Cuba, the FSLN communiqués at that time described the movement as 'pluri-ideological' and 'pluri-classist'. Militants saw themselves as acting as a 'bridge between socialist ideas and the movement of the peasant labour masses'.

In 1977 the FSLN split into three factions. The prolonged popular war faction favoured rural actions and was close to Havana and led by Tomás Borge Martínez. The proletarian tendency, led by Jaime Wheelock, Luis Carrión Cruz and Carlos Nuñez Téllez, believed in a dual strategy of rural and urban-based terrorist operations. The third line favoured direct military attacks on towns, and was accused of compromising revolutionary orthodoxy for the sake of attracting reformists to the FSLN. They were led by the brothers Daniel and Humberto Ortega Saavedra and Tirado López.

That year the guerrillas mounted a handful of carefully prepared attacks upon small towns — the lakeside port of San Carlos, Masayo, and Dilipito, where the armed presence of guerrillas in albeit limited and largely unsuccessful operations was for the first time felt nationally. Smaller operations took place in the capital. Of the October 1977 casualties none was felt more keenly than the loss of Pedro Aranz Palacios, who only a year earlier had succeeded Fonseca as leader.

Two occurrences directly favoured the cause of the Sandinists. In September 1977 President Somoza suffered a heart attack, and although he recovered in 1978 public attention was focused on the need for a peaceful transfer of power to a successor. Secondly, in January 1978 the right murdered Dr Chamorro Cardenal, a leading but respected opposition spokesman and editor of *La Prensa*. As Church-backed protest and agitation spread, the FSLN took advantage of new recruits who in a few months swelled its ranks from dozens to hundreds. By the end of 1978 the Sandinists may have numbered 1500; by the time of Somoza's fall, several thousand were fighting.

In August 1978 the FSLN launched its most spectacular attack, upon the Congressional Palace itself. No more than two dozen Sandinists took the building, holding eventually 100 people hostage in return for the release of jailed colleagues. The occupation ended with the departure for Panama of 59 prisoners, whose liberty the Archbishop of Managua and the Costa Rican and Panamanian Ambassadors guaranteed. Edén Pastora Gómez led the attack, and subsequently became FSLN military commander.

An FSLN call for a general insurrection in September 1978 failed, despite heavy fighting in Masaya, León, Esteli, Chinandega and Diramba. Possibly 5000 died in the conflict, and a further 16,000 were injured.

By this time the FSLN enjoyed the support of broad sections of the established classes, as well as sympathy from abroad of Venezuela, Panama and Costa Rica in particular. From raising their funds from bank robbery, the Sandinists turned to floating loans in Puerto Rico, Mexico,

Costa Rica, Panama and Venezuela, backed by the word of Ernesto Cardenal, the former priest and internationally renowned poet.

The 1978 offensive failed. Yet in 1979 the Sandinists won power, due partly to a new unity between the three factions and to an improved and expanded military performance, but also because of the US pressure on Somoza and the National Guard to relinquish control and seek exile. It is also true that the military struggle had contributed to an economic undermining of the regime. Although arms and training had come from Cuba, condemnation of Somoza had been forthcoming from all neighbouring countries, so that at the time of victory the FSLN enjoyed the support of a broad section of national and international opinion. The government that took power in July 1979 was led by Daniel Ortega and Moisés Hassan Morales, both Sandinists. Later, FSLN founder member, Tomás Borge Martínez, took over the ministry of the interior, adding to Sandinist control of Nicaraguan destinies.

As the Sandinist movement had in the first place been devoid of ideological content, it was open to the Marxists within the movement to provide it. Increasingly in the course of 1981 Daniel Ortega swung the revolution away from pluri-party democracy towards Marxism-Leninism. Reliant upon Cuba for help, the regime antagonised the USA and the business community which had finally sided with revolution against Somoza. Such a stance alienated many former Sandinists, including Edén Pastora, who resigned from the administration, returned to Costa Rica, and finally in April 1982 declared his determination to revert to armed action against a regime which in his view had fallen into the undemocratic hands of a Marxist-Leninist clique dependent upon Cuban and Soviet intentions.

Paraguay

General Alfredo Stroessner (b. 1928) has prevented the emergence of political violence since being elected president in 1954. After a period of political instability following a short civil war in 1947, he took office with the backing of the armed forces, which he commanded. Stroessner identified his personal rule with that of the Colorado Party, which since coming to power he has successfully manipulated. The Liberal Party opposition neither from within nor from outside the country ever succeeded in threatening his rule. When it contested elections for a Constituent Assembly in 1967, the party made a poor showing.

In Paraguay the Cuban revolution was allowed no impact at all in the 1960s, nor were the 1970s troubled by the indigenous urban insurgencies that afflicted neighbouring Argentina and Uruguay. In the Church lay the seeds of political movement, which she encouraged by giving support to the Agrarian Peasant Leagues, that fostered a sense of decency and responsibility side by side rural poverty. From radical Catholicism too came the stimulus that provided a weak echo in the 1970s to revolutionary movement in Argentina — manifested in the First of March Organisation. In the 1980s only Stroessner's longevity prevented change in Paraguay: as with all military dictatorships, succession raises a problem and there is no guarantee that change, when it comes, will benefit the people.

Bibliography

George Pendle wrote a good general introduction to Paraguay in *Paraguay: A Riverside Nation* (London, 1956), but for the politics of the Stroessner era, see Paul Lewis, *Paraquay under Stroessner* (North Carolina, 1980) and for a leftist review the Latin American Bureau's *Paraguay: Power Game* (London, 1980).

Agrarian Peasant Leagues
(Ligas Agrarias Campesinas — LAC)

The rural peasantry, with the support of the Church, has provided the only serious opposition to President Stroessner's regime. In the early 1960s a grass-roots social movement, the Agrarian Leagues, emerged to challenge the inequitable system of land tenure. Originally non-violent, the Leagues received considerable backing from the Church and by 1969

membership was estimated at over 20,000, organised into local communities and operating small cooperative ventures.

By the mid-1970s, the Leagues began to threaten the Colorado Party's
traditional hold over the peasantry; accordingly the government denounced them, claiming they were communist-inspired and linked to
the OPM guerrilla movement. A crack-down followed when some 50
peasant leaders died, several thousand were arrested and hundreds fled
to exile. Cooperatives were broken up and families relocated in distant
parts of the country.

Thereafter little was heard of the Leagues until 1980, when they were
behind the most serious disturbances of Stroessner's 26-year rule. The
Leagues had become active once more, opposing Brazilian economic
penetration in the east of the country, where massive hydroelectric
development (mostly financed by Brazil) was taking place. On 8 March 30
armed peasants hijacked a tourist bus with the intention of driving to
Asunción to publicise their grievances. A shoot-out with a road patrol
forced the peasants to flee and 1000 troops were immediately despatched. Two days later most had been surrounded at the village of
Guyrúa-gúa, where 19 peasants were killed. Subsequently, the army
clashed with some 300 League members under their leader, Víctor Centurión; 95 peasants were reported killed. Centurión escaped and was
granted asylum in the Panamanian embassy.

First of March Organisation, also known as Politico-Military Organisation
*(Organización l Marzo or Organización Político-Militar —
OPM)*

Paraguay's only true guerrilla group was formed in 1974 by radical
Catholic students. Influenced by events in Argentina, it maintained
links with the Argentinian ERP. OPM membership was drawn from
peasant activists of the Agrarian Leagues as well as the student body, and
support was believed to have come from some radical sections of the
Church, notably the Jesuits.

In April 1976 police moved against the group, which was still in
embryonic form, raiding its headquarters in Asunción. They met determined opposition and five policemen were killed, but when the shooting
ended 30 guerrillas were dead. The leaders of the group, Juan Carlos de
Costa and Mario Schaerer, were wounded and were alleged to have died
subsequently under police torture.

There followed an intensive police investigation, and over 1500 suspects were detained. Police raided the Jesuit-run Cristo Rey College and
the offices of the Episcopal Conference, and a number of Jesuits were
subsequently expelled. OPM never recovered from this set-back, although some peasant members remained active within the Agrarian
Leagues; other members fled to Argentina.

Peru

Guerrilla actions in the 1960s were but brief sparks, the product of Trotskyism in the case of the Left Revolutionary Front (FIR) and of fashionable Castroism in the case of the National Liberation Army (ELN) and the Movement of the Revolutionary Left (MIR). Of these the more important were the ELN and the MIR, which attempted to open four fronts. The MIR's leader, Luis de la Puente Uceda, was active in the Convention Zone in Cuzco department; Hector Béjar of the ELN led the so-called Javier Heraud group in the Sea Zone in Ayacucho department; MIR supporters, Guillermo Lobatón and Máximo Velando, were active in Concepción and Jauja provinces in Junín department; Gonzalo Fernández Gasco and Helio Portocarrero of MIR never actually launched the northern MIR front in Ayabaca in Piura department.

These guerrilla groups cost the lives of only a handful of people, but their importance lay in their outrageous daring at a time of intellectual ferment and peasant agitation for land. There is no doubt that the Cuban revolution powerfully influenced the Peruvian ultra-left, not least in the training of a handful of recruits whom agents had selected from radical university circles. They found their way back to Peru so as to contribute to the guerrilla episodes, yet their participation never amounted to control of these miniscule organisations.

The 1960s guerrilla failure in Peru needs explaining. Tactically it was due to lack of mobility — they could not move swiftly enough to escape the path of advancing troops. In the longer term it is true that trained bands of men working to a plan can cause havoc to provincial government, but not unless they speak the local language. The guerrilla leaders spoke Spanish exclusively, the Indians Quechua or Aymara. There could therefore be little contact with, much less motivation of, the peasantry. The success which attended Hugo Blanco, the Trotskyist peasant leader, lay almost entirely in the fact that he was encouraging peasants to occupy the property of landowners they knew and hated. But this was not guerrilla warfare.

Nor did these activities prompt the military to assume power under General Velasco, who displaced the political elite and proclaimed the Land Reform Act of 1969, which in scope was breath-taking, leaving the 1200 proprietors who owned 60 per cent of the best cultivatable land with little more than government bonds. The large estates were to be run as cooperatives on a profit-sharing basis by those who had previously worked for landlords. In part the fact that Peru later escaped leftist political violence of an organised nature throughout the 1970s can be attributed to the determined radicalism of the Peruvian military, although as always military rule had to hand immediate force, a compulsion it was prepared to and did in fact use.

In an unusual development the military returned power to the civilian politicians in July 1980, at the very moment when a new Maoist guerrilla group, Shining Path (SL), took up a campaign of rural sabotage and later city bombings. Unlike earlier insurgents, SL cadres, although initially the product of the university world, quickly learned native languages and recruited Indians whose subsequent campaign threatened the survival of civilian government.

Bibliography

David Scott Palmer provided an excellent general introduction to the problems of the country in *Peru: The Authoritarian Tradition* (Praeger, 1980). Whilst George Philip discussed how the military preempted revolution in *The Rise and Fall of the Peruvian Military Radicals 1968-1976* (London, 1978). The most well-known Peruvian revolutionary writer is the Trotskyist, Hugo Blanco, whose concern for land reform is clearly expressed in *Land or Death: The Peasant Struggle in Peru* (Pathfinder Press, New York, 1972). At the time he published *El Camino de Nuestra Revolución* (Lima, 1964). For the impact he made, consult Víctor Villanueva's *Hugo Blanco y la Rebelión Campesina* (Editorial Juan Mejía Baca, Lima, 1967).

The land seizures of the late 1950s and early 1960s are analysed in a University of Texas publication *Struggle in the Andes: Peasant Political Mobilisation in Peru* (Austin, 1975). David Collier describes the evolution of authoritarian politics in *Squatters and Oligarchs* (Johns Hopkins, London, 1976). Héctor Béjar, an important intellectual leader and one-time guerrilla, published from Havana *Perú: Apuntes sobre una Experiencia Guerrillera*, which Editions Maspero in Parish translated in 1969, and which the following year the New York *Monthly Review* published in English.

The journalist, Hugo Neira, although committed to the left, can be trusted to provide an informed guide in many journals and newspapers. He described the life of an activist in *Huillca: Habla un Campesino Peruano* (Ediciones Peisa, Lima, 1974). The FIR can be researched in *Historia Secreta de las Guerrillas* (Ediciones Más Allá, Lima, 1967) by Gonzalo Añi Castillo, and in *Perú: Revolución, Insurrección, Guerrillas* by Ricardo Letts. For MIR tenets, see the unique article in the *Monthly Review* (November 1965) entitled 'The Peruvian Revolution: Concepts and Perspectives' by Luis de la Puente Uceda, himself the protagonist of the MIR. More widely, R. Mercado wrote of MIR activities in *Las Guerrillas del MIR*. The Peruvian government provided its own account in *Las Guerrillas en el Peré y su Repressión* (War Ministry, Lima, 1966). Because of its recent origins SL was badly documented in 1982 with the exception of Roger Mercado's *El Partido Comunista del Perú: Sendero Luminoso* (Ediciones de Cultura Popular, Lima, 1982).

Front of the Revolutionary Left
(Frente de la Izquierda Revolucionaria — FIR)

In conjunction with smaller revolutionary groups, the Trotskyist Revolutionary Workers' Party (POR) set up the FIR in the leftist city of Cuzco in December 1961. The principal organisers were Trotskyists — the Peruvian, Hugo Blanco (b. 1933), the Argentinian, Arturo 'Che' Pereyra, and the Spaniard, José Martorell. The Fourth International gave its backing to FIR, which had some 60 urban members.

Within months disagreement broke out between Blanco's supporters in Cuzco and Hugo Bressano's supporters in Lima. Short of money, FIR robbed two banks. But on 28 April Pereyra was captured by police outside Cuzco, and the next day Bressano fled to Argentina. On 4 May Hernano Boggio, an FIR Central Committee member and chief recipient of the stolen money, turned himself over to the authorities. Blanco remained at large, fired with enthusiasm to work for a rural revolution among the Peruvian peasants, until captured on 29 May 1963. He received a prison sentence of 20 years, but was subsequently pardoned and became a senator on behalf of radicalism.

Movement of the Revolutionary Left
(Movimiento de la Izquierda Revolucionaria — MIR)

The MIR was born in June 1962 from a rebel faction led by Luis de la Puente Uceda (1926-65) of the reformist American Popular Revolutionary Alliance (APRA), founded in 1924 by the veteran politician, Víctor Raúl Haya de la Torre. Its name was identical to that taken earlier by dissidents who split from Romulo Betancourt's reformist Democratic Action (AD) in Venezuela.

Luis de la Puente had Cuban contacts, but in origin the MIR was an indigenous Peruvian development. True, de la Puente succeeded in obtaining Castro's help for his revolutionary objectives, which were to provide radical peasantry with armed backing. For two years de la Puente undertook little but theoretical work; in mid-1964 he went underground to promote a 'people's war' prompted by the extraordinary ferment at the time in favour of land reform, a movement which led to many spontaneous seizures by peasants of large estates.

In addition to de la Puente, the MIR's rural activity was directed by Guillermo Lobatón, Máximo Velando, Gonzalo Fernández Gasco, Elío Portocarrero Ríos and Rubén Tupayachi. They organised three rural

focuses, the first in June 1965 in mountainous terrain near the Anda-
marca river. They stole dynamite from a local mine, blew up a bridge and
sacked an estate.

Further actions of a similar kind followed the same month. Troops
moved in, and by August contacts were taking place with the guerrillas,
who withdrew, only to reappear in other areas. But within weeks guerrilla tactics turned into a desperate attempt to evade military pursuit.
During November and December they suffered a number of casualties;
finally, near the river Sotziqui, Lobatón was throught to have died on 7
January 1966. The whole guerrilla episode had lasted no more than six
months.

De la Puente was still more unfortunate. His group commenced action
in August 1965, clashed with the army for the first time on 9 September,
and after surviving intense surveillance and attack from the air a month
later found itself surrounded. The end was thought to have come on 23
October. None escaped with their lives. The third focus never functioned
at all.

National Liberation Army
(Ejército de Liberación Nacional — ELN)

The ELN had a slightly longer history than the MIR or the FIR, dating
back to 1962, when it had organised a guerrilla episode at Puerto Mal-
donado in May 1963. A small band led by Javier Heraud, a young
Peruvian intellectual who had spent time in Cuba, crossed from Bolivia
into Peru. Within days they clashed with police and were killed.

For two years the ELN remained dormant, during which time its
leader, Héctor Béjar, prepared for guerrilla action. In September 1965, the
ELN publicly pledged itself to aid the MIR, but it was in no position to
prevent the eradication of MIR guerrilla activity that year. Béjar, it is true,
committed the ELN to its first terrorist acts that month when the group
murdered the joint owners of a large country estate in Ayacucho. The
army moved in, and by December had made contact with the guerrillas,
who did not survive the month. Béjar was captured and imprisoned in
February 1966. He later received an amnesty and became assistant
director of *El Comercio* in Lima.

Peruvian Communist Party — Red Flag
(Partido Comunista Peruano — Bandera Roja)

In 1982 Red Flag was led by lawyer Saturnino Paredes, who in 1964 had
headed a pro-Chinese faction which broke with the Moscow-line Peruvian Communist Party. Members started a paper, *Red Flag*, which advocated armed struggle. From this group split a further faction known as
Red Fatherland in 1967, and in 1970 Shining path split from Red Flag.

Although Red Flag believes in the armed struggle it does not in fact practise it, and is accused by Shining Path of collaborating with the government. Its main front organisations are the Peasant Confederation of Peru (CCP) and the Popular Democrat Front (FDP).

Shining Path
(Sendero Luminoso — SL)

Shining Path first came to public attention in 1980 after a decade of dogmatic self-examination and rigorously selected recruitment. Its origins go back to 1970, when a faction led by Abimael Guzmán split from the Peruvian Communist Party Red Flag group. Guzmán was professor in the University of Huamanga in Ayacucho, where he worked assiduously on party propaganda and cultivated a circle known as the Revolutionary Student Front for the Shining Path of Mariátegui. Both Red Flag and Shining Path entertained no doubts about the correctness of armed struggle in the countryside in order to bring to power the new communist order. Subsequently Shining Path Maoist convictions were challenged by Professor Luis Kawata Makabe, who championed the Albanian heresy of Enver Hoxha, which gave equal weight to pursuing the armed struggle in town and country, and which, if adopted as policy, would bring Shining Path closer to Red Flag.

The originality of Shining Path lies in its taking as examples former Indian rebel leaders, particularly Juan Santos Atahualpa and Tupac Amaru. By so doing SL attracted rural Indian supporters, thereby awakening a longstanding ethnic resentment against the white coloniser, who for so long had robbed them of language, philosophy, wealth and power. Thus communist revolution was wedded to reversing the imposed ethnic order of centuries and allied itself with a trend likely to grow irresistibly.

Violence began in July 1980, for the most part in the departments of Lima and Ayacucho, and by the end of the year some 240 incidents had been recorded. Actions included the destruction of local tax records, bombings of administrative offices and the sabotage of electricity pylons. In 1981 the incidence of 40 attacks a month grew and on many occasions a score of guerrillas took part in raiding banks, quarries, mines, and police posts. Their most spectacular action, which involved 150 guerrillas, was to spring 300 prisoners from Ayacucho jail in late February 1982. Subsequently SL included kidnapping as a tactic, and the harsh punishment of mutilation and death was meted out to some who informed upon terrorist movements.

Tupac Amaru

Allied with Shining Path, Tupac Amaru operates in northern departments of La Libertad, Cajamarca, Jaen, Lambayeque and Amazonas. In 1982 prominent names included Ernesto Montas Aliaga and Marcos Rojas. Some of those involved had been active with Luis de la Puente Uceda in 1965. The name Tupac Amaru recalls the Peruvian Indian leader who revolted against the Spaniards and was put to death in the late eighteenth century, and whose memory a decade earlier the Uruguayan National Liberation Movement had revived.

Uruguay

Serious political violence was unknown in modern Uruguay before the appearance in the early 1960s of the Tupamaros, and has been unknown since the uprooting in 1972 of that movement. Prior to their appearance the country was renowned for its political stability, its free press, civil liberties and honest elections; after it, in a tough reaction which the Tupamaros themselves sought to bring about, Uruguay has been characterised by military rule.

The terrorist phenomenon undoubtedly had to do with the country's declining economic performance, which was tied to the export of wool, leather and meat. But significant too was creeping corruption in the financial sphere, widespread smuggling, tax evasion and speculative and fraudulent transactions. Inflation in the 1960s bit into the social fabric — taking the cost of living index in 1963 as 100, by 1969 it topped 2000 and by 1973 was nearly 6000. Unemployment and under-employment contributed to the scepticism which convinced a tiny section of the professional elite to opt for an armed struggle to bring down the democratic system. At the time labour unrest was high, culminating in a general strike in 1966. In the years following, large demonstrations brought about the occasional death from police fire.

The political system had been devised by Uruguay's greatest statesman, José Batlle y Ordóñez, in the first decade of the twentieth century. Through the Blanco and Colorado parties he put an end to nineteenth-century civil strife. By mid-century however it was in need of reform, for the Colorados had held office consistently until 1958. The political task confronting the military after 1973 was to devise a new system of government which would not resurrect old inadequacies, and which would not open the door to a further guerrilla campaign.

Bibliography

The initial success of the Tupamaros, who dedicated a great deal of attention to publicity, led to the publication of much documentary evidence. Best of all is *Tupamaros: Antología Documental* (Centro Intercultural de Documentación, Cuernavaca, Mexico, 1971) edited by Ernesto Mayans, who provides a good introduction, a useful chronology and an excellent bibliography. Also of value is *Tupamaros: Estrategia y Acción* (Montevideo, 1969) by two objective Uruguayan journalists, Antonio Mercader and Jorge de Vera, who, among other documents, include important interviews. The *Actas Tupamaras* (Schapire, Buenos

Aires, 1971) can also be consulted, as well as Omar Costa's *Los Tupamaros* (Ediciones Era, Mexico, 1971), and in English *Terror and Urban Guerrillas: A Study of Tactics and Documents* (Coral Gables, 1971) edited by Jay Mallin.

The most complete statistics and valuable documentation from government sources is available in the three-volume *Testimonio de una Nación Agredida* (Montevideo, 1978). The MLN urban strategy was largely the work of the veteran Spanish Civil War activist, Abraham Guillén, whose *Teoría de la Violencia* (1965) and *Estrategia de la Guerrilla Urbana* (1966) are essential reading and are available in English in *Philosophy of the Urban Guerrilla* (New York, 1973). María Gilio's much vaunted *The Tupamaros* (London, 1972) looks at the sociological background, whilst Alain Labrousse provided a fair account in French, *Les Tupamaros* (Éditions du Seuil, Paris, 1971). For a quick and useful summary, together with the main chronology, see *Urban Guerrilla Warfare in Latin America* (Cambridge, Mass. and London, 1974) by James Kohl and John Litt. Régis Debray analysed the Tupamaro failure in his indispensable *The Revolution on Trial* (Penguin, 1978). For accounts by two Tupamaro victims, see that of the British Ambassador, Geoffrey Jackson, *Peoples Prison* (London, 1973), and the American Claude Fly, *No Hope But God* (New York, 1973).

National Liberation Movement
(Movimiento de Liberación Nacional — MLN)

Raúl Sendic Antonaccio founded the Tupamaros in the early 1960s, having earlier been active in rural trade union militancy through the Artigas Sugar Workers' Union. The first action for which the MLN claimed responsibility was an attack in July 1963 on a rifle club; thereafter sporadic attacks were made, which in 1964 were coupled with bank robberies. Bomb attacks were carefully selected — diplomatic vehicles, especially those belonging to Brazilian and US personnel, and the houses of a handful of government advisers and parliamentarians. As early as September 1964 the government severed relations with Cuba, on account of Castro's alleged support for MLN activity.

In January 1966 Sendic convened the MLN's first national convention and decided to formalise Tupamaro action in the city: henceforth the MLN broke with the Castroite tradition of rural guerrilla warfare, becoming urban-based in the capital, Montevideo, a city of one million inhabitants. They took their name from a Peruvian Indian leader, Tupac Amaru, whom the Spaniards had burned in 1782.

In December 1966 the MLN lost its first members in two shoot-outs with police, who uncovered a printing shop, a training centre, a target range and two safe houses. For twelve months as a result of these setbacks the MLN was unable to launch an attack. But in January 1968 the group stole 500 kilos of explosives and that year a series of bomb attacks and nine large bank robberies followed. Thereafter for three years Tupamaro audacity scarcely knew any bounds in its systematic attack upon Uruguayan democracy. In effect it had taken three years to build from nothing a well organised and impenetrable subversive network. Next to Sendic, Julio Angel Marenales Saenz, Gabino Falero Montes de Oca, Jorge Amílcar Manera Lluveras and Heraclio Jesús Rodríguez Recalde were the principal leaders.

During those years the MLN was intent upon disclosing the rotten aspects of the political and economic system, then in decline largely as a result of world economic trends. In February 1969 the Tupamaros exposed financial irregularities by seizing ledgers as well as cash in the Financiera Monty company. They undertook a similar operation on the Mailhos estate. They stole from the Casino San Rafael and turned over the gambling money to the poor. They advertised on radio stations, which members occupied for brief periods, and eventually set up their own twice weekly clandestine station.

Foreign investment became a target in the form of multinational companies; individual members of the security forces were selected for assassination. International ramifications stemmed from the abduction of the US AID officer, Dan Mitrione, reputedly a CIA agent, in July 1970, for whose release they demanded the freedom of 150 jailed colleagues. He was murdered on 9 August, following the capture of the Tupamaro leadership, including Sendic and Raúl Bidegain Greissing, the second in command.

The following year the British Ambassador, Geoffrey Jackson, was abducted in January and held for eight months undiscovered in a 'people's prison'. Three days earlier 106 Tupamaros, including Sendic, Manera Lluveras and Marenales Saenz had escaped from Punta Carretas jail. In 1972 the Tupamaros began to murder individuals whom it considered responsible for the growth of right-wing death squad victims, a practice which had begun in 1970 and quickened horribly in 1971. The military saw in these tactics a direct challenge to its authority and prestige; it was indeed the first time that the Tupamaros had killed an officer. It provoked a declaration of internal war, which allowed any part of the country to be put under military jurisdiction. This step proved the beginning of the end.

In May, June and July 1972 a major security breakthrough unravelled the subversive network. It showed that the MLN had recruited at every level of society, from prostitutes and common criminals to high-ranking members of the administration. Active in student and trade union circles, the movement was nonetheless primarily composed of well established professional people in the upper- and middle-income brackets. These included many teachers and lecturers, lawyers, doctors, surgeons, dentists, accountants, bankers, architects and engineers, a model, a radio announcer and a well-known actress. By the end of November 1972, 2600 people had been jailed and 42 killed.

Of the 200 safe houses and hideouts discovered, some had air conditioning, food storage capacity, books and television. Their ingenious construction and design showed them to be the work of highly trained and imaginative engineers. Besides the capture of an electronics laboratory, a laboratory used for forging documents and a hospital complete with operating table and X-ray equipment, a foundry with a furnace and industrial equipment for making grenades was discovered in Fray Bentos city. *Matériel* sufficient to maintain on a war footing an army of at least 2000 had been captured.

The MLN had never been a popular movement, despite its carefully fostered Robin Hood image. At the height of its power in 1971, the Uruguayan people rejected the Broad Front, which the MLN tacitly supported, voting massively for the two traditional parties. Thus isolated from the people, the Tupamaros crumbled quickly before the consistent security pressure of military-backed measures.

Captured intelligence material proved the existence of seven provincial columns, each of which constructed hideouts according to the terrain, and enjoyed medical, printing and information services. These columns were seriously restricted by the dispersal in August 1972 of the supporting units, consisting of men and women who did not actually contravene the law. The mastermind, Amílcar Manera Lluveras, was captured on 22 June, while the MLN founder, Raúl Sendic, was retaken on 1 September after a gunfight in which he was wounded. Like a number of prominent guerrillas, he had undergone plastic surgery to change his appearance.

From 1973 to the present day the MLN has proved unable to reorganise. In its day Cuba gave it copious propaganda support, and provided a handful of its recruits with training. The MLN had contacts with Argentina's People's Revolutionary Army (ERP) and with the Chilean Movement of the Revolutionary Left (MIR). Its relationship with the Uruguayan Communist Party was friendly, although in the end the party was thought to have contributed to breaking the MLN.

Venezuela

As in many countries in Latin America, the Venezuelan guerrilla experience of the 1960s derived in spirit from the 1959 victory in Cuba of Fidel Castro, but action would not have followed had it not been for the active participation of the Venezuelan Communist Party (PCV) and the practical aid provided by Cuba.

At first the Armed Forces of National Liberation (FALN) and their allies in the Movement of the Revolutionary Left (MIR) attempted through urban activity in 1963 to prevent the election of President Leoni. They failed, and following Cuban advice, particularly that put forward by Che Guevara and Régis Debray, turned to a programme of rural revolution.

This too was unsuccessful, for four main reasons: the PCV in 1964 and then Cuba in 1969 defected from its support for guerrilla activity; throughout the campaign the government security forces remained loyal, and with US counter-insurgency training their performance improved; paying with oil exports, the government introduced social reform; and, finally, political amnesty was offered realistically, at times when the guerrilla movement was wracked by internal dissension.

During the 1970s political violence did not revive in a form which threatened the state. True, it was an irritant, but one which did not call into question the development of responsible political processes. The left-wing parties, the PCV, the MIR and others improved their electoral standing and seemed to challenge the traditional position of Democratic Action as the party of reform.

Bibliography

The best analysis of the early urban tactics of the Armed Forces of National Liberation (FALN) and the Movement of the Revolutionary Left (MIR) is to be found in a 1970 Georgetown Research Project published by Atlantic Research Corporation in Alexandria, Virginia, entitled *Castro-Communist Insurgency in Venezuela: A Study of Insurgency and Counter-Insurgency Operations and Techniques in Venezuela 1960-64*. For more detailed guidance to articles, the student should turn to the basic bibliography of Charles Russell, James Miller and Robert Hildner in *Latin America Research Review*, Vol. 9, No. 1, 1974.

The guerrilla leader, Moisés Moleiro, wrote an inside account of the MIR, *El MIR de Venezuela* (Havana, 1967), also of interest for the early period is *Venezuela Okey* (Ediciones del Litoral, Santiago, 1963) by

Manuel Cabieses Donoso, but more important, because of his own role, is Fabricio Ojeda's *Hacía el Poder Revolucionario* (Havana, 1967). Useful documentary material is found in French translation in *Avec Douglas Bravo dans les Maquis Vénézuéliens* (Dossiers Partisans, Maspero, Paris, 1968). Régis Debray analysed the Venezuelan guerrilla failure in *The Revolution on Trial* (Penguin, 1978).

Armed Forces of National Liberation
(Fuerzas Armadas de Liberación Nacional — FALN)

The FALN grew out of a conviction within the hierarchy of the Moscow-line Venezuelan Communist Party (PCV) that the political situation called for resorting to guerrilla warfare in order to seize political power. To launch the campaign the PCV chose exceptionally talented younger members, particularly Douglas Bravo (b. 1933), son of a minor land-owner, and a former law student, Eloy Torres, and Teodoro Petkoff, of Bulgarian/Russian extraction.

These men joined with activists from the Movement of the Revolutionary Left (MIR), a splinter group of the ruling Democratic Action Party, to form in 1961 the nucleus of the future FALN. Preparations were made that year; some were uncovered in early 1962, but not sufficient to prevent the first guerrilla attacks on stores in the countryside. Rather than concentrate its forces, the FALN distributed them in some 20 small detachments in half the states of Venezuela, of which the most important were the Chirinos Guerrilla Front in Falcón, and El Charal in Portuguesa State. Little or no contact between them took place, and there was no unified command. Those who took part were enthusiastic amateurs, untrained for the most part in guerrilla warfare. By the end of the year military action had snuffed out most of these revolutionary sparks.

Yet during the year a few military officers, who had raised the standard of revolt, but failed to find any response, deserted to the mountains and through their professionalism strengthened the guerrilla structure. It resulted in the formalisation of the FALN on 20 February 1963, with the full participation of the PCV and with a view to provoking wholesale military desertion. Alongside the FALN was a communist-backed political organisation — the National Liberation Front (FNL).

From early on emphasis was laid upon sabotaging US interests in retaliation for American pressure on Cuba during the October 1962 missile crisis. Saboteurs attacked four power stations and blew up pipe lines belonging to US companies. In February 1963 an arson attack caused damage estimated at US $2,500,000 million to Sears Roebuck in Caracas.

With an eye for publicity, militants carried off world famous canvasses from an important exhibition of French painting, only to return them three days later. In February 1963 armed stowaways captured the 3000-ton *Anzoategui* as it steamed towards New Orleans, and took it to Brazil.

Later in August members disguised as policemen abducted the Argentinian footballer, Alfredo di Stefano, for two days. A similar indignity occurred to the deputy head of the United States Military Mission in Venezuela, Colonel James Chenault, in Caracas. Still more outrageous, six teenage students hijacked an airliner on a domestic flight and, after scattering leaflets, forced the pilot to fly to Trinidad.

Whilst these stunts caught the attention of the world, the FALN pursued the business of revolution in the capital, where armed engagements, although unsuccessful in the end, for a brief spell were a daily occurrence. In November a large collection of arms for the FALN from Cuba was intercepted on the coast.

That December, the left suffered a resounding defeat in the presidential and congressional elections, a fact which led the PCV to reconsider its support for FALN guerrilla actions, especially when the new President offered to legalise the party's activities if it renounced violence. Gradually the party back-tracked, so that by 1967 it was firmly opposed to the armed path it had originally encouraged.

Douglas Bravo, after the 1963 defeat of the FALN in the capital, was left at large in the countryside, and increasingly opposed the PCV, which in 1966 expelled him from the Central Committee and from the party the following year. Castro, did not desert him, and with Cuban support the FALN engaged in a further wave of urban terrorism in 1966, based on student support at the Central University. It proved less disruptive than the first wave, but its defeat and the consequent loss of urban support cells did not dislodge the FALN from its mountainous retreats.

To recover from the withdrawal of PCV support, a new directorate was appointed — for the political work of the FLN Fabricio Ojeda, until his death in a police cell in June 1966, and Américo Martín were responsible; Douglas Bravo and Elías Manuit Camero commanded in the guerrilla field. Ojeda was generally thought to have been murdered, but his death did not stop a landing in July on the coast of Falcón state by a group of Cuban-trained FALN cadres under the command of Luben Petkoff, who joined Bravo in September. The group continued to receive Cuban support until 1969, but without achieving any striking successes. That year Soviet pressure compelled Castro to abandon the FALN; the USSR was interested in establishing relations with the Venezuelan government and Cuban supported guerrilla activity was an embarrassment and hindrance to this plan.

By this time the Democratic Action party had lost power to the Christian Democrat COPEI party in December 1968 elections and President Caldera had legalised the PCV in a pacification programme which extended to an amnesty for guerrillas. Some returned to legality; those that remained at large fell to quarrelling — the MIR left the FALN and splintered. Differences were patched up in 1970 with the creation of a Committee of Revolutionary Integration, but there was no disguising the guerrilla weakness. Having lost its Cuban patron, actively opposed by the PCV, and with social reform, rural counter-insurgency and oil wealth at the government's disposal, the FALN fell into inactivity after 1972.

Bravo left the country and spent some time in Europe, before returning to help release his colleagues from San Carlos jail in a dramatic escape in 1975. Little further activity was recorded and in October 1979 Bravo ended 18 years of clandestinity by accepting a presidential pardon.

Movement of the Revolutionary Left
(*Movimiento de la Izquierda Revolucionaria — MIR*)

The MIR, led by Américo Martín and Alberto Rangel, consisted of a dissident faction of the Venezuelan reformist Democratic Action (AD) party in 1960. They took their cue from Fidel Castro's victory in Cuba the previous year, and defined the MIR as a Marxist party. In the legislature 14 of the 73 AD deputies joined the new party, which in November called for a mass uprising. Fighting took place in the streets, and particularly on the university campus, but the insurrection failed.

In 1961 MIR activists such as Moisés Moleira worked closely with the Venezuelan Communist Party (PCV) in forming the nucleus of what became the Armed Forces of National Liberation (FALN). Unlike the PCV, the MIR stuck by the FALN, despite its defeat in Caracas in 1963 and again in 1966, and continued to receive aid and encouragement from Havana.

However, in the first half of 1967 the MIR broke away to form in April a new front in the mountain range of El Bachiller in eastern Venezuela. Ideological disagreement lay at the root of that split. A further weakening of the MIR occurred in 1968, when the imprisoned leadership —Américo Martín and Simón Saenz Mérida — called for a suspension of the armed struggle, a stand resisted by those in the field led by Julio Escalona.

More significant still in contributing to the decline in MIR activity was the decision taken by Cuba in 1969 to cease support for armed struggle, a policy forced upon Castro by Moscow. Out on a limb, the MIR attempted to reconcile its differences with the FALN, also dropped by Cuba. In January 1970 a Committee of Revolutionary Integration was set up, which consisted of Julio Escalona, Carlos Betancourt and Gabriel Puerta, who had split from the MIR to form the Red Flag (BR) faction, and FALN leader, Douglas Bravo.

Even if no ideological agreement was forthcoming from the new committee, the MIR guerrillas at least solved their financial problems in 1972 by cooperating in the joint kidnapping of millionaire canning manufacturer Carlos Domínquez Chavez near Caracas, for whom a ransom of US $1 million was paid in June and shared between the various groups.

In March 1973 President Caldera furthered his policy of canalising left-wing activity into the legitimate mainstream of national politics by legalising the MIR, which had refused to take advantage of the 1969 amnesty. Thereafter, instead of disrupting elections the MIR competed in the electoral process.

Popular Revolutionary Movement
(Movimiento Popular Revolucionario — MPR)

The MPR appeared in late 1977 in eastern Venezuela near Trujillo, and claimed responsibility for a clutch of minor actions in 1978. Nothing further was heard of the group, and it was assumed that it operated as a splinter group of the Armed Forces of National Liberation (FALN) or of Red Flag. It did not survive the amnesty offered by the government to guerrillas in 1979.

Red Flag
(Bandera Roja)

Red Flag splintered from the Venezuelan Movement of the Revolutionary Left (MIR) in 1969, when at the behest of the Russians Cuba dropped support for guerrilla warfare in Venezuela. The group, active in eastern Venezuela, was led by Carlos Betancourt and Gabriel Puerta, who financed themselves by a spectacular kidnap demand in 1972. Both leaders were subsequently apprehended in the summer of 1973 and imprisoned in Caracas' top security jail, from which they made a dramatic escape in January 1975. It was estimated that their tunnel had taken months to dig — it stretched for 60 metres.

Their escape was followed by a joint communiqué with the Armed Forces of National Liberation (FALN) and a similar splinter group to itself, Zero Point, rejecting the Venezuelan constitutional left, which included the Venezuelan Communist Party (PVC) and the MIR. In March 1975 the group issued a death list condemning 20 men prominent in the agricultural sector. It was also set upon the abduction of politicians, but resorted instead to holding wealthy businessmen to ransom.

Thus financed, some terrorist activity by Red Flag occurred in 1976 and more in 1977. Activists were able to ambush the occasional military vehicle and for short periods to take over small towns whilst they re-stocked with provisions. The recapture of Betancourt that year reduced Red Flag activity in 1978 and little or no action occurred in 1979. Gabriel Puerta and Julio Escalona remained at large until the latter accepted a presidential pardon in May 1979. It was assumed that Puerta went to Cuba. True or not, the group resurfaced dramatically in December 1981, when it hijacked three domestic flights and demanded a ransom and the release of prisoners. The government did not succumb to intimidation and in a remarkable action in April 1982 police captured Puerta in

Caracas. Six months later police killed some 25 militants in a shoot-out south-east of the capital.

Zero Point
(Punto Cero)

Zero Point was a Venezuelan splinter group of the Movement of the Revolutionary Left (MIR). It attacked a National Guard post in 1972, after which a number of militants were arrested. In May 1973 the group hijacked a Venezuelan aircraft demanding the release of 79 prisoners, but faced by a government hard-line no-negotiation policy it merely flew the aircraft to Cuba. Some of those behind bars escaped from jail in January 1975 in a dramatic spring, thought to have been organised by FALN leader Douglas Bravo. But no further activity resulted in the late 1970s, despite the rejection of a presidential amnesty in 1979.

Index of Groups

List of More Widely Used Acronyms

AAA	*Alianza Apolstólica Anticomunista*, or *Alianza Anticomunista Argentina*
AD	*Action Directe*
ANC	African National Congress, or African National Council
ANE	*Acción Nacional Española*
AOC	*Aliança Operária e Camponesa*
ARA	*Acção Revolucionária Armada*
ARC	*Action pour la Renaissance de la Corse*, or *Action Révolutionnaire Corse*
APC	*Associo di Patrioti Corsi*
ASALA	Armenian Secret Army for the Liberation of Armenia
BR	*Brigate Rosse*, or *Brigadas Revolucionárias*
BRF	*Brigades Révolutionnaires Françaises*
BVE	*Batallón Vasco Español*
COREMO	*Comitê Revolucionário de Moçambique*
DA	*Deutsche Aktionsgruppen*
EGP	*Ejército Guerrillero de los Pobres*, or *Ejército Guerrillero del Pueblo*
ELA	*Epanastatikos Laikos Agonas*
ELF	Eritrean Liberation Front
ELN	*Ejército de Liberación Nacional*
EOKA	*Ethniki Organosis Kyprion Agoniston*
EPL	*Ejército Popular de Liberación*
EPLF	Eritrean Peoples Liberation Front
ERP	*Ejército Revolucionario del Pueblo*
ESEMA	*Ethnikos Syndesmos Ellinon Monimon Axiomatikon*
ETA	*Euskadi ta Askatasuna*
EZ	*Euzkal Zuzentasuna*

FAC	*Front d'Alliberament Català*
FAL	*Fuerzas Armadas de Liberación*
FALN	*Fuerzas Armadas de Liberación Nacional*
FANE	*Fédération d'Action Nationale Européenne*
FAP	*Fuerzas Armadas Peronistas*
FAR	*Fuerzas Armadas Revolucionarias,* or *Fuerzas Armadas Rebeldes*
FARC	*Fuerzas Armadas Revolucionarias de Colombia*
FARN	*Fuerzas Armadas de Resistencia Nacional,* or *Fuerzas Armadas Revolucionarias de Nicaragua*
FLA	*Frente da Libertação das Açores*
FLAMA	*Frente da Libertação do Arquipélago de Madeira*
FLB	*Front de Libération de la Bretagne*
FLEC	*Frente de Libertação do Enclave de Cabinda*
FLN	*Front de Libération Nationale*
FLNC	*Front de la Libération Nationale de la Corse,* or *Front de Libération Nationale du Congo*
FLNF	*Front de Libération Nationale Française*
FLOSY	Front for Liberation of Occupied Yemen
FLQ	*Front de Libération du Québec*
FNE	*Faisceaux Nationaux Européens*
FNLA	*Frente Nacional da Libertação de Angola*
FP-25	*Forças Populares do 25 Abril*
FPCL	*Front Paysan Corse de Libération*
FPL	*Fuerzas Populares de Liberación*
FRANCIA	*Front d'Action Nouvelle contre l'Indépendence et l'Autonomie*
FRAP	*Frente Revolucionario Antifascista y Patriótico,* or *Fuerzas Revolucionarias Armadas del Pueblo*
FRELIMO	*Frente da Libertação de Moçambique*
FRETILIN	*Frente Revolucionária Timorense de Libertação e Independência*
FROLINAT	*Front de Libération Nationale du Tchad*
FSLN	*Frente Sandinista de Liberación Nacional*
FUP	*Força de Unidade Popular*
GAP	*Gruppi d'Azione Partigiana*
GARI	*Grupos de Acción Revolucionaria Internacionalista*
GD	*Guerilla Diffusa*
GRAPO	*Grupo de Resistencia Antifascista Primero de Octubre*

HIRO	*Hrvatska Ilegalna Revolucionarna Organizacija*
HOP	*Hrvatski Oslobodilučki Pokret*
HNV	*Hrvatsko Narodno Vijeće*
HNO	*Hrvatski Narodni Otpor*
HRB	*Hrvatsko Revolucionarno Bratsvo*
HUKS	*Hukbong Bayan Laban Sa Hapon*
IMG	*International Marxist Group*
INLA	*Irish National Liberation Army*
IRA	*Irish Republican Army*
IRSP	*Irish Republican Socialist Party*
JCR	*Jeunesse Communiste Révolutionnaire*
JVP	*Janatha Vimukthi Peramuna*
KKK	*Ku Klux Klan*
LUAR	*Liga de União e Acção Revolucionária*
M-19	*Movimiento 19 Abril*
MAR	*Movimento d'Azione Rivoluzionaria*
MIR	*Movimiento de la Izquierda Revolucionaria*
MLN	*Movimiento de Liberación Nacional*
MOULINAKA	National Liberation Movement of Kampuchea
MPAIAC	*Movimiento para la Autodeterminación e Indepen-dencia del Archipiélago de las Canarias*
MPLA	*Movimento Popular para a Libertação de Angola*
MRM	*Movimento da Resistência Moçambicana*
MRNB	*Mouvement de Résistance Nationaliste Bretonne*
MRPP	*Movimento Reorganizativo do Partido do Prole-tariado*
NAP	*Nuclei Armati Proletari*
NAPAP	*Noyaux Armés pour l'Autonomie Populaire*
NAR	*Nuclei Armati Rivoluzionari*
NF	National Front
NWLF	New World Liberation Front
OAS	*Organisation de l'Armée Secrète*
OEA	*Organismos Ethnikis Anorthosoos*
OLla	*Organització Lluita Armada*
ORPA	*Organización Revolucionaria del Pueblo en Armas*
PAC	Pan Africanist Congress

PAIGC	*Partido Africano da Independência da Guiné e Cabo Verde*
PFLO	Popular Front for the Liberation of Oman
PFLOAG	Popular Front for the Liberation of Oman and the Arab Gulf
PFLP	Popular Front for the Liberation of Palestine
PIRA	Provisional Irish Republican Army
PL	*Prima Linea*
PLO	Palestine Liberation Organisation
POLISARIO	Peoples Front for the Liberation of Saguiat al Hamra and Rio de Oro
RAF	*Rote Armee Fraktion*
RH	*Rode Hulp*
RJ	*Rode Jeugd*
RNM	*Resistência Nacional Moçambicana*
RVZ	*Rood Verzetsfront*
RZ	*Revolutionäre Zellen*
SALF	Somali-Abo Liberation Front
SDSF	Somali Democratic Salvation Front
SLA	Symbionese Liberation Army
SUV	*Soldados Unidos Vencerão*
SWP	Socialist Workers' Party
TOM	Troops Out Movement
TPLA	Turkish People Liberation Army
TPLF	Tigre People's Liberation Front
UDA	Ulster Defence Association
UFF	Ulster Freedom Fighters
UHRO	*Ustaša Hrvatska Revolucionarna Organizacija*
UJC	*Union des Jeunesses Communistes*
UNITA	*União Nacional para a Independência Total de Angola*
UPV	Ulster Protestant Volunteers
UVF	Ulster Volunteer Force
UWC	Ulster Workers' Council
WRP	Workers' Revolutionary Party
WSLF	Western Somali Liberation Front
ZANU	Zimbabwe African National Union
ZAPU	Zimbabwe African People's Union